Fifth
Edition

THE ECONOMICS
OF WOMEN, MEN,
AND WORK

Francine D. Blau
Cornell University

Marianne A. Ferber
University of Illinois at Urbana–Champaign

Anne E. Winkler
University of Missouri–St. Louis

PEARSON

Prentice
Hall

Upper Saddle River, NJ 07458

Library of Congress Cataloging in Publication Division
Blau, Francine D.
  The economics of women, men, and work / Francine D. Blau, Marianne A.
Ferber, Anne E. Winkler.-- 5th ed.
    p. cm.
  Includes bibliographical references and index.
  ISBN 0-13-185154-3 (pbk. : alk. paper)
  1. Women--United States--Economic conditions. 2. Feminist
economics--United States. 3. Women--Employment--United States. 4. Sexual
division of labor--United States. 5. Labor market--United States.
6. Women--United States--Social conditions. I. Ferber, Marianne A., [date] II.
Winkler, Anne E., [date] III. Title.
  HQ1421.B56 2006
  305.42'0973--dc22

                                                              2005005877

VP/Editorial Director: Jeff Shelstad
AVP/Executive Editor: David Alexander
Acquisitions Editor: Jon Axelrod
Assistant Editor: Francesca Calogero
Editorial Assistant: Michael Dittamo
AVP/Executive Marketing Manager: Sharon Koch
Marketing Assistant: Tina Panagiotou
Associate Director: Judy Leale
Production Editor: Suzanne Grappi
Permissions Supervisor: Charles Morris
Manufacturing Buyer: Michelle Klein
Cover Design Manager: Jayne Conte
Composition: Laserwords
Full-Service Project Management: Jennifer Welsch, BookMasters, Inc.
Typeface: 10/12 Times Ten

Credits and acknowledgments borrowed from other sources and reproduced, with
permission, in this textbook appear on appropriate page within text.

Pearson Education LTD.
Pearson Education Singapore, Pte. Ltd
Pearson Education, Canada, Ltd
Pearson Education–Japan

Pearson Education Australia PTY, Limited
Pearson Education North Asia Ltd
Pearson Educación de Mexico, S.A. de C.V.
Pearson Education Malaysia, Pte. Ltd

10 9 8 7 6 5 4 3
ISBN 0-13-185154-3

For
Lawrence M. Kahn
Daniel Blau Kahn
Lisa Blau Kahn

and

Bob Ferber
Don Ferber
Ellen Ferber Rogalin

and

Michael Joseph Kowalkowski
Henrik Francis Kowalkowski
Andrew Joseph Kowalkowski

With love

Brief Contents

Preface   xvii

Chapter 1   Introduction   1

Chapter 2   Women and Men: Changing Roles in a Changing Economy   13

Chapter 3   The Family as an Economic Unit   35

Chapter 4   The Allocation of Time between the Household and the Labor Market   85

Chapter 5   Differences in Occupations and Earnings: Overview   136

Chapter 6   Differences in Occupations and Earnings: The Human Capital Model   158

Chapter 7   Differences in Occupations and Earnings: The Role of Labor Market Discrimination   202

Chapter 8   Recent Developments in the Labor Market: Their Impact on Women and Men   256

Chapter 9   Changing Work Roles and the Family   289

Chapter 10   Policies Affecting Paid Work and the Family   326

Chapter 11   Gender Differences in Other Countries   371

Author Index   421

Subject Index   431

Contents

Preface   xvii

CHAPTER 1   Introduction   1

What Economics Is About   3

Uses of Economic Theory   4

The Scope of Economics   5

Individuals, Families, and Households   6

A Note on Terminology   7

Outline of the Book   7

Appendix: A Review of Supply and Demand in the Labor Market   8

Questions for Review and Discussion   12

**CHAPTER 2   Women and Men: Changing Roles in a Changing
Economy   13**

The Nature of Males and Females   14

The Role of Sociobiology in Explaining Gender Differences   15

Factors Influencing Women's Relative Status   18

Women's Roles and Economic Development   19

The U.S. Experience   21

The Preindustrial Period   21

Industrialization   22

Industrialization and the Evolution of the Family   23

Women in the Labor Market   28

Conclusion   33

Questions for Review and Discussion   34

Suggested Readings   34

CHAPTER 3   The Family as an Economic Unit   35

The Simple Neoclassical Model: Specialization and Exchange   37

Comparative Advantage   37

Specialization and Exchange: Numerical Examples   38

Gains to Specialization and Exchange   40

Other Advantages of Families   42

Economies of Scale   42

Public Goods   42

Externalities in Consumption   42

Marriage-Specific Investments   43

Risk Pooling   43

Institutional Advantages   43

Disadvantages of Specialization   43

Sharing of Housework   44

Life Cycle Changes   45

Costs of Interdependence   45

Tastes and Bargaining Power   46

Domestic Violence   48

Disadvantages of Specialization: A Summary   49

Transaction Cost and Bargaining Approaches   49

Marxist and Radical Feminist Views of the Family   53

Nonmarket Work   55

Housework   56

Volunteer Work   63

Estimating the Value of Nonmarket Production   66

The American Family in the Twenty-First Century   70

Conclusion   74

Appendix: Specialization and Exchange: A Graphical Analysis   75

Questions for Review and Discussion   83

Suggested Readings   83

**CHAPTER 4   The Allocation of Time between the Household
and the Labor Market   85**

The Labor Force: Some Definitions   86

Trends in Labor Force Participation   88

Trends in Labor Force Attachment   92

Trends in Hours Worked   95

The Labor Supply Decision   96

The Budget Constraint   98

Indifference Curves   99

The Participation Decision   102

The Value of Nonmarket Time (w)   104*

The Value of Market Time (w)   109

The Hours Decision   113

Empirical Evidence on Income and Substitution Effects   113

Economic Conditions   115

*Some Applications of the Theory: Taxes, Child Care Costs,
     and Labor Supply   116*

Analyzing Trends in Women's Participation: An Overview   118

Factors Influencing the Value of Market Time (w)   118

Factors Influencing the Value of Nonmarket Time (w)   120*

The World War II Experience   122

The Post–World War II Baby Boom   124

The 1960s to the 1980s: Increased Participation of Married Mothers   125

The 1990s and Early 2000s: Diverging Participation Trends
     for Married and Single Mothers   127

Analyzing Trends in Men's Participation   128

Black and White Participation Differentials: A Closer Look   129

Conclusion   132

Appendix: The Income and Substitution Effects: A Closer Look   131

Questions for Review and Discussion   134

Suggested Readings   134

CHAPTER 5   Differences in Occupations and Earnings: Overview   136

Occupational Differences   137

Occupational Segregation   141

Hierarchies Within Occupations   143

Evaluating the Extent of Occupational Segregation   143

Trends in Occupational Segregation   144

Female-Male Earnings Ratio   147

Conclusion   156

Questions for Review and Discussion   157

**CHAPTER 6   Differences in Occupations and Earnings: The Human
Capital Model   158**

What Is Human Capital?   160

Gender Differences in Educational Attainment   161

The Educational Investment Decision   165

Education and Productivity   170

Gender Differences in Educational Investment Decisions: The Human
Capital Analysis   171

Expected Work Life   171

Gender Differences in Educational Investment Decisions:
Other Factors   174

Socialization   174

Gender-Appropriate Traits and Competencies   177

Biased Evaluations   179

Discrimination by Educational Institutions   179

Subtle Barriers   180

Policy Issue: The Role of Government in Combating Discrimination
in Educational Institutions   182

Explaining Women's Rising Educational Attainment   183

On-the-Job Training   184

Gender Differences in Labor Market Experience   185

The On-the-Job Training Investment Decision   186

General Training   186

Firm-Specific Training   187

Experience and Productivity   189

Gender Differences in Training Investment Decisions   190

Expected Work Life   190

Discrimination   192

Occupations and Earnings   193

Other Supply-Side Factors   194

The Human Capital Explanation: An Assessment   196

Conclusion   200

Questions for Review and Discussion   200

Suggested Readings   201

CHAPTER 7 Differences in Occupations and Earnings: The Role of Labor Market Discrimination 202

Labor Market Discrimination: A Definition 203

Empirical Evidence of Labor Market Discrimination 204

Earnings Differences 204

Occupational Differences 211

Models of Labor Market Discrimination 218

Tastes for Discrimination 218

Statistical Discrimination 226

The Overcrowding Model 228

Institutional Models 231

Feedback Effects 233

Policy Issue: The Government and Equal Employment Opportunity 234

Equal Employment Opportunity Laws and Regulations 235

Effectiveness of the Government's Antidiscrimination Effort 240

Affirmative Action 242

Comparable Worth 245

Conclusion 249

Appendix: Regression Analysis and Empirical Estimates of Labor Market Discrimination 250

Questions for Review and Discussion 254

Suggested Readings 255

CHAPTER 8 Recent Developments in the Labor Market: Their Impact on Women and Men 256

Trends in Female and Male Wages 257

The Declining Gender Pay Gap 259

Determinants of Trends in the Gender Pay Gap 259

Empirical Results for the 1980s 260

Empirical Results for the 1990s 264

The Rising Payoff to Education 265

Changing Labor Market Dynamics 267

The High-Churning U.S. Labor Market 267

Unemployment 268

Other Indicators of Employment Problems 270

Trends in the Gender Difference in Unemployment 272

Future Labor Market Prospects 273

The Rise of the Nonstandard Workforce   274

Definition and Characteristics of the Nonstandard Workforce   274

Explanations Behind the Rise of Nonstandard Workers   276

Consequences for Workers and Their Families   277

The Growth in Women's Self-Employment   278

The Changing Face of Labor Unions   281

Trends in Labor Union Membership   281

Benefits of Union Membership for Workers and the Impact of Deunionization   282

Reasons for the Historic Underrepresentation of Women in Unions   283

The Glass Ceiling in Union Leadership   284

Prospects for Women in Unions   285

Conclusion   286

Questions for Review and Discussion   287

Suggested Readings   287

CHAPTER 9   Changing Work Roles and the Family   289

Economic Explanations for Family Formation   290

Marriage   290

Divorce   294

Cohabitation: Opposite-Sex, Unmarried Couples   299

Cohabitation: Gay and Lesbian Couples   301

Fertility   303

Changing Family Structure and Economic Well-Being   310

Dual-Earner Families   310

Maternal Employment and Children's Outcomes   314

Single-Parent Families   316

Family Structure and Children's Outcomes   322

Conclusion   323

Questions for Review and Discussion   324

Suggested Readings   324

CHAPTER 10   Policies Affecting Paid Work and the Family   326

Policies to Alleviate Poverty   326

AFDC: Our Former Welfare Program   327

The Iron Triangle of Welfare   329

Employment Strategies 330

TANF: Our Current Welfare Program 331

The Earned Income Tax Credit 336

Child Support Enforcement 338

Taxes, Specialization, and Marriage 340

Income Taxation Policy 341

The Social Security System 345

The Competing Demands of Work and Family 348

Who Is Responsible for Children? 350

Family-Friendly Policies 352

Family Leave 353

Child Care 356

Alternative Work Schedules 362

Flexible Benefits 364

Policies to Assist Couples 364

Conclusion 367

Questions for Review and Discussion 368

Suggested Readings 369

CHAPTER 11   Gender Differences in Other Countries   371

The Economic Status of the World's Women: Overview 372

Labor Force Participation 372

Occupations 377

Earnings 378

Educational Attainment 379

Fertility 380

Housework 382

Women's Role in Government and Their Standing Before the Law 383

Interpretations and Implications 383

A Comparison of the United States to Other Economically
      Advanced Countries 386

Labor Force Participation 389

Occupations 390

The Gender-Wage Gap 393

Demographic Trends 398

Housework 402

Summary on Economically Advanced Countries 402

Developing Countries   403

  Education as the Pathway to Empowerment   *403*

  Fertility and Population Control   *405*

  Child Labor   *408*

  Microcredit for Women: Lifeline or Mirage?   *410*

  Summary on Women in Developing Countries   *413*

Countries of the Former Soviet Bloc   414

Conclusion   417

Questions for Review and Discussion   417

Suggested Readings   418

Author Index   **421**

Subject Index   **431**

Preface

We wrote *The Economics of Women, Men, and Work* because we saw a need for a text that would acquaint students with the findings of research on women, men, and work in the labor market and the household. We are extremely gratified on the publication of the fifth edition to reflect that this belief was justified, and hope that this fully revised and updated edition will serve as effectively as the earlier editions.

OVERVIEW OF THE TEXT

The book is written at a level that should both utilize and enhance students' knowledge of economic concepts and analysis but do so in terms intelligible to those not versed in advanced theory. Even though we assume a knowledge of introductory economics on the part of the reader, an interested and determined individual wanting to learn more about the economic status of women as compared to men could benefit considerably from the material offered here. The book also draws upon research in the other social sciences. The text, used in its entirety, is primarily intended for courses specifically concerned with the economic status of women. However, this book could be used to good advantage in interdisciplinary women's studies courses, as well as introductory-level courses in economic problems. Selected readings would also make a useful supplement to round out a general labor economics course. In addition, it would serve as a useful reference work for those not familiar with the rapidly growing body of literature on women, men, and work as well as for practicing economists looking for a single volume on this topic.

SIGNIFICANT FEATURES OF THE FIFTH EDITION

The fifth edition reflects the numerous changes in the labor market and in the family that have occurred in recent years. All data and tables have been updated and discussions and references take into account the most recent research on each subject covered. As in the fourth edition, questions are provided at the end of each chapter to review major concepts and to stimulate further discussion among students and instructors. Key features of the fifth edition include the following:

- As in the past, we thoroughly review trends in the labor supply of women and men to the market. In Chapter 4, we summarize these trends and provide some analysis of important recent developments including the large increase in labor force participation of single mothers since the mid 1990s. The leveling off of the participation rates of married women is also highlighted.

- We present an updated analysis of the reasons for the gender-wage gap in Chapter 7, as well as a summary of new research on the slowing convergence in the gender-wage gap in the 1990s in Chapter 8.

- We also highlight other important recent developments in the labor market and their consequences for women and men. These developments include the increasingly divergent outcomes for individuals and families by level of educational attainment, including the continuing employment problems of less educated men, as well as growing wage inequality, and changes in welfare policy that moved greater numbers of welfare recipients, largely single mothers, into the labor force. Each chapter reflects these changes as relevant, and Chapter 8, "Recent Developments in the Labor Market," as well as Chapter 10, "Policies Affecting Paid Work and the Family," focus specifically on these developments.

- We devote considerable attention to changes within married-couple families as well as to changing family structure and the implications of these shifts for labor market outcomes. Chapter 3, which focuses on nonmarket work, includes new data on the allocation of housework between women and men and provides an expanded discussion of the usefulness and importance of collecting time use data on nonmarket activities. It also discusses trends in time spent with children, which is of interest, both in terms of its implications for time spent in nonmarket work and its potential implications for children's development. Further, as in earlier editions, this chapter considers alternatives to the standard economic approach, including the transaction cost approach and bargaining models, as well as a discussion of the Marxist and radical feminist views of decision making in the family.

- In keeping with the times, Chapter 9 examines trends in marriage, divorce, and overall fertility, along with trends in births to unmarried mothers, teen births, cohabitation, and same-sex relationships. The chapter also devotes considerable attention to the implications of the large increases in the number of dual-earner, married-couple families and single-parent families for children's outcomes. The new edition also discusses the state of marriage in the United States in the 2000s, including the recent court decision in Massachusetts to permit same-sex marriage.

- All discussions concerning policy have been thoroughly revised. In Chapter 7, we discuss recent developments concerning affirmative action and findings regarding the effectiveness of antidiscrimination legislation. Updated discussions of policies that affect paid work and the family in Chapter 10 focus on three broad policy areas: (1) policies to alleviate poverty, including the Temporary Assistance for Needy Families (TANF) program, the Earned Income Tax Credit (EITC), and child support enforcement; (2) government tax policies; and (3) policies expected to help workers and their families balance the dual demands of paid work and family responsibilities. The chapter includes new evidence on the effects of welfare reform on labor market and family outcomes, as well as a discussion of recent government efforts to promote marriage. In addition, the text discusses tax changes made by the George W. Bush administration, and how they affect the marriage penalty and labor force participation.

- Finally, Chapter 11 offers extensive revisions of the discussion of gender differences from an international perspective. As in the earlier editions, it considers differences in women's status across broad regions of the world, then compares the United States with a number of other economically advanced nations, especially Sweden and Japan, with respect to labor force participation, the gender-wage gap, occupations, sharing of housework, and demographic trends. This chapter also specifically looks at the situation of women in developing countries, highlighting the difficulties they face as well as the progress they have made, and briefly considers the problems of women living in the countries of the former Soviet bloc.

ACKNOWLEDGMENTS

All of us have taught a course on women in the labor market for some time, and we wish to acknowledge that this book benefited from the experience and the insights we gained from our students. We are also greatly indebted to a rather large and diverse group of colleagues, from a number of disciplines, who contributed material and provided valuable comments on the various editions:

Deborah Anderson, University of Arizona
Orley C. Ashenfelter, Princeton University
Nancy S. Barrett, Western Michigan University, Kalamazoo
Andrea H. Beller, University of Illinois, Urbana–Champaign
Lourdes Beneria, Cornell University
Barbara R. Bergmann, American University
Charles Brown, University of Michigan
Clair Brown, University of California, Berkeley
Michael Brun, University of Illinois, Urbana–Champaign and Illinois State University
Greg J. Duncan, Northwestern University
Margaret C. Dunkle, American Association of University Women, Educational Foundation
Kathleen M. Early, University of Missouri–St. Louis
Cristina Echevarria, University of Saskatchewan
Paula England, Stanford University
Robert Fairlie, University of California, Santa Cruz
Belton M. Fleisher, Ohio State University
Claudia D. Goldin, Harvard University
Janet Gornick, Baruch College, City University of New York
Ulla Grapard, Colgate University
Shoshana Grossbard–Schechtman, San Diego State University
Daniel S. Hamermesh, University of Texas, Austin
Michele Hoyman, University of North Carolina–Chapel Hill
Joan A. Huber, Ohio State University
Randy Ilg, Bureau of Labor Statistics

Thomas R. Ireland, University of Missouri–St. Louis
John Johnson IV, University of Illinois, Urbana–Champaign
Heather Joshi, City University, London
Joan R. Kahn, University of Maryland
Lawrence M. Kahn, Cornell University
Lisa Blau Kahn, Harvard University
Kristen Keith, University of Toledo
Mark R. Killingsworth, Rutgers University
Marcia Brumit Kropf, Girls Incorporated
Fidan Kurtulus, Cornell University
Pareena Lawrence, University of Minnesota
Phil Levine, Wellesley College
Shelly J. Lundberg, University of Washington, Seattle
Julie A. Matthaei, Wellesley College
Joan Moriarty, UNITE HERE
Janet Norwood, Urban Institute
Elizabeth Peters, Cornell University
Leila Pratt, University of Tennessee at Chattanooga
Harriet B. Presser, University of Maryland
Barbara B. Reagan, Southern Methodist University
Barbara F. Reskin, University of Washington, Seattle
Patricia A. Roos, State University of New York, Stony Brook
Elaina Rose, University of Washington, Seattle
Steven H. Sandell, U.S. Department of Health and Human Services
Lisa Saunders, University of Massachusetts, Amherst
Richard Stratton, University of Akron
Myra H. Strober, Stanford University
Louise A. Tilly, New School University
Donald J. Treiman, University of California, Los Angeles
Jane Waldfogel, Columbia University
Alison Wellington, The College of Wooster
Herbert D. Werner, University of Missouri–St. Louis
H. F. (Bill) Williamson, University of Illinois, Urbana–Champaign
Frances Woolley, Carleton University, Ottawa

Without their help, this book would have had many more deficiencies. For those that remain, as well as for all opinions expressed, we, of course, take complete responsibility. This list of acknowledgments would be incomplete if we did not also thank Fidan Kurtulus, Kathleen Early, and Majana Burazovic, the research assistants who helped us track down sources and references and prepare tables and graphs for this edition. Finally, we are immensely grateful to the exceptionally helpful team that worked with us on this edition: at Prentice Hall, David Alexander, executive editor; Francesca Calogero, assistant editor; Suzanne Grappi, production editor; and acquisitions editor, Jon Axelrod; and, at BookMasters, Jennifer Welsch, project director.

F.D.B.
M.A.F.
A.E.W.

CHAPTER
1 ‖ INTRODUCTION

Chapter Highlights

■ What Economics Is About

■ Uses of Economic Theory

■ The Scope of Economics

■ Individuals, Families, and Households

■ A Note on Terminology

■ Outline of the Book

■ Appendix: A Review of Supply and Demand in the Labor Market

Courses in economics abound at universities and colleges, along with an ample supply of texts focusing on the many facets of this discipline. These courses and books increasingly recognize that women play an important role in the economy as workers and consumers and that in many ways their behavior and their problems differ from those of men. However, male patterns often receive the major emphasis, just as patterns of the majority racial and ethnic groups do, while gender differences are, at best, just one of many topics covered. For example, workers are often assumed to enter the labor market after completing their education and to remain until their retirement. Similarly, institutions studied are mainly those involved in traditional labor markets, from businesses to labor unions and relevant government agencies. Although women in growing numbers are spending an increasing proportion of their time working for pay, their lives and their world continue to be significantly different from those of men, and more of their time continues to be spent in nonmarket activities.

In recent years, much attention has been focused on the rising labor force participation rates of women and particularly on the changing economic roles of married women. Much has been made, especially in the popular media, of the often large percentage increases in the number of women in nontraditional

1

occupations, not to mention the publicity received by "the first woman" in a given field, whether it be stockbroker, jockey, or prime minister. All this focus tends to obscure both the continued responsibility of most women for the bulk of nonmarket work and the large occupational differences between men and women that remain, despite considerable progress. As long as this situation persists, there is a need to address these issues in depth, as is done in this book.

Although economic behavior is clearly not isolated from the remainder of human existence, the primary focus of this book is on the economic behavior of women and men, on economic institutions, and on economic outcomes. To refresh the memory of students who have some acquaintance with economics, and to provide a minimal background for those who do not, we begin with a brief introduction to the tools of this discipline. Neoclassical or mainstream economic theory provides the major emphasis of this book. However, students need to be aware that we endeavor to constantly stretch and challenge the existing theories to shed light on issues related to gender and work. So, in addition to presenting conventional analyses, we sometimes offer critiques of existing approaches. Further, we tend to emphasize the importance and implications of gender inequities in the labor market and in the household to a greater extent than some of our colleagues might and also take more note of diversity by race and ethnicity. In addition, we point to the increasingly divergent outcomes for individuals and families by level of educational attainment. Finally, we attempt to take account of institutional factors, alternative perspectives, and the insights of other disciplines where relevant.[1]

Throughout this book, but especially in those segments where we deal with policy, we are confronted by a dilemma common to the social sciences. On the one hand, much of what we present is positive, rather than normative, in the sense that we present facts and research results as we find them. Furthermore, we try to avoid value judgments and prescriptive attitudes; personal values should not be permitted to intrude upon objective analysis. On the other hand, it is unrealistic to claim that the choice of topics, the emphasis in discussions, and the references provided are, or even can be, entirely value free. A reasonable solution is to try to present various sides of controversial questions, while making clear that different premises will lead to different conclusions and that the policies one should adopt depend on the goals one wants to reach. We attempt to follow this approach.

At the same time, the tenor of this book is undoubtedly colored to some extent by our feminist perspective. Thus, we recognize, for instance, the extent to which persons of the same sex may differ, and persons of the opposite sex may be similar. And, like other feminists, in considering gender differences, we are increasingly aware of how these differences vary by race and ethnicity. Our feminist perspective also means we believe that, as much as possible, individuals should have the opportunity to live up to their potential, rather than be forced to conform to stereotypical roles. Most of all, it means that, while recognizing differences between women and men, some possibly caused by biological factors and others by the way girls and boys are reared in our society, we are less

---

[1]For a feminist critique of neoclassical economics, see Julie A. Nelson, *Feminism, Objectivity and Economics* (London: Routledge, 1996).

inclined to emphasize the differences between them than the common humanity that unites them.

WHAT ECONOMICS IS ABOUT

Neoclassical economics is concerned with decision making under conditions of **scarcity**, which means not enough resources are available to satisfy everyone's wants, and choices have to be made about their use. Given this constraint, it is crucial to recognize that using labor, capital, and land to produce one good means that fewer of these inputs will be available for producing other goods. Hence, the real cost of having more of one good is forgoing the opportunity of having more of another.

This concept of **opportunity cost** is fundamental to an understanding of the central economic problem—how to allocate scarce resources so as to maximize well-being. In order to make a rational decision whether to spend money to buy a new coat or whether to spend time going for a hike, it is not sufficient to know how much utility or satisfaction will be derived from each. Because the amount of money and time is limited, and we cannot buy and do everything, it is crucial also to be aware of how much satisfaction is lost by giving up desirable alternatives. **Rationality**, as economists use the term, involves some knowledge of available opportunities and the terms on which they are available. Only on the basis of such information is it possible to weigh the alternatives and choose those that provide more utility than any others.

One of the most fundamental assumptions in traditional economics is that people may be expected to behave rationally in this sense. It does not mean, as critics have occasionally suggested, that only monetary costs and benefits are considered. It is entirely rational to take into account nonpecuniary factors because *satisfaction,* not, say, money income, is to be maximized. This definition is so broad that almost everyone might be expected to behave this way. Nonetheless, rationality cannot be taken for granted. It is not satisfactory simply to argue that whatever a person does must provide more satisfaction than any alternative course of action because he or she would otherwise have made a different choice. Such an argument amounts to a mere tautology. An individual who blindly follows the traditional course of action without considering costs and benefits, or who fails to consider long-run implications or indirect effects is not necessarily rational. Nor is it uncommon to find persons who, with surprising regularity, make choices that they presently appear to regret. Most of us have probably known someone whose behavior fits one or more of these patterns.

These facts should be kept in mind, lest we accept too readily that whatever people do must be for the best. On the other hand, as a first approximation it is probably more realistic to assume that people tend to try to maximize their well-being rather than that they are indifferent to it. We shall, for the most part, accept this as a reasonable generalization, while recognizing that it is not necessarily appropriate in every instance. Specifically, it must be kept in mind that the knowledge needed to make optimal decisions is often difficult and costly to obtain. When this cost is likely to exceed the gain derived, it is rational to *satisfice* rather than to insist on maximization.[2] By the same

---

[2]This concept was first proposed by Herbert Simon in *Models of Man* (New York: Wiley, 1957). He argued that when the knowledge needed to make optimal decisions is difficult and costly to obtain, an individual may be content with selecting a "satisfactory" alternative—one that meets a minimum standard of acceptability.

token, however, when additional information can be provided relatively cheaply and easily, it is likely to be useful in improving decision making.

USES OF ECONOMIC THEORY

Assuming that individuals are rational is only one of the many simplifying assumptions economists tend to make in formulating **theories** and building **models**. The justification for making such assumptions is that, much like laboratory experiments in the biological and physical sciences, these abstractions help to focus attention on the particular issue we are attempting to clarify and on the main relationships we want to understand.

In many instances, the approach is to examine the effects of changes in a single variable, such as price or income, while assuming that all else remains the same. This approach does not suggest that economists believe the real world actually works in such a simple way. An aerospace engineer finds it useful to test a plane in a tunnel where everything except wind speed is artificially stabilized, even though the vehicle will later have to fly in an environment where temperature, atmospheric pressure, and humidity vary. Similarly, the social scientist finds it helpful to begin by abstracting from numerous complications.

A theory is not intended to be a full description of the underlying reality. A description is like a photograph, which shows reality in all its details. A theory may be likened to a modern painting, which at most shows the broad outlines of its subject but may provide deeper insight than a more realistic picture would. Hence, a theory or model should not be judged primarily on its detailed resemblance to reality, but rather in terms of the extent to which it enables us to grasp the salient features of that reality. Thus, economic theory, at its best, can help us to understand the present and to correctly predict the future.

Economists should not, therefore, be faulted for making simplifying assumptions or using abstractions, as long as they are aware of what they are doing and test their conclusions against empirical evidence, which is drawn from the real world with all its complexities. Unfortunately, such testing is not always easy to do. Computers now enable us to process vast amounts of information, and econometricians have made substantial progress in developing better methods for doing so. The availability, timeliness, and quality of the data, however, often still leave much to be desired.

Collecting data is a slow, expensive, and generally unglamorous undertaking. The U.S. government does more and better work in this respect than governments of many other countries. Even so, collecting, compiling, and publishing the information may take quite some time. Some data are, in any case, collected only intermittently, other data not at all. For a variety of reasons, including the government's appropriate reluctance to invade certain areas, as well as lack of interest in pursuing topics with no strong political constituency, some substantial gaps occur in official data collection. Private research organizations endeavor to fill these holes to a degree, but they are even more likely to be constrained by lack of necessary funds. The data from such special surveys are particularly likely to be collected sporadically or at lengthy intervals. Despite these difficulties, the possibilities for empirical work have improved beyond the wildest dreams of economists of even one or two generations ago.

When suitable data are available, evidence for some relationships can be obtained using such simple devices as averages and cross-tabulations. In other instances, however, sophisticated statistical methods are required to analyze the data. Such studies are time consuming, and rarely are conclusions from any one study regarded as final. At times ambiguities occur, with different sets of data or various approaches producing inconsistent results. Even so, such studies enhance the progress of science and help us to identify important areas for future research.

Because of these difficulties of data collection and analysis, timely and definitive answers are simply not available for every question. We have, however, done our best to summarize existing knowledge on each topic considered in this book.

THE SCOPE OF ECONOMICS

Traditionally, and for the most part even today, economics has focused on the market and on the government. In the market, goods and services are sold. Government is itself a major buyer and seller of goods and services and is also an agent that regulates and otherwise influences the economy. Only in recent decades have mainstream economists devoted any significant attention to the allocation of time within the household itself, and even now such material is not always included in general economics courses. Also, for the most part, the value of nonmarket household production is ignored when aggregate indicators of economic welfare, such as gross domestic product (GDP), are computed. This exclusion is a matter for concern, in part because women play the dominant role in the nonmarket sector. The U.S. government, following the lead of many other countries, has recently initiated a national survey that collects data on time spent in nonmarket activities that could be used in the future for this purpose. It also promises to provide greater insight into a number of issues related to how people allocate their nonmarket time. We point to data from this survey in our discussion of the division of labor within the family in Chapter 3.

In its microeconomics section, the typical introductory economics course puts primary emphasis on the analysis of product market transactions with the firm as seller, concerned with maximizing profits, and the household as buyer, concerned with maximizing satisfaction or utility. Later it introduces markets for factors of production, specifically labor, in which the household is generally the supplier and the firm the purchaser. As a rule, however, this discussion is a brief portion in the section on factors of production, and most students may well come away with a view of the market as chiefly an institution where goods and services are supplied by businesses, and the demand for them comes from the household.

In this book, our interest is most specifically in women and men, their work in the labor market and in the household, and the interdependence among individuals within the household. Therefore, we briefly review supply and demand in this context in the appendix to this chapter.

In a market economy, the forces of supply and demand for labor determine both the jobs that will be available and how much workers will be paid for doing them. Much of our analysis throughout this book will be concerned with the determinants of the supply of labor. We shall examine how individuals and their families decide to allocate their time between housework and market work and how women's changing roles in this regard are affecting their own well-being and that of their families.

Demand is essentially determined by the behavior of employers, who are in turn influenced by the business climate in which they operate. In the simplest case, their goal is to maximize profits, and their demand for labor is related to its productivity in making the goods or producing the services sold by the firm. Thus, the firm's demand for labor is *derived* from the demand of consumers for its final product. It is, however, possible that employers depart from the dictates of profit maximization and consider aspects of workers that are not directly related to their productivity. Discrimination is one such aspect. In this text, discrimination against women in the labor market and its role in producing wage and occupational differences between women and men is another topic that we shall explore in some depth. In doing so, we also take note of the fact that differences exist within each of these groups, most notably by race and ethnicity.

On the supply side, workers may influence their productivity by attending school or getting training on the job. We shall also consider the determinants of such human capital investment decisions and their role in producing gender differences in labor market outcomes.

INDIVIDUALS, FAMILIES, AND HOUSEHOLDS

Throughout this book, we shall at times focus on the behavior of families and, at other times, on that of individuals. A **family** is officially defined as consisting of two or more persons, related by blood, marriage, or adoption, living in the same household.[3] It is, of course, the individual who, in the last analysis, consumes commodities and supplies labor. Nonetheless, it is often appropriate to treat the family as the relevant economic unit because decisions of various members within a family are interdependent, much of their consumption is joint, and it is common for them to pool income. At the same time, it is important not to lose sight of the fact that the composition of families changes as individuals move in and out and that the interests of family members may diverge to a greater or lesser extent. We shall return to these issues throughout this book as we discuss the status of women and men within the family and in the labor market.

The broader concept of the **household** is also relevant to economic decision making and is becoming increasingly more so. A household consists of one or more persons living in one dwelling unit and sharing living expenses. Thus, all families are households, but one-person households, or those composed of unrelated individuals, are not families. The term *household* is more general than *family* and does greater justice to the increasing prevalence of alternative living arrangements; however, because families still constitute a substantial majority of households that include more than one person, and because the term *family* is more familiar and connotes a more uniform set of relationships, in this book we choose to use it primarily.

---

[3]This official definition is used in government statistics. The typical **nuclear family** is composed of married parents and children, but single-parent families are becoming increasingly common. An **extended family**, a type of unit more common in some other societies, may include grandparents, uncles, aunts, and other relatives. Cohabiting couples, who are also growing more prevalent, are not included in the official definition of a family. Also, as of 2004, with the exception of Massachusetts and a few localities, same-sex couples are not permitted to be legally married and hence are not recognized as a "family" in government statistics.

A NOTE ON TERMINOLOGY

Traditionally the terms *sex* and *gender* were used interchangeably to refer to the biological and social differences between women and men. More recently, it has become increasingly common to use the term *sex* to refer to the biological differences between males and females, and *gender* to encompass the distinctions society has erected on this biological base.[4] Thus, *gender* connotes a cultural or social construct, including distinctions in roles and behaviors as well as mental and emotional characteristics.[5] We see enough merit in this distinction between *sex* and *gender* that we have generally observed it in writing this book.

The question of appropriate language also arises with respect to racial and ethnic groups. Historically, people of African origin in the United States were generally called Negroes. Several decades ago the term *black* came into use, followed more recently by *African American*. For purposes of this book, we generally use *black*, mainly because *black* is the term that continues to be used in the official government statistics on which we frequently rely. For the same reason, and to keep terminology consistent in the text, we use the term *Hispanic* rather than other alternatives such as *Latino*.

OUTLINE OF THE BOOK

As suggested earlier, the primary focus of this book is on "economic woman," as she interacts and competes with "economic man." Economic behavior is not, however, treated in isolation from the remainder of human existence. To provide a more comprehensive picture, subsequent chapters will reflect insights from other social sciences, which enhance our understanding of a variety of factors. Such noneconomic factors help to determine economic behavior and how that behavior, in turn, shapes other aspects of life.

Chapter 2 deals with the historical evolution of the roles of women and men, focusing particularly on the United States. Chapter 3 considers the gender division of labor within the family, with special attention paid to the allocation of household tasks between men and women, as well as to alternative approaches to family decision making such as bargaining models. Chapter 4 analyzes the individual's decision about how to allocate his or her time between the household and the labor market, with emphasis placed on explaining the factors behind recent trends in women's and men's labor force participation.

The next four chapters deal specifically with women's position in the labor market as compared to that of men, beginning with an overview of gender differences in occupations and earnings in Chapter 5, followed by an in-depth examination of the various explanations of the existing situation. Specifically, Chapter 6 reviews the human capital approach, and Chapter 7 concentrates on discrimination as a possible cause of women's less favorable labor market outcomes. Chapter 8 rounds out the picture by considering some significant recent developments in the labor market. We especially focus on describing and explaining the substantial decrease in the gender pay gap that has occurred in recent years. We also examine a number of other recent developments

---

[4]Francine D. Blau, "Gender," in John Eatwell, Murray Milgate, and Peter Newman, eds., *The New Palgrave: A Dictionary of Economic Theory and Doctrine,* vol. 2 (London: MacMillan Press, 1987), p. 492.
[5]Helen Tierney, ed., *Women's Studies Encyclopedia* (New York: Greenwood Press, 1989), p. 153.

and their effects on women and men, including trends in real wages and growing wage inequality, the increasing payoff to education, trends in unemployment by gender, the growth of the nonstandard workforce, the rising self-employment of women, and the declining rate of unionization.

In Chapters 9 and 10 we return to the family. Chapter 9 examines the impact of women's employment on family structure and on the well-being of family members, with special attention paid to the growing number of dual-earner and single-parent families. Chapter 10 looks at a variety of policies affecting paid work and families, including those designed to alleviate poverty, government tax policies, and the growing number of "family-friendly" policies designed to assist individuals in balancing paid work and family responsibilities.

Finally, in Chapter 11, we compare the economic status of women relative to men throughout the world, with special emphasis on similarities and differences between the United States and other economically advanced nations. We also consider the particular problems and issues facing women in developing nations and in the countries of the former Soviet bloc. Substantial differences in the behaviors and economic status of men and women across countries suggest that particular outcomes are not inevitable but rather are subject to choice. In instances where a country appears to have impressive achievements in gender equality to its credit, we may be able to learn from the experiences there.

APPENDIX 1A

A Review of Supply and Demand in the Labor Market

As we explained in Chapter 1, supply and demand provide economists with a framework for analyzing labor markets. We briefly review these concepts here in the context of a particular type of labor, clerical workers.

Curve *DD* in Figure 1-1 shows the typical downward-sloping **demand curve**. Wage rate (price) is on the vertical axis, and quantity (number of workers) is on the horizontal axis. The demand curve represents the various amounts of labor that would be hired at various prices by firms in this labor market over a given period of time. If all else remains the same, including methods of production and prices of other inputs, changes in the wage rate cause movements along this curve. In this case, a change occurs

in the *quantity demanded,* but demand (i.e., the demand curve) remains the same. If, on the other hand, other factors do not remain the same, the entire demand curve may shift.

Demand curves are normally expected to slope downward to the right, which means that the firm will hire more workers at a lower wage rate and fewer at a higher wage rate. There are several reasons for this. The first is that in the short run there is **diminishing marginal productivity** of labor, meaning that additional units of labor provide progressively less additional output when combined with fixed amounts of capital (plant and equipment). Capital can only be expanded or contracted over a longer period of time, which means that the only way to immediately increase output is to hire additional workers or have workers put in longer hours. The second is the **substitution**

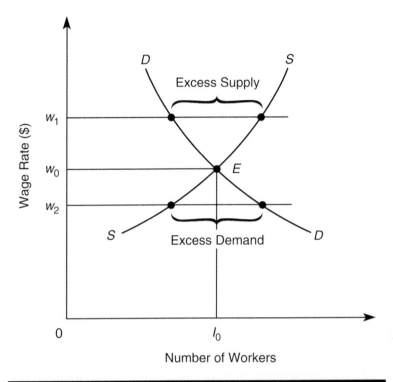

FIGURE 1-1 The Market for Clerical Workers

effect. When the price of a particular input changes, while prices of potential substitutes remain the same, the tendency is for profit-maximizing employers to use more of the input that is now relatively cheaper and less of the input that is now relatively more expensive. In the short run, for example, less-skilled labor may be substituted for more-skilled workers. In the long run, it may be possible to substitute capital for labor. Last, the **scale effect** can operate in both the short and long run. As wages increase, the price of the product will go up, less of it will be purchased, and fewer workers will be employed. The scale effect is likely to be especially large when wages constitute a substantial part of the costs of production, as is usually the case for services. These factors cause the quantity of labor hired to decrease as the wage rate increases, but the movements are along the given demand curve and do not involve a shift of the demand curve.

The **supply curve**, shown by *SS* in Figure 1-1, slopes upward and to the right. It shows the number of workers who would be willing to do clerical work at all possible prices. The supply curve is upward sloping because, if rewards for one type of job increase while those for all others remain the same, additional workers will be attracted from related occupations. So, for example, an increase in the wages of clerical workers may induce individuals who are currently employed in other jobs to improve their clerical skills and compete for clerical positions. Similarly, if pay for clerical work declines relative to others, the quantity of labor supplied to clerical jobs is expected to decline as workers move to other sectors.

It is important to emphasize that the supply curve depicted in Figure 1-1 represents the number of individuals available for a particular line of work. As we shall see in greater detail in Chapter 4, the number of hours supplied to the market by any particular individual may not increase when wages rise. This situation may happen because, at a higher wage rate, an individual who participates in the labor market may choose to allocate more of his or her time to nonmarket activities and the satisfactions they bring.

The intersection of the supply and demand curves shown in Figure 1-1 represents a **stable equilibrium**. An equilibrium exists when all persons willing to work at the going rate are able to find employment and all employers willing to hire someone at the going rate are able to find workers. In other words, the quantity demanded and the quantity supplied are equal at E, and no forces are causing the wage to move from its present level as long as no external shocks take place. In this case, the equilibrium wage is w_0, and the equilibrium quantity of labor employed is l_0. To illustrate why point E represents a *stable* equilibrium, let us assume that, for whatever reason, the wage rate is initially set higher than w_0, say at w_1. At this point, the quantity of labor supplied would exceed the quantity of labor demanded and push wages down toward E. Conversely, if wages were initially set at w_2, the opposite would be true. In short, we have a stable equilibrium when there is no tendency to move away from E. If an external shock were to cause a deviation, the tendency would be to return to E.

External shocks may, of course, also cause shifts in demand, supply, or both, leading to a new equilibrium. Such shocks may come from changes in markets for goods, for nonlabor inputs, or for other types of labor, and they are extremely common. Therefore, a stable equilibrium is not necessarily one

that remains fixed for any length of time. It merely means that at any given time the tendency is toward convergence at the point where the quantity of labor supplied equals the quantity of labor demanded, until conditions cause this point to shift.

It may be instructive to consider a couple of examples of shifts in the supply or demand curves. These sample situations can help to clarify the difference between factors that cause a movement along an existing supply or demand curve and those that cause a shift in the entire curve. We shall also be able to see how the new equilibrium position is established.

Suppose that the government issues a report on the dangers of credit spending and that it is effective enough to cause a reduction in the demand for such services provided by the banking industry. That is, at any given price of these services, consumers demand less of them. Because this industry employs a substantial number of clerical workers, such a change would cause a marked inward shift in the marketwide demand curve for clerical workers, from DD to $D'D'$ in Figure 1-2a. At any given wage rate, then, firms are willing to hire fewer clerical workers. This example illustrates that the demand for labor is a *derived* demand: It is derived from consumer demand for the goods and services that the workers produce. A new equilibrium will occur at E_1, where the quantity of labor supplied again equals the (new) quantity of labor demanded. At E_1, fewer individuals are employed as clerical workers and a lower wage rate is determined for that occupation.

Shifts in supply curves can also alter the market equilibrium, as shown in Figure 1-2b. For instance, suppose that the government's antidiscrimination policies increase opportunities for women in managerial jobs, raising their wages and making it easier for them to obtain such employment. This change will result in a reduction in the

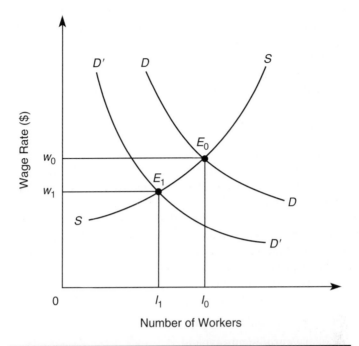

FIGURE 1-2a   A Shift in Demand

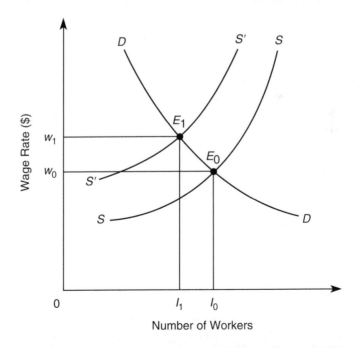

FIGURE 1-2b   A Shift in Supply

supply (inward shift in the supply curve) of clerical workers, an occupation staffed primarily by women. At any given wage, fewer women would be available to work in clerical jobs than previously. At the new equilibrium (E_1), the wages are higher, and the number of workers employed is lower than in the initial situation (E_0). This example illustrates that improved opportunities for women in traditionally male jobs can potentially improve the economic welfare even of those women who remain in traditionally female pursuits.

Questions for Review and Discussion

1. Define scarcity and explain why the concept is so central to neoclassical economics.
2. In everyday language *cost* generally means the amount of money it takes to purchase a commodity. Can this meaning be tied to the concept of opportunity cost and, if so, how?
3. Discuss the uses and abuses of simplifying assumptions in economic models.
4. Using a graph, show how each of the following labor markets (assumed to be competitive and initially in equilibrium) is affected by the following changes. Clearly explain your reasoning.
   a. Labor market for math and science teachers.

   Wages available in private industries utilizing these skills rise.

   b. Labor market for university professors.

   College enrollments expand.

   c. Labor market for low-skilled workers.

   The 1996 federal welfare legislation requires that a much larger fraction of welfare recipients work than in the past.

   d. Labor market for workers who completed high school only.

   The workplace becomes more computerized and technically sophisticated.

   e. Labor market for workers who completed college or more.

   The workplace becomes more computerized and technically sophisticated.

2

WOMEN AND MEN: CHANGING ROLES IN A CHANGING ECONOMY

Chapter Highlights

■ The Nature of Males and Females

■ The Role of Sociobiology in Explaining Gender Differences

■ Factors Influencing Women's Relative Status

■ Women's Roles and Economic Development

■ The U.S. Experience

It seems to me that an economic interpretation of history is an indispensable element in the study of society, but it is only one element. In layers below it lie geography, biology and psychology, and in layers above it the investigation of social and political relationships and the history of culture, law and religion.

—JOAN ROBINSON
*Freedom and Necessity**

We are constantly told today that we live in an era of rapid change—change in economic conditions, in economic and social institutions, in mores and beliefs. And so we do. Changes in the roles of women and men, their relations to each other, and the nature of the families in which most of them continue to live take place at an unprecedented speed. This situation inevitably creates stresses and strains. Not surprisingly, people who feel insecure

---

*Joan Robinson, *Freedom and Necessity: An Introduction to the Study of Society* (London: George Allen and Unwin, 1970), p. 5.

in a world of shifting boundaries and values are prone to look back with nostalgia to the "good old days" when women were women and men were men, and both "knew their proper place."

How realistic is this picture some hold of traditional gender roles, unchanging for all time and pervasive for all places, which is supposed to have existed before the recent era of turmoil and upheaval? The answer to this question has substantial practical implications. If the same roles of women and men have existed always and everywhere, some may conclude that these roles are biologically determined and that they probably cannot, and perhaps should not, be changed. If, on the other hand, the roles of men and women experienced a good deal of variation over time, it is likely that there is also room for flexibility now and in the future.

For this reason, gaining some insight into the nature of changing gender roles through the course of human development is very valuable. Further, awareness of the complexities of history is indispensable for an understanding of the present. It is also crucial if we are to make any progress toward correctly anticipating the future. The following brief historical review shows that, although the rate may have been a great deal slower in the past, change is the one constant. Furthermore, societies throughout time have been characterized by a diversity of economic and social institutions.

We begin by briefly considering the biological and anthropological evidence about the nature of males and females and the sociobiologist's explanation for gender differences. This discussion takes us away from traditional economics somewhat, but provides valuable background for the historical analysis that follows. Here we consider the changing roles of men and women in the household and in the economy, and the evolution of the family, in the course of economic development through the period of industrialization that started in the nineteenth century. Although other factors are not ignored, economic causation is assigned the predominant role in shaping these changes. The focus is primarily on the United States.

THE NATURE OF MALES AND FEMALES

As late as the 1970s, a common interpretation of the behavior of, and relation between, men and women emphasized the importance of "man the hunter" and of the biological maternal function of the female in determining the nature and content of her being.[1] In this view, a woman's early life is a preparation for becoming, and her later life is devoted to being, a successful wife and mother. Accordingly, her nature is compliant, not competitive; nurturant, not instrumental. Her activities, though not necessarily confined to the home, at least center around it, for her primary mission is to be a helpmate to her husband and to provide a warm and safe haven for her family. If she does work for pay, she will do best in jobs compatible with her household responsibilities and her "feminine" personality. Men, on the other hand, are not constrained by their paternal function from fully entering the world outside the home. On the contrary, their natural role as provider and protector spurs them on to greater efforts.

Based on this early work, the popular perception was often that investigations of male and female roles among nonhuman species provided support for the view that

---

[1] See, for example, Lionel Tiger, *Men in Groups* (New York: Random House, 1969).

biology is destiny.[2] However, more recent research suggests that no generalization holds for all species and that extrapolation from animal studies does not support the traditional view of male dominance and aggressiveness, and of female passivity and nurturance. Many of the new studies of various animal groups show evidence of "female dominance, autonomy, and power; of male nurturance and cooperation; and of monogamous behavior as well as promiscuity in both males and females."[3] This evidence signals caution about the argument that any attribute or behavior is always male or female, even if generalizing from animals to humans were otherwise acceptable. Such generalization is itself debatable. An alternative approach suggests that what distinguishes Homo sapiens from other species is that, for humans, it is primarily the norms and expectations of their societies, not blind animal instincts, that are important in shaping their actions and their relations. In this view, biology constrains, but does not determine, human behavior. Human gender roles are no more limited to those of animals than is human behavior otherwise limited to that of animals.[4]

There are, to be sure, physiological and psychological differences between men and women but, it is argued, they fail to adequately explain all existing variations in behavior or why female traits are so often viewed as socially inferior to male traits. Biological nature, which determines the difference between the sexes, is seen as a broad base upon which a variety of structures, with respect to socially determined gender differences, can be built. This hypothesis is consistent with the diverse male and female roles that sprang up under varying conditions in early societies, in spite of the fact that some differentiation of the work and roles of men and women seems to have been present in all known instances. Anthropologists of this school point out that women vary in their social roles and powers, their public status, and their cultural definitions, and that the nature, quantity, and social significance of women's activities are far more varied and interesting than often assumed. At the same time, other scientists emphasize biology, and particularly the biological origin of differences between men and women, and nature as well as nurture. As a result, sociobiology is once again enjoying a great deal of attention.

THE ROLE OF SOCIOBIOLOGY IN EXPLAINING GENDER DIFFERENCES

Since the publication in 1975 of Edward O. Wilson's *Sociobiology: The New Synthesis*, sociobiologists have followed Darwin's theory of natural selection and have argued that genes determine human as well as animal traits.[5] Their views created a good deal of uneasiness among social scientists, because, in the past, social Darwinism had been

---

[2] Foremost among these were Robert Ardrey, *The Territorial Imperative* (New York: Atheneum Press, 1966); Desmond Morris, *The Human Zoo* (New York: McGraw-Hill, 1969); and Lionel Tiger and Robin Fox, *The Imperial Animal* (New York: Holt, Rinehart & Winston, 1971).

[3] Cynthia F. Epstein, *Deceptive Distinctions: Sex, Gender, and the Social Order* (New Haven, CT: Yale University Press, 1988), p. 59.

[4] This view was first emphasized by anthropologists such as Ernestine Friedl, *Women and Men: An Anthropologist's View* (New York: Holt, Rinehart & Winston, 1975); and Michelle Z. Rosaldo and Louise Lamphere, eds., *Women, Culture and Society* (Stanford: Stanford University Press, 1974).

[5] Edward O. Wilson, *Sociobiology: The New Synthesis* (Cambridge, MA: Belknap Press of Harvard University Press, 1975). For a critique see, Betty Rosoff and Ethel Tobach, "Introduction," in *Challenging Racism and Sexism: Alternatives to Genetic Explanations*, edited by Ethel Tobach and Betty Rosoff (New York: Feminist Press of the City University of New York, 1994), pp. 1–30.

used to justify such causes as colonialism, imperialism, racism, sexism and, at its worst, mass murder.[6] Selective criteria were frequently employed to indicate superiority and inferiority in order to justify the exploitation and subjection of particular groups. For instance, it was after Africans were enslaved to further the economic well-being of their owners that criteria such as skull volume and brain size were constructed to rationalize and justify this practice, while criteria that did not favor white men were discarded.[7]

Recent decades saw much change in this way of thinking. On the one hand, sociobiology today differs from the social Darwinism of the nineteenth century. On the other hand, social scientists who were reluctant to incorporate biological variables in their models are now increasingly ready to embrace the notion that many patterns of human behavior have a basis in evolution. They also make room for the possibility that male and female brains, although similar, may function differently.[8] Similarly, they recognize that although measured attributes of individual boys and girls reveal few consistent sex differences, children show a powerful tendency to seek out playmates of the same sex, and groups of boys and of girls are different from each other. Further, they accept that such differences greatly influence their development.[9] Nonetheless, significant unresolved questions remain. The sociobiological explanation of existing differences between women and men in preferences for mates provides a good example.

Research in the 1960s and 1970s showed that women placed considerable emphasis on finding good providers, while men were looking for relatively young women who would bear children and be good homemakers. This behavior is seen as the result of differential selection pressures experienced by ancestral humans. Women needed mates who were able and willing to support them and their children, while men wanted partners who would bear and nurture their children, as well as tend home and hearth. By virtue of their youth, women at the beginning of their childbearing age were also likely to possess physical characteristics that came to be accepted as standards of beauty. Women who conformed to these standards tended to experience greater reproductive success than those who did not, passing their genes on to their offspring. Similarly, intelligence, aggression, and territoriality, "all characteristics of the stereotypical male,"[10] were qualities that enabled the men who possessed them to leave more offspring than others. Hence these attributes, inherited by sons from their fathers who were more successful at surviving and reproducing, increased in frequency during subsequent generations.

---

[6]Melwin Konner, "Darwin's Truth, Jefferson's Vision: Sociobiology and the Politics of Human Nature," *American Prospect* 45 (July 1999): 30–38.

[7]Ruth Hubbard, "Race and Sex as Biological Categories," in *Challenging Racism and Sexism: Alternatives to Genetic Explanations*, edited by Ethel Tobach and Betty Rosoff (New York: Feminist Press of the City University of New York, 1994), pp. 11–21.

[8]Deborah Blum, *Sex on the Brain: The Biological Differences Between Men and Women* (New York: Viking Penguin, 1997); Doreen Kimura, "Sex Differences in the Brain," Scentific American.com (May 13, 2002); and Natalie Angier and Kenneth Chang, "Gray Matter and the Sexes: Still a Scientific Gray Area," *New York Times* (January 24, 2005).

[9]Eleanor Maccoby, *The Two Sexes: Growing Up Apart, Coming Together* (Cambridge, MA: Harvard University Press, 1998), p. 287.

[10]Gisela Kaplan and Lesley J. Rogers, "Race and Gender Fallacies: The Paucity of Biological Determinist Explanations of Difference," in *Challenging Racism and Sexism: Alternatives to Genetic Explanations,* edited by Ethel Tobach and Betty Rosoff (New York: Feminist Press of the City University of New York, 1994), p. 76.

Thus, preferences that served their purpose well in the past presumably became part of men's and women's sexual natures and are maintained throughout the world to this day. Therefore, while fully recognizing the complex interaction between biology and voluntarily chosen behavior,[11] sociobiologists generally conclude that, in spite of some psychological differences among individuals, the basic characteristics of the sexes are extremely difficult to change. This view is supported by the finding of one study that women who are financially independent are as likely as those who are not to have a preference for good providers.[12] This finding would clearly not be expected if women were merely motivated by rational economic concerns. At the same time, men particularly value physical appearance and prefer mates who are a few years younger than they are, while women seek somewhat older men who are arguably more reliable providers.

This sociobiological view of differences between the sexes does shed a good deal of light on the behavior and social organization of animals—including humans. It is not surprising, then, that it has been widely accepted not only among researchers in natural history and animal behavior, but also among many psychologists and other social scientists. Even so, critical reservations about this interpretation deserve to be taken seriously. Further, neo-Darwinist theory, accepted by Wilson and his followers, often leads to oversimplifications, which is most likely a major reason why it has not replaced other behavioral sciences, but has rather become a small, albeit significant, part of the whole field.

One of the objections to this explanation of human behavior is that it views gene replication as the main or even sole purpose of life,[13] with reproduction taking precedence even over survival.[14] Moreover as a number of authors point out,[15] the tendency is to exaggerate biological differences between women and men, to emphasize distinctions rather than to recognize the many similarities, and to ignore the great diversities within each group. It is, for example, common to stress the difference in means of height, strength, math SATs, and so forth, rather than the fact that the range for each substantially overlaps. The same attitude is indicated by use of the phrase "the opposite sex" rather than "the other sex."

An alternative to the uncritical acceptance or rejection of sociobiology is a middle course. This new approach embraces many elements of evolutionary theory, but no longer imposes rigid limits on social change as early theories did;[16] it accepts the importance of biology without ignoring the possibility that function may to some extent influence structure.[17] It leaves room for adaptation in behavior to changing circumstances. For instance, in earlier days men may have looked for women who would make good mothers, while women generally looked for men who would make good providers, but this observation does not preclude the possibility that men today increasingly prefer

---

[11]Maccoby, *Two Sexes.*

[12]Michael W. Wiederman and Elizabeth Rice Allgeier, "Mate Selection," in *Human Sexuality: An Encyclopedia,* edited by Vern L. Bullough and Bonnie Bullough (Buffalo, NY: Garland Publishing, 1994), pp. 386–90.

[13]Kaplan and Rogers, "Race and Gender Fallacies."

[14]Konner, "Darwin's Truth."

[15]Hubbard, "Race and Sex"; and Blum, *Sex on the Brain.*

[16]Discussed in Cynthia Russett, *Sexual Science: The Victorian Construction of Womanhood* (Cambridge, MA: Harvard University Press, 1989).

[17]Blum, *Sex on the Brain,* p. 41.

women able to share in supporting the family, and that women search for men who are likely to become nurturing fathers and partners in homemaking. This view is supported by findings that male and female preferences for characteristics of mates are slowly becoming more similar.[18]

In sum, all differences in the roles of men and women are not likely to disappear. This statement is supported by the evidence that women tend to spend a significantly larger share of their time and income on their children.[19] Importantly, however, recognition of differences need not mean that superiority and dominance is assigned to characteristics of one sex, and inferiority and submissiveness to those of the other. It is, for instance, now acknowledged that in some species among primates, males are dominant by virtue of their strength and aggressiveness, but in other species females dominate over individualistic males by virtue of having formed strong group bonds.[20] Nor is there any reason to accept traits of males as the standard and the traits of women as deviant. For example, devoting time to care of the young and the old at the expense of maximizing earnings in the labor market need not be viewed as aberrant behavior. In other words, the most realistic and also the most constructive approach is likely to be one that recognizes the role of both biology and the environment, of limitations imposed by heredity and the opportunities for overcoming them, and of the importance of history as well as the possibility for progress.

FACTORS INFLUENCING WOMEN'S RELATIVE STATUS

In their studies of human societies, anthropologists, particularly women anthropologists who began to focus on this issue in the 1970s, agree that the relative status of women has varied over time and across societies. There is less agreement regarding the factors determining their relative position. Although it may not be possible to definitively answer this question at present, some important insights can be gained by considering existing theories.

Ernestine Friedl was one of the first anthropologists to emphasize the importance of environmental constraints in shaping human organization.[21] She argues that the technology employed by a society to produce the necessities of life has tended, in the past, to determine the division of labor on the basis of gender. She also believes that the more important women's role is in production and in controlling distribution outside the family, the higher their status compared to men. Friedl and others espousing this view point to the relatively egalitarian situation in primitive societies where men and women shared in providing food, clothing, and shelter for their families or, in modern days, when both earn an income. In contrast, the status of men and women was unequal in societies where men provided all the needed resources and women devoted

---

[18]Wiederman and Allgeier, "Mate Selection."

[19]Rae L. Blumberg, "Income Under Female versus Male Control: Hypotheses from a Theory of Gender Stratification and Data from the Third World," *Journal of Family Issues* 9, no. 1 (March 1988): 51–84; and Shelly J. Lundberg, Robert A. Pollak, and Terence J. Wales, "Do Husbands and Wives Pool Their Resources? Evidence from the U.K. Child Benefit," *Journal of Human Resources* 32, no. 3 (Summer 1997): 463–80.

[20]Blum, *Sex on the Brain*, p. 73.

[21]Friedl, *Women and Men*. See also Joan Huber and Glenna Spitze, *Sex Stratification: Children, Housework, and Jobs* (New York: Academic Press, 1983).

themselves to transforming these resources into usable form and creating a pleasant atmosphere in which they could be used.

Others tend to disagree, at least with the emphasis on the importance of production roles in determining status. In past epochs, slaves did a great deal of productive work without achieving correspondingly high status, and members of the upper class derived their power and prestige from ownership of wealth rather than from any work they did. Few dispute, however, the fact that property gives owners power over distribution and that this power helps to determine status.

We are inclined toward the view that the structure of social relationships and participation in productive work both play a role. Specifically, in the case of women, it appears that sharing in the provision for the family's needs is a necessary, though not a sufficient, ingredient in achieving a greater degree of equality.[22] Clearly, the extent to which women's activities are confined to the home, while men monopolize the public sphere, also plays an important role.[23]

In the remainder of this chapter, we explore how changing technology and changing property relations affect the nature and perception of gender roles, focusing primarily on the United States. First, however, we briefly consider the issue of the relationship between women's roles and economic development in more general terms.

WOMEN'S ROLES AND ECONOMIC DEVELOPMENT

In technologically primitive **hunting and gathering societies**, men and women shared in providing food, clothing, and shelter for their families. Men hunted large animals and defended the tribe, whereas women gathered a variety of vegetable foods, occasionally hunted small animals,[24] and had the main responsibility for food preparation and care of children. Such a division of labor was undoubtedly expedient when women were pregnant or nursing most of their adult lives, and thus could not participate in activities that would have taken them far from home. The greater strength of men also gave them a considerable advantage for such activities as hunting large animals and fighting.

The extent to which men and women contributed to the necessities of life was determined by the availability of various resources, and women's status appeared to vary accordingly. In general, the fact that men provided for the safety of the tribe and furnished most of the meat, always regarded as the prestige food, gave them the advantage. Nonetheless, the common payment of the bride price suggests that women were also valued for their contributions.

In the somewhat more advanced **horticultural societies**, plants were cultivated in small plots located near the home. Men continued to conduct warfare and also prepared the ground by slashing and burning; women prepared the food and cared for infants.

[22]Joyce M. Nielsen, *Sex and Gender in Society: Perspectives and Stratification,* 2nd ed. (Prospect Heights, IL: Waveland Press, Inc., 1990).

[23]Michelle Z. Rosaldo, "Women, Culture, and Society: A Theoretical Overview," in *Women, Culture, and Society,* edited by Michelle Z. Rosaldo and Louise Lamphere (Stanford: Stanford University Press, 1974). See also Julie A. Matthaei, *An Economic History of Women in America* (New York: Schocken Books, 1982).

[24]Some evidence suggests that women may have participated in hunting more than was acknowledged earlier, especially in tribes where group hunting was common. See, for instance, Agnes Estioko-Griffin and P. Bion Griffin, "Woman the Hunter: The Agta," in *Woman the Gatherer,* edited by Frances Dahlberg (New Haven, CT: Yale University Press, 1981), pp. 121–52.

Virtually all other activities were shared. Accordingly, men and women tended to be considerably more equal during this stage than in the agricultural societies that would follow.

In **pastoral societies**, on the other hand, men tended to monopolize the herding of large animals, an activity that often took them far from home. Herding provided the bulk of what was needed for subsistence. Women's contributions were largely confined to tending the primitive equivalent of hearth and home, and females never reached more than a subservient status.

The situation changed radically when horticultural societies were superseded by **agricultural societies**, which arrived with the introduction of the plow. Although women "helped" in the fields,[25] looked after small animals and gardens, and worked in the now permanent homes taking care of large families, only men owned and worked the land, and the disparity in power and influence became great indeed. The **dowry**, paid by the father of the bride to the groom, who henceforth undertakes her support, and **purdah**, the practice of hiding women from the sight of men, came into use during that period in some of these societies. Both may be viewed as ways of subordinating women as well as signs of their subjugation.

One factor helped to offset this lowly position for at least a small minority of women. As ownership of land and other assets created an upper class of landed gentry, membership in that class entailed great wealth and power. Under these conditions, birth in the right family conferred status even on women. Property was generally owned and inherited by men, but in the absence of a male heir in a ruling family, a woman might even become head of state.[26] For example, ruling queens included the well-known Elizabeth I of England. In general, however, while upper-class females enjoyed a rather luxurious lifestyle, they were mainly seen as producers of children, rarely had influence except as behind-the-scenes manipulators, and were typically used as pawns in political and economic alliances. Only in exceptional cases did women achieve important roles in the economy and in the development of culture, aided by achieving high rank in religious orders in some instances or by the extended absence of fighting men in others.

Women were also more likely to be partners, though not equal ones, among the growing class of merchants and artisans in the urban centers that began to grow along with developing agriculture. They participated in what were, in those early days, truly family enterprises, generally took charge when the men traveled on business, and often continued to be in charge after the husband died. Household and workplace were not rigidly separated, nor were consumption and production. Father, mother, children, perhaps other relatives, and often apprentices lived and worked together. Yet their tasks and responsibilities were determined by their age and by their sex. Whenever the father was present, he was the head of the family enterprise.

As we have seen, women tended to have a higher status in horticultural societies than in agricultural ones, in which women's activities came to be increasingly centered within the home. Nonetheless, because much production was concentrated in the household, and because women were active participants, they continued to be perceived as productive

---

[25]Very poor women also worked as hired laborers and domestic servants.

[26]Only recently have any women become heads of state who were not born into the position, and even today they tend to come from the upper classes.

members of the family, albeit not equal partners.[27] During the early stages of **industrialization**, on the other hand, much of the production previously concentrated in the household was shifted from the home to the factory and the office. This shift reduced the burden of housekeeping but did little to advance the status of women, who, for the most part, continued to center their activities around the home. Indeed, the perceived importance of their productive role initially tended to decline, as did their relative status. In time, however, continued industrialization began to draw ever-increasing numbers of women into the paid labor force, paving the way for a "subtle revolution" in gender roles.[28] In the following sections, we review this process in greater detail, focusing upon the situation in the United States.

The case of the United States is in some respects unique, even in comparison to other economically advanced countries. In particular, the frontier experience was shared by only a few of these countries, such as Canada and Australia. Nonetheless, the broad contours of the shifts outlined here are to some extent applicable to many of them. Indeed, the alteration of men's and women's work roles occurring in the United States today may be seen as part of a transformation taking place in much of the industrialized world. (Recent developments in other countries are discussed in greater detail in Chapter 11.)

THE U.S. EXPERIENCE

The Preindustrial Period

In colonial America, as in other preindustrial economies, the family enterprise was the dominant economic unit, and production was the major function of the family.[29] Most of the necessities for survival were produced in the household, though some goods were generally produced for sale, the proceeds of which were used to purchase some market goods and to accumulate wealth. Cooking; cleaning; care of the young, the old, and the infirm; spinning; weaving; sewing; knitting; soap and candle making; and simple carpentry were carried on in the home. Much of the food and other raw materials were grown on the farm. All members of the family capable of making any contribution participated in production, but there was always some specialization and division of labor.

Among the nonslave population, men were primarily responsible for agriculture and occasionally trade, whereas women did much of the rest of the work, including what would today be characterized as "light manufacturing" activity. But gender-role specialization was by no means complete. Slave women were used to work in the fields. Widows tended to take over the family enterprise when the need arose, and in early days, single women were on occasion given "maidplots." Even though men and women often had different tasks, and men were more often involved in production for the market and

---

[27]Nancy Folbre, *Who Pays for the Kids?* (London: Routledge, 1994), p. 135.

[28]Ralph E. Smith, "The Movement of Women into the Labor Force," in *The Subtle Revolution: Women at Work,* edited by Ralph E. Smith (Washington, DC: Urban Institute, 1979), pp. 1–29.

[29]A more detailed account of the position of women during the colonial era and the early years of the Republic may be found in Alice Kessler-Harris, *Out to Work: A History of America's Wage Earning Women* (New York: Oxford University Press, 1982), pp. 3–45.

generally owned all property, everyone participated in productive activity. Even aged grandparents would help with tasks that required responsibility and judgment and would perhaps also supervise children in carrying out small chores they could adequately perform from an early age.

All family members, except for infants, had essentially the same economic role. They either contributed goods and services directly or earned money by selling some of these in the market. The important economic role of children, as well as the plentiful availability of land, encouraged large families. High infant mortality rates provided a further incentive to bear many children. In the eighteenth century, completed fertility may have averaged as many as 8 to 10 births per woman.[30]

Wealthy women were primarily managers, not workers, within the household. Their work was, no doubt, less arduous and possibly more rewarding, but no less absorbing. Most women, regardless of their affluence, experienced little role conflict. The ideal of the frugal, industrious housewife working alongside her family corresponded closely to reality. The only women for whom this picture was not true were the poorest women, who often became indentured servants, and, of course, black women, who were generally slaves. The former were, as a rule, not permitted to marry during their years of servitude; the latter might potentially have their family entirely disrupted by their owners' choice. Both had to work very hard, and slaves did not even have the modest legal protection of rights that indentured servants enjoyed.

The one thing all these diverse groups had in common was that they were productive members of nearly self-sufficient households. Government played a minimal role, and although some exchange of goods and services, chiefly barter, took place, it was not until well into the nineteenth century that production outside the home, for sale rather than for direct use, came to dominate the economy.

Industrialization

During the early period of industrialization in the late eighteenth and early nineteenth centuries, women (and children) in the United States, as elsewhere, worked in the textile mills and other industries that sprang up in the East. Initially, primarily young farm girls were employed in the factories, often contributing part of their pay to supplement family income and using some to accumulate a "dowry" that would make them more desirable marriage partners. The employment of these young women in factories may have appeared quite natural to observers at the time. They were doing much the same type of work they had done in the home, only in a new location and under the supervision of a foreman rather than the head of the household.[31] Once married, women generally left their jobs to look after their own households, which would soon include children.

The earliest available data show that at the end of the nineteenth century, when the labor force participation rate for men was 84 percent, only 18 percent of all women were in the paid labor force, and the percentage of married women who worked outside the

---

[30]For a description of demographic trends during this period, see Karl E. Taeuber and James A. Sweet, "Family and Work: The Social Life Cycle of Women," in *Women and the American Economy: A Look to the 1980s,* edited by Juanita M. Kreps (Englewood Cliffs, NJ: Prentice Hall, 1976), pp. 31–60.
[31]This similarity was pointed out by Edith Abbott, *Women in Industry* (New York: Appleton and Company, 1910). For a recent discussion, see Dora L. Costa, "From Mill Town to Board Room: The Rise of Women's Paid Labor," *Journal of Economic Perspectives* 14, no. 4 (Fall 2000): 101–22.

home was only 5 percent.[32] The situation was different for black women. About 23 percent of black wives were employed. Most of these women worked either as domestics or in agriculture in the rural South. Although such early industries as textiles, millinery, and cigars did employ women, mainly young single ones, the new, rapidly growing sophisticated industries relied from the beginning almost entirely on male workers.

Among some immigrant groups, however, who in the course of the nineteenth century increasingly replaced American-born workers in factories, it was not uncommon even for married women to be employed.[33] Most of these people came to the New World determined to improve their economic condition and particularly to make sure that their children would get a better start than they did. At times, the whole family worked. Often if a choice needed to be made between the children leaving school to supplement family income or the mother seeking employment, the latter choice was made even among groups traditionally reluctant to have women work outside the home. By the same token, maternal employment was associated with dire need and was viewed as a temporary expedient to give the family a better start. Few wives remained in the labor force once the husband earned enough for an adequate living. The immigrants' goal of achieving the desired standard of living included what by then was widely considered the American ideal of the family—the male breadwinner who supported his family and the female homemaker who cared for his domestic needs.

Industrialization and the Evolution of the Family

As an increasingly larger segment of the population began living in urban centers rather than on farms, and family shops were replaced by factories, women found that their household work increasingly came to be confined to the care of children, the nurturing of the husband, and the maintenance of the home. They no longer had responsibility for tending a garden, caring for farm animals, or providing seasonal help with the crops. Further, they less often had an opportunity to participate in a family business. As husbands left the home to earn the income needed to support their families, a more rigid division developed between the female domestic sphere and the male public sphere.

Thus, along with industrialization in the nineteenth century arose the concept of the **traditional family**, which lingered to a greater or lesser degree well into the twentieth century.[34] The family shifted from a production unit to a consumption unit, and the

---

[32]All labor force participation figures cited here are from Claudia Goldin, *Understanding the Gender Gap: An Economic History of American Women* (New York: Oxford University Press, 1990), with the exception of the overall male and female participation rates, which are from U.S. Census Bureau, *Historical Statistics of the United States: Colonial Times to 1970,* part 1 (1975), pp. 131–32. As discussed later, official figures undoubtedly underestimate the proportion of women who worked for pay. Not only was seasonal work frequently ignored, but work done in the home, such as taking in boarders and bringing home piecework, was often overlooked as well.

[33]Milton Cantor and Bruce Laurie, eds., *Class, Sex and the Woman Worker* (Westport, CT: Greenwood Press, 1977) contains a great deal of interesting information on immigrant women during the early years.

[34]Historian Carl N. Degler termed this shift the "first transformation." In his view, the second transformation came in the 1940s, when married women began to enter the labor market in large numbers. See his *At Odds: Women and the Family in America from the Revolution to the Present* (New York: Oxford University Press, 1980). It was also during this period that women's work in the household came to be officially classified as unproductive, as pointed out by Nancy Folbre, "The Unproductive Housewife: Her Evolution in Nineteenth-Century Economic Thought," *Signs: Journal of Women in Culture and Society* 16, no. 3 (Spring 1991): 463–84.

responsibility for earning a living came to rest squarely on the shoulders of the husband. Wives (and children) grew to be dependent on his income. Redistribution became an important function of the family, as it provided a mechanism for the transfer of income from the market-productive husband to his dependent wife and children. Not only did specific *tasks* differ between men and women, as was always the case, but men and women now had different *economic roles* as well. Many workers and social reformers explicitly advocated that a man should be paid a "family wage," adequate to support not only him but also his wife and children.

As we have seen, among the poor, particularly blacks and immigrants, it was often necessary for wives to enter the labor market. But for the middle-class white wife, and even for the working-class wife whose husband had a steady income, holding a job was frowned upon as inconsistent with her social status. If the wife entered the labor market, it was assumed that she was either compensating for her husband's inadequacy as a breadwinner or that she was selfishly pursuing a career at the expense of her household responsibilities.

The status of children also changed. Only in very poor families would they be expected to help to raise the family's standard of living, though some might work to earn spending money or because their parents thought it would be good for their moral fiber. Furthermore, the age when children came to be considered young adults and were supposed to become productive members of the family increased considerably. By the end of the nineteenth century, child labor laws were passed that prohibited employment of "minors."

As a consequence of industrialization and urbanization, more and more goods and services used by households came to be produced outside the home. Nonetheless, much time and effort were still expended to purchase and maintain these commodities and to use them to attain the desired standard of living. With soap and bleach purchased at the store, and the washing machine doing the scrubbing, laundry became far less of a chore, but it was done far more frequently, and housewives came to take pride in making it "whiter than white." Groceries bought at the supermarket and a gas or electric range made cooking much easier, but homemakers would now serve elaborate meals rather than a pot of stew. To do otherwise would not be consistent with the role of dedicated mother and wife, whose every thought was for the well-being of her family. The husband might help her, but this assistance was never to interfere with his "work." The children, too, particularly girls, might be expected to assist their mothers, but the basic responsibility for the household rested with the wife.

The net result of these developments was that the number of hours that full-time homemakers devoted to housework, more than 50 per week, did not change from the beginning of the twentieth century to the 1960s.[35] Two additional trends contributed to this situation. One was the decline in the number of household servants, whose presence was not uncommon in middle-class households in the nineteenth and early twentieth centuries. Probably more important was the tendency to use the time no longer

---

[35]Joann Vanek found that even as late as 1966, full-time homemakers were devoting as much time to their work as their grandmothers had in the 1920s. See Vanek, "Time Spent in Housework," *Scientific American* 231, no. 5 (November 1974): 116–20. It was not until the seventies that this situation changed; see our discussion in Chapter 3.

needed to produce essentials to raise the standard of cleanliness and comfort the family could enjoy, not to increase the wife's leisure time.[36]

Fertility declined with industrialization, in part because of the diminished economic value of children. With far less opportunity for children to participate in production in urban households and growing immigration, hired workers were more readily available as a source of farm labor.[37] Further, the number of years of schooling grew in both towns and rural areas, so that children remained dependent for a longer period of time. Consequently, women born in the early nineteenth century averaged somewhat fewer than five births, considerably below the rate of their eighteenth-century predecessors, and those born toward the end of the nineteenth century averaged only about three births.[38] However, as the number of children declined, the amount of maternal care per child increased greatly, and the number of years of such care was extended substantially.

Responsibility for spending the family's money and for determining the amount to be saved was not as clear, but certain norms were generally accepted. The wife made most of the everyday purchases but was expected to comply with her husband's wishes and to try to please her family. Thus, to some extent, she might be viewed as the purchasing agent rather than an independent decision maker when she did the shopping. The husband generally determined where the family would live and what major items should be bought, such as larger durables and, particularly, the house.

The man's authority as "head of the household" was supposed to be absolute in all important matters, because he basically determined the family's lifestyle by providing the money income on which it depended.[39] Further, the husband's decisions defined the parameters within which the other family members operated. Thus, he was dominant within the household as well as in the outside world. It was, however, generally assumed that, within the family, he would see to it that benefits were distributed equally or according to need, as deemed appropriate.

As the economic role of women changed within the family, so too did the image of the ideal wife. Whereas the colonial wife was valued for her industriousness, the growing **cult of true womanhood** that developed with industrialization in the nineteenth century equated piety, purity, domesticity, and submissiveness with the femininity to

---

[36]Newly available information has suggested the importance of cleanliness to raising a healthy family; see Joel Mokyr, "Why 'More Work for Mother?' Knowledge and Household Behavior, 1870-1945," *The Journal of Economic History* 60, no. 1 (March 2000): 1–41. And, as Bonnie J. Fox points out, advertisements tended to emphasize improved housekeeping standards and better service to the family rather than liberation from household chores; see "Selling the Mechanized Household: 70 Years of Ads in the *Ladies Home Journal*," *Gender and Society* 4, no. 1 (March 1990): 25–40.

[37]Improved methods of birth control are often credited for the declining birth rate, but significant decreases occurred in much of the industrialized world before any major breakthroughs in contraceptive techniques. See Joan Huber, "Toward a Sociotechnological Theory of the Women's Movement," *Social Problems* 23, no. 4 (April 1976): 371–88.

[38]For an interesting analysis of these trends, see Jeremy Greenwood and Ananth Seshadri, "The U.S. Demographic Transition," *American Economic Review* 92, no. 2 (May 2002): 153–59.

[39]See, for instance, Janet R. Wilkie, "Marriage, Family Life, and Women's Employment," in *Women Working*, edited by Ann H. Stromberg and Shirley Harkess (Mountain View, CA: Mayfield Publishing Company, 1988), pp. 149–66. She suggests that "the husband's occupation affected where the family lived, whether they moved, how they spent disposable income, whether the wife worked, and so forth. In fact, the husband's primacy went well beyond this. Men enjoyed greater power in other non-job related spheres of the marital relationship" (p. 151).

which all women were expected to aspire.[40] Their role was in the now consumption-oriented home—as daughter, sister, but most of all as wife and mother. This ideal particularly extolled the lifestyle of affluent middle- and upper-class women, who were to a great extent freed even from their domestic chores by the servants their husbands' ample incomes could provide. Understandably, overburdened working-class women, who often contributed to family income, if not through wage labor then by taking in boarders or doing piecework at home, might come to look longingly at such a leisurely existence as something to hope for and strive toward. For men of all social classes, it came to be a mark of success to be the sole wage earner in the family.

This image of the family was fostered not only by the example of the middle and upper middle classes, which was the envy of the poor woman bearing the double burden of paid and unpaid work or toiling at home to make ends meet on a limited budget,[41] but also by male workers and their trade unions. Initially, the availability of women and children for work in industry was welcomed by national leaders because they provided cheap, competitive labor, while agricultural production could be maintained by men.[42] However, attitudes changed as workers became more plentiful with the growing influx of immigrants. Working men were particularly eager to get married women out of the labor force entirely and women out of all but the lowest-paid jobs. Their goals were to reserve the better positions for themselves, make sure they would not be underbid, and give greater force to the argument that a "living wage" for a man had to be sufficient to support a dependent wife and children. Thus, women received little, if any, support from organized labor in trying to improve their own working conditions and rewards.[43]

This was the genesis of the traditional family, once accepted as the backbone of American society. As we have seen, it is in fact comparatively recent in origin, dating back only to the mid-nineteenth and early twentieth centuries. Even in its heyday, it was never entirely universal. Many poor, black, and immigrant married women worked outside their homes; in addition, many others earned income at home, taking in boarders or doing piecework. Moreover, the historical record indicates that single-parent families were not all that uncommon; in 1900, 9 percent of children lived in such families, in most cases with a widowed parent. As a point of comparison, the same proportion of children lived with a single parent in 1960.[44]

Throughout this period, market work was quite common among single women, and a relatively small number of women, particularly college graduates, chose careers

---

[40]Barbara Easton, "Industrialization and Femininity: A Case Study of Nineteenth Century New England," *Social Problems* 23, no. 4 (April 1976): 389–401; and Barbara Welter, "The Cult of True Womanhood, 1820–1860," in *The American Family in Social-Historical Perspective,* edited by Michael Gordon (New York: St. Martin's Press, 1978), pp. 313–33.

[41]As Louise Tilly and Joan Scott, *Women, Work and Family* (New York: Holt, Rinehart & Winston, 1978) forcefully point out, mothers found it very difficult to combine employment outside the home with housework and child care.

[42]George Washington is quoted as writing to Lafayette, "I conceive much might be done in the way of women, children and others [producing yarn and cloth] without taking one really necessary hand from tilling the earth." Cited in Alice Kessler-Harris, *Women Have Always Worked* (New York: McGraw-Hill, 1981), p. 8.

[43]Alice Kessler-Harris, "Organizing the Unorganizable: Three Jewish Women and Their Union," in *Class, Sex and the Woman Worker,* edited by Milton Cantor and Bruce Laurie (Westport, CT: Greenwood Press, 1977) is eloquent on this point.

[44]For an interesting historical perspective on the family, see Linda Gordon and Sara McLanahan, "Single Parenthood in 1900," *Journal of Family History* 16, no. 2 (April 1991): 97–116.

over marriage as a lifelong vocation. Nonetheless, exclusive dedication to the role of mother and wife was widely accepted as the only proper and fulfilling life for a woman. It was not long, however, before this orthodoxy was challenged. Progressive modernization brought about dramatic changes in conditions of production and in the economic roles of men and women, followed by changes in ideas and aspirations.

As family size continued to shrink, the amount of time and energy needed for childbearing and childrearing declined. At the same time, women were living longer. Although, as previously noted, full-time homemakers continued to work long hours, thus achieving ever higher standards of homemaking, women had the choice of devoting time to other activities, especially during the years after their children grew up. More and more of the goods and services that were previously provided within the household for its own use were now mass-produced and available for purchase. New appliances facilitated faster and easier production of many of the others. Increasingly, the market also provided many new goods and services desired by consumers that could not readily be produced in the home. This reason likely explains why increasing numbers of women and men decided that a second paycheck would make a greater contribution to the family's standard of living than additional time devoted to upgrading the quality of homemaking. Other factors, to be discussed in Chapter 4, such as increased education and changes in the demand for labor, were important in facilitating the influx of women into the labor market. However, the shrinking household and household sphere were among the basic developments that made it possible.

Economic Incentives: An Engine of Change for Women's Property Rights

In 1848, in the Declaration of Sentiments and Resolutions issued at the Seneca Falls Convention, Elizabeth Cady Stanton and other prominent women's rights activists set forth a list of demands.* One of the best known was a demand for the right to vote, which women ultimately gained in 1920 when the 19th amendment of the U.S. Constitution was passed. Another demand was for the right for women to own their own wages and property. For instance, as of 1840, in the 27 U.S. states at that time, with few exceptions, wives were not able to buy, sell, or own property, nor did they did have ownership of their own labor market earnings. Once women were married, their husbands had legal claim to their earnings and property, under a system known as patriarchal property rights. Only in the middle to later part of the 1890s did states begin to extend to married women property rights to their earnings and property holdings. By 1920 married women in all but three states had such rights. What precipitated these changes in state laws governing married women's property rights? This inset discusses recent research by Rick Geddes and Dean Lueck that points to the pivotal role of economic incentives as the catalyst for change in women's property rights.**

Geddes and Lueck argue that prior to industrialization, economic incentive to change existing property laws for women was minimal because they had few opportunities to buy or sell goods or to get paid jobs. However, by the latter part of the nineteenth century, industrialization was in full swing, cities were growing, wealth was increasing, and a larger proportion of women had some education. As opportunities in the market economy expanded, the existing set of patriarchal property rights became, in the authors' words, a "relatively costly institution." That is, without legal ownership of their own earnings, married women had little economic incentive to participate in the growing economy, which in turn, constrained families' potential income. Hence, Geddes and Lueck argue, it was in the interests of both women and men to extend property rights to married women. Further, as one might suspect, once married women were given the legal ownership of their wages, this further increased their incentive to get an education, invest in market skills, and participate in the market economy.

Claudia Goldin's research on marriage bars—rules created by firms that prohibited married women from employment in teaching and clerical jobs—provides another example of how economic incentives serve as an engine of change for women. She points to the fact that marriage bars fell to the wayside in the 1940s when schools and firms faced a shortage of the young, single women they had traditionally hired into these positions. This shortage increased employers' demand for the labor services of married women. In both cases, we are reminded that economic incentives can be an important force in changing long-standing, seemingly immutable institutional arrangements. Moreover, these examples illustrate that improvements in women's rights and opportunities can benefit society at large.

*Elizabeth Cady Stanton, "Declaration of Sentiments and Resolutions," Seneca Falls Convention, 1848.
** Rick Geddes and Dean Lueck, "The Gains from Self-Ownership and the Expansion of Women's Rights," *American Economic Review* 92, no. 4 (September 2002): 1079–92. This inset also draws on Elissa Braunstein and Nancy Folbre, "To Honor and Obey: Efficiency, Inequality, and Patriarchal Property Rights," *Feminist Economics* 7, no. 1 (March 2001): 25–44; and Claudia Goldin, *Understanding the Gender Gap: An Economic History of American Women* (New York: Oxford University Press, 1990).

Women in the Labor Market

As suggested previously, some women were always economically active beyond taking care of family and home.[45] Official statistics cited earlier indicate that 84 percent of men, but only 18 percent of women and less than 5 percent of married women, were in the labor force in 1890. Even though the census did not severely undercount the paid work of married women outside the home in the early years of collecting separate data for men and women, it did considerably understate paid work in the home (such as taking in boarders or doing piecework) and on the farm. One estimate of women's labor force participation, more broadly defined to include paid work done within the household, is as high as 26 percent in 1890; but participation rates decreased thereafter with

---

[45]Much useful information on the economic status of women in the United States prior to World War II is found in Goldin, *Understanding the Gender Gap;* Matthaei, *Economic History;* and Costa, "From Mill Town to Board Room."

the decline in the family farm and in paid work done at home, not to reach the previous high again until around 1940.[46] Interestingly, these trends are consistent with the notion, discussed earlier in this chapter, that women's participation in productive activity is likely first to decline, but to rise once more as the economy moves from one dominated by agriculture through early, and then advanced, industrialization.

Each of the two definitions of labor force participation has merit, depending on whether one is primarily interested in the extent to which women are independent wage earners or in their productive contributions to the household. The issue is mainly relevant for wives because, throughout the period for which data have been available, single women were considerably more likely to be gainfully employed outside the home. As late as 1940, the labor force participation of married women was only 14 percent, while it was 46 percent for single women. One reason for the low rates for married women was the so-called *marriage bar* prohibiting the employment of married women instituted in the late 1800s and lasting into the mid-1900s. Marriage bars were particularly prevalent in teaching and clerical work, two occupations that were to become among the most common for married women in later years. Another obstacle to married women's employment outside the home was the lack of availability of part-time work at a time when women's household responsibilities were quite demanding.[47]

Not only were relatively few women employed during the early years of the twentieth century, but they also tended to work in different occupations than men and were concentrated in relatively few jobs. As shown in Table 2-1, at the turn of the century, 42 percent of men were in agricultural jobs and 38 percent were in manufacturing jobs. Of

TABLE 2-1 Distribution of Workers by Occupation, Race and Gender, 1890/1900

	Men	*Women*		
	Total (%)	*Total (%)*	*White (%)*	*Nonwhite (%)*
Professional	10.2	9.6	12.5	0.9
Clerical	2.8	4.0	5.2	0.4
Sales	4.6	4.3	5.7	0.1
Service*	3.1	35.5	31.3	48.2
Manufacturing	37.6	27.7	34.7	6.4
Agricultural	41.7	19.0	10.8	44.0
Total Employed	100.0	100.0	100.0	100.0

*For women, service primarily refers to domestic service.

Source: From Claudia Dale Goldin, *Understanding the Gender Gap: An Economic History of American Women*, (New York: Oxford University Press, 1990), tables 3.2 and 3.3.

---

[46]This figure reflects Goldin's estimate that including undercounted workers would lead to a 7 percentage point increase in her calculation of the overall labor force participation rate for women. For white married women, in particular, including such workers would raise their rate by as much as 10 percentage points, from 2.5 to 12.5 percent. See Goldin, *Understanding the Gender Gap,* pp. 44–45. See also Claudia Goldin, "The U-Shaped Female Labor Force Function in Economic Development and Economic History," in *Investments in Women's Human Capital,* edited by T. Paul Schultz (Chicago: University of Chicago, 1995), pp. 61–90.
[47]Goldin, *Understanding the Gender Gap,* chap. 6, pp. 159–84.

the 18 percent in white-collar jobs, the largest share was in the professional category (which included managers and proprietors) followed by sales and clerical occupations. Relatively few men, 3 percent, were in service jobs (e.g., waiter or barber).

In contrast, among women nearly 36 percent were in the service sector, the majority employed in domestic service. As many as 28 percent were in manufacturing, virtually all in textiles, clothing, and tobacco. Another 19 percent were in agriculture. Table 2-1 further shows that more than 90 percent of black women worked as either domestic servants or as farm laborers, as compared with only 42 percent of white women. It was also the case that foreign-born white women were overrepresented in manufacturing and domestic service, as compared with U.S.-born white women, though these figures are not shown separately here. Another 10 percent of all women were in professional positions; almost all were schoolteachers or nurses. These professions, like domestic service, may be regarded as extensions of women's domestic role, though initially almost all schoolteachers were men. The remainder of women workers (8.3%) were in clerical work and sales occupations. Like teaching, clerical work was originally a primarily male occupation. As late as the turn of the century, 85 percent of clerical workers were men. It was not until after 1900, when such positions gradually ceased to be viewed as apprenticeships, that women entered this field to any significant extent; in time, as more women entered the labor market, clerical work became predominantly female and absorbed a substantial proportion of employed women.

A wide variety of factors undoubtedly contributed to the rapid growth of female clerical employment. Among these was the growth of large corporations, which greatly increased the volume of paperwork and thus the demand for clerical workers. The large proportion of women with a high school education who needed little or no on-the-job training to perform such work provided an inexpensive labor pool to satisfy this expanding demand. Employers were willing to hire these women, even when they were not expected to stay for a long time; this practice became all the more common after these positions came to serve a purely clerical function rather than serving as a training ground for advancement. Women, in turn, were likely to find these jobs attractive because relevant skills did not tend to depreciate much during periods out of the labor force and reentry was relatively easy. It is also possible that many preferred clean white-collar jobs to the dirtier, noisier, and at times more physically demanding blue-collar jobs, and they had few other such alternatives.[48]

Women's labor force participation has been rising ever since the 1890s, the first year for which official data are available. It rose only from 18 percent to 28 percent over the next 50 years until 1940. However, between then and 2003, it increased considerably more rapidly to 60 percent.[49] The causes of this increase are considered in greater detail in Chapter 4; however, the growth in the demand for clerical workers undoubtedly facilitated the rapid influx of women into the labor force that began in the 1940s.

---

[48]For analyses of women's occupational choices and of their entry into clerical work, see Claudia Goldin, "Historical Evolution of Female Earnings Functions and Occupations," *Explorations in Economic History* 21, no. 1 (January 1984): 1–27; and Margery Davies, "Woman's Place Is at the Typewriter: The Feminization of the Clerical Labor Force," in *Labor Market Segmentation,* edited by Richard C. Edwards, Michael Reich, and David M. Gordon (Lexington, MA: D.C. Health, 1975), pp. 279–96.

[49]For more detailed data, including differences by race and marital status, see Goldin, *Understanding the Gender Gap,* chap. 2.

The steady increase in women's earnings, both in absolute terms and relative to men's, was also likely a contributing factor. Recent research provides evidence on the historical trend in women's earnings relative to men's. Available data from the manufacturing as well as the agricultural sector indicate that the gender earnings ratio rose from 1815, around the start of early industrialization, through the turn of the century. Later data, which are available for the economy as a whole, indicate that the ratio increased from .46 in 1890 to .56 by 1930. The trend over these 40 years was largely due to an increase in the relative earnings of women within broad occupations, though it also reflects some movement of women into higher-paying sectors.[50] Subsequently, little change took place until about 1980, but since then the ratio has risen to .76. We present recent trends in the gender earnings ratio in greater detail in Chapter 5.

Nonwage benefits, on the other hand, provided little incentive for women to enter the labor force. Because the foundations of the modern welfare state were laid during the time when the traditional family was still accepted as the norm, these programs generally addressed the needs of such families rather than those of two-earner or one-adult households. The focus on the traditional family applied both to the benefits employers began to provide early in the twentieth century, including health insurance, disability coverage, and pensions, and to those introduced by government in the 1930s, most notably Social Security.

By the dawn of the twenty-first century, substantial change had occurred. Three-fourths of all employed married men and more than 90 percent of employed married women had a spouse in the labor force. In addition, more than 13 percent of employed women maintained families (with no husband present).[51] These figures reflect the long secular increase in women's labor force participation as well as the much higher divorce and nonmarital birth rates of recent decades. With these changes, programs and policies are emerging to assist the growing number of employed single-parent and dual-earner families. These recent trends, as well as others, will be discussed in greater detail in subsequent chapters.

College-Educated Women over the Last 100 Years: Work, Family, or Both?

Recent research by economic historian Claudia Goldin points to dramatic changes over the twentieth century in the ability of women who are relatively career-oriented—those who are college-educated—to combine paid work and family.* Her work provides a useful historical context for understanding the challenges faced by career-oriented women today.

Goldin begins with a cohort of women who graduated from college about 1910. She finds that they were expected to make a choice between a career (most often teaching) and having a family. Indeed, fully 50 percent did not marry or, if married, did not have children compared to only 22 percent of their contemporaries who did not attend college. Their experience suggests that prevailing social norms strongly discouraged married women from working outside the home.

---

[50]Goldin, *Understanding the Gender Gap,* pp. 58–63.
[51]U.S. Census Bureau, "Historical Income Tables–Families," www.census.gov; and Bureau of Labor Statistics, *The Employment Situation: January 2004.*

The cohort of women who graduated from college about 1955 was more demographically similar to other women in the general population. During a time when Americans were generally marrying younger and having more children, college women were part of the trend, with only 17.5 percent not married or, if married, childless. Moreover, in contrast to their predecessors, many were able to have both a family *and* a job, though for the most part they did these activities in stages. Like many other women at that time, they first had a family and took a job later. For this group, college provided an economic reward, not only because it increased their potential earnings, but also because college women were more likely to marry college men (who outnumbered them 2 to 1). Thus, they reaped the added benefit of a higher-earning husband. Even though the experience of this cohort suggests that it was becoming more acceptable for married women to work for pay, even the college-educated generally had "jobs" rather than "careers," which require substantial human capital investment and more continuous labor force participation.

Among the cohort of women graduating college about 1972, a larger share sought to have careers, rather than simply jobs. Because of the investment required in undertaking a career, many women in this cohort delayed childbearing and pursued the route of career first, family later. Still, Goldin's data suggest that the proportion of them who have been able to "have it all," that is, family and career, is surprisingly small. Only 13 to 18 percent of women in this cohort achieved both goals by about age 40, when family is defined as having given birth to at least one child and career as having earnings over a certain amount during the two to three preceding years.** The latest cohort for which data are available are women about age 40 who graduated college in the early 1980s. Using a consistent definition, Goldin finds that 21 to 27 percent of these women attained family and career, certainly an improvement over the earlier cohort.

Of course, career is a difficult concept to define and the proportion found to have careers varies with the definition. Moreover, the estimates of career may be low among the age group surveyed because of the presence of young children among a substantial proportion of the women who had families. Yet even this qualification suggests that women face the need to make decisions and trade-offs seldom confronted by their male counterparts. Goldin's findings regarding the difficulty of combining family and career are reinforced by considerable evidence suggesting that, among women as a group, children have a negative effect on earnings and employment.

Nonetheless, there is reason to be optimistic about prospects for future cohorts. Access to family leave, for instance, has been found to substantially mitigate the negative effect of children on women's wages. Thus, the difficulties that women face in achieving career and family are likely to continue to decrease as more firms adopt such policies. Moreover, as discrimination in the labor market continues to decline, marriages gradually become more egalitarian, and various other family-friendly policies are offered on a more widespread basis in the workplace, more women who want to "have it all" will be able to do so.

*Claudia Goldin, "Career and Family: College Women Look to the Past," in *Gender and Family Issues in the Workplace*, edited by Francine D. Blau and Ronald G. Ehrenberg (New York: Russell Sage Foundation, 1997), pp. 20–59; and Claudia Goldin, "The Long Road to the Fast Track: Career and Family," *The Annals of the American Academy of Political and Social Science* 596, no. 1 (2004): 20–35. Evidence on the impact of children and the availability of maternity leave on women's earnings is from Jane Waldfogel, "Understanding the 'Family Gap' in Pay for Women with Children," *Journal of Economic Perspectives* 12, no. 1 (Winter 1998): 157–70.
**Specifically, having income or average hourly earnings at least as high as a man at the 25th percentile of the college-educated male earnings distribution. When Goldin, instead, defines career as working full-time during the preceding three years, she obtains a somewhat higher estimate of 22 percent. In related work, Marianne A. Ferber and Carole Green examined a sample of women predominately in their fifties and found a larger share who meet the definition of career and family; see "Career or Family: What Choices do College Women Have?" *Journal of Labor Research* 24, no. 1 (Winter 2003): 143–51.

Conclusion

The overview provided here, though general, permits us to draw some conclusions. The roles of men and women and the social rules that prescribe appropriate behavior for each are not shaped by biology alone. Rather, they are determined by the interaction of technology, the role of women in production, and a variety of social and political factors. The evidence provides some reason to believe that women are less likely to be seen as dependents, defined solely in terms of their maternal and family role, when they participate in "productive" work.

It is also likely that the roles of men and women, which developed initially as a rational response to conditions that existed at one time in the course of economic development, continue their hold long after they ceased to be functional.[52] Thus, the view that women should devote themselves to homemaking, once a full-time occupation when life was short, families were large, and housekeeping was laborious, lingered long after these conditions changed substantially. Jobs originally allocated to men because they required great physical strength often continued as male preserves when mechanization did away with the need for muscle power. The possibility that such lags in adjustment are not uncommon should be kept in mind when we come to analyze the current situation.

Our review also suggests that neither the role of housewife nor that of working woman is without significant problems for women. Men's work in the public sphere (i.e., outside the family) has usually enjoyed higher status than women's domestic work within the family circle. Even when women succeeded in entering the world beyond the household to a greater or lesser extent, men failed to show much inclination to share in household work. This situation, in turn, makes it difficult for women to achieve substantial equality in the public sphere. Many of those who tried found themselves

---

[52]"Although stereotypes are often initially based on fact, they are seldom revised as quickly as the facts change." Smith, "The Movement of Women," p. 3.

confronted by the problem of "the double burden" of responsibility for home and market work, or felt forced to choose between a career and marriage. In modern times, machines eliminate much of the need for muscle, and physical strength is no longer required for the most highly valued work. At the same time, childbearing absorbs an increasingly smaller proportion of a woman's adult life and can, for the most part, be timed at will. It is entirely possible that, under these conditions, it is the unequal distribution of labor in the home rather than women's lesser ability to perform other types of work that increasingly poses the main obstacle to equality.

Questions for Review and Discussion

1. Explain how women's and men's roles in production changed between the colonial period and early industrialization.
2. From a historical perspective, how has the labor market experience of black and white women differed?
3. Compare and contrast the role of women in the following stages:
   a. hunting and gathering
   b. horticulture
   c. agriculture
   d. early industrialization
   e. today
4. In view of what we have learned from sociobiologists, to what extent can traditional roles of men and women be expected to change with changing economic conditions?
5. Discuss possible relationships between economic development and women's rights.

Suggested Readings

Blum, Deborah. *Sex on the Brain: The Biological Differences Between Men and Women.* New York: Viking Penguin, 1997.

Costa, Dora L. "From Mill Town to Board Room: The Rise of Women's Paid Labor," *Journal of Economic Perspectives* 14, no. 4 (Fall 2000): 101–22.

Friedl, Ernestine. *Women and Men: An Anthropological View.* New York: Holt, Rinehart & Winston, 1975.

Goldin, Claudia. *Understanding the Gender Gap: An Economic History of American Women.* New York: Oxford University Press, 1990.

———. "The U-Shaped Female Labor Force Function in Economic Development and Economic History." In *Investments in Women's Human Capital,* edited by T. Paul Schultz, pp. 61–90. Chicago: University of Chicago, 1995.

Matthaei, Julie A. *An Economic History of Women in America.* New York: Schocken Books, 1982.

Nielsen, Joyce M. *Sex and Gender in Society: Perspectives and Stratification,* 2nd ed. Prospect Heights, IL: Waveland Press, Inc., 1990.

O'Kelly, Charlotte G. *Women and Men in Society.* New York: D. Van Nostrand Co., 1980.

Rosaldo, Michelle Z., and Louise Lamphere, eds. *Women, Culture and Society.* Stanford: Stanford University Press, 1974.

Tiger, Lionel, and Robin Fox. *The Imperial Animal.* New York: Holt, Rinehart & Winston, 1971.

Tilly, Louise, and Joan Scott. *Women, Work and Family.* New York: Holt, Rinehart & Winston, 1978.

Welter, Barbara. "The Cult of True Womanhood, 1820–1860." In *The American Family in Social-Historical Perspective,* edited by Michael Gordon, pp. 313–33. New York: St. Martin's Press, 1978.

Wilson, Edward O. *Sociobiology: The New Synthesis.* Cambridge, MA: Belknap Press of Harvard University Press, 1975.

CHAPTER

3

THE FAMILY AS AN ECONOMIC UNIT

Chapter Highlights

■ The Simple Neoclassical Model: Specialization and Exchange

■ Other Advantages of Families

■ Disadvantages of Specialization

■ Transaction Cost and Bargaining Approaches

■ Marxist and Radical Feminist Views of the Family

■ Nonmarket Work

■ The American Family in the Twenty-First Century

■ Appendix: Specialization and Exchange

For a long time, neoclassical economics, the dominant school of economics in the United States and most of the rest of the world today, and the approach we primarily draw on in this text, concerned itself largely with the behavior of "economic man." It was, of course, acknowledged that this man interacted with others, in competition or in cooperation, but it was his individual well-being that he would attempt to maximize. Consumer economics had long recognized the existence of the family and its importance as a unit of consumption. However, it was not until the 1960s, with the path-breaking work of Gary Becker and Jacob Mincer, that mainstream economists began to concern themselves with the issues confronted by men and women in allocating their time and wealth so as to maximize family well-being.[1] Since then, using sophisticated theory and advanced econometric methods, economists have developed and tested

---

[1]See Gary S. Becker, "A Theory of the Allocation of Time," *Economic Journal* 75, no. 299 (September 1965): 493–517; and Jacob Mincer, "Labor Force Participation of Married Women," in *Aspects of Labor Economics,* edited by H. Gregg Lewis, Universities National Bureau of Economic Research Conference Series, no. 14

models that have produced important insights in this area. Yet, many of these models are not altogether satisfactory, because the tendency is still to treat even this multiperson family as a single-minded, indivisible, utility-maximizing unit.

In this chapter, we draw heavily upon neoclassical economic analysis, with appropriate simplifying assumptions, to better understand the determinants of the division of labor in the family. Because a substantial majority of people continues to live in married-couple families, we focus largely on the division of labor between husbands and wives. At the same time, it would be a mistake to overlook the considerable increase in the number of cohabiting heterosexual couples, or the presence of gay and lesbian couples, some of them married as of 2004. We shall examine both of these types of couples in Chapter 9.

Our focus on economic analysis does not mean that we believe families are established or dissolved entirely, or even primarily, for economic reasons. On the contrary, human need for companionship, sexual attraction, affection, and the desire to have children all play a substantial part in family formation. Human need for independence and privacy, as well as incompatibilities and preference for a variety of partners, all play a large part in family breakups. Nonetheless, it is our belief that economic factors are important and that focusing upon them considerably enhances our understanding of the determinants of the division of labor in the family.

After presenting the neoclassical model of the family, we provide an evaluation and critique of this approach and introduce a more complex reality. In particular, the simple neoclassical model points to potential efficiency gains arising from the traditional division of labor in which the husband specializes in market work and the wife specializes in home work. Nevertheless, such an arrangement is less and less prevalent. Moreover, individuals continue to form families despite this decrease in specialization. We shed light on the reasons for these developments by extending the simple model in two ways.[2]

- We point out other types of economic benefits to forming families besides specialization. Thus, couples may discard specialization and still reap economic gains from living in families.
- We examine the disadvantages of the traditional division of labor, particularly for women, which are not considered in the simple neoclassical model. These disadvantages help to explain the decline of the traditional division of labor.

(Princeton, NJ: Princeton University Press, 1962), pp. 63–97. An early pioneer was Margaret G. Reid, *Economics of Household Production* (New York: Wiley, 1934). A large number of authors contributed to the growing literature of the "New Home Economics" in recent decades, but much of this work has been conveniently summarized by Gary S. Becker in *A Treatise on the Family* (Cambridge, MA: Harvard University Press, 1981, enlarged edition, 1991). For theoretical critiques and extensions of Becker's work, see, for instance, Robert A. Pollak, "Gary Becker's Contributions to Family and Household Economics," *Review of Economics of the Household* 1, no. 1–2 (January/April 2002): 111–141; and Paula England, "Separate and Soluble Selves: Dichotomous Thinking in Economics," in *Feminist Economics Today*, edited by Marianne A. Ferber and Julie A. Nelson (Chicago: University of Chicago, 2003), pp. 61–80.
[2]Much of this material was first developed in Marianne A. Ferber and Bonnie G. Birnbaum, "The New Home Economics: Retrospect and Prospects," *Journal of Consumer Research* 4, no. 4 (June 1977): 19–28. For an updated discussion, see Marianne A. Ferber, "A Feminist Critique of the Neoclassical Theory of the Family," in *Women, Family, and Work,* edited by Karine S. Moe (Oxford: Blackwell, 2003), chap. 1.

We then briefly discuss alternative neoclassical approaches of transaction costs and bargaining models, as well as the radical feminist and Marxist feminist approaches.

Next, we examine available evidence on the allocation of time to market work, housework, and volunteer work by men and women, as well as changes in this allocation during recent decades. This discussion will provide some indication as to the extent that husbands and wives specialize and to what extent we are moving toward egalitarian marriages, in which both spouses equally share the responsibility for earning a living and for homemaking. Here we focus on trends in nonmarket work and in Chapter 4 we examine trends in female labor force participation.

Finally, the chapter concludes by looking at the American family in the twenty-first century. As we shall see, married couples, who are the focus of this chapter, have been declining as a share of all households. We briefly summarize the changes that have occurred and point to the increasing complexity of families in the United States and elsewhere. More detailed analyses of these trends are provided in Chapter 9.

THE SIMPLE NEOCLASSICAL MODEL: SPECIALIZATION AND EXCHANGE

The neoclassical analysis of the family relies on the following basic underlying assumption: The family is a unit whose adult members make informed and rational decisions that result in maximizing the utility or well-being of the family. Beginning with this premise, economists have applied the tools of their discipline to the analysis of the division of labor within the family. Models employing these basic economic concepts have also been used to explain women's increasing labor force participation rates, growing divorce rates, and declining fertility; the family's greater emphasis on education of children; and a number of other aspects of human behavior.

As noted earlier, the simplest model of the family assumes that the family's goal is to maximize its utility or satisfaction by selecting the combination of **commodities** from which it derives the greatest possible amount of utility. These commodities are produced by combining the home time of family members with goods and services purchased in the market, using labor market earnings.

Virtually all market-purchased goods and services require an infusion of home time to transform them into the commodities that provide utility—from food that needs to be bought and prepared and furniture that needs to be purchased, arranged in the home, and maintained, to day care centers, which must be carefully chosen and where children must be dropped off and picked up. Similarly, even time spent in leisure generally requires the input of market goods and services to be enjoyable—from television sets and CD players to concerts and baseball games. Thus, time spent on paid work produces the income necessary to purchase market goods, which in turn are needed together with home time to produce commodities. A crucial question for the family is how time should be allocated between home and market most efficiently in order to maximize satisfaction.

Comparative Advantage

Under certain conditions, commodity production is carried out most efficiently if one member of the family specializes, at least to some extent, in market production while the other specializes, at least to some extent, in home production. They may then exchange their output or pool the fruits of their labor to achieve their utility-maximizing combination of market-purchased goods and home-produced goods. For there to be gains from this arrangement, it is necessary for the two individuals to have differing **comparative advantages** for home and market production. That is to say, the ratio of the value of time spent at home to the value of time spent in the market must be higher for one individual than the other.[3]

Is it generally the case that women are relatively more productive in the home and men are relatively more productive in the market? Whether or not one assumes that women are biologically better suited for housework because they are the ones who bear children, it will frequently be the case that women have a comparative advantage in household production and that men have a comparative advantage in market work. The reason is that men and women are traditionally raised with different expectations and receive different education and training. It may also be the case that women have been discriminated against in the labor market, lowering their market earnings. Moreover, the traditional division of labor itself is likely to magnify differences in the household and market skills of men and women because both types of skills tend to increase with experience "on the job." Thus, even a small initial gender difference in comparative advantage may increase considerably over time.

Although each of the preceding factors tends to produce gender differences in comparative advantage for homemaking as compared to market work, it is not necessarily the case that the traditional division of labor is the optimal arrangement. Treating children according to gender rather than individual talents and discriminating against women workers in the labor market clearly introduce distortions. Even more obvious is the fact that circular reasoning is involved when women supposedly specialize in housework because they do it better, but, in fact, they do it better because they specialize in it. To the extent that women's relative advantage for homemaking is socially determined and reflects unequal access to market opportunities, the traditional division of labor is not always efficient, let alone desirable, particularly when, as we shall see, it entails many disadvantages for women.

In the following discussion we assume that women have a comparative advantage in housework relative to men because the reality that we seek to explain is one in which women generally assume primary responsibility for homemaking. We do not mean to imply, however, that the traditional division of labor is inevitable or that it will persist indefinitely into the future. Indeed, we are also concerned with better understanding the reasons why traditional patterns are changing.

Specialization and Exchange: Numerical Examples

Two simple examples will help to clarify the notion of comparative advantage and to illustrate the efficiency of specialization and exchange. The analysis is analogous to the standard proof of gains from international trade and is illustrated in Tables 3-1a and 3-1b.

---

[3]The case for specialization as a way to maximize the well-being of the family is similar to that for international trade, where each country specializes in production for which it has a relative advantage. Among the important differences between the two situations, however, is that countries generally need not rely on a single trading partner, allowing somewhat less opportunity for the stronger partner to take advantage of the weaker one. Another difference is that couples, unlike countries, must also share a good deal of consumption.

TABLE 3-1   An Illustration of the Gains from Specialization and Exchange

(a) CASE 1: ABSOLUTE ADVANTAGE

Separate Production

	Value of Market Goods	Value of Home Cooking	Total Income
John	(6 hrs. × $10) $60	(2 hrs. × $5) + $10	= $70
Jane	(7 hrs. × $5) $35	(1 hr. × $10) + $10	= $45
Total (John and Jane)	$95	$20	$115

(b) CASE 2: COMPARATIVE ADVANTAGE

Separate Production

	Value of Market Goods	Value of Home Cooking	Total Income
Dave	(6 hrs. × $10) $60	(2 hrs. × $5) + $10	= $70
Diane	(7 hrs. × $15) $105	(1 hr. × $15) + $15	= $120
Total (Dave and Diane)	$165	$25	$190

Specialization and Exchange

	Value of Market Goods	Value of Home Cooking	Total Income
John	(8 hrs. × $10) $80	(0 hrs. × $5) + $0	= $80
Jane	(5 hrs. × $5) $25	(3 hrs. × $10) + $30	= $55
Total (John and Jane)	$105	$30	$135

Specialization and Exchange

	Value of Market Goods	Value of Home Cooking	Total Income
Dave	(8 hrs. × $10) $80	(0 hrs. × $5) + $0	= $80
Diane	(6 hrs. × $15) $90	(2 hrs. × $15) + $30	= $120
Total (Dave and Diane)	$170	$30	$200

Absolute Advantage

The simplest case is when one individual has an absolute advantage in market work while the other individual has an absolute advantage in household production. Suppose John could earn $10 for working one hour in the labor market or could produce a mediocre dinner worth about $5 at home during the same period of time. A second individual, Jane, would earn only $5 an hour in the labor market but is able to prepare an excellent dinner at home worth about $10 in one hour. In this case, it is clear that John and Jane's combined level of economic well-being can be increased if they each specialize. John, who has an absolute advantage in market work, can spend all his time in the labor market earning money while Jane, who has an absolute advantage in cooking, prepares the dinners.

This scenario is illustrated in the top section of Table 3-1a. Initially, John and Jane are each self-sufficient and both allocate some time to market work and some time to the preparation of home-cooked meals. John devotes six hours to earning income and two hours to cooking. His total income (including the value of home-cooked meals) is $70. Jane spends seven hours in the market and one hour on cooking. Her total income is $45. The sum of their two incomes (although they are not necessarily sharing at this point) is $115. If they collaborate, they have the option of each specializing to a greater extent in the activity they do better and exchanging (or pooling) their output, as shown in the bottom section of Table 3-1a.

Through specialization and exchange, John and Jane can produce a higher value of both market goods and home-cooked meals and, thus, increase their total income. The concept of opportunity cost is useful in understanding the benefits of specialization. As we explained in Chapter 1, opportunity cost is the benefit forgone in the next best alternative. John's opportunity cost of obtaining $10 worth of market goods in terms of the value of meals forgone ($5) is lower than Jane's ($20). On the other hand, a home-cooked meal valued at $10 is cheaper for Jane to produce in terms of the value of market goods forgone ($5) than it is for John ($20). Suppose John decides to devote all his time to the market, and Jane transfers two additional hours from market work to cooking. By reallocating their time, the couple is able to raise their total income from $115 to $135.

Comparative Advantage

Less obvious is the fact that specialization can also raise the income of the couple when one individual not only earns more in the labor market but is also a better cook. In other words, one individual has an absolute advantage in both types of work. In this situation, the crucial question is whether each has a *comparative advantage* for doing one type of work.

As illustrated in Table 3-1b, Dave earns $10 per hour for time spent in the labor market or can produce a meal worth, say, $5 for an hour spent cooking. Diane is more efficient than Dave in both activities. Her market wage is $15, while she can produce a meal worth $15 in an hour's time. The important point here is that, although Diane is a bit more efficient than Dave in the labor market, she is a far better cook than he is. The opportunity cost (in terms of market goods forgone) of a home-cooked meal worth $10 is lower when Diane produces it than when Dave does. It takes Dave two hours (valued at $20) to produce such a meal, and Diane can do so in 40 minutes (valued at $10). Table 3-1b shows that through specialization and exchange, the couple can increase their total output of both market goods and home-cooked meals and raise their total income from $190 to $200.

Gains to Specialization and Exchange

These examples illustrate the potential gain in output of specialization and exchange. They do not, however, tell us how much time John and Jane will spend on each type of work. The goal of the family is to maximize utility or satisfaction. Thus, the value attached to various commodities and the time allocation actually chosen by each couple will depend on their preferences for market- versus home-produced goods. Many outcomes are possible. For example, perhaps Jane and John have such a strong preference for market goods that their well-being would be maximized by both of them only working for pay and purchasing all the goods and services they consume rather than producing any at home. Or Diane and Dave might have such a strong preference for home production that she would entirely specialize in housework, and he would divide his time between market and home. In the appendix to this chapter, we present a fuller treatment of the decision-making process that explicitly takes into account both the production possibilities available to the couple and their preferences for each type of good.

In any case, however, each couple will seek to produce their desired combination of market and home goods in the most efficient way. Thus, as long as they produce some of each type of good, if the wife has a comparative advantage in housework (relative to the husband) and the husband has a comparative advantage in market work (relative to the wife), the analysis suggests that they will choose to specialize at least to some extent in the activities generally associated with women and men.

It would appear, then, that this analysis provides a perfect explanation for the traditional family with a male breadwinner and a female homemaker. Each may help the other if demand is high for the production he or she is not particularly qualified for, but each has a clearly defined sphere of primary responsibility. For whenever such specialization does not take place, the couple will fail to maximize their output and, potentially, their well-being.

Yet, as we know, the traditional family has become much less common in recent years, as families in which both husband and wife work in the labor market have become the norm. Within the context of the model, this shift may be traced in part to trends that narrow differences in women's and men's comparative advantage. As discussed in greater detail in Chapters 6 and 7, women's educational attainment and labor market experience have substantially increased and it is likely that the extent of labor market discrimination against women has declined. These factors raise the wages that women earn in the market. At the same time, the relative value of nonmarket time has fallen, as substitute goods such as microwaves and "fast food" have become a part of families' everyday lives. In addition, more out-of-home child care is available than in the past, though issues of access, affordability, and quality remain, as discussed further in Chapter 10.

The direction of causality for such changes may be difficult to establish and effects may be mutually reinforcing. For example, rising educational attainment of women may reduce their comparative advantage for household work, but at the same time women's reduced desire to adhere to the traditional division of labor in the family may motivate, at least in part, their rising educational attainment. As another example, greater availability of fast food may reduce women's comparative advantage for household work, but may also be a result of growing demand for easy-to-prepare meals due to women's rising labor force participation. However, the important point from the perspective of the issues we are considering here is that such shifts in comparative advantage of women and men substantially reduce the gains to marriage. Thus, it is not surprising that marriage rates have fallen somewhat and divorce has become considerably more common, as discussed in Chapter 9. Nevertheless, the vast majority of couples continue to marry.

Part of the reason for the continued prevalence of marriage is that gender differences in comparative advantages have not completely disappeared. Women continue to earn less than men in the labor market and data that we present later in this chapter show that they continue to do the bulk of the housework, even when they are employed outside the home. Moreover, even if wives and husbands have identical comparative advantages, other economic gains can be realized in marriage, in addition to important noneconomic advantages. It is also important to recognize that even when there are substantial gains from the traditional division of labor, this arrangement has a number of disadvantages, particularly for the wife. In the following sections we extend the simple analysis by pointing to other economic advantages of marriage, as well as the disadvantages of complete specialization.

OTHER ADVANTAGES OF FAMILIES

When husbands and wives do not differ in their relative abilities in the market and in the household or do not differ significantly, other reasons may motivate their economic self-interest to form families. These reasons include economies of scale, externalities in consumption, public goods, the opportunity to make marriage-specific investments, risk pooling, as well as institutional factors. Arguably, these benefits do not necessarily require a husband-wife family per se, but they are likely to be enhanced when individuals expect to have a long-term relationship with a strong degree of commitment.

Economies of Scale

Economies of scale exist when an increase in the scale of operation of a productive unit can result in increased output at decreasing incremental cost. To the extent that a couple is able to benefit from such economies of scale, both in the production of some home goods and in purchasing market goods and services, economic gains result from living together. For example, ample housing for two is likely to cost less than the combined amount each would pay for their housing separately. Meals for two generally take less than twice as much time to prepare as meals for one, and so forth.[4]

Public Goods

A public good has the unique characteristic that the consumption or enjoyment of the item by one person does not diminish the consumption or enjoyment of the same item by others. Within the family, many goods are likely to have this characteristic. For example, one partner's enjoyment of a television program is unlikely to be reduced at all by the fact that the other partner is also watching. Similarly, the delight of a parent in his or her child's adorable antics is not apt to be diminished by the other parent's pleasure. Many aspects of housing—the views from the windows, the decoration of the rooms—also have public goods aspects. In fact, the enjoyment of these goods by one partner may even enhance that of the other. To the extent that public goods are important, the gains from joint consumption are increased because two individuals derive more total satisfaction from sharing a given stock of public goods and services by living together than they would by living separately.

Externalities in Consumption

Externalities in consumption occur when the consumption of a good or service by one of the partners affects the well-being of the other. To the extent that these externalities are positive—one person derives enjoyment from the other's consumption—gains will be greater than indicated by the simple model. For example, a husband's purchase of a new suit may increase his wife's utility as well as his own. Both members of a couple may enjoy their summer vacation more because they are traveling together than they would if each were traveling alone. When two people care for one another, one partner may even derive satisfaction simply from the enjoyment and happiness of the other, which also greatly enhances the gains from joint consumption.

---

[4]Economies of scale also explain the advantages of larger groups living together. The fact that such arrangements are not common in affluent societies suggests that most people value additional privacy highly once they can afford it.

Marriage-Specific Investments

Marriage-specific investments refer to skills and knowledge developed in marriage and other investments made during a marriage that are worth far more within the marriage than they would be if the marriage were terminated.[5] Examples of such investments include learning to cook each other's favorite meals or learning to do the same recreational activities, such as skiing or rock climbing. Perhaps the prime example of a marriage-specific investment is the rearing of children. Parents devote considerable time and energy to nurturing their children and fostering the same values that they themselves have. Thus, children generally provide considerable satisfaction to parents within the marriage. They may, however, not provide such satisfaction to a different partner and their presence may even be an obstacle to forming and maintaining a new relationship.

Risk Pooling

Married-couple families, particularly those consisting of two earners, have the added advantage that if one of the spouses becomes unemployed, they may be able to rely on the earning power of the other partner to cover at least part, if not all, of their family's expenses. In bad economic times, if the husband loses his job or his earnings decline, even a traditional homemaker may enter the labor market to maintain family income. This "added worker" effect is discussed in Chapter 4. In addition, couples have much greater flexibility to switch jobs, change careers, or pursue additional education or job training because they can rely on the other spouse's earning power, whether she or he is already in the labor market.

Institutional Advantages

In the United States today, married couples also frequently enjoy institutional advantages including, for instance, coverage by a spouse's health insurance, pension rights, and Social Security benefits. Some employers extend benefits such as health insurance to the live-in partners of unmarried heterosexual workers, as well as gay and lesbian workers, but to date this practice is far from universal. Also, since 2000 Vermont has permitted civil unions, which extend a wide range of legal protections to gay and lesbian partners, and since 2004 Massachusetts has permitted gay marriage. Nevertheless, the vast majority of gay and lesbian couples do not live in these two states. Even in Massachusetts, where gay marriage is permitted, these married spouses are ineligible for spousal benefits in federal programs. These issues are discussed later in the chapter in an inset on the state of unions in the United States.

DISADVANTAGES OF SPECIALIZATION

As we have just seen, significant economic advantages derive from forming families, even in the case of couples whose comparative advantage in market work and home production is similar, so that they gain little from specialization and exchange. We now return to the issue of specialization and exchange itself, which the simple model suggests is the economic foundation of marriage. Here we consider the possibility that

---

[5]See Becker, *A Treatise on the Family;* and Robert A. Pollak, "A Transaction Cost Approach to Families and Households," *Journal of Economic Literature* 23, no. 2 (June 1985): 581–608.

such specialization and a gender-based division of labor may not always be desirable, particularly for women, even when specialization and exchange does yield some economic gains to the family. The potential disadvantages of specialization are generally not discussed in the standard models but are nonetheless important.

Sharing of Housework

Even if an employed wife still has a comparative advantage in doing housework as compared to her husband, a fuller consideration of the issues suggests a number of reasons why a couple might often find it desirable to share the housework rather than for each spouse to specialize completely. First, the sweeping assumption that women have a comparative advantage in all household tasks is unrealistic. The problem is that the simple model assumes only one type of home good. In our numerical example, it was home-cooked meals; more generally it is an aggregate category of home goods. In fact, tasks typically performed within the household vary from child care, house cleaning, cooking, and shopping to gardening, home repairs, car maintenance, and taking care of the family finances. It is not likely that the wife will have a relative advantage in performing all of these tasks as compared to the husband; rather it is likely that he will have a comparative advantage in at least some of them, even taking his larger market earnings into account. Of course, once the wife is at home because she is better at some, or many, of the household tasks, it may be more efficient for her to undertake other related work as well. The husband also spends a good bit of time in the home, and not all household tasks are performed in or around the house (e.g., shopping, dropping off a child at day care, or going to the bank). Therefore, even a traditional family will generally find it efficient for the husband to do a bit more housework than suggested by the simple model.

Second, it is worthwhile to consider the utility or disutility that people derive from work itself. The simple model considers only the utility derived from the consumption of market-produced and home-produced goods. Yet most people spend much of their time working, and their well-being is influenced by the satisfaction or dissatisfaction associated directly with their work. If everyone always enjoyed more (or disliked less) the kind of work they do more efficiently, the gains from specialization would be even greater than indicated by the simple model; and that may to a degree be the case. However, this line of reasoning ignores the possibility that how we feel about doing particular tasks depends on how much time we have to spend on them. Persons who dislike market or home work to begin with are likely to hate additional time spent on it even more as they do increasingly more of it. Even those individuals who like what they do are, nonetheless, likely to become less enthusiastic.[6] The stronger this effect, the less likely are gains in utility from specialization suggested by the simple model.

A similar issue arises with respect to the utility each individual derives from leisure. The model fails to consider adequately that leisure is likely to be more highly valued by the partner who has less of it and that the one who has a great deal of leisure may become bored and also come to feel useless. Thus, the situation in which the wife works in the market and retains full responsibility for housework is not likely to be

---

[6]The reasoning is analogous to diminishing marginal utility as additional units of the same good are consumed.

optimal if it results in considerably less leisure for her than for her husband; this situation is especially likely to occur during the childrearing years. Alternatively, when the husband holds a demanding full-time position, while the responsibilities of the full-time homemaker become rather modest because the children are growing up or may even have left home, he will be short of leisure, whereas the wife may have more of it than she finds desirable.

Finally, some tasks are more efficiently performed by two people together, and many people may enjoy housework more when they do not have to do it alone. Frequently, homemakers spend much of their time isolated with little possibility for interaction with other adults.

For all these reasons, complete specialization by the husband in market work, regardless of whether the wife specializes completely in housework, may not maximize utility for the family. Nonetheless, the simple model does seem to square with reality to the extent that, on average, husbands devote substantially less time to housework.

Life Cycle Changes

A serious shortcoming of the simple model is that it ignores the fact that the comparative advantage of an individual does not necessarily remain the same over the life cycle. The value of home production for women peaks during the childrearing years and then declines as children grow up and become more self-sufficient. At the same time, labor market earnings and career opportunities tend to increase with work experience, and decline during years out of the labor force. If a woman withdraws from the labor force for a considerable period of time for childrearing, she is likely to pay a high price in terms of career advancement and earnings when she reenters the labor market. Hence, specializing entirely in homemaking may not be advantageous to the wife or to her family in the long run, even if it maximizes family well-being in the short run. Couples who are aware of this trade-off may decide it is worthwhile for the family to make some sacrifices of utility during the early years so that the wife can remain in the labor market in order to improve her long-run career prospects and enhance her lifetime earnings. As women increasingly value career achievement as an end in itself, the costs of work disruptions are apt to loom even larger. These issues are considered in greater detail in Chapter 6.

It might be argued that offsetting these disadvantages for the wife's career and the lifetime income of the family is the higher quality of children produced when the mother is at home full time. However, as discussed later in this chapter, differences in the amount of time that employed and nonemployed mothers spend with children appear to be quite modest. Also, maternal care is only one factor, of many, that affects children's well-being and achievement, as discussed further in Chapter 9.

Costs of Interdependence

Whatever the probability that the well-being of husband and wife will be maximized by specialization under existing circumstances, they will be less well-prepared to deal with unforeseen developments. When each spouse is able to manage a household and to earn a living if the need arises, the family will not be devastated if the husband is laid off or does not get a promotion or if the wife becomes ill and needs care instead of providing it for the rest of the family. Each will also be better equipped to manage alone in the event of divorce, separation, or death.

The difficulties encountered by the wife who has specialized in housework are related to her financial dependency and the negative effect on her potential earnings of time spent out of the labor force. As long as the relationship lasts, both husband and wife may gain from the greater proficiency each acquires in the area in which he or she specializes. However, their skills in the other area are likely to deteriorate or, at best, may fail to improve.

This problem will be especially serious for the homemaker. The husband who has concentrated on market work may be seriously inconvenienced by a lack of household skills, but his market earnings can be used to purchase household services. The woman who has specialized in household production, on the other hand, is left with no earnings and market skills that may be obsolete. In view of the high divorce rate and the substantially higher life expectancy of women than men, the risk of becoming a "displaced homemaker" is serious. The special problems of female-headed families are discussed more fully in Chapter 9.

Other potential difficulties exist for a full-time homemaker even if the partnership lasts until her death or until a time when she is adequately taken care of by a pension or inheritance. As pointed out earlier, the value of the homemaker's contribution to the family is greatest while the children are young. Now that the average number of children is about two and female life expectancy is nearly 80, this period would be relatively early in a woman's life. After that, the value of her contribution at home, assuming traditional childbearing patterns, would decline. Because her earning ability (generally lower than her husband's to begin with) would also decline during the time she was out of the labor market, her contribution during the latter part of her life would be considerably smaller than her partner's.

One way of looking at this scenario is that the husband's increasing earnings in the market may compensate for her declining productivity, so that she can now enjoy her share of the family's total income and a good deal of leisure. Yet, even if her partner is fond of her, is happy to share his largesse, and is grateful to her for the considerable contributions she made earlier, she may come to wonder about her present worth to the family. It is the reason we used to hear so much about the empty nest syndrome. On the other hand, she may not be so lucky. Her spouse may ask what she has done for him lately; he may take advantage of his increasingly greater bargaining power by appropriating a larger share of family income for commodities only he uses or only he wants and, in general, by adopting a lifestyle that conforms to his, but not necessarily to her, preferences.

Tastes and Bargaining Power

In our development of the simple model, we did not consider how the couple determines the allocation of income and of time to various commodities the family would enjoy. The decision will be relatively easy to make if they both have the same tastes and preferences. Then they will each opt for the same combination of goods and services to be shared. However, if their tastes differ significantly, the question arises as to how they will decide on the combination of commodities to be produced and consumed. Phrasing this point somewhat differently, whose preferences (husband's or wife's) will receive greater weight? These issues are first considered here in general terms and then, in the next section, are examined in light of alternative approaches to analyzing family decision making that have been developed more recently: transaction cost and bargaining models.

Considerable flexibility exists in the case where the partners pool production but then each can choose different bundles of commodities for individual consumption, although even here the share of the total going to each partner could be a matter of dispute. In fact, as we shall see, the assumption of income pooling within the household is not entirely realistic. More difficult problems arise in the case of public goods or commodities that have significant externalities. We saw earlier that for people with similar tastes, public goods and positive externalities increase the gains from joint consumption and collaboration. However, where one person's public good is another's public "bad" or where negative externalities in consumption exist, consumption of the commodity by one individual may reduce the well-being of the other. For example, one partner may derive enormous satisfaction from the presence of children, whereas the other may dislike having them around. Or one individual listening to loud music may reduce the enjoyment of the evening for the other.

These difficulties are relevant to the conclusions we derived from the simple model regarding the benefits of specialization. They suggest that conflicts of interest may arise between husband and wife and that relative bargaining power would likely play a role in resolving these conflicts.

Because in the traditional family the husband earns the money, he may be viewed as having the "power of the purse" and, therefore, be accorded a greater say in spending decisions. However, as might be expected, this situation is less likely when wives are employed.[7] A number of sociologists also suggest that decision making and allocation of responsibilities are built into the traditional husband-wife roles based on cultural norms and are unrelated to individual skills and interests. Accordingly, it is still often the case that the husband makes the important decisions. For instance, he may determine the make of the car they will buy, although the wife may decide on the color. On the other hand, in dual-earner couples, especially those in which both spouses are highly educated with similar earning power, spouses tend to make decisions concerning purchases of large-ticket items jointly, including the purchase of cars.[8]

Further, in a money economy, adherence to the traditional division of labor results in the wife being financially dependent on her husband. Because she stands to lose more if the marriage breaks up, she is likely to be under greater pressure to subordinate her wishes to her husband's than vice versa. Finally, the lesser outside contacts of the full-time homemaker in comparison to her employed husband may make her more dependent on his counsel and judgment than he is on hers. In fact, as noted earlier, a number of studies tend to confirm the dominance of the husband in decision making in marriages with the traditional division of labor.

---

[7]For studies of allocation and decision making within marriage, see Philip Blumstein and Pepper Schwartz, *American Couples* (New York: William Morrow, 1983); and Edward P. Lazear and Robert T. Michael, *Allocation of Income within the Household* (Chicago: University of Chicago Press, 1988). See also Marianne A. Ferber, "Labor Market Participation of Young Married Women: Causes and Effects," *Journal of Marriage and Family* 44, no. 2 (May 1982): 457–68.

[8]See, for instance, Philip Blumstein and Pepper Schwartz, "Money and Ideology: Their Impact on Power and the Division of Household Labor," in *Gender, Family, and the Economy: The Triple Overlap,* edited by Rae L. Blumberg (Newbury Park, CA: Sage, 1991), pp. 261–88; and Diane Crispell, "Dual-Earner Diversity," *American Demographics* 17, no. 7 (July 1995): 32–37.

Domestic Violence

An additional disadvantage of specialization is that it will tend to limit opportunities for women to get out of an abusive, harmful situation.[9] This issue gained substantial attention following the arrest in 1994 of O.J. Simpson, a well-known media figure and former star football player, who was accused of murdering his ex-wife, Nicole Brown Simpson, following a pattern of domestic abuse. Although he was acquitted of the murder charge in criminal court, he was later convicted in civil court. In any event, Simpson's case served to focus considerable attention on the issue of domestic violence and on the question of why abused spouses so often stay in such situations. It has been suggested that Nicole Brown Simpson felt trapped because her opportunities outside of marriage would not be good enough to enable her to maintain the lifestyle she had been accustomed to while she was married.[10] If that was the case for Nicole Brown Simpson, who was part of an affluent family, it would be all the more true for women with considerably worse prospects than hers. This outcome is also what bargaining models of economic behavior predict.[11] That is, women who are not employed themselves are less likely to have the financial means to leave an abusive relationship or to effectively persuade their husbands to stop the battering while still remaining in the marriage. Therefore it is not surprising that research identifies a link between improvements in women's economic status and reduced domestic violence. Similarly, changes in factors external to the family, such as states' adoption of unilateral divorce, have been found to reduce domestic violence, presumably because these options also improve women's bargaining power in the family. The availability of services for victims of domestic violence such as shelters, counseling, and legal advice would be expected to have the same effect.[12]

Dealing with spousal abuse, whether the aggressor be a husband or occasionally a wife, is often made more difficult by the ambivalent attitudes of society. Many believe that such battering is a "family matter" and should stay outside the realm of the legal system or suggest that the victim might have "asked for it" in some way. Another complication is that children in the household may further add to the emotional as well as the financial difficulty of leaving.

The consequences of domestic violence likely vary, depending on the length and severity of the abuse, but may include both psychological difficulties and physical injuries. Domestic violence may also affect employment and earnings. Interestingly, studies find that labor force participation rates of women who are victims of domestic violence are the same or even higher than of otherwise similar women who are not victims. This finding could be because battered women seek employment outside the home as a refuge or as a means to achieving economic independence (in preparation for leaving).

---

[9]For a discussion on trends in domestic violence, see Francine D. Blau, "Trends in the Well-Being of American Women, 1970–1995," *Journal of Economic Literature* 36, no. 1 (March 1998): 112–65.

[10]Michele Ingrassia and Melinda Beck, "Patterns of Abuse," *Newsweek,* July 4, 1994.

[11]For sociological theories regarding domestic violence, see Murray A. Strauss and Richard J. Gelles, *Physical Violence in American Families* (New Brunswick, NJ: Transaction Publishers, 1990). An economist, Robert Pollak, formalizes the notion of a cycle of domestic violence in "An Intergenerational Model of Domestic Violence," *Journal of Population Economics* 17, no. 2 (June 2004): 311–29.

[12]For evidence on these points, see Amy Farmer and Jill Tiefenthaler, "An Economic Analysis of Domestic Violence," *Review of Social Economy* 55, no. 3 (Fall 1997): 337–58; Helen V. Tauchen, Ann Dryden Witte, and Sharon K. Long, "Domestic Violence: A Nonrandom Affair," *International Economic Review* 32, no. 2 (May 1991): 491–521; and Betsey Stevenson and Justin Wolfers, "Bargaining in the Shadow of the Law: Divorce Laws and Family Distress," National Bureau of Economic Research Working Paper No. 10175 (December 2003).

On the other hand, some evidence indicates that battering negatively affects women's job performance and may consequently lower their wages.[13]

Disadvantages of Specialization: A Summary

Thus, we find that the traditional family, in which husband and wife each specialize in a separate sphere, is not as advantageous as the simple economic model presented at the beginning of this chapter suggests. Specializing in homemaking is a particularly high-risk undertaking, for the value of home production peaks early in the life cycle; market skills tend to decline when a person is out of the labor market; and women are often socially isolated in the home. Therefore, the homemaker's bargaining power within the family is likely to decline over time, and she will find it difficult to manage on her own if the need arises. However, the wage earner encounters some risks as well. If the marriage breaks up, he may be confronted with the need to pay alimony or face the problem of avoiding it. Also, he may lack even the minimal skills to keep house for himself, let alone his children. Last, but not least, children of divorced parents may have to live in poverty with a mother unable to earn a decent living or, in some cases, with a father relatively inexperienced in child care.

One may speculate as to why so many couples opted for so long for a lifestyle that raises so many potential problems, even as conditions grew less favorable for traditional marriages. A number of obvious answers come to mind. First, many young people, fully aware of the high divorce rate, nonetheless expected their own marriages to succeed. This mindset is not so different from the person who starts a small business, fully expecting to make a go of it in spite of the formidable bankruptcy rate. Second, important initial decisions tended to be made at a relatively young age, when concerns for well-being in middle and old age generally do not loom large. Third, pressures from relatives and peers toward adoption of traditional family arrangements likely played a role. Among some groups it may still take a strong-willed, confident, young person to withstand these pressures. Without a doubt, however, these factors changed considerably, which surely helps to account for the rising proportion of couples who are rejecting the old breadwinner-homemaker dichotomy.

Before leaving the subject of the disadvantages of specialization, it is also worth noting that public policies, some of them the subject of lively public debate, can also influence the decision as to whether the wife should be a full-time homemaker. These factors include tax and Social Security provisions that favor one-earner as opposed to two-earner couples, which are discussed in some detail in Chapter 10, as well as divorce laws that may or may not adequately protect the interests of partners with little or no labor market experience in cases of marital dissolution.

TRANSACTION COST AND BARGAINING APPROACHES

One of the shortcomings of the neoclassical model of the family highlighted by the preceding discussion is that it ignores the internal decision-making structure of the family. It simply assumes that the family operates efficiently and frictionlessly either because of a consensus on preferences within the family or because decisions are made by an

---

[13]Amy Farmer and Jill Tiefenthaler, "The Employment Effects of Domestic Violence," *Research in Labor Economics* 23 (2004).

altruistic family head and accepted by all other members.[14] In this view of the family, power has no relevance.

However, more recently developed alternative approaches emphasize transaction costs and bargaining. These approaches endeavor to unlock the "black box" of the family and look more deeply into how families are organized and make decisions.[15] The transaction cost approach, for instance, focuses on the role of institutions in structuring complex, long-term relationships so as to minimize transaction costs. That is, just as a merger between firms eliminates the costs of negotiating repeated contracts and ensures that the initially separate firms will do business together for years to come, a marriage fosters a long-term relationship between partners. Marriage incorporates both rules about the nature of the ongoing relationship and about the rights of each individual should the union break up. Hence, it might be seen as a contractual affiliation that is "flexible enough to allow adaptive sequential decision making in the face of unfolding events."[16]

Marriage as an implicit contract provides incentives for couples to make substantial marriage-specific investments. Hence, they are likely to invest more time and effort in activities that produce "commodities" more highly valued within the marriage than they would be otherwise. Most importantly, they often devote much effort to raising their children, who are likely to be particularly valued by their own parents, but may not be valued by another partner and may be a liability in the search for a new spouse.[17] Women, especially traditional homemakers, are more likely than men to make such marriage-specific investments, which puts them at a greater disadvantage if the marriage should end.

Because marriage is intended to be a long-term relationship, it is not realistic to specify everything in advance, that is, to provide for all possible contingencies.[18] At the same time, it is quite unlikely that husbands and wives share the same preferences regarding all consumption and production decisions. These factors serve to make bargaining between the partners particularly important. A class of models has been developed that allows for husbands and wives to have different preferences with outcomes determined through a process of bargaining.[19]

---

[14]The consensus model was proposed by Paul Samuelson, "Social Indifference Curves," *Quarterly Journal of Economics* 70, no. 1 (February 1956): 1–22. The altruist model was introduced by Gary S. Becker, "A Theory of Marriage: Part II," *Journal of Political Economy* 82, no. 2 (March/April 1974): 11–26.

[15]Even though this section focuses on decision making among spouses, bargaining models have been applied to decisions made by a parent and an adult child as well. See, for instance, Lilliana E. Pezzin and Barbara Steinberg Schone, "Intergenerational Household Formation, Female Labor Supply and Informal Caregiving: A Bargaining Approach," *Journal of Human Resources* 34, no. 3 (Summer 1999): 475–503.

[16]For a discussion of the transaction cost approach, see Pollak, "A Transaction Cost Approach"; quote is from p. 595.

[17]For instance, see Evelyn Lehrer, "On Marriage-Specific Human Capital: Its Role as a Determinant of Remarriage," *Journal of Population Economics* 3, no. 3 (October 1990): 193–213.

[18]For a discussion, see Paula England and George Farkas, *Households, Employment and Gender* (New York: Aldine Publishing Co., 1986).

[19]For reviews of the literature, see Shelly J. Lundberg and Robert A. Pollak, "Bargaining and Distribution in Marriage," *Journal of Economic Perspectives* 10, no. 4 (Fall 1996): 139–58; Bina Agarwal, "'Bargaining' and Gender Relations: Within and Beyond the Household," *Feminist Economics* 3, no. 1 (March 1997): 1–51; and Theodore Bergstrom, "Economics in a Family Way," *Journal of Economic Literature* 34, no. 4 (December 1996): 1903–34. For early work in this area, see Mary Jean Horney and Marjorie B. McElroy, "Nash-Bargained Household Decisions: Toward a Generalization of the Theory of Demand," *International Economic Review* 22, no. 2 (June 1981): 333–49; and Marilyn Manser and Murray Brown, "Marriage and Household Decision Making," *International Economic Review* 21, no. 1 (February 1980): 31–44. In related work, Pierre-Andre Chiappori developed a "collective" model that nests the cooperative bargaining model and common preference model within it as special cases in "Collective Labor Supply and Welfare," *Journal of Political Economy* 100, no. 3 (June 1992): 437–67.

In these models, the bargaining power of each spouse is determined by his or her *threat point*—the level of well-being that each would attain if they cannot reach agreement within the marriage. In the most common type of family bargaining model, termed *divorce-threat* bargaining models, the threat point depends on the amount of income controlled by each party if the marriage were to terminate.[20] As in the case of negotiations between a vendor and a customer, the final solution is likely to more closely reflect the preferences of the party with the stronger threat effect, who is better able to "walk away" from the deal. Apart from each individual's control of resources outside the marriage, factors external to the family may also affect one or both of the partners' threat points. Such factors might include laws defining the division of marital property, the probability of remarriage, as well as eligibility rules for and benefit levels under welfare.[21]

To make the discussion concrete, let's reconsider the example of John and Jane, one of the married couples discussed earlier. They maximized total family income by specializing; Jane split her time between home production and market work while John did only market work, with no time spent in home production. Once total income is maximized, the next issue is to decide how to allocate this joint income among different commodities the family might use. For instance, even if parents agree on a basic level of support for their children, they may differ on the amount and quality of items such as children's clothing or "extras" such as music lessons and gymnastics classes. As another example, one spouse may prefer to spend discretionary income on expensive cars, while the other may prefer travel. The simple model assumes either that John and Jane have the same preferences or that John is an altruistic head and so only his preferences matter.

In some instances one of these assumptions may be reasonable, but bargaining models more realistically allow for the possibility that John's and Jane's preferences may differ, and that both matter. In this view, whether the amount spent, say, on their children's clothing ultimately favors John's or Jane's preferences depends, in large part, on their relative bargaining power. Assuming a traditional division of labor, Jane is expected to have less power because she has a weaker threat point. That is, if the couple were to divorce, she would probably not fare as well as John; for even if she were to receive child support and perhaps a small divorce settlement, she would likely have more difficulty supporting herself (and their children) because she has mainly invested in marriage-specific rather than market skills. Other factors that affect her relative bargaining power would be the level of welfare benefits and food stamps available to her if she were divorced, her labor market opportunities, and her chances for remarriage. John, on the other hand, is likely to be in a much stronger bargaining position because, during the marriage, he remained fully attached to the labor market. However, it is also the case that once divorced, he may have considerably less contact with his children, depending in part on the provisions of the child custody agreement. John may also need to pay alimony

---

[20]As an alternative, Shelly J. Lundberg and Robert A. Pollak suggest a noncooperative threat point within the marriage itself, in which the partners fully specialize in the provision of public goods according to traditional gender roles; thus, the wife may provide all the child care, while the husband may do all the outdoor work. In this scenario, an individual has a stronger threat point if the noncooperative solution is closer to his or her desired level of public goods. See "Separate Spheres Bargaining and the Marriage Market," *Journal of Political Economy* 101, no. 6 (December 1993): 988–1010.

[21]Marjorie B. McElroy, "The Empirical Content of Nash-Bargained Household Behavior," *Journal of Human Resources* 25, no. 4 (Fall 1990): 559–83.

and child support. In addition, he is likely to have to purchase some household services formerly obtained from his wife, and it may be difficult, for instance, to find restaurants and caterers willing and able to provide meals equally convenient and suited to his personal tastes.

One way of determining whether husbands' and wives' preferences differ significantly is to see whether they spend their personal income in the same way. A good deal of research shows that they generally do not. One study specifically examined the effect of a policy change in the United Kingdom in the 1970s that transferred receipt of income, in the form of a child benefit, from the father to the mother. It found that this change led to an *increase* in expenditures on children's clothing.[22] This study, among others, suggests that the "common preference" assumption of the simple model does not hold up. Indeed, consistent with bargaining models, mounting evidence shows that who controls family resources affects a wide array of outcomes beyond consumption expenditures, including decisions as to how couples allocate their time, as well as how much they give to charities and who should receive these donations.[23] In addition, as discussed earlier, women who have greater economic resources tend to experience lower levels of domestic violence, again showing that the distribution of resources in a marriage affects family outcomes. These findings do not directly prove that bargaining takes place, nor indicate what specific form it might take, but they are consistent with a bargaining framework rather than either the consensus or altruist models.

In our preceding discussion, we focused on expenditures on children's clothing as an illustrative example of a case in which husbands and wives may disagree about expenditures on children. In fact, a growing body of research suggests that mothers allocate more resources and place greater emphasis on their children's well-being than do fathers. Notably, in developing countries where resources are scarce, children's health and survival probabilities have been found to improve when mothers have greater control over family resources.[24]

One implication of the research evidence we have reviewed is that the government has the *potential* to promote certain outcomes, to the extent that its policies and laws affect the distribution of resources between men and women, both inside and outside of marriage.[25] For instance, in the United Kingdom, when the government paid the child benefit to mothers rather than fathers, it was found to improve children's well-being. Another way that government may affect families is through laws that govern the distribution of

---

[22]Shelly J. Lundberg, Robert. A. Pollak, and Terence J. Wales, "Do Husbands and Wives Pool Their Resources? Evidence from the U.K. Child Benefit," *Journal of Human Resources* 32, no. 3 (Summer 1997): 463–80.

[23]Regarding married couple labor supply, see Paul Schultz, "Testing the Neoclassical Model of Family Labor Supply and Fertility," *Journal of Human Resources* 25, no. 4 (Fall 1990): 599–634; and for cohabitors see Anne E. Winkler, "Economic Decision Making Among Cohabitors: Findings Regarding Income Pooling," *Applied Economics* 29, no. 8 (August 1997): 1079–90. Regarding charitable contributions, see James Andreoni, Eleanor Brown, and Isaac Rischall, "Charitable Giving by Married Couples: Who Decides and Why Does It Matter?" *Journal of Human Resources* 38, no. 1 (Winter 2003): 111–33.

[24]See, for instance, Duncan Thomas, "Intra-Household Resource Allocation: An Inferential Approach," *Journal of Human Resources* 25, no. 4 (Fall 1990): 635–64; Duncan Thomas, "Like Father, Like Son: Like Mother, Like Daughter: Parental Resources and Child Height," *Journal of Human Resources* 29, no. 4 (Fall 1994): 950–88; and Rae L. Blumberg, "Income Under Female versus Male Control: Hypotheses from a Theory of Gender Stratification and Data from the Third World," *Journal of Family Issues* 9, no. 1 (March 1988): 51–84.

[25]Agarwal, "'Bargaining' and Gender Relations."

marital assets in case of divorce. For example, adopting community property law (which mandates equal division of property) would give the wife a larger share of marital assets and hence increase her bargaining power within marriage. Interestingly, one study found that marital property laws that favor women are associated with increased labor supply of wives, and in turn, less time spent in housework.[26] Similarly, as discussed earlier, the adoption of unilateral divorce laws have been found to reduce domestic violence, again most likely by increasing women's bargaining power. It has been further suggested that changes in men's and women's relative bargaining power may affect not only decisions *within* existing marriages, but even the decisions of unmarried individuals, such as whether to get married, and if so, to whom.[27]

MARXIST AND RADICAL FEMINIST VIEWS OF THE FAMILY

Up to now we have focused on the mainstream neoclassical model of the family, first developed by Gary S. Becker, followed by a discussion of the transaction cost and bargaining variations of the neoclassical model. Now we turn to the so-called heterodox views of Marxists and radical feminists, who offer substantially different interpretations of the division of labor within the family and of its relation to the position of women and men in the family and in the labor market.[28] Like proponents of bargaining models, adherents of both the Marxist and radical feminist schools of thought emphasize the role of power relationships. And, both emphasize the potential for exploitation of the weaker party. Beyond that, however, their views differ fundamentally from each other. Marxists focus on the role of class and capitalism, while radical feminists focus on the role of gender and patriarchy.[29]

Capitalism describes an economy where the preponderance of capital is privately owned and controlled, even though government may also play a large part, as is the case in all capitalist countries, including the United States. Marxists see such an economy as one in which capitalists, who own the means of production, wield power over workers who do not, that is, who lack income-yielding property. Workers are therefore forced to sell their labor to capitalists for wages. Women, whether they are workers or

---

[26]Jeffrey S. Gray, "Divorce-Law Changes and Married Women's Labor Supply," *American Economic Review* 88, no. 3 (June 1998): 628–51.

[27]Robert A. Pollak, "Empowering Women, Bargaining in Families, and Marriage Markets," unpublished working paper, Washington University in St. Louis (January 2003).

[28]See, for example, Heidi I. Hartmann, "Capitalism, Patriarchy, and Job Segregation by Sex," *Signs: Journal of Women in Culture and Society* 1, no. 3 (Spring 1976, pt. 2): 137–70; Heidi I. Hartmann, "The Family as the Locus of Gender, Class and Political Struggle: The Example of Housework," *Signs: Journal of Women in Culture and Society* 6, no. 3 (Spring 1981): 366–94; and Nancy Folbre, *Who Pays for the Kids? Gender and the Structures of Constraint* (London: Routledge, 1994). For an institutional approach to the family, see Clair Brown, "Consumption Norms, Work Roles, and Economic Growth," in *Gender in the Workplace*, edited by Clair Brown and Joseph A. Pechman (Washington, DC: Brookings Institution, 1987); and Daphne Greenwood, "The Economic Significance of 'Women's Place' in Society: A New-Institutionalist View," *Journal of Economic Issues* 18, no. 3 (September 1984): 663–80.

[29]The following analysis draws on the explications of Nancy Folbre, "Socialism, Feminist and Scientific," in *Beyond Economic Man*, edited by Marianne A. Ferber and Julie A. Nelson (Chicago: University of Chicago Press, 1993), pp. 94–110; Julie A. Nelson, "The Study of Choice or the Study of Provisioning? Gender and the Definition of Economics," in *Beyond Economic Man*, edited by Marianne A. Ferber and Julie A. Nelson (Chicago: University of Chicago Press, 1993), pp. 23–36; and Therese Jefferson and John E. King, "Never Intended to be a Theory of Everything: Domestic Labor in Neoclassical and Marxian Economics" *Feminist Economics* 7, no. 3 (November 2001): 71–101.

not, supply unpaid labor, including reproductive services in the family, thereby reducing the wages capitalists have to pay. Thus they are viewed as being exploited by capitalists, indirectly as housewives, as well as directly if they are workers. In addition, Marxists recognize that women are often oppressed by their wage-earning husbands.

Engels,[30] Marx's collaborator and close friend, whose ideas about the family were widely accepted by Marxists, argued that women's inferior position came about as a result of men gaining control over private property over long years of pre-industrial history. In this view, married women, who had been publicly recognized household administrators, became a kind of private servant. Later, with the rise of large-scale industry, working women did regain some access to the public sphere—as workers—but also remained responsible for housework. Marxists promised that they would relieve women of this burden by "socializing housework," providing such services as day care for children, nursing home care for the elderly and infirm, and public dining rooms for workers. However, even the former Soviet Union was slow to provide these facilities and gave priority to rapid industrialization, while arguing that the fall of capitalism, which was the cause of women's oppression, would bring about their liberation.[31] In the meantime, they never questioned that the household was women's responsibility, nor were men hired to do jobs that were previously performed by women in the household.[32]

Other socialists have often been more sympathetic to women's concerns, with views that are much closer to those of feminists than are those of doctrinaire Marxists. For instance, one of the best-known early British socialists, Robert Owen, wanted to eliminate the rigid boundary drawn by both neoclassical and Marxist economists between the dog-eat-dog economy where all people single-mindedly pursue their own self interest, and the family, where everyone is dedicated to the common good. Owen further viewed allegiance to family as basically another version of self-interest.[33] And, the early German socialist August Bebel provided an extensive account of legal injustices, with emphasis on women's lack of control over their own lives.[34] These authors, while sharing Marxists' concern with class, were clearly concerned with patriarchy as well.

Patriarchy refers to a system where men's dominance as a group over women as a group is the real source of gender inequality.[35] Radical feminists generally see the family as the true locus of women's oppression. In addition, although they recognize both

---

[30]Friedrich Engels, *The Origin of the Family, Private Property, and the State* (New York: International Publishers, 1884 [1972]).

[31]In practice, however, their promises to socialize housework had been only partially fulfilled by the time of the dissolution of the Soviet Union.

[32]Some exceptions include Clara Zetkin, "Dialogue with Clarra Zetkin," reprinted in Robert C. Tucker, *The Lenin Anthology* (New York: W.W. Norton and Company, 1975). Another was one of the greatest Marxian economic theorists, Rosa Luxemburg, "Women's Suffrage and Class Struggle," in *Selected Political Writings of Rosa Luxemburg,* edited by Dick Howard (New York: Monthly Review Press, 1912 [1971]), pp. 216–22. Both of these women argued that the Soviet Union should make greater efforts to provide services that would take the place of household labor.

[33]Robert Owen, *Lectures on the Marriages of the Priesthood of the Old Immoral World . . . with an Appendix Containing the Marriage System of the New Moral World* (Leeds: J. Hobson, 1840).

[34]August Bebel, *Women and Socialism* (New York: Schocken Books, 1971).

[35]Folbre suggests that it is also based on age and sexual preference in *Who Pays for the Kids*? Other useful discussions of patriarchy are to be found in Nancy Holmstrom, "The Socialist Feminist Project," *Monthly Review* 54, no. 10 (March 2003): 38–48; and Julie Matthaei, "Marxist-Feminist Contributions to Radical Economics," in *Radical Economics*, edited by Robert and Susan Feiner (Boston: Kluwer, 1992), pp. 117–44.

the existence of emotional ties and of some unified interests within the family, they nonetheless see the family as the locus of struggle. Radical feminists were also the ones who originated the slogan "the personal is political." In this view, Jane's responsibility for taking care of the household and the children, while John "helps her" by clearing the table, taking out the garbage, and putting the children to bed, is not merely the result of a private decision of these individuals, but is to a considerable extent influenced by patriarchal tradition. Adherence to this patriarchal tradition serves in turn to perpetuate it. Further, radical feminists assert that the patriarchal tradition existed long before capitalism and would, absent other changes, continue even if capitalism disappeared. In fact, they believe that the particular economic system is largely irrelevant to their concern with patriarchy, just as Marxists believe that patriarchy is irrelevant to their concern with the economic system.

The Marxist feminist interpretation of the situation is somewhat different from either of the other two. Adherents of this view believe that the present status of women is the result of a long process of interaction between patriarchy and capitalism. They argue that patriarchy preceded capitalism and helped to shape its present form, but that capitalism in turn has helped to shape patriarchy as it exists today. Specifically, they claim that the primary mechanism for maintaining male superiority in the capitalistic economy has been occupational segregation, the restriction of women in the labor market to a relatively small number of predominantly female jobs.[36] This job segregation, caused and perpetuated not only by capitalists but also by male workers and their unions, depresses wages for women and thus makes them economically dependent on men. At the same time, the traditional division of labor in the home reinforces occupational segregation in the labor market. Therefore, Marxist feminists argue that if women's subordination is to end, and if working men are to escape class oppression, occupational segregation and the traditional division of labor in the household will both have to end. In their view, in order to achieve freedom for everyone, men must be persuaded, or forced if need be, to join with women in the struggles against patriarchal capitalism, the embodiment of the stratified society par excellence.

NONMARKET WORK

Economists have traditionally focused their analyses and interests on market work; however, much work is performed outside the market, both in the household and in the voluntary sector. Such unpaid work substantially contributes to the well-being of individuals, their families, and society at large. In this section we consider both types of nonmarket work and how women's and men's involvement in these activities has changed with women's rising labor force participation. By examining the available evidence, it is possible to estimate how much time husbands and wives spend on market work, home production, and volunteer work, and the extent to which changes have occurred in recent decades in the allocation of time to each of them. In addition, we consider the complex issues involved in estimating the value of unpaid nonmarket contributions.

---

[36]Some Marxist feminists go so far as to analyze the household itself in class terms, seeing the husband as the capitalist who appropriates the surplus value of the worker-wife. See, for instance, Harriet Fraad, Stephen Resnick, and Richard Wolff, *Bringing It All Back Home: Class, Gender and Power in the Modern Household* (London: Pluto Press, 1994).

Housework

Estimates of hours spent in housework vary considerably. A review of the individual studies suggests reasons for these differences. They are based on different samples, drawn from different populations, the information is collected in different ways, and definitions of housework are not always the same.[37] For instance, some studies collect information based on retrospective questions about particular activities such as "How many hours did you spend doing laundry last week?" while other studies ask respondents to record in a "time diary" what they do during specific blocks of time. It turns out that estimates of hours spent in housework obtained from retrospective reports tend to be quite a bit higher. In terms of definitions, some studies explicitly include child care, others do not; some include only work done around the house, while others include household-related activities performed elsewhere.[38]

It is only as recently as 2003 that the U.S. government launched its first-ever time use survey, the American Time Use Survey (ATUS), following the lead of many other countries, including Canada, Australia, and the countries in the European Union.[39] This survey collects time diary reports from one respondent per household using a subsample of households who were interviewed for the Current Population Survey (CPS). (The CPS is the U.S. government survey used to collect data on unemployment and *paid* work and is the source of much of the data provided in this book.) Because these data have only just become available, we rely on other surveys to provide information about trends in housework.

Notably, data from various sources indicate similar trends in time spent in housework. They show that wives, both employed and nonemployed, did substantially less housework in the 1970s than was the case in the 1960s, while time spent by husbands in housework did not change much.[40]

Table 3-2, which provides data for more recent years, shows that while the division of labor remained quite unequal in 2000, the difference in the allocation of time to market work and nonmarket work between husbands and wives nonetheless narrowed considerably since the late 1970s.[41] An interesting feature of these data is that they show trends in paid work and housework disaggregated by marital status and by employment

---

[37]For a discussion of methodological issues, see National Research Council, *Time-Use Measurement and Research* (Washington, DC: National Academy Press, 2000); and Beth Anne Shelton and Daphne John, "The Division of Household Labor," *Annual Review of Sociology* 22, no. 1 (1996): 299–322.

[38]See, for instance, Suzanne Bianchi, Melissa A. Milkie, Liana C. Sayer, and John P. Robinson, "Is Anyone Doing the Housework? Trends in the Gender Division of Household Labor," *Social Forces* 79, no. 1 (September 2000): 1–39; W. Keith Bryant, Hyojin Kang, Cathleen D. Zick, and Anna Y. Chan, "Measuring Housework in Time Use Surveys," *Review of Economics of the Household* 2 (2004): 23–47; and Anne E. Winkler, "Measuring Time Use in Households with More Than One Person," *Monthly Labor Review* 125, no. 2 (February 2002): 45–52.

[39]A description of the ATUS can be found on the U.S. Bureau of Labor Statistics' Web site, www.bls.gov and in Michael Horrigan and Diane Herz, "Planning, Designing, and Executing the BLS American Time-Use Survey," *Monthly Labor Review* 127 no. 10 (October 2004): 3–19. Regarding international efforts, see National Research Council, *Time-Use Measurement and Research.*

[40]See Joseph H. Pleck, "Husband's Paid Work and Family Roles: Current Research Issues," *Research in the Interweave of Social Roles: Jobs and Families,* edited by Helena Lopata and Joseph H. Pleck (Greenwich, CT: JAI Press, 1983), pp. 251–333; and Francine D. Blau, Anne E. Winkler, and Marianne A. Ferber, *The Economics of Women, Men, and Work,* 3rd ed. (Upper Saddle River, NJ: Prentice Hall, 1998), table 3.2, p. 52.

[41]The table and discussion here draw on Blau, "Trends in the Well-Being of American Women." See also John P. Robinson and Geoffrey Godbey, *Time for Life: The Surprising Ways Americans Use Their Time,* 2nd ed. (University Park: Pennsylvania State University Press, 1999).

TABLE 3-2   Average Weekly Hours of Housework and Market Work, Selected Years

	1978		*1988*		*2000*		*Change in Housework Hours*		
	Market Work	*House-Work*	*Market Work*	*House-Work*	*Market Work*	*House-Work*	*1978–1988*	*1988–2000*	*1978–2000*
Women	20.1	26.7	26.4	21.3	28.9	16.3	−5.4	−5.0	−10.4
Nonmarried	27.2	17.2	32.1	13.4	32.3	12.3	−3.8	−1.1	−4.9
Married	18.3	29.1	24.9	23.6	27.5	17.9	−5.5	−5.7	−11.2
Not employed	0.3	37.1	0.3	33.0	0.2	27.4	−4.1	−5.6	−9.7
Employed	29.3	24.3	32.2	20.8	34.3	15.5	−3.5	−5.3	−8.8
Men	42.5	6.1	43.3	7.4	41.3	7.2	1.3	−0.2	1.1
Nonmarried	38.3	8.2	41.2	7.0	37.1	8.0	−1.2	1.0	−0.2
Married	43.1	5.8	43.7	7.5	42.6	7.0	1.7	−0.5	1.2
Wife not employed	42.5	5.0	41.3	6.4	42.0	6.3	1.4	−0.1	1.3
Wife employed	43.5	6.4	44.4	7.8	42.7	7.1	1.4	−0.7	0.7

Note: Time spent on housework may be understated because respondents were not specifically queried about child care or time spent on household chores away from home (e.g., shopping). Omitting these hours implies a corresponding understatement of total work time. Data are drawn from the Panel Study of Income Dynamics.

Source: Figures for 1978 and 1988 are from Francine D. Blau, "Trends in the Well-Being of American Women: 1970–1995," *Journal of Economic Literature*, 36, no.1 (March 1998): 112–65. Figures for 2000 were calculated by authors. In each year, the sample excludes respondents and spouses with missing values for hours of market work and housework. For earlier years, but not for 2000, respondents with missing values for education are also excluded.

status of the wife. As seen in Table 3-2, women's average hours of housework declined at a steady and rapid pace from the late 1970s to 2000. In fact, their time spent in housework declined by 10.4 hours, substantially more so for married than unmarried women, and, surprisingly, somewhat more for nonemployed than for employed wives. Over the same period of time, women increased their market work by 8.8 hours, on average, largely as a result of the rise in the proportion of married women in the labor force, but also as a result of an increase in hours of paid work among employed wives.[42]

For men, the data in Table 3-2 suggest a different picture. Their hours of market work decreased and hours of housework increased from the late 1970s to 2000, and both these changes were uneven and far more modest than for women. For instance, husbands' hours of housework increased by 1.7 hours from the late 1970s to late 1980s and decreased by .5 hours in the 1990s, leading to an overall increase in housework for the full period of 1.2 hours. The lack of further increase in husband's time spent in housework in the 1990s identified in Table 3-2 is corroborated by data from other sources.[43] Because it is not yet clear why this stalling occurred, it is difficult to project future trends.

---

[42]Trends in market hours for women workers are also discussed in Chapter 4. The trends reported here differ somewhat; among the reasons for this difference is that the underlying data differ as do the subgroups analyzed. Table 3-2 provides trends in hours worked for all women (including employed and nonemployed) and for employed married women; Chapter 4 discusses trends for all employed women.

[43]Robinson and Godbey, *Time for Life*, chap. 22; and Bianchi et al., "Is Anyone Doing the Housework?"

For unmarried men, housework hours declined between the late 1970s to late 1980s (as did housework hours for all groups except married men), but subsequently increased in the 1990s. This recent increase, albeit small, is rather puzzling in light of the fact that housework hours have decreased or have remained virtually unchanged for all other groups. It could reflect the rising share of single-father households or it may simply be a small random fluctuation.

Overall, women's time spent in housework decreased from about four times to three times that of men from the late 1970s to the late 1980s. This decrease was the result of the sizable reduction in housework done by women combined with a small increase in housework by men. By 2000, women's time spent in housework was two times that of men, though this further decrease was mainly due to women's reduction in time spent in housework.[44]

Several developments documented in Table 3-2 stand out. First, as already noted, the increase in housework for married men observed from the late 1970s to the late 1980s stands in sharp contrast to the decline for all other groups. The trend toward smaller families, changes in household technology, and the increasing availability of market substitutes probably help to explain this decline. Therefore, absent some reallocation between husbands and wives, we would have expected husbands' housework to have declined also. The fact that it increased suggests some reallocation of tasks during the 1980s, though as noted earlier, it did not continue after that. The rise in real wages for women, which increased the opportunity cost of their time spent in nonmarket activities, is likely one of the factors that contributed to the decrease in the time they spend on housework. A dynamic process may be going on in which rising market wages induce women to allocate more time to market work and less time to housework. As they do so, they accumulate more labor market experience, further enhancing their wages and resulting in further decreases in their housework time. It would also explain why women's housework hours continued to decline through the 1990s.

A second striking development seen in Table 3-2 is that although nonemployed wives continue to do more housework than employed wives, the time they spend on it decreased somewhat more than for employed wives during the entire period examined. This trend is particularly notable in light of the fact that, during the first half of the twentieth century, the amount of time that full-time homemakers spent on housework remained virtually unchanged.[45] A third interesting trend is that from the late 1970s to the late 1980s, time spent on housework increased not only for husbands with employed wives but also for those whose wives were not employed. A possible explanation is that women's rising earnings potential may have altered the balance of bargaining power in the household, regardless of wives' employment, and that wives may have used their increased bargaining power to insist on some reallocation of housework.

Recent research also points to several other interesting patterns in the allocation of housework. For instance, based on Gary Becker's theory, we would especially expect to see husbands spend more time doing housework in families in which the wife brings

---

[44]The 2:1 figure reported here is also consistent with 2003 findings from the American Time Use Survey (ATUS). See U.S. Bureau of Labor Statistics, "Time-Use Survey—First Results Announced by BLS," *News* (USDL 04-1797), September 14, 2004.

[45]As noted in Chapter 2, until the mid-1960s housewives continued to spend as many hours on housework as their grandmothers had at around the turn of the century. See Joann Vanek, "Time Spent in Housework," *Scientific American* 231, no. 5 (November 1974): 116–20.

home the majority of the earnings (as compared to families in which the husband does). The available evidence, however, suggests that even in these families, wives still do the lion's share of the housework, though the division of labor is a bit more equal as compared with households in which the husband is the main earner. Available data also indicate that nonemployed husbands spend surprisingly little time on housework. Taken together, these findings suggest that time spent in housework continues to remain tied to traditional notions of women's and men's expected gender roles.[46]

Time spent in housework also depends on the presence and ages of children. Men tend to do the most housework in families with young children, though not necessarily child care, and do far less when their children are older, especially if there is a daughter age 12 or older. Moreover, not only do teenage girls do more housework than teenage boys, but this gender gap appears to widen over the course of high school.[47]

Interesting differences are also evident in the allocation of housework between married spouses and cohabiting men and women. In both types of living arrangements, women do considerably more housework than men, but the gender gap is wider among married couples. On average, cohabiting men spend 7 percent more time in housework than married men, while cohabiting women spend 18 percent less time on housework than married women.[48] These findings are consistent with Becker's theory of specialization. Cohabitation, by definition, involves fewer legal protections. Consequently, specialization is particularly risky. Evidence also shows less specialization among partners in gay and lesbian couples, perhaps for this reason, among others.[49]

A serious limitation of the data presented in Table 3-2 is that respondents were not specifically asked about time spent on child care or on household chores away from home. Child care in any case raises measurement problems because it is not clear which child care activities should be included. In cases such as going for a walk with a child, it is difficult to separate nonmarket work from leisure. In addition, counting time spent with children accurately is complicated because parents often watch them while they are doing another activity such as cleaning the house or reading the newspaper. Nonetheless, given the considerable interest in how much time parents and children spend together, we review recent trends.

It should come as no surprise that nonemployed mothers spend more time with their children than employed mothers do. One study, which defined children's time spent with mothers quite broadly to include time their mother was directly engaged

---

[46]Richard B. Freeman, "The Feminization of Work in the U.S.: A New Era for (Man)kind?" *Gender and the Labor Market: Econometric Evidence on Obstacles in Achieving Gender Equality,* edited by Siv Gustafsson and Danièle Meulders (New York: MacMillan, 2000); Michael Bittman, Paula England, Nancy Folbre, Liana Sayer, and George Matheson, "When Does Gender Trump Money? Bargaining and Time in Household Work," *American Journal of Sociology* 109, no. 1 (July 2003): 186–214; and Julie Brines, "Economic Dependency, Gender, and the Division of Labor at Home," *American Journal of Sociology* 100, no. 3 (November 1994): 652–88.

[47]Constance T. Gager, Teresa M. Cooney, and Kathleen Thiede Call, "The Effects of Family Characteristics and Time Use on Teenagers' Household Labor," *Journal of Marriage and Family* 61, no. 4 (November 1999): 982–95.

[48]Scott J. South and Glenna Spitze, "Housework in Marital and Nonmarital Households," *American Sociological Review* 59 (June 1994): 327–47.

[49]Lisa A. Giddings, "Political Economy and the Construction of Gender: The Example of Housework within Same-Sex Households," *Feminist Economics* 4, no. 2 (Summer 1998): 97–106; and M.V. Lee Badgett, *Money, Myths and Change: The Economic Lives of Lesbians and Gay Men* (Chicago: University of Chicago Press, 2001), chap. 6.

with them or when she was just present, found that, in 1997, children of employed mothers spent about 83 percent as much time with their mothers as did children of nonemployed mothers. This figure is down somewhat from 86 percent in 1981, not because employed mothers and their children are now spending less time together, but because time children spent with nonemployed mothers increased somewhat more than did time children spent with employed mothers.[50]

The time that children spend with employed compared to nonemployed mothers may sound higher than one might have expected. However, Suzanne Bianchi, among others, offers a number of plausible explanations. For instance, a considerable fraction of employed women work less than full-time, full year. In addition, even women who are employed full-time may be able to juggle their schedules to pick their children up after school and occasionally take an afternoon off from work. Also, school-age children spend a good part of their day in school and preschool has become quite common even for children with nonemployed mothers. These factors, as well, reduce the difference in the total amount of time children of employed and nonemployed mothers spend together.[51]

There has also been substantial interest in how the amount of "quality time" shared by children and their mothers compares, depending on the mother's employment. Perhaps not surprisingly, however, it is difficult to measure quality time, let alone draw meaningful comparisons. On the one hand, nonemployed mothers engage in a variety of nonmarket activities such as cooking, organizing family schedules, running errands or doing volunteer work, which may limit the time that they can engage in direct activities with their children even when they are together, such as playing with them or helping them with their homework. Of course, employed mothers engage in these types of nonmarket activities as well, though often to a lesser degree. On the other hand, value may be derived from having a mother in close proximity, even when she is primarily focused on her own activities. The time spent together may be enjoyable for children and they may learn new skills.[52]

Some recent research also indicates that, despite concerns about maternal employment, whether children live with two parents or only one is a more important determinant of time spent with their mother than whether their mother is employed. This finding is largely due to the fact that two parents can often coordinate their schedules to allow for more time with their children. Additional evidence indicates the amount of time that mothers and children spend together in two-parent families increased from at least the mid-1980s to the late 1990s, while virtually no change occurred for single-mother families. Regarding fathers, although they continue to spend considerably less time with children than mothers, it appears that in recent decades those in two-parent families substantially increased the amount of time spent with their children, both in

---

[50]These estimates, which are based on children's time use data, are from John F. Sandberg and Sandra L. Hofferth, "Changes in Children's Time with Parents, U.S. 1981–1997," *Demography* 38 (August 2001): 423–36, fig. 4.

[51]See Suzanne M. Bianchi, "Maternal Employment and Time with Children: Dramatic Change or Surprising Continuity?" *Demography* 37, no. 4 (November 2000): 401–14; and Suzanne M. Bianchi and Sara Raley, "Changing Work and Family Demographics," unpublished working paper, University of Maryland (2003). Also, see David Blau and Janet Currie, "Preschool, Day Care, and Afterschool Care: Who's Minding the Kids," National Bureau of Economic Research Working Paper 10670 (August 2004).

[52]Bianchi, "Maternal Employment and Time with Children."

absolute terms and relative to mothers, whether measured as time spent on one-on-one activities with children or more broadly defined. Married fathers have even increased their participation in routine child care tasks, such as giving children a bath, further evidence of their changing family role. Although comparable data on trends are not available for noncustodial divorced and never-married fathers, their average level of involvement with their children tends to be much lower.[53]

Recent trends regarding the allocation of work and child care in two-parent families are generally heartening, but more egalitarian families face many challenges, including determining what is a fair share of housework for each partner and how specific housework tasks are to be allocated. In addition, many men were raised in traditional homes where boys only did "male chores" such as raking leaves or shoveling snow and were not expected to do the laundry or cook dinner. Two-earner couples, who often face a "time squeeze," must also learn how to "make do" and be willing to accept less than perfection from each other when it comes to housekeeping and taking care of children.[54]

As for the problems of women, it is important to note that the data we examined tend to underestimate the difficulties of both nonemployed and employed women. Full-time homemakers may have a great deal more leisure than either other women or men, but it is unequally distributed over the life cycle. In addition, they tend to have less bargaining power within the family and, most seriously, they will often be in dire straits if the need arises, for whatever reason, for them to manage on their own. As for employed women, the problems they face differ greatly, depending on whether they are part-time or full-time workers, a fact that cannot be readily discerned from data on "employed" women. Those employed part-time, often because they have primary responsibility for their family, are likely to confront a smaller and less attractive choice of jobs, frequently lower earnings, scant fringe benefits, and fewer opportunities for promotion, while those who work full-time must deal with a considerably heavier workload. Finally, employed women who are responsible for very young children or other family members who need personal care are likely to confront particular problems. The difficulties of mothers of infants and toddlers are particularly serious because many are also at the age when workers need to prove themselves on the job if they are to make much progress. Their extra responsibilities are apt to make it more difficult for them to compete with their male counterparts. Thus, whatever route employed wives choose, the unequal division of labor in the home is likely to adversely affect their success in the labor market.[55]

On the other hand, it has been argued that the unequal division of household and market labor is in some ways less of a problem for women than it superficially seems to be. First, many tasks women perform are no longer as physically exacting as those their

---

[53]This paragraph draws from Sandberg and Hofferth, "Changes in Children's Time"; Bianchi, "Maternal Employment"; Liana C. Sayer, Suzanne M. Bianchi, and John P. Robinson, "Are Parents Investing Less in Children? Trends in Mothers' and Fathers' Time with Children," *American Journal of Sociology* 110, no. 1 (July 2004): 1–43; and Joseph H. Pleck, "Balancing Work and Family," *Scientific American Presents* 10, no. 2 (Summer 1999): 38–43.

[54]Sue Shellenbarger, "More Men Move Past Incompetence Defense to Share Housework," *Wall Street Journal,* February 21, 1996, sec. B, p. 1.

[55]For further discussion, see Barbara R. Bergmann, *The Economic Emergence of Women* (New York: Basic Books, 1986).

grandmothers did. Second, as discussed earlier, such activities as shopping and, to a considerable extent, child care may be enjoyable enough to be regarded as quasi-leisure. However, much of paid work has also become less onerous, and such time on the job as interacting with fellow workers and entertaining clients is as likely to be quasi-leisure as any family work. In fact, an extensive study of people's preferences indicates that, on the whole, they enjoy child care more than any other activities included in a comprehensive list, but enjoy their jobs far more than any other types of housework and considerably more than many leisure activities.[56]

The question also arises as to what has happened to all of the housework that used to be done in past years.[57] In part, "norms" about how much time should be devoted to housework as well as what sort of housework needs to be done have changed. For instance, one study finds that while women's overall satisfaction with the cleanliness of their homes has changed little during the past two decades, sales have declined for products like furniture polish and carpet cleaner, indicating that individuals are spending less time on "discretionary" cleaning.[58] Another part of the answer is that homemakers take advantage of conveniences such as washing machines and dishwashers, microwaves and food processors. These appliances considerably reduce the effort required for many basic housekeeping activities, though not necessarily the time in all cases. Further, many items that were previously produced at home are now often purchased, including frozen dinners, restaurant meals, clothing, and child care. Another strategy for families is to hire firms or individuals to come into their homes to do regular tasks such as house cleaning. As might be expected, the research evidence indicates that family income matters, especially the wife's earnings, in determining whether a family purchases market substitutes such as those just mentioned. This strategy is not simply an issue of affordability, however, because even with the same income, African-Americans have been found to be less likely to use market substitutes than other groups.[59]

In spite of the many changes, it is likely that for the foreseeable future, the ultimate locus of responsibility for homemaking in most instances will continue to rest with women. So, when unexpected problems and small emergencies come up, it will still be women who are expected to give family needs greater priority relative to market work than men do. Part of the explanation for the slow pace of change is that, as noted, the role of homemaker continues to be associated with femininity but is seen as in conflict with masculinity. To the extent that these cultural roles persist, it is likely that even wives who are employed full-time will continue to do a considerable amount of housework and that nonemployed men will likely continue to spend little time on housework. Nevertheless,

---

[56]F. Thomas Juster, "Preferences for Work and Leisure," in *Time, Goods and Well-Being,* edited by F. Thomas Juster and Frank P. Stafford (Ann Arbor: Institute for Social Research, University of Michigan, 1985).

[57]Bianchi et al., "Is Anyone Doing the Housework?"

[58]John P. Robinson and Melissa Milkie, "Dances with Dust Bunnies: Housecleaning in America," *American Demographics* 19, no. 1 (January 1997): 37–59.

[59]Philip N. Cohen, "Replacing Housework in the Service Economy: Gender, Class, Race-Ethnicity in Service Spending," *Gender and Society* 12, no. 2 (April 1998): 219–31. See also Horacio Soberon-Ferrer and Rachel Dardis, "Determinants of Household Expenditures for Services," *Journal of Consumer Research* 17, no. 4 (March 1991): 385–97; and R. S. Oropesa, "Using the Service Economy to Relieve the Double Burden: Female Labor Force Participation and the Service Purchases," *Journal of Family Issues* 14, no. 4 (September 1993): 438–73.

as men assume more homemaking responsibilities, these cultural definitions may be expected to erode and hasten the decline in the traditional gender division of labor.

Volunteer Work

In addition to market work and housework, many people also spend an appreciable amount of time on volunteer work. Before examining how much time men and women spend in volunteer work, such activities must be distinguished from other work. Volunteer activities are defined as tasks performed without direct reward in money or in kind that mainly benefit others rather than the individuals themselves or their immediate family.

Thus, volunteer work is neither a way of earning a living nor an integral part of homemaking. Nevertheless, much business is transacted and many profitable contacts are made at Rotary club meetings. People participate in labor unions at least in part to improve their own working conditions, and in the symphony guild so that they will be able to attend concerts. They are also more likely to participate in the PTA or scouting when they have children who are involved. Further, anything that enhances life in the community influences the well-being of the family at least indirectly, and often the connection is a fairly close one. In principle, the distinction is made in terms of which is the dominant purpose, but in practice it is by no means easy to decide where the line should be drawn.

The issue also arises as to how to distinguish volunteer work from leisure activities individuals undertake simply because they derive gratification or enjoyment from doing them. One such example might be bringing over meals to a sick neighbor. Another might be taking a Brownie troop on a museum outing. This problem is sometimes solved by including only services rendered as part of an organized program. However, in that case, valid volunteer activities may be excluded. Given these ambiguities, it is not surprising that estimates of the amount of volunteer work done vary widely, depending on the definition used, the questions asked, and the respondent who answers the questions.

An alternative view of volunteer work is that, rather than indirectly enhancing either the income or direct enjoyment of the participants, it is mainly a "conscience good." This interpretation is based on the finding that people most often do volunteer work in response to a request, rather than of their own accord.[60] To the extent that this view is realistic, volunteer work is distinct both from other work and from recreation.

In any case, much valuable volunteer work is performed in this country, though the fraction of the population that does so has varied somewhat over time. As shown in Table 3-3, a national survey conducted in 2003 found that nearly 29 percent of adults volunteered for some type of organization, whether it be serving food at a shelter or serving as a board member.[61]

---

[60]Richard B. Freeman, "Working for Nothing: The Supply of Volunteer Labor," *Journal of Labor Economics* 15, no. 1, pt. 2 (January 1997): S140–66; and John Wilson, "Volunteering," *Annual Review of Sociology* 26 (2000): 215–40.

[61]Survey estimates vary considerably depending on respondent age, and how the question is worded. For instance, the Independent Sector reports that as many as 44 percent of adults over age 21 volunteered for a formal organization. See Independent Sector, *Giving and Volunteering in the United States: Findings from a National Survey* (Washington, DC, 2000). Data on volunteering are now also available from the new American Time Use Survey (ATUS), as reported in Bureau of Labor Statistics, "Time Use Survey—First Results Announced by BLS."

TABLE 3-3   Participation Rates in Volunteer Work, 2003[a]

	Women (%)	Men (%)	Total (%)
Total	32.2	25.1	28.8
Race/Ethnicity[b]			
White	34.4	26.6	30.6
Black	22.2	17.2	20.0
Asian	19.5	17.7	18.7
Hispanic origin	19.6	12.0	15.7
Educational Attainment[c]			
Less than HS diploma	11.3	8.4	9.9
HS graduate only	25.0	18.0	21.7
Some college	38.6	28.8	34.1
College graduate	49.9	41.3	45.6
Employment Status			
Employed full-time	33.3	26.9	29.6
Employed part-time	42.3	30.5	38.4
Unemployed	33.2	20.9	26.7
Not in labor force	27.3	20.0	24.6

Note: Figures are computed for individuals age 16 and over for period September 1, 2002, to September 1, 2003.

[a]Figures on volunteers count those individuals who performed unpaid volunteer activities for an organization; figures exclude informal volunteer work such as helping a neighbor.

[b]The categories for race/ethnicity do not sum to 100% because the figures for "other races" are not included and because a person of Hispanic origin may be of any race.

[c]Data on educational atttainment are computed for those age 25 and over.

Source: U.S. Bureau of Labor Statistics, "Volunteering in the United States, 2003," *News,* USDL 03-888 (December 17, 2003), table 1. Available at www.bls.gov/cps.

A notable gender difference that can be seen in Table 3-3 and identified in other sources is that women volunteer at higher rates than men.[62] In 2003, the rates were 32 percent for women and 25 percent for men. Part of the explanation for this difference is that women are more likely to be part-time workers, a group with a much higher volunteer rate, though notably, even women who are employed full-time volunteer at a higher rate than their male counterparts. On the other hand, both women and men who are out of the labor force are less likely to do volunteer work than those who are employed either full-time or part-time, in part because they tend to be considerably older, but also because volunteer work is frequently job-related, as when people are active in a labor union or a local business association. For this group as well, women volunteer at higher rates than men. These data and others also indicate that women and men tend to differ in the kinds of volunteer work they do. Women have been found to contribute more time to health organizations and educational institutions, while men have been

---

[62]Other evidence is provided in regular surveys conducted by the Independent Sector as well as the 2003 American Time Use Survey, conducted by the Bureau of Labor Statistics.

found to do more voluntary work for civic and political organizations, as well as sport and recreational organizations. Substantial differences are not found in the proportions of women and men involved in social welfare organizations and religious institutions.[63]

Rates of volunteerism to organizations also differ by race and ethnicity. The participation rate for the population as a whole was 29 percent, while it was only 20 percent for African Americans and just under 16 percent for Hispanics. The lower figures for these groups are likely explained by the fact that volunteerism is greater, on average, for more highly educated, higher-income individuals.

Due to changes in the designs of the major surveys used to collect volunteer data, only limited information is available on *trends* in women's and men's rates of volunteerism. One data source, which allows for such comparisons, indicates that women's participation rate in volunteer activities increased more than men's between 1987 to 1998, which may be rather surprising in light of the fact that women's labor force participation also increased during the same years. On the other hand, these data also indicate a decline in average hours spent volunteering by both women and men over the same period. Thus, the question of how women's entry into the labor market has affected volunteerism has no simple answer.[64]

In sum, many reasons explain why people do work that, by definition, brings few or no direct material rewards. True altruism (or conscience), contact with congenial people, dedication to a particular cause, desire for recognition, furthering business, and advancing one's own or a spouse's career or the well-being of one's children all may play a part to a greater or lesser extent.[65] Research also suggests that volunteer activities may help women who are out of the labor force get better jobs when they reenter. Indeed, some recent research finds that volunteer work confers economic benefits in the form of higher earnings and greater occupational achievement, perhaps by providing the individual with valuable human capital or networking opportunities that the individual would otherwise not have. Although experience gained in volunteer work is probably not as valuable, in general, as that acquired on the job, women with demanding family responsibilities, such as caring for young children or elderly relatives, may value the more flexible schedule, and others may enjoy the greater ability to choose the type of work they do.[66] Experience in volunteer work is also likely to be particularly

---

[63]"A Vast Empirical Record Refutes the Idea of Civic Decline," Special issue of *Public Perspective* 7, no. 4 (June/July 1996); and Stephanie Borass, "Volunteerism in the United States," *Monthly Labor Review* (August 2003): 3–11.

[64]The surveys on volunteering regularly conducted by the Independent Sector and the U.S. Census Bureau (figures from this latter survey are reported in Table 3-3) underwent major changes in the 2000s, and so the most recent data are not comparable with earlier years. The information on trends reported in the text is based on earlier survey data from the Independent Sector, *Giving and Volunteering in the United States.*

[65]Notably, Richard Freeman finds that the opportunity cost of time as reflected by the wage, an important determinant of labor force participation, explains only a minor part of the decision to volunteer in "Working for Nothing."

[66]See, for instance, John Wilson and Marc Musick, "Doing Well by Doing Good: Volunteering and Occupational Achievement Among American Women," *Sociological Quarterly* 44, no. 3 (August 2003): 433–50; Kathleen M. Day and Rose Anne Devlin, "The Payoff to Work Without Pay: Volunteer Work as an Investment in Human Capital," *Canadian Journal of Economics* 31, no. 5 (November 1998): 1179–91; Marnie W. Mueller, "Economic Determinants of Volunteer Work by Women," *Signs: Journal of Women in Culture and Society* 1, no. 2 (Winter 1975): 325–38; and Francine D. Blau, "How Voluntary Is Volunteer Work? Comment on 'Economic Determinants of Volunteer Work by Women,'" *Signs: Journal of Women in Culture and Society* 21, no. 1 (Autumn 1976): 251–54.

useful for persons interested in running for political office, both because of the skills acquired and the valuable contacts often made.

From the point of view of society, voluntary organizations also serve a number of useful functions. They offer the opportunity for mediation, integration of subgroups, affirmation of values, and distribution of power. All of these functions are important, especially in a democratic society. Beyond the benefits listed, volunteers provide free services. It is frequently argued that as more and more women enter the labor market and have less time to spend on unpaid work, their contributions to worthy causes will be greatly missed. However, as noted, even though women's average hours of volunteerism appear to have declined, along with those of men, the available data suggest that a greater fraction of women are participating in volunteer work. Further, it must not be overlooked that an increasing number of women now earn an income. They are, therefore, able to contribute more money to worthy causes. Employed women also pay taxes, thus making additional expenditures on public services possible. Hence, workers could be hired to do some of what was earlier done by volunteers.

Estimating the Value of Nonmarket Production

No one doubts that unpaid productive activities like housework and at-home child care are valuable to households and to the community. At present, however, these contributions are not included in U.S. **gross domestic product (GDP)**. GDP is the total money value of all the goods and services produced by factors of production within a country over a one-year period. The consequences of the omission of nonmarket production from GDP in the United States and elsewhere are potentially serious. For instance, comparisons of GDP between countries are distorted to the extent that the relative sizes of household and market sectors differ. Further, within a country, the growth in GDP is overstated if women reduce home production as they work more in the labor market, as has been the case in the United States.[67]

Estimating the value of nonmarket activities, and ultimately including this value in GDP, poses a number of challenges. Many of these difficulties are well-known to forensic economists—economists called upon to estimate the value of lost household services in court cases involving wrongful death and permanent injury. Most recently, such estimates were needed in the aftermath of September 11, 2001, as discussed in a subsequent inset.

One challenge, only recently surmounted, has been the lack of a national U.S. government survey on how Americans spend their time. These data should be useful in future efforts to value unpaid work, though national time use data, in and of itself, is not enough. The complex issue of what nonmarket activities should be included remains to be determined. As just one example, should time spent producing a gourmet meal at home be counted fully as work or is it partly leisure?

---

[67]These distortions have been recognized for some time. For instance, in 1946, economist A. C. Pigou observed that "... the services rendered by women enter into the dividend [Britain's measure of GDP at the time] when they are rendered in exchange for wages ... but do not enter into it when they are rendered by mothers or wives. ... Thus, if a man married his housekeeper or his cook, the national dividend is diminished." This quote is cited in Statistics Canada, "Households' Unpaid Work: Measurement and Valuation," *Studies in National Accounting* (December 1995), p. 3.

Perhaps the greatest challenge in estimating the value of nonmarket production is the lack of agreement regarding the preferable method.[68] There are two fundamentally different methods, each with its own strengths and drawbacks. Economists, for the most part, tend to use the **opportunity cost approach**, which sets the value of unpaid work equal to the income the person could earn in the labor market. It meshes well with the theory of labor supply, which will be discussed in detail in Chapter 4, in which individuals who participate in the labor force equate the value of nonmarket time to the market wage rate. For individuals who do not participate in the labor market, the value of nonmarket time must be at least as great as the potential market wage.

However, despite its theoretical appeal, a number of difficulties arise with this approach. First, there is the nontrivial problem of estimating potential market earnings for those who are out of the labor force. Second, although the market wage is known for those who are employed, the presumption that it accurately represents the value of nonmarket time may not be correct. Many workers do not have the option of working precisely as long as they wish but must work a specified number of hours or forgo an otherwise desirable job. Hence, they may not be able to divide their time so that the value of the last hour spent at home is exactly equal to their wage rate.

In addition to these problems, although correct application of the opportunity cost approach may identify the value of the nonmarket production to individuals and their families, it results in a higher value being placed on the nonmarket production of those whose (potential) market productivity is higher. So, for example, an hour spent scrubbing floors by a college graduate is valued more highly than an hour spent by a high school graduate in the same activity, even when the quantity and quality of their nonmarket production is identical.

The main alternative to the opportunity cost approach is the so-called **market cost approach**, which sets the value of nonmarket production equal to the cost of hiring someone to do it. This method is not free of difficulties either. The main difficulty is the need to make sure that the purchased item is of equal quality and, for that matter, that it is possible to purchase it. What qualifications must a housecleaner, a cook, a gardener, and a baby-sitter have to adequately replace the services of a homemaker and parent? Is it possible to delegate such tasks as directing children's upbringing and planning and budgeting for the household?

One way to estimate market cost is to first determine how much time is spent on each individual activity, itself a difficult task, and then to use the wages of such specialists as cooks, home decorators, chauffeurs, and even child psychologists to estimate the value of nonmarket time. This estimation may be unrealistic in that it is unlikely that the typical homemaker has all these skills to the same extent that such specialists do. Another alternative is to value unpaid home work at the wage of a domestic worker. However, the elements of "personal and emotional care" in much nonmarket work, such as caring for one's own children, would not be fully captured in such market-based estimates, suggesting that estimates for some types of activities might be too low.[69]

---

[68]See, for instance, Barnet Wagman and Nancy Folbre, "Household Services and Economic Growth in the U.S., 1870–1930," *Feminist Economics* no. 1 (Spring 1996): 43–66; and Statistics Canada, "Households' Unpaid Work: Measurement and Valuation."

[69]Nancy Folbre and Julie A. Nelson emphasize that some nonmarket work has a caring component. "For Love or Money—Or Both?" *Journal of Economic Perspectives* 14, no. 4 (Fall 2000): 123–40.

Despite the many difficulties in calculating an estimate of the value of unpaid work to adjust standard U.S. GDP figures, some preliminary efforts have been made. For instance, one recent study (which valued an hour of time spent in unpaid work at a housekeeper's wage) determined that by ignoring nonmarket output, U.S. GDP was underestimated by 24 percent in 1997. Estimates for earlier years are even higher because a larger fraction of women were full-time homemakers and household technology was less advanced.[70] Such estimates could be used to supplement existing data on GDP, or GDP could even be redefined to include the value of unpaid work, though this inclusion might raise comparability issues with past GDP data. Thus, this issue remains a controversial one.

Another question that might be raised about including the value of unpaid work in GDP is whether it would affect the status of women as a group, because they are of course disproportionately involved in this activity. Here too, we encounter some considerable controversy. Some argue that the exclusion of unpaid work from GDP in some sense brands it as "unproductive." In this view, assigning money value to housework would favorably affect women's status because it would gain recognition for the activities of women in the home and validate their economic contributions.[71] Others dispute this contention and believe that the inclusion of housework in GDP would not fundamentally affect the status of women because it would not make housewives more independent, nor raise the wages of women who perform these services for pay.[72]

Looking to the future, given that national time use data is now being regularly collected in the United States, and the fact that other economically advanced countries are collecting such data and estimating adjusted measures of GDP (along with the standard measure), the United States is likely to follow suit. In light of the many methodological challenges, however, it will likely be some time before a standard method is widely accepted.

The September 11th Victim Compensation Fund of 2001: Just Compensation?

The terrorist attacks that occurred in the United States on September 11, 2001, took the lives of a diverse cross-section of individuals: U.S. citizens and noncitizens; males and females, both old and young; spouses, significant others, parents, and children; food workers, investment bankers, flight crews, and nonemployed persons. In some instances, more than one family member was killed. In the wake of the attacks, Congress set up a special fund called the September 11th Victim Compensation Fund of 2001 to provide some measure of financial compensation for the families of the victims. Those who accepted awards from the Fund had to agree not to sue the airlines involved or the U.S. government. The U.S. government

---

[70]J. Steven Landefeld and Stephanie H. McCulla, "Accounting for Nonmarket Household Production within a National Account Framework," *Review of Income and Wealth Series* 46, no. 3 (September 2000): 289–307.

[71]See Susan Himmelweit, "The Discovery of 'Unpaid Work': The Social Consequences of the Expansion of 'Work,'" *Feminist Economics* 1, no. 2 (Summer 1995): 1–19; and Nancy Folbre, *Who Pays for the Kids? Gender and the Structures of Constraint* (London: Routledge, 1994).

[72]Barbara R. Bergmann, "The Economic Risks of Being a Housewife," *American Economic Review* 71, no. 2 (May 1981): 81–86.

appointed a "Special Master" to be in charge of the disbursement of monies. He faced the difficult task of deciding how much compensation each family would receive, within the guidelines specified by Congress. The final ruling by the Special Master could not be disputed. Families were eligible to receive monies for the loss of their loved one, independent of economic considerations (to reflect the loss of enjoyment of life and to compensate for the pain and suffering their loved one experienced during the attacks). They were also to be compensated for the "presumed economic loss" of their loved one, which is the focus here. The Final Rules, promulgated March 13, 2002, reflect input from a wide array of groups, including the National Organization for Women (NOW) Legal Defense and Education Fund.*

In the Victim Compensation Fund, economic loss was computed as lost income and benefits less consumption expenditures. For those who were employed at the time of the attack, income loss was calculated as lost future earnings potential. That is, how much they *would have* earned, given their recent earnings stream, if they had been employed until the end of their projected worklife. Early on, when the Fund's rules were first set forth, the value of household work was not counted as lost income for *full-time* workers, while it was measured at "replacement value" for homemakers and part-time workers. As noted in NOW's memo to the Special Master, excluding the value of household services for full-time workers particularly understates women's economic contribution because many women who work full-time for pay also work a "second shift" when they get home: they make dinner and clean up, do laundry, and take care of their children's needs. Husbands who work full-time also do some housework, but as we have seen, women continue to do the majority of household work. As a result of NOW's argument, the Final Rules gave the Special Master the discretion to include the value of lost household services for full-time workers as well. Even with this modification, however, the question remains as to whether wives' household services, whether performed on a full- or part-time basis, are adequately rewarded, particularly the "managerial" function that many wives provide.** Moreover, family members offer more than just household labor; as discussed in the text, their services include a "caring" component that cannot be readily quantified in the market.

Another concern raised in the NOW memo was that the income loss for women workers was based on their lost earnings, which may be too low as a result of gender discrimination. The Final Rules did not make a specific adjustment for women's earnings in this regard, nor is this adjustment presently made in tort litigation involving wrongful death or permanent injury. However, in the Final Rules, estimates of men's average worklife were used in calculating women's as well as men's economic loss. Because men's average worklife estimates are longer than women's, this factor should work to many women's advantage. In addition, to the extent that women's lowered earnings are a result of greater time and effort in household activities, the inclusion of household services in the economic loss estimate addresses this concern to some extent.

Apart from issues of gender equity, other equity concerns have been raised about the methodology used by the Victim Compensation Fund. For instance, the use of labor market earnings to estimate economic loss has made many uncomfortable because this method confers substantially higher dollar awards to families of top executives than to those working in lower-level positions (though both get identical compensation for noneconomic losses). Indeed, total awards have varied from $250,000 to $6 million, principally as a result of differences in estimates of economic loss. However, it should be noted that the approach followed by the Fund in this regard is quite standard in other cases in which an economic value is placed on loss of life or injury.†

Some concern also centers around the difficulties that long-term unmarried partners, whether opposite-sex or same sex, faced in receiving monies from the Fund. The Final Rules did not alleviate this concern: State law determined who could seek compensation for the loss of a loved one. In 2003, the lesbian partner of one September 11th victim received monies from the Fund, so at least some precedent was set, but other unmarried partners may have been deterred by the lengthier hearings process required, or by the publicity.‡

This inset points to the fact that issues related to valuing housework (in addition to lifetime labor market contributions) have important practical applications. In addition, it highlights the considerable challenges faced by those charged with the task of estimating such values.

*This inset draws on "Victim Compensation Fund, Frequently Asked Questions" (May 21, 2003), www.usdoj.gov/victimcompensation/faq5.pdf; Memo from NOW Legal Defense and Education Fund to Mr. Kenneth Feinberg (February 11, 2002), www.nowldef.org/html/news/unpaidmemo.pdf; Final Rules, Victim Compensation Fund of September 11th, 2001 (March 13, 2001), www.usdoj. gov/victimcompensation/civil_01.html; and Interim Final Rules, Victim Compensation Fund of Semptember 11th, 2001 (December 21, 2001), www.usdoj.gov/victimcompensation/civil_01.html.
** Thomas R. Ireland, "Economic Loss in the Case of a Full-Time Mother and Homemaker: When Lost Services Are the Only Pecuniary Loss," *Assessing Family Loss in Wrongful Death Litigation: The Special Roles of Lost Services and Personal Consumption*, edited by Thomas R. Ireland and Thomas O. Depperschmidt (Tucson, AZ: Lawyers & Judges Publishing Co., 1999).
†Figure is from "Judge Affirms 9/11 Fund; Finds Award Process Is Fair," *Newsday*, May 9, 2003. See also Steven Brill, "A Tragic Calculus," *Newsweek*, December 31, 2001, p. 28; and Thomas R. Ireland and John O. Ward, *Assessing Damages in Injuries and Deaths of Minor Children* (Tucson, AZ: Lawyers & Judges Publishing Co., 2001).
‡ "U.S. Awards Lesbian 9/11 Compensation for Loss of Partner," *Washington Post*, January 23, 2003. See also, Jennifer Barrett, "Shut Out," *Newsweek*, February 15, 2002.

THE AMERICAN FAMILY IN THE TWENTY-FIRST CENTURY

Although this chapter focused on married-couple families, it is important to discuss to what extent this type of family is still predominant in the United States, to what extent even this type of family has changed in recent decades, and what the increasingly common alternatives are. Such changes in the United States did not occur in isolation, but rather arose as part of a wave of similar changes that have taken place in other economically advanced nations to a greater or lesser extent. Here we provide an overview of the developments in the United States, with a more detailed examination reserved for Chapter 9, and some discussion of demographic trends in other countries in Chapter 11.

Demographic changes are both a cause and a consequence of changes in labor force activity among women. Chapter 4 considers the substantial impact of changes in the family on women's labor market activity and outcomes. Chapter 9 then "turns the tables" and explores the economic factors, including women's rising labor force participation, that have led to changes in the American family.[73]

The most fundamental shift in the family in recent years relates to the "declining significance of marriage."[74] The once strong links between marriage, sexual activity, and childbearing have become substantially weaker as indicated by falling marriage rates and increases in unmarried, opposite-sex couples, often termed *cohabitors*. As of the mid-1990s, just over 40 percent of women age 15 to 44 had cohabited with a person of the opposite sex at some time in their lives, and this figure was as high as 50 percent for women in their thirties.[75] Also, a substantial increase occurred in the proportion of births to unmarried mothers, from slightly more than 1 in 10 births in 1970 to just over 1 in 3 by 2002.[76] Furthermore, the divorce rate rose considerably from the 1970s through the 1980s, although it then leveled off and even declined somewhat.

These demographic patterns can be seen in children's living arrangements. In 2002, just 69 percent of all children were living with two married parents. The majority of the remaining children were living with a single parent, while a much smaller fraction were living in households with cohabiting parents, or with a grandparent, other relative, or nonrelative. Even married, two-parent families have changed over time, with many more children today living in a blended (or step) parent family rather than in a traditional nuclear family.[77]

The definitions used by the U.S. Census Bureau to categorize family structure and children's living arrangements have failed to fully keep pace with recent demographic changes. For instance, the government defines "family" as any two or more individuals living together who are related by blood, marriage, or adoption. Under this definition, a household consisting of an unmarried mother and one or more children living with the children's father may be included in the count of single-parent families. As rates of cohabitation increase, government statistics become increasingly misleading regarding the extent to which children live with one parent or both. Indeed, one recent study finds that nearly 40 percent of all children born to unmarried mothers in the early 1990s went home to households that included both parents. All told, it is estimated that 40 percent of all children will spend some time in a cohabiting family before they reach age 16.[78]

---

[73]Who should be defined as a family is increasingly complex. Teresa J. Rothausen further argues that the current notion of "family" may be biased toward a "white middle-class" reality in "'Family' in Organizational Research: A Review and Comparison of Definitions and Measures," *Journal of Organizational Behavior* 20, no. 6 (November 1999): 817–36.

[74]Larry Bumpass, "The Declining Significance of Marriage: Changing Family Life in the U.S." NSFH Working Paper No. 66 (University of Wisconsin-Madison, Center for Demography and Ecology, 1995).

[75]U.S. Census Bureau, *Statistical Abstract of the United States: 1999* (Washington, DC: GPO, 2000), table 66.

[76]U.S. Department of Health and Human Services, "Births: Final Data for 2002," *National Vital Statistics Reports* 52, no. 10 (December 15, 2003).

[77]See U.S. Census Bureau, "Children's Living Arrangements and Characteristics: March 2002," *Current Population Reports* P20-547 (June 2003).

[78]Larry Bumpass and H.-H. Lu, "Trends in Cohabitation and Implications for Children's Family Context in the United States," *Population Studies* 54, no. 1 (March 2000): 29–41.

How to classify opposite-sex cohabitors, whether to include them in the definition of family or as a distinct category, and how to incorporate gay and lesbian couples into government statistics, are highly charged issues (see the following inset on the state of marriage). Nevertheless, it is important to accurately quantify these living arrangements and their characteristics given the increasing numbers of children growing up in them.

Along with and related to changing family structure, the demographic "mix" of the U.S. population continues to change. Changes in race and ethnicity are a consequence of shifts in immigration, both in terms of source countries and absolute numbers, as well as of differences in birthrates among various groups in the U.S. born population. The largest increase is projected among Hispanics, both white and black, from 12.6 percent of the population in 2000 to 17.8 percent by 2020. The black population is also expected to increase over the same period, but only from 12.7 percent to 13.5 percent, while it is anticipated that the share of the non-Hispanic white population will decrease from 69.4 percent to 61.3 percent of the total population.[79]

How to classify individuals of mixed races and ethnicities is another issue receiving substantial attention. Regarding race, individuals have generally been limited to choosing a single category in government surveys. For the 2000 U.S. census, five major race groups were identified: white; black or African American; Asian; American Indian or Alaska native; and Native Hawaiian or Other Pacific Islander. One significant difference between the 2000 census and earlier ones is that individuals were allowed to select as many of these categories as apply, rather than being restricted to choosing a single race. In the 2000 census, just under 2.5 percent of the population designated that they were of more than one race group.[80] Although a long time in coming, the opportunity to "check more than one box" raises questions about how minorities will be counted for statistical purposes in identifying discrimination in housing, education, and employment on the basis of race or color.

The previous discussion suggests that the American family at the start of the twenty-first century is quite different from that of the 1950s' characterization of an invariably white family, comprised of a homemaker wife and breadwinner husband with two or three children and a dog as immortalized in television, movies, and American lore. A historical perspective indicates that this family was, to some extent, a demographic aberration. In fact, fertility rates were lower and the average age of marriage was higher in earlier times than in the 1950s, and divorce was, even then, by no means unheard of.[81] And, of course, considerable racial and ethnic diversity existed at that time as well. Nonetheless, without a doubt, the changes that occurred since then greatly affected both how people live and how they make a living. These issues will be discussed further in subsequent chapters.

---

[79]U.S. Census Bureau, "U.S. Interim Projections by Age, Sex, Race and Hispanic Origin," Table 1a (March 18, 2004), from www.census.gov.

[80]Reynolds Farley, "Racial Identities in 2000," *The New Race Question: How the Census Counts Multiracial Individuals,* edited by Joel Perlmann and Mary C. Waters (New York: Russell Sage Foundation, 2002), pp. 33–61.

[81]Catherine A. Fitch and Steven Ruggles, "Historical Trends in Marriage Formation: The United States 1850–1990," in *The Ties That Bind: Perspectives on Marriage and Cohabitation,* edited by Linda Waite (New York: Aldine de Gruyter, 2000), pp. 59–90; and Julie DaVanzo and M. Omar Rahman, "American Families: Trends and Correlates," *Population Index* 59, no. 3 (Fall 1993): 350–86.

The State of Unions in the United States

In the last few years, it has been hard to read a newspaper or a magazine that does not have at least one article on some aspect of marriage. Part of the reason is that strengthening marriage has come to be viewed by some as an important solution to many of America's ills.* For instance, as discussed in Chapter 9, a number of academic studies, though importantly not all, show that children do better in married families with both biological parents present than in single-parent families. Some advocate marriage as a potential antipoverty solution, as discussed further in Chapter 10. Finally, marriage continues to make headlines as gay and lesbian couples seek to have the same rights and privileges as opposite-sex couples, and especially since some localities began permitting same-sex marriages. In this inset, we discuss the state of marriage in the 2000s.

The U.S. federal government and many state governments began actively promoting marriage starting in the mid 1990s. This involvement is partly due to a lesser-known goal of the 1996 federal welfare legislation, which is to "encourage the formation and maintenance of two-parent families." To this end, the legislation provided funds for states to use toward promoting healthy marriages. More recently, legislation to reauthorize welfare (pending as of 2004) included a Bush Administration proposal to promote marriage. State policies have run the gamut from making changes in their welfare programs such as reducing marriage penalties to funding premarital education classes for couples. Several states, including Louisiana, Arizona, and Arkansas, enacted legislation permitting an alternative, stricter form of marriage called "covenant marriage." Couples who choose to enter a covenant marriage must obtain marriage counseling prior to marriage, must seek counseling if their marriage is in trouble, and must provide a specific reason for divorce.** Because these programs are fairly new, conclusive evidence is not yet available on their effectiveness in stabilizing marriage as compared with traditional marriage. At the federal level, changes made in various rules in the individual income tax somewhat alleviate marriage penalties faced by some two-earner couples as well as increase the marriage bonus received by single-earner couples.

Also, in 1996, the U.S. Congress passed the Defense of Marriage Act, which defines marriage as the "legal union between one man and one woman" and defines a spouse as a husband or wife of the opposite sex. The act also specifies that if a state were to permit same-sex marriage, other states do not have to provide the same legal recognition.† At the time the 1996 legislation was passed, same-sex marriage appeared to be on the horizon in Hawaii, but no state had yet permitted same-sex marriage and quite a few states prohibited it. However, starting in 2004, same-sex couples were granted marriage licenses in Massachusetts, as well as in some localities in other states. Also, countries such as the Netherlands, Canada, and Belgium permit same-sex marriage and quite a few countries including France, Denmark and Germany allow for legal partnerships for same-sex couples.†† Recent opinion polls indicate that even though the majority of Americans remain opposed to marriage for same-sex couples, considerably more support can be found for civil unions, such as permitted in Vermont since 2000. In Vermont, a civil union grants the couple "all the same benefits, protections and responsibilities under Vermont law . . . as are granted to spouses in a marriage."‡ For instance, without legal marriage or a civil union, an unmarried partner may not be permitted to make health decisions in the event that his or her partner is incapacitated. However, given the Defense of Marriage Act, same-sex couples who marry (as well as those who enter civil unions) are not eligible for federal benefits as married couples or spouses under federal programs such as Social Security.

In the United States, permitting marriage among gay and lesbian couples has generated a firestorm of debate. On the one hand, some argue that gay and lesbian couples should not only be legally entitled to precisely the same rights and protections as opposite-sex couples, but also enjoy the same status in society.‡‡ On the other hand, others argue that the extension of marriage to gay and lesbian couples is a harbinger of the demise of marriage. As of 2004, a number of states had passed constitutional amendments to ban same-sex marriage, though efforts to pass a similar amendment at the federal level had not been successful.

*See, for instance, Wade F. Horn, "Wedding Bell Blues: Marriage and Welfare Reform," *The Brookings Review* 19, no. 3 (Summer 2001), pp. 3–42.
**Karen N. Gardiner, Michael E. Fishman, Plamen Nikolov, Asaph Glosser, and Stephanie Laud, *State Policies to Promote Marriage,* Final Report (U.S. Department of Health and Human Services, Assistant Secretary for Planning and Evaluation, September 2002), aspe.hhs.gov.
†"Jerry Gray, "House Passes Bar to U.S. Sanction of Gay Marriage," *New York Times* (July 13, 1996), p. 1.
††Sarah Lyall, "In Europe, Lovers Now Propose: Marry Me, A Little," *New York Times* (February 14, 2004), p. 3.
‡"The Vermont Guide to Civil Unions," Vermont Secretary of State Web site, www.sec.state.vt.us (2004).
‡‡ Katharine B. Silbaugh, "After Goodridge: Will Civil Unions Do?" *Jurist* (February 11, 2004), jurist.law.pitt.edu.

Conclusion

We saw in Chapter 2 how the concept of the traditional family evolved with the man as the breadwinner and the woman as the homemaker, combining her time and the goods and services purchased with the husband's earnings to satisfy the family's needs and wants. The simple neoclassical model explains how such a division of labor may be advantageous under appropriate conditions. However, it cannot be taken for granted that these conditions are satisfied at any given point in time, let alone that they will be for the rest of each person's life.

The traditional specialization came about during a time when cloth was spun, bread was baked, and soap was produced at home, the family was large, and market wages in jobs available to women were low, so that her relative advantage for home work was great. With many children and a shorter life expectancy, the problem of the decline in the value of housework after the children grew up was far less serious. Also, with severe social and religious sanctions against divorce, women were less likely to find themselves and their children dependent on a recalcitrant ex-husband for a living. However, as these factors changed, the advantages of the traditional division of labor decreased and the costs associated with it, particularly for women, increased.

Growing recognition of the drawbacks of the traditional division of responsibilities between husband and wife is thought to be one of the factors contributing to the increase in women's labor force participation and the decline of the married-couple family comprised of a homemaker wife and breadwinner husband. Furthermore, the lessening economic gains from marriage, women's increasing awareness of the risks associated with full specialization in the home, and improvements in women's labor market opportunities are also likely related to the decline in marriage, the increase in divorce, and the rise in cohabitation. Related to these changes is a noticeable, though modest, reallocation of household tasks between married men and women. Even so, unless major changes take place in the availability and affordability of day care and elder care, and in the attitudes of men and women, women are likely to continue to shoulder the lion's share of home responsibilities for quite some time to come.

APPENDIX 3A

Specialization and Exchange: A Graphical Analysis

As discussed in Chapter 3, a complete analysis of the division of labor between the individuals who make up a couple takes into account both their production possibilities and their preferences for different goods. This appendix provides a fuller examination of the simple neoclassical model in the context of a graphical analysis and reaches the same conclusions as to the value of specialization and exchange as those based on the examples presented in Tables 3-1a and 3-1b.

For simplicity, we assume that individuals derive utility from only two types of goods—home goods, produced with inputs of home time, and market goods, purchased with market income. In Figure 3-1, H and M measure the dollar value of household output and market goods, respectively. Two persons, Kathy and Jim, each allocate their time between market work (M production) and housework (H production).[82]

If Kathy and Jim are each dependent on their own output, their consumption opportunities are limited to their individual *production possibility frontiers*. The production possibility frontier shows the largest feasible combinations of the two outputs that can be produced with given resources (in this case, time inputs) and know-how. M_1H_1 indicates the combinations of household and market outputs available to Jim, while M_2H_2 shows the options from which Kathy can choose. For example, if Jim devotes full time to market work (M production), he can produce a maximum of $80 worth of market goods. If he spends all his

---

[82]We also assume fixed proportions production functions for H and M for each individual. For example, an additional hour spent on the production of H by Kathy increases output by the same amount, regardless of how much H she already produced. This simplifying assumption results in the straight-line production possibility frontiers shown in Figure 3-1. For a discussion of this point, along with a consideration of other ways in which the standard theoretical model might be made more realistic, see Pollak, "Gary Becker's Contributions to Family and Household Economics."

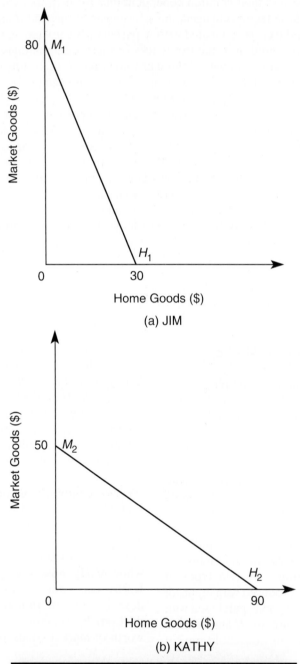

(a) JIM

(b) KATHY

FIGURE 3-1 Separate and Combined Production
Possibility Frontiers

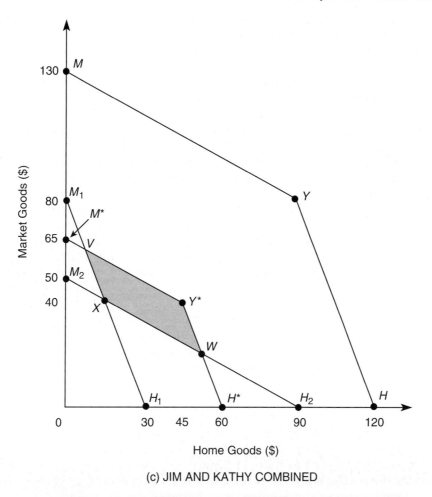

(c) JIM AND KATHY COMBINED

FIGURE 3-1   Continued

time on household activities, he can produce $30 worth of home goods.

The slope of the line $M_1 H_1$ tells us the money value of the market goods Jim must give up to get an additional dollar of home goods. The fact that $M_1 H_1$ is more steeply sloped than $M_2 H_2$ means that Jim must give up more market goods to get an additional dollar of home goods than Kathy. Specifically, Jim must give up $2.67 of market goods to get an additional dollar of home goods ($80/$30), whereas Kathy needs to give up only $.56 of market goods to get an additional dollar of

home goods ($50/$90). Viewing the matter somewhat differently, Kathy must forgo more home goods to get an additional dollar of market goods than Jim. Kathy would have to give up $1.80 worth of home goods to get an additional dollar of market goods ($90/$50), while Jim needs to give up only $.38 worth of home goods to get an additional dollar of market goods ($30/$80). Thus, Jim has a comparative advantage in market work and Kathy has a comparative advantage in home production.

If Jim and Kathy decide to collaborate, their combined production possibility curve will be *MYH,* as shown in panel c. At point *M* both Jim and Kathy specialize entirely in market work, producing $130 ($80 + $50) of market goods. If they prefer to have some home goods, it will pay for only Kathy to do housework, up to the point where she does no market work at all (point *Y*), because she adds more to home production ($1.80) for every dollar of market goods given up than Jim would add ($.38). Therefore, the segment *MY* has the same slope as M_2H_2, showing that as long as only Kathy is dividing her time between market and home, it is Kathy's slope that is relevant. Jim will do some housework only if a mix of more household production and fewer market goods are desired than segment *MY* represents. Beyond that point, the slope of M_1H_1 becomes relevant, as it is only Jim who is dividing his time between home and market. At the extreme, at point *H,* both Jim and Kathy work only in the home, producing $120 ($30 + $90) of home goods.

The combined production possibility frontier (*MYH*) makes feasible some combinations of *M* and *H* that would not be attainable by Kathy and Jim on their separate production possibility frontiers. These gains from specialization and exchange may be illustrated by putting the output combinations represented by production possibility frontier *MYH* on a per capita or per person basis. This is shown by production possibility frontier *M*Y*H** that is obtained by dividing *MYH* by 2. (For instance, point Y reflects $90 worth of home goods and $80 worth of market goods, while point Y* reflects $45 worth of home goods and $40 worth of market goods). *M*Y*H** may be compared to the options represented by Jim and Kathy's individual production possibility frontiers, M_1H_1 and M_2H_2 (panel c). The shaded area *WXVY** represents the increased per capita output that is now available. This gain in output may potentially be distributed between Jim and

Kathy so as to make them both better off than they would have been separately. To obtain the gains represented by *WXVY**, the couple must produce a nontrivial amount of both market and home goods, for it is the production of both commodities that gives each of them the opportunity to specialize in the area of their comparative advantage.

This analysis also illustrates that the gains from specialization will be larger the more the two individuals differ in their comparative advantages. To see this relationship, imagine the extreme case in which Kathy and Jim both have the same production possibility frontier, say M_1H_1. The combined production possibility frontier would then be $2 \times M_1H_1$. On a per capita basis (dividing the combined production possibility frontier in half), we would simply be left with M_1H_1. Kathy and Jim would do no better combining forces than they would each do separately. Based on this simple analysis alone, it is not clear what the economic gains of collaborating are for such a couple. However, as we saw in Chapter 3, economic gains are likely even in this case, mainly because two people can use many goods and services more efficiently than a single person can. Here, however, we focus on a couple that can potentially increase its income through joint production.

To provide a link between the potential increase in output due to collaboration and the goal of maximizing satisfaction, we need to introduce an additional tool of economic analysis and pursue our inquiry one step further. So far we established the various combinations of the two types of outputs that Kathy and Jim could produce. Which of these they would choose depends on their tastes, that is to say, on their preferences for market goods compared to home goods. To considerably simplify the analysis, we will assume that they have identical tastes. If home goods are valued more highly than market goods, the couple will be willing to give up a considerable amount of market goods in order to get an additional dollar of home goods, and vice versa if market goods are valued more highly. This relationship can be illustrated using indifference curves, as seen in Figure 3-2.

Let us assume that Kathy and Jim have been told that they could have the combination of market and home goods represented by point *A* in panel a. They are then asked to find various other combinations of *H* and *M* from which they would derive exactly the same amount of satisfaction or utility. These other points can all be connected into one indifference curve, U_2, called that because the couple is indifferent about being at various points on the curve. The U_2 curve is *negatively sloped;* the reason for the negative slope is that if the amount of market or home goods is decreased, the amount of the other good must be increased for the couple to remain equally well off.

Notice too that indifference curve U_2 is convex to the origin. That is, it gets steeper as we move to the left and flatter as we move to the right. What this means is that at a point like *C*, where *M* goods are relatively plentiful and *H* goods are relatively scarce, it takes a fairly large amount of *M* ($15 worth) to induce the couple to give up a fairly small amount of *H* ($5 worth) and still remain equally well off. On the other hand, at a point like *E,* where *M* goods are relatively scarce and *H* goods are relatively plentiful, the couple is willing to give up a fairly large amount of *H* ($20 worth) to get even a small additional amount of scarce *M* ($2 worth). The convex shape depicted here is generally realistic to the extent that relatively scarce goods are valued more highly.

However, Kathy and Jim do not have just one indifference curve, but rather a whole family of higher and lower indifference curves. For it is possible to choose a point like *G* on curve U_3 that offers more

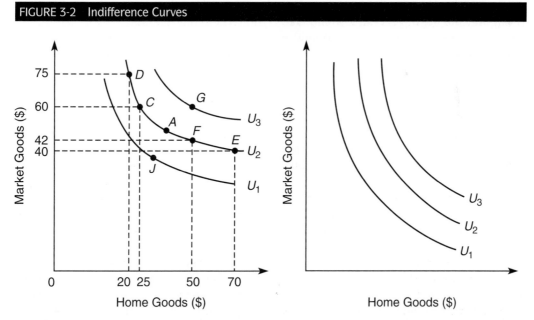

FIGURE 3-2   Indifference Curves

(a) RELATIVELY STRONG PREFERENCES
FOR MARKET GOODS

(b) RELATIVELY STRONG PREFERENCES
FOR HOME GOODS

of both M and H and is therefore clearly preferable to point A on curve U_2. Hence, all points on curve U_3 will, by extension, be preferable to (give more satisfaction than) all points on curve U_2. Similarly, it is possible to choose a point like J on curve U_1 that offers less of both M and H than at point A. Point J is clearly less desirable than point A and, by extension, all points on curve U_1 are less desirable (give less satisfaction) than all points on curve U_2. It should be clear that indifference curves can never intersect. All points on any one curve represent an equal amount of utility, while any point above (below) represents a larger (smaller) amount of utility. At the point where two curves intersect, they clearly represent the same amount of utility, yet at all other points they do not. This is a logical impossibility.

On the other hand, another couple's preferences might look like those depicted in panel b of Figure 3-2. These indifference curves are steeper and show that this couple places a relatively higher value on home goods, compared with market goods, than Kathy and Jim do. In general, it would take a larger amount of market goods to induce them to give up a dollar's worth of home goods while remaining equally well off.

To determine the division of labor (or time allocation) a couple will actually choose, we must consider both their production possibilities and their tastes or preferences. In Figure 3-3, we superimpose the couple's hypothetical indifference map on the production possibility frontier shown in Figure 3-1, panel c. It is then readily possible to determine the combination of home-produced and market-produced goods that a rational couple with those tastes (indifference curves) will choose. It will always be the point where the production possibility curve just touches the highest indifference curve it reaches. The reason is simple—the couple always prefers to be on a higher indifference curve (by definition,

as we have seen), but because they are constrained to the possible combinations of output represented by the production possibility frontier, they cannot realistically reach an indifference curve that at all points lies above the frontier.

In Figure 3-3, we illustrate the impact of the couple's preferences on their time allocation. The combined production possibility curve for the couple, MYH, shows the various combinations of H and M the couple can produce while taking full advantage of their combined resources and the comparative advantage each has in producing one of the goods. Let us continue to assume that the wife has a comparative advantage in home production and that the husband has a comparative advantage in market work.

As may be seen in panel a, a couple with relatively strong preferences for market goods will maximize satisfaction at point A along segment MY. The husband will specialize entirely in market production and the wife will do all the housework and also supply some time to the market. They will consume M_a dollars of market goods and H_a dollars of home goods.

Panel b shows a couple with stronger preferences for home-produced goods. They will maximize utility at point B. The wife will devote herself entirely to household production, while the husband will do some housework as well as supplying time to the market. Such a couple will consume fewer market goods (M_b) and more home goods (H_b) than a couple with stronger preferences for market goods.

Finally, panel c shows a couple with intermediate tastes. They will maximize utility at point Y. Both wife and husband will each fully specialize in home and market production, respectively, and will consume M_c dollars of market goods and H_c dollars of home goods.

Couples may differ in their allocation of tasks within the family, not solely due to

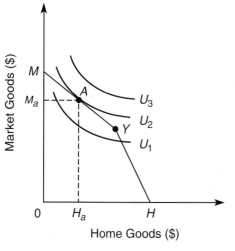

(a) RELATIVELY STRONG PREFERENCES
FOR MARKET GOODS

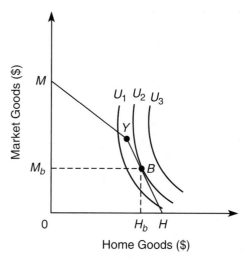

(b) RELATIVELY STRONG PREFERENCES
FOR HOME GOODS

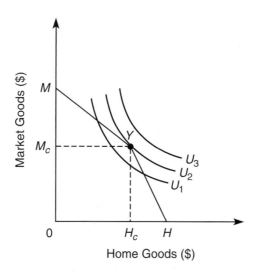

(c) INTERMEDIATE PREFERENCES

FIGURE 3-3   The Role of Tastes in Determining the Household Division of Labor

differences in tastes. The relative productivity of each member of the family in the production of market and home goods will also be an important factor. We already noted that if both husband and wife are equally productive in each endeavor, they will not realize any gains from specialization or division of labor within the family. However, even if we assume that the wife has a comparative advantage in household production and that the husband has a comparative advantage in market work, the relative productivities of

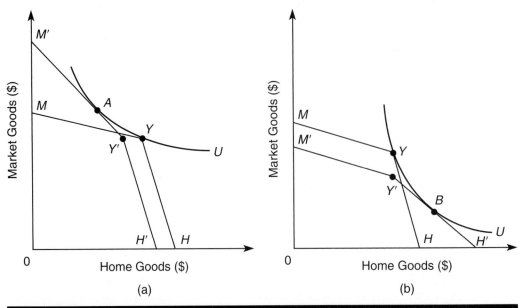

FIGURE 3-4   The Role of the Production Possibility Frontier in Determining the Household
Division of Labor

each individual in home and market production are still relevant, which is illustrated in Figure 3-4.

Panel a shows two hypothetical production possibility frontiers. In *MYH,* the segment corresponding to the wife's frontier (*MY*) is relatively flat, indicating that she is considerably more productive in the home than in the market. For given tastes (represented by indifference curve *U*), the couple maximizes utility at point *Y,* where the wife specializes entirely in home production and the husband specializes completely in market work. However, if the couple's production possibility frontier were *MY′H′,* even with the same tastes (indifference curve), they would choose point *A* along segment *M′Y′*. Here the wife will continue to do all the housework but will do some market work as well. This is because *MY′* is steeper than *MY,* indicating a higher ratio of the wife's market productivity relative to her home productivity. The opportunity cost of home goods in terms of market goods forgone has

increased and as a result the family consumes less home goods.

Similarly, as shown in panel b, the couple's time allocation may also depend on the husband's relative productivity in the home and the market. For given tastes (represented by indifference curve *U*), the couple will choose point *Y* when the husband's productivity in the home is extremely low relative to his market productivity. (This is indicated by the relatively steep slope of segment *YH* on frontier *MYH.*) They are more likely to choose a point like *B* along the flatter segment *Y′H′* on frontier *M′Y′H′,* where the husband does some housework as well as market work, when his market productivity is lower relative to his home productivity. At *B,* the couple consumes more of the now relatively cheaper home-produced goods than at *Y.*

Figure 3-4 shows how the relative productivity of the husband and the wife in the home and the market influences the division of labor in the family and the combination of home- and market-produced goods that they choose to consume. Nonetheless, as long as the comparative advantages of husband and wife differ in this simple model, some degree of specialization will be efficient. As we have seen, the greater the difference between the two in their comparative advantage, the greater the gains to specialization and exchange.

Thus, the fuller analysis presented here supports the conclusions reached on the basis of the numerical example provided in Chapter 3. In this case too, however, the same qualifications hold. First, potential economic benefits to marriage include more than just specialization and exchange, and, second, the traditional division of labor is not without its disadvantages, particularly for women.

Questions for Review and Discussion

1. Explain why husbands and wives benefit from specialization and exchange. Under what conditions are these benefits likely to be large?
2. Jason and Jennifer are married. If Jason works in the labor market, he can earn a wage of $20 per hour, while Jennifer can earn a wage of $10 per hour.
   a. Who has an absolute advantage in the labor market? How do you know?
   b. Suppose we want to know who has a comparative advantage in the labor market. What specific information do we need to know? Discuss.
3. In view of the advantages of specialization and exchange pointed out by Becker, why are families increasingly moving away from the traditional division of labor?
4. To what extent is the presumption that women have a comparative advantage in housework justified?
5. Explain under what conditions it would be rational for a woman who could earn more than her husband in the labor market to specialize in housework.
6. For a long time, economists did not include housework in their analyses. In what respect was this omission justified or not?
7. Why have women been so eager to increase their participation in the labor market, and why have men been so reluctant to increase their participation in housework?
8. Clearly nonmarket production has some value. Discuss the merits of estimating its value.
9. It is frequently pointed out that each method of valuing nonmarket production is far from perfect. Explain what the main advantages and deficiencies of each method are.
10. What is a "bargaining approach" to decision making? Why is this approach more realistic than the standard neoclassical model?
11. Suggest some factors that would improve the bargaining power of married women.

Suggested Readings

Becker, Gary S. *A Treatise on the Family.* Cambridge, MA: Harvard University Press, 1981, enlarged edition, 1991.

Bianchi, Suzanne. "Maternal Employment and Time with Children: Dramatic Change or Surprising Continuity?" *Demography* 37, no. 4 (November 2000): 401–14.

Blau, Francine D. "Trends in the Well-Being of American Women, 1970–1995." *Journal of*

Economic Literature 36, no. 1 (March 1998): 112–65.

Ferber, Marianne A., and Bonnie G. Birnbaum. "The New Home Economics: Retrospects and Prospects." *Journal of Consumer Research* 4, no. 1 (June 1977): 19–28.

Ferber, Marianne A., "A Feminist Critique of the Neoclassical Theory of the Family." In *Women, Family, and Work,* edited by Karine S. Moe. Oxford: Blackwell, 2003, chap. 1.

Ferber, Marianne A., and Julie A. Nelson, eds. *Beyond Economic Man.* Chicago: University of Chicago Press, 1993.

Ferber, Marianne A. and Julie A. Nelson, eds. *Feminist Economics Today.* Chicago: University of Chicago Press, 2003.

Folbre, Nancy. *Who Pays for the Kids? Gender and the Structures of Constraint.* London: Routledge, 1994.

Folbre, Nancy, and Julie A. Nelson. "For Love or Money—Or Both?" *Journal of Economic Perspectives* 14, no. 4 (Fall 2000): 123–40.

Fuchs, Victor R. *Women's Quest for Economic Equality.* Cambridge, MA: Harvard University Press, 1988.

Hartmann, Heidi I. "The Family as the Locus of Gender, Class and Political Struggle: The Example of Housework." *Signs: Journal of Women in Culture and Society* 6, no. 3 (Spring 1981): 366–94.

Jefferson, Therese, and John E. King. "Never Intended to be a Theory of Everything: Domestic Labor in Neoclassical and Marxian Economics" *Feminist Economics* 7, no. 3 (November 2001): 71–101.

Juster, F. Thomas, and Frank P. Stafford. "The Allocation of Time: Empirical Findings, Behavioral Models, and Problems of Measurement." *Journal of Economic Literature* 29, no. 2 (June 1991): 471–522.

Lazear, Edward P., and Robert T. Michael. *Allocation of Income Within the Household.* Chicago: University of Chicago Press, 1988.

Lundberg, Shelly, and Robert A. Pollak. "Bargaining and Distribution in Marriage." *Journal of Economic Perspectives* 10, no. 4 (Fall 1996): 139–58.

Perlmann, Joel, and Mary C. Waters, eds. *The New Race Question: How the Census Counts Multiracial Individuals.* New York: Russell Sage Foundation, 2002.

Robinson, John P., and Geoffrey Godbey. *Time for Life: The Surprising Ways Americans Use Their Time*, 2nd ed. University Park: Pennsylvania State University Press, 1999.

4

THE ALLOCATION OF TIME BETWEEN THE HOUSEHOLD AND THE LABOR MARKET

Chapter Highlights

■ Labor Force Participation and Attachment: Definitions and Trends

■ The Labor Supply Decision

■ Analyzing Trends in Women's Participation: An Overview

■ The World War II Experience

■ The Post–World War II Baby Boom

■ The 1960s to the 1980s: Increased Participation of Married Mothers

■ The 1990s and Early 2000s: Diverging Trends for Married and Single Mothers

■ Analyzing Trends in Men's Participation

■ Black and White Participation Differentials: A Closer Look

■ Appendix: The Income and Substitution Effects: A Closer Look

The rapid growth in women's labor force participation has been one of the most significant economic and social developments in the post–World War II period, in this country and elsewhere. One reason for our interest in women's participation trends is that they underlie the transformation in gender roles that has occurred in much of the world in recent years. However, other reasons also prompt an examination of women's labor force participation.

First, the economic well-being of women and their families is obviously significantly influenced by whether they participate in the labor force and their earnings levels, given participation. Such issues have gained in importance with the increase in the incidence of female-headed families and the growing dependence of married-couple families on the contributions of employed wives. Second, the family bargaining models reviewed in Chapter 3 suggest that, in married-couple families, women's participation in the labor force and their level of earnings while employed may affect the distribution of resources within marriage. According to these models, a woman who works outside the home will have a higher utility at the threat point and, hence, a more favorable distribution within marriage. Third, shifts in participation are of importance for women's wages in that they influence the average levels of labor market experience of women and, as we shall see in Chapter 6, experience is an important determinant of wages.

In this chapter, we first review the definition of the labor force and summarize trends over time in female and male labor force participation. We shall see that, while female participation rates have been increasing, male rates have been declining, albeit not as dramatically. As a consequence of both types of changes, men's and women's labor force participation rates and their patterns of involvement in market work over the life cycle are becoming increasingly similar. We then turn to the development of some economic concepts for analyzing these trends and use them to provide a better understanding of the reasons for the remarkable influx of women into the labor market. Next we use economic theory to analyze the decrease in male labor force participation and conclude with an examination of factors contributing to differences in labor force participation trends between blacks and whites.

THE LABOR FORCE: SOME DEFINITIONS

Each month, the U.S. Census Bureau conducts a survey to gather statistics on the labor force. According to the official definition, the **labor force** includes all those individuals 16 years of age and over who worked for pay or profit during the reference week or actively sought paid employment during the four weeks prior to the reference week. That is, the labor force is comprised of both the *employed* and the *unemployed.*

The **employed** group includes all those who worked one hour per week or more as paid employees or were self-employed in their own business or profession or on their own farm. This definition includes part-time workers who worked fewer than 35 hours per week, as well as those who worked full-time, 35 hours or more. It also includes all those temporarily absent from paid employment because of bad weather, vacation, family leave, labor-management disputes, or personal reasons, whether or not they were paid. An exception to the emphasis on paid employment is that those who worked at least 15 hours as unpaid workers in an enterprise operated by a family member are also included.[1] The **unemployed** include those who do not have a job but who have made specific efforts to find a job within the past four weeks, as well as those not working but waiting to be called back to work or to report for a new job within 30 days. The relationships among these labor force concepts are illustrated in Figure 4-1.

---

[1] The labor force excludes people engaged in illegal activities such as prostitution and drug trafficking. Furthermore, employment ranging from baby-sitting to yard work, which is paid for in cash and not reported for tax purposes (the so-called "underground economy"), is likely to be underreported in labor force statistics.

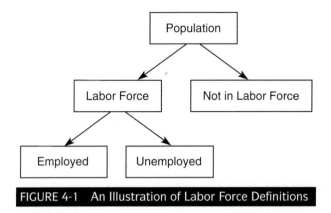

FIGURE 4-1   An Illustration of Labor Force Definitions

The **labor force participation rate** of a particular group is equal to the number of its members who are in the labor force divided by the total number of the group in the population. Thus, for example, a labor force participation rate of 60 percent for women means that 60 percent of women 16 years of age and over are labor force participants.

A careful reading of the definition of the labor force makes it clear that being in the labor force is not synonymous with working. Individuals who work fewer than 15 hours a week as unpaid family workers and those who only do unpaid work in the household or as volunteer workers—no matter how many hours—are excluded. On the other hand, persons temporarily not working, or unemployed, are included. In large part, this results from the emphasis in the official definition of the labor force on being employed in or seeking *market* work. Because women have tended to have primary responsibility for nonmarket work, they constitute a high proportion in the categories that are left out. Thus, their share of the labor force considerably understates their share of work. This understatement was particularly true in earlier days when family enterprises were more common and when most married women were homemakers.[2] In fact, as discussed in the following inset, until surprisingly recently the official definitions were not even applied in the same way to men and women. In spite of these reservations, women's labor force participation rate is considered to be an important indicator of their status in a market economy.

Other aspects of the official definition of the labor force have also been the object of criticism at various times. For example, the definition of the unemployed excludes those who would like a job but who have given up searching because they believe no work is available. Although no definition is likely to be equally satisfactory to all, adherence to a reasonably consistent definition over a long period of time provides useful data for analyzing trends. In some cases, as is further discussed in Chapter 8, criticism has been accommodated by considering alternative measures of labor market difficulties.

---

[2]It has been suggested that, historically, such activities of married women as taking in boarders, piecework done at home, and even seasonal work done in factories frequently went unreported, especially when it was the husband who was interviewed. (See, for instance, Milton Cantor and Bruce Laurie, eds., *Class, Sex, and the Woman Worker* [Westport, CT: Greenwood Press, 1977].) How important this undercount may have been is suggested by the fact that when, in 1910, census enumerators were given instructions to take special care not to overlook women workers, especially unpaid family workers, the participation rate was found to be about 4 percentage points higher than would be expected based on earlier and immediately subsequent decades. It is due to this incomparability that 1910 is normally omitted from historical series on women's labor force participation. We follow this practice in Table 4-1.

No More Guessing About Who Is a Homemaker

It has only been since January 1994 that the Current Population Survey, the major survey used by the Bureau of Labor Statistics to collect data on work activity in the home and in the labor market, asked men and women the same questions regarding their activity in the previous week. Prior to this time, if an adult woman opened the door, it was assumed that she might well be a homemaker. Accordingly, she was asked the question, "What were you doing most of last week—working, keeping house, or something else?" If an adult man opened the door, he was asked about "working, or something else." As a consequence of this type of stereotyping, women were more likely to be classified as out of the labor force (i.e., keeping house) rather than as unemployed (currently without a job, but searching). Now all individuals are asked the same questions, thus avoiding any potential bias from this source.

The Current Population Survey was also reworded to distinguish hours spent at home-based work for pay from hours spent doing unpaid work around the house. Specifically, the question asking "Did you do any work at all last week, not counting work around the house?" was changed to "Last week did you do any work for pay?"

Because the revised survey better captures the full range of women's paid work activities and their unemployment, these changes result in higher estimates of women's labor force activity than found with the previous survey. During a test period in 1993 when the old and new sets of questions were used, the estimate of women's employment-to-population rate (i.e., the number of women who were employed as a share of the female population) was 54.2 percent based on the old questions, and 54.9 percent using the new set. This might seem like a small difference, but it translates into thousands of women who were previously uncounted.

SOURCE: U.S. Department of Labor, Bureau of Labor Statistics, "Revisions in the Current Population Survey Effective January 1994," *Employment and Earnings* (February 1994).

TRENDS IN LABOR FORCE PARTICIPATION

The purpose of this section is to briefly review the trends in female and male labor force participation. The reasons for the observed changes are considered later, but here we may obtain an overview of how substantial these changes have been. Labor force participation rates for selected years since 1890 are shown in Table 4-1.[3] The figures indicate a relatively slow rate of increase in the labor force participation rates of women in the pre-1940 period. After 1940, however, considerably larger changes occurred. In 1940, 28 percent of women were in the labor force; by 2003, the figure had risen to 60 percent of women 16 years of age and over, and more than three-quarters (76 percent) of women between the ages of 25 and 54 were labor force participants. During this time, women workers increased from 25 to 47 percent of the labor force.

Table 4-1 also indicates the sizable effect that the mobilization for World War II had on female labor force participation. As males left their civilian jobs to join the

---

[3]Until 1890, published census volumes contained few tabulations of the labor force participation and occupations of women; see Claudia Goldin, *Understanding the Gender Gap: An Economic History of American Women* (New York: Oxford University Press, 1990), p. 186.

TABLE 4-1   Labor Force Participation Rates of Men and Women, 1890–2003

Year	Men in the Labor Force (%)	Women in the Labor Force (%)
1890	84.3	18.2
1900	85.7	20.0
1920	84.6	22.7
1930	82.1	23.6
1940	82.5	27.9
1945	87.6	35.8
1947	86.8	31.5
1950	86.4	33.9
1960	83.3	37.7
1970	79.9	43.3
1980	77.4	51.5
1990	76.4	57.5
1995	75.0	58.9
2000	74.8	59.9
2003	73.5	59.5

Notes: Based on the total population prior to 1950 and the civilian population thereafter. Rates are computed for individuals 14 years of age and over before 1947, and 16 years and over thereafter.

Sources: U.S. Department of Commerce, Census Bureau, *Historical Statistics of the United States Colonial Times to 1970*, Bicentennial Edition, Part 1, 1975, pp. 131–32; and *Employment and Earnings*, various issues.

armed forces, women entered the labor force in unprecedented numbers. Between 1940 and 1945, the female participation rate increased from 28 to 36 percent. As suggested by the 1947 figures, some decline occurred in the immediate post–World War II period, but the upward trend in female participation quickly resumed. As may be seen in Figure 4-2, however, the steep rise in female participation rates slowed in the early 1990s, and female participation rates have been roughly constant since the mid-1990s.

In contrast to the long-term increase in labor force participation for women, male participation rates began to decline in the 1950s, from 86 percent in 1950 to 74 percent in 2003. As a consequence of these opposing trends, the *difference* between the male and female participation rates has declined sharply from 55 percentage points in 1940 to 14 percentage points in 2003. This growing convergence is also illustrated in Figure 4-2.

We gain a fuller picture of labor force participation patterns by examining them separately for different subgroups. Table 4-2 shows trends in labor force participation since 1955 by race and Hispanic origin. (Because data only recently became available for Asians, only data since 1995 are provided for this group in the table.) The participation rate declined for all groups of men except Asians (for whom we observe only a few years of data), but much more so for blacks. For instance, in 1955, participation rates for white and black men were roughly equal, but in recent years the rate for blacks is considerably lower. In contrast, in recent years, Hispanic men are considerably more likely, and Asian men somewhat more likely, to be in the labor force than whites.

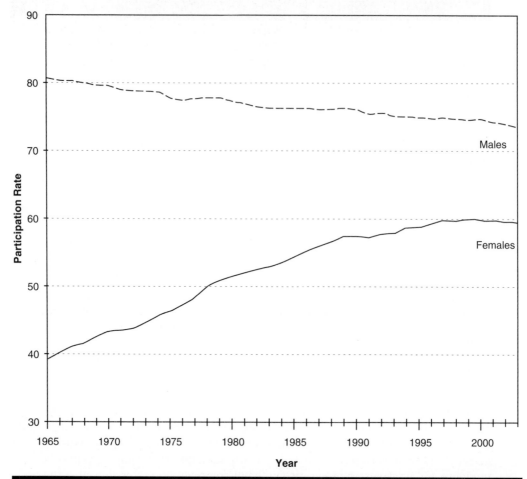

FIGURE 4-2   Trends in Female and Male Labor Force Participation Rates, 1965–2003

The participation rate rose for all groups of women except Asians (for whom we observe only a few years of data), but substantially more so for whites and Hispanics than for blacks. Thus, while black women traditionally had far higher labor force participation rates than white women, this race gap in participation had closed by the mid-1980s. Black women's participation rates drew ahead of those of white women again in the late 1990s, due to a substantial increase in black women's participation rates during that period. Hispanic women's participation rates remained consistently lower than those of whites. And, for years when data are available, Asian women's participation rate was about the same or slightly lower than whites'.

The growth in female labor force participation that occurred since World War II was accompanied by pronounced changes in the patterns of women's employment over the life cycle. Before 1940, the typical female worker was young and single; most women tended to leave the labor force permanently upon marriage and childbearing. As Figure 4-3 shows, at that time, the peak age-specific participation rate occurred

TABLE 4-2   Labor Force Participation Rates of Men and Women by Race and Hispanic Origin, 1955–2003

	Males (%)				Females (%)			
Year	*Whites*	*Blacks*	*Hispanics*	*Asians*	*Whites*	*Blacks*	*Hispanics*	*Asians*
1955	85.4	85.0	n.a.	n.a.	34.5	46.1	n.a.	n.a.
1965	80.8	79.6	n.a.	n.a.	38.1	48.6	n.a.	n.a.
1975	78.7	70.9	80.7	n.a.	45.9	48.8	43.1	n.a.
1985	77.0	70.8	80.3	n.a.	54.1	53.1	49.3	n.a.
1990	76.9	70.1	81.2	n.a.	57.5	57.8	53.0	n.a.
1995[a]	75.7	69.0	79.1	73.6	59.0	59.5	52.6	58.6
2000	75.4	69.0	80.6	74.0	59.8	63.2	56.9	59.3
2003	74.2	67.3	80.1	75.6	59.2	61.9	55.9	58.3

[a]Data for Asians are for 1996.

Notes: Civilian labor force; includes population aged 16 and over. Hispanics may be of any race. Prior to 1975, other nonwhites are included with blacks; and prior to 2003, Pacific Islanders are included with Asians. Also, prior to 2003, persons who reported more than one race (white, black, Asian) were included in the group they identified as the main race. In 2003, whites, blacks, and Asians are defined as persons who selected this race group only; persons who selected more than one race group are not included.
n.a. = Not available.

Sources: U.S. Department of Labor, Bureau of Labor Statistics, *Working Women: A Databook*, 1977, pp. 44–5; U.S. Department of Labor, *Handbook of Labor Statistics* (August 1989), pp. 25–30; and U.S. Department of Labor, *Employment and Earnings* (various issues). Asian data for 1996 and 2000 are from U.S. Census Bureau, Current Population Survey, available at www.census.gov/population/www/socdemo/race/api.html.

among women 20 to 24 years of age and declined for each successive age group after that.[4] Over the next 20 years, older married women with school-age or grown children entered or reentered the labor force in increasing numbers, while little change occurred in the labor force participation rates of women between the ages of 20 and 34. The proportion of women workers who were married increased from 30 percent in 1940 to 54 percent in 1960. The World War II experience may have played a part in encouraging this shift in the behavior of married women, because during the war, for the first time, large numbers of older married women worked outside the home.

Since 1960, participation rates increased for all age groups of women, but particularly among women ages 25 to 44. This increase in part reflects declines in the birthrate and increases in the divorce rate over this period. Most notable, however, is the large increase in the participation rates of married women with small children. Among those with children less than 6 years old, only 19 percent worked outside the home in 1960, compared to 61 percent in 2002. More than half (55 percent) of married mothers who had a child in the last year were in the labor force.

As a result of these changes, the pattern of age-specific participation rates among women has come to more closely resemble the male pattern shown in Figure 4-4. This

---

[4]Note that when labor force participation rates are changing, cross-sectional data on participation rates by age, as shown in Figure 4-3, may give a misleading impression of the actual experiences of individual women over the life cycle. For a fuller explanation of this issue, as well as an interesting analysis of cohort patterns of married women's participation, see Goldin, *Understanding the Gender Gap*, pp. 21–23.

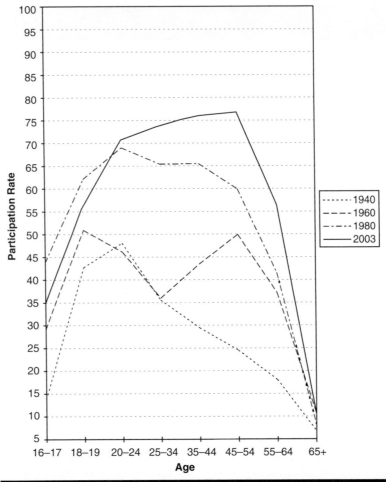

FIGURE 4-3   Civilian Labor Force Participation Rates of Women by Age

figure also shows that the decline in male labor force participation rates that occurred during the post–World War II period was concentrated among younger men, those under 20, and among older men, aged 55 and over. Since the 1960s, smaller but notable decreases also occurred in the participation rates of men in the so-called prime work-ing ages, not only those 45 to 54 but even those 25 to 44. Participation rates for these age groups remain relatively high, however, with over 90 percent of 25- to 44-year-olds, and 88 percent of 45- to 54-year-olds in the labor force.

TRENDS IN LABOR FORCE ATTACHMENT

The changes in the pattern of women's labor force participation by age that oc-curred since 1940 suggest that rising female participation rates are associated with an increase in the labor force attachment of women over the life cycle. That is,

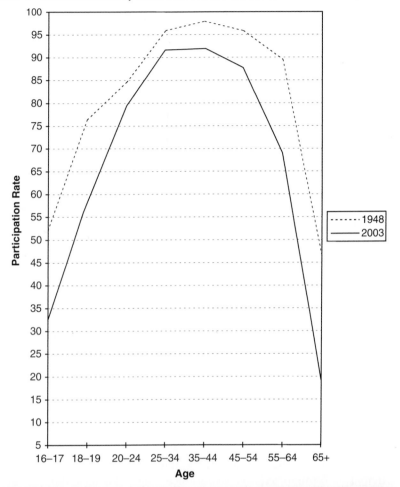

FIGURE 4-4   Civilian Labor Force Participation Rates of Men by Age

women tend to remain in the labor force more consistently over a period of time. This impression is reinforced by data on increases in the labor force attachment of women over the course of a year. So, for example, in 1970, 53 percent of women worked at some time during the year. Of these women with work experience, only 41 percent were employed full-time and year round. By 2002, 63 percent of women worked at some time during the year, and 59 percent of them were employed full-time and year round.[5] Women's increased commitment to the labor force can also be seen by comparing women's labor force attachment near the time of a first birth

[5]"Work Experience of the Population in 2002," U.S. Department of Labor, Bureau of Labor Statistics, *News Release*, December 19, 2003, www.bls.gov/news.release/work.toc.htm, accessed September 21, 2004; and *Women in the Labor Force: A Databook*, U.S. Department of Labor, Bureau of Labor Statistics, www.bls.gov/cps/wlf-databook.htm, accessed September 21, 2004.

in the early 1960s with the early 1990s. One notable difference between the two periods is that women are now substantially more likely to work while pregnant. Of women who gave birth to their first child in the early 1960s, only 44 percent worked during their pregnancy, compared to 67 percent of women who had a first birth in the early 1990s. In addition, women are now much more likely to return to work soon after a first birth. For instance, of those who worked during pregnancy in the early 1960s, only 17 percent returned to work within 3 months and just 21 percent within 6 months, while in the early 1990s, these figures were 58 percent and 70 percent, respectively.[6]

This growing labor force attachment of women contributed to the increase in their labor force participation rate. The labor force group is increased by entries into the labor force and decreased by exits from the labor force. When the number of entrants exceeds the number of those who leave the labor force, the size of the labor force is increased. Thus, both *increases* in flows of *entrants* and *decreases* in flows of *exits* potentially contribute to the growth of the female labor force. Both of these factors appear to have played a role in increasing the female participation rate.

As we shall see in greater detail in Chapter 6, work experience is an important determinant of labor market earnings. The lesser amount of work experience of women relative to men has traditionally been cited as an important reason for their lower earnings. It is not immediately obvious, however, whether recent increases in women's labor force participation are associated with increases or decreases in the *average* amount of work experience of the female labor force. Two changes that would tend to have opposite effects are taking place here. On the one hand, the growing number of new entrants, with little work experience, negatively affects the average labor market experience of women workers. On the other hand, the growing tendency for women to remain in the labor force for longer periods of time has a positive effect.

Unfortunately, the usual published statistics on labor force participation do not help to answer the question about the net effect of women's increased labor force participation on their average experience. This is because data on work experience are not routinely collected. However, estimates are made from time to time based on special surveys that explicitly ask respondents about their labor market experience, as well as less directly from information on labor force entry and exit rates. The evidence suggests that before the late 1960s, rising female labor force participation rates were associated with constant or slowly increasing average levels of work experience among women workers, but since then, notable gains in women's average experience levels occurred.[7] These trends are discussed in greater detail in Chapter 6.

---

[6]Kristin Smith, Barbara Downs, and Martin O'Connell, "Maternity Leave and Employment Patterns: 1961–1995," *Current Population Reports* P70-79, U.S. Census Bureau, Washington, DC (2001). The early 1960s refer to 1961–1965 and the early 1990s refer to 1991–1995.

[7]Goldin, *Understanding the Gender Gap*, pp. 37–41; James P. Smith and Michael P. Ward, "Time Series Changes in the Female Labor Force," *Journal of Labor Economics* (January 1985, supp.); June O'Neill and Solomon Polachek, "Why the Gender Gap in Wages Narrowed in the 1980s," *Journal of Labor Economics* 11, no. 1, pt. 1 (January 1993): 205–28; Francine D. Blau and Lawrence M. Kahn, "Swimming Upstream: Trends in the Gender Wage Differential in the 1980s," *Journal of Labor Economics* 15, no. 1, pt. 1 (January 1997): 1–42; and Francine D. Blau and Lawrence M. Kahn, "The U.S. Gender Pay Gap in the 1990s: Slowing Convergence," National Bureau of Economic Research Working Paper No. 10853 (October 2004).

TRENDS IN HOURS WORKED

The main focus of this chapter is on labor force participation. However, another important aspect of the labor supply decision is *hours worked*. In Chapter 3 we considered trends in the allocation of time of women and men between housework and market work. Here we focus on trends in hours among the employed. Hours worked can be measured as hours worked per day, per week, or annually. One particularly notable trend is that the full-time workweek declined from 60 hours at the turn of the century to about 40 hours in the 1940s and, notably, remains at about that level today. Similarly, the average number of paid hours worked per week for male and female workers showed considerable stability; male workers averaged about 42 hours per week since the 1940s, while women averaged about 36 hours, since at least the 1970s.[8] The lower figure for women in part reflects their continued greater likelihood of working part time than men. For example, in 2002, 28 percent of women usually worked part time (fewer than 35 hours per week) compared to 13 percent of men.[9] As already noted, the proportion of employed women working full time and year round increased over time; however, even among this group, women tend to be employed fewer hours than men.

Trends in annual work hours are more difficult to measure because they may be influenced by workers' difficulty obtaining a job (spells unemployed or out of the labor force), decisions to work part time or part year, and how paid vacation time is counted. Not surprisingly then, there has been some controversy about these trends and how they should be measured, with some studies finding little change in annual hours for women and men and others modest positive or negative trends.[10]

While in the aggregate relatively little change occurred in weekly and annual work hours, an important recent development is that work hours of both men and women have diverged by skill level, with a rising trend for more highly skilled workers and a declining trend for workers with fewer skills.[11] For instance, the length of the workweek generally decreased for employees with less than a high school education, while it rose for those who completed four or more years of college, as well as for those in professional, managerial, and technical occupations. Similarly, average annual hours worked increased for well-educated workers and decreased for the less educated. This increase in work hours for some individuals, combined with the fact that many Americans are single parents with responsibility for children or are members of a dual-earner family, leads to more families facing a growing "time squeeze," a topic discussed further in Chapter 10.

---

[8]See Thomas J. Kniesner, "The Full-Time Work Week in the U.S.: 1900–1970," *Industrial and Labor Relations Review* 30, no. 1 (October 1976): 3–15; Mary T. Coleman and John Pencavel, "Changes in Work Hours of Male Employees, 1940–1988," *Industrial and Labor Relations Review* 46, no. 2 (January 1993): 262–83; Mary T. Coleman and John Pencavel, "Trends in Market Work Behavior of Women Since 1940," *Industrial and Labor Relations Review* 46, no. 4 (July 1993): 653–76; and Jerry A. Jacobs and Kathleen Gerson, "Who Are the Overworked Americans?" *Review of Social Economy* 54, no. 4 (Winter 1998): 442–59.

[9]"Work Experience of the Population in 2002," U.S. Department of Labor, Bureau of Labor Statistics, *News Release*, December 19, 2003, www.bls.gov/news.release/work.toc.htm, accessed September 21, 2004.

[10]For reviews, see Deborah M. Figart and Lonnie Golden, "The Social Economics of Work Time: Introduction," *Review of Social Economy* 54, no. 4 (Winter 1998): 411–24; and Jerry A. Jacobs and Kathleen Gerson, *The Time Divide: Work, Family, and Gender Inequality* (Cambridge, MA: Harvard University Press, 2004).

[11]Coleman and Pencavel, "Changes in Work Hours of Male Employees, 1940–1988"; Coleman and Pencavel, "Trends in Market Work Behavior of Women Since 1940"; and Jacobs and Gerson, "Who Are the Overworked Americans?" See also Jacobs and Gerson, *The Time Divide.*

THE LABOR SUPPLY DECISION

In Chapter 3, we examined the division of housework and market work between husband and wife. Here we focus upon the closely related question of how an individual, whether married or single, decides on the allocation of his or her time between the home and the labor market. We again use a neoclassical model and assume that the individual's goal is to maximize utility or satisfaction.[12] A brief preview of our conclusions may be helpful in understanding the more detailed analysis that follows. The economic model suggests that individuals decide whether to participate in the labor force by comparing the value of their time in the market given by their hourly wage rate (w) to the value they place on their time spent at home (w^*). If the value of time in the market is greater than the value of time spent at home ($w > w^*$), they choose to participate in the labor force. Alternatively, if the value of home time is greater than or equal to the value of market time ($w^* \geq w$), they choose to remain out of the labor force. After tracing out the reasoning behind this decision rule in this section, in the next section we analyze the long-run increase in women's labor force participation in terms of factors that increased the value of their market time and lowered the value of their home time.

Individuals are viewed as deriving utility from the consumption of *commodities* (goods and services) that are produced using inputs of market goods and nonmarket time.[13] For example, the commodity, a family dinner, is produced using inputs of market goods (groceries, cooking equipment, etc.) and the individual's own time in preparing the meal. In order to keep this model reasonably simple, we make the following three additional assumptions.

First, we assume that all income earned in the labor market is spent on market goods. This assumption avoids the need to consider the determinants of savings and also means that we may use the terms *market income* and (the money value of) *market goods* interchangeably.

Second, we assume that all nonmarket time is spent in the production of commodities, whether the output is a loaf of bread, a clean house, a healthy child, or a game of golf. This approach not only avoids the need for analyzing a three-way choice among market work, housework, and leisure but also makes the often difficult distinction between nonmarket work (including volunteer work) and leisure unnecessary.[14] We do

---

[12]As before, the underpinnings of the analysis are derived from the work of Gary S. Becker; see "A Theory of the Allocation of Time," *Economic Journal* 75, no. 299 (September 1965): 493–517; and Jacob Mincer, "Labor Force Participation of Married Women," in *Aspects of Labor Economics,* edited by H. Gregg Lewis, Universities National Bureau of Economic Research Conference Studies, no. 14 (Princeton, NJ: Princeton University Press, 1962), pp. 63–97. James Heckman and Reuben Gronau, among others, also made significant contributions to the development of statistical techniques for estimating the theoretical relationships; for an excellent review, see Mark R. Killingsworth, *Labor Supply* (Cambridge: Cambridge University Press, 1983).

[13]Students who have read the appendix to Chapter 3, where a graphical analysis of specialization and exchange was presented, will recognize the basic approach employed here as quite similar. However, in this analysis, we do not need to make the rigid distinction between home goods (produced exclusively with inputs of home time) and market goods (produced entirely with market-purchased goods) that was used to simplify the analysis in the appendix to Chapter 3. Indeed, not only can we recognize that market goods and nonmarket time are both inputs into the production of commodities, but also that more than one way may be used to produce the same commodity.

[14]Market work is relatively easy to distinguish as any activity that results in material, usually monetary, reward. However, it is quite problematic to determine whether preparation of a gourmet meal, going to a League of Women Voters meeting, growing flowers, or taking a child for a walk is work or leisure.

not wish to suggest, however, that in reality no difference separates the two. Indeed, one of the concerns about the impact of married women's increased labor force participation on their welfare is that it was not accompanied by a comparable real-location of household chores. As a result, women are often saddled with the "double burden" of home and market work. This "working a double shift" may reduce the leisure time available to them, impede their ability to compete with men in the labor market, or both. Data on housework were presented in Chapter 3.

Third, and perhaps even more crucially, we focus here on the individual rather than on the family as a whole. This focus is quite realistic when the individual is the only adult in the family. However, as we saw in Chapter 3, where more than one adult is present, the division of labor among them, and thus the labor supply decision of each, is reasonably expected to be a family decision. We do not introduce all the complexities of family decision making here, which would cause the exposition to become unduly complex. We do, however, view the individual in a family context by taking into account the impact of the earnings of other family members on each person's labor supply decision, but the labor supply of other members of the household is taken as given and is assumed not to be influenced by the individual's own choice. This assumption is probably less unreasonable when we consider women's labor supply decisions since, in most American families, husbands are still likely to remain in the labor market full time regardless of their wives' participation decision. However, some research suggests that the husband's labor supply does respond to the wife's decision under certain circumstances and it is of course possible that this responsiveness increased in recent years as the two-earner family has become more the norm.[15]

Now that we have reviewed some of the assumptions of the model, we are ready to turn to analysis of the labor supply decision itself. In this model, both market goods and nonmarket time are used in the production of the commodities from which the individual derives satisfaction. Thus, the goal of the individual is to select the utility-maximizing combination of market goods and nonmarket time. Because market goods are purchased with income earned through market work, and all time available is spent either on market work or nonmarket activities, this choice is the basis of the labor supply decision. In making this choice, the individual must take into account both the options that are open to him or her, given by the *budget constraint* shown in panel a of Figure 4-5, and his or her tastes or preferences expressed in the family of *indifference curves* shown in panel b of Figure 4-5. Let us trace out this decision for the hypothetical case of a married woman named Mary.

The Budget Constraint

The budget constraint in panel a shows the various combinations of nonmarket time and market goods from which Mary can choose, given her market wage rate and the nonlabor income available to her. The **wage** is the amount of money an individual earns

---

[15]The empirical evidence regarding the dependence of husbands' labor supply decisions and earnings on the decisions of their wives is mixed. For example, a study by Thomas Mroz found no evidence of such dependence; see "The Sensitivity of an Empirical Model of Married Women's Hours of Work to Economic and Statistical Assumptions," *Econometrica* 55, no. 4 (July 1987): 765–800. On the other hand, Shelly J. Lundberg finds that the presence of children is a crucial variable, with each spouse acting independently of the other's decision except when young children are present; see "Labor Supply of Husbands and Wives: A Simultaneous Equations Approach," *Review of Economics and Statistics* 70, no. 2 (May 1988): 224–35.

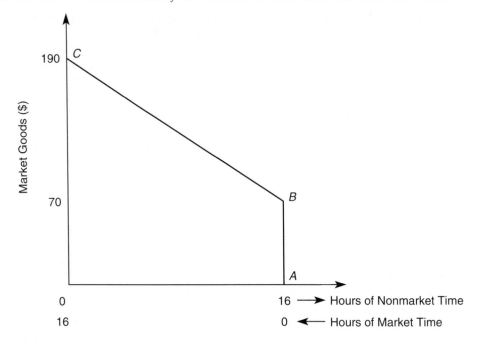

(a) THE BUDGET CONSTRAINT

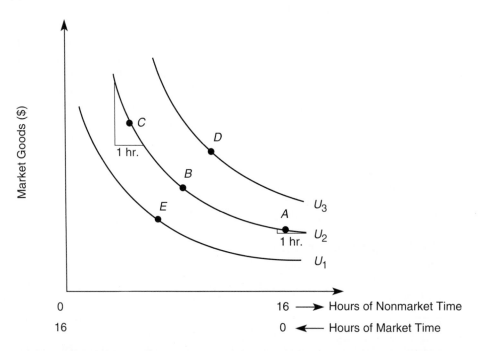

(b) INDIFFERENCE CURVES

FIGURE 4-5   The Budget Constraint and the Indifference Curves

for each hour he or she works; the wage is an hourly rate of pay. **Nonlabor income** is any income an individual receives, apart from his or her own labor market earnings. The amount of nonlabor income is thus unrelated to the amount of time the individual devotes to the labor market. Nonlabor income may include the earnings of a spouse, as well as any income received from interest, dividends, or rental property. For simplicity, government transfer payments, such as welfare or unemployment insurance, may also be considered nonlabor income, although the amount of income received from such sources is influenced by the amount of time a person supplies to the labor market. Hours of *nonmarket time* are measured from left to right along the horizontal axis.

We assume that Mary has a total of 16 hours available to her in a day to allocate between market and nonmarket activities (allowing 8 hours for nondiscretionary activities like sleeping). Since any of this time that Mary does not spend in nonmarket activities is spent in the market, hours of *market time* are measured from right to left along the horizontal axis.

Mary's nonlabor income is $70 a day. The vertical segment *BA* of the budget constraint shows that Mary has this income available to her even if she supplies no time to the labor market. She may further increase her money income by participating in the labor force. For each additional hour she supplies to the market, she must give up an hour of nonmarket time. In return she receives $7.50, her hourly market wage (*w*). Thus, segment *CB* is negatively sloped. Its slope is equal to –7.50 or –*w*. If Mary devotes all her time to the market, her total earnings will be $120 ($7.5 x 16). Her total daily income, including her nonlabor income, will be $190 ($120 + $70).

Indifference Curves

Mary's preferences for market goods and nonmarket time are represented by her indifference map, shown in panel b. As discussed previously, we can incorporate the family context of decision making into the budget constraint by including the income of other family members as part of the individual's nonlabor income. This issue is more difficult when we consider the indifference curves. One possibility would be to view the indifference curves in Figure 4-5 as representing the family's preferences for various combinations of market goods and Mary's nonmarket time. We do not adopt this approach because, as we saw in Chapter 3, preferences among family members may differ, and the process of arriving at family decisions is complex. However, it is important to recognize that our discussion of indifference curves as representing the individual's preferences is only an approximation. In fact, we expect that the individual's decisions are made in the context of the family and that the preferences of other family members are taken into account in the decision-making process. Bearing this point in mind, we now take a closer look at the indifference curves.

Suppose Mary is told that she could have the combination of market goods and nonmarket time represented by point *B*. She is then asked to find various other combinations of market goods and nonmarket time from which she would get exactly the same amount of satisfaction or utility and identifies the combinations represented by points *A* and *C*. These and other points, which represent equal satisfaction, can all be connected into one indifference curve, so named because Mary is indifferent about being at various points on the curve. Thus, each indifference curve indicates the various combinations of market goods and nonmarket time that provide Mary with the same amount of utility or satisfaction.

However, Mary has not just one indifference curve, but a whole family of higher and lower curves. A point like D on indifference curve U_3 is clearly preferable to B because it offers more of both market goods and nonmarket time. Thus, by extension, all points on U_3 are preferred to all points on U_2. Similarly, B is preferred to E and, thus, all the points on U_2 are preferred to all the points on U_1.[16] As we move out from the origin in a northeasterly direction, consumption possibilities, and thus potential satisfaction, increase.

Indifference curves are generally assumed to be convex to the origin. That is, they become flatter as we move from left to right and steeper as we move from right to left. This shape occurs because it is believed that individuals generally value additional units of relatively scarcer commodities more highly than additional units of relatively more plentiful ones. At point A, where nonmarket time is relatively plentiful and market goods are relatively scarce, Mary would be willing to exchange an hour of nonmarket time for a relatively small amount of income (market goods) and still feel equally well off. However, at a point like C, where market goods are relatively plentiful and nonmarket time is relatively scarce, it would take a lot of income (market goods) to induce her to give up an additional hour of scarce nonmarket time.

It is interesting to consider more closely the way in which an individual like Mary may substitute market goods for nonmarket time (or vice versa) along an indifference curve while still remaining equally well off. It is important to recognize that we assume she does not derive satisfaction directly from market goods and nonmarket time. Rather, she values them only insofar as they can be used to produce commodities.[17] Thus, broadly speaking, two types of substitution are involved.

Substitution in Consumption

Some commodities are relatively *goods intensive* to produce. That is, they are produced using relatively large amounts of market goods and relatively little nonmarket time. Examples include buying expensive antiques, furniture, and clothing or recreational activities such as dining at an elegant restaurant or flying to the Caribbean for a short vacation.

Other commodities are relatively *time intensive*. That is, they are produced using relatively large inputs of nonmarket time and relatively fewer inputs of market goods. Examples of these commodities include recreational activities like hiking, bird watching, going to a baseball game, or taking a cycling trip. Also, as anyone who has spent time caring for youngsters can attest, small children are a relatively time-intensive "commodity."

Substitution in consumption involves choosing among commodities so as to substitute goods-intensive commodities for time-intensive ones or time-intensive commodities for goods-intensive ones. When such substitutions are made along a given indifference curve, the implication is that the individual is indifferent between the two alternatives. So, for example, an individual may be indifferent between a goods-intensive vacation like staying for a short time at an expensive resort or a more time-intensive one of spending

---

[16]It should be clear that indifference curves can never intersect. All points on any one curve represent an equal amount of utility, while any point above (below) represents a larger (smaller) amount of utility. At the point where two curves intersect, they represent the same utility. Yet at all other points they do not. This is a logical impossibility.

[17]The indifference curves used in this chapter are a graphical representation of what has been termed the individual's *indirect utility function;* see Becker, "A Theory of the Allocation of Time." Students who read the appendix to Chapter 3 will recognize that we took a different approach in the analysis presented there and simply assumed that families derive utility *directly* from market and home goods.

an extensive period hiking and backpacking. Or, more broadly, an individual might be indifferent between having a large family of time-intensive children and spending more time in recreational activities that are more goods intensive.

Substitution in Production

In many instances, the same commodity can be produced using a relatively time-intensive technique or a relatively goods-intensive technique. For example, a meal may be prepared from scratch at home, made using convenience foods, or purchased at a restaurant. A clean house may be produced by individuals doing the work themselves or by hiring cleaning help. A small child may be cared for entirely by a parent, have a baby-sitter for a few hours a day, or spend all day at a child care center.

Substitution in production involves choosing among various ways of producing the same commodity so as to substitute goods-intensive production techniques for time-intensive ones or time-intensive production techniques for goods-intensive ones. Again, when such substitutions are made along a given indifference curve, the implication is that the individual is indifferent between the two alternatives. Examples here include those already described: preparing a meal at home versus eating out, hiring cleaning help versus doing it oneself, taking a child to a child care center versus taking care of the child oneself.

Substitution between Market Goods and Nonmarket Time

As an individual like Mary moves from point A to point B to point C along indifference curve U_2 in Figure 4-5, she is likely to exploit opportunities for substitution in both consumption and production. That is, she will substitute goods-intensive commodities for time-intensive commodities in consumption, and goods-intensive for time-intensive production techniques. As she continues to do so, she will exhaust many of the obvious possibilities. It will take larger increments of market goods to induce her to part with her scarcer nonmarket time, which explains why indifference curves are believed to get steeper as we move from right to left.

Comparing across individuals, the steepness of the indifference curve is influenced by how easy or difficult it is for them to substitute market goods for nonmarket time while remaining equally well off. This ease or difficulty, in turn, will depend on their opportunities for substituting one for the other in production or consumption or both. For example, those who enjoy hiking a great deal will not easily be induced to decrease the time they spend on it. They will have steeper indifference curves, reflecting that they have greater difficulty in substituting market goods for nonmarket time in consumption than those who care less for such time-intensive activities.

Similarly, we would expect those whose services are in greater demand in the home (say, because small children are present) to have steeper indifference curves, reflecting their greater difficulty in substituting market goods for nonmarket time in production. Tastes and preferences will be a factor here, too. People who feel strongly that children should be cared for full time by their own parent and that alternative care is an extremely poor substitute will have steeper indifference curves than those who believe that adequate alternative care can be provided.

This analysis assumes a degree of substitutability between market goods and nonmarket time. However, some commodities cannot be purchased in the market. Various personal services and management tasks provided in the home may be of this nature.

Similarly, some commodities available in the market cannot be produced at home. Examples range from sophisticated medical care and advanced education to means of transportation and communication, insurance, and many consumer durables.[18] Nonetheless, it is highly likely that when all commodities are aggregated together (as in the indifference curves shown in Figure 4-5) some substitution possibilities between market goods and nonmarket time exist. The ease or difficulty of substitution, then, is represented by the steepness of the indifference curves.

Tastes

Beyond considerations of this kind, economists generally do not analyze the determinants of individuals' preferences for income (market goods) versus nonmarket time. However, it is important to point out that individuals do not operate in a social vacuum. Their tastes and behaviors are undoubtedly influenced by social attitudes and norms.[19] For example, the willingness of a woman to substitute purchased services for her own time in child care is undoubtedly influenced by the social acceptability of doing so. Yet it is probably true that attitudes follow behavior to some extent, as well. Thus, it is likely, for example, that it is more acceptable for mothers of small children to work outside the home in part because it is more common for them to do so.

A woman's relative preference for income (market goods) versus nonmarket time also reflects a variety of other factors not generally emphasized by economists. As we saw in Chapter 3, women may value earning their own income for the economic independence it brings and to enhance their relative power position in the family. An increasing number of women value career success in much the same way their male counterparts do, which also affects the shape of their indifference curves.

Although such considerations do not invalidate the use of this model in analyzing women's labor supply decisions, they do serve to make us aware that the term *tastes* (or preferences), as economists use it, covers a lot of ground. This awareness is particularly important as we attempt to explain women's rising labor force participation over time.

The Participation Decision

Let's suppose that Mary's indifference curves and her budget constraint are those shown in panel a of Figure 4-6. Mary will maximize utility or satisfaction at point Y where the budget constraint just touches the highest attainable indifference curve, U_2. At Y, the amount of income needed to induce her to give up an additional hour of nonmarket time, given by the slope of the indifference curve at Y, exactly equals the market wage she is offered for that hour, given by the slope of the budget constraint. That is, the budget constraint is tangent to the indifference curve at Y. Mary, therefore, supplies 8 hours per day to the market and spends 8 hours on nonmarket activities. Her daily earnings of \$60 (\$7.50 × 8) plus her daily nonlabor income of \$70 give her (and her family) a total income of \$130 per day.

It is interesting to consider in greater detail why Mary does not select point A, where she would supply no time to the labor market. At A, where indifference curve

---

[18]Nancy Folbre and Julie A. Nelson, "For Love or Money—Or Both?" *Journal of Economic Perspectives* 14, no. 4 (Fall 2000): 123–40; and Clair (Vickery) Brown, "Home Production for Use in a Market Economy," in *Rethinking the Family: Some Feminist Questions,* edited by Barrie Thorne (New York: Longman, Inc., 1981).

[19]The importance of social norms is particularly emphasized by Clair Brown, "An Institutional Model of Wives' Work Decisions," *Industrial Relations* 24, no. 2 (Spring 1985): 182–204.

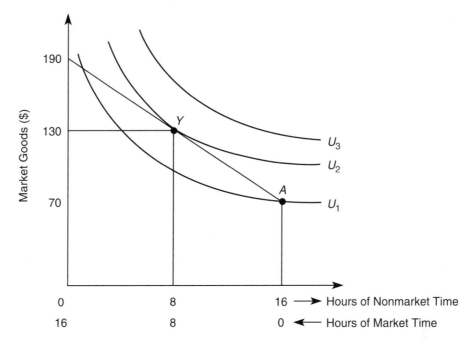

(a) $w > w^*$ PARTICIPATES IN THE LABOR MARKET

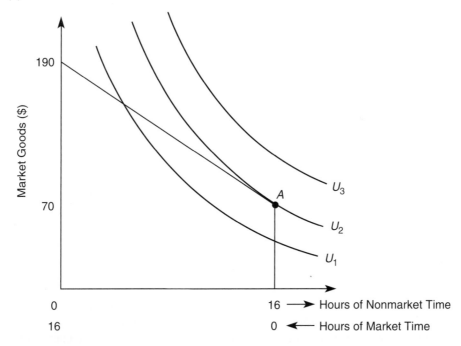

(b) $w < w^*$ DOES NOT PARTICIPATE IN THE LABOR MARKET

FIGURE 4-6 The Labor Force Participation Decision

U_1 intersects the budget constraint, it is *flatter* than the negatively sloped portion of the budget constraint (which passes through point A and point 190 on the market goods axis). This means that, at point A, Mary values her nonmarket time *less* than the wage the market is willing to pay her for it. Thus, she will certainly choose to supply some time to the market.

Another woman, Joyce, faces the same budget constraint as Mary but has steeper indifference curves (shown in panel b of Figure 4-6). Perhaps she has more young children to care for than Mary. In Joyce's case, the budget constraint touches the highest attainable indifference curve at point A. At A, the indifference curve is steeper than the budget constraint. This means that Joyce sets a *higher* value on her nonmarket time than the wage rate she is offered in the market. She will maximize her utility by remaining out of the labor force, spending all 16 hours available to her on nonmarket activities. Her consumption of market goods will be limited to her nonlabor income of $70 per day.

The slope of the indifference curve at zero hours of market work (point A in panels a and b of Figure 4-6) is termed the **reservation wage** (w^*). It is equal to the value the woman places on her time at home. If the market wage is greater than the reservation wage (i.e., $w > w^*$), as in panel a, the individual will choose to participate in the labor market. If the reservation wage is greater than or equal to the market wage ($w^* \geq w$), as in panel b, the individual will choose not to participate. This decision rule can be summarized by the following simple equations:

$$w > w^* \Rightarrow \text{in the labor force}$$
$$w^* \geq w \Rightarrow \text{out of the labor force}$$

This economic analysis suggests that factors that increase the value of market time (w) tend to increase the probability that the individual will choose to participate in the labor force, all else equal. In other words, labor force participation is *positively related* to the wage or the value of market time. On the other hand, factors that increase the value of nonmarket time (w^*) tend to lower the probability of labor force participation, other things being equal. Therefore, labor force participation is *negatively related* to the reservation wage or the value of nonmarket time.

The Value of Nonmarket Time (w^*)

As our previous discussion suggests, the value of nonmarket time is influenced by tastes and preferences and also by the demands placed on an individual's nonmarket time. Given adherence to the traditional division of labor in most families, the presence of small children, and other circumstances that increase the need for housework, particularly influence women's participation decisions.

Another factor that influences the value placed on nonmarket time is the availability of income from sources other than the individual's own work efforts. Figure 4-7 shows the impact of changes in nonlabor income on the labor force participation decision. Let's suppose that the figure represents the budget constraint and indifference curves for Susan, a married woman with two small children. Suppose that her husband is unemployed and that initially her budget constraint is ABC. This represents $30 of nonlabor income (from interest on some bonds the family owns) and her market wage of $7.50. She maximizes utility at point D, where she supplies five hours a day to the market and earns $37.50. This brings the family's total daily income to $67.50. Now suppose Susan's

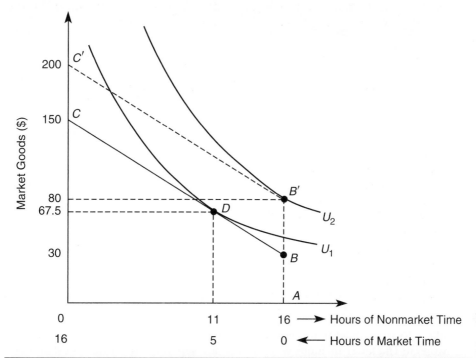

FIGURE 4-7   The Impact of Nonlabor Income on Labor Force Participation

husband finds a job. When his earnings ($50) are added to the interest received from the bonds ($30), her nonlabor income becomes $80. Her new budget constraint is $AB'C'$. Note that segment $B'C'$ is parallel to segment BC. This is because Susan's market wage rate, which is the slope of segment BC, remains unchanged at $7.50.

At the higher income level, Susan's consumption possibilities increase, and she is able to reach a higher indifference curve. She maximizes utility at B' where she has more of both market goods and nonmarket time, and supplies less time to the market; in fact, in this example, she withdraws from the labor force entirely. This example represents the impact of the **income effect**. Ordinarily, when individuals' incomes go up, they demand more of all commodities from which they derive utility. To the extent that nonmarket time is used to produce these commodities, an increase in income will increase the value of nonmarket time and result in less time spent in the labor market. The income effect will be relatively large when the demand for time-intensive commodities increases sharply with income. The individual then needs to transfer more time from market to nonmarket activities in order to produce them. This shift is likely to occur when market goods are not considered to be good substitutes for home-produced items. So Susan, whose wage rate has not changed while her income increased, may choose to consume more recreation or spend more time caring for her children.

Table 4-3 illustrates the impact of the value of nonmarket time (w^*) on women's labor force participation decisions, using actual data on female participation rates by marital status and presence and age of children. Marital status reflects in part the availability and level of alternative sources of income. Thus, we see that, in 2002, within children's age categories, women who are married, with spouse present, are generally less

TABLE 4-3 Labor Force Participation Rates of Women by Marital Status, and Presence and Age of Children, 1960 and 2002

Marital Status	Total[a]	With Children		
		Under Age 18	*6 to 17 only*	*Under 6*
1960				
Never married	44.1	n.a.	n.a.	n.a.
Married, husband present	30.5	27.6	39.0	18.6
Other ever-married	40.0	56.0	65.9	40.5
2002				
Never married	67.1	75.3	81.7	71.0
Married, husband present	61.5	69.6	76.8	60.8
Other ever-married	49.3	82.1	83.6	77.9

[a]Includes women with and without children present.

Notes: Data are for March of each year and include women 16 years of age and over in 2002, 14 years of age and over in 1960.

n.a. = Not available.

Sources: U.S. Census Bureau, *Statistical Abstract of the United States: 2003*, Table 597; and U.S. Census Bureau, *Statistical Abstract of the United States: 1995*, Table 638.

likely to work outside the home than never-married women and other ever-married women. The latter includes women who are separated from their husbands, divorced, or widowed. Further evidence for the importance of the value of home time is provided by studies that find that, among married women, labor force participation is negatively related to husband's income, all else equal.[20] Recall here that we expect an increase in the wife's nonlabor income to raise the value of her nonmarket time (w^*).

The impact of children on women's labor force participation may be discerned by comparing the participation rates of women with small children (children under 6) to the rates for women with school-age children (children 6–17), within each marital status category. We see that the presence of small children has a negative effect on women's participation, no doubt because they greatly increase the value of time spent at home. Of course, the causation may, to some extent, run in the opposite direction: Women who are more committed to the labor market or who face more attractive labor market opportunities may choose to have fewer children. It is difficult to distinguish between these two possible explanations for the negative association between women's labor force participation and the presence and age of children.[21]

---

[20]See, for example, the studies reported in James P. Smith, ed., *Female Labor Supply: Theory and Estimation* (Princeton, NJ: Princeton University Press, 1980).

[21]See, for example, Robert Willis, "What Have We Learned from the Economics of the Family?" *American Economic Review* 77, no. 2 (May 1987): 68–81; and Martin Browning, "Children and Household Economic Behavior," *Journal of Economic Literature* 30, no. 3 (September 1992): 1432–75. The statistical problem in identifying the causal effect of children on labor supply is that, as in any problem of this type, it is necessary to find a variable that determines the number of children but does not directly influence labor supply. For an interesting new approach using variation in the sex mix of the first two children as well as twin births as predictors of fertility, see Joshua D. Angrist and William N. Evans, "Children and Their Parents' Labor Supply: Evidence from Exogenous Variation in Family Size," *American Economic Review* 88, no. 3 (June 1998): 450–77; see also Joyce P. Jacobsen, James Wishart Pearce III, and Joshua L. Rosenbloom, "The Effects of Childbearing on Married Women's Labor Supply and Earnings: Using Twin Births as a Natural Experiment," *Journal of Human Resources* 34, no. 3 (Summer 1999): 449–74.

Note that participation rates in the "total" column (which include women with and without children under age 18 present) tend to be lower than for the group of women with children present. One reason is that married and other ever-married women with no children under 18 tend to be older, in some cases widows, whose children have left home. These women tend to have lower participation rates. Another reason is that never-married women with no children present tend to be younger women, who may still be attending school and thus out of the labor force for that reason.

The data in the table also illustrate some interesting trends in the impact of marital status and the presence of children on labor force participation. Although the presence of small children was an important determinant of women's labor force participation throughout this period, women with small children were considerably more likely to work outside the home in 2002 than in 1960. For example, in 2002, 61 percent of married women with children under six years old were in the labor force, compared to only 19 percent in 1960. Similarly, 77 percent of married women with children between the ages of six and seventeen were labor force participants in 2002, compared to 39 percent in 1960.[22]

The differences in participation rates by marital status are also considerably smaller today than they were 30 years ago. In addition, within the group of married women, wives' participation decisions are less sensitive to their husbands' income than they were in the past.[23] In other words, today wives' labor force participation rates are quite high, even for those married to husbands with successful careers. In this way too, married women's behavior is now more similar to that of their nonmarried counterparts.

Figures 4-8a and b show trends in participation rates of women with children by marital status in more detail. Figure 4-8a gives the participation rates for women with children under age 18 and Figure 4-8b shows the participation rates for women with children under age 6 separately. Broadly similar patterns hold for both groups, but the differences in trends by marital status are especially dramatic for those with children under 6. Prior to 1990, increases in the labor force participation rates of married mothers were especially large compared to those of never-married and other ever-married mothers. For example, in the early 1960s, participation rates of married mothers of small children were 22 percentage points lower than those of other ever-married mothers, but by 1991 the participation rates of the two groups were the same. Published data on never-married mothers have only been available since 1975. At that time their participation rates were about the same as those of married mothers; however, by 1990 married mothers were *considerably more* likely to be in the labor force than never-married mothers with children in the same age category.

In contrast, after 1990, the growth in labor force participation of married mothers slowed and their participation rates began to level off in the mid-1990s; among those with preschool children present, participation rates actually declined somewhat in the late 1990s and early 2000s. At the same time participation increased sharply among never-married

---

[22]Statistical analyses controlling for other factors affecting the labor force participation of wives, including husband's income and education, confirm that very young children exert a smaller negative influence on wives' participation than formerly; see, for example, Arleen Leibowitz and Jacob Klerman, "Explaining Changes in Married Mothers' Employment Over Time," *Demography* 32, no. 3 (August 1995): 365–78.
[23]Chinhui Juhn and Kevin M. Murphy, "Wage Inequality and Family Labor Supply," *Journal of Labor Economics* 15, no. 1, pt. 1 (January 1997): 72–97.

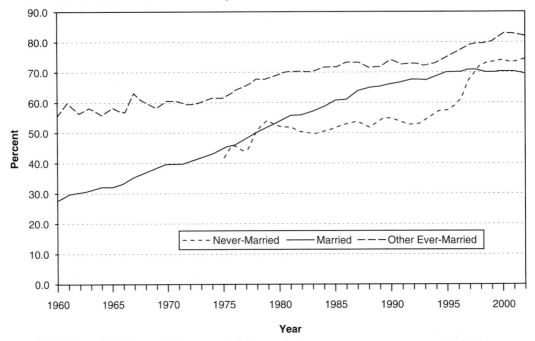

FIGURE 4-8a Labor Force Participation Rates of Women with Children Under Age 18, 1960–2002

Sources: U.S. Statistical Abstract: 2004, Table 597; Bureau of Labor Statistics, *Handbook of Labor Statistics,* Bulletin 2340 (August 1989); Bernan Press, *Handbook of U.S. Labor Statistics,* 1st ed. (1997).

and other ever-married mothers.[24] As a consequence, both never-married and other ever-married mothers are now more likely to be in the labor force than married mothers. The factors behind these various recent trends are explored further later in this chapter.

Even though most attention has focused on the effect of the presence of children on women's labor supply, some research has examined the impact of children on male labor supply. Perhaps not surprisingly given traditional gender roles, fatherhood has been found to *increase* the labor supply of men. What is perhaps surprising is that men increased their labor supply more in response to the birth of sons than daughters.[25] Although, as discussed in Chapter 11, preference for male children is quite pronounced in a number of Asian countries including India, China, and Korea, this and other recent research suggests it is by no means entirely absent in the United States.[26]

---

[24]See also, Rebecca M. Blank, "Distinguished Lecture on Economics in Government—Fighting Poverty: Lessons from Recent U.S. History," *Journal of Economic Perspectives* 14, no. 2 (Spring 2000): 3–19; and Bruce D. Meyer and Dan T. Rosenbaum, "Making Single Mothers Work: Recent Tax and Welfare Policy and Its Effects," *National Tax Journal* 53 (December 2000): 1027–62.

[25]Shelly Lundberg and Elaina Rose, "The Effects of Sons and Daughters on Men's Labor Supply and Wages," *Review of Economics and Statistics* 84, no 2 (May 2002): 251–68.

[26]For example, in addition to having stronger effects on men's labor supply, the birth or expected birth of a son increased the probability that unmarried biological parents will marry, and the presence of sons reduced the probability that married couples will divorce. Studies also find that in families with at least two children, the probability of having another child is higher in all-girl families than in all-boy families. See Gordon B. Dahl and Enrico Moretti, "The Demand for Sons: Evidence from Divorce, Fertility, and Shotgun Marriage," National Bureau of Economic Research Working Paper No. 10281 (January 2004); and Shelly Lundberg and Elaina Rose, "Child Gender and the Transition to Marriage," *Demography* 40, no. 2 (May 2003): 333–49.

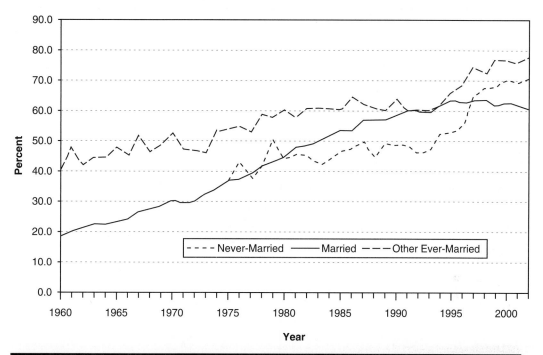

FIGURE 4-8b   Labor Force Participation Rates of Women with Children Under Age 6, 1960–2002

Sources: U.S. Statistical Abstract: 2004, Table 597; Bureau of Labor Statistics, *Handbook of Labor Statistics*, Bulletin 2340 (August 1989); Bernan Press, *Handbook of U.S. Labor Statistics*, 1st ed. (1997).

The Value of Market Time (*w*)

In addition to the impact of the value of nonmarket time, the labor force participation decision is influenced by the labor market opportunities an individual faces, particularly the wage rate available in the labor market. To see this effect in greater detail, let us consider the case of Ellen, who initially faces the budget constraint, *ABC,* shown in Figure 4-9. Her potential market wage is $8.00 per hour, while her nonlabor income (say, equal to her husband's earnings) is $100 per day. Given her tastes (represented by her indifference map), she maximizes utility at point *B* where she devotes all her time to nonmarket activities. Note that at point *B* the indifference curve (U_1) is steeper than the budget line (*BC*)—Ellen's reservation wage (*w**) is higher than the wage rate offered to her by the market (*w*).

Now suppose that Ellen's market opportunities improve and her potential market wage increases to $12.00. Her new budget constraint is *ABC′*. Segment *BA* of her budget constraint remains unchanged because it is still the case that if she remains out of the labor market entirely, she (and her family) will receive $100 a day of nonlabor income. However, *BC′* is steeper than *BC* because she now receives $12.00 for each hour she supplies to the market rather than $8.00. Another way to see it is to realize that *C′* must lie above *C* because, if Ellen devotes all her time to market work, her total income at a wage of $12.00 per hour ($292) will be higher than it would have been at a wage of $8.00 per hour ($228).

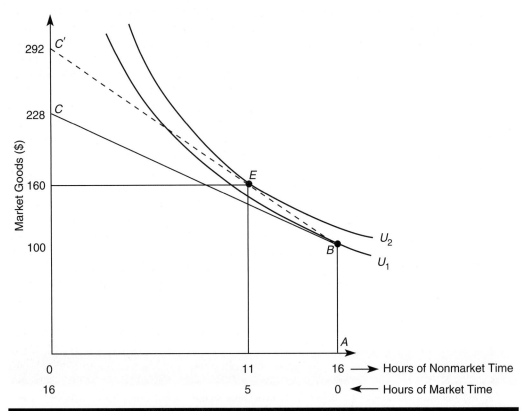

FIGURE 4-9   The Impact of the (Potential) Market Wage on Labor Force Participation

At the higher wage, the budget constraint (BC') is now steeper than the indifference curve at point B—the market wage (w) is greater than the reservation wage (w^*), and Ellen maximizes her utility at point E on indifference curve U_2, where she supplies 5 hours to the market. Thus, Ellen now chooses to participate in the labor force.

This example illustrates the **substitution effect**. An increase in the wage rate, all else being equal, raises the opportunity cost of time spent in nonmarket activities and, hence, the "price" of nonmarket time. Individuals are expected to respond by supplying more time to the market and substituting market goods for nonmarket time in consumption or production. Because the wage increase clearly enables Ellen to reach a higher indifference curve, we may conclude that she feels better off with the combination of commodities represented by point E, even though she has less nonmarket time available at E than at B.

Published data are not readily available on participation rates of individuals by the wage they could potentially earn in the labor market. However, some indication of the impact of the potential market wage on labor force participation may be gained by examining the association between educational attainment and labor force participation. As we shall see in greater detail in Chapter 6, education is strongly positively associated with labor market earnings. A common interpretation of this empirical relationship is that education increases market productivity and hence market earnings, which would lead us to expect education to be positively associated with labor force participation. One qualification worth noting, however, is that, especially for women, the positive effect of education on labor force participation may be reduced to the extent that additional education also raises the productivity of women's nonmarket time. For example, the time that more-educated women spend with their children could potentially contribute more to their children's achievement levels than time spent by less-educated women.

Nonetheless, as may be seen in panel a of Figure 4-10, a positive relationship exists between education and labor force participation among women. Women with higher levels of education are more likely to be in the labor force. Therefore, the impact of education on labor market earnings is greater than its impact on the value of home time. We may interpret this positive relationship between education and labor force participation as reflecting a positive relationship between wages and labor force participation. However, the positive relationship between education and participation may also reflect self-selection: Women who plan to spend a relatively high proportion of their adult years in the labor force are more likely to invest in education. Finally, we may note that the jobs held by more educated individuals usually offer greater nonpecuniary (or nonmonetary) attractions—such as a more pleasant environment, more challenging work, and so on—as well as higher wages. Consideration of such job features serves to emphasizes that the value of market work should ideally take into account not only pecuniary benefits but also other aspects of the job.

Panel a of Figure 4-10 also shows that even though education was a determinant of labor force participation in both 1970 and 2003, participation rates of high school graduates and of college-educated women increased substantially more over the period than they did for women who did not complete high school. These differential increases resulted in a stronger relationship between participation and education in 2003 than existed in 1970. Panel b of Figure 4-10 indicates that a similar trend occurred among men. Although participation fell for all education groups, it decreased more for less-educated men.

At the same time that the participation of less-educated men and women decreased relative to their more educated counterparts, their relative labor market wages also fell. A trend toward widening wage inequality in the United States and to a lesser extent in many other economically advanced nations resulted in widening wage differentials between more-skilled and less-skilled workers. Some evidence indicates that the declining relative labor force participation of less-educated women and men is due at least in part to their declining market wage opportunities.[27] The trend toward rising wage inequality is considered in more detail in Chapter 8, where we review recent labor market developments. In addition to declining relative participation and wages, a considerably faster increase in single headship among less-educated women than among their more highly educated counterparts also adversely affected their economic status.[28] Chapter 9 discusses the considerable economic disadvantages faced by such families.

---

[27]Chinhui Juhn, "Decline of Male Labor Market Participation: The Role of Declining Market Opportunities," *Quarterly Journal of Economics* 107, no. 1 (February 1992): 79–121; and Juhn and Murphy, "Wage Inequality and Family Labor Supply."

[28]Francine D. Blau, "Trends in the Well-Being of American Women: 1970–1995," *Journal of Economic Literature* 36, no. 1 (March 1998): 112–165.

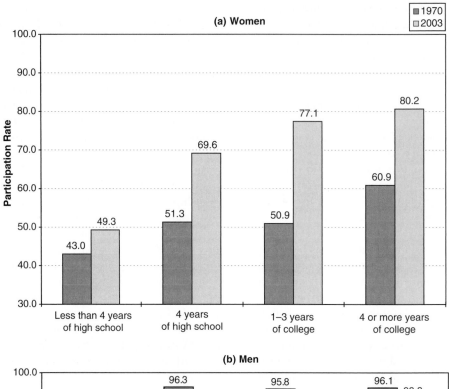

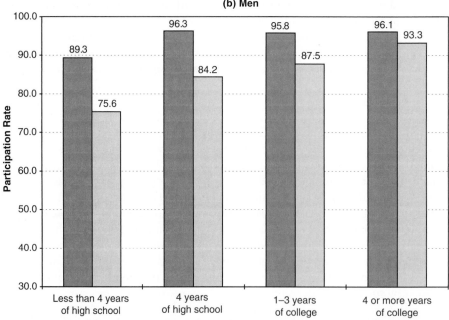

FIGURE 4-10   Labor Force Participation by Education, 1970 and 2003, Ages 25–64

Note: Educational categories are defined somewhat differently in 2003.

Sources: U.S. Department of Labor, *Handbook of Labor Statistics*, 1989; and author's tabulations from the 2003 microdata file of the March Current Population Survey.

The Hours Decision

The impact of a change in the wage rate on the number of *hours* supplied to the market by those who are already labor force participants is a bit more complex than the impact of a wage change on *labor force participation*. This complexity is illustrated in Figure 4-11. As we saw in Figure 4-9, an increase in the wage rate corresponds to an outward rotation of the budget constraint, because more market goods can now be purchased for every hour worked, shown as a rotation from *CD* to *CD'* in Figure 4-11. In both panels a and b, the individual initially maximizes utility at point *A* on indifference curve U_1. At a higher wage, he or she is able to reach a higher indifference curve and selects point *B* on indifference curve U_2, resulting in either an increase (shown in panel a) or a decrease (shown in panel b) in hours supplied to the market.[29] These outcomes illustrate that, for those who are labor force participants, an increase in the wage rate produces two distinct effects.

On the one hand, the increase in the wage is like an increase in income. For any given amount of time supplied to the market *greater than 0 hours,* income is higher along *CD'* than along *CD*. This gives rise to an *income effect* that, other things being the same, increases the demand not only for most market goods, but also for nonmarket time, and hence lowers hours supplied to the market. On the other hand, the increase in the wage also raises the opportunity cost of nonmarket time, resulting in a *substitution effect* that, all else equal, causes a reduction in nonmarket time and an increase in the supply of hours to the market.

Thus, when the wage rate rises, the substitution effect operates to increase labor hours supplied, but the income effect operates to reduce labor hours supplied. The net effect is theoretically indeterminate. If the substitution effect dominates the income effect, work hours increase (panel a). If the income effect dominates the substitution effect, work hours are reduced (panel b). Again, recall that a wage increase unambiguously raises the probability of labor force participation because, in this case, no offsetting income effect occurs, only a positive substitution effect.

Empirical Evidence on Income and Substitution Effects

Our analysis of the labor force participation decision and the hours of work decision of participants suggests the importance of distinguishing between these two types of decisions. In recent years economists have found that this distinction is indeed quite important empirically. For both men and women, the participation decision is much more responsive to income and wages than the hours of work decision of labor force participants. Early studies of labor force participation suggested that married women's labor supply was much more sensitive to wages and income than men's labor supply. Economists now realize that this impression arose in good part because the responsiveness of women's *participation* decisions, which tends to be rather large, was being compared to the responsiveness of men's *hours of work* decisions, which tends to be rather small. Women's overall labor supply response is influenced by their participation decisions to a greater extent than men's because a considerably higher fraction of women than men are out of the labor force.[30] It is,

---

[29]The diagrammatic representation of the effect of a wage change on work hours is shown in greater detail in the appendix to this chapter.
[30]James J. Heckman, "What Has Been Learned About Labor Supply in the Past Twenty Years," *American Economic Review* 83, no. 2 (May 1993): 116–21.

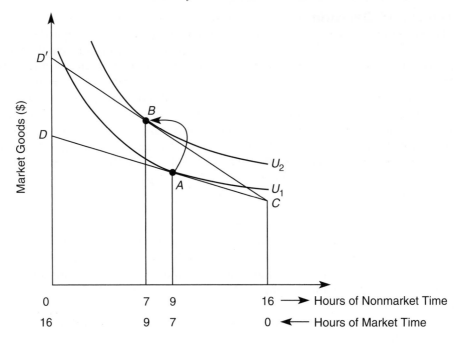

(a) THE SUBSTITUTION EFFECT DOMINATES THE INCOME EFFECT

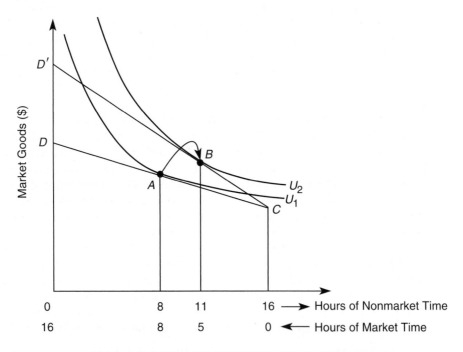

(b) THE INCOME EFFECT DOMINATES THE SUBSTITUTION EFFECT

FIGURE 4-11   The Impact of the Market Wage on Labor Hours

however, also true that even for the hours of work decision, married women's responsiveness to wages and income tends to exceed men's.[31]

Traditional gender roles may be one reason for the gender difference in the responsiveness to wage changes. As a group, men traditionally worked full-time in the market and devoted most of their nonmarket time to recreation rather than household production. Although it is possible to substitute market goods for nonmarket time in recreational activities, these possibilities are necessarily limited. The situation is quite different for women, most of whom spend a great deal of nonmarket time doing housework. Because purchased goods and services are in many cases useful substitutes for nonmarket time in producing the commodities the family wants, the substitution effect is more likely to dominate the income effect for women than for men.[32]

Economic Conditions

Fluctuations in economic conditions also affect labor force participation. These effects are likely to be largest among demographic groups that contain a relatively high proportion of individuals who are loosely attached to the labor force. These groups would include teenagers and older individuals of both sexes and adult women in the so-called prime working ages. Economists view the response of labor force participation to changes in the level of economic activity as being the net result of two opposing effects.

The **added worker effect** predicts that during economic downturns, if the primary earner becomes unemployed, other family members may enter (or postpone their exit from) the labor force in order to maintain family income. The decline in their nonlabor income due to the unemployment of the primary earner lowers the value of other family members' nonmarket time (w^*). (This effect is shown as a movement from point B' to point D in Figure 4-7.) Such individuals may leave the labor force when economic conditions improve and the primary earner is again employed on a regular basis.

At the same time, the **discouraged worker effect** holds that during times of high unemployment, when individuals lose their jobs, they may become discouraged and drop out of the labor force after a fruitless period of job search. Others who are outside the labor market may postpone labor force entry until economic conditions improve. Discouragement is due to the decline in the perceived reward to market work (w) because of the difficulty of locating an acceptable job. (This effect is shown as a movement from point E to point B in Figure 4-9.) As economic conditions improve, previously discouraged workers may renew their job search and enter the labor force.

Both these effects can operate at the same time for different households. The *net* effect of economic conditions on labor force participation depends on whether the discouraged or added worker effect predominates in the aggregate. It is an empirical question. The data suggest that for the labor force as a whole, the discouraged worker effect is dominant. Thus, the labor force tends to shrink or grow less rapidly in recessions and to expand or grow more rapidly during upturns in the economy. One study

---

[31]See the survey in Killingsworth, *Labor Supply.*
[32]This difference was first emphasized by Mincer, "Labor Force Participation of Married Women."

finds that cyclical sensitivity is particularly pronounced for teenagers, older men, and women under 35.[33]

Some Applications of the Theory: Taxes, Child Care Costs, and Labor Supply

Taxes and the Decision to Work

Not all money earned is actually at the disposal of the worker. Some of it has to be paid out in taxes. Because earnings are taxed and the value of home production is not, labor force participation among married women is discouraged. This effect is increased by the progressive nature of the tax system. Because the family (rather than the individual) is the tax unit, married women, often regarded as secondary earners within the family, face relatively high tax rates on the first dollar of their labor market earnings. In general, we expect that the higher the tax rate (the lower the after-tax wage), the more likely a woman is to decide not to participate in the labor force.

These points may be illustrated by Figure 4-9. Suppose Joan earns $12.00 per hour and faces budget constraint ABC'. If she has to pay out, say, one-third (33.3 percent) of her income in taxes, her after-tax wage (or hourly take-home pay) will be only $8.00. This situation is represented by budget constraint ABC. At this lower wage, Joan chooses to stay out of the labor market.[34]

One interesting study used the reduction in the top marginal tax rates under the Tax Reform Act of 1986 to obtain empirical evidence about the labor supply response of married women to changes in the tax rate. In that legislation, the top rate was lowered from 50 to 28 percent. It was found that the reduction in the tax rate increased the labor supply of married women from high-income families (who were most affected by the change) relative to women from somewhat less-affluent families (whose marginal tax rates were not affected). The reduction in taxes was estimated to have increased the participation rates of the high-income women by 8.4 percent.[35] Further consideration of the impact of the federal income tax on the labor supply of wives is provided in Chapter 10.

Government Subsidies of Child Care and Women's Labor Force Participation

Young children are still a significant deterrent to the entry of their mothers into the labor market. Child care subsidies by the government could lower the cost of child

---

[33]Kim B. Clark and Lawrence H. Summers, "Demographic Differences in Cyclical Employment Variation," *Journal of Human Resources* 16, no. 1 (Winter 1981): 61–79. Some evidence indicates that the added worker effect also exists, though it is small; see Shelly Lundberg, "The Added Worker Effect," *Journal of Labor Economics* 3, no. 1 (January 1985): 11–37. Recent work suggests that one reason the added worker effect has been found to be so small empirically is that receipt of unemployment insurance helps to counteract the negative effect on family income that would otherwise occur when the primary breadwinner becomes unemployed. See Jonathan Gruber and Julie Berry Cullen, "Does Unemployment Insurance Crowd Out Spousal Labor Supply?" *Journal of Labor Economics* 18, no. 3 (July 2000): 546–72.

[34]We simplified the representation of a progressive tax in Figure 4-8 in that we show only one tax rate—the one Joan faces given her level of family income—and assume that additional hours worked do not push her into a higher tax bracket. In fact, as long as individuals are below the maximum rate, it is possible that as they work more hours their higher total income will push them into a higher tax bracket. Thus, the after-tax budget constraint may be "kinked," its slope becoming flatter each time the individual enters a higher tax bracket.

[35]Nada Eissa, "Taxation and Labor Supply of Married Women: The Tax Reform Act of 1986 as a Natural Experiment," National Bureau of Economic Research Working Paper No. 5023 (February 1995).

care. What would be the expected effect on women's labor supply? We can use economic theory to see that a reduction in child care costs is expected to increase women's labor force participation.

Recall that so far we have assumed that individuals do not value market goods and nonmarket time in themselves, but rather because they can be used to produce commodities. This framework yields valuable insights into the possibilities of substitution in consumption and in production, which help determine the steepness of the indifference curves. However, to examine the impact of the cost of child care explicitly, it will be more convenient to simply assume that the indifference curves represent the individual's preferences for market goods (income) versus nonmarket time.

Suppose Figure 4-9 represents the situation of Nancy, a woman with small children. To examine the impact of child care costs, we may view the hourly cost of child care that Nancy must pay if she works as a "tax" on her market earnings. If the budget constraint shows the wage Nancy receives after child care costs are subtracted out, it is clear that a decrease in child care costs is equivalent to an increase in the wage rate. For example, suppose Nancy can earn $14.00 an hour but must pay $6.00 an hour in child care costs. This results in a *net* wage of $8.00 per hour ($14.00 − $6.00 = $8.00), given by segment *BC*. At this wage, she chooses not to participate in the labor market. However, if her child care costs were to fall to $2.00 per hour, her net wage rises to $12.00 per hour ($14.00 − $2.00 = $12.00), given by segment *BC'*, and she would participate.

In this example, the decrease in child care costs results in Nancy deciding to enter the labor force. In general, we would expect the availability of child care at a lower price to increase the labor force participation rate of women with small children. The empirical evidence supports this expectation. For example, one study using data from the mid-1980s found that, for married mothers with children under 13, participation would increase from 58.8 percent to 64.0 percent if child care were subsidized by 50 percent. If universal no-cost child care were available, the participation rate of this group would rise to 68.7 percent.[36] A recent study using data from the early to mid-1990s sheds further light on this relationship. This study found that the labor force participation of the least skilled women is most responsive to the market price of child care, suggesting that the price of child care is a particularly strong determinant of labor force participation for this group.[37]

A decline in child care costs is also likely to have long-run effects on women's labor supply and wages. Because women would experience shorter (and possibly fewer) labor force interruptions, they would accumulate longer and more continuous labor market experience. This factor would be expected to have a favorable effect on the types of jobs they are able to obtain and on their earnings, and would in turn further reinforce

---

[36]Rachel Connelly, "The Effect of Child Care Costs on Married Women's Labor Force Participation," *Review of Economics and Statistics* 74, no. 1 (February 1992): 83–90. See also David M. Blau and Philip K. Robins, "Child-Care Costs and Family Labor Supply," *Review of Economics and Statistics* 70, no. 3 (August 1988): 374–81; and Jean Kimmel, "The Effectiveness of Child-Care Subsidies in Encouraging the Welfare-to-Work Transition of Low-Income Single Mothers," *American Economic Review* 85, no. 2 (May 1995): 271–75.

[37]Patricia M. Anderson and Phillip B. Levine, "Child Care and Mothers' Employment Decisions," in *Finding Jobs: Work and Welfare Reform*, edited by David Card and Rebecca Blank (New York: Russel Sage Foundation, 2000).

the tendency toward spending more time in the labor market.[38] Therefore, in the long run, a reduction in child care costs is likely not only to raise women's labor force participation, but also to enhance their occupational attainment and earnings. Thus, child care subsidies could contribute to a reduction in labor market inequality between men and women. Whether such subsidies are desirable on other grounds is considered in greater detail in Chapter 10.

ANALYZING TRENDS IN WOMEN'S PARTICIPATION: AN OVERVIEW

In the remaining sections of this chapter we apply the theoretical model of labor supply to analyze some of the major trends in labor force participation described at the beginning of this chapter. In this section, we provide an overview of the factors responsible for the long-term increase in women's labor force participation over the twentieth and into the early twenty-first century. In the following sections, we take a closer look at a number of subperiods of particular interest. We first consider explanations for the dramatic rise in female labor force participation during World War II and the further increase that occurred during the post–World War II baby boom. We then analyze the period of the 1960s to the 1980s when especially sharp increases occurred in the labor force participation rates of married mothers of young children and then the 1990s to early 2000s when growth in the participation rates of this group slowed but that of single mothers with young children increased substantially. Next, we consider explanations for the long-term decrease in men's labor force participation rates and conclude with an examination of some of the reasons for differences in labor force participation trends of blacks and whites.

Why did female labor force participation rise over the course of the twentieth and early twenty-first century? Drawing upon the analysis presented earlier in this chapter, the obvious answer is a rise in the wage rate (w), a decrease in the value of time spent in the home (w^*), or both. Considerable evidence shows various developments that would be expected to cause each of these effects, as well as complex interactions that reinforce the original results.[39]

Factors Influencing the Value of Market Time (w)

A variety of factors caused the real (inflation-adjusted) wages of women to increase over time. The result was an outward rotation of the budget constraint, as shown in Figure 4-9. Under these circumstances, more women are expected to find that the wage offered them by the market exceeds their reservation wage and to choose to enter the labor force. This process does not require that women's wages increase relative to men's wages. During the 1950s and 1960s both men's and women's real wages were rising and the gender gap remained roughly constant. For much of the period since the early 1970s, men's real wages were stagnant or declining, while women's real wages increased overall and rose particularly sharply in the 1980s. During this time the gender pay gap narrowed.

---

[38]For evidence that current work experience increases the probability of future participation due to its effect on wages, see Zvi Eckstein and Kenneth I. Wolpin, "Dynamic Labour Force Participation of Married Women and Endogenous Work Experience," *Review of Economic Studies* 56, no. 3 (July 1989): 375–90.
[39]See Goldin, *Understanding the Gender Gap,* for an interesting econometric analysis of these trends in labor force participation.

Rising Qualifications: Education and Experience

As young women received more education, the wage rate they were able to earn by working in the market went up and they were more likely to work outside the home. At the same time, once women were more inclined to work for pay, they would want to obtain more market-oriented schooling in order to be able to obtain better-paying jobs.

The magnitude of this phenomenon can be gauged by the enormous increases in the proportion of the population that graduated from high school or obtained college degrees. Between 1940 and 2002, the proportion of women who completed at least four years of high school increased from 26 to 84 percent. The increase for men was even greater, from 23 to 84 percent, because initially women were more likely to graduate high school than men.[40] During this same period, the proportion of women who completed four or more years of college increased from 3.8 to 25.1 percent, whereas for men the proportion rose from 5.5 to 28.5 percent.

The statistics for higher education reflect the fact that traditionally more young men than young women completed college and pursued graduate study. However, this gender differential began to decline in the late 1960s. Women have increased their share of college, graduate, and professional degrees, as well as their representation in traditionally male fields of study. (Data on this trend are presented in Chapter 6.) Hence, although men's educational attainment also increased over time, gender differences in higher education in the general population narrowed substantially, and, in fact, young women are now more likely to graduate college than young men.

Women's increased expectation of participating in the labor force over the life cycle increased their incentives to invest in education and helped to narrow the gender gap in educational attainment at the college and graduate level. An additional factor increasing the returns to education was the growing number of years women could expect to live. Life expectancy at birth for women went up from 48 years around 1900 to nearly 80 years at the beginning of the new century. Though most individuals retire by age 65, this increase in life expectancy meant that women were able to reap considerably higher rewards from education and on-the-job training over their lifetime, even if they took some time out for homemaking.

As women accumulated more labor force experience and responded to the increased incentives to invest in market-related education and on-the-job training, their potential market wages were further increased, raising the opportunity cost of nonmarket activities and, thus, further increasing their labor force participation.

The Demand for Female Labor

It is also frequently suggested that, first with industrialization and then with the movement to the postindustrial economy, the demand for workers in traditionally female clerical and service jobs increased and caused their wages to be higher than they otherwise would have been.[41] As discussed in Chapter 2, married women were

---

[40]The gender difference was quite pronounced earlier in the century. In 1900 only two-thirds as many boys as girls graduated from high school. Note that the statistics presented on educational attainment here, which are from the *Statistical Abstract of the United States*, differ somewhat from those presented in Chapter 6. This discrepancy is due to the age range, which is 25 years or over here, but 25–64 in Chapter 6.

[41]Valerie Oppenheimer, *The Female Labor Force in the United States: Demographic and Economic Factors Governing Its Growth and Changing Composition* (Westport, CT: Greenwood Press, 1976; originally published 1970); and Goldin, *Understanding the Gender Gap.*

barred from clerical employment by many large firms in the 1920s and 1930s, and they did not fully benefit from this expansion in demand until marriage bars were abandoned in the 1950s.[42] It is also quite likely that antidiscrimination legislation increased the demand for women in traditionally male jobs since its passage in the mid-1960s.

Overall Productivity Increases

Female as well as male workers benefited from increases in labor productivity due to growth over time in the capital stock and technological change, which exerted upward pressure on wages, all else equal.

Factors Influencing the Value of Nonmarket Time (w^*)

It would be a mistake, however, to ascribe the impetus for the persistent influx of women into the labor market solely to higher wage rates and to overlook those changes that influenced the relative value of nonmarket time. Even though changes in w^* are not directly measurable, our review of the changes in the various factors influencing w^* suggests that their net effect was to decrease the value of nonmarket time. In any case it seems clear the value of nonmarket time did decline *relative to* market time and, thus, the proportion of women working for pay increased.

Availability of Market Substitutes and Technological Change

Among the most obvious changes was the increase in the availability of goods and services previously produced in the home but that became increasingly available for purchase in the market. Not only did fruits and vegetables, in earlier days grown in the family garden, come to be available at the grocery, but in time they were cleaned, canned, frozen, and eventually often included in prepared dishes or meals. First yarn, earlier spun at home, became commonly available; next it was cloth, and then ready-made clothing. Schools extended the hours and years of care provided for older children. For young children, nursery schools and, more recently, day care centers became more prevalent, while hospitals increasingly cared for the sick, and various types of care for the infirm and aged became more common. These examples show only a few commodities that in earlier days were produced with large inputs of home time but that today require mainly expenditures of money.

At the same time, technological changes made housework easier and less time consuming. These important innovations included indoor plumbing and electrification of houses, as well as appliances, from vacuum cleaners, washing machines, and refrigerators to dishwashers and microwave ovens, which became increasingly common in U.S. households.[43]

To be sure, some changes did have the opposite effect, such as the considerably higher cost and greater difficulty of finding domestic help. By and large, however, market goods offered more substitutability for nonmarket time, and technological change made doing housework less taxing. As a result, women would be expected to be more

---

[42]Goldin, *Understanding the Gender Gap*. Both Oppenheimer and Goldin attribute the increased willingness of employers to hire older married women in the 1950s to a decrease in the supply of young, single female workers, caused by the small size of the cohort born during the 1930s coupled with the decline in the marriage age that occurred during the 1950s.

[43]For evidence on the impact of the increased availability of consumer durables on female labor force participation, see Jeremy Greenwood, Ananth Seshadri, and Mehmet Yorukoglu, "Engines of Liberation," *Review of Economics and Statistics* (forthcoming).

willing to give up time at home in order to be able to do more market work, a change illustrated in Figure 4-6 by the flatter indifference curves shown in panel a as compared to the steeper indifference curves shown in panel b.

Thus, we see that the greater availability of goods and services for purchase as well as labor-saving technological change in the home resulted in a decrease in the value of women's nonmarket time (w^*) and caused their labor force participation to increase. At the same time, women's rising labor force participation tended to increase the demand for market goods and services that substitute for their time in the home or make housework tasks easier, further encouraging development and production of such products.

Demographic Trends

Another important change that influenced relative preferences for home versus market time was the long-run decline in the birthrate, from 30.1 births per 1,000 population in 1910 to 14.1 per 1,000 by 2001. Because the rearing of young children, generally considered to be women's responsibility, is extremely time intensive, especially in the absence of adequate provision for their care outside the home, their presence used to be one of the strongest barriers to women's entry into the labor market. As already described, only since the 1960s have mothers of preschoolers worked outside the home to any significant extent, and even now their participation remains lower than that of mothers with school-age children.

Not only is the period during which young children are present in the home more protracted as their numbers rise, but the longer the woman is at home, the less favorable the terms she is likely to encounter in the labor market upon her return, and the more likely she is to remain out permanently. Women are, of course, aware of this cost and to some extent adjust family size to their work plans, as well as vice versa.

Just as women's labor force participation is influenced by, and in turn influences, their fertility, the same is true of marital stability. The divorce rate per 1,000 population per year went from 0.9 in 1910 to 4.0 in 2001. The divorce rate influences women's labor force participation in part due to its impact on the composition of the female population: Divorced women have considerably less nonlabor income than married women and are thus more likely to participate in the labor force. However, married women's behavior is affected by rising divorce rates as well. As married women become aware of the increasing probability of divorce, their participation increases as a means of safeguarding their standard of living in case of a marital breakup.[44] The other side of the coin is that a two-earner couple can more readily afford to get divorced. The woman can count on her own income, rather than being completely dependent on the often uncertain support of an ex-husband; the man need not spend resources to fully support, or to avoid support of, an ex-wife.

Rising Husband's Income

Not all changes operated in the direction of lowering the value of nonmarket time. In particular, earnings of men increased more rapidly than the cost of living for most of

---

[44]William R. Johnson and Jonathan Skinner, "Labor Supply and Marital Separation," *American Economic Review* 76, no. 3 (June 1986): 455–69. The terms under which divorce is available can also affect the labor supply of married women; see, for example, H. Elizabeth Peters, "Marriage and Divorce: Informational Constraints and Private Contracting," *American Economic Review* 76, no. 3 (June 1986): 437–54; and Jeffrey S. Gray, "Divorce-Law Changes, Household Bargaining, and Married Women's Labor Supply," *American Economic Review* 88, no. 3 (June 1998): 628–42.

the twentieth century. As their husbands' real income goes up, all else equal, married women's labor force participation is reduced due to the income effect (Figure 4-7). For women, however, the positive substitution effect of their own rising real wages tends to more than offset the negative income effect due to the increasing real incomes of their husbands.[45] Also, perhaps due to changing gender roles, married women's participation shows less sensitivity to their husbands' income in recent years. Finally, since the 1970s, men's real wages in general stagnated, and those of the less educated and unskilled declined in real terms.[46]

Tastes

Over time, the development of many desirable market products that could not be produced in the home, like automobiles, air conditioning, television, CD players, and personal computers, likely increased people's preferences for market-produced goods and reduced the relative value placed on nonmarket time.[47] Such changes in tastes may be related to broader trends such as the growing urbanization of the population. The movement from country to city reduced the opportunity for household production (e.g., growing and processing fruits and vegetables) and increased the convenience of market purchases as well as access to market work. Even leisure activities changed from those that mainly required time—hiking, swimming in the waterhole, and chatting on the front porch—to others that required substantial expenditures, such as going to the theater, concerts, and sporting events, watching television, listening to CDs, and surfing the Web.

It is also entirely possible that the trend toward rising female participation rates itself was responsible for further changes in tastes. It was probably far more difficult for women to enter the labor force in the past when it was the exception rather than the rule as it is today. Shifting cultural norms, encouraged in part by the example of more women working in the market, led women to place a higher value on the independence and autonomy that their own earnings bring, and, increasingly, many value career success in much the same way as their male counterparts. In addition, to the extent that people want to keep up with the Joneses in their consumption standards, it takes two paychecks to keep pace today.[48]

THE WORLD WAR II EXPERIENCE

As we saw in Table 4-1, a sharp rise in the female labor force participation rate occurred during World War II, particularly among married women. The rate declined in the immediate post–World War II period, but it remained above prewar levels and

---

[45]This phenomenon was first pointed out by Mincer in "Labor Force Participation of Married Women." Claudia Goldin, *Understanding the Gender Gap,* presents evidence of a declining income elasticity of married women's labor supply over the twentieth century.

[46]See, for example, Chinhui Juhn, Kevin M. Murphy, and Brooks Pierce, "Wage Inequality and the Rise in Returns to Skill," *Journal of Political Economy* 101, no. 3 (June 1993): 410–42; and Lawrence F. Katz and Kevin M. Murphy, "Changes in Relative Wages, 1963–87: Supply and Demand Factors," *Quarterly Journal of Economics* 107, no. 1 (February 1992): 35–78. For an analysis of the impact of these developments on labor supply, see Juhn and Murphy, "Wage Inequality and Family Labor Supply."

[47]This factor is particularly emphasized by Brown, "An Institutional Model of Wives' Work Decisions."

[48]For evidence suggesting that women's labor force participation decisions are influenced by those of other women, see David Neumark and Andrew Postlewaite, "Relative Income Concerns and the Rise in Married Women's Employment," *Journal of Public Economics* 70, no. 1 (October 1998): 157–83.

began its long-term rise shortly after that. In this section we explain these changes by considering factors influencing the value of market time (w) and nonmarket time (w^*). Overall, the World War II experience illustrates the importance of both economic and social factors in causing changes in female labor force participation.

As men were mobilized for the armed forces and the need for workers rose at the same time, the demand for women to fill the available positions increased greatly. This surge in labor market opportunities, which included relatively high-paying, traditionally male jobs, drove up the potential market wages of women. At the same time, married women were urged to work outside the home to contribute to the war effort, raising the nonpecuniary benefits of market work for women and lowering their subjective assessment of the value of nonmarket time. In addition, the birthrate, already relatively low in the Depression years of the 1930s, remained low during the war because many young men were away in the armed forces. In addition, many of the women whose husbands joined the military experienced a decrease in their nonlabor income, because working for "Uncle Sam" often did not pay as much as civilian employment.

A further factor that worked to lower the value of home time for married women was that the government and some employers opened day care centers for children of employed mothers.[49] Even though not enough places were available for all youngsters whose mothers were employed, this action increased both the supply, and the acceptability, of alternative care of children, at least for the duration of the war. Thus, the combination of an increase in the value of market time and a reduction in the value of nonmarket time induced a large increase in the proportion of women working outside the home.

In the immediate postwar period, each of these factors was reversed, helping to bring about the observed decline in women's participation rates. As men returned to the civilian labor force, many were able to reclaim their former jobs from the women who held them during the war. For example, many union contracts reserved their former jobs for men who had left them for military service. Even in the absence of union agreements, some employers voluntarily restored veterans' jobs because they felt it was the appropriate recompense for the veteran's wartime contribution. Moreover, whether a returning veteran claimed a specific job held by a woman during the war, the influx of returning males into the labor market certainly lowered the demand for women workers. Also, the increase in earnings as husbands resumed civilian employment boosted wives' nonlabor income.

In addition, social values changed and the employment of married women outside the home was once again frowned upon, now that the wartime emergency was over. Indeed, after enduring the major dislocations of the Great Depression of the 1930s followed by a world war of unprecedented proportions, there may understandably have been a desire to return to "normalcy," including traditional gender roles. This swing in attitudes likely also played a part in producing the upsurge in birthrates during the postwar period, discussed in the next section. Finally, when the wartime labor shortage

---

[49]Given public concern, both about stimulating maternal employment in war industries and about possible neglect of children, during the 1941–1943 period the federal government provided matching funds to induce states to provide day care centers. An estimated 1.6 million children attended these programs. The best-known centers established by large private employers were those by Curtiss-Wright in Buffalo and by Kaiser in Portland. See Bernard Greenblatt, *The Changing Role of Family and State in Child Development* (San Francisco: Jossey Bass, 1977), pp. 58–60.

was over, day care centers were perceived to be no longer needed and were closed. These changes combined to lower the benefits of market work relative to the value of home time and to reduce women's labor force participation rate in the immediate post–World War II period.

The operation of the long-term factors discussed in the preceding section meant that the postwar participation rate, while lower than the wartime peak, exceeded prewar levels. The rise in participation rates that followed the war was primarily due to fundamental economic and social factors. Yet the wartime experience may have hastened this process by helping to break down the attitudinal barriers to married women's employment outside the home and giving many women a taste of earning their own income. For example, historian William H. Chafe argues that the notion that woman's appropriate sphere was in the home was so deeply embedded that it took a cataclysmic event like World War II to break down this normative barrier.[50] On the other hand, economic historian Claudia Goldin gives less weight to the influence of World War II on later trends, presenting evidence that the war had little *direct* effect on women's participation in the postwar years. Goldin found that more than half of the women working in 1950 had been employed in 1940 (i.e., before the United States entered the war). Just 20 percent of those working in 1950 entered the labor force during the war, and about half of the wartime entrants left the labor force sometime after December 1944. However, Goldin acknowledges that this evidence does not rule out *indirect* effects of the war, such as on views of women's roles or on the subsequent behavior of young women who were employed during the war and later returned to the labor force after dropping out for a time.[51]

THE POST–WORLD WAR II BABY BOOM

As noted previously, the long-run downward trend in birthrates was interrupted by the post–World War II baby boom. From 1946 to the mid-1950s, birthrates rose steadily, and remained at relatively high levels until the early 1960s. Although some of this rise in birthrates was simply a result of the postponement of childbearing that occurred during the Depression and the war years, much of it did indeed reflect an increase in family size in comparison to earlier periods. At the height of the baby boom, women averaged three births, considerably more than the replacement-level fertility rates of their Depression-era mothers. The decline in the birthrate, which contributed to the rise in female labor force participation over the long run, does not help to explain the increase in participation that occurred during the baby boom era.

How did participation rates increase in the face of the negative effect of high birthrates? The first point to be made is that the increase in birthrates would principally affect younger women (under age 35) in the prime childbearing ages, who would be

---

[50]William H. Chafe, *The American Woman: Her Changing Social, Economic, and Political Role, 1920–1970* (Oxford: Oxford University Press, 1972). Similarly, Dorothy Sue Cobble emphasizes the dramatic impact the war years had on the attitudes of women workers, particularly the emergence of a new consensus on equal pay and a breakdown of the formerly near-universal consensus in favor of protective legislation for women; see Dorothy Sue Cobble, "Recapturing Working-Class Feminism: Union Women in the Postwar Era," in *Not June Cleaver: Women and Gender in Postwar America, 1945–1960,* edited by Joanne Meyerowitz, (Philadelphia: Temple University Press, 1994), pp. 57–83.

[51]Claudia Goldin, "The Role of World War II in the Rise of Women's Work," *American Economic Review* 81, no. 4 (September 1991).

most likely to have small children present. Recall that it was precisely this group for whom labor force participation rates did *not* increase over the 1940–1960 period (Figure 4-3). Rising participation rates were primarily due to the entry of older women (over age 35) with school-age or grown children. They were desirable workers from the employer's perspective, because they were from a generation that benefited from considerably more education than their elders had received: The rate of high school completion increased from 29 percent in 1930 to 49 percent in 1940.[52] Further, even though the baby boom meant that young children would cause mothers to stay home. This was not the case as the children grew older and more self-sufficient. Indeed, it might be argued that teenagers, and especially college students, need more money rather than time, especially now that young people tend to stay in school so much longer.

Second, during this period, economic factors were particularly favorable for rising female participation rates. Real wages were steadily increasing and economic conditions were relatively good.[53] Thus, both the continued rise in participation rates in this period and its concentration among older women can be explained in significant part by economic and demographic factors.

THE 1960s TO THE 1980s: INCREASED PARTICIPATION OF MARRIED MOTHERS

Female labor force participation rates rose sharply from the 1960s to the 1980s, and, as we saw in Figures 4-8a and 4-8b, the increases in participation were especially large for married mothers, including those with small children. In this section, we again use the tools of economic analysis to understand the factors responsible for this increase.

We begin by considering demographic factors that are expected to affect the value of home time (w^*). The post–World War II baby boom was followed by a baby bust, when birthrates fell. By the late 1970s, total fertility rates had fallen below the replacement level and relatively low rates continued after that time. This decrease in fertility would be expected to lower w^* and thus increase the labor force participation of women. In addition, increasing numbers of women began to postpone marriage and childbirth into their late twenties, thirties, or even early forties. This pattern of childbearing appears to be associated with stronger attachment to the labor market and a reduction in time spent out of the labor force for childrearing. A further demographic trend that encouraged rising participation rates was the sharp increase in the divorce rate; divorced women are more likely to be in the labor force than married women. This trend likely also contributed to the increase in married women's participation as they sought to protect their family income in the face of a rising probability of a marital breakup. Although the divorce rate began to level off and even to fall slightly in the 1980s, it remains at a high level.

These demographic shifts, particularly the decline in fertility, would most affect the labor force participation of younger women, and it was exactly this group, women under

---

[52]Goldin, *Understanding the Gender Gap.*
[53]Goldin, *Understanding the Gender Gap,* finds that demand factors, in conjunction with the particularly large wage elasticity of supply that prevailed at that time for married women, largely account for the increase in participation that occurred during this period.

age 45, who posted the largest gains in participation rates over this period.[54] Nonetheless, even though these demographic factors undoubtedly are important,[55] a major factor contributing to rising female labor force participation rates during this period was the increase in participation rates among married mothers, including those with small children present.

Economic conditions are another possible factor contributing to the rising labor force attachment of married mothers during this period, but here the picture is mixed. During much of the 1960s, real wages were rising and unemployment was relatively low, favorable conditions for increases in female labor force participation rates. However, during the 1970s and the early 1980s, the situation was more complex. A stagnating economy resulted in frequent bouts of high unemployment and little increase in real wages.[56] Moreover, while the economy expanded during the mid to late 1980s, overall real wages did not increase. This factor raises the question of why married women's participation rates continued to rise despite these unfavorable economic conditions.

One obvious explanation is that, although real wages were not rising overall, they were increasing for women, particularly well-educated women. This increase may help to explain not only rising participation rates for women as a group, but also why participation rates increased more slowly for less-educated women whose real wages lagged. It further points to rising educational attainment of women as an additional factor increasing the wages they could earn in the labor market and hence their labor force participation. It is also possible that stagnating male incomes increased the impetus of married women to enter the labor force. However, recent research suggests that, just as rising real incomes of husbands did not forestall the rise in participation of their wives during earlier, more prosperous, times, the poor income performance of husbands does not explain much of the increase in wives' participation during the 1970s and 1980s. In both cases, the dominant factor was women's own labor market prospects.[57]

Rising real wages for a large proportion of women in conjunction with the demographic factors discussed previously and the continued increase in women's educational attainment all contributed to the rise in participation rates over this period. However, a number of studies suggest that the increase in married women's participation during this time cannot be fully explained by changes in such measurable factors. It also reflects, in part, changes in women's responses to these factors, perhaps due to

---

[54]One reason for the decline in marriage rates for the baby boom cohort was the so-called "marriage squeeze." During the early part of the baby boom, from 1946 to 1955, the birthrate for each successive year was higher than the previous year's. It meant that women born during this period faced a worse "marriage market," that is, a shortage of men two years older whom they would traditionally marry. Some evidence suggesting that this development contributed to the rise in female participation is presented in Shoshana Grossbard-Schechtman and Clive W. Granger, "Women's Jobs and Marriage, Baby-Boom versus Baby-Bust," *Population* 53 (September 1998): 731–52 (in French).

[55]Jacobsen, Pearce, and Rosenbaum, "The Effects of Childbearing," estimate that declining fertility explains between 6 and 13 percent of the increase in married women's labor supply between 1970 and 1980.

[56]The unstable economic conditions of the 1970s and early 1980s perhaps contributed to the growth in participation by giving married women an incentive to enter the labor market as soon as possible rather than waiting to supply labor in a more uncertain future; see Francine D. Blau and Adam J. Grossberg, "Wage and Employment Uncertainty and the Labor Force Participation Decisions of Married Women," *Economic Inquiry* 29, no. 4 (October 1991): 678–95.

[57]Juhn and Murphy, "Wage Inequality and Family Labor Supply."

changing social attitudes, as women's participation has become less sensitive to the presence of small children and to their husband's income and more responsive to their own market opportunities (wages).[58]

One may speculate that changes in the work expectations of younger women help to explain some portion of the participation increase not due to changes in measurable factors. It may be recalled that prior to World War II, most women left the labor force permanently upon marriage and childbearing. It is quite likely that the older married women who entered or reentered the labor force during World War II and the early postwar period had not anticipated working during this stage of the life cycle but were drawn into the labor market by prevailing economic and social conditions.

As the reentry pattern became firmly established, younger women could increasingly anticipate spending a substantial portion of their mature years in the labor force. They likely also learned, by observing the experiences of older women, that time spent out of the labor force was costly in terms of career advancement and earnings. To maximize their labor market earnings and to secure the more attractive jobs that were increasingly becoming available to women, they would have to increase their investment in market-oriented human capital and keep work force interruptions to a minimum. The development and dissemination of more effective contraceptive techniques, most importantly the birth control pill, was undoubtedly important in enabling women to achieve these goals because they gave women greater control over the timing as well as the number of children.[59] As young women entered the labor force with greater training and higher work expectations, they were more likely to remain employed after the birth of a child or to return shortly thereafter. Further, once it was socially acceptable for mothers of older children to work outside the home, it was not long before it was socially permissible for women with increasingly younger children to do so as well.

THE 1990s AND EARLY 2000s: DIVERGING PARTICIPATION TRENDS FOR MARRIED AND SINGLE MOTHERS

Another important trend discussed earlier and illustrated in Figures 4-8a and 4-8b is that labor force participation rates of single and married mothers of small children diverged considerably during the 1990s and early 2000s. Participation rates of single mothers expanded rapidly during the 1990s, especially during the latter part of the decade. At the same time, growth in the participation rate of married mothers slowed, and participation rates of this group began to level off in the mid-1990s and declined somewhat in the late 1990s and early 2000s. How do we explain these trends?

Starting with the trends for single mothers of small children, analyses suggest that the increasing participation of this group reflects the impact of some important changes

---

[58]See Goldin, *Understanding the Gender Gap;* David Shapiro and Lois Shaw, "Growth in the Labor Force Attachment of Married Women: Accounting for Changes in the 1970s," *Southern Economic Journal* 50, no. 2 (October 1983): 461–73; Juhn and Murphy, "Wage Inequality and Family Labor Supply"; and Leibowitz and Klerman, "Explaining Changes."

[59]See Claudia Goldin and Lawrence F. Katz, "The Power of the Pill: Oral Contraceptives and Women's Career and Marriage Decisions," *Journal of Political Economy* 110, no. 4 (August 2002): 730–70; and Claudia Goldin, "From the Valley to the Summit: The Quiet Revolution That Transformed Women's Work," National Bureau of Economic Research Working Paper No.10335 (March 2004).

in government policy combined with a buoyant economy.[60] By the time of its peak in March 2001, the record U.S. economic expansion that began in the 1990s had lasted 10 years. Single female family heads are disproportionately low skilled, and an expanding economy disproportionately benefits less-skilled individuals. However, it is unlikely that economic expansion alone can fully account for the participation gains of single mothers over this decade. Shifts in government policies that occurred at the same time reinforced the positive effects of the booming economy on the employment of this group.

As explained in greater detail in Chapter 10, changes in welfare policies, including a new work requirement for welfare recipients, led to an increase in single mothers' labor force participation, and also contributed to a substantial decline in the welfare rolls. In addition, the Earned Income Tax Credit (EITC) was expanded several times in the 1990s. These expansions raised the subsidy received by low income families with a working adult, and thus increased the incentive of single mothers to work outside the home.

The reasons for the slowing growth in the participation rates of married mothers with small children during the 1990s and early 2000s have not yet been analyzed. It would be tempting to attribute this development, at least in part, to favorable economic conditions as well. That is, given better employment prospects for their husbands, some women who might otherwise have entered the labor force may have chosen not to do so. However, during the 1970s and 1980s, the dominant economic factor explaining the increase in married women's labor force participation was their *own* labor market opportunities. Moreover, as already noted, empirical studies suggest that married women's participation behavior shows less sensitivity to their husbands' incomes over time. This decreased responsiveness makes it unlikely that husbands' employment prospects would provide the entire explanation for the slowing growth in married mothers' participation, but we must await empirical studies of this period to resolve this issue. In any case, it is perhaps not surprising that growth in the participation rates of married mothers would eventually taper off as those women who could most readily participate in the labor force, and had the greatest incentives to do so, were already in the labor force.

ANALYZING TRENDS IN MEN'S PARTICIPATION

The changes in men's labor force participation patterns, while less dramatic than women's, are nonetheless quite significant. The decline in the participation rates of younger men (Figure 4-4) is mainly due to their tendency to remain in school longer. This trend in turn reflects the ever-increasing skills demanded by our advanced economy. Expenditures on education are more profitable to the individual when they are made relatively early in the life cycle, resulting in a longer period over which to reap the returns of this investment in the form of higher earnings. Moreover, with rising real incomes, families were better able to keep their children in school longer because they could afford to pay the bills and also to forgo the contribution their children might otherwise make to family income.

---

[60]This section draws heavily on Blank, "Fighting Poverty"; and Rebecca Blank, "Evaluating Welfare Reform in the United States," *Journal of Economic Literature* 60, no. 4 (December 2002): 1105–66. See also Meyer and Rosenbaum, "Making Single Mothers Work"; and Nada Eissa and Jeffrey B. Liebman, "Labor Supply Response to the Earned Income Tax Credit," *Quarterly Journal of Economics* 111, no. 2 (May 1996): 605–37.

The declining participation rates of older males are often viewed as evidence of the dominance of the income effect over the substitution effect. As real wages rose over the course of the last century, men's demand for nonmarket time increased. This is suggested by the decline (and subsequent stability) of the average full-time work-week discussed earlier. The increased propensity of men to retire at earlier ages is also seen as part of this pattern. In addition, the provision of Social Security and the growing coverage of private pension schemes, while in part a transfer of income from earlier to later years, also created an income effect that encouraged older males to retire.[61]

We may note that the same factors that influenced the labor force participation of younger and older men also affected the participation of women in these age groups. As shown in Figure 4-3, the long-term increase in the participation rates for women over 65 remains quite modest. In addition, the participation of younger women recently declined somewhat as greater numbers of them remain in school for longer periods.

Figure 4-4 also shows a decline in the participation rate of prime-age males (25 to 54), which is smaller than that for younger and older men, but is nonetheless notable. This development appears closely connected to the declining relative demand for less-skilled workers, which depressed their relative wages.[62] This trend is suggested by Figure 4-10b, which shows that participation rates dropped most markedly for less-educated males. The decrease in participation of prime-age males also reflects expansions of government programs that provide disability income to men below conventional retirement age.[63] In the absence of such programs, more men with disabilities would probably be forced to seek work. Less-skilled men are disproportionately affected by the provision of disability income because the opportunity cost of leaving the labor force is less for low-wage workers.

The decline in the labor force participation of men in the prime working years may also, to some extent, reflect the impact of the increased employment of women outside the home. As the two-earner family becomes the norm, the additional income may induce some (still relatively few) males to leave the labor force for periods of time, say, to retool for a midlife career change.

BLACK AND WHITE PARTICIPATION DIFFERENTIALS: A CLOSER LOOK

As we saw in Table 4-2, since the 1950s, black male participation rates declined faster than those of white males, while black female participation rates increased at a slower pace than those of white females (though the period from 1995 to 2000 is a recent

[61]See Patricia M. Anderson, Alan L. Gustman, and Thomas L. Steinmeier, "Trends in Male Labor Force Participation and Retirement: Some Evidence on the Role of Pensions and Social Security in the 1970s and 1980s," *Journal of Labor Economics* 17, no. 4, pt. 1 (October 1999): 757–83.

[62]See Juhn, "Decline of Male Labor Market Participation." A smaller role for wage changes in explaining the trends is found by Paul Devereux, "Changes in Male Labor Supply and Wages," *Industrial and Labor Relations Review* 56, no. 3 (April 2003): 409–28.

[63]Donald Parsons, "The Decline in Male Labor Force Participation," *Journal of Political Economy* 88, no. 1 (February 1980): 117–34; and David H. Autor and Mark G. Duggan, "The Rise in the Disability Rolls and the Decline in Unemployment," *Quarterly Journal of Economics* 118, no.1 (February 2003): 157–205. These programs expanded first in the 1960s and 1970s and then again since the mid-1980s.

exception). The result is that now black male participation rates are considerably below those of white males, while black female participation rates, which used to greatly exceed those of white women, are now only a few percentage points higher.

One explanation for the differential trend in black and white participation rates is that since blacks obtain less education, on average, and are more likely to drop out of high school than whites, they are disproportionately affected by the overall trends toward lower participation among less-educated individuals. However, even when comparing participation rates of less-skilled white and black men, these trends are less favorable for blacks. This observation suggests that while declining labor market opportunities for the less educated in general may explain a portion of the race trends in participation among men, other factors also play a role.[64] One such factor may be the expansion of government disability programs. Because black men are less-educated and less-skilled, on average, they would be particularly affected by the expansion of these programs—and, to the extent that, due to discrimination, their wages are lower than those of white men with similar education, the attractiveness of these programs to them is further increased. In addition, the black unemployment rate is considerably higher than the white rate: Even in the midst of a boom year like 1999, for example, when the white unemployment rate stood at 3.7 percent, the black rate was 8.0 percent, and as we saw earlier, the net effect of high unemployment rates is to discourage labor force participation.

Two other factors are also identified in recent research as contributing to the decrease in employment of less-educated, young black men (ages 16 to 34) relative to their white counterparts.[65] One is the dramatic increase in incarceration rates, which have been rising more rapidly for blacks than whites. Individuals who are incarcerated are not included in statistics on labor force participation and employment, implying that such statistics may actually understate the employment problems of blacks in this respect. However, ex-offenders are included in the statistics and are likely to have poorer employment prospects than nonoffenders due both to the negative effect of incarceration itself (e.g., loss of work experience) as well as employer reluctance to hire ex-offenders. Another factor that may contribute to relatively lower employment rates of less-educated young African-American men is the stronger enforcement of child support laws in recent years. Although this policy may be desirable on other grounds, mandated child support payments are equivalent to a "tax" on the income of noncustodial fathers. This "tax" is expected to reduce work incentives, especially for those with low incomes. Here again, young black males are likely to be disproportionately affected, because they are a low income group and female headship is much more pronounced in the black than in the white community.

As may be seen in Table 4-2, the relative participation picture for black women is considerably more favorable than that for black men because they have higher participation rates than white women. As noted earlier, even though white and black women

---

[64]Juhn, "Decline of Male Labor Market Participation"; and Chinhui Juhn, "Black-White Employment Differential in a Tight Labor Market," in *Prosperity for All? The Economic Boom and African Americans,* edited by Robert Cherry and William M. Rodgers III (New York: Russell Sage Foundation, 2000), pp. 88–109.
[65]This discussion is based on Harry J. Holzer, Paul Offner, and Elaine Sorensen, "Declining Employment among Young Black Less-Educated Men: The Role of Incarceration and Child Support," Institute for Research on Poverty, Discussion Paper No. 1281-04 (May 2004). See also, Amitabh Chandra, "Labor-Market Dropouts and the Racial Wage Gap: 1940–1990," *American Economic Review* 90, no. 2 (May 2000): 333–38.

had about the same participation rates in 1995, black women's labor force participation rates increased substantially more since that time, largely due to an increase in participation among less-educated black women.[66] This increase was likely tied to the growth in participation rates of single mothers during this period that we discussed previously, because within each education category, black women are more likely to be single-family heads than are white women.[67] In addition, given their extremely high unemployment rates, blacks as a group are likely to have benefited disproportionately from the decline in unemployment that occurred over the late 1990s. Notably, however, as the economy cooled and recession set in, the increase in black female labor force participation halted and a small reduction actually occurred in black women's participation rate between 2000 and 2003. Most likely, this recent development reflects the fact that unemployment rates remained relatively high even after the official recession ended in November 2001.[68]

Conclusion

We began by reviewing the trends in male and female participation rates. We found that while female labor force participation rates increased over the course of the last century—from 20 percent in 1900 to 28 percent in 1940 and 60 percent in 2003—male participation rates declined from 87 percent in 1950 to 74 percent in 2003. We then turned to the economic theory of labor supply to gain insight into the determinants of labor force participation in order to better understand these trends, as well as differences in participation across various groups.

After decades of substantial increase, growth in female labor force participation slowed in the early 1990s and overall female participation rates remained roughly constant since then, with some decreases in participation rates among married mothers with small children. What does this development portend for the future? Taking into account the recent slowing of the increase in female labor force participation, as well as shifts in the age composition of the population and other factors, the Bureau of Labor Statistics (BLS) projects that 62 percent of adult women will be in the labor force by the year 2012, an increase of 2 percentage points over the 2003 level of 60 percent.[69]

This projection of continued increase in the female labor force participation rate, albeit at a fairly modest rate, seems reasonable to us. Now that 76 percent of women in the prime working ages (25–54) are labor force participants, it is perhaps to be expected that the female labor force will grow more slowly. We expect a modest rise in participation nonetheless, as women continue to accumulate more market-oriented education and increasingly enter nontraditional fields with higher earnings. In addition, today's young women who have far higher labor force participation during their childrearing years than earlier cohorts are more likely to remain employed continuously up to retirement age. Of course, some women have always chosen to forsake market work for

---

[66]See Francine D. Blau, Marianne A. Ferber, and Anne E. Winkler, *The Economics of Women, Men, and Work,* 4th ed. (Upper Saddle River, NJ: Prentice Hall, 2002), Table 4-5, p. 127.

[67]Blau, "Trends in the Well-Being of American Women."

[68]The dating of the peak and trough of the recessions is that determined by the Business Cycle Dating Committee of the National Bureau of Economic Research; see www.nber.org/cycles/main.html, accessed on September 15, 2004.

[69]Mitra Toossi, "Labor Force Projections to 2012: The Graying of the U.S. Labor Force," *Monthly Labor Review* 127, no. 2 (February 2004): 37–57.

traditional homemaking roles, at least for a period of time, and we expect that practice to continue. Most recently, as noted previously, there has even been a small decline in the participation rates of married mothers of small children. But we consider it extremely unlikely that women's overall participation rate will decline appreciably in the foreseeable future.

As for the labor force participation of men, the BLS projects an additional decrease of 1 percentage point in the male participation rate, from 74 percent in 2003 to 73 percent in 2012, and this prediction too seems reasonable. Should a dramatic shift toward acceptance of men and women as equally responsible for earning income and homemaking occur, the decline may be larger, but we do not anticipate such a change in the foreseeable future.

Combining the two projections, we expect a further reduction in the differential in labor force participation between men and women, though we do not expect it to disappear entirely for a long time to come. Under the BLS projections, the gap between the male and female participation rates would decline from 14 percentage points in 2003 to 11 percentage points in 2012. The full magnitude of the change becomes clear when we remember that this differential was 66 percentage points at the turn of the century.

APPENDIX 4A

The Income and Substitution Effects: A Closer Look

As discussed in Chapter 4, for labor force participants, an increase in the wage rate causes an uncertain effect on hours supplied, all else equal. This is illustrated in greater detail in Figure 4-12 . The *overall* effect of the wage change is shown (in panels a and b) by the move from point *A* to point *C.* It may be broken down into two distinct components, attributable to the income and substitution effects.

The income effect is represented by a hypothetical increase in income just large enough to get the individual to the higher indifference curve, U_2, leaving the wage rate unchanged. This move takes the individual from point *A* to point *B.* For the reasons discussed earlier, the effect of the increase in income, all else equal, is unambiguously to reduce labor hours supplied to the market. The substitution effect is given by the impact of a hypothetical change in the wage (the slope of the budget constraint) along a given indifference curve, U_2, resulting in a move from *B* to *C.* The substitution effect of an increase in the opportunity cost (or price) of nonmarket time, all else being equal, is unambiguously to increase labor hours supplied.

As may be seen in panel a, if the substitution effect is large relative to the income effect, *the substitution effect dominates the income effect* and the wage increase results in an *increase* in hours worked. Alternatively, as seen in panel b, if the income effect is large relative to the substitution effect, *the income effect dominates the substitution effect* and the wage increase results in a *decrease* in hours worked.

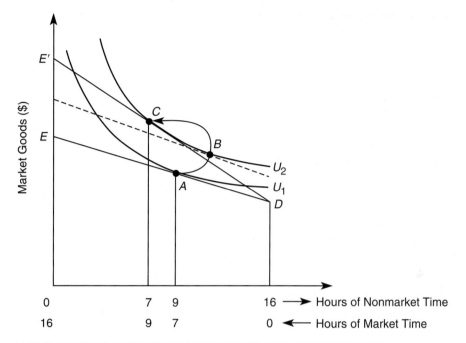

(a) THE SUBSTITUTION EFFECT DOMINATES THE INCOME EFFECT

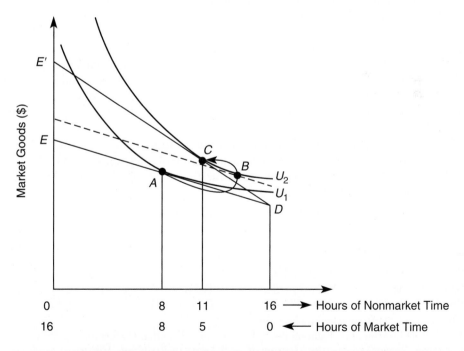

(b) THE INCOME EFFECT DOMINATES THE SUBSTITUTION EFFECT

FIGURE 4-12   The Impact of the Market Wage on Labor Hours: A Closer Look

Questions for Review and Discussion

> * Indicates that the question can be answered using an indifference curve frame-work as well as verbally. Consult with your instructor about the appropriate approach for your class.

1. Suppose that you have the following information for Country X:

Population:	100,000
Employed:	60,000
Unemployed:	3,000
Not in labor force:	37,000

   a. Calculate the size of the labor force, the labor force participation rate, and the unemployment rate.
   b. Provide examples of individuals who would be classified as "not in the labor force."
   c. What economic factors might shift a woman from "not in the labor force" to in the labor force? Discuss.
   d. Suppose an economic downturn occurred. How would you expect this change to affect the number employed, the number of unemployed, and the number classified as "not in the labor force"? Explain.

2. Explain the reasons why men's labor force participation decreased. Why do these same factors not cause women's labor force participation to decline as well?

3. Use economic reasoning (economic theory) to explain why the labor force participation rate for married women and never-married women might differ.*

4. Suppose the government were to provide a $2-per-hour subsidy for families with an employed mother who purchases child care.
   a. Consider a mother with a preschool-age child who is currently not employed. How would this subsidy affect her decision to work, all else equal?*
   b. Consider a mother with a preschool-age child who is currently employed. How would this subsidy affect the number of hours that she chooses to work (assuming she can vary them), all else equal?*

5. Now suppose that the government provides a subsidy of $300 per month for all families with children. Answer part a and part b of question 4 again under this scenario. How would your answers to question 4 change? Explain fully.*

6. Do you expect that sometime in the future labor force participation rates for men and women will be equal? Discuss.

Suggested Readings

Becker, Gary S. "A Theory of the Allocation of Time." *Economic Journal* 75, no. 299 (September 1965): 493–517.

Blank, Rebecca M. "Distinguished Lecture on Economics in Government—Fighting Poverty: Lessons from Recent U.S. History." *Journal of Economic Perspectives* 14, no. 2 (Spring 2000): 3–19.

Costa, Dora. "From Mill Town to Board Room: The Rise of Women's Paid Labor." *Journal of Economic Perspectives* 14, no. 4 (Fall 2000): 101–22.

Goldin, Claudia. *Understanding the Gender Gap: An Economic History of American Women.* New York: Oxford University Press, 1990.

Heckman, James J. "What Has Been Learned About Labor Supply in the Past Twenty Years." *American Economic Review* 83, no. 2 (May 1993): 116–21.

Jacobs, Jerry A., and Kathleen Gerson. *The Time Divide: Work, Family, and Gender Inequality.* Cambridge, MA: Harvard University Press, 2004.

Juhn, Chinhui. "Decline of Male Labor Market Participation: The Role of Declining Market Opportunities." *Quarterly Journal of Economics* 107, no. 1 (February 1992): 79–121.

Juhn, Chinhui, and Kevin M. Murphy. "Wage Inequality and Family Labor Supply." *Journal of Labor Economics* 15, no. 1, pt. 1 (January 1997): 72–97.

Killingsworth, Mark R. *Labor Supply.* Cambridge: Cambridge University Press, 1983.

Leibowitz, Arleen, and Jacob Klerman. "Explaining Changes in Married Mothers' Employment Over Time." *Demography* 32, no. 3 (August 1995): 365–78.

Mincer, Jacob. "Labor Force Participation of Married Women." In *Aspects of Labor Economics,* edited by H. Greg Lewis. Universities National Bureau of Economic Research Conference Studies, no. 14. Princeton, NJ: Princeton University Press, 1962, pp. 63–97.

Smith, James P., ed. *Female Labor Supply: Theory and Estimation.* Princeton, NJ: Princeton University Press, 1980.

5

DIFFERENCES IN OCCUPATIONS AND EARNINGS: OVERVIEW

Chapter Highlights

- Occupational Differences
- Trends in Occupational Segregation
- Female-Male Earnings Ratio

Chapter 4 reviewed the large increase in women's labor force participation that occurred since World War II. This increase, in conjunction with a decline in male labor force participation rates, resulted in a steady narrowing of gender differentials in involvement in paid work. Further, as women became more committed to market work, their labor force attachment increased and they were employed more continuously over the life cycle. We now shift to the question of how women fare in the labor market. In this chapter, we review the extent of gender differences in the two main indicators of labor market status—occupational attainment and earnings. As we shall see, despite important recent gains, substantial differences between men and women remain.

In Chapters 6 and 7, we consider alternative theoretical explanations for the observed differences in labor market outcomes between men and women. In Chapter 6, we focus on supply-side explanations, particularly the human capital model, which emphasizes the role of women's preferences and the choices that they may make to invest less in job-related education and training, as well as to spend a smaller share of their adult years in the labor force. These explanations can also include premarket discrimination, or societal discrimination, in which various types of social pressures influence women's choices adversely.

In Chapter 7, we consider demand-side explanations of the gender differences in outcomes. We focus on the results of gender discrimination in the labor market, which occurs when men and women with equal qualifications are treated differently. We also point out that labor market discrimination can indirectly lower women's earnings and occupational attainment by reducing their incentives and opportunities to acquire education and training.

In Chapter 8, we use what we learned in Chapters 6 and 7, as well as some additional insights, to explain the reasons for the narrowing of the gender earnings gap in recent years. This trend is considered in the context of other recent changes that profoundly affected the labor market.

OCCUPATIONAL DIFFERENCES

We can get a general idea of the differences in occupations between men and women by comparing the distribution of male and female workers across the 10 broad categories shown in Table 5-1 for 2003. (These major occupational classifications include more than 400 detailed occupations.[1]) Traditionally, women tended to be concentrated in **office and administrative support** and **service** occupations. In 2003, 42.6 percent of all women workers were in these two categories, compared to only 19.3 percent of men. Office and administrative support occupations include clerical jobs like secretary and administrative assistant, file clerk, data-entry keyer, and bookkeeper, as well as other support jobs such as computer operator, customer service representative, postal service clerk, and reservation and transportation ticket agent. Examples of service occupations include child care workers, firefighters and police, waiters and waitresses, hairdressers and cosmetologists, cooks, and maids and housekeeping cleaners.

Women were also considerably more likely than men to be in **professional** jobs — 24.5 percent of women were in such jobs compared to 16.6 percent of men. Examples

TABLE 5-1   Distribution of Men and Women by Major Occupation, 2003

Occupation	Men (%)	Women (%)
Management, business, and financial operations occupations	15.7	13.0
Professional and related occupations	16.6	24.5
Service occupations	12.9	19.6
Sales and related occupations	11.1	12.1
Office and administrative support occupations	6.4	23.0
Farming, fishing, and forestry occupations	1.1	0.4
Construction and extraction occupations	10.8	0.3
Installation, maintenance, and repair occupations	6.6	0.3
Production occupations	9.1	4.7
Transportation and material moving occupations	9.6	2.0
Total employed	100.0	100.0

Note: Data refer to civilian workers 16 years of age and older.

Source: U.S. Department of Labor, Bureau of Labor Statistics, *Employment and Earnings* (January 2004), Table 10.

---

[1] A listing of most of the detailed categories included in each major occupation is provided in U.S. Department of Labor, *Employment and Earnings* (January 2004), Table 11.

of jobs in this category are architects, engineers, lawyers, physicians, teachers, registered nurses, pharmacists, librarians, and social workers.

Men, on the other hand, were considerably more likely than women to be in "blue-collar" occupations, which span skilled production, craft and repair work as well as semiskilled and unskilled manual jobs. In 2003, 36.1 percent of male workers were employed in such jobs, as compared to 7.3 percent of women. These include **construction and extraction occupations** such as electricians, carpenters, plumbers, and mining machine operators; **installation, maintenance, and repair occupations** such as automotive service technicians and mechanics, computer, automated teller and office machine repairers, and telecommunications line installers and repairers; **production occupations** such as bakers, butchers, machinists, tool and die makers, and sewing machine operators; and **transportation and material moving occupations** such as truck, taxi, and bus drivers, aircraft pilots, parking lot and service station attendants, and refuse and recyclable material collectors.

In contrast, women and men were about equally likely to work in **sales occupations**, with 11 percent of employed women in sales occupations, as compared with 12 percent of employed men. Examples of occupations in this varied category include cashiers; retail salespersons; securities, commodities, and financial services sales agents; travel agents; wholesale and manufacturing sales representatives; and telemarketers. There is more of a gender difference for **management, business, and financial occupations**, though differences are not nearly as extreme as for clerical and administrative occupations or blue-collar occupations. As shown in Table 5-1, 13 percent of all employed women were in such positions as compared with 15.7 percent of employed men. Examples of such jobs include chief executives, financial managers, human resources managers, education administrators, medical and health services managers, accountants and auditors, insurance underwriters, and wholesale and retail buyers.

Some notable changes have occurred over time in the extent of gender differences in occupations. These changes can be seen by comparing the percentage of women in a given occupation at an earlier point in time with the percentage in 2003. For instance, women are substantially less concentrated in office, administrative support, and service occupations than they were in 1972, when 53 percent of women held such jobs compared to 43 percent in 2003. On the other hand, women are much more likely to be in management, business, and financial operations occupations than they were in the past; the female share of workers in these jobs rose from 20 to 42 percent between 1972 and 2003.[2]

The industries in which men and women work also differ considerably. As may be seen in Table 5-2, in 2003, men were more heavily concentrated in mining, construction,

---

[2]Substantial changes occurred in the Census occupational classifications in 2000, which were adopted by the Current Population Survey (the data source for the figures reported in the text) in 2003. Therefore, the figures cited in the text for 1972 and 2003 are not strictly comparable. However, data for 2002 are available in both the new (2000) occupational categories and in categories more comparable to those used in 1972. For the tabulations cited in the text, the figures are quite similar for both sets of occupational classifications. Specifically, in 2002, the percentage of women who were in office, administrative support, and service occupations was 41 percent using the old categories and 43 percent using the new (2000) categories; similarly, the female share of management, business, and financial operations occupations was 46 percent using the old categories and 41 percent using the new categories. (See U.S. Department of Labor, *Employment and Earnings,* January 2003 and 2004.) These data do suggest, however, that female gains in managerial positions are somewhat understated by the change in occupational classifications.

Industry	Men (%)	Women (%)
TABLE 5-2 Distribution of Men and Women by Major Industry, 2003		
Agriculture, forestry, fishing, and hunting	2.3	0.9
Mining	0.6	0.1
Construction	12.5	1.5
Manufacturing	16.0	8.0
Wholesale and retail trade	15.6	14.4
Transportation and utilities	7.2	2.6
Information	2.8	2.5
Financial activities	5.9	8.4
Professional and business services	10.8	9.3
Education and health services	9.5	33.0
Leisure and hospitality	7.7	9.3
Other services	4.5	5.4
Public administration	4.6	4.5
Total employed	100.0	100.0

Note: Data refer to civilian workers 16 years of age and over.

Source: U.S. Department of Labor, Bureau of Labor Statistics, *Employment and Earnings* (January 2004), Table 17.

manufacturing, and transportation and utilities—36.3 percent of men worked in those industries, as compared to 12.3 percent of women. In contrast, women were considerably more likely to be employed in education and health services and in financial activities—41.4 percent of women were in these industries, compared to 15.4 percent of men. To some extent, these differences in distribution by industry reflect gender differences in occupations. For example, men are more likely to hold blue-collar jobs than women, and a high proportion of such jobs are in construction and manufacturing. However, substantial differences exist in the employment of men and women by firm or industry *within* occupational categories,[3] further contributing to the observed industry differences by gender.

In order to examine occupational differences by race and ethnicity as well as by gender, Table 5-3 provides data separately for black, white, Asian, and Hispanic workers. Black and Hispanic men and women were less likely than whites of the same sex to be employed in higher-paying managerial and professional positions. At the other end of the pay scale, they were overrepresented in service occupations, as well as in production and transportation and material moving occupations. The occupational distribution of Asian men and women compares much more favorably to that of whites than

[3]See, for example, Francine D. Blau, *Equal Pay in the Office* (Lexington, MA: Lexington Books, 1977); Erica L. Groshen, "The Structure of the Female/Male Wage Differential: Is It Who You Are, What You Do, or Where You Work?" *Journal of Human Resources* 26, no. 3 (Summer 1991): 457–72; and Kimberly Bayard, Judith Hellerstein, David Neumark, and Kenneth Troske, "New Evidence on Sex Segregation and Sex Difference in Wages from Matched Employee-Employer Data," *Journal of Labor Economics* 21, no. 4 (October 2003): 887–922. For historical evidence, see Claudia Goldin, *Understanding the Gender Gap: An Economic History of American Women* (New York: Oxford University Press, 1990).

TABLE 5-3   Distribution of Workers by Occupation, Race, Hispanic Origin, and Gender, 2003

Occupation	*Whites* Men (%)	Women (%)	*Blacks* Men (%)	Women (%)	*Asians* Men (%)	Women (%)	*Hispanics* Men (%)	Women (%)
Management, business, and financial operations	16.6	13.5	8.5	10.0	15.6	13.7	6.6	7.1
Professional and related	16.4	24.9	13.2	20.9	31.7	29.2	7.5	14.0
Service occupations	12.0	18.6	19.6	26.2	13.4	19.1	20.1	30.0
Sales and related	11.5	12.4	8.4	10.7	11.3	11.4	7.7	12.2
Office and administrative support	5.9	23.5	10.0	22.5	7.4	15.6	6.4	21.7
Farming, fishing, and forestry	1.2	0.4	0.6	0.1	0.3	0.4	3.1	1.4
Constuction and extraction	11.4	0.4	8.2	0.2	2.6	0.1	18.1	0.5
Installation, maintenance, and repair	6.9	0.3	5.3	0.4	3.9	0.2	6.1	0.5
Production occupations	9.0	4.2	10.4	6.2	8.7	9.1	12.5	9.1
Transportation and material moving	9.1	1.9	15.9	2.7	5.2	1.3	11.9	3.4
Total employed	100.0	100.0	100.0	100.0	100.0	100.0	100.0	100.0

Notes: Data refer to civilian workers 16 years of age and older. Racial affiliation indicates persons who selected the respective racial group only; persons who selected more than one racial group are not included. Hispanics may be of any race.

Source: U.S. Department of Labor, Bureau of Labor Statistics, *Employment and Earnings* (January 2004), Table 10.

is the case for the other minority groups. Asians were about as likely as whites of the same sex to be employed in management, business, and financial operations occupations and more likely than whites to be employed as professionals. They were only slightly more likely than whites to be in service jobs, and less likely to be in blue-collar occupations.

Within each race or ethnic group, however, the broad outlines of occupational differences by gender show considerable similarities. Women were heavily overrepresented in office and administrative support, as well as service occupations, and, except among Asians, more likely than men to be in professional jobs. Black and Hispanic women were also more likely than their male counterparts to be in sales jobs. At the same time, women tended to be underrepresented in blue-collar occupations compared to men—though Asian women were slightly more likely to be in production occupations than Asian men. However, in contrast to the situation among whites and Asians, black and Hispanic women were more likely than black and Hispanic men to be managerial workers.[4]

---

[4]Based on analyses of detailed occupational categories, the occupational differences by race (i.e., between blacks and whites) are considerably less pronounced than by sex, and declined more rapidly between 1960 and 1990. See Victor Fuchs, *Women's Quest for Economic Equality* (Cambridge, MA: Harvard University Press, 1988); and Joyce P. Jacobsen, "Trends in Work Force Sex Segregation, 1960–90," *Social Science Quarterly* 75, no. 1 (March 1994): 204–11.

Occupational Segregation

So far, we have discussed gender differences in occupational distributions for broadly defined occupational categories, but data on these major occupations do not reveal the full extent of occupational differences by gender. For example, while Table 5-1 indicates that about the same proportion of men and women are in sales and related occupations, women are more likely to be employed as cashiers, retail salespersons, travel agents, and telemarketers, whereas men are more likely to be securities, commodities, and financial services sales agents and wholesale and manufacturing sales representatives. Information is, in fact, available on the large set of detailed occupations that underlie these broad categories. The precise number varies over time but, as already noted, is generally well in excess of 400. Women's representation in these more narrowly defined occupations does indeed tend to vary considerably. This is illustrated in Table 5-4, which shows percent female (i.e., the percentage of workers in the occupation who are women) for a selection of professional occupations, chosen because we tend to be familiar with the nature and function of the various professions and because both men and women are substantially represented in the category as a whole.

As evident from the table, many of the jobs in the professional category are either predominantly female or predominantly male. In 2003, women comprised more than 80 percent of workers in five of the professions shown in the table—dietitians and nutritionists, librarians, preschool and kindergarten teachers, elementary and middle school teachers, and registered nurses. Men comprised more than 80 percent of the workers in the engineering occupations listed and among clergy, as well as more than three-quarters of architects and dentists. Although considerable occupational differences by gender remain within the professional category, it is important to note that women have made considerable inroads into traditionally male professions since 1970. By 2003, women constituted more than 20 percent of workers in such formerly highly male occupations as architects, chemists, computer scientists and systems analysts, dentists, lawyers, pharmacists, and physicians and surgeons.

One way to assess the magnitude of differences in the distribution of women and men across occupational categories is the **index of segregation**.[5] It gives the percentage of female (or male) workers who would have to change jobs in order for the occupational distribution of the two groups to be the same. The index would equal zero if the distribution of men and women across occupational categories were identical; it would equal 100 if all occupations were either completely male or female.

A number of studies have calculated the index of occupational segregation for various years using a detailed breakdown of all occupations. For much of the twentieth century, these studies showed levels of occupational segregation well in excess of 60 percent. Significant declines in the index began in the 1970s, and we shall consider this important trend in greater detail later. Nonetheless, the extent of occupational

---

[5]Otis Dudley Duncan and Beverly Duncan, "A Methodological Analysis of Segregation Indexes," *American Sociological Review* 20, no. 2 (1955): 210–17. The index of occupational segregation by sex is defined as:

$$\text{Segregation index} = 1/2 \, \Sigma_i \, |M_i - F_i|$$

where M_i = the percentage of males in the labor force employed in occupation i, and F_i = the percentage of females in the labor force employed in occupation i.

TABLE 5-4   Percent Female in Selected Professional and Related Occupations, 1970 and 2003

Occupations	1970	2003
Architects, except naval	4.0	22.1
Biological scientists	37.8	46.1
Chemists and materials scientist	11.7	36.4
Clergy	2.9	13.9
Computer scientists and systems analysts[a]	13.6	30.4
Dentists	3.5	23.7
Dietitians and nutritionists	92.0	91.1
Engineering occupations[b]		
Aerospace engineers[a]	1.8	11.0
Chemical engineers	1.3	14.9
Civil engineers	1.3	8.7
Electrical and electronics engineers	1.7	7.1
Industrial engineers, including health and safety	2.6	19.2
Mechanical engineers	1.0	5.5
Lawyers	4.9	27.6
Librarians	82.1	84.4
News analysts, reporters and correspondents, editors[c]	41.6	50.7
Pharmacists	12.1	51.5
Physicians and surgeons	9.7	29.9
Psychologists	38.8	65.8
Public relations specialists	26.6	66.5
Registered nurses	97.3	92.1
Social workers	63.3	79.5
Teaching occupations[b]		
Preschool and kindergarten teachers	97.9	97.8
Elementary and middle school teachers	83.9	81.7
Secondary school teachers	49.6	55.2
Postsecondary teachers	29.1	44.9

Notes: Substantial changes occurred in the Census occupational categories in 2000. Thus, the 2003 and 1970 occupational categories are not strictly comparable. 1970 data are from the 1970 Census and are for the experienced civilian labor force aged 16 and over. 2003 data are annual averages from the *Current Population Surveys* and are for employed civilians aged 16 and over.
[a]Especially large changes occurred in the definition of this occupation in the 2003 data compared to 1970.
[b]Occupations listed are illustrative and do not include all those in this category.
[c]In the 1970 occupational categories "Editors and reporters" is one category, but in the 2000 occupational categories "Editors" and "Reporters" are separate categories, thus we combine the two categories here.

Sources: U.S. Census Bureau, *Detailed Occupation of the Experienced Civilian Labor Force by Sex for the United States and Regions: 1980 and 1970*, Supplementary Report PC80-S1-15 (March 1984); and U.S. Department of Labor, Bureau of Labor Statistics, *Employment and Earnings* (January 2004), Table 11.

segregation remains substantial: the comparable segregation index for 2000 was estimated to be 52 percent, indicating that more than half of women (or men) would have had to change their jobs for the occupational distribution of the two groups to be the same.[6] Moreover, measures like the segregation index likely underestimate the full extent of employment segregation by sex. Job categories used by employers are far more detailed than the census occupational categories, and researchers find that particular firms often employ mostly men or mostly women, even in occupations where both sexes are substantially represented. Restaurants, for instance, commonly employ only waiters or waitresses, but not both.[7]

Hierarchies Within Occupations

Not only do men and women tend to work in different occupations, they also tend to be employed at different levels of the hierarchy within occupations. No adequate data are available that would enable us to construct economy-wide quantitative measures, but such hierarchical differences are undoubtedly substantial. A good example is the hierarchy on university faculties because universities generally use a clear and widely understood set of titles. Despite considerable growth in the representation of women in academia over the past 25 years, in academic year 2003–2004, women constituted 58 percent of instructors and 46 percent of assistant professors (the lowest ranks), compared to 39 percent of associate and 23 percent of full professors at the upper ranks.

The academic case is not unique. Although women markedly increased their share of managerial jobs, their representation in top positions is still extremely sparse. According to a report by Catalyst on *Fortune* 500 companies, only 15.7 percent of all corporate officers and 7.9 percent of top-level executives were women in 2002; and women held just 5.2 percent of top-earner spots comprised of the five highest-paid executives in the company. These figures did, however, represent a substantial increase from 8.7 percent of officers, 2.4 percent of top-level executives, and 1.2 percent of top earners in 1995.[8] These types of disparities prompt the claim that women face a "glass ceiling," or a set of subtle barriers impeding their attempts to move up the hierarchy. We return to this issue in Chapter 7, where we more closely examine the evidence on women's representation at the upper levels of industry, government, and academia, as well as possible explanations for the observed gender differences.

Evaluating the Extent of Occupational Segregation

However segregation is measured, and whatever the numerical value of the index arrived at, how can any figure in excess of zero and short of 100 be classified as modest or excessive? The answer depends in part on one's perception of how great the differences are in men's and women's talents, tastes, and motivations and how relevant they are to occupational distribution and achievements.

On one side are those who argue that occupational segregation is natural and appropriate. In this view, efforts to change the existing situation will merely lead to economic inefficiency and personal frustration. Its proponents emphasize the similarities among individuals within each sex and the differences between the two groups. Those who emphasize the similarities between men and women and the variations among individuals within each sex

---

[6]Jerry A. Jacobs, "Detours on the Road to Equality: Women, Work and Higher Education," *Contexts* 2, no. 1 (Winter 2003): 32–41.

[7]Blau, *Equal Pay*; Groshen, "The Stucture of the Female/Male Wage Differential"; and Bayard et al., "New Evidence on Sex Segregation."

[8]Top-level or "clout" positions include CEO, chair, vice chair, president, COO, senior VP, and executive VP; see *2002 Catalyst Census of Women Corporate Officers and Top Earners in the Fortune 500* (New York).

group are on the other side. In this view, if men and women were not constrained by gender stereotyping and various barriers to individual choice but were free to follow their own inclinations, they would be far less concentrated in separate occupations. The fact that some occupations are predominantly male in some countries but female in others lends support to the view that socially imposed restrictions play a role in the sex typing of jobs.[9] In this case, removing existing barriers would presumably increase efficiency and decrease frustration because individuals could seek work more suited to their particular aptitudes.

However, even if the present level of Ç occupational segregation is deemed excessive, it would be unreasonable to conclude that the optimal situation would necessarily be a precisely proportional distribution of men and women. Apart from whatever innate differences may exist, past socialization and the prevalent allocation of household responsibilities would make such an outcome unlikely for some time to come.

In addition, the rate of change is limited by the time it takes for new people to be trained and hired. Large numbers of people cannot be expected to change jobs on short notice, as the computation of the segregation index perhaps implies. The most that could reasonably be expected is that the underrepresented group would be more highly represented among new hires, to the extent that they are qualified for the available positions, than among those presently employed in the occupation—at best, a slow process.

TRENDS IN OCCUPATIONAL SEGREGATION

The same issues confronted in measuring current occupational segregation arise in determining the extent to which it has changed over time. However, in addition to the concern over how detailed the categories are, and whether women are included in the upper ranks of occupational hierarchies, there is also the question of whether the same occupational categories are used for the various periods to be compared. The main difficulty is that the definition and number of occupational categories often undergo significant changes. Given constant flux in the economy, this shift in definitions and included occupations is inevitable. For example, if the Census Bureau rigidly adhered to the occupational categories of an earlier era, jobs such as computer scientist and computer programmer would not be included. Thus, regardless of the best efforts of those who compile the data and the researchers who use them, data are not entirely comparable over the years and are less so as the years get further apart.

In spite of these limitations, the unanimous findings of numerous studies that point to little change in the degree of segregation over a number of decades prior to 1960 are still persuasive. The index of segregation by detailed occupation was actually reported to have increased by 1.1 percentage points between 1950 and 1960, as predominantly female clerical and professional jobs grew in relative size. Between 1960 and 1970, however, an inflow of men into female professions and of women into male sales and clerical jobs produced a modest drop in the segregation index of 3.1 percentage points.[10]

---

[9]This subject will be discussed at greater length in Chapter 11.

[10]For the pre-1960 period, see Edward Gross, "Plus Ça Change? The Sexual Structure of Occupations over Time," *Social Problems* 16, no. 1 (Fall 1968): 198–208; for 1950 to 1970, see Francine D. Blau and Wallace E. Hendricks, "Occupational Segregation by Sex: Trends and Prospects," *Journal of Human Resources* 14, no. 2 (Spring 1979): 197–210. The changes in the index presented for the 1950s and 1960s are not strictly comparable to those given for later years because of changes in the number and composition of occupational categories that are included.

		Current Population
		Survey (CPS)

TABLE 5-5 Trends in Occupational Segregation by Sex, 1970–2000

Year	Census	Current Population Survey (CPS)
1970	67.7	
1980	59.3	
1990	53.0	56.4
2000		52.4

Sources: Francine D. Blau, Patricia Simpson, and Deborah Anderson, "Continuing Progress? Trends in Occupational Segregation over the 1970s and 1980s," *Feminist Economics* 4, no. 3 (Fall 1998): 29–71; and Jerry A. Jacobs, "Detours on the Road to Equality: Women, Work, and Higher Education," *Contexts* 2, no. 1 (Winter 2003): 32–41.

Table 5-5 shows the larger declines in the index in the 1970s and 1980s. Estimates based on detailed census data indicate that the index fell from 67.7 in 1970 to 59.3 in 1980 and 53.0 in 1990.[11] Even though the level of segregation that remained was considerable, the cumulative reduction of nearly 15 percentage points over the two decades is substantial, especially when considered in light of the stability of the index in earlier decades. Some indication of trends over the 1990s may be obtained using *Current Population Survey* data based on a somewhat different set of detailed occupations and workers. The index of segregation computed from this source decreased from 56.4 in 1990 to 52.4 in 2000,[12] yielding a 4 percentage point decrease over the 1990s, compared to 8 and 6 percentage point decreases in the 1970s and 1980s, respectively. Thus, in sum, the figures indicate that a substantial decline in the amount of segregation by occupation occurred since 1960, with the pace of change accelerating markedly over the 1970s and 1980s and continuing at a slower pace in the 1990s.

Changes in the extent of segregation may be due to changes in the sex composition of individual occupations, as a result of the integration of previously male or female jobs, or to shifts in the occupational mix of the economy, through greater employment growth in occupations that are already integrated relative to growth in segregated male and female jobs. Changes in the sex composition of occupations were the principal cause of the reduction in segregation over the 1970s and 1980s, though changing occupational mix also played a role. Although such shifts in sex composition could have been due either to women entering formerly male jobs or men entering previously

---

[11]These figures are for a comparable set of occupations in each of the years. See Francine D. Blau, Patricia Simpson, and Deborah Anderson, "Continuing Progress? Trends in Occupational Segregation over the 1970s and 1980s," *Feminist Economics* 4, no. 3 (Fall 1998): 29–71. See also Andrea H. Beller, "Changes in the Sex Composition of U.S. Occupations, 1960–1981," *Journal of Human Resources* 20, no. 2 (Spring 1985) 235–50; Jacobsen, "Trends in Workforce Sex Segregation"; and David A. Macpherson and Barry T. Hirsch, "Wages and Gender Composition: Why Do Women's Jobs Pay Less?" *Journal of Labor Economics* 13, no. 3 (July 1995): 426–71.

[12]Jerry A. Jacobs, "The Sex Segregation of Occupations: Prospects for the 21st Century," in *Handbook of Gender in Organizations,* edited by Gary N. Powell (Newbury Park, CA: Sage Publications, 1999), pp. 125–41; and Jerry A. Jacobs, "Detours on the Road to Equality: Women, Work and Higher Education," *Contexts* 2, no. 1 (Winter 2003): 32–41.

female jobs or a combination of both, it was in fact movements of women into pre-dominantly male jobs that played the major role. As women entered formerly male jobs, these occupations became more integrated and the degree of segregation in the labor market overall was diminished. Women were especially successful in entering formerly male white-collar jobs, particularly professional and managerial occupations. Examples of the gains for women in the professional category are shown in Table 5-4 where women significantly increased their representation in a number of formerly highly segregated male professions. The impact of these changes in the sex composition of occupations was supplemented by some important shifts in the occupational mix of the economy that also decreased segregation. Employment in integrated jobs in-creased compared to employment in predominately female and predominately male jobs. Examples of segregated jobs that declined in relative importance include a num-ber of female administrative support jobs (e.g., secretary, typist, bookkeeper, and tele-phone operator) and male farm and blue-collar occupations.[13]

Despite recent gains, numerous predominantly single-sex occupations remain. Many of the predominantly male jobs are blue-collar occupations; examples include carpenters, electricians, highway maintenance workers, and plumbers, occupations in which women comprise less than 5 percent of workers. The predominantly female categories include, in addition to the traditionally female professions, a number of jobs in the administrative support and service areas; examples include bookkeepers, child care workers, and file clerks, occupations where women comprise more than 90 percent of workers.

The areas with substantial occupational integration and those that tended to re-main segregated are linked to differential trends in the reduction of occupational seg-regation by gender across education groups. More substantial progress was made by highly educated women, who showed increasing success moving into formerly male managerial and professional occupations. Gains were smaller for less-educated women, reflecting the slower progress in integrating blue-collar occupations. So, for ex-ample, as recently as 1971, the extent of occupational segregation was fairly similar across education groups. However, between 1971 and 1997, while the segregation index declined by 20 percentage points among college graduates and 18 percentage points among those with some post-college education, it fell by 12 percentage points among high school dropouts and only 5 percentage points among high school graduates.[14] The finding that gender differences in occupations narrowed less for less-educated groups is one of a growing number of labor market disadvantages for women with less educa-tion. As discussed in Chapter 4, like less-educated men, the labor force participation rates of less-educated women fell substantially relative to the more highly educated, and, as we shall see in Chapter 8, again like less-educated men, their wages relative to the more highly educated also declined. A considerably faster increase in single head-ship among less-educated women than among their more highly educated counterparts also negatively affected their economic status; as we shall see in Chapter 9, such fami-lies face considerable economic problems.

---

[13]See Blau, Simpson, and Anderson, "Continuing Progress?"
[14]Jacobs, "The Sex Segregation of Occupations: Prospects for the 21st Century." These same patterns are identified in other industrialized countries, as discussed in Chapter 11.

In considering the overall long-term decrease in occupational segregation, it is also important to consider whether the observed trends reflect real improvements in opportunities for women. In some cases, firms responded to government pressures by placing women into nominal management positions that involve little responsibility and little contact with higher levels of management. In other instances, jobs became increasingly female when skill requirements declined because of technological changes. In such cases, integration may turn out to be a short-run phenomenon, as resegregation occurs and women increasingly come to dominate such jobs. One example of this phenomenon is the case of insurance adjusters and examiners. One study found that although women dramatically increased their share of this occupation since 1970, they were employed primarily as "inside adjusters" whose decision making was, to a considerable extent, computerized and involved little discretion. "Outside adjusters," a better-paid and more prestigious job, remained largely male. In yet other instances, women may gain access to a sector of an occupation that was always low paying. For example, the same study found that even though the representation of women among bus drivers increased substantially since 1970, men continued to comprise the majority of full-time workers in metropolitan transportation systems, whereas women were concentrated among part-time school bus drivers.[15]

At the same time, it is important to point out that women are expected to benefit from the increase in the demand for female labor that results when they are able to enter additional occupations from which they were previously excluded, even when the new jobs are qualitatively similar to those formerly available to them. Moreover, it is highly likely that much of the observed decline in occupational segregation does indeed represent enhanced labor market opportunities for women.

FEMALE-MALE EARNINGS RATIO

For many years, the single best-known statistic relevant to the economic status of women in this country probably was that women who worked full-time, year-round, earned about 59 cents to every dollar earned by men working full-time, year-round.[16] One reason for the public awareness of this figure was that the same earnings ratio persisted for two decades with only modest fluctuations and no significant trend. Although it was actually somewhat higher in the 1950s, as shown in Table 5-6 and Figure 5-1, the female-to-male earnings ratios based on annual data hovered close to the 59 percent figure throughout the 1960s and 1970s.[17] In the early 1980s,

---

[15]These examples are from Barbara F. Reskin and Patricia A. Roos, *Job Queues, Gender Queues: Explaining Women's Inroads into Male Occupations* (Philadelphia: Temple University Press, 1990). See also Paula England, Paul Allison, Su Li, Noah Mark, Jennifer Thompson, Michelle Budig, and Han Sun, "Why Are Some Academic Fields Tipping Toward Female? The Sex Composition of U.S. Fields of Doctoral Degree Receipt, 1971–1998," Stanford University (December 2003).

[16]*Full-time* is defined as 35 hours or more per week; *year-round* is defined as 50 weeks or more per year. The focus on full-time, year-round workers is an effort to adjust published government data on annual earnings for gender differences in hours and weeks worked. However, because even women who are employed full time work an average 8 to 10 percent fewer hours per week than male full-time workers, a finer adjustment for hours would raise the earnings ratio; see June O'Neill, "Women & Wages," *American Enterprise* 1, no. 6 (November/December 1990): 25–33.

[17]Median rather than mean earnings are shown because more government data are presented that way. The definition of the median is that half the cases fall above it and half below. In this case, half the individuals have higher earnings and half have lower. The mean, or arithmetic mean, is calculated by adding up the total earnings of all the individuals concerned and dividing by their number. Because a relatively small number of persons report extremely high earnings, the mean tends to be higher than the median.

TABLE 5-6   Female-to-Male Earnings Ratios of Full-Time Workers, Selected Years, 1955–2003

Year	Annual Earnings of Full-Time Year-Round Workers[a]	Usual Weekly Earnings of Full-Time Workers[b]
1955	63.9	
1960	60.8	
1965	60.0	
1970	59.4	62.3
1975	58.8	62.0
1980	60.2	64.4
1985	64.6	68.2
1990	71.6	71.8
1995	71.4	75.5
2000	73.3	76.0
2003	75.5	79.4

[a]Workers aged 16 and over. Prior to 1979, workers aged 14 and over.
[b]Workers aged 16 and over.

Sources: U.S. Department of Labor, Women's Bureau, *Time of Change: 1984 Handbook on Women Workers*, Bulletin 298; U.S. Census Bureau, Population Reports, *Money Income of Households, Families, and Persons in the United States*, Consumer Income Series P-60; U.S. Census Bureau, Population Reports, *Money, Income, and Poverty Status in the United States*, Consumer Income Series P-60, various issues; Earl F. Mellor, "Investigating the Differences in Weekly Earnings of Women and Men," *Monthly Labor Review* 107, no. 6 (June 1984); Bureau of Labor Statistics, *Handbook of Labor Statistics*, Bulletin 2340 (August 1989); Bureau of Labor Statistics, *Employment and Earnings*, various issues.

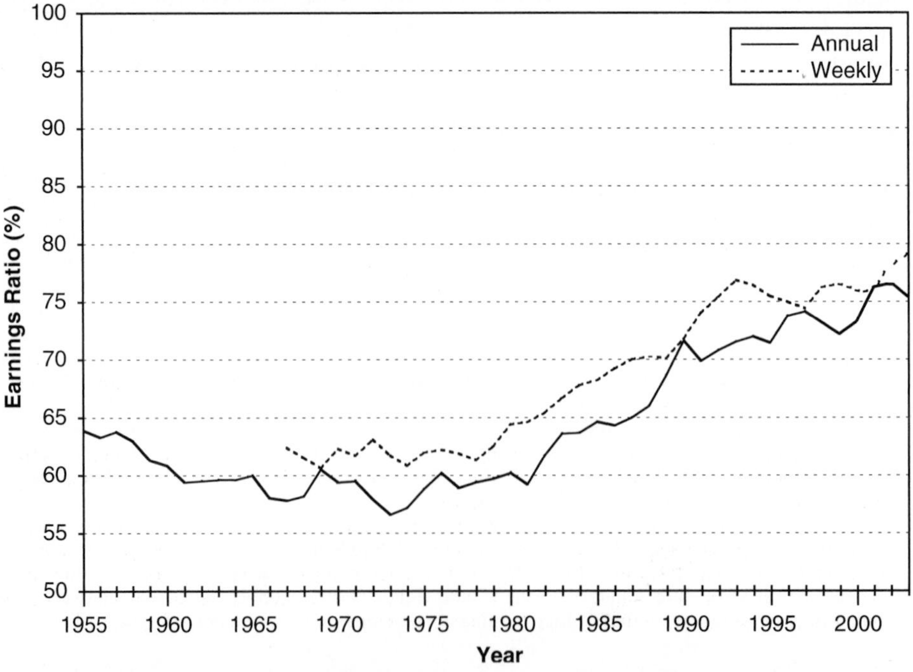

FIGURE 5-1   Female-to-Male Earnings Ratios of Full-Time Workers, 1955–2003

however, the ratio began to rise. Between 1981 and 2003 it increased from 59 percent to 76 percent.[18]

Table 5-6 and Figure 5-1 also show the female-to-male earnings ratio calculated using data on the usual weekly earnings of full-time workers. For a variety of reasons, the earnings ratio computed on the basis of weekly earnings is generally higher than the annual figure.[19] Of more interest, however, is that the data for weekly earnings also show an upward trend dating from the late 1970s. Between 1978 and 2003, the earnings ratio, defined in these terms, increased from 61 to 79 percent.

Looking more closely at the trends in Figure 5-1, we see a substantial and steady narrowing of the gender earnings gap over the 1980s. However, during the 1990s, the pace of convergence in both the annual and the weekly earnings series slowed and both series behaved more erratically. The pace of change picked up again in the early 2000s.[20] The long-run significance of this recent experience is unclear. It may signal a resumption of a strong, long-run trend toward convergence in male-female earnings or may prove to be of only short duration. One short-term factor could be the recession of 2001 and the relatively high unemployment rates that lingered in its aftermath. The demand for male workers tends to be more cyclically sensitive than that for female workers due to their greater concentration in blue-collar jobs and durable manufacturing industries. Nonetheless, the renewed growth in the gender earnings ratio at the start of the new century is an encouraging development.

Evidence on changes in the gender earnings ratio over the life cycle is shown in Table 5-7 for the 1970 to 2003 period. Data are presented on mean earnings ratios of

TABLE 5-7   Female-to-Male Ratios of Mean Earnings for Full-Time, Year-Round Workers by Age, 1970–2003

Age	1970	1980	1990	2000	2003
25–34	64.9	68.5	76.9	74.4	85.4
35–44	53.9	55.3	64.4	66.1	69.4
45–54	56.3	52.0	58.2	60.4	65.8
55–64	60.3	54.9	57.1	53.6	60.0

Sources: 1970: June O'Neill, "Women & Wages," *American Enterprise* 1 (November/December 1990): 29; 1980 and 1990: U.S. Census Bureau, *Money Income of Households, Families, and Persons in the United States,* Consumer Income Series P-60, 1981 and 1991; 2000: PINC04 Tables of the Current Population Survey Annual Social and Economic Supplement, 2001, available at ferret.bls.census.gov/macro/032001/perinc/toc.htm; 2003: PINC04 Tables of the Current Population Survey Annual Social and Economic Supplement, 2004, available at ferret.bls.census.gov/macro/032004/perinc/toc.htm.

---

[18]Focusing on all workers, rather than simply those employed full-time, year-round, Francine D. Blau and Andrea H. Beller found evidence of some earnings gains for women during the 1970s, after adjustment for hours and weeks worked; see "Trends in Earnings Differentials by Gender, 1971–1981," *Industrial and Labor Relations Review* 41, no. 4 (July 1988): 513–29.

[19]For example, annual earnings include overtime pay and bonuses. Men tend to receive greater amounts of this type of pay; see Nancy Rytina, "Comparing Annual and Weekly Earnings from the Current Population Survey," *Monthly Labor Review* 106 (April 1983): 32–38.

[20]Between 1980 and 1990, the average annual increase in the ratio was 1.14 percentage points for annual earnings and .74 percentage points for weekly earnings, while, between 1990 and 2000, it was only .16 percentage points for annual earnings and .42 percentage points for weekly earnings. Relative earnings growth in the early 2000s was more robust: between 2000 and 2003, the average annual increase in the ratio was .75 percentage points for annual earnings and 1.14 percentage points for weekly earnings.

full-time, year-round workers for four age groups: 25–34, 35–44, 45–54, and 55–64. The age range 25–64 was selected because individuals in this age group have generally completed their formal schooling but have not yet retired from paid employment. The data in the table indicate that women earn less than men in all age categories. However, as may be seen in Figure 5-2, the ratio tends to decrease with age, though increasing a bit in the oldest age group in some years. This decrease in the gender earnings ratio with age is partially due to women accumulating less work experience than men, on average, as they age, particularly for earlier cohorts. It may also reflect greater barriers to women's advancement at higher levels of the job hierarchy, an issue we will discuss further in Chapter 7 when we consider evidence on the glass ceiling.

As was the case for the overall earnings ratio, we see that the gender earnings ratio within age groups also rose substantially in the 1980s. Little further change occurred over the 1990s, but gains resumed again in the early 2000s. The earnings ratio began to rise as early as the 1970s for younger women (especially the youngest group aged 25 to 34), although the gains in the 1980s were considerably larger. Younger women also experienced the largest cumulative increases: Between 1970 and 2003, the earnings ratio rose by about 21 percentage points for 25- to 34-year-olds and 16 percentage points for 35- to 44-year-olds, while the ratio for 45- to 54-year-olds increased by 10 percentage points. As indicated in Figure 5-2, the pattern of declining gender earnings ratios with age remained the same, but the whole curve shifted to the right as the earnings of women relative to men increased within each age group.

One question we may address with these data is what happens to the gender ratio as women age. Interestingly, gains in relative earnings of women over the 1980s were

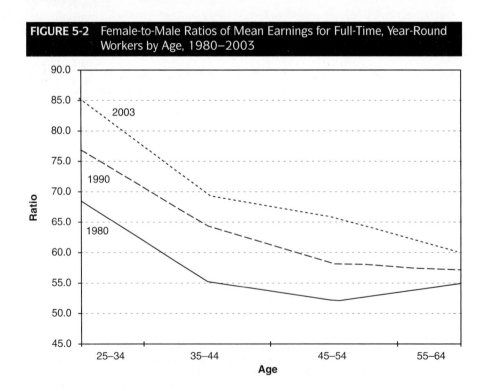

FIGURE 5-2   Female-to-Male Ratios of Mean Earnings for Full-Time, Year-Round Workers by Age, 1980–2003

large enough so that younger female cohorts did not experience a large decrease in the ratio with age as might be expected based on the data for 1980 or 1990 alone. If we compare the earnings ratio for 25- to 34-year-olds in 1980 to the ratio for 35- to 44-year-olds 10 years later in 1990, we find that the ratio fell only slightly from 69 to 64 percent. Further, the earnings ratio of 58 percent for the 45- to 54-year-old age group in 1990 was 3 percentage points greater than that of 35- to 44-year-olds 10 years earlier.

This same pattern does not hold in the 1990s. The 2000 figures strongly suggest a fairly substantial fall-off in earnings as women who were 25–34 years old in 1990 aged to 35–44, with the ratio declining from 77 to 66 percent. Similarly, the earnings ratio for 45- to 54-year-olds in 2000 was four percentage points lower than the figure for 35- to 44-year-olds in 1990. It is unclear what will happen in the future. Even taking into account the more favorable 2003 data, the earnings of younger women appear to be declining relative to men's as they age. In interpreting data like those presented in Table 5-7 it is important to bear in mind that comparisons of this type may be influenced by which men and women choose to seek paid employment in each year, as well as by their success in locating jobs. Due to this problem of "selection bias," we cannot be completely certain that data on those who are employed accurately measure shifts in labor market opportunities for all women.[21]

Table 5-8 provides information on the earnings of workers by level of education. Although education has a strong positive effect on the earnings of both men and women, men continue to earn substantially more than women within each educational category. Nonetheless, as was the case for the overall earnings gap and the earnings differentials by age, the gender gap within educational categories also narrowed over time. In 1974 and indeed through much of the 1970s, the gap was so large that it was often noted that women college graduates earned less than male high school dropouts.

TABLE 5-8 Ratio of Female-to-Male Mean Earnings by Education for Workers 18 Years and Older, 1974 and 2003

Education	*1974*	*2003*
High school:		
1–3 years	55.1	73.6
4 years	57.5	72.9
College:		
1–3 years	57.0	71.0
4 or more years	54.6	65.7

Notes: Definitions of educational categories are not exactly comparable for the two years. In 2003, mean earnings for 1–3 years of college is computed as a weighted average of the means for "some college, no degree" and "associate degree." Full-time, year-round workers are used.

Sources: 1974: U.S. Census Bureau Historical Income Tables, People Series, Table P-35, available at www.census.gov/hhes/income/histinc/p35.html; 2003: CPS Annual Demographic Survey, March Supplement, PINC04 Series, available at ferret.bls.census.gov/macro//032004/perinc/toc.htm.

---

[21]Seminal work by Nobel Prize–winning economist James J. Heckman greatly increased economists' awareness of this problem; see, for example, James J. Heckman, "Sample Selection Bias as a Specification Error," *Econometrica* 47, no. 1 (January 1979): 153–61.

Now, that is no longer true, and the earnings of women college graduates are roughly comparable to those of males with some college (1–3 years).

Table 5-9 reviews the trends in the income of women relative to men separately by race and Hispanic origin.[22] Within each group, women earned less than men in 2003, but the female-to-male income ratio was considerably higher among blacks (84 percent) and Hispanics (86 percent) than among whites (76 percent) and Asians (72 percent). Not surprisingly, the trends in income ratios by gender among whites closely mirror the overall trends because whites still comprise a substantial majority of the population. This group showed little tendency toward an increase in the gender ratio until the 1980s when considerable progress in narrowing the gender gap occurred; progress was slower in the 1990s but picked up a bit in the early 2000s. In contrast, the female-to-male income ratio among blacks increased considerably from the mid-1950s, by 29 percentage points. A sizable increase in the gender income ratio (17 percentage points) is also apparent among Hispanics since the mid-1970s when data first became available for this group. Like white

TABLE 5-9   Female-to-Male Ratios of Median Income by Race and Hispanic Origin for Full-Time, Year-Round Workers, 1955–2003

Year	Whites	Blacks	Asians	Hispanics
1955	65.3	55.1	n.a.	n.a.
1960	60.6	62.2	n.a.	n.a.
1965	57.9	62.5	n.a.	n.a.
1970	58.6	70.5	n.a.	n.a.
1975	57.5	75.1	n.a.	68.6
1980	59.3	78.7	n.a.	71.7
1985	64.1	81.2	n.a.	78.0
1990	69.3	86.3	80.7	83.6
1995	72.4	85.0	79.6	86.9
2000	73.5	83.3	76.6	84.0
2003[a]	75.6	83.7	71.9	85.7

[a]Data are for median earnings.
Notes: Prior to 1970, blacks include blacks and other nonwhites; prior to 2003, Asians include Asians and Pacific Islanders. For 2003, whites refer to white alone, blacks are defined as black alone or in combination with other races, Asians are defined as Asian alone or in combination with other races. In all years, Hispanic individuals may be of any race. Data for 1980 onwards refer to workers 15 years of age and older; and for 1955–1975 to workers 14 years of age and older.
n.a. = Not available.
Sources: 1955–1985: U.S. Census Bureau, *Current Population Reports*, Consumer Income Series P-60, various issues; 2000: U.S. Census Bureau Historical Income Tables - People, Tables P-36a through P-36d, available at www.census.gov/hhes/income/histinc/incperdet.html; 2003: PINC05 Tables of the CPS Annual Social and Economic Supplement 2004, available at ferret.bls.census.gov/macro/032004/perinc/ new05_117.htm.

---

[22]The reason for using income data here and in Table 5-10 is that no comparable earnings data are available for the full period examined. Income includes such items as interest, dividends, and transfer payments, as well as earnings. However, because these amounts are relatively small for the great majority of year-round, full-time workers, income ratios tend to be quite similar to earnings ratios. For 2003, only median earnings data were available and so they are reported for this year.

women, however, neither black nor Hispanic women made much progress in closing the pay gap with men of the same race or ethnicity over the 1990s. The data on Asians not only show a relatively high gender gap compared to the other minority groups but also show no trend toward narrowing since data became available in 1990.[23]

Table 5-10 provides income comparisons for male and female minority group members relative to their white counterparts. Note that the data in the table for whites are presented for all whites (including those of Hispanic origin), rather than for non-Hispanic whites separately because information on the broader group has been available for a longer period of time. Because most Hispanics are white, an important caveat to keep in mind is that the inclusion of this growing low-income group among whites in Table 5-10 may artificially inflate the relative progress of minority groups.[24]

In terms of the racial and ethnic differences shown in the table, we see that, except for Asians, minority individuals of both sexes earned less than whites in 2003, but the differential was considerably smaller among women than among men. In 2003, the median income of black males was 78 percent of white males' median income, and the figure for Hispanic males was 63 percent. These figures were considerably lower than the

TABLE 5-10 Minority-to-White Ratios of Median Income by Gender for Full-Time, Year-Round Workers, 1955–2003

	Black-to-White Ratios		*Asian-to-White Ratios*		*Hispanic-to-White Ratios*	
Year	*Males*	*Females*	*Males*	*Females*	*Males*	*Females*
1955	60.9	51.4	n.a.	n.a.	n.a.	n.a.
1960	66.1	67.8	n.a.	n.a.	n.a.	n.a.
1965	62.8	67.9	n.a.	n.a.	n.a.	n.a.
1970	68.1	81.9	n.a.	n.a.	n.a.	n.a.
1975	73.2	95.5	n.a.	n.a.	71.2	85.0
1980	70.4	93.3	n.a.	n.a.	70.0	84.5
1985	70.0	88.5	n.a.	n.a.	67.5	82.0
1990	71.4	89.0	90.7	105.7	64.4	77.6
1995	74.0	86.9	95.6	105.1	61.3	73.6
2000	76.5	86.8	103.2	107.6	62.1	70.9
2003[a]	78.3	86.6	109.4	104.1	63.3	71.7

[a]Data are for median earnings.

Notes: Prior to 1970, blacks include blacks and other nonwhites. Prior to 2003, Asians include Asians and Pacific Islanders. For 2003, whites refer to white alone; blacks are defined as black alone or in combination with other races; Asians are defined as Asian alone or in combination with other races. In all years, Hispanic individuals may be of any race. Data for 1980 and later refer to workers 16 years of age and older; and for 1955–1975 to workers 14 years of age and older.
n.a. = Not available.

Sources: 1955–1985: U.S. Census Bureau, *Current Population Reports*, Consumer Income Series P-60, various issues; 2000: U.S. Census Bureau Historical Income Tables, People, Tables P-36a through P-36d, available at www.census.gov/hhes/income/histinc/incperdet.html; 2003: PINC05 Tables of the CPS Annual Social and Economic Supplement 2004, available at ferret.bls.census.gov/macro/032004/perinc/new05_11.

[23]Trends for this group should be regarded with some caution, however, because underlying sample sizes are small and, prior to 2003, the government data on Asians also included Pacific Islanders.
[24]For example, when income for blacks is compared to that of non-Hispanic whites, the income ratio was 74 percent for men and 86 percent for women in 2003, lower than the ratios shown in Table 5-10 of 78 percent for men and 88 percent for women.

income ratios of 87 percent for black women and 72 percent for Hispanic women, both compared to white women. Finally, since 2000 for men and since data became available in 1990 for women, the median income of Asians has been higher than their white counterparts. This may reflect their higher educational attainment than whites, which will be discussed in Chapter 6.

Among women, black-to-white income ratios increased substantially from the mid-1950s, when the ratio was only 51 percent, to the mid-1970s, when it was 96 percent. Black men also gained relative to white men, although not nearly as rapidly, from 63 percent of white men's income in 1965 to 73 percent in 1975. Between 1975 and 1990, however, income differentials between blacks and whites widened. Since then, the data show signs of a renewed convergence between black and white men. However, some caution is warranted in interpreting the trends for black males in Table 5-10, including recent gains, because the data are based on measured earnings of employed individuals. As discussed earlier in Chapter 4, the participation and employment rates of black relative to white males decreased substantially since the 1950s, and it is likely that it is individuals with the least favorable labor market opportunities who dropped out of the labor force. If the least successful blacks are leaving the labor force at a faster rate than comparable whites, observed black-white earnings ratios may rise, even in the absence of any changes in the relative earnings prospects of all blacks (including both the employed and nonemployed). Putting this point somewhat differently, the observed black-white earnings ratio may rise simply because of a change in the composition of employed blacks rather than due to a true improvement in labor market opportunities for blacks. Existing research suggests that this factor is important but the general outlines of the trends remain: The black-white earnings ratio among males increased considerably from the mid-1960s to the late 1970s, but few further increases occurred in the ratio during the 1980s and only moderate signs of further convergence since then.[25]

A similar issue potentially affects trends in the black-white earnings ratio among women, because, although black women traditionally had higher labor force participation rates than white women, the participation gap narrowed considerably since the 1950s. However, the participation decision of women is considerably more complex than men's, and researchers find it more difficult to estimate the likely effects of shifting participation patterns on the black-white earnings ratio for women.[26] Earnings trends by race will be considered further in Chapter 8.

In contrast to the trends for blacks, data on Hispanics show declining income ratios for this group relative to whites since this information first became available in the

[25]This is another example of selection bias; and again, James Heckman was the first to call it to the attention of economists in his work with Richard Butler, "The Impact of the Economy and State on the Economic Status of Black Americans: A Critical Review," in *Equal Rights and Industrial Relations,* edited by Farrell E. Bloch (Madison, WI: Industrial Relations Research Association, 1977), pp. 235–81. Other work includes Charles Brown, "Black-White Earnings Ratios Since the Civil Rights Act of 1964: The Importance of Labor Market Dropouts," *Quarterly Journal of Economics* 99, no. 1 (February 1984): 31–44; Chinhui Juhn, "Labor Market Dropouts and Trends in the Wages of Black and White Men," *Industrial and Labor Relations Review* 56, no. 4 (July 2003): 643–63; James J. Heckman, Thomas M. Lyons, and Petra E. Todd, "Understanding Black-White Wage Differentials, 1960–1990," *American Economic Review* 90, no. 2 (May 2000): 344–49; and Amitabh Chandra, "Labor-Market Dropouts and the Racial Wage Gap: 1940–90," *American Economic Review* 90, no. 2 (May 2000): 333–38.
[26]For a study that does include women, see Francine D. Blau and Andrea H. Beller, "Black-White Earnings over the 1970s and 1980s, Gender Differences in Trends," *Review of Economics and Statistics* 74, no. 2 (May 1992): 276–86.

mid-1970s. Hispanic-to-white income ratios are also considerably lower tha to-white income ratios for both men and women. One reason may be that a large an growing proportion of Hispanics are recent immigrants to the United States. Hence their earnings are reduced because they tend to be relatively young, may not speak English well, and face other difficulties in adjusting to their new environment. Of course discrimination may also play a role in Hispanic-white income differences, just as it may for black-white differences.

The Gender Pay Gap in the News

We are bombarded in the press with a multitude of figures regarding how much women earn relative to men. Compounding this information overload are often inaccurate or misleading interpretations of the data presented. This inset provides a source and context for two figures that received particular media attention.

The most common figure cited is based on the median earnings of year-round, full-time workers. It is readily available from the Census Bureau web site and is shown in Figure 5-1 and Table 5-6. This figure, which was 76 percent in 2003, pertains to men and women who work full-time and year-round, but may well differ, on average, in terms of their age, educational attainment, seniority, occupation, industry, and other characteristics related to earnings. Nevertheless, it is frequently misunderstood, as in a recent *Los Angeles Times* article that referred to this ratio as being for men and women "doing the same work."[*] In fact, the pay ratio for men and women in the same occupation may be considerably higher than the overall ratio in some jobs, though gender pay ratios vary considerably across occupations.

Another figure that received substantial media attention, for instance by columnist George Will and in a recent book entitled *Women's Figures* by Diane Furchtgott-Roth and Christine Stolba, is the estimate of a 98 percent female-male earnings ratio for women and men ages 27 to 33 who have never had a child.[†] Should we take this statistic to mean that discrimination is virtually eliminated, as these authors do? This conclusion is probably not warranted. First, it represents women's and men's earnings at the start of their careers. Hence, it does not reflect later pay differences that may arise as a result of gender differences in promotion and advancement. As we saw in Table 5-7 and Figure 5-2, the gender earnings ratio tends to decrease with age. Second, the 98 percent statistic compares men and women who do not have children. As we shall see in Chapters 6 and 9, recent research indicates that mothers incur a wage penalty compared to other women, even when they have the same measured qualifications such as education and experience. Researchers do not find a similar wage penalty for fathers, and some find a wage premium for them. Thus the gender pay gap is smaller when comparing men and women without children.

Based on this evidence, some contend that the gender pay gap is largely due to differences between men and women in "preferences, motivations, and expectations," and "experience, education, and skills."[‡] Although these factors may well explain part of the gender pay gap, it is also possible that employers treat men and women differently, even when no productivity differences exist between them. Our extensive review of the evidence in Chapter 7 suggests that discrimination against women in the labor market does exist and, while it may not be as severe as in the past, represents more than an occasional anomaly.

It is also critical to keep in mind the assumptions that are made in interpreting any statistic on the gender pay gap and what can reasonably be concluded based on any particular piece of data. It matters a great deal, for instance, whether we assume that occupation represents solely an individual's choice or that it may be influenced by past or anticipated discrimination; or whether we assume that all mothers tend to prefer less-demanding "mommy-track" positions or that they may sometimes be channeled into them. Similarly, we must be cautious in interpreting an aggregate figure like "76 percent" as evidence of discrimination, when it does not take into account valid reasons why male and female pay may differ. At the same time it may not be reasonable to conclude that discrimination has virtually disappeared simply because young women and men at the beginning of their careers have similar starting salaries. Rather, it may be more appropriate to obtain information about a broader and more representative group of workers before reaching such a conclusion. Individuals on both sides of the debate must be careful not to oversimplify complex issues or cite a statistic without fully explaining its strengths and limitations. The bottom line is that, even though pinpointing discrimination is difficult, ample evidence indicates that, despite recent progress, it has not gone away entirely.

*Renee Tawa, "Who's in Charge? With More Women Working and Bringing Home Bigger Paychecks, Some Men Are Staying Home to Rear the Kids. Now Couples Must Struggle with Touchy Issues of Identity and Balance of Power," *Los Angeles Times*, September 27, 1999, p. E1.
†George Will, "Lies, Damned Lies," *Newsweek*, March 29, 1999, p. 84; Diana Furchtgott-Roth and Christine Stolba, *Women's Figures: An Illustrated Guide to the Economic Progress of Women in America* (Washington DC: AEI Press: 1999); and June O'Neill, "The Shrinking Pay Gap," *Wall Street Journal*, October 7, 1994.
‡Furchtgott-Roth and Stolba, *Women's Figures*, p. 4.

Conclusion

In this chapter, we presented data on gender differentials in occupations and earnings in general, as well as for various subgroups. Although occupational and earnings differences remain substantial, both declined significantly over the past 25 to 35 years. Reductions in occupational segregation by gender actually date back to the 1960s, though more rapid progress occurred in subsequent decades. The overall gap in the earnings of male and female full-time workers started to narrow in the late 1970s or early 1980s. The trend toward earnings convergence was particularly dramatic during the 1980s, slowed in the 1990s, but picked up again in the early years of the twenty-first century. The next two chapters will thoroughly investigate the possible explanations for the gender differences described here, while Chapter 8 focuses in part on explaining the reasons for the long-term convergence in the gender gap.

Questions for Review and Discussion

1. Why have women been increasingly eager to move into men's occupations? Why do you think men generally show less enthusiasm about moving into women's occupations?

2. Consider the following hypothetical information about the occupational distribution of Country Y. Assume that 100 employed men and 100 employed women work in either Occupation A or Occupation B.

	Employed Women	*Employed Men*
Occupation A	70%	20%
Occupation B	30%	80%
Total	100%	100%

   a. Calculate the index of occupational segregation by sex using the formula given in footnote 5, Chapter 5.
   b. Explain exactly what the number you obtained in (a) means in light of the verbal definition of the sex segregation index.

3. When the occupational segregation index is calculated for the 10 major occupational categories shown in Table 5-1 it is found to be 32.2. (You can verify this figure, again using the formula given in the text.) Why is this figure lower than the values obtained when a large set of detailed occupations are considered as in Table 5-5?

4. Explain why the female-male earnings ratio is higher for full-time, year-round workers than for all workers.

6

DIFFERENCES IN OCCUPATIONS AND EARNINGS: THE HUMAN CAPITAL MODEL

Chapter Highlights

- What Is Human Capital?
- Gender Differences in Educational Attainment and Investment Decisions
- Gender Differences in Labor Market Experience and Training Investment Decisions
- Occupations and Earnings
- Other Supply-Side Factors
- The Human Capital Explanation: An Assessment

In this chapter, we present supply-side explanations for the gender differences in occupations and earnings described in Chapter 5. We first summarize the arguments of scholars who emphasize this point of view, beginning with a consideration of the determinants of the decision to invest in formal education and on-the-job training and an analysis of the sources of gender differences in these decisions within the human capital framework. Next we apply these concepts to understanding gender differences in occupations and earnings. We then consider other supply-side factors that may produce gender differences in economic outcomes. We conclude by presenting an evaluation of the contributions of the human capital approach. In Chapter 7 we consider labor market discrimination, which provides an alternative explanation for gender differences in occupations and earnings. It is our view that these two sets of explanations are not mutually exclusive and that both provide valuable insights into the sources of male-female differences in occupations and earnings.

Supply-side explanations focus on the observation that men and women may come to the labor market with different tastes and with different qualifications, such as education, formal training, or experience. Gender differences in tastes might mean, for example, that one group or the other shows greater tolerance for an unpleasant, unhealthy, or dangerous work environment, for longer work hours or inflexible work schedules, for physical strain, or for repetitive tasks, and is more willing to accept any or all of these working conditions in return for higher wages. An example of a gender difference in qualifications would be a woman having a college degree in English and a man having a college degree in engineering. Or, as another example, a woman might move in and out of the labor force as her family situation changes, whereas a man's attachment might be more continuous.

To the extent such differences in men's and women's tastes and qualifications exist, they could cause women to earn less and to be concentrated in different occupations. Little is known about tastes and their effects on occupational choices and rewards; however, a great deal of research looks at job-related qualifications. Hence, we too shall concentrate on those qualifications.

Before considering the effects of gender differences in qualifications on earnings and occupations, one issue that arises is whether such differences in qualifications should be viewed as the result of the voluntary choices men and women make or as the outcome of what is termed *prelabor market* or **societal discrimination.** Societal discrimination denotes the multitude of social influences that cause women to make decisions that adversely influence their status in the labor market. Because we are all products of our environments to a greater or lesser extent, it is often difficult to draw the line between voluntary choice and this type of discrimination.

This distinction may in part reflect disciplinary boundaries. The discipline of economics tends to view individual decision making as determined by economic incentives and individual preferences (or tastes). It generally does not analyze the formation of preferences, and choices are generally viewed as being at least to some extent voluntary. In contrast, sociologists and social psychologists are more apt to examine the role of socialization and social-structural factors in producing what economists classify as individual preferences.[1] Thus, within the context of sociology or social psychology, individual choices are more likely to be seen as stemming from social conditioning or constraints rather than as voluntary.

The tendency to emphasize the role of choice versus societal discrimination may also reflect an implicit value judgment. Those who are reasonably content with the status quo of gender differences in economic outcomes tend to speak mainly of voluntary choices, whereas those who decry gender inequality in pay and occupations are more likely to focus on societal discrimination.

We tend toward the view that at least some of the gender differences in qualifications that currently exist stem from undesirable societal discrimination, although we acknowledge that, particularly in the past and to a lesser extent

---

[1]Sociologists might question the appropriateness of the term *discrimination* in the context of gender socialization. We use it here only to the extent that the socialization process adversely affects the labor market success of young women.

today, many individuals regarded this type of gender differentiation as perfectly appropriate. The most important point is that even if societal discrimination is a problem, it is essentially different from **labor market discrimination** (which is discussed in Chapter 7), and a different set of policies is required to deal with it.

A second issue that deserves attention is that distinguishing between supply- and demand-side factors is not as easy as it appears at first. Labor market discrimination can affect women's economic status *indirectly* by lowering their incentives to invest in themselves and to acquire particular job qualifications. Thus, gender differences in productivity-related characteristics may reflect not only the voluntary choices of men and women and the impact of societal discrimination but also the indirect effects of labor market discrimination. This last point will also be developed further in Chapter 7.

WHAT IS HUMAN CAPITAL?

Within the economics literature, the human capital model provides the major supply-side explanation for gender differentials in economic outcomes. Most of us are familiar with the notion of investments in physical capital. For example, businesspeople expend resources today to build new plants or to purchase new machinery. This augments their firms' productive capabilities and increases output in future years. They make such decisions based upon a comparison of the expected costs and benefits of these investments. Economists such as Theodore Schultz, Gary Becker, and Jacob Mincer pointed out that individuals and their families make analogous decisions regarding **human capital** investments.[2] In this case, resources are invested in an individual today in order to increase his or her future productivity and earnings. Examples of human capital investments include formal education, on-the-job training, job search, and geographic migration.

Although the analogy between physical and human capital is compelling, some differences between the two are important. Chiefly, an individual's human capital investment decisions will be influenced to a greater extent by nonpecuniary (nonmonetary) considerations than is typically the case for physical capital investment decisions. Some people enjoy going to school; others do not. Some find indoor, white-collar work attractive; others would prefer to do manual work in the fresh air. Another important difference is that, in the absence of government intervention, it is generally more difficult to borrow to finance human capital investments than to finance physical ones, primarily because one does not have collateral to offer if the loan for human capital is not repaid. These differences between physical and human capital illustrate the general point that although labor markets are similar to other markets, they are not identical to them—in large part because labor services cannot be separated from the individuals who provide them. This distinction does not invalidate the use of economic analysis in the study of labor markets, but it does require us to be aware of the significant differences between labor markets and other markets.

---

[2]See, for example, Theodore W. Schultz, "Investment in Human Capital," *American Economic Review* 51, no. 1 (March 1960): 1–17; Gary S. Becker, *Human Capital: A Theoretical and Empirical Analysis, With Special Reference to Education,* 3rd ed. (Chicago: University of Chicago Press, 1993); and Jacob Mincer; "On-the-Job Training: Costs, Returns and Some Implications," *Journal of Political Economy* 70, no. 5, pt. 2 (October 1962): 50–79.

We first focus upon the pecuniary aspects of the human capital investment decision and then consider how nonpecuniary factors might influence the analysis. We emphasize two major kinds of human capital investments: formal schooling and on-the-job training. According to the work of Jacob Mincer, Solomon Polachek, and others, gender differences in these areas—in both the amount and type of investments made—can produce substantial differences in the pay and occupations of men and women in the labor market.[3]

GENDER DIFFERENCES IN EDUCATIONAL ATTAINMENT

Gender differences in educational attainment in the United States are not large. They are, for example, considerably smaller than educational differences between minorities and whites in the United States or than gender differences in educational attainment in many parts of the developing world. However, there are some significant gender differences in the *pattern* of educational attainment of men and women. Historically, women were more likely to complete high school than men, but higher proportions of men than women completed college and went on to postgraduate education. These tendencies are reflected in the data for 1970 and 2003 shown in Table 6-1.

In both years, higher proportions of men than women were high school dropouts, although gender differences were quite small. In 1970, differences between men and women in college completion were considerably larger; men were 1.7 times as likely to complete four or more years of college as were women. However, the gender difference in higher education declined as men and women in younger cohorts acquired more similar educational attainment. By 2003, women were nearly as likely to complete four or more years of college as men; among 25- to 34-year-olds, women were

---

TABLE 6-1 Educational Attainment of the Population by Gender: 1970 and 2003 (Ages 25–64)

	1970		2003	
	Males (%)	*Females (%)*	*Males (%)*	*Females (%)*
Less than 4 years of high school	39.3	38.2	12.1	10.4
4 years of high school only	33.5	42.3	32.4	32.5
Some college	11.9	10.5	25.5	28.4
4 or more years of college	15.3	9.0	30.1	28.8
Total	100.0	100.0	100.0	100.0

Notes: Some changes occurred in the coding of education in the CPS data so that the 1970 and 2003 data are not strictly comparable. In making the two series as compatible as possible we follow the suggestions of David A. Jaeger, "Reconciling the Old and New Census Bureau Education Questions: Recommendations for Researchers," *Journal of Business and Economic Statistics* 15, no. 3 (July 1997): 300–309. In particular, as recommended by Jaeger, both individuals with a high school degree, as well as those with 12 years of high school but no degree, are coded as having 4 years of high school.

Source: Tabulated from the 1970 and 2003 microdata files of the March *Current Population Survey (CPS).*

---

[3]Jacob Mincer and Solomon W. Polachek, "Family Investments in Human Capital: Earnings of Women," *Journal of Political Economy* 82, no. 2, pt. 2 (March/April 1974): 76–108; and Solomon W. Polachek, "Occupational Self-Selection: A Human Capital Approach to Sex Differences in Occupational Structure," *Review of Economics and Statistics* 63, no. 1 (February 1981): 60–69.

actually more likely to be college graduates than men—in this age group 32 percent of women were college graduates compared to 28 percent of men.

The data in Table 6-1 also show rising educational attainment of both men and women over the period. A typical individual of either sex was much less likely to drop out of high school in 2003 than in 1970, and considerably more likely to obtain some schooling beyond high school.

Educational attainment is shown separately by race and Hispanic origin in Table 6-2. With the exception of Asians, women were less likely to be high school dropouts than men, although these differences are small for all groups. There were sharper differences across groups in college completion. Among whites, men and women were nearly equally likely to complete college whereas among Asians, men showed a clear edge in college completion. In contrast, among blacks and Hispanics, women were somewhat more likely to be college graduates.

Some noticeable differences are also evident in educational attainment across minority groups. Blacks and Hispanics had lower educational attainment than whites: they were more likely to drop out of high school and less likely to graduate from college. The differences between blacks and whites were considerably smaller than the differences between Hispanics and whites, reflecting a substantial increase in the relative educational attainment of blacks since the 1960s. The large influx of immigrants with low levels of education may explain some of the sizable Hispanic-white difference in educational attainment; however, the numbers also reflect considerably higher high school dropout rates even of native-born Hispanic students.[4] Asians, on the other hand, had higher educational attainment than whites, with an especially high proportion graduating college among both men and women.

The trends in higher education by gender, shown in greater detail in Table 6-3, reinforce our impression of declining gender differences in educational attainment

TABLE 6-2 Educational Attainment of the Population by Gender, Race, and Hispanic Origin, 2003 (Ages 25–64)

	Whites		Blacks		Hispanics		Asians	
	Males (%)	Females (%)	Males (%)	Females (%)	Males (%)	Females (%)	Males (%)	Females (%)
Less than 4 years of high school	12.0	9.9	14.0	12.9	39.2	36.8	7.6	9.1
4 years of high school only	31.9	32.4	40.8	36.5	31.0	30.8	19.1	22.6
Some college	25.5	28.4	27.5	31.1	18.3	20.1	18.1	18.8
4 or more years of college	30.6	29.3	17.7	19.5	11.4	12.3	55.2	49.6
Total	100.0	100.0	100.0	100.0	100.0	100.0	100.0	100.0

Notes: Whites are defined as white only; blacks are defined as black only as well as black in combination with another race; Asians are defined as Asian only as well as Asian in combination with another race. Hispanics may be of any race. As in Table 6-1, the category of 4 years of high school includes those with a high school degree as well as those with 12 years of high school but no degree.

Source: Tabulated from the 2003 microdata file of the March *Current Population Survey (CPS)*.

[4]Steven A. Holmes, "Education Gap between Races Closes," *New York Times,* September 6, 1996, p. A18 and George J. Borjas, "Assimilation and Changes in Cohort Quality Revisited: What Happened to Immigrant Earnings in the 1980s?" *Journal of Labor Economics* 13, no. 2 (April 1995): 201–45.

TABLE 6-3 Degrees Awarded to Women by Level for Selected Years				
Years	*Associate* (%)	*Bachelor's* (%)	*Master's* (%)	*Ph.D.* (%)	*First Professional* (%)
1929–1930	n.a.	39.9[a]	40.4	15.4	n.a.
1960–1961	n.a.	38.5	31.7	10.5	2.7
1970–1971	42.9	43.4	40.1	14.3	6.3
1980–1981	54.7	49.8	50.3	31.1	26.6
1990–1991	58.8	53.9	53.6	37.0	39.1
2000–2001	60.0	57.3	58.5	44.9	46.2

[a]Includes first professional degrees.
n.a.=Not available.

Source: U.S. Department of Education, National Center for Education Statistics, *Digest of Education Statistics*, 2002.

among younger cohorts. In the early 1960s, women received 39 percent of bachelor's degrees, about the same as their share in 1930. By 2001, 57 percent of bachelor's degrees were awarded to women, as were 59 percent of master's degrees. Similarly, although women received 43 percent of associate degrees in the early 1970s, they received a majority of such degrees by the 1980s and 60 percent by 2001. Women still were awarded fewer than half (45–46 percent) of doctorate (Ph.D.) and first professional degrees in 2001, but this percentage represented a substantial increase in their share since the 1960s. First professional degrees are those awarded in postcollege professional training programs, including those in medicine, law, dentistry, pharmacy, veterinary medicine, and theology.[5]

The figures on educational attainment reveal only part of the story of gender differences in formal schooling, however. Beginning in high school, male and female students tended to differ in the types of courses taken and fields of specialization. This difference was especially true in the past and remains the case to some extent even today.

For example, at the secondary level, girls traditionally took fewer courses in mathematics and natural sciences than boys. Such differences are potentially important. Although differences in the number of courses taken in these fields have little effect on gender differences in pay for high school graduates, taking more high school math increases the wages of female college graduates, as well as the likelihood of their entering technical and nontraditional fields.[6] Considerable progress has been made in reducing gender differences in high school courses in recent years. A recent government report found that "overall, females' high school academic programs in mathematics and science are at least as challenging as those taken by males." However, some differences remain. Males made up a higher proportion of students taking advanced placement (AP) exams in science and calculus and obtained higher average scores on these examinations. They were also more likely than girls to take physics, though girls were more likely than boys

---

[5]Master's degrees in business are also generally thought of as first professional degrees, however, the Department of Education, which provides the data for Table 6-3 includes them with master's degrees. In Table 6-5 we include business master's degrees with first professional degrees.
[6]See Charles Brown and Mary Corcoran, "Sex-Based Differences in School Content and the Male/Female Wage Gap," *Journal of Labor Economics* 15, no. 3, pt. 1 (July 1997): 431–65; and Phillip B. Levine and David J. Zimmerman, "The Benefit of Additional High-School Math and Science Classes of Young Men and Women," *Journal of Business and Economic Statistics* 13, no. 2 (April 1995): 137–49.

to take algebra II, biology, and chemistry.[7] Interestingly, boys and girls are about equally likely to have access to a computer at home or to use the Internet.[8]

Differences between men and women in fields of specialization at the college level are more substantial, as illustrated in Table 6-4. Here too, however, the gender difference narrowed considerably since the mid-1960s. For example, in 1964, the index of segregation by college major was 51.4, indicating that more than half of college women (or men) needed to change majors in order for the distribution of women and men across majors to be the same. By 1990, this figure declined substantially to 29.4.[9] Similarly, the considerable

TABLE 6-4 Bachelor's Degrees Awarded to Women by Field, 1965–1966 and 2000–2001 for Selected Fields

Field	1965–1966 (%)	2000–2001 (%)
Agriculture and natural resources	2.7	45.1
Architecture and related programs	4.0	40.0
Biological sciences/life sciences	28.2	59.5
Business management, administrative sciences, and marketing	8.5	49.6
Computer and information sciences	13.0[a]	27.7
Education	75.3	76.7
Engineering	0.4	19.9
English and English literature	66.2	68.4
Foreign languages	70.7	70.9
Health	76.9	83.8
Home economics	97.5	87.6
Mathematics	33.3	47.7
Physical sciences and science technologies	13.6	41.2
Psychology	41.0	77.5
Social sciences	35.0	51.8
Economics	9.8	34.1
History	34.6	41.5
Sociology	59.6	70.7

[a]Data are for 1969, the earliest year available.

Sources: U.S. Department of Health, Education and Welfare, Office of Education, *Earned Degrees Conferred: 1965–66*; U.S. Department of Education, National Center for Education Statistics, *Digest of Education Statistics*, 2002.

[7]See, Catherine E. Freeman, *Trends in Educational Equity of Girls and Women*, National Center for Educational Statistics (NCES) NCES 2005-016, November 2004 (quotation is from p. 7). See also, American Association of University Women *Gender Gaps. Where Schools Still Fail Our Children* (Washington, DC: American Association of University Women, 1998). For an analysis of gender differences in mathematics, see Sheila Tobias, *Overcoming Math Anxiety* (New York: W.W. Norton, 1993), chap. 3.
[8]Eric C. Newburger, Home Computers and Internet Use in the United States: August 2000, *Current Population Reports* P23–207, U.S. Census Bureau (September 2001).
[9]Jerry A. Jacobs, *Revolving Doors: Sex Segregation and Women's Careers* (Stanford: Stanford University Press, 1989); and Jerry A. Jacobs, "Gender and Academic Specialties: Trends Among Recipients of College Degrees in the 1980s," *Sociology of Education* 68, no. 2 (April 1995): 81–98. Jacobs reports that the trend toward gender integration in fields of study was especially strong in the 1970s and slowed markedly in the late 1980s.

TABLE 6-5 First Professional Degrees Awarded to Women by Field, 1966, 1981, and 2001 for Selected Fields			
Field	*1966 (%)*	*1981 (%)*	*2001 (%)*
Business[a]	3.2[b]	23.8	40.6
Dentistry	1.1	14.4	38.6
Medicine	6.7	24.7	43.3
Pharmacy	16.4	42.6	66.1
Veterinary medicine	8.0[c]	35.2	69.8
Law	3.8	32.4	47.3
Theology	4.1	14.0	32.0

[a]Master's degrees in business administration and management.
[b]Data are for 1964–65.
[c]Data are for 1967–68.

Sources: U.S. Department of Health, Education and Welfare, Office of Education, *Earned Degrees Conferred: 1965–66*; U.S. Department of Education, National Center for Educational Statistics, *Digest of Education Statistics*, 1983 and 2002.

increase in the percentage of women receiving first professional degrees, which we saw in Table 6-3, reflected large gains in their representation among students in traditionally male fields such as medicine, law, and business (a specific breakdown is shown in Table 6-5).

In summary, while the educational attainment of men and women is fairly similar, there are still some important gender differences in education that may have an impact on women's earnings and occupational attainment. Historically, women were more likely than men to complete high school, but higher proportions of men than women completed four or more years of college. Further, traditionally, women took fewer math and science courses than men in high school, and college men and women tended to differ in their fields of study. However, all these differences narrowed in recent years, and the high school academic programs of girls and boys in math and science tend to be equally challenging, although some important differences remain as to the specific courses taken, and, among young adults, women are actually more likely to graduate college than men.

We now turn to the explanation provided by the human capital model for the historical tendency of men and women to acquire different amounts of education and to specialize in different fields. We then consider some of the other factors that may account for these differences.

THE EDUCATIONAL INVESTMENT DECISION

We begin by considering an individual's decision of whether to invest in formal education, as illustrated in Figure 6-1. Here we consider Daniel's choice between going to college or ending his formal education with high school. Initially, we focus solely upon the pecuniary costs and benefits of investing in education, although later we consider nonpecuniary costs and benefits as well. This investment decision entails a comparison between the expected **experience-earnings profiles** (the annual earnings at each level of labor market experience) associated with each type of schooling.

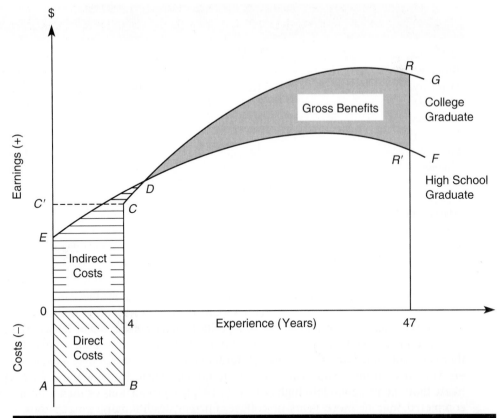

FIGURE 6-1 The Educational Investment Decision

In this case, Daniel expects his profile to be *EF* if he enters the labor market after completing high school. Alternatively, if he goes on to college, he will incur out-of-pocket expenses on tuition and books of *OA* dollars per year (negative "earnings") for the four-year period. (He does not anticipate taking a job while he goes to school.) Upon graduation, he expects to earn *OC'* dollars. The investment in a college education is believed to increase his productivity and, hence, his earnings above what he could have earned entering the labor force directly after high school (*OE*). In this hypothetical example, he initially earns less than if he worked for four years rather than going to college, but over his work life his expected earnings are higher. His experience-earnings profile, if he goes to college, is *ABCG*.

As indicated in Figure 6-1, the earnings of both high school and college graduates are expected to increase with labor market experience over much of the individual's work life. Human capital theory attributes this increase to the productivity-enhancing effects of on-the-job training, which we discuss later in this chapter. Note that Figure 6-1 shows the college graduate's profile as rising more steeply than the high school graduate's. As we shall see later, this has indeed been found to be the case empirically and suggests that college graduates acquire more training informally on the job as well as formally in school.

Now let us consider how Daniel can use the information in Figure 6-1 to make his investment decision. To do so he considers both the incremental costs and the incremental benefits associated with graduating from college. He must take into account two types of costs of schooling. **Direct costs** are expenditures on such items as tuition, fees, and books. Less obvious, but no less important than direct costs, are the earnings forgone during the time an individual is in school. These **indirect costs** correspond to the opportunity costs of schooling. We assumed that Daniel does not work for pay while attending college, but even if he did, his forgone earnings are still likely to be substantial—college students are seldom employed for as many hours or for as high a wage as workers not enrolled in school. The full costs of a college education are equal to the sum of the direct and indirect costs, or area *EABCD*.

The gross benefits of a college education are given by the excess of the expected earnings of a college graduate over those of a high school graduate over the individual's work life. Other things being equal, the size of these benefits depends on the length of the expected work life. If Daniel expects to work 43 years after college until retirement at age 65, his benefits are equal to the shaded area *DRR'*.

For Daniel to decide in favor of a college education (on an economic basis), the *gross benefits* of this investment must exceed the costs; that is, the *net benefits* must be positive. Further, gross benefits must exceed costs by an amount sufficient to give him an adequate return on his investment. Individuals may differ on the rate of return required to induce them to undertake this investment, but all are likely to require a positive rate of return.

For one thing, instead of investing resources in human capital, Daniel could have put his money into a savings bank or invested it in other assets. Those alternatives provide a positive rate of return and, thus, his human capital investment must also do so in order to be competitive. More fundamentally, Daniel, like most people, prefers income (and the opportunity to spend it) now to income (and the opportunity to spend it) later. To induce him to delay his gratification and receive his income later rather than sooner, the labor market has to offer him (and others like him) an inducement in the form of a positive rate of return. In Daniel's case, the investment does appear profitable, although we cannot tell simply by looking at the diagram because even though the benefit area appears to exceed the cost area, we do not know what the resulting rate of return is or whether Daniel will find it acceptable. If indeed he deems the investment sufficiently profitable, he is likely to decide to go on to college.[10]

Estimates of the average private rate of return to a college education range from 5 to 15 percent.[11] Interestingly, the rate of return to education tends to be higher than for

---

[10]Some additional details may be of interest to advanced students. It is possible to express the **present value** of an income or cost stream today by discounting future income or costs by the interest rate. Based on such a calculation, an individual would undertake the investment in education if the present value of benefits is greater than or at least equal to the present value of the costs. Alternatively, one can solve for the discount rate that exactly equates the present value of costs to the present value of benefits. If this rate, called the **internal rate of return**, represents an adequate rate of return from the individual's perspective, the individual will choose to invest in education.

[11]See, for example, George Psacharopoulos, "Returns to Education: A Further International Update and Implications," *Journal of Human Resources* 20, no. 4 (Fall 1985): 583–604. Calculating the rate of return involves estimating the increase in earnings attributable to additional education as well as all the costs involved in acquiring it, including both forgone earnings and out-of-pocket expenses. A number of difficulties arise in statistically estimating the returns to schooling; for a discussion, see David Card, "Earnings, Schooling, and Ability Revisited," *Research in Labor Economics,* edited by Solomon W. Polachek (Greenwich CT: JAI Press, 1995).

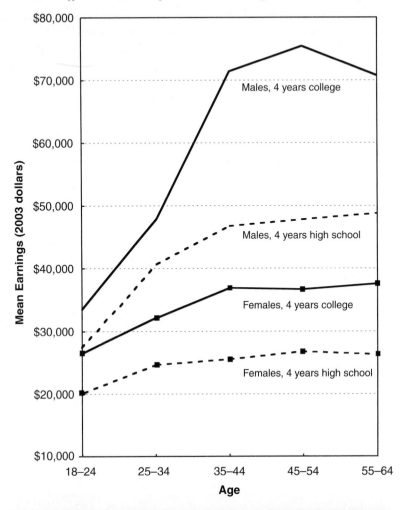

FIGURE 6-2a Age-Earnings Profiles of Year-Round, Full-Time Workers by Gender and Education, 1974

various types of financial investments. One possible reason is that investment in human capital is riskier in that everything depends on how well the specific individual fares in the labor market.

Numerous studies confirm that, as the theory predicts, earnings tend to rise with additional education for both men and women. This relationship is illustrated in Figures 6-2a and b, which show age-earnings profiles of high school and college graduates for 1974 and 2003. In each year the earnings of college graduates lie above those of high school graduates of the same sex. Moreover, the earnings profiles of college graduates of both sexes are steeper than those of their high school counterparts, as noted previously. Nonetheless, within each education group, women earn less than men and their earnings

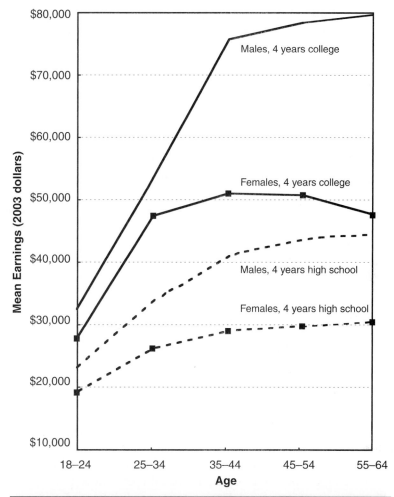

FIGURE 6-2b Age-Earnings Profiles of Year-Round, Full-Time Workers by Gender and Education, 2003

profiles tend to be flatter than men's. We consider these gender differences in greater detail later in this chapter.

Despite the general similarity of the profiles in each of the two years, there have been some changes that illustrate important labor market developments over the past 25 to 30 years. Earnings are shown in terms of 2003 dollars in both years (i.e., they are adjusted for inflation) so levels of earnings and differences across groups are comparable in each year. One striking difference between the mid-1970s and the early 2000 is that, for each sex, the earnings of college graduates rose relative to high school graduates, which means that the rate of return to education increased. This increase is part of a trend toward rising returns to skills over this period.[12] As a consequence, college graduates experienced more favorable trends in real earnings than high school graduates or high school dropouts, with young, less-educated men particularly losing ground in real terms. These recent trends are considered in more detail in Chapter 8.

EDUCATION AND PRODUCTIVITY

Human capital theory postulates that earnings rise with additional education because of the productivity-enhancing effects of education. Intuitively, it seems reasonable that education imparts a variety of skills and knowledge that would potentially be useful on the job, ranging from specific skills, such as computer programming and accounting, to general skills such as reasoning ability, writing skills, and proficiency in solving mathematical problems. Educational institutions may also teach certain behaviors that are valued on the job, such as punctuality, following instructions, and habits of predictability and dependability.

Others suggest an alternative interpretation of the positive relationship between education and earnings in which education functions solely as a **screening device** or a **signal**.[13] In this view, employers have imperfect information on worker productivity and, thus, seek ways to distinguish more productive applicants from less productive applicants before hiring them. At the same time, it is assumed that more able (productive) individuals find the (psychic and monetary) costs of acquiring additional schooling lower than the less able, perhaps because they find their studies less arduous or because they are awarded scholarships. If the more able incur lower costs, an educational investment may be profitable for them when it would not be for the less able. In an extreme version of the signaling model, education is rewarded *solely* because it *signals* higher productivity to the employer and *not* because of any skills it imparts.

Unfortunately, this theoretical disagreement between the human capital and signaling models has proved difficult to resolve empirically. This is the case because the issue is a particularly thorny one—*not* whether or not more education is correlated with higher productivity and earnings, but *why*. From the individual's perspective, however, it does not matter whether education raises earnings by increasing productivity or by signaling greater ability. Thus, the decision-making process illustrated in Figure 6-1 would be unaffected.

Nonetheless, one potential consequence of the signaling model for gender differences in labor market outcomes is worth noting. If employers believe that a given level of education signals lower productivity for a woman than for a man, women may have to have higher educational credentials than men to obtain the same job. So, for example, suppose an employer who is hiring for entry-level management positions believes that a bachelor's degree signals a lower commitment to the labor market for women

---

[12]Rising educational differentials and other increases in the returns to skill over this period have been widely reported in the literature. See, for example, Chinhui Juhn, Kevin M. Murphy, and Brooks Pierce, "Wage Inequality and the Rise in Returns to Skill," *Journal of Political Economy* 101, no. 3 (June 1993): 410–42; and Lawrence F. Katz and Kevin M. Murphy, "Changes in Relative Wages, 1963–87: Supply and Demand Factors," *Quarterly Journal of Economics* 107, no. 1 (February 1992): 35–78. To be fully confident that the return to college has risen, we should also look at trends in out-of-pocket costs, but any changes there are likely to be dwarfed by the large shifts in earnings profiles.

[13]See, especially, Michael Spence, *Market Signalling* (Cambridge, MA: Harvard University Press, 1974).

than for men. The employer may require a woman to have, say, an MBA degree in order to obtain employment, while being perfectly willing to hire a man with only a bachelor's degree. This is quite similar to the notion of **statistical discrimination** to be discussed in Chapter 7.

GENDER DIFFERENCES IN EDUCATIONAL INVESTMENT DECISIONS: THE HUMAN CAPITAL ANALYSIS

Does our analysis of the human capital investment decision suggest any reasons why men and women might decide to acquire different amounts or types of formal education? According to the analysis already presented, the major factors to consider are the expected costs and benefits of the investment. The definitions of costs and benefits may be extended to include nonpecuniary, as well as pecuniary, costs and benefits, and we do so later. In addition, because individuals may find it hard to borrow to finance their human capital investments, access to funds is a further consideration of some importance. Thus, we will want to consider why men and women might differ in these respects.

Expected Work Life

The major factor emphasized by human capital theorists as producing gender differences in human capital investments is that, given traditional roles in the family, many women anticipate shorter, more disrupted work lives than men. Such women reach the point sooner when additional investment is no longer worthwhile. Furthermore, it will not pay for them to make the types of human capital investments that require sustained, high-level commitment to the labor force to make them profitable and that depreciate rapidly during periods of work interruptions.

The impact of these factors is illustrated in Figure 6-3, which reproduces the earnings profiles shown in Figure 6-1. Note that the horizontal axis now refers to potential experience or the total time elapsed since completing high school. We present it in this way in order to be able to represent periods of time out of the labor force on this diagram.

A career-oriented woman who anticipates working the same number of years as Daniel will find it equally profitable to invest in a college education, assuming she faces similar costs and has the opportunity to reap the same returns. However, a woman who expects to spend fewer years in the labor market will find her benefits correspondingly reduced.

For example, suppose Adele plans to be in the labor force for a time — 6 years — after college and then to drop out for 10 years, say, for childrearing. If she, like Daniel, expects to retire at age 65, her expected work life is 33 years in comparison to his 43 years. Her shorter work life reduces the benefits of her human capital investment because she does not earn income during the time she spends out of the labor force. Further, it is generally believed that skills depreciate during time spent out of the labor force when they are not used. It is thus expected that, upon her return to the labor force after an interruption of 10 years, Adele's earnings of e_2 will be less in real terms than she was making when she left (e_1) and that she will be faced with profile GH rather than profile CD. We show profile GH as approaching CD over time, as

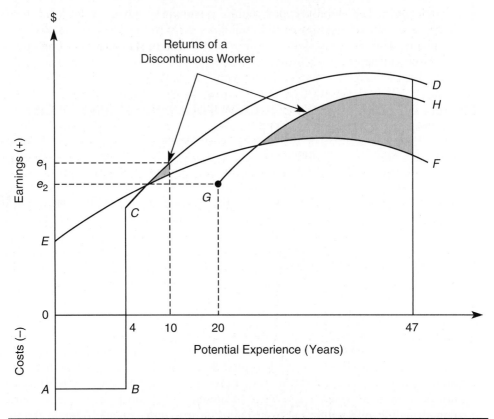

FIGURE 6-3 The Impact of Expected Work Life on the Education Investment Decision

Adele retools or becomes less rusty.[14] Nonetheless, the time out of the labor force costs her a reduction in earnings over the remainder of her working life. In this example, the benefits of the investment in a college education, the sum of the two shaded areas, may not be large enough to make it worthwhile.

A complication that we did not show in Figure 6-3 is that a break in experience would also affect *EF,* the high school earnings profile. Specifically, a portion of the *EF* line would be shifted down to represent Adele's options after she returns from her work-force interruption. However, taking this consideration into account is unlikely to affect our conclusion that a workforce interruption reduces the returns to investing in a college education because a major factor reducing the returns to the investment in college is simply the interruption itself and the loss of returns for that period. In addition, because the skills of high school graduates are less than those of college graduates, the loss due to depreciation is likely to also be less for them. Thus, we omitted this shift in *EF* from Figure 6-3 to keep our diagram as simple as possible while still capturing the major points.

---

[14]For evidence that earnings tend to "rebound" after workforce interruptions, see Jacob Mincer and Haim Ofek, "Interrupted Work Careers: Depreciation and Restoration of Human Capital," *Journal of Human Resources* 17, no. 1 (Winter 1982): 3–24; and Joyce P. Jacobsen and Laurence M. Levin, "Effects of Intermittent Labor Force Attachment on Women's Earnings," *Monthly Labor Review* 118, no. 9 (September 1995): 14–19.

One factor that might somewhat offset the conclusions we arrived at from considering Figure 6-3 is that education may increase productivity in some nonmarket activities as well as in market work. For example, the time that more highly educated parents spend with their children may have a larger positive effect on their offspring's cognitive ability than the time of less well educated parents. Were we to factor in these potential benefits in the home, the loss of returns due to labor force withdrawals would be reduced. However, it is unlikely that our conclusion would be altered: Higher anticipated time spent out of the labor force is likely to lower the amount of educational investments that the individual finds profitable.

Thus, the human capital model shows how an adherence to traditional gender roles in the family can explain why women traditionally were less likely than men to pursue college and graduate study. It also suggests one reason for the decline in gender differences in college attendance. As we saw in Chapter 4, women have increased their labor force participation substantially. As young women anticipate longer and more continuous working lives, it will be profitable for them to increase their investment in formal education. Furthermore, Figure 6-3 suggests that once women decide to acquire higher education, for whatever reason, their attachment to the labor force is reinforced because the opportunity cost of time spent out of the labor force is increased.

Although our application of the human capital model suggests a plausible explanation for the historical tendency of men to be more likely to pursue college and graduate study, it does not explain why in the past women were considerably *more* likely than men to complete high school. For example, in 1900, only two-thirds as many boys as girls graduated from high school. A likely explanation for this difference is that the opportunity cost of remaining in high school was lower for young women than for young men, because their potential labor market earnings were less. As job opportunities for young men who have not finished high school have declined, so too has the gender differential in high school completion.

The human capital model also suggests that discontinuity of expected labor force participation may help to explain gender differences in fields of specialization. In some fields, such as science and engineering, technological change progresses rapidly. A woman returning from a labor force interruption will not only have to contend with her depreciation of skills over the interim but also with the advancement of the field during her absence. On the other hand, in such fields as teaching history or English, the pace of change is slower. A woman returning from a workforce interruption is likely to find that her earnings fall less steeply. Women anticipating traditional gender roles are, therefore, expected to avoid fields where the rate of technological change is rapid and to concentrate in fields where the cost of workforce interruptions is lower.[15] Thus, women's increasing labor force attachment may partially explain their increased representation in traditionally male fields of study.

Some studies cite gender differences in mathematical ability, as indicated, for example, by differences between young men and women in scores on standardized tests such as the SAT, as a factor in the gender differences in majors.[16] Although the gender

---

[15]Solomon W. Polachek, "Sex Differences in College Major," *Industrial and Labor Relations Review* 31, no. 4 (July 1978): 498–508; Arthur F. Blakemore and Stuart A. Low, "Sex Differences in Occupational Selection: The Case of College Majors," *Review of Economics and Statistics* 66, no. 1 (February 1984): 157–63; and Daniel E. Hecker, "Earnings of College Graduates, 1993," *Monthly Labor Review* 118, no. 12 (Dec. 1995): 3–17. Another issue is that some fields more easily accommodate part-time work, thus facilitating reentry.
[16]Morton Paglin and Anthony M. Rufolo, "Heterogeneous Human Capital, Occupational Choice, and Male–Female Earnings Differences," *Journal of Labor Economics* 8, no. 1, pt. 1 (January 1990): 123–44.

gap in math scores remains substantial, it has declined as the high school course work of young men and women has grown more similar. In 1977 when the gender difference in SAT math scores was at its highest level in recent years, girls' scores lagged 46 points below boys' scores, on average. By the mid-1990s, the difference was 35 points and remained at about that level through 2003. The SAT verbal scores of boys also exceed those of girls, though these differences (9 points as of 2003) are much smaller and also declined through the mid-1990s.[17]

Whatever their source, gender differences in college major are strongly related to the gender wage gap among college graduates. One study found that they accounted for 40 to 45 percent of the overall male-female wage differential among this group in the mid-1980s, with about one-third to one-half of this effect due to job characteristics, that is, to the occupational and industrial differences associated with the gender differences in major.[18] Another study found that the growing similarity in college majors between men and women contributed to a narrowing of the gender wage gap over the 1980s.[19]

GENDER DIFFERENCES IN EDUCATIONAL INVESTMENT DECISIONS: OTHER FACTORS

Although expected working life is a factor that has been particularly emphasized by human capital theorists, societal discrimination may also cause gender differences in educational attainment and field of specialization. To see this, we must consider the nonpecuniary as well as the pecuniary costs and benefits of human capital investments. Societal influences may raise the costs of, or lower the returns to, specific types of education for women relative to men. Given these higher costs or lower returns, the investment in education may not prove profitable for many women. This situation is particularly apt to arise in traditionally male-dominated fields.

It is also important to bear in mind that social pressures may help to cause the gender differences in labor force participation patterns, which are identified as being the primary cause of gender differences in educational investment decisions in the human capital model. In addition, women's lower labor force participation may to some extent be due to the discrimination they face in the labor market, which reduces their opportunities and lowers their earnings. Such feedback effects of labor market discrimination are considered in greater detail in Chapter 7.

Socialization

Socialization is the name given to the process by which the influence of family, friends, teachers, and the media shapes an individual's attitudes and behavior.[20]

---

[17]See "College Board Reports Continuing Upward Trend in Average Scores on SAT 1" Press Release, College Board, August 22, 1996; and the College Board Web site at www.collegeboard.org. There was virtually no difference in the mean ACT scores of young men (21) and women (20.8) in 2003. The ACT score represents a combined assessment of English, math, reading, and science reasoning; see the ACT web site at www.act.org.
[18]Brown and Corcoran, "Sex-Based Differences." Gender differences in high school courses, however, were found to have little effect on the wage gap.
[19]Eric Eide, "College Major Choice and Changes in the Gender Wage Gap," *Contemporary Economic Policy* 12, no. 2 (April 1994): 55–64.
[20]See, for example, Cynthia Fuchs Epstein, *Deceptive Distinctions: Sex, Gender, and the Social Order* (New Haven, CT: Yale University Press, 1988); and Margaret M. Marini and Mary C. Brinton, "Sex Stereotyping in Occupational Socialization," in *Sex Segregation in the Work Place: Trends, Explanations, and Remedies,* edited by Barbara Reskin (Washington, DC: National Academy Press, 1984), pp. 192–232.

A later inset points out how even something as seemingly innocuous as children's games can reinforce stereotypical views of appropriate gender roles. As another example, studies show that male characters traditionally dominated children's television programming.[21] Also, even though the 2000s brought TV and film heroines who were strong, athletic, and powerful in shows such as *Buffy the Vampire Slayer* and films such as *Charlie's Angels* and *Kill Bill,* conventional beauty and scanty dress generally remain part of the equation. In general, both television and films contain more male than female characters. Moreover, female characters tend to be younger and are more often portrayed in domestic roles, while male characters are more likely to be defined by their workforce occupations, and more often are corporate heads or political leaders.[22]

The socialization process influences the self-esteem of men and women, as well as their perceptions of gender-appropriate competencies and behavior. It also helps to shape the role they expect work to occupy in their lives and the types of jobs to which they aspire. We have already seen how gender differences in the expected importance of market work in their lives may influence men's and women's human capital investment decisions. The consequences of gender differences in occupational orientation are also important. To a great extent in the past, and even today, boys and girls are taught from an early age to aspire to and train for gender-appropriate lines of work. These messages tend to result in gender differences in fields of specialization. Further, even if, despite these influences, a young woman shows an interest in entering a traditionally male field, the disapproval of her family, teachers, or friends represents a nonpecuniary cost that lowers her subjective evaluation of the net value of this investment.[23] Familial attitudes may also pose practical problems for a young woman if her family is more reluctant to finance her education than her brother's.[24] It is likely that these types of problems diminished with the growing social acceptance of women's employment outside the home and their participation in what were formerly viewed as male occupations, but it is unlikely that such gender differences have disappeared entirely.

Children's Toys: The Selling of Stereotypes

Children's toys expose both boys and girls to gender stereotypes from an early age,* whether as a result of their parents' selection of toys for them; what they see when they go to toy stores, look through catalogs, or watch television; or the kinds of toys that they see at the homes of friends and relatives.

---

[21]Bill Carter, "Children's TV, Where Boys Are King," *New York Times,* May 1, 1991, pp. 1, B6.

[22]For information on television, see, Felicia R. Lee, "Networking on TV: A Feminine Touch," *New York Times,* November 29, 2003, sec. B, pp. 9, 11; for information on film, see the report of Martha M. Lauzen, Ph.D., School of Communication, San Diego State University "The Celluloid Ceiling: Behind-the-Scenes and On-Screen Employment of Women in the Top 250 Films of 2002, Executive Summary," posted at www.moviesbywomen.com.

[23]One study found that women graduate students in the biological and physical sciences received less moral support from their mothers than either the male students in the same field or students of either sex in education. See Helen M. Berg and Marianne A. Ferber, "Men and Women Graduate Students: Who Succeeds and Why?" *Journal of Higher Education* 54, no. 6 (November–December 1983): 629–48.

[24]Some evidence indicates that sibling sex composition affects women's but not men's educational attainment. Controlling for household size, women with any sisters show lower educational attainment than women raised only with brothers; see Kristin Butcher and Anne Case, "The Effect of Sibling Sex Composition on Women's Education and Earnings," *Quarterly Journal of Economics* 109, no. 3 (August 1994): 531–65. The authors suggest that their finding is consistent with a "reference group" model in which the presence of a sister affects either parents' educational goals for their daughters or the skills that the young woman develops.

For girls, toy stores, of course, offer ubiquitous dolls: babies they can take care of, children they can dress up, and glamorous young women they can try to emulate, and, of course, Barbie, the most popular doll ever. Even though Barbie is now available with wardrobes and accessories for various careers, she still has a body that few girls will ever have; to be exact, only 1 young woman out of 100,000 will have such a shape. Ken's proportions, though also rare in the general population, are more realistic; 1 in 50 young men will have his shape.**

When it comes to dress-up for occasions such as Halloween, toy store aisles and catalogs are still replete with ballerina and princess costumes, but now costumes are also available for girls wanting to be superheroes. This available variety might suggest progress toward gender equity except that they tend to be highly form-fitting feminine outfits, a stark contrast to the macho black ninja costumes marketed for boys. Other toys intended for girls include kitchen accessories and makeup. Most recently, a number of specialty stores are marketing parties for little girls where they and their friends can dress up as princesses for the afternoon or have a "fantasy makeover."†

The message that comes through loud and clear is that girls want to be pretty, and that they are interested in having boyfriends, even at an early age. They also want to prepare themselves for a life in which being a good mother and competent household manager is primary. The few toys that show a connection to careers come in a poor second. Video games, cartoons, and movies assign girls the same role. As just one example, *Powerpuff Girls* on the Cartoon Network has Bubbles, Blossom, and Buttercup who are "cute little preschoolers with big eyes and a tendency to play house."†† Finally, of course, *the* girl toy colors—pink and light purple—are strictly off limits to boys.

Enter a "boy aisle" in the toy store and you will be barraged by light sabers, swords, and the TV and movie action figures that go with them. Traditional superheroes Batman, Superman, and Spiderman are joined by Teenage Mutant Ninja Turtles, Power Rangers, Yugioh characters, and others. Watch a cartoon or movie directed at boys and you will see plenty of violence as good battles evil. These characters are far from the nurturing role models given girls. Moreover, it remains far less socially acceptable for boys to cross the gender barrier in stores and choose a Barbie than it is for a girl to choose a Batman figure.

It is unlikely that sex-stereotyping of toys will abate anytime soon. Toys R Us, for instance, has girl and boy zones in their stores, with dolls, homemaking toys, and makeup at one end, and superhero action figures, trucks, train sets, and Lego building kits at the other. There are those who argue that merchants are merely responding to children's preferences, that placing toys for girls and boys in distinct areas is more convenient for shoppers, and that playing with these toys does no real harm to boys and girls. Also, some gender-neutral toys and games such as Monopoly and roller blades are quite popular with children of both sexes. Nonetheless, separate toy aisles for girls and boys help to perpetuate traditional gender roles by limiting children's visions of who they can be and what they should do at an early age.

* This inset draws on Crispin Sartwell, "The Gender Gap Remains—For Boys," *Baltimore Sun*, May 28, 2000; Megan Rosenfeld, "Games Girls Play: A Toy Chest Full of Stereotypes," *Washington Post*, December 22, 1995, p. A1; and C. Estelle Campenni, "Gender Stereotyping of Children's Toys: A Comparison of Parents and Nonparents," *Sex Roles: A Journal of Research* 40, no. 1 (January 1999): 121–39.
** Kevin I. Norton, Timothy S. Olds, Scott Olive, and Stephen Dank, "Ken and Barbie at Life Size," *Sex Roles: A Journal of Research* 34, no. 3–4 (February 1996): 287–94.
† Gary Strauss, "Princesses Rule the Hearts of Little Girls," *USA Today,* March 2, 2004, p. 1D.
†† Sartwell, "The Gender Gap Remains."

Gender-Appropriate Traits and Competencies

Another way in which social influences may operate to affect women's labor market outcomes is that women may be socialized to emphasize appropriate "feminine" personality traits, such as being subordinate, nurturing, and emotional. Traditionally male fields may be stereotyped as requiring "masculine" personality traits such as dominance, competitiveness, and rationality.[25] Having internalized the idea of what is properly female, women may then avoid male fields because they perceive a nonpecuniary cost in acting in an "unfeminine" manner or because they feel unequipped to do so. In the latter case, they might expect to be less successful in the field, thus lowering their anticipated returns. Similarly, if women are reared to believe they lack competence in "masculine" subjects like math and science, this belief would raise their perceived costs and lower their perceived returns to entry into fields emphasizing this knowledge. Men may see traditionally female fields as inappropriate for similar reasons. As suggested in the following inset, stereotypes may adversely affect the performance of women, further compounding their negative effects.

Women, Math, and Stereotype Threat

Recent research by psychologists Diane M. Quinn, Steven J. Spencer, and Claude M. Steele suggests that cultural stereotypes, such as the belief that girls and women have better verbal skills while boys and men are better at mathematics and science, may negatively affect girls' performance on math exams. Quinn explains how such "stereotype threat" situations can adversely affect girl's test performance and summarizes some of their findings:

> In the case of gender and math, imagine a boy and girl sitting down to take the SAT for the first time. They have equivalent math experience. Taking the SAT is a tense, sometimes frustrating experience for both of them.

[25] As one interesting new example, it has been found that men's and women's propensities to negotiate differ—with women being much less likely to do so. In *Women Don't Ask: Negotiation and the Gender Divide* (Princeton: Princeton University Press, 2003), Linda Babcock and Sara Laschever document these differences, which they attribute to a variety of social factors, present evidence that they are costly to women, and provide guidance on developing and exercising negotiating skills.

However, as the girl is taking the test she has an extra worry to contend with that the boy does not: A stereotype that she, as a girl, has inferior math skills. As she experiences frustration and difficulty with the problems, she has the burden of knowing that her difficulty could be judged as proof of the veracity of the stereotype. The boy has none of these doubts or thoughts to interrupt his performance. It is important to note that in this situation neither the girl nor the boy have to believe that the stereotype is true. . . . Just the knowledge of the stereotype itself is enough to affect performance in the situation. How do we know this occurs?

My colleagues and I have tested the stereotype threat hypothesis in a series of studies. . . . In all of our experiments we bring university men and women matched for equivalent math backgrounds and interest into the laboratory. In the first of these studies we simply gave participants an easy or difficult math test. We found that women only performed worse than men on the difficult math test. To demonstrate that it was the threat of the stereotype that caused this underperformance, we gave a second group of men and women the same difficult math test. In order to make stereotypes about math explicit, half of the participants were told that the test had shown gender differences in the past. In order to eliminate a stereotype based interpretation of the situation, the other half of the participants were told that the test had been shown to be gender fair—that men and women performed equally on this test. In line with our predictions, when the stereotype was not applicable to the situation, when men and women were simply told that they were taking a gender fair test, men and women performed equally on the test. When told that the exact same test had shown gender differences in the past, women scored lower on the test than men. Just a simple change in the situation—a different line in the instructions—changed an outcome that many believed intractable. . . . We have also conducted studies where we have a condition in which we do not mention gender at all—we simply describe the math test as a standardized test. In this situation, women also score lower on the test than men, suggesting that standardized mathematical testing situations are implicitly stereotype threat situations. . . .

When we look at what women and men are actually doing when working on the difficult test, we found that women and men primarily used the same strategies to solve the problems, however, women in stereotype threat situations were less likely to think of any way to solve a problem. That is, women were more likely to "blank out" or "choke" on a problem when they were in a stereotype threat condition. Thus research results so far point to the following scenario: When women with a strong interest and identification with math are in a situation in which their math skills could be negatively judged, their performance is undermined by the cognitive activation of gender stereotypes combined with some feelings of stress or anxiety. Women are not alone in being affected by negative stereotypes. Research on stereotype threat has demonstrated its effect on

African–Americans and Latinos in intellectual situations, on the elderly in memory testing situations and even on White men in sports situations.*

Quinn also offers some suggestions to reduce stereotype threat and level the playing field for all students. For instance, stereotype threat is likely to be reduced in situations in which women (or minorities) are reassured that everyone struggles with difficult concepts, and are assured that the exam is fair. Even small measures, such as these, may make a real difference.

*Reprinted from Diane M. Quinn, "Women, Math, and Stereotype Threat," *Newsletter of the American Economic Association Committee on the Status of Women in the Economics Profession* (Winter 2004), pp. 10–11, available at www.cswep.org. Reprinted by permission of the author. See also, Diane M. Quinn and Steven Spencer, "The Interference of Stereotype Threat on Women's Generation of Mathematical Problem-Solving Strategies," *Journal of Social Issues* 57, no.1 (Spring 2001): 55–71; and Steven J. Spencer, Claude M. Steele, and Diane M. Quinn, "Stereotype Threat and Women's Math Performance" *Journal of Experimental Social Psychology* 35, no. 1 (1999): 4–28.

Biased Evaluations

Even women's possession of "male" traits or competencies and their willingness to display them may not guarantee them equal success. Studies find that, among both female and male college students, identical papers were given higher ratings on such dimensions as value, persuasiveness, profundity, writing style, and competence when respondents believed the author to be male rather than female. Similar findings were obtained in studies requiring both women and men to evaluate the qualifications of applicants for employment.[26] The expectation of inferior performance may eventually cause that inferior performance. Even if it does not, it would lower the expected return to investments in educational credentials.

Discrimination by Educational Institutions

Discrimination against women in the course of their studies, particularly in traditionally male fields, may increase the nonpecuniary costs of obtaining education or lower the returns to their investment. It is well to remember that overt discrimination against women in admission to college and professional school was pervasive in the not-too-distant past. American women were not admitted to higher education until 1837 when Oberlin College opened its doors.[27] Women did not gain entrance to medical school until 1847, and it was not until 1915 that the American Medical Association accepted women members. As late as 1869, the U.S. Supreme Court upheld the refusal of the Illinois State Bar to admit a woman. One of the justices declared that "the natural and proper timidity and delicacy which belongs to the female sex evidently unfit it

---

[26]See the studies reviewed in Virginia Valian, *Why So Slow? The Advancement of Women* (Cambridge, MA: MIT Press, 1998), chap. 7, pp. 125–44. See also, R.E. Steinpreis, K.A. Anders, and D. Ritzke, "The Impact of Gender on the Review of the Curricula Vitae of Job Applicants and Tenure Candidates: A National Empirical Study," *Sex Roles* 41, no. 7–8 (October 1999): 509–28.

[27]Mount Holyoke College was another pioneer in higher education for women. The information on admissions of women is from Michelle Patterson and Laurie Engleberg, "Women in Male-Dominated Professions," in *Women Working: Theories and Facts in Perspective,* edited by Ann H. Stromberg and Shirley Harkess (Mountain View, CA: Mayfield, 1978), pp. 266–92.

for many of the occupations of civil life."[28] Nonetheless, a year later, in 1870, the first woman did succeed in graduating from an American law school.

Even after these "firsts," women were not universally admitted to all institutions of higher education in all fields for a long time. The prestigious Harvard Medical School did not admit women until 1945, while Harvard Law School excluded women until 1950. Similarly, many highly respected undergraduate institutions, like Princeton and Yale, remained male only until the late 1960s or early 1970s. Others, like Harvard, granted women access to classes and some facilities but officially restricted them to a separate college.

Moreover, the opening of doors to women did not necessarily mean that the doors opened as widely for them as for men. Women continued in many cases to be discriminated against in admissions and financial aid policies long after they gained formal admittance. In some cases, women were held to higher standards than men; in others, overt or informal quotas limited the number of places available to them.[29] Often course requirements for male and female high school students were different, and, at all levels, gender-based counseling was prevalent.

Subtle Barriers

Although most of these overt barriers are gone, it is important to bear in mind that they did place serious limits on the educational options of older women. Thus, their impact continues to be reflected in the *current* occupational distribution of women. Further, subtle barriers to women's success in the study of traditionally male fields remain a problem. In Chapter 7, we shall consider how these subtle barriers also block women's upward progression in the workplace.

The male dominance of a field can itself discourage young women from attempting to enter. In this way, past discrimination continues to have an impact on younger women. Lacking contact with or firsthand knowledge of successful women, they may assume (quite possibly erroneously) that they too would be unable to succeed. Even if they believe that times have changed and that their prospects for success are greater than indicated by the present low representation of women, the scarcity of women may still pose problems for them, limiting their eventual success and lowering the returns to entering predominantly male fields. For example, without older women to serve as **role models**, female entrants lack adequate information about acceptable (or successful) modes of behavior and dress. They also lack access to the knowledge acquired by older women about successful strategies for combining work roles and family responsibilities. Thus, they are forced to be pioneers, and blazing a new trail is undoubtedly more difficult than following along a well-established path.

Women students may also be excluded from the informal relationships desirable for eventual career success. Older individuals who are well established in the field (mentors) often take promising young students (protégés) under their wing—informally socializing them into the norms of the field, giving them access to the latest research in the area, and tying them into their network of professional contacts.

---

[28]Cited in Patterson and Engleberg, "Women in Male-Dominated Professions," p. 277.
[29]See, for example, Ann Sutherland Harris, "The Second Sex in Academe," *AAUP Bulletin* 56, no. 3 (Fall 1970): 283–95; and Mary Frank Fox, "Women and Higher Education: Gender Differences in the Status of Students and Scholars," in *Women: A Feminist Perspective,* 3rd ed., edited by Jo Freeman (Palo Alto, CA: Mayfield, 1984), pp. 217–35.

The **mentor-protégé system** is generally the result of the older individual identifying with the younger person. Male mentors may simply not identify with young women. Or they may fear that the development of a close relationship with a young woman would be misunderstood by their colleagues or their wives. Thus, women students are likely to be at a disadvantage in predominantly male fields. Their problems will be aggravated if male students neglect to include them in their **informal network**. Such informal contacts among students include study groups and discussions over lunches, sports, coffee breaks, or a Friday afternoon beer, where important information about coursework, the field, and career opportunities may be exchanged.

Thus, women often lack the support, encouragement, and access to information and job opportunities provided by informal contacts between teachers and students and among students, as well as female role models to emulate. The absence of these elements raises the nonpecuniary costs to them in comparison to otherwise similar male students, lowering their incentives to enter traditionally male fields. It may also result in their being less successful than comparable men when they complete their studies. To the extent that they foresee this, their entry into predominantly male fields is further discouraged.

Although it is widely believed that a lack of female role models and mentors is a significant problem for women students, quantitative evidence is difficult to gather. One approach uses self-reports and perceptions of young women, often, although not always, finding evidence that female role models and mentors are important.[30] Other studies use a different approach, examining the impact of the presence of women faculty on indicators of performance or choices of female students. One study finds that the percentage of female faculty at their undergraduate college or university is positively related to the probability that female students attain an advanced degree.[31] Another reports that the race, gender, and ethnicity match between high school students and their teachers does not appear to affect how much students learn, but it does sometimes positively affect the teacher's subjective evaluation of the students, suggesting, for example, that same-sex teachers might better serve as mentors.[32] On the other hand, for a sample of three schools, no evidence was found that an increase in the proportion of female college or university faculty in a department was associated with an increase in the proportion of majors that were women.[33]

Finally, labor market discrimination itself can adversely affect the incentives of women to invest in formal schooling insofar as it results in a lower return on their investment. Some studies find that female college seniors expect lower earnings than their male counterparts, even after controlling for any differences in future work expectations.[34] We consider the possibility of discrimination in greater detail in the next chapter.

---

[30]See, for example, Berg and Ferber, "Men and Women Graduate Students"; and Nancy E. Betz and Louise F. Fitzgerald, *The Career Psychology of Women* (Orlando, FL: Academic Press, 1987) and the references therein.

[31]Donna S. Rothstein, "Do Female Faculty Influence Female Students' Educational and Labor Market Attainments?" *Industrial and Labor Relations Review* 48, no. 3 (April 1995): 515–30.

[32]Ronald G. Ehrenberg, Daniel D. Goldhaber, and Dominic J. Brewer, "Do Teachers' Race, Gender, and Ethnicity Matter? Evidence from NELS," *Industrial and Labor Relations Review* 48, no. 3 (April 1995): 547–61.

[33]Brandice Canes and Harvey Rosen, "Following in Her Footsteps? Women's Choices of College Majors and Faculty Gender Composition," *Industrial and Labor Relations Review* 48, no. 3 (April 1995): 486–504.

[34]Jerry A. Jacobs, "Gender and the Earnings Expectations of College Seniors," Working Paper, University of Pennsylvania (April 2000); and Francine D. Blau and Marianne A. Ferber, "Career Plans and Expectations of Young Men and Women," *Journal of Human Resources* 26, no. 4 (Fall 1991): 581–607.

POLICY ISSUE: THE ROLE OF GOVERNMENT IN COMBATING DISCRIMINATION IN EDUCATIONAL INSTITUTIONS

To remedy discrimination in educational institutions, in 1972 Congress passed Title IX of the Educational Amendments (to the Civil Rights Act of 1964). It prohibits discrimination on the basis of sex in any educational program or activity receiving federal financial assistance and covers admissions, financial aid, and access to programs and activities, as well as employment of teachers and other personnel.

The main provisions relevant at the high school level are that all courses and programs, except sex instruction, chorus, and contact sports, must be available to both males and females. At the university level, the most important provisions are for nondiscrimination in admissions and in faculty hiring, and for equal availability of scholarships and fellowships, assistantships, research opportunities, and housing. Private, single-sex undergraduate schools are exempt from the nondiscrimination in admission requirements; however, once any women (or men) are admitted, no discrimination in admissions is permitted. Even though enforcement has not always been rigorous, it is likely that this legislation contributed to the substantial changes in the extent and type of participation of women in the educational system.

Title IX has had a particularly dramatic impact on high school and collegiate athletics. Since its passage, support and facilities for women athletes greatly increased, as did women's participation in athletic programs.[35] When the legislation was enacted in 1972, 50 percent of American boys participated in school sports compared to only 4 percent of girls. By the mid-1990s, one-third of girls participated in sports, and almost one-half of college varsity players were female.[36] The transformation in women's athletics is especially highlighted in the Olympics. In the 1976 Olympics, the first Olympic games after the passage of Title IX, only one out of seven athletes representing the United States was female. By the 2004 games, more than 48 percent of the athletes competing for the United States were women.[37]

Some research suggests that athletics has a positive effect on girls who participate. Girls do better academically and are less likely to drop out of school, take drugs, or become pregnant, although it is unclear to what extent these results might be due to a self-selection of more successful girls into athletics. Leading female athletes can also serve as role models for young women, just as male athletes have long served as role models for young men.

A controversial issue that has arisen regarding educational institutions is the desirability and legality of single-sex education. Some claim that, due to classroom issues,

---

[35]Title IX has not been without controversy. In some cases, for example, institutions cut men's sports (rather than expanding women's athletic opportunities). Nonetheless, in 2003, the Department of Education reviewed the rules of Title IX and reaffirmed them.

[36]For evidence on the remaining disparities, see Welch Suggs, "Uneven Progress for Women's Sports: A *Chronicle* Survey Finds Gains at Big-Time Football Powers, Struggles at the 'Have-Nots'," *Chronicle of Higher Education,* April 7, 2000, pp. A52–A57. Ironically, the expansion in women's collegiate sports has been accompanied by a decline in the proportion of women's teams coached by women; see Mireya Navarro, "Women in Sports Cultivating New Playing Fields," *New York Times*, February 13, 2001, at www.nytimes.com.

[37]The proportion of women on the 2004 Olympic team is from "From A (Athens) to Z (Zeus)," *The San Diego Union-Tribune*, August 13, 2004, at www.signonsandiego.com. See also Frank Deford, "The Women of Atlanta," *Newsweek,* June 10, 1996, pp. 62–83; and Amy Shipley, "Female Athletes Continue to Gain Ground," *The Washington Post,* April 22, 2004.

such as the tendency for males to dominate class discussion, women may benefit from single-sex schooling. Similar arguments favor predominantly black institutions. At the same time, two elite, state-financed, all-male military schools claimed that the benefits of their educational experience depended on an all-male environment.

From a legal perspective, different issues are raised depending on whether the educational institution involved is publicly funded. Single-sex, privately funded institutions are exempt from Title IX's admission requirements. However, constitutional issues come into play in single-sex, publicly funded schools. In 1996, the United States Supreme Court found that the exclusion of qualified women from the Virginia Military Institute (V.M.I.), a state-run, all-male military school, was not permissible. This case is important, and the reasoning behind it is particularly instructive. Writing for the majority, Justice Ruth Bader Ginsburg explained that the state must demonstrate an "exceedingly persuasive justification" for any official action that treats men and women differently. "The justification must be genuine, not hypothesized or invented *post hoc* in response to litigation. . . . And it must not rely on overbroad generalizations about the different talents, capacities, or preferences of males and females." This decision resulted in the admission of women into V.M.I. and a similar institution, the Citadel in South Carolina, which was not explicitly involved in the case.[38]

Private schools were unaffected by the Supreme Court decision. As of the mid-1990s, only three all-male private colleges operated in the United States, with a total enrollment of fewer than 5,000 students. Interestingly, all-female private colleges were much more prevalent; the 84 in operation included enrollment of 120,000 students. Profiting from the view that women's schools can benefit and motivate female students, and the high-profile success of some of their graduates, enrollments at women's schools rose over the 1990s.[39] However, controversy still surrounds the issue of single-sex public schools at the elementary and high school level. Despite concerns by some critics that single-sex schools are in violation of Title IX, the Bush administration supported giving public school districts freedom to create same-sex classes and schools as long as "substantially equal" opportunities are provided for the excluded sex. The National Association for Single Sex Public Education (NASSPE) reports that for the 2004–2005 school year at least 143 public schools planned to offer gender-separate educational opportunities, with 36 of these being entirely single-sex institutions; this increase is substantial from only 8 years previously when four public schools offered single-sex educational opportunities.[40]

EXPLAINING WOMEN'S RISING EDUCATIONAL ATTAINMENT

Whatever the past barriers to women's access to higher education or the remaining gender differences in fields of study and in the acquisition of first professional and Ph.D. degrees, the increase in women's representation in college and postgraduate

---

[38]Linda Greenhouse, "Military College Can't Bar Women, High Court Rules," *New York Times,* 27 June 1996, pp. A1, B8.

[39]Mike Allen, "Separatism Is In, Except for White Men," *New York Times,* Sunday, June 30, 1996, p. E5. For some evidence on the effects of single-sex female schools, see Sara J. Solnick, "Changes in Women's Majors from Entrance to Graduation at Women's and Coeducational Colleges," *Industrial and Labor Relations Review* 48, no. 3 (April 1995): 505–14.

[40]See, "Single-Sex Public Schools in the United States," at www.singlesexschools.org, accessed January 11, 2005; and Diana Jean Schemo, "Administration Proposes Same-Sex-School Option," *New York Times,* March 4, 2004, p. A16.

study that we documented earlier is truly remarkable. How do we explain this change that began in earnest in the 1970s? As we noted previously, the human capital model provides one explanation. As women anticipated spending longer periods in the labor market, the return on their investment in higher education increased and with it their motivation to secure higher levels of education and more market-oriented education as well. Rising labor market opportunities for women, resulting in part from the passage of antidiscrimination legislation, which we discuss in Chapter 7, undoubtedly also played a role. Shifting social attitudes toward women's work roles and their capabilities likely played a part too. Finally, passage and enforcement of Title IX which specifically banned discrimination in educational institutions, led to changes in the admission practices of educational institutions facilitating and reinforcing the impact of these other developments.

A recent study by Claudia Goldin and Lawrence F. Katz points to an additional factor that may have importantly influenced women's educational decisions and most particularly their increasing participation in professional programs: the development of oral contraception, otherwise known as "the pill," and especially its growing availability to young, unmarried women beginning in the late 1960s and early 1970s.[41] The availability of the pill was associated with and facilitated a delay in marriage and childbearing, which in turn enabled women to pursue professional training after college. The authors argue that the pill led to important *direct* and *indirect* effects on women's career investments. The direct effect of the pill was that it increased the reliability of contraception and the ease of using it, thereby enabling women to postpone marrying and starting a family and more confidently embark on a lengthy professional education.[42] The indirect effect of the pill was that, because it encouraged the delay of marriage for *all* young people (not just those acquiring professional training), a woman who postponed marriage to pursue professional studies would find a larger pool of eligible bachelors to choose from. Had this not occurred, a woman who put off marriage for professional studies would have faced a much smaller pool of potential mates and, given this smaller selection, would have had to settle for a lesser match if she wanted to marry. This would have raised the cost to women of professional study.[43]

ON-THE-JOB TRAINING

One of the major insights of human capital theory is the observation that individuals can increase their productivity not only through their investments in formal education but also by learning important work skills while they are on the job.[44] Sometimes workers participate in formal training programs sponsored by their employers. More often,

---

[41]Claudia Goldin and Lawrence F. Katz, "Career and Marriage in the Age of the Pill," *American Economic Review* 90, no. 2 (May 2000): 461–75.

[42]As the authors point out, in the absence of reliable contraception, a young woman entering a professional program was forced to choose abstinence or cope with considerable uncertainty regarding pregnancy.

[43]One puzzle regarding the trends in educational attainment is that not only did women become 50 percent of those receiving bachelor's degrees in 1981–1982, but their representation continued to increase steadily to 57.3 percent in 2000–2001. One study attributes this trend to gender differences in the trends in anticipated earnings dispersion; see Kerwin Kofi Charles and Ming-Ching Luoh, "Gender Differences in Completed Schooling," *Review of Economics and Statistics* 85, no. 3 (August 2003): 559–77.

[44]See, for example, Becker, *Human Capital;* Mincer, "On-the-Job Training"; and Walter Oi, "Labor as a Quasi-Fixed Factor," *Journal of Political Economy* 70, no. 6 (December 1962): 538–55.

they benefit from informal instruction by their supervisors or coworkers and grow proficient at their jobs through repetition and trial and error. Human capital theory suggests that the weaker attachment to the labor force of women who follow traditional gender roles means that they will acquire less of this valuable on-the-job training. As will be discussed in Chapter 7, women may also be denied equal access to this type of training due to employer discrimination.

GENDER DIFFERENCES IN LABOR MARKET EXPERIENCE

Before developing these ideas further, let us look at the actual extent of gender differences in work experience. Unfortunately, this information is not collected by government agencies on a regular basis but must be pieced together from various special surveys. The available data indicate that, on average, women in the labor market have less work experience than men, but that gender differences have narrowed considerably since 1980.

For example, employed women in all age groups increased their average labor market experience over the 1950–1980 period taken as a whole, with much of the gains occurring in the 1970s.[45] Despite an increase in average experience within most age groups over the 1970s, however, the *average* level of experience for all women workers fell slightly because of the large increases in labor force participation of younger women (discussed in Chapter 4). This shift resulted in a decrease in the average age of women workers. Even with women in each age group working more years than previously, because younger women have less experience than older women, this change in age mix resulted in a small decline in average experience for women as a whole.[46] Yet, it is precisely this pattern of growing labor force attachment of women during the childbearing years that would increase women's average experience in the long run. By the 1980s, overall female experience levels unambiguously began to rise relative to males'. Indeed, the gender gap in full-time experience decreased by more than 2 years (from 6.6 to 4.3 years) between 1979 and 1989, and declined nearly another year (to 3.5 years) by 1998.[47]

---

[45]James P. Smith and Michael P. Ward, "Women's Wages and Work in the Twentieth Century," RAND, R-3119-NICHD, 1984. These estimates are based on data on women's labor force participation and labor force turnover (entries and exits) rather than on direct information on actual work experience. However, direct data on experience, where available, suggest these estimates are reasonable. For complementary estimates that also include an earlier period, see Claudia Goldin, *Understanding the Gender Gap: An Economic History of American Women* (New York: Oxford University Press, 1990), chap. 2.

[46]Goldin, *Understanding the Gender Gap,* p. 41.

[47]Data are for full-time workers and are from Francine D. Blau and Lawrence M. Kahn, "The U.S. Gender Pay Gap in the 1990s: Slowing Convergence," National Bureau of Economic Research Working Paper No. 10853 (October 2004). A number of other studies also report rising experience levels for women; see, for example, Francine D. Blau and Lawrence M. Kahn, "Swimming Upstream: Trends in the Gender Wage Differential in the 1980s," *Journal of Labor Economics* 15, no. 1, pt. 1 (January 1997): 1–42; June O'Neill and Solomon W. Polachek, "Why the Gender Gap in Wages Narrowed in the 1980s," *Journal of Labor Economics* 11, no. 1, pt. 1 (January 1993): 205–28; and Alison J. Wellington, "Changes in the Male/Female Wage Gap, 1976–85," *Journal of Human Resources* 28, no. 2 (Spring 1993): 383–411. Another way to look at the experience gap is to cumulate it over the work life. For example, in a sample of men and women aged 51–61 in 1992, mean labor market experience at age 50 was 9.6 years less for women than for men; see Phillip B. Levine, Olivia S. Mitchell, and John W. Phillips, "Worklife Determinants of Retirement Income Differentials between Men and Women," in *Innovations in Financing Retirement*, edited by Z. Bodie, B. Hammond, and O. S. Mitchell (Philadelphia, PA: University of Pennsylvania Press, 2002), pp. 50–76. Of course, the lifetime gap would be expected to be smaller for later cohorts of women who were more consistently attached to the labor force.

Another dimension of labor market experience is tenure, time spent with a specific firm. Recent evidence also shows a decline in the gender difference in tenure. So, for example, between 1966 and 2002, the gender gap in tenure decreased by almost 2 years (from 2.4 to .5 years).[48]

To summarize, the view that women have, on average, less work experience than men is borne out by the evidence. However, the differences between men and women in the extent of involvement in paid employment have narrowed considerably since 1980. We examine next how, according to the human capital model, gender differences in labor force attachment and experience could lower women's pay and cause differences in occupational choices between men and women.

THE ON-THE-JOB TRAINING INVESTMENT DECISION

We begin with a general analysis of the training investment decision. On-the-job training may be divided into two types:

- General training
- Firm-specific training

General training increases the individual's productivity to the same extent in all (or a large number of) firms. For example, an individual may learn to operate an office machine that is widely used by many firms. On the other hand, **firm-specific** training, as its name implies, increases the individual's productivity only at the firm that provides the training. For example, one may learn how to get things done within a particular bureaucracy or deal with the idiosyncrasies of a particular piece of equipment. Most training probably combines elements of both general and firm-specific training. However, for simplicity we assume that training may be classified as being entirely general or entirely firm specific.

General Training

General training is, by definition, completely transferable from the firm providing the training to other firms. The employer would presumably not be willing to foot any part of the bill for such training because, in a competitive labor market, the employer has no way to collect any of the returns. After workers obtain training, employers must pay them what they are worth elsewhere, or they would simply leave the firm. Thus, if general training is to occur, the employee must be willing to bear all the costs, since he or she will reap all the returns. As in the case of formal education, an individual decides whether to invest in general training by comparing the costs and benefits.

Let us consider Lisa's investment decision, illustrated in Figure 6-4. She will contrast the experience-earnings profile she can expect if she takes a job with no training (UU') to the profile she can expect if she receives general training (GG'). On-the-job training, although often informal, still entails costs just as does formal schooling. Some of these costs may be direct. For example, in the cases with formal programs, expenses are incurred for instructors or for materials used in the training. Another portion of the

---

[48]See, U.S. Department of Labor, Bureau of Labor Statistics, "Job Tenure of Workers, January 1966," *Special Labor Force Report* No. 77 (1967); and U.S. Department of Labor, Bureau of Labor Statistics, "Employee Tenure in 2002 Summary," *News* (September 19, 2002).

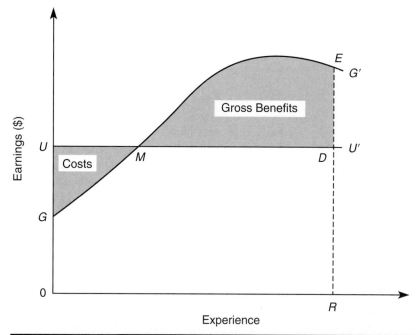

FIGURE 6-4   The On-the-Job Training Investment Decision: General Training

costs is indirect, as the worker and his or her coworkers or supervisor transfer their attention from daily production to training activities. Such expenses arise even when, as is frequently the case, no formal program is in place. The resulting decline in output represents the opportunity cost to the firm of the training activity.

How does Lisa go about "paying" such costs if she decides to invest in general training? She does so by accepting a wage below what she could obtain elsewhere. This lower wage corresponds to her productivity (net of training costs) to the firm during the training period. The costs of the investment in general training are given by the area UGM. As Lisa becomes more skilled, her earnings catch up to and eventually surpass what she could earn without training. Assuming a total of OR years of labor market experience over her work life, her gross benefits will be equal to the area MED. As in the case of formal schooling, she is likely to undertake the investment if gross benefits exceed costs by a sufficient amount to yield the desired rate of return (as appears to be the case in Figure 6-4).

Firm-Specific Training

Figure 6-5 illustrates Don's decision of whether to invest in firm-specific training. His productivity on the job is shown by the profile GG'. It is also what his earnings profile would be in the case of general training. However, because firm-specific training is not transferable, Don will not be willing to bear all the costs of the training; his ability to reap the returns depends on continued employment at the firm that initially provided the training. If he were to lose his job, his investment would be wiped out. (The earnings profile available to him at another firm is UU'.) If Don paid for all his training, he would experience a strong incentive to remain with his employer, but his employer would have no particular reason to accord him any special protection from layoffs.

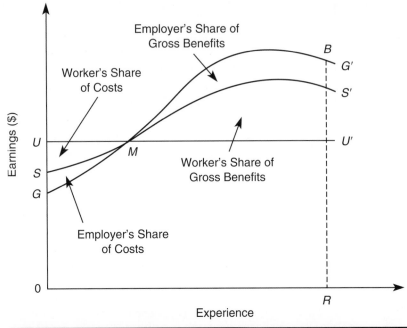

FIGURE 6-5   The On-the-Job Training Investment Decision: Firm-Specific
Training

Similarly, the employer is unwilling to shoulder all the costs of firm-specific training because if Don were to quit, the firm would lose its investment. If the employer were to pay all the costs and receive all the returns, Don's profile would be *UU'*. He would have no special incentive to remain with the firm because he would be earning no more than he could get elsewhere. A temporary shift in demand that resulted in higher wages in another industry or even just more favorable working conditions at another firm might be sufficient to lure him away.

The solution is for the worker and the employer to share the costs of, and returns to, firm-specific training. In this case the specifically trained worker's profile is *SS'*. The worker (Don) has an incentive to remain with the firm after completing training because he earns more there than he can get elsewhere (given by profile *UU'*). The firm also has an incentive to retain a worker who completed specific training, even in the face of, say, a dip in the demand for the firm's product. This incentive results because the specifically trained worker (Don in this case) is actually being paid less than his productivity—after point *M, SS'* lies below *GG'*.

Two important implications come from this analysis of firm-specific training. First, a relatively permanent attachment is likely to develop between the firm and the specifically trained worker. Such workers are less likely either to quit or to be laid off their jobs than untrained or generally trained workers. Second, because employers pay part of the costs of firm-specific training, they will be concerned about the expected employment stability of workers hired into jobs where such training is important. (We develop this point in greater detail later.)

As Figures 6-4 and 6-5 suggest, earnings will increase with experience for workers who invested in training. Considerable empirical evidence does indeed show a positive relationship between labor market experience and earnings for workers of both sexes. Although the return to experience was lower for women than for men in the 1960s and 1970s, the return to experience for women subsequently increased relative to men's and currently little gender difference is found.[49]

EXPERIENCE AND PRODUCTIVITY

Human capital theory suggests that the reason why earnings tend to increase with experience in the labor market is that a worker's productivity is augmented by on-the-job training. However, critics of the human capital explanation argue that it is not clear that the productivity-enhancing effects of on-the-job training actually *cause* these higher earnings.[50]

For example, the rise in earnings with experience may simply reflect the widespread use of seniority arrangements, which appear to govern wage setting to some extent in the nonunion as well as the union sector. Of course, this reasoning does not explain why firms would adhere to this practice, if more senior workers were not also generally more productive.

Another alternative explanation is that upward-sloping earnings profiles, which reward experience with the firm (tenure), raise workers' productivity because employees are motivated to work hard so as to remain with the firm until retirement and, thus, reap the higher earnings that come with longer tenure.[51] This relationship is in the interest of both workers and firms because the resulting increased productivity makes possible both higher earnings and higher profits. Note that, in this model, even though workers are induced to put forth extra effort and be more productive, higher productivity is *not* due to training and productivity does *not* rise with experience. Such alternative explanations focus on the return to tenure (experience with a particular employer), however, and do not necessarily challenge the human capital explanation for the return associated with *general* labor market experience.

It is difficult to obtain data to shed light on this controversy, because information on actual productivity of workers is seldom available. Available empirical evidence is mixed, with some studies supporting the human capital explanation and others refuting it.[52]

---

[49]For evidence of higher returns to experience for men in earlier years, see for example, Mincer and Polachek, "Family Investments in Human Capital." For studies pointing to a reduction or elimination of this gender difference over the 1980s and 1990s, see for example, Blau and Kahn, "Swimming Upstream," and "The U.S. Gender Pay Gap in the 1990s"; and O'Neill and Polachek, "Why the Gender Gap in Wages Narrowed in the 1980s."

[50]See, for example, James L. Medoff and Katherine G. Abraham, "Are Those Paid More Really More Productive? The Case of Experience," *Journal of Human Resources* 16, no. 2 (Spring 1981): 186–216.

[51]Edward P. Lazear, "Why Is There Mandatory Retirement?" *Journal of Political Economy* 87 (December 1979): 1261–84. Another suggestion is that the observed return to tenure is just a statistical artifact: "Good matches" between workers and firms tend to last longer. So, at any point in time, workers with longer tenure will be higher paid, not because their earnings have risen with seniority but rather because workers with good, high-paying jobs are likely to keep them. See Katherine G. Abraham and Henry Farber, "Job Duration, Seniority, and Earnings," *American Economic Review* 77, no. 3 (June 1987): 278–97.

[52]Studies that do not support the training explanation include Medoff and Abraham, "Are Those Paid More?"; and Abraham and Farber, "Job Duration." Those providing support for the training hypothesis include Robert Topel, "Specific Capital, Mobility and Wages: Wages Rise with Job Seniority," *Journal of Political Economy* 99, no. 1 (February 1991): 145–76; and James Brown, "Why Do Wages Increase with Tenure?" *American Economic Review* 79, no. 5 (December 1989): 971–91.

From the perspective of the individual, the factors influencing the investment decision are not affected by the reasons for the upward-sloping experience-earnings profile. It is the magnitude of costs *versus* benefits that is the individual's principal concern. When the upward-sloping experience-earnings profile reflects an incentive structure offered to the worker by a particular firm, the situation is similar to firm-specific training in that the higher earnings will only be available to the worker if he or she remains at that firm.

GENDER DIFFERENCES IN TRAINING INVESTMENT DECISIONS

Expected Work Life

Does our analysis of the training investment decision suggest that women will be less likely to invest in on-the-job training than men? Or, to put the question somewhat differently, would they be less willing to spend time in relatively low-paid, entry-level positions in order to reap a return in terms of higher earnings later? Again, human capital theory suggests that adherence to traditional gender roles would lower women's incentives to invest.

The impact of women's shorter work lives is illustrated in Figure 6-6. Let us assume *TT'* represents the earnings profile of a worker with general training. Here we see that, just as in the case of formal education, the gross return to on-the-job training depends upon the number of years over which the return is earned. Jane, who plans to be in the labor market for a shorter period of time than Lisa, will find the investment in on-the-job

FIGURE 6-6   The Impact of Expected Work Life on the Training Investment Decision

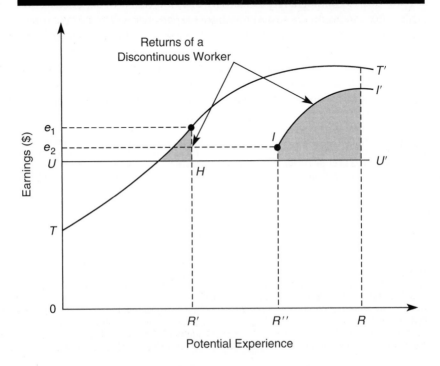

training less profitable. For example, suppose she expects to work R' years, and then return after an interruption of $R''-R'$ years. Her benefits are reduced by the time spent out of the labor force when her earnings are zero. Further, it is expected that, due to depreciation of skills, the workforce interruption will lower her earnings profile when she returns from TT' to II', resulting in a further loss of benefits. Although we have again shown the postinterruption profile (II') as approaching the profile of a continuous worker (TT'), a lifetime loss in earnings still occurs.

Jane's gross return to her investment in general training is equal to the sum of the two shaded areas, considerably less than Lisa's return shown in Figure 6-4. Given these reductions in benefits, women following traditional gender roles are likely to find it less profitable to make large investments in general training than will career-oriented men or women. Moreover, as we noted in our discussion of field of educational specialization, if occupations differ in the amount of depreciation associated with them, women who anticipate discontinuous work careers are likely to be attracted to fields in which such depreciation is relatively small.[53]

Figure 6-6 may also be used to illustrate the consequences of the shorter and more discontinuous labor force participation of women following a traditional path for their incentives to invest in *firm-specific* training. Assume now that TT' is the earnings profile of a worker who obtained firm-specific training. The impact of work interruptions is potentially even more serious in this case, depending crucially on whether a woman is able to return to her initial employer.

Suppose Jennifer left the labor force for a substantial period of time and is unable to get her old job back. The firm-specific skills she acquired are useless in other firms. Her earnings upon her return to the labor force will be only U dollars (the earnings of an individual without training), and her new earnings profile will be UU' (the profile of an individual without training). The returns to Jennifer's investment in firm-specific training were completely wiped out by her withdrawal from the labor force! That is, the second shaded area shown in Figure 6-6 is eliminated, although she will still receive some returns for the brief period before she leaves the labor force. Of course, this conclusion depends on our assumption that she could not return to her original employer. Unless a woman is guaranteed reemployment, she must always face this risk. Thus, human capital theory suggests that women who anticipate workforce interruptions of long or uncertain duration will particularly avoid jobs where firm-specific training is important. Women who seek shorter, fixed-duration interruptions may, however, be covered by an employer's leave policy.

Considerable empirical evidence supports the prediction of the human capital model that women will receive less on-the-job training than men.[54] This finding is consistent with employer and worker decisions based on a lower expected probability of

[53]See, especially, Solomon W. Polachek, "Occupational Self-Selection."

[54]Greg J. Duncan and Saul Hoffman, "On-the-Job Training and Earnings Differences by Race and Sex," *Review of Economics and Statistics* 61, no. 4 (November 1979); Joseph G. Altonji and James R. Spletzer, "Worker Characteristics, Job Characteristics, and the Receipt of On-the-Job Training," *Industrial and Labor Relations Review* 45, no. 1 (October 1991): 58–79; Lisa M. Lynch, "Private Sector Training and the Earnings of Young Workers," *American Economic Review* 82, no. 1 (March 1992): 299–312; Reed Neil Olsen and Edwin A. Sexton, "Gender Differences in the Returns to and the Acquisition of On-the-Job Training," *Industrial Relations* 35, no. 1 (January 1996): 59–77; and John Barron and Dan A. Black, "Gender Differences in Training, Capital and Wages," *Journal of Human Resources* 28, no. 2 (Spring 1993): 342–64.

women remaining with the firm or in the workforce. Interestingly, however, one study that explicitly examined the determinants of obtaining training found that, even though women's higher probability of turnover can explain some of the gender training difference, a major portion remains unexplained even after this and other determinants of training are taken into account.[55] This finding suggests that differences in the amount of training men and women acquire may not be fully explained by factors emphasized in the human capital model, and that discrimination (discussed next) potentially plays a role.

As women's labor force attachment and career orientation increase, the profitability of on-the-job training investments for them, both general and firm specific, will increase; so too should their representation in jobs requiring such investments. Moreover, as more women are employed in jobs with training opportunities, the opportunity cost of workforce interruptions is increased and their labor force attachment is further reinforced. The most important factor in the case of firm-specific training is attachment to a particular firm. Such an attachment most likely requires that women keep any workforce interruptions within the limits of their employers' leave policy and also raises the question of what such policies should be. We consider this issue in Chapter 10.

Discrimination

The explanation for gender differences in on-the-job training investment decisions suggested by human capital theory stresses differences between men and women in anticipated labor force participation over the life cycle. It is, however, important to point out that, just as in the case of men's and women's formal education decisions, societal discrimination may also be a factor increasing the (pecuniary and nonpecuniary) costs or decreasing the (pecuniary and nonpecuniary) returns to entry into traditionally male fields. Further, labor market discrimination, which is discussed in greater detail in Chapter 7, may also play a part in reducing women's representation in jobs where training is important. That is, overt or subtle discrimination on the part of employers, coworkers, or customers may prove an obstacle to women gaining access to jobs in such areas or reduce the pay of those who are able to obtain employment.

Consideration of firm-specific training introduces a particular rationale for employer discrimination that may be important. As illustrated in Figure 6-5, the employer is expected to share some of the costs of firm-specific training. The returns to the firm's (as well as to the worker's) investment depend on how long the individual remains with the firm. Thus, if employers believe that women are less likely to stay at the firm than men, on average, they may prefer men for jobs that require considerable specific training. Employers' differential treatment of men and women on the basis of their perceptions of average gender differences in productivity or job stability has been termed **statistical discrimination**. Such behavior on the part of employers can restrict opportunities for career-oriented as well as noncareer-oriented women, if employers cannot easily distinguish between them.

---

[55] Anne Beeson Royalty, "The Effects of Job Turnover on the Training of Men and Women," *Industrial and Labor Relations Review* 49, no. 3 (April 1996): 506–21.

Finally, labor market discrimination may indirectly lower women's incentives to invest in themselves by decreasing the rewards for doing so. The possibility of such "feedback effects" is considered in greater detail in the next chapter.

OCCUPATIONS AND EARNINGS

The analysis of gender differences in occupations and earnings based on the human capital model is quite straightforward. It is assumed that, given the traditional division of labor in the family, most women do indeed anticipate shorter and less continuous work careers than men. Thus, women are expected to select occupations requiring less investment in education and on-the-job training than those chosen by men. They will particularly avoid jobs in which firm-specific training is important, and employers will be reluctant to hire them for such jobs. Further, they will seek jobs where depreciation of earnings for time spent out of the labor force is minimal.

Hypothetical earnings profiles for predominantly male and predominantly female jobs are shown in Figure 6-7. For simplicity, we assume all workers have the same amount of formal schooling. Earnings profiles in predominantly male jobs are expected to slope steeply upward as does profile MM', because men are expected to undertake substantial investments in on-the-job training. Women, on the other

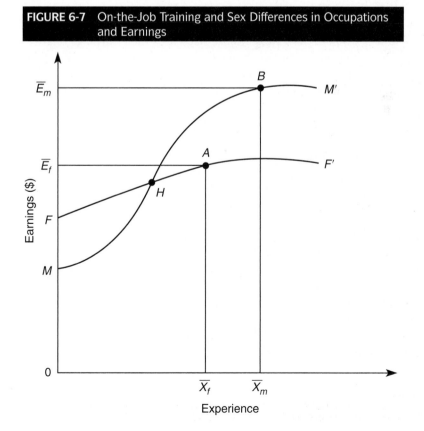

FIGURE 6-7   On-the-Job Training and Sex Differences in Occupations and Earnings

hand, are expected to choose the flatter profile *FF'*, representing smaller amounts of investment in on-the-job training. The existence of the crossover point, *H,* is crucial to this argument. Before *H,* profile *FF'* lies above profile *MM'*. It is argued that women choose higher earnings now in preference to higher earnings in the future because they do not expect to be in the labor market long enough for the larger human capital investment to pay off. Thus, we see that the human capital analysis of on-the-job training decisions, in conjunction with our previous discussion of formal education, can provide an explanation for the occupational segregation by gender detailed in Chapter 5.

The human capital analysis can also provide an explanation for gender differences in earnings. We already looked at why the human capital model implies that women are less likely to make large investments in formal schooling. To the extent that women in the labor force were less likely than men to obtain a college or graduate education, their earnings would be reduced relative to men's. Because, even in the past, gender differences in educational attainment were fairly small, differences between men and women in fields of specialization would be of potentially more importance in explaining gender differences in earnings, to the extent that men are likely to enter more lucrative areas.

For given levels of formal education, our consideration of on-the-job training investments also gives us reasons to expect women to earn less, on average, as illustrated in Figure 6-7: Mean female earnings are $\overline{E}_f$ dollars and are less than male mean earnings of $\overline{E}_m$ dollars. Why do women earn less? First, on average they have less labor market experience than men—$\overline{X}_f$ is less than $\overline{X}_m$. Because earnings tend to increase with experience, women's lesser experience decreases their earnings relative to men's. Second, for reasons given earlier, males have steeper profiles; they experience larger increases in earnings for additional years of experience. After crossover point *H,* this difference in returns produces a widening gap between male and female earnings with increasing labor market experience.

OTHER SUPPLY-SIDE FACTORS

Traditional gender roles, which result in women being viewed as the secondary earner in the family, may work to produce differences in economic outcomes in a variety of other ways. For example, a study found that wives in dual-earner couples who have the "secondary" career in their family tend to earn lower wages than those who have the "primary" career, even controlling for any differences in levels of education or actual work experience, and the presence of children.[56] We briefly consider a number of ways in which adherence to traditional gender roles in the family could reduce women's wages relative to men's. This issue receives considerably more attention in Chapters 9 and 10.

First, the longer hours that women tend to spend on housework may reduce the effort that they put into their market jobs and may thus decrease their hourly wage

---

[56]Anne E. Winkler and David C. Rose, "Career Hierarchy in Dual-Earner Families," *Research in Labor Economics,* edited by Solomon W. Polachek (Greenwich, CT: JAI Press, 2000), pp. 147–72.

compared to men with similar qualifications.[57] Indeed, additional hours spent in housework by workers are associated with lower wages, all else equal.[58] Also consistent with women placing a greater priority on family responsibilities to the detriment of their labor market outcomes is the empirical evidence that women are more likely to quit their jobs for family-related reasons, which negatively affects their subsequent earnings.[59] Interestingly, some evidence shows that this gender difference in the pattern of quits is concentrated among workers with a high school education or less, while little gender difference is found for those who have attended college.[60] This finding suggests that workforce attachment of the latter group may be more nearly equal to their male counterparts.

Further evidence suggesting that women's nonmarket responsibilities may negatively affect their labor market outcomes is the finding that the presence of children negatively affects the wages of women.[61] To some extent this finding reflects the labor force disruptions such women may experience. However, even after adjusting for differences in experience, mothers earn less. One explanation for this finding is that, in the past, the birth or adoption of a child often resulted in women severing their tie to the firm. They would thus lose the returns to any firm-specific training acquired and forgo what might have been an exceptionally good job match. Some evidence indicates that the availability of maternity leave significantly mitigates this negative effect, most likely because it enables women to take a short amount of time out but still maintain their attachment to the firm.[62]

In contrast to the finding that children negatively affect the wages of women, married men tend to earn a wage premium compared to single men, whether or not children are present.[63] While the positive association between marriage and wages for men might reflect a selection of men with higher earnings potential into marriage, or even discrimination in favor of married men by employers, the evidence suggests higher productivity is an important factor. This may in turn reflect the greater motivation or commitment of married men to their jobs, given some adherence to traditional gender roles in the family.

---

[57]See Gary S. Becker, "The Allocation of Effort, Specific Human Capital, and the Differences Between Men and Women in Earnings and Occupations," *Journal of Labor Economics* 3, no. 1, pt. 2 (January 1985): 33–58.

[58]For evidence that housework reduces wages, see Joni Hersch and Leslie S. Stratton, "Housework, Fixed Effects and Wages of Married Workers," *Journal of Human Resources* 32, no. 2 (Spring 1997): 285–307. In other work, Leslie S. Stratton suggests that time spent in housework may reduce wages, not because of less effort, but because of time constraints created by the demands of household responsibilities; see "Why Does More Housework Lower Women's Wages? Testing Hypotheses Involving Job Effort and Hours Flexibility," *Social Science Quarterly* 82, no. 1 (March 2001): 67–76.

[59]Kristen Keith and Abagail McWilliams, "The Wage Effects of Cumulative Job Mobility," *Industrial and Labor Relations Review* 49, no. 1 (October 1995): 121–37.

[60]Anne Beeson Royalty, "Job-to-Job and Job-to-Nonemployment Turnover by Gender and Education Level," *Journal of Labor Economics* 16, no. 2 (April 1998): 392–443.

[61]See, for example, Victor R. Fuchs, *Women's Quest for Economic Equality* (Cambridge, MA: Harvard University Press, 1988); and Jane Waldfogel, "Understanding the 'Family Gap' in Pay for Women with Children," *Journal of Economic Perspectives* 12, no. 1 (Winter 1998): 157–70.

[62]See, Waldfogel, "Understanding the 'Family Gap' in Pay for Women with Children." Considerably smaller effects of maternity leave are reported by Masanori Hashimoto, Rick Percy, Teresa Schoellner, and Bruce A. Weinberg, in "The Long and Short of it: Maternity Leave Coverage and Women's Labor Market Outcomes," IZA Discussion Paper No. 1207 (July 2004).

[63]David C. Ribar, "What Do Social Scientists Know About the Benefits of Marriage? A Review of Quantitative Methodologies," IZA Discussion Paper No. 998 (January 2004).

Second, to the extent that families place priority on the husband's, rather than the wife's, career in determining the location of the family, her earnings are likely to be decreased. She may be a "tied mover," relocating when it is not advantageous for her to leave a job where she has accumulated considerable seniority and firm-specific training. Alternatively, she may be a "tied stayer," unable to relocate despite good opportunities elsewhere.[64] Anticipation of a lesser ability to determine the geographic location of the family may also lead women to select occupations in which jobs are likely to be readily obtained in any labor market, thus constraining their occupational choices.

Third, if women tend to give greater priority than men to family concerns, they may restrict the amount of daily commuting they are willing to do,[65] their hours and work schedules, or their availability for work-related travel. Such constraints could adversely influence women's employment and occupational choices and reduce their earnings relative to men's.

Finally, if women anticipate a shorter work life than men, they may invest less time in searching out the best possible job and, as a consequence, receive lower earnings.[66]

As with the other supply-side influences we discussed, it is important to bear in mind that women's decisions with regard to the priority they place on their own versus their husbands' careers, the adaptations they make in response to family responsibilities, and so on may reflect social pressures as well as voluntary choices. Further, to the extent that women face discrimination in the labor market that decreases their wages relative to their husbands', traditional gender roles in the family are reinforced. This is the case because the opportunity cost of wives sacrificing their career objectives to family demands is reduced relative to their husbands'.

THE HUMAN CAPITAL EXPLANATION: AN ASSESSMENT

The human capital model provides a clear, consistent theoretical explanation for gender differences in earnings and occupations in terms of the voluntary choices women and men make. In assessing the contribution of the model, however, it is important to consider the extent to which the data support it. Specifically, we want to know the answers to two questions: Do the factors emphasized by human capital theorists help to explain gender differences in labor market outcomes? If so, do they provide the *full* explanation? A voluminous literature in economics has grown up around investigating these questions. Actual estimates vary depending on the sources of the data used and the types of qualifications examined. Nonetheless, most studies find that human capital factors, particularly women's lesser labor market experience, are important in explaining the gender pay gap. In addition to gender differences in overall experience, other

---

[64]See, for example, Jacob Mincer, "Family Migration Decisions," *Journal of Political Economy* 86, no. 5 (October 1978): 749–73; and Joyce P. Jacobsen and Laurence M. Levin, "Marriage and Migration: Comparing Gains and Losses from Migration for Couples and Singles," *Social Science Quarterly* 78, no. 3 (September 1997): 688–709.

[65]Janice Madden suggested that the lesser willingness of women to commute increases the monopsony power of firms over their wages, thus decreasing their wages relative to men's; see "A Spatial Theory of Sex Discrimination," *Journal of Regional Science* 17, no. 3 (December 1977): 369–80. The monopsony model is discussed further in Chapter 7.

[66]Some evidence consistent with this possibility is found in Steven H. Sandell, "Is the Unemployment Rate of Women Too Low? A Direct Test of the Economic Theory of Job Search," *Review of Economics and Statistics* 62, no. 4 (November 1980): 634–38.

important dimensions of work history include length of time employed on a particular job (tenure), work interruptions, and the timing of past work experience.[67] However, most studies also find that a substantial portion of the pay gap cannot be explained by gender differences in qualifications. The portion of the pay gap that is not explained by gender differences in qualifications is generally presumed to be due to labor market discrimination, although important measurement problems need to be taken into account before reaching such a conclusion. We discuss this evidence at greater length in Chapter 7. Here we briefly sketch some of the reasoning and evidence underlying this conclusion.

One way to examine the explanatory power of the human capital model is to consider how well it explains gender differences in earnings at a point in time. We begin by returning to Figure 6-2, which presents the **age-earnings profiles** in real (2003) dollars for male and female high school and college graduates in 1974 and 2003. The age-earnings profiles shown in the figure indicate how earnings vary with age. When comparing the profiles for males and females shown in Figure 6-2, it is important to remember that women's greater likelihood of workforce interruptions means that, at any given age, they have, on average, less actual labor market experience than men.

The profiles in Figure 6-2 suggest that gender differences in earnings are not fully explained by differences in educational attainment of men and women because, within each educational category, women tend to earn less than men. Of course, gender differences in labor market experience and investments in on-the-job training may also be a factor.

To consider this factor, let us compare Figure 6-2 to Figure 6-7. We see that, as predicted by the human capital model, women's age-earnings profiles tend to be flatter than men's. This flatter profile is consistent with less investment in on-the-job training for women than for men. Note, however, that in the hypothetical diagram, Figure 6-7, a crossover point H occurs between the male and female profiles. This crossover point implies that during their early years in the labor market, women should actually earn more than men with the same education, because men are investing in on-the-job training and women are not, or are doing so to a lesser extent. However, the actual data seen in Figure 6-2 do not show such a crossover point. On the contrary, within educational categories, men generally earn more than women at every age, even among the youngest workers who are recent entrants to the labor force. These findings suggest that gender differences in years of formal education and on-the-job training do not fully explain gender differences in earnings.

Another piece of evidence that women's human capital investment decisions reflect the types of considerations emphasized by the human capital analysis is the finding that young women who expect to work at age 35 have experience-wage profiles that "begin at a lower point and have a steeper (initial) slope than those of their no-work-plans counterparts."[68] That is, the women who were more committed to the labor market were moving along an earnings profile like MM' in Figure 6-7, whereas the less

---

[67]See, for example, Mincer and Polachek, "Family Investments in Human Capital"; Blau and Kahn, "Swimming Upstream"; O'Neill and Polachek, "Why the Gender Gap"; Wellington, "Changes in the Male/Female Wage Gap"; and Audrey Light and Manuelita Ureta, "Early-Career Work Experience and Gender Wage Differentials," *Journal of Labor Economics* 13, no. 1 (January 1995): 121–54.

[68]Steven H. Sandell and David Shapiro, "Work Expectations, Human Capital Accumulation, and the Wages of Young Women," *Journal of Human Resources* 15, no. 3 (Summer 1980): 335–43.

committed women were moving along a profile like *FF'*. However, the data presented in Figure 6-2 (as well as other evidence reviewed in Chapter 7) suggest that *both* groups of women earn less than comparable men.

A comparison of the age-earnings profiles for 1974 and 2003 also discloses some interesting trends in gender differentials. First, while in the mid-1970s female college graduates earned less than male high school graduates, by the early 2000s their earnings clearly exceeded those of male high school graduates. A significant part of this change represents an increase in the real wages of women college graduates, but a good bit of it also reflects falling real wages of male high school graduates; their real wages decreased across all age groups, with particularly sharp declines among younger men. Female high school graduates did better than male high school graduates, with young workers experiencing only small real wage declines and older workers actually experiencing small real wage increases. This difference illustrates a general trend, discussed in Chapter 8, showing that women tended to fare better than men in terms of real wage changes over this period. Second, the age-earnings profiles of women, particularly of college graduates, became steeper over this period, suggesting that they were remaining in the labor force more consistently and investing more in on-the-job training.

As suggested by our discussion of Figure 6-7, the human capital model also provides an explanation for occupational segregation by gender in terms of women's optimizing behavior, given the traditional division of labor by gender within the family. Women are believed to choose occupations characterized by flatter experience-earnings profiles—illustrated by *FF'* in Figure 6-7. Men, on the other hand, are willing to undertake the larger human capital investments represented by profile *MM'*. This reasoning implies that women who do enter predominantly male occupations should be those who anticipate more continuous labor force participation and are willing to undertake the larger investments in on-the-job training required in male jobs. In return, they should reap higher returns to each year of their labor market experience. In other words, the human capital analysis suggests that women in predominantly male jobs should be moving along profile *MM'*, whereas women in predominantly female jobs should be moving along profile *FF'*. Further, women who anticipate more work interruptions should enter predominantly female jobs where depreciation of earnings due to time spent out of the labor force is less than in predominantly male jobs.

The research investigating the implications of the human capital theory as an explanation for gender differences in occupations has produced mixed results. On the one hand, women in predominantly male jobs were found to earn more than women in predominantly female jobs at every age; that is, there is no evidence of the crossover point *H* in Figure 6-7 between the earnings profiles in predominantly male and predominantly female jobs, even when we look just among women. Further, women in predominantly male jobs were not found to earn greater returns to each year of experience than women in predominantly female occupations, as would be expected based on the hypothetical figure. Nor was it found that the earnings of women in predominantly female jobs depreciate less during periods of time spent out of the labor force than do the earnings of women in predominantly male jobs. Finally, women with discontinuous work histories were not more likely to be in a predominantly female occupation than women employed more continuously.[69] These findings are surprising in light of the results

---

[69]See, Paula England, "The Failure of Human Capital Theory to Explain Occupational Sex Segregation," *Journal of Human Resources* 17, no. 3 (Summer 1982): 358–70.

discussed earlier that women who are more committed to the labor market *do* appear to have lower entry wages and steeper experience-earnings profiles than women who are less committed. It appears that labor force commitment and participation in predominantly male and predominantly female jobs are not as closely associated as the human capital explanation for occupational segregation would lead us to expect.

On the other hand, some support for the human capital explanation is provided by empirical evidence that a substantial portion of the lower pay in female jobs is accounted for by differences in the skills required in male and female jobs.[70] Moreover, although there is no evidence that women in predominantly female jobs experience lower earnings penalties for the total amount of time spent out of the labor force, one study found that married women have lower penalties for having *recently reentered* the labor force in female than in male occupations.[71] This latter finding is consistent with the predictions of the human capital model. Finally, the finding in one study that women with more limited expected future labor force participation select occupations with lower job skills is also consistent with the human capital model of occupational choice.[72]

Given the mixed evidence on this question, it is difficult to reach firm conclusions regarding the importance of the factors identified by the human capital model in explaining occupational segregation by sex. Even though the human capital explanation may account for a portion of the occupational differences between men and women, it appears unwarranted, based on the evidence, to conclude that the model could fully account for these differences.

Another type of test of the explanatory power of the human capital explanation for gender differences in earnings is provided by an examination of the trends in the gender-pay differential. As we saw in Chapter 5, virtually no progress was made in closing the overall male-female pay gap during the 1960s and 1970s. Beginning in the late 1970s or early 1980s, the female-to-male earnings ratio began to increase. Gains were particularly marked over the 1980s. How do these trends correspond to shifts in women's qualifications, particularly their relative educational attainment and experience? In general, women's qualifications increased as the pay gap declined. Though overall differences in educational attainment were never large, women's fields of study and propensity to pursue college and graduate education are now more similar to men's. And, although women on average continue to have less labor market experience than men, the gender differential declined here as well. As previously noted, the average experience levels of women within age groups started to increase in the 1970s, but the average level of experience of the female labor force as a whole did not start to rise relative to men's until the 1980s. This shift corresponds to the period of the fastest narrowing of the pay gap. The decline in the gender pay gap also slowed in the 1990s when the gender difference in experience narrowed at a slower pace. Thus, both the

---

[70]Skills are generally measured by government data on occupational requirements. Among the higher estimates for the effect of skills are those found in David A. Macpherson and Barry T. Hirsch, "Wages and Gender Composition: Why Do Women's Jobs Pay Less?" *Journal of Labor Economics* 13, no. 3 (July 1995): 426–71. For a review of the evidence, see also Elaine Sorensen, "The Crowding Hypothesis and Comparable Worth Issue," *Journal of Human Resources* 25, no. 1 (Winter 1990): 55–89.

[71]John Robst and Jennifer VanGilder "Atrophy Rates in Male and Female Occupations," *Economic Letters* 69, no. 3 (2000): 407–13.

[72]Evelyn L. Lehrer and Houston Stokes, "Determinants of the Female Occupational Distribution: A Log Linear Analysis," *Review of Economics and Statistics* 67, no. 3 (August 1985): 395–404. See also Polachek, "Occupational Self-Selection."

rrowing of the male-female pay gap and the time pattern of the trend are roughly nsistent with the human capital model.

This broad consistency of the human capital explanation with the observed trends in the female-to-male earnings ratio strongly suggests that human capital factors account for at least part of the male-female pay gap. Its consistency does not necessarily mean, however, that the human capital model provides the *sole* explanation of pay differences. Other factors, such as a decrease in discrimination against women, may well have contributed to the observed trends. We consider the sources of the declining gender pay gap more fully in Chapter 8. We generally conclude from our examination that decreasing human capital differences between men and women were an important part of the story, but do not appear to be the only reason for the fall in the pay gap.

Conclusion

In this chapter, we examined supply-side explanations for gender differences in occupations and earnings, chiefly focusing upon the human capital model and its explanation for gender differences in investment in formal education and on-the-job training. Although the evidence suggests that such factors are important, they explain only part of the story. Discrimination against women in the labor market is also an important factor, to which we turn in the next chapter. In Chapter 10, we broadly consider the conflicts that female and increasingly male workers face in coping with the dual demands of family and paid work and the policies that government or private employers pursue, or might consider pursuing, to increase women's human capital and labor force attachment.

Questions for Review and Discussion

* Indicates that the question can be answered using a diagram illustrating the individual's human capital investment decision as well as verbally. Consult with your instructor about the appropriate approach for your class.

1. What are the main economic factors that underlie the decision to go to college?
2. Carefully explain how the following hypothetical situations would affect the cost-benefit calculation of going to college:
   a. It is increasingly the case that full-time undergraduate students need 5 years to complete all of the requirements for a bachelor's degree.*
   b. The real earnings of college-trained workers increase while those for high school–trained workers decrease.*
3. As a future worker, explain the costs and benefits to you of obtaining highly specialized training from a particular firm.
4. What are the main reasons why women frequently invested less in their human capital than men? What changed this tendency? What government or employer policies would be likely to accelerate this change?
5. To what extent and how did economic factors influence the following:
   a. Your decision to attend college?
   b. Your choice of major?
   c. Your plans to go on or not to go on to graduate work?
      Would you expect any of these considerations to differ between men and women, and if so why?

6. It is claimed that employers are reluctant to hire women for some jobs because of their higher expected quit rates. Assuming women are more likely to quit, use human capital theory to explain what kind of jobs an employer would be especially reluctant to hire women for. Explain the reasons for the employer's reluctance.* How valid do you think such employer assumptions about women are today?

Suggested Readings

American Association of University Women. *Gender Gaps: Where Schools Still Fail Our Children.* Washington, DC: American Association of University Women, 1998.

Becker, Gary S. *Human Capital: A Theoretical and Empirical Analysis, With Special Reference to Education,* 3rd ed. Chicago: University of Chicago Press, 1993.

Blau, Francine D., and Lawrence M. Kahn. "Gender Differences in Pay." *Journal of Economic Perspectives* 14, no. 4 (Fall 2000): 75–99.

England, Paula. "The Failure of Human Capital Theory to Explain Occupational Sex Segregation." *Journal of Human Resources* 17, no. 3 (Summer 1982): 358–70.

Freeman, Catherine E. *Trends in Educational Equity of Girls and Women*, National Center for Educational Statistics (NCES) NCES 2005-016, November 2004.

Mincer, Jacob, and Solomon W. Polachek. "Family Investments in Human Capital: Earnings of Women." *Journal of Political Economy* 82, no. 2, pt. 2 (March/April 1974): S76–S108.

Neumark, David. *Sex Differences in Labor Markets.* London: Routledge, 2004.

O'Neill, June, and Solomon W. Polachek. "Why the Gender Gap in Wages Narrowed in the 1980s." *Journal of Labor Economics* 11, no. 1, pt. 1 (January 1993): 205–28.

Reskin, Barbara F., and Heidi I. Hartmann. *Women's Work, Men's Work: Sex Segregation on the Job.* Washington, DC: National Academy Press, 1986.

Tobias, Sheila. *Overcoming Math Anxiety.* New York: W.W. Norton, 1993.

Waldfogel, Jane. "Understanding the 'Family Gap' in Pay for Women with Children." *Journal of Economic Perspectives* 12, no. 1 (Winter 1998): 157–70.

7

DIFFERENCES IN OCCUPATIONS AND EARNINGS: THE ROLE OF LABOR MARKET DISCRIMINATION

Chapter Highlights

- Labor Market Discrimination: A Definition

- Empirical Evidence of Labor Market Discrimination

- Models of Labor Market Discrimination

- Policy Issue: The Government and Equal Employment Opportunity

- Appendix: Regression Analysis and Empirical Estimates of Labor Market Discrimination

In the preceding chapter, we examined the role of supply-side factors in producing the gender differences in earnings and occupational attainment that we observe in the labor market and that were described in Chapter 5. We now focus upon the demand side, specifically the role of labor market discrimination. As we explained at the end of Chapter 6, the available evidence suggests that both supply- and demand-side influences are responsible for gender differences in economic outcomes.

In this chapter, we begin by providing a definition of labor market discrimination. Next, we examine the empirical evidence on the extent of gender discrimination in the labor market with respect to earnings and occupations. We then turn to a detailed consideration of the various explanations that economists offer for the existence and persistence of such discrimination. Although our focus is on gender discrimination, much of the analysis is equally applicable to discrimination based on other factors, such as race, ethnicity, age, or disability.

In fact, most of the models of discrimination that we discuss were initially developed to explain racial discrimination.

Our primary concern here is to determine to what extent discrimination exists and its possible effects on women's status in the labor market. This is partly an issue of equity or fairness. However, there is also an issue of misallocation of resources when workers are not hired, promoted, or rewarded on the basis of their qualifications. Thus, efficiency, as well as considerations of equity, provides an important rationale for government intervention to combat labor market discrimination. We conclude by reviewing the government's antidiscrimination policies and examining their possible effects.

LABOR MARKET DISCRIMINATION: A DEFINITION

Labor market discrimination exists when *two equally qualified individuals are treated differently solely on the basis of their gender* (race, age, disability, etc.).[1] As we saw in Chapter 1, in the absence of discrimination, profit-maximizing employers in a competitive labor market pay workers in accordance with their productivity. For similar reasons, they also find it in their economic self-interest to make other personnel decisions, such as hiring, placement, or promotion, on the same objective basis. An individual's gender (or race, age, disability, etc.) would be an irrelevant consideration.

If labor market discrimination nonetheless exists, it is expected to adversely affect the economic status of women *directly* by producing differences in economic outcomes between men and women that are *not* accounted for by differences in productivity-related characteristics or qualifications. That is, men and women who, in the absence of discrimination, would be equally productive and would receive the same pay (or be in the same occupation) do not receive equal rewards. As we shall see, in some economic models of discrimination, this inequality occurs because women are paid less than their marginal product due to discrimination. In other views of this process, labor market discrimination *directly* lowers women's productivity as well as their pay, as for instance, when a woman is denied access to an employer-sponsored training program or when customers are reluctant to patronize a female salesperson.

If such gender differences in *treatment* of equally qualified men and women are widespread and persistent, the behavior of women themselves may be adversely affected. As we saw in the preceding chapter, productivity differences among workers reflect, in part, the decisions they make as to whether to continue their schooling, participate in a training program, remain continuously in the labor market, and so on. Faced with discrimination in the labor market that lowers the returns to such human capital investments, women are likely to have less incentive to undertake them. To the extent that such *indirect* or **feedback effects** of labor market discrimination exist, they are also expected to adversely affect the economic outcomes of women compared to men.

---

[1]This definition is derived from the work of Gary S. Becker, *The Economics of Discrimination*, 2nd ed. (Chicago: University of Chicago Press, 1971).

Much of the theoretical and virtually all of the empirical work on labor market discrimination has focused on its more readily measured *direct* effects, that is, on pay or occupational differences between equally well-qualified (potentially equally productive) men and women. We shall follow that emphasis in this chapter. However, it is important to recognize that the *full* impact of discrimination also includes any feedback effects on women's behavior that result in their being less well qualified than men.[2] Thus, we also discuss such feedback effects.

EMPIRICAL EVIDENCE OF LABOR MARKET DISCRIMINATION

Having defined labor market discrimination, we now consider the empirical evidence as to the existence and extent of such discrimination. We restrict ourselves entirely to the direct effects of such discrimination and, thus, take as given any gender differences in qualifications. We seek to address more fully the types of questions raised at the end of Chapter 6. Are gender differences in labor market outcomes *fully* explained by gender differences in qualifications or (potential) productivity? If not, how large is the unexplained portion of the gender differential? It is this differential that is commonly used as an estimate of the impact of labor market discrimination. Unfortunately, as we shall see, though the questions are relatively straightforward, the answers are not so easily obtained. We turn first to a consideration of gender differences in earnings and then to an examination of gender differences in occupations.

Earnings Differences

Economists and other social scientists have studied the sources of the earnings gap between men and women workers extensively. Actual estimates vary depending on the data used and the types of qualifications examined. However, virtually all studies find that a substantial portion of the pay gap cannot be explained by gender differences in qualifications.[3]

Representative findings from analyses of this type may be illustrated by results from a recent study using data from the Panel Study of Income Dynamics (PSID), which contains information on actual labor market experience for a large, nationally representative sample.[4] The data are for full-time workers aged 18 to 65 in 1999. (Information on wages relates to the preceding calendar year, 1998.) The restriction to

---

[2]Note that the argument is *not* that *all* differences in qualifications between men and women are due to the indirect effects of discrimination, but, rather, that *some* of these differences may be a response to such discrimination.

[3]For summaries of this literature, see for example, Joseph G. Altonji and Rebecca M. Blank, "Race and Gender in the Labor Market," in *Handbook of Labor Economics,* edited by Orley C. Ashenfelter and David Card (Amsterdam: North-Holland, 1999), pp. 3C: 3143–259; Francine D. Blau and Lawrence M. Kahn, "Gender Differences in Pay," *Journal of Economic Perspectives* 14, no. 4 (Fall 2000): 75–99; and T. D. Stanley and Stephen B. Jarrell, "Gender Wage Discrimination Bias? A Meta-Regression Analysis," *Journal of Human Resources* 33, no. 4 (Fall 1998): 947–73. Similar statistical techniques are employed to study discrimination on the basis of sexual orientation. For an example, see Dan A. Black, Hoda R. Makar, Seth G. Sanders, and Lowell J. Taylor, "The Earnings Effects of Sexual Orientation," *Industrial and Labor Relations Review* 56, no. 3 (April 2003): 449–69 and references therein.

[4]Francine D. Blau and Lawrence M. Kahn, "The U.S. Gender Pay Gap in the 1990s: Slowing Convergence," National Bureau of Economic Research Working Paper No. 10853 (October 2004).

full-time workers is designed to focus on male and female workers who are as similar as possible.[5]

The impact of gender differences in characteristics on the male-female wage differential are shown in Table 7-1. The results in the table are based on a statistical analysis of the contribution of each variable to explaining the gender wage differential of 20 percent. This procedure is explained in detail in the appendix. The variables considered include indicators of "human capital," that is, those relating to education and experience, as well as measures of occupation, industry and union status. (Race is also included as a control variable, but its effect is small because the proportion of each race group in the full-time sample is about the same for men and women.)

As would be expected based on our discussion in Chapter 6, women's lesser amount of labor market experience is found to be a significant determinant of the gender wage differential, explaining 11 percent of the gender gap in wages. This proportion reflects a 3.5-year difference in full-time experience between men and women, which, though smaller than in previous years, is still a substantial factor explaining the wage gap.[6]

Interestingly, women in this sample had higher educational attainment than men, which (as indicated by the negative sign in the table) works to *lower* the gender wage

TABLE 7-1   Contribution of Measured Characteristics to the Gender Wage Differential, 1998

Characteristics	*Percent Explained*
Educational attainment	–6.7
Labor force experience	10.5
Race	2.4
Occupational category	27.4
Industry category	21.9
Union status	3.5
Unexplained	41.1
Total	100.0
Wage differential (%)	20.3

Source: Calculated from data presented in Francine D. Blau and Lawrence M. Kahn, "The U.S. Gender Pay Gap in the 1990s: Slowing Convergence," National Bureau of Economic Research Working Paper No. 10853 (October 2004).

---

[5]In addition to gender differences in qualifications and the extent of discrimination, the gender earnings differential may also be affected by the self-selection of women and men into full-time employment, and, more generally, into the labor force. In other words, those choosing to participate—or to work full-time—may differ from those outside the labor force or part-time workers in terms of both their measured and unmeasured characteristics. One possibility, for example, is that labor force participants are a positively selected group of those who received higher wage offers. Similarly, full-time workers may be more highly qualified and more committed to market work. Blau and Kahn find that, at a point in time, the gender pay gap is smaller if only full-time workers are considered than if part-timers and nonparticipants are included; in their paper, they examine the impact of changes in female and male selection into the labor force for trends in the gender pay gap. Other research that examined the earnings differential for white and black women found that, if self-selection is not accounted for, the race differential is underestimated; see Derek Neal, "The Measured Black-White Wage Gap Among Women Is Too Small," *Journal of Political Economy* 112, no. 1, pt. 2 (February 2004): S1–S28.

[6]Although women do have a bit more part-time experience than men, part-time experience has been found to have a very low payoff in terms of current wages.

gap by 7 percent. In other words, gender differences in educational attainment do not help to explain the gender wage gap, but rather work slightly in the opposite direction. As we saw in Chapter 6, traditionally women were less likely to go on to college and graduate and professional school than men. However, since the early 1980s, women comprised more than half of college graduates and master's degree recipients And, the gender difference in professional and Ph.D. degrees, while favoring men, decreased considerably. Thus, even though men's educational attainment is still somewhat higher than women's in the population as a whole (including earlier cohorts), when we focus on a sample of the population which is not only employed, but employed full time, women have a slight edge.[7]

Finally, as we would expect based on the data presented in Chapter 5, gender differences in occupation and industry are substantial and help to explain a considerable portion of the gender wage gap. Recall that men are more likely to be in blue-collar jobs and to work in mining, construction, durable manufacturing, or transportation and utilities; they are also more likely to be in unionized employment. Women are more likely to be in clerical or professional jobs and to work in education and health services and financial activities. Taken together, these variables explain 53 percent of the gender wage gap—27 percent for occupation, 22 percent for industry, and an additional 4 percent for union status.[8]

Although these findings suggest that gender differences in work-related characteristics are important, they also indicate that qualifications are only part of the story. The proportion of the wage differential that is *not* explained by these types of productivity-related characteristics serves as an estimate of the impact of labor market discrimination. In this case, 41 percent of the gender gap cannot be explained even when gender differences in education, experience, industries, occupations, and union status are taken into account. The portion of the pay gap that remains unexplained is potentially due to discrimination, though as we shall see shortly, the matter is not quite so simple.

We can consider the results of this study somewhat differently by focusing on the gender wage ratio. The actual ("unadjusted") gender wage ratio is 80 percent; that is, women's wages are, on average, 80 percent of men's wages. If women had the same human capital characteristics (i.e., education and experience), industry and occupational distribution, and union coverage as men, the "adjusted" ratio would rise to 91 percent of men's wages. Thus, although measured characteristics are important, women still earn less than similar men even when all measured characteristics are taken into account.

How conclusive are such estimates as indicators of labor market discrimination? Certainly not entirely so; a number of problems associated with these types of analyses may result in either upward or downward biases in the estimate of discrimination. One difficulty is that we lack information on all the qualifications of individuals that are associated with their (potential) productivity. Some of the factors that affect earnings,

---

[7]As we saw in Chapter 4, female labor force participation is positively correlated with education. This relationship is also true of male participation, but it is stronger for women. Thus, women in the labor force tend to be more highly educated relative to men than is the total female population. Note that the educational variables employed in this study include years of education and dummy variables for being a college graduate and having an advanced degree. Thus these variables do not distinguish between master's degrees on the one hand and Ph.D. and professional degrees on the other.

[8]The study controls for 19 occupations and 25 industries.

such as motivation or work effort, cannot easily be quantified. Others (for example, college major) are frequently unavailable in a particular data set. Hence, in general, it is not possible to include all relevant job qualifications in a study of gender differences in wages.

For instance, although the study reported in Table 7-1 accounts for differences between men and women in many important work-related factors, it lacks data on others that are potentially relevant. If men are more highly qualified with respect to the factors that are omitted from the analysis, the extent of labor market discrimination is likely to be *overestimated.* Some portion of the "unexplained" gender differential in Table 7-1 may, in fact, be due to men being more highly motivated or to gender differences in college major. However, it is also possible that women are more highly qualified in some respects not taken into account. They may possess greater interpersonal skills, for example. In that case, discrimination would be underestimated. In general, more attention has been focused on the possibility that discrimination may be overestimated due to omitted factors.[9]

At the same time, some of the lower qualifications of women may be a direct result of labor market discrimination. For example, qualified women may be excluded from particular jobs due to discrimination in hiring or promotion. The results reported in Table 7-1 include controls for variables such as occupation and industry, which could themselves be affected by such discrimination. To the extent that studies of discrimination control for qualifications that themselves reflect the direct effects of discrimination, the impact of discrimination on the pay gap will be *underestimated.*[10]

Analyses of the type presented in Table 7-1 also neglect the feedback effects of labor market discrimination on the behavior and choices of women themselves. For example, women traditionally received lower returns to labor market experience than men. The lesser amount of work experience that they accumulated may be due in part to their response to these lower returns. As another example, women were perhaps less likely to pursue college study in traditionally male fields because of their perception that they would encounter job discrimination in these areas.

Given the problems with traditional statistical studies, some particularly persuasive evidence of discrimination comes from other types of studies that take a different approach to the question than most previous research. First, two studies applied the same statistical techniques as those discussed previously to especially homogeneous groups and employed particularly extensive controls for qualifications, thus minimizing

---

[9]This problem is a bit less serious than it appears at first glance in that the included factors likely capture some of the effects of those that cannot be controlled for because of lack of information. For example, it is likely that more highly educated individuals are also more intelligent and more able, on average, than the less educated. For an interesting explication of the statistical issues raised by imperfect measures of productivity in empirical analyses, see Arthur Goldberger, "Reverse Regression and Salary Discrimination," *Journal of Human Resources* 19, no. 3 (Summer 1984): 293–318.

[10]For a consideration of such issues, see Alan Blinder, "Wage Discrimination: Reduced Form and Structural Estimates," *Journal of Human Resources* 8, no. 4 (Fall 1973): 436–55; and Ronald Oaxaca, "Male-Female Wage Differences in Urban Labor Markets," *International Economic Review* 14, no. 3 (October 1973): 693–709. For evidence on the issue of discrimination against women in access to on-the-job training, see Greg J. Duncan and Saul Hoffman, "On-the-Job Training and Earnings Differences by Race and Sex," *Review of Economics and Statistics* 61, no. 4 (November 1979): 594–603; John M. Barron, Dan A. Black, and Mark A. Lowenstein, "Gender Differences in Training, Capital and Wages," *Journal of Human Resources* 28, no. 2 (1993): 342–64; and Anne Beeson Royalty, "The Effects of Job Turnover on the Training of Men and Women," *Industrial and Labor Relations Review* 49, no. 3 (April 1996): 506–21.

the effect of gender differences in unmeasured characteristics. The first focused on graduates of the University of Michigan Law School classes of 1972 to 1975, 15 years after graduation.[11] The gap in pay between women and men was found to be relatively small at the outset of their careers, but 15 years later, women graduates earned only 60 percent as much as men. Some of this difference reflected choices that workers themselves made, including the propensity of women lawyers to work shorter hours. However, even after accounting for differences in current hours worked, as well as an extensive list of worker qualifications and other factors, including family status, race, location, grades while in law school, and detailed work history data, such as years practiced law, months of part-time work, and type and size of employer, men still earned 13 percent more. In a similar vein, another study examined gender wage differences in 1985 among recent college graduates (who graduated 1–2 years earlier).[12] After controlling for narrowly defined college major, college grade point average, and specific educational institution attended, this study still found an unexplained pay gap of 10 to 15 percent between men and women.

In addition to providing evidence of unexplained pay differentials between men and women, the results of the study of lawyers suggest the danger in placing too much weight on how younger women fare relative to their male counterparts in assessing whether discrimination against women in the labor market exists. Even though the exceptionally large decreases in the gender pay gap among young workers that we reviewed in Chapter 5 are a welcome sign, it is important to realize that gender pay differences tended in the past to increase over the work career.

A second set of studies used an experimental approach. One analyzed the results of a hiring "audit" in which male and female pseudo–job seekers were given similar résumés and sent to apply for jobs waiting on tables at the same set of 65 Philadelphia restaurants.[13] The results provided statistically significant evidence of discrimination against women in high-priced restaurants where earnings of workers are generally higher. In these restaurants, a female applicant's probability of getting an interview was 40 percentage points lower than a male's and her probability of getting an offer was 50 percentage points lower. A second study examined the impact of the adoption of "blind" auditions for musicians by symphony orchestras in which a screen is used to conceal the identity of the candidate.[14] The screen substantially increased the probability that a woman would advance out of preliminary rounds and be the winner in the final round. The switch to blind auditions was found to explain one quarter of the increase in the percentage female in the top five symphony orchestras in the United States, from less than 5 percent of all musicians in 1970 to 25 percent in 1996.

Third, a recent study that focused on the manufacturing sector attempted to more directly estimate the productivity of women relative to men and then compare the magnitude

---

[11]Robert G. Wood, Mary E. Corcoran, and Paul Courant, "Pay Differences Among the Highly Paid: The Male-Female Earnings Gap in Lawyers' Salaries," *Journal of Labor Economics* 11, no. 3 (July 1993): 417–41.

[12]Catherine J. Weinberger, "Race and Gender Wage Gaps in the Market for Recent College Graduates," *Industrial Relations* 37, no. 1 (January 1998): 67–84.

[13]David Neumark, with the assistance of Roy J. Blank and Kyle D. Van Nort, *Quarterly Journal of Economics* 111, no. 3 (August, 1996): 915–42. Such hiring audits also find evidence of discrimination against minorities; for a summary, see U.S. Department of Labor, *Affirmative Action Review: Report to the President,* 1995.

[14]Claudia Goldin and Cecilia Rouse, "Orchestrating Impartiality: The Impact of 'Blind' Auditions on Female Musicians," *American Economic Review* 90, no. 4 (September 2000): 715–41 See also Blair Tindall, "Call Me Madame Maestro," *New York Times*, January 14, 2005, at www.nytimes.com.

of the productivity gap to the magnitude of the gender wage gap. It was found that women's estimated marginal product was somewhat lower than men's. However, women's wages fell short of men's by considerably more than could be explained by their lower marginal productivity. This finding is consistent with discrimination against women in the labor market.[15]

Further evidence that labor market discrimination exists is provided by the many employment discrimination cases in which employers were found guilty of discrimination in pay or reached out-of-court settlements with the plaintiffs. A number of employment practices that explicitly discriminated against women used to be quite prevalent, including marriage bars restricting the employment of married women[16] and the intentional segregation of men and women into separate job categories with associated separate and lower pay scales for women.[17] Although many such overt practices have receded, recent court cases still provide evidence of employment practices that produce discriminatory outcomes for women.

One recent high-profile case is the $54 million settlement of a sex discrimination lawsuit against Morgan Stanley in 2004, in which plaintiffs claimed that the firm underpaid and did not promote women. Allegations of sexist practices reportedly included claims that Morgan Stanley withheld raises and desirable assignments from women who took maternity leave, and that it condoned a hostile workplace where men made sexist comments and organized trips to topless bars and strip clubs.[18] Another example of a major case was the $31 million settlement of sex bias charges against American Express Financial Advisors, where it was also claimed that female employees were underpaid and given fewer job opportunities. According to the plaintiffs, the company steered the most profitable accounts to male financial advisers and, corporate-wide, men were given preferential treatment in training, mentoring, and promotion. It was claimed that these gender differences were "the product of a stereotype—pervasive both inside Amex and throughout the industry—that women do not have what it takes to succeed in the financial planning business and that only young males have the temperament and the ability to achieve aggressive sales."[19] Similar issues were raised in another high-profile case involving State Farm Insurance, which agreed in 1997 to pay $250 million to a group of women whose lawsuit claimed they were denied or deterred from positions as insurance agents. As yet another example, in 2000, the U.S. Information Agency agreed to pay $508 million to settle a case in which the Voice of America rejected women who applied for high-paying positions in the communications field. A lawyer representing

---

[15]See Judith K. Hellerstein, David Neumark, and Kenneth R. Troske, "Wages, Productivity, and Worker Characteristics: Evidence from Plant-Level Production Functions and Wage Equations," *Journal of Labor Economics* 17, no. 3 (July 1999): 409–46. See also Jonathan S. Leonard, "Antidiscrimination or Reverse Discrimination: The Impact of Title VII, Affirmative Action, and Changing Demographics on Productivity," *Journal of Human Resources* 19 no. 2 (Spring 1984): 145–84.

[16]Claudia Goldin, *Understanding the Gender Gap: An Economic History of American Women* (New York: Oxford University Press, 1990).

[17]See, for example, *Bowe* v. *Colgate-Palmolive Co.,* 416 F.2d 711 (7th Cir., 1969); and *IUE* v. *Westinghouse Electric Co.,* 631 F.2d 1094 (3rd Cir., 1980).

[18]"Sex Suit Costs Morgan Stanley $54M," July 12, 2004, at www.cbsnews.com. See also, Patrick McGeehan, "Discrimination on Wall St.? Run the Numbers and Weep," *New York Times* (July 14, 2004), Section C, pp. 1, 7.

[19]Bureau of National Affairs, "American Express Financial Advisors Reach $31 Million Agreement on Sex Bias Charges," *Employment Discrimination Report* 18, no. 9 (February 27, 2002), p. 251.

the plaintiffs said that the women were told things such as, "These jobs are only for men," or "We're looking for a male voice."[20]

A number of sex discrimination suits have been filed against grocery chains. In 1994, a major chain, Lucky Stores, agreed to a settlement of $107 million after the judge found that "sex discrimination was the standard operating procedure at Lucky with respect to placement, promotion, movement to full-time positions, and the allocation of additional hours." Similar lawsuits against several other grocery chains also ended in settlements, including Publix Super Markets of Florida, which, in 1997, agreed to pay $81.5 million to settle a sex discrimination lawsuit that accused the chain of keeping women in dead-end, low-wage jobs. Although women comprised half the company's workforce, fewer than 5 percent of its 535 store managers were women.[21] Also of interest, it was found in one recent case against a regional grocery chain that clear signs of improvement in the status of female employees occurred as a result of the filing of a lawsuit and the subsequent trial, even before court-mandated remedies were implemented.[22] We provide a review of the provisions of the employment discrimination laws and regulations later in this chapter.

Finally, it is suggestive that the perceptions of Americans, both women and men, are consistent with the existence of gender discrimination. For example, a 2003 Gallup poll reported that 56 percent of women and 44 percent of men did not believe women had equal job opportunities to men; and 62 percent of women and 56 percent of men favored affirmative action programs for women. Similarly, a CBS News poll conducted in 1999 found that 67 percent of women and 58 percent of men thought that it was easier for men than women to get top executive jobs in business or government, while 70 percent of women and 59 percent of men believed that if a man and a woman are doing the same work, the man generally earns more than the woman.[23] Other perceived barriers are noted later in the section on the "glass ceiling."

Where do these findings, taken as a whole, leave us? They suggest that pinpointing the exact portion of the pay gap that is due to labor market discrimination is difficult. Nonetheless, the findings of traditional statistical studies provide strong evidence of pay differences between men and women that are *not* accounted for by gender differences in measured qualifications, even when the list of qualifications is quite extensive. The inference from these results that discrimination exists is backed up by the results of studies that take a different approach, as well as by evidence from court cases and opinion polls. We conclude that discrimination does indeed exist. Although precisely estimating its magnitude is difficult, the evidence suggests that the *direct* effects of labor market discrimination may explain 40 percent or more of the pay differential between men and women.

---

[20]*Federal Human Resources Week* 6, no. 47 (5 April 2000); and Ronette King, "Women Taking Action Against Many Companies," *Times-Picayune,* April 27, 1997.

[21]*Stender v. Lucky Stores, Inc.,* 803 F. Supp. 259 (N.D. Cal., 1992); and King, "Women Taking Action."

[22]Michael R. Ransom and Ronald L. Oaxaca, "Intrafirm Mobility and Sex Differences in Pay," *Industrial and Labor Relations Review* 58, no. 2 (January 2005): 219–37.

[23]Gallup poll data are from www.nationaljournal.com; CBS poll data are from www.pollingreport.com. Interestingly, it has been found that younger women are much more likely than older women to report that they encountered discrimination, perhaps because they are more likely to see a given gender difference as discriminatory; see Heather Antecol and Peter Kuhn, "Gender as an Impediment to Labor Market Success: Why Do Young Women Report Greater Harm?" *Journal of Labor Economics* 18, no. 4 (October 2000): 702–28.

Occupational Differences

As we saw in Chapter 5, not only do women earn less than men, they also tend to be concentrated in different occupations. In this section, we address two questions.

- What are the consequences for women of such occupational segregation? In particular, what is its relationship to the pay gap between men and women?
- What are the causes of these gender differences in occupational distributions? Specifically, what role does labor market discrimination play? Does the evidence indicate a "glass ceiling" that limits the upward mobility of women?

From a policy perspective, an understanding of the consequences of segregation is crucial for assessing how important a problem it is, and an analysis of its causes helps us to determine the most effective tools for attacking it.

Consequences of Occupational Segregation

In Chapter 5, we saw that women are more likely than men to be concentrated in clerical and service jobs, whereas men are more likely than women to work in higher-paying jobs such as skilled craft occupations. Similarly, although the representation of women in the professional category actually exceeds men's, men are more likely to work in lucrative professions such as law, medicine, and engineering, whereas women are more often employed in lower-paying ones such as elementary and secondary school teaching and nursing. Such observations suggest that women are concentrated in relatively low-paying occupations and that this gender difference in occupations helps to explain the male-female pay gap.

On the other hand, factors other than gender composition may help to account for pay differences between male and female jobs. For example, male jobs may tend to require more education and training than female jobs or call for the exercise of skills, such as supervisory responsibility, that are more valuable to the employer. Also, some require more physical strength, inconvenient hours, and so on.

Such characteristics are important, but occupational differences appear to be a significant factor in explaining the earnings gap, even when productivity-related characteristics of workers are held constant. The findings of the study reported in Table 7-1, for example, suggest that differences in the employment of men and women across the 19 occupational categories included in the study account for 27 percent of the pay difference between men and women. Other research that takes account of even more detailed occupational categories suggests that the lower pay in predominantly female jobs accounts for 14 to 23 percent of the gender wage gap, even when the analysis includes a variety of occupational-level and industrial-level characteristics that might help to account for the occupation pay differences.[24]

The findings based on detailed occupations use in excess of 400 occupational categories distinguished by the census—an impressive number. Nonetheless, employers

---

[24]The 23 percent figure is from Elaine Sorensen, "The Crowding Hypothesis and Comparable Worth Issue," *Journal of Human Resources* 25, no. 1 (Winter 1990): 55–89. The 14 percent figure is from George Johnson and Gary Solon, "Estimates of the Direct Effects of Comparable Worth Policy," *American Economic Review* 76, no. 5 (December 1986): 1117–25. The Sorensen article provides an extremely useful summary of the empirical findings in this area; see also David A. Macpherson and Barry T. Hirsch, "Wages and Gender Composition, Why Do Women's Jobs Pay Less?" *Journal of Labor Economics* 13, no. 3 (July 1995): 426–71.

use considerably finer breakdowns. It is likely that, were such extremely detailed categories available for the economy as a whole, an even higher proportion of the pay gap would be attributed to occupational segregation.[25] Moreover, within the same occupational category, women tend to be employed in low-wage firms and industries, whereas men tend to be employed in high-wage firms and industries. In the study reported in Table 7-1, for example, gender differences in industry and union status together account for an additional 25 percent of the gender gap. Other research suggests that, even when controls for detailed occupational category are included, industry differences account for 12 to 17 percent of the pay gap among equally qualified male and female workers.[26]

In evaluating the negative consequences of occupational segregation for women, it is important to bear in mind that the focus upon earnings does not take into account any adverse nonpecuniary consequences of such segregation. For one, it is likely that occupational segregation reinforces cultural notions of exaggerated differences between men and women in capabilities, preferences, and social and economic roles. Such beliefs may adversely affect the opportunities and outcomes even of women in predominantly male jobs.

Causes of Occupational Segregation

As with earnings differences, the causes of occupational segregation may be classified into supply-side versus demand-side factors. It is only the latter—differences in treatment—that represent *direct* labor market discrimination. Of course, here again, the anticipation of, or experience with, labor market discrimination may indirectly influence women's choices via feedback effects.

In the preceding chapter, we considered human capital theory, which suggests that, because women generally anticipate shorter and less continuous work lives than men, it will be in their economic self-interest to choose female occupations, which presumably require smaller human capital investments and have lower wage penalties for time spent out of the labor market. We also discussed a variety of other supply-side factors that could influence women's occupational choices, including the socialization process and constraints placed by traditional gender roles on women's ability to work long hours, travel extensively as part of their jobs, and relocate to new labor markets; and considered various subtle barriers that may impede women's access to training in traditionally male fields. On the demand side, employers may contribute to occupational segregation by discriminating against equally qualified women in hiring, job placement, access to training programs, and promotion for traditionally male jobs.

---

[25]See, for instance, Francine D. Blau, "Occupational Segregation and Labor Market Discrimination," in *Sex Segregation in the Workplace: Trends, Explanations, Remedies,* edited by Barbara Reskin (Washington, DC: National Academy Press, 1984), pp. 117–43.

[26]Sorensen, "The Crowding Hypothesis." For evidence of the importance of gender differences in employment by firm, see Francine D. Blau, *Equal Pay in the Office* (Lexington, MA: Lexington Books, 1977); Erica L. Groshen, "The Structure of the Female/Male Wage Differential: Is It Who You Are, What You Do, or Where You Work?" *Journal of Human Resources* 26, no. 3 (Summer 1991): 457–72; and Kimberly Bayard, Judith Hellerstein, David Neumark, and Kenneth Troske, "New Evidence on Sex Segregation and Sex Difference in Wages from Matched Employee-Employer Data," *Journal of Labor Ecnomics* 21, no.4 (October 2003): 887–923.

Considerable evidence supports the belief that gender differences in preferences play some role in gender differences in occupations.[27] The claim that discrimination is also important is more controversial, but here too quite a bit of evidence suggests that discrimination plays a role as well. Of course, it is not an easy matter to distinguish between preferences and discrimination empirically especially when, as is likely, both contribute to observed differences.

Some persuasive evidence of the importance of discrimination comes from descriptions of institutional barriers that historically excluded women from particular pursuits or impeded their upward progression.[28] In addition, many studies, although not all, find that women are less likely to be promoted, all else equal.[29] Another finding is that a major portion of the gender difference in on-the-job training remains unexplained, even after gender differences in the probability of worker turnover and other variables are taken into account.[30] This finding suggests that women may encounter discrimination in access to on-the-job training; such training may be valuable in providing an entrée to higher-paying jobs.

Although such findings regarding promotion and training are certainly consistent with discrimination, it is important to note that they suffer from the same problems raised earlier in our analysis of the determinants of the gender pay gap. They may overstate discrimination if other important nondiscriminatory factors are omitted from the analysis, such as tastes for particular types of work, availability for travel, and so forth, which could help to account for the observed gender differences. On the other hand, discrimination would be understated to the extent some of the variables that are controlled for, such as initial job category in a promotion study, reflect the impact of labor market discrimination.

Given these types of concerns, it is not possible to use these findings to ascribe a specific portion of gender differences in occupations to the choices individual men and women make versus labor market discrimination (i.e., to supply-side vs. demand-side factors).[31] However, as in the case of our review of evidence on the pay gap, the evidence

---

[27]Morley Gunderson, "Male-Female Wage Differentials and Policy Responses," *Journal of Economic Literature* 27, no. 1 (March 1989): 46–72.

[28]Barbara F. Reskin and Heidi I. Hartmann, eds., *Women's Work, Men's Work: Sex Segregation on the Job* (Washington DC: National Academy Press, 1986).

[29]For examples of studies that find evidence of lower promotion rates, see Deborah A. Cobb-Clark, "Getting Ahead: The Determinants of and Payoffs for Internal Promotion for Young U.S. Men and Women," in *Worker Wellbeing in a Changing Labor Market*, edited by Solomon W. Polachek, *Research in Labor Economics*, vol. 20 (Amsterdam: Elsevier Science, JAI, 2001), pp. 339–72; and Kristin McCue, "Promotions and Wage Growth," *Journal of Labor Economics* 14, no. 2 (1996): 175–209. For an example of a study that does not find evidence of discrimination, see Joni Hersch and W. Kip Viscusi, "Gender Differences in Promotions and Wages," *Industrial Relations* 35, no. 4 (October 1996): 461–72.

[30]Royalty, "The Effects of Job Turnover"; see also Barron, Black, and Lowenstein, "Gender Differences"; and Duncan and Hoffman, "On-the-Job Training."

[31]For additional evidence on the sources of gender differences in occupations, see Barbara F. Reskin and Patricia A. Roos, *Job Queues, Gender Queues: Explaining Women's Inroads into Male Occupations* (Philadelphia: Temple University Press, 1990); Virginia Valian, *Why So Slow? The Advancement of Women* (Cambridge MA: MIT Press, 1998); Paula England, "Socioeconomic Explanations of Job Segregation," in *Comparable Worth and Wage Discrimination: Technical Possibilities and Political Realities*, edited by Helen Remick (Philadelphia: Temple University Press, 1984), pp. 28–46; Patricia A. Roos and Barbara F. Reskin, "Institutional Factors Contributing to Occupational Sex Segregation," in *Sex Segregation in the Workplace: Trends, Explanations, Remedies*, edited by Barbara Reskin (Washington, DC: National Academy Press, 1984), pp. 235–60; and Reskin and Hartmann, *Women's Work, Men's Work*.

suggests that both are important. And, as in the case of pay differences, evidence of discrimination may be found not only in statistical analyses but also in the audit studies discussed earlier and discrimination cases in which employers were found guilty of gender discrimination or settled the cases out of court.

Two recent studies are especially suggestive of the importance of discrimination, including the types of subtle barriers that we consider in our discussion of the glass ceiling that follows. One, a study of small firms, found that male employers paid higher wages and employed fewer women than did female employers.[32] The second, a study of managers in the California savings and loan industry, found that employing more women at specific levels of the firm hierarchy creates more opportunities for women. Specifically, women's chances of being hired and promoted were greater when a higher proportion of women were employed at the level of the job being filled.[33]

Is There a Glass Ceiling?

The *glass ceiling* is the name given to the set of subtle barriers believed by many to inhibit women and minorities from reaching the upper echelons of corporate America, government, and academia. To the extent such barriers exist, they constitute a form of labor market discrimination. Is there a glass ceiling impeding women's occupational advancement? Disparities in the representation of women at the upper levels of many professions are easy to document. As our preceding discussion suggests, however, the reasons behind them may be harder to pin down. In this section, we consider the extent of the gender differences in representation at the higher levels of the job hierarchy, focusing first on management jobs and then academia, and summarize what is known about the reasons for women's underrepresentation at the upper levels, as well as steps recommended to promote women's advancement.

Looking first at the senior ranks of management, we noted in Chapter 5 the extremely low representation of women in these jobs. According to a report by Catalyst on *Fortune* 500 companies, only 15.7 percent of all corporate officers and 7.9 percent of top-level executives were women in 2002. Further, women held just 5.2 percent of the top five most highly paid executive positions in the company. These findings did, however, represent a substantial increase from 8.7 percent of officers, 2.4 percent of top-level executives, and 1.2 percent of top earners in 1995.[34] Women were also sparsely represented on corporate boards of directors in these firms, holding 13.6 percent of board seats, up from 8.3 percent in 1993.[35]

It is difficult in general to determine whether these disparities are simply due to the fact that women are relative newcomers and it takes time to move up through the ranks or whether they represent particular barriers to women's advancement. This issue is particularly thorny in areas such as management, where data on the available candidates for

---

[32]William J. Carrington and Kenneth R. Troske, "Gender Segregation in Small Firms," *Journal of Human Resources* 30, no. 3 (Summer 1995): 503–33.

[33]Lisa E. Cohen, Joseph P. Broschak, and Heather Haveman, "And Then There Were More? The Effect of Organizational Sex Composition on the Hiring and Promotion of Women," *American Sociological Review* 63, no. 5 (October 1998): 711–27.

[34]Top-level or "clout" positions include CEO, chair, vice chair, president, COO, senior VP, and executive VP; see Catalyst, *2002 Catalyst Census of Women Corporate Officers and Top Earners in the Fortune 500.* For international evidence on the extent of such disparities, see Linda Wirth, *Breaking Through the Glass Ceiling: Women in Management* (Geneva: International Labour Office, 2001).

[35]Catalys*t, 2003 Catalyst Census of Women Board Directors,* and previous issues.

these positions do not exist and where norms regarding the speed of upward movement are not well defined. However, a recent study of executives does highlight the substantial impact on pay of gender differences in level of the job hierarchy and firm, although it does not shed light on the causes of such differences.[36] In a sample of the five highest-paid executives among a large group of firms, the study found that the 2.5 percent of the executives who were women earned 45 percent less than their male counterparts. Female executives were younger and thus had less seniority, a factor in the gender pay difference. However, three-quarters of the gender pay gap was due to the fact that women managed smaller companies and were less likely to be the CEO, chair, or president of their company. Consistent with the Catalyst data, this study found that over the 1992–1997 sample period, the representation of women in these top-earner executive jobs rose somewhat and women's representation at larger corporations increased as well.

Even though the evidence is not sufficient to fully resolve the issue of how disparities of the type we outlined here arise, it is important to understand that, to the extent discrimination plays a role, it certainly need not manifest itself through overt and conscious acts of discrimination against women. The barriers women face are often subtle and difficult to document, let alone remove. One example is recruiting practices in which the use of personal contacts from the "old boys' network" can leave women "out of the loop." In addition, women often remain outsiders to a "male" workplace culture. A study of female executives found that women who do break through the glass ceiling are successful because "they've developed styles that make men comfortable." A prime example is that, because sports have traditionally been a male domain, successful women are often those who learn to play golf and talk sports.[37]

There may also be stereotyped views about women's qualifications that result in able women receiving fewer opportunities. For example, it may be believed that women are not aggressive enough, are unwilling to relocate for higher positions, and, when they have families, are less committed to their jobs than their male counterparts. In the increasingly important arena of international business, a number of preconceptions limit women's access to these jobs and, in turn, may restrict their corporate opportunities. Among these preconceptions are that women are not as geographically mobile as men, that international clients are not as comfortable doing business with women as with men, and that women would find it more difficult than men to balance the dual demands of job-related international travel with home responsibilities.[38]

Another subtle barrier that may limit women's advancement is the perception that men make better bosses. A 2003 survey of female executives from *Fortune* 1000 companies by Catalyst reported that 40 percent believed that men have difficulty being managed by women.[39] Because men have traditionally staffed upper-level positions in

---

[36]Marianne Bertrand and Kevin F. Hallock, "The Gender Gap in Top Corporate Jobs," *Industrial and Labor Relations Review* 55, no.1 (October 2001): 3–21. Blau and Kahn, "The U.S. Gender Pay Gap in the 1990s," present some evidence consistent with a greater negative effect of glass ceiling barriers on women's relative wages in the 1990s than in the 1980s, and speculate that women's 1980s gains placed more of them into the higher-level positions where glass-ceiling barriers hinder their further upward progression.
[37]"Women's Success Linked to Their Ability to Adapt," *St. Louis Post-Dispatch,* February 28, 1996.
[38]Catalyst, *Passport to Opportunity: U.S. Women in Global Business,* news release, October 18, 2000.
[39]See Catalyst, *Women in U.S. Corporate Leadership,* New York, 2003, p. 6. Alice H. Eagly and Steven J. Karau argue that a perceived incongruity between the female gender role and leadership roles results in women being viewed less favorably than men as potential leaders and being evaluated less favorably than men for behavior that fits with a leadership role; see "Role Congruity Theory of Prejudice Toward Female Leaders," *Psychological Review* 109, no. 3 (July 2002): 573–98.

most firms, many men and women make this assessment without any previous opportunity to compare. One study found that when workers are exposed to women bosses, preexisting stereotypes tend to break down; both men and women who ever worked for a female boss were considerably less likely to prefer a male boss.[40]

When asked about the major barriers to women's advancement in general, the female executives cited the same types of barriers in 2003 as respondents had in 1996; the three mentioned most frequently were: lack of general management or line experience (the latter refers to positions tied to the firm's "bottom line"); exclusion from informal networks; and stereotyping and preconceptions of women's roles and abilities. They did, however, see these barriers as somewhat less pervasive than 1996 respondents. Women's underrepresentation in line positions is a disadvantage because these jobs tend to provide greater opportunities for upward progression in the corporate hierarchy than the staff positions that women are more likely to hold. The female executives were also asked about the barriers they personally faced in moving up. One factor that they mentioned, not cited in the preceding discussion, is a lack of role models.[41]

The status of women in academia, discussed briefly in Chapter 5, is a subject that has attracted a great deal of attention among researchers. This attention may in part be due to the role faculty members can play as potential mentors and role models for students. Another reason is that a clear hierarchy for faculty exists, along with relatively well-defined criteria for progressing within this hierarchy. These factors make the status of women in academia a particularly instructive case.

Table 7-2 provides data on the distribution of men and women in academia by rank in the mid-1970s and the early 2000s. In its broad outlines, the situation is quite clear. In each year, women were concentrated at the lower end of the occupational hierarchy as lecturers, instructors and assistant professors, whereas men were more highly represented at the upper ranks, as professors and associate professors—the categories that tend to provide job security in the form of tenure. Women were especially heavily represented as instructors and lecturers, job categories that tend to be considerably less desirable in terms of pay, promotion prospects, and job continuity. Other data indicate substantial differences by level of institution, with women tending to be underrepresented at the most highly ranked research universities and much more heavily represented at smaller, liberal arts institutions and two-year colleges.[42] Women also tend to be concentrated in less lucrative fields in the humanities, while men tend to dominate in the higher-paying scientific and technical fields.

Disparities in the representation of women and men by level of the academic hierarchy may be due in whole or part to the more recent entry of women into academia and the time it takes to move up the ladder. The data in Table 7-2 do suggest some female gains over time, consistent with the "pipeline" argument. So, although women are

---

[40]See "Bias Alive in Workplace," *St. Louis Post-Dispatch,* March 27, 1996; and Marianne Ferber, Joan Huber, and Glenna Spitze, "Preference for Men as Bosses and Professionals," *Social Forces* 58, no. 2 (1979): 466–76.

[41]Catalyst, *Women in U.S. Corporate Leadership*, New York, 2003, p. 16.

[42]For example, in 1998–1999, women constituted 46.6 percent of faculty at two-year colleges but were only 28.8 percent of the faculty at research universities that grant doctorates (*Academe,* March–April 1999, table 12, p. 32). See also Marianne A. Ferber and Jane W. Loeb, "Introduction," in *Academic Couples, Problems and Promise,* edited by Marianne A. Ferber and Jane W. Loeb (Champaign, IL: University of Illinois Press, 1997).

TABLE 7-2 Percent Female of Faculty in Institutions of Higher Education by Academic Rank, 1976–1977 and 2003–2004

Academic Rank	1976–1977	2003–2004
Professors	8.4	23.0
Associate professors	16.7	38.5
Assistant professors	29.7	46.2
Instructors	49.0	58.3
Lecturers	41.9	54.2
All Ranks	22.4	37.2

Sources: *Academe*, August 1981 and March–April 1993: 2003–2004 figures calculated from *Academe* (March–April 2004), Table 12.

underrepresented at the higher ranks in both years, their representation increased markedly over time with the progression of women up through the ranks.

Detailed studies suggest, however, that despite recent changes, discrimination does play a role in academia. For example, a recent study of faculty promotion in the economics profession found that, controlling for quality of Ph.D. training, publishing productivity, major field of specialization, current placement in a distinguished department, age, and post-Ph.D. experience, female economists were still significantly less likely to be promoted from assistant to associate and from associate to full professor—although some evidence also indicates that women's promotion opportunities from associate to full professor improved in the 1980s.[43] Moreover, women appear to face obstacles to their efforts to accumulate the publications and other credentials necessary to move up in the ranks. For example, some evidence indicates that women in predominantly male fields are likely to have greater difficulty than men finding collaborators and in getting their papers accepted for publication. And, once published, their publications are less likely to be cited.[44] Other types of disparities in treatment may adversely affect the success of women in academia. For example, a 1999 report on faculty at MIT found evidence of differential treatment of senior women that may encompass not simply differences in salary but also in space, awards, and resources, "with women receiving less despite professional accomplishments equal to those of their male colleagues."[45]

[43]John M. McDowell, Larry D. Singell Jr., and James P. Ziliak, "Cracks in the Glass Ceiling: Gender and Promotion in the Economics Profession," *American Economic Review* 89, no. 2 (May 1999): 392–96. See also Shulamit Kahn and Donna K. Ginther, "Women in Economics: Moving Up or Falling Off the Academic Career Ladder," *Journal of Economic Perspectives* 18, no. 3 (Summer 2004): 193–214; Massachusetts Institute of Technology, "A Study on the Status of Women Faculty in Science at MIT," *The MIT Faculty Newsletter* 11, no. 4 (March 1999); Donna K. Ginther and Kathy J. Hayes, "Gender Differences in Salary and Promotion in the Humanities," *American Economic Review* 89, no. 2 (May 1999): 397–402; and Sharon G. Levin and Paula E. Stephan, "Gender Differences in the Rewards to Publishing in Academe: Science in the 1970s," *Sex Roles* 38, no. 11–12 (June 1998): 1049–64.

[44]Marianne A. Ferber and Michelle L. Teiman, "Are Women Economists at a Disadvantage in Publishing Journal Articles?" *Eastern Economic Journal* 6, nos. 3–4 (August–October 1980): 189–94; and Marianne A. Ferber, "Citations and Networking," *Gender and Society* 2, no. 1 (March 1988): 82–89. However, one study of a major economics journal did not find evidence of a gender difference in acceptance rates; see Rebecca M. Blank, "The Effects of Double-Blind versus Single-Blind Reviewing: Experimental Evidence from the *American Economic Review*," *American Economic Review* 81, no. 5 (December 1991): 1041–67.

[45]Massachusetts Institute of Technology, "A Study on the Status of Women Faculty," p. 4.

In 1995, a bipartisan Federal Glass Ceiling Commission made several recommendations to address these various concerns.[46] The commission's report recommended that government "lead by example" and strengthen enforcement of antidiscrimination laws. Later in this chapter, we summarize these laws and consider what is known about their effectiveness. The report also stressed a variety of actions employers can take voluntarily to promote the advancement of women and minorities in the organization, including ensuring strong leadership at the top, linking pay and promotions of managers to meeting goals of workplace diversity, and expanding recruitment practices to cast a wider net for minorities and women, as well as providing additional training and mentoring opportunities for new hires. Finally, the report noted that society at large helps to perpetuate the glass ceiling. The commission recommended that the media carefully examine how they portray minorities and women, and that educators take steps to encourage minority and female students to pursue nontraditional careers.

MODELS OF LABOR MARKET DISCRIMINATION

The empirical evidence suggests that there are indeed pay and occupational differences between men and women that are not accounted for by (potential) productivity differences. We now turn to an examination of how labor market discrimination can produce such gender differences in economic outcomes and why this inequality has persisted over time. Economists have developed a variety of models that may be used to analyze these issues. Empirical research in this area does not, however, establish which of these approaches most accurately describes the labor market. Indeed, for the most part, these explanations are *not* mutually exclusive and each may shed some light on how labor market discrimination affects women's economic outcomes.

Unless otherwise indicated, the analyses presented here assume that male labor and female labor are perfect substitutes in production. That is, it is assumed that male and female workers are equally well qualified and, in the absence of discrimination, would be equally productive and receive the same pay. Of course, we know that this assumption is not an accurate description of reality—gender differences in qualifications exist and explain some of the pay gap. However, this assumption is appropriate in that models of discrimination are efforts to explain the portion of the pay gap that is *not* due to differences in qualifications; that is, they are intended to explain pay differences between men and women who are (potentially) equally productive.

Tastes for Discrimination

The foundation for the modern neoclassical analysis of labor market discrimination was laid by Gary Becker.[47] Becker conceptualized discrimination as a personal prejudice, or what he termed a *taste,* against associating with a particular group. In his model, employers, coworkers, and customers may all potentially display such discriminatory

[46]See "The Glass Ceiling," *CQ Researcher,* Congressional Quarterly Inc. 3, no. 40, (October 29, 1993): 937–59; and "A Solid Investment: Making Full Use of the Nation's Human Capital," Recommendations of the Glass Ceiling Commission, Washington, DC (November 1995).

[47]Becker, *The Economics of Discrimination.* In our presentation of the tastes for discrimination model, we incorporate some of the insights of Kenneth Arrow; see "The Theory of Discrimination," in *Discrimination in Labor Markets,* edited by Orley Ashenfelter and Albert Rees (Princeton, NJ: Princeton University Press, 1973), pp. 3–33.

tastes. In contrast to the case of racial discrimination that Becker initially analyzed, it may at first seem odd to hypothesize that men would not like to associate with women when, in fact, they generally live together in families. The issue here may be more one of socially appropriate roles than of the desire to maintain social distance, as Becker postulated was the case with race.[48]

Employers who show no reservations about hiring women as secretaries may be reluctant to employ them as plumbers. Men who are willing to work with women in complementary or subordinate positions may dislike interacting with them as equals or superiors. Customers who are delighted to purchase pantyhose from female clerks may avoid women who sell cars or are attorneys. If such discriminatory tastes reflect a dislike for interacting with women in these positions, rather than beliefs that women are less qualified than men for traditionally male pursuits, they are appropriately analyzed here.[49] The latter possibility is considered later under notions of statistical discrimination.

In order for such discriminatory tastes to result in important consequences for women's earnings and employment, they must actually influence people's behavior. According to Becker, individuals with tastes for discrimination against women act as if there were nonpecuniary costs of associating with women—say, in what is viewed as a socially inappropriate role.[50] The strength of the individual's discriminatory taste is measured by his or her **discrimination coefficient** (i.e., the size of these costs in money terms). We now examine the consequences of discrimination based on employer, employee, and customer preferences, respectively.

Employer Discrimination

If an employer has tastes for discrimination against women, he or she will act as if there were a nonpecuniary cost of employing women equal in dollar terms to d_r (the discrimination coefficient). To this employer, the costs of employing a man will be his wage, w_m, but the *full* costs of employing a woman will be her wage *plus* the discrimination coefficient ($w_f + d_r$). A discriminating employer will hire a woman only if the full cost of employing her ($w_f + d_r$) is no greater than the cost of employing a man (w_m) and will be indifferent between hiring a man or a woman if the full cost of a woman exactly equals the cost for a man. This implies that the discriminating employer will hire a woman only at a lower wage than a man ($w_f = w_m - d_r$). Further, if we assume that men and women are equally productive, that is, their marginal products *(MP)* are

---

[48]The notion of socially appropriate roles may also be a factor in racial discrimination, as when blacks experience little difficulty in gaining access to menial jobs but encounter discrimination in obtaining higher-level positions.

[49]However, as we shall see, such discriminatory preferences on the part of workers or customers for men will cause women to be less productive from the point of view of the employer. For further consideration of the origin and persistence of occupational segregation, see Reskin and Roos, *Job Queues, Gender Queues;* and Myra H. Strober, "Toward a General Theory of Occupational Sex Segregation: The Case of Public School Teaching," in *Sex Segregation in the Workplace: Trends, Explanations, Remedies,* edited by Barbara F. Reskin (Washington, DC: National Academy Press, 1984), pp. 144–56.

[50]Throughout, we assume that employers, coworkers, or customers have tastes for discrimination against women. It is also possible that they have positive preferences for employing, working with, or buying from men. This may be termed a kind of *nepotism.* See Matthew Goldberg, "Discrimination, Nepotism, and Long-Run Wage Differentials," *Quarterly Journal of Economics* 97, no. 2 (May 1982): 307–19 for an interesting analysis of the consequences of nepotism for the persistence of discrimination in the long run. See also David Neumark, "Employers' Discriminatory Behavior and the Estimation of Wage Discrimination," *Journal of Human Resources* 23, no. 3 (Summer 1988): 279–95.

the same, and that men are paid in accordance with their productivity, then women will be hired only if they are paid less than their productivity.[51]

Becker's analysis showed that the consequences of this situation for female workers depend on the prevalence and size of discriminatory tastes among employers, as well as on the number of women seeking employment. Nondiscriminatory employers are willing to hire men and women at the same wage rate (i.e., their discrimination coefficient equals 0). When the number of such nondiscriminatory employers is relatively large or relatively few women are seeking employment, women workers may all be absorbed by the nondiscriminatory firms. In this case, no discriminatory pay differential occurs based on gender, even though some employers have tastes for discrimination against women.

However, if discriminatory tastes are widespread, or the number women seeking employment is relatively large, some women will have to find jobs at discriminatory firms. These women obtain such employment only if w_f is less than w_m. If we assume that the labor market is competitive, all employers will pay the (same) going rate established in the market for workers of a particular sex. No employer would be willing to pay more than the going rate, because additional workers are always available at that wage. No worker will accept less than the going rate, because jobs at other firms are always available to him or her at that wage. In equilibrium, then, the market wage differential between men and women must be large enough so that all the women who are looking for employment obtain it—including those who must find work at discriminatory firms. Thus, the more prevalent and the stronger employers' discriminatory tastes against women and the larger the number of women seeking employment, the larger will be the marketwide wage gap $(w_m - w_f)$ between men and women.

This model of employer tastes for discrimination is consistent with the inequalities between men and women that we observe in the labor market. Under this model, a wage differential may exist between equally qualified male and female workers because discriminatory employers will hire women workers only at a wage discount.[52] Further, because less discriminatory employers will hire more women workers than more discriminatory employers, male and female workers may be segregated by firm—as also appears to be the case. Finally, if, as seems likely, employer tastes for discrimination vary across occupations, occupational segregation by sex can also occur.

However, one problem that economists have identified with this model is that discrimination is not costless to the employer who forgoes the opportunity to hire more of the lower-priced female labor and less of the higher-priced male labor. Therefore, less discriminatory firms should have lower costs of production. Such a competitive advantage would enable them to expand and drive the more discriminatory firms out of business in the long run. As the less discriminatory firms expand, the demand for female labor would

---

[51]That is, if $w_m = MP$, where MP is equal to the marginal productivity of men (or women), then women will be paid $w_m - d_r$, which is less than their productivity.

[52]Some studies have proposed testing the employer discrimination model by comparing the gender pay gap among self-employed workers and employees. The claim is that if *employer* discrimination is responsible for the pay differential, female self-employed workers should fare relatively better than female employees, all else being equal. See Victor R. Fuchs, "Differences in Hourly Earnings Between Men and Women," *Monthly Labor Review* 94, no. 5 (May 1971): 9–15; and Robert L. Moore, "Employer Discrimination: Evidence from Self-Employed Workers," *Review of Economics and Statistics* 65, no. 3 (August 1983): 496–501. Although such studies do not support the employer discrimination model, they do not provide an ideal test because self-employment and wage and salary employment differ in a number of important dimensions. Among these dimensions, self-employment requires access to capital, and there may be discrimination against women by lenders. Discrimination by customers is another possibility.

be increased and the male-female pay gap would be reduced. If there were enough *entirely* nondiscriminatory firms to absorb all the women workers, the pay gap would be eliminated. Hence, the question is how discrimination, which represents a departure from profit-maximizing behavior, can withstand the impact of competitive pressures.

One answer to this question is that discrimination may simply result from a lack of such competitive pressures in the economy. Becker hypothesized that, on average, employer discrimination would be less severe in competitive than in monopolistic industries, and some research supports this prediction. For example, with the deregulation of the banking industry beginning in the mid-1970s, the gender pay gap in banking declined and the representation of women in managerial positions increased.[53] These findings suggest that employers in banking were able to discriminate in part due to the monopolistic nature of the industry, but that their ability to do so was reduced when competition was increased (by deregulation).

Also consistent with Becker's reasoning is another recent study that finds that, among plants with high levels of product market power (and hence an ability to exercise their tastes for discrimination in the Becker model), those employing relatively more women were more profitable.[54] This correlation suggests that, among these firms, there is some discrimination against women and that less discriminatory firms benefit from the lower costs of production resulting from hiring more women.

Finally, unions may also, to some extent, be considered a barrier to competition in that wages may be set above the competitive level in the union sector. Unions are also more likely to arise in less competitive industries, and it is indeed the case that women are less highly represented in unionized employment. Thus, women do not benefit from the wage advantage of unionism to the same extent as men.[55] However, as we shall see in greater detail in Chapter 8, the gender difference in union representation has been narrowing.

It has also been suggested that *monopsony* power by employers in the labor market plays a role in producing and perpetuating the gender pay differential. One way in which a firm gains monopsony power is when it is a large buyer of labor relative to the size of a particular market.

To see how monopsony power can adversely affect women, consider the not uncommon case of a one-university town. In the past, when the husband's job prospects usually determined the location of the family, the faculty wife with a Ph.D. had little choice but to take whatever the university offered her—most considered themselves fortunate if they were able to obtain employment at all. Even the growing numbers of egalitarian Ph.D. couples cannot entirely avoid this problem. Although an increasing number of two-career couples, in academia and elsewhere, work in different locations

---

[53]Sandra E. Black and Philip E. Strahan, "The Division of Spoils: Rent-Sharing and Discrimination in a Regulated Labor Market" *American Economic Review* 91, no. 4 (September 2001): 814-31. See also Sandra E. Black, "Investigating the Link Between Competition and Discrimination," *Monthly Labor Review* 122, no. 12 (December 1999): 39–43; and Orley Ashenfelter and Timothy Hannan, "Sex Discrimination and Product Market Competition: The Case of the Banking Industry," *Quarterly Journal of Economics* 101, no. 1 (February 1986): 149–73. Another possible reason for the persistence of employer discrimination in the long run is that it is based on a positive preference by employers for male workers (or "nepotism") rather than a disutility for employing female workers; see Goldberg, "Discrimination, Nepotism, and Long-Run Wage Differentials."
[54]Judith K. Hellerstein, David Neumark, and Kenneth Troske, "Market Forces and Sex Discrimination," *Journal of Human Resources* 37, no. 2 (Spring 2002): 353–80.
[55]For an analysis of the impact of unions on gender pay differences, see William E. Even and David A. MacPherson, "The Decline of Private-Sector Unionism and the Gender Wage Gap," *Journal of Human Resources* 28, no. 2 (Spring 1993): 279–96.

and see each other, say, on weekends, most seek jobs in the same location. In order to change jobs, such couples must find *two* acceptable alternatives in a single location. This will obviously be harder to do than to find *one* desirable alternative. Thus, the Ph.D. couple will have fewer options than those with only one Ph.D. in the family. (Similar problems can arise for two-career couples in other fields.)

This situation gives the employer a degree of monopsony power and is likely to lower the pay of both members of the couple relative to Ph.D.s who can relocate more easily. Note that among Ph.D. couples, both the husband's *and* the wife's salary may be adversely affected. However, because women with Ph.D.s are more likely than male Ph.D.s to have a Ph.D. spouse (still considerably fewer women than men obtain Ph.D.s), this factor is likely to have a larger adverse effect on academic women as a group than on academic men.[56]

The monopsony model has been offered as a general explanation for the gender pay gap. Some argue that employers hold greater monopsony power over women than men due to such factors as occupational segregation that may limit women's options. Further, as we saw in Chapter 6, women who adopt more traditional gender roles will tend to engage in less job search than men and to seek jobs that are closer to home.[57]

Consideration of job search suggests that another way in which firms may gain monopsony power is if workers lack perfect information about employment opportunities.[58] In a competitive model with perfect information, even a slightly higher wage at another firm will induce workers to move to that better opportunity. However, when information is imperfect, workers must search among employers for a good job match, thus incurring "search costs." These costs include the opportunity cost of the time spent looking for a job, as well as out-of-pocket costs for printing up a resume, transportation expenses to employment interviews, and so on. Because search is costly, workers will be less mobile across firms than they would be if information was perfectly and costlessly available and it will take larger wage premiums at other firms to bid them away. The presence of search costs gives employers a degree of monopsony power over workers. If we further assume that some employers discriminate against women and are not willing to hire them, we see that women face higher search costs than men. As a consequence employers will exploit this greater monopsony power over women and offer them lower wages than men. Thus, when information is imperfect and search costs exist, it is more credible that employer discrimination can persist in the long run.[59]

---

[56]Evidence indicates, at least for one institution, that both men and women in academic couples were paid less; see Marianne A. Ferber and Jane W. Loeb, "Professors, Performance and Rewards," *Industrial Relations,* 13, no. 1 (February 1974): 67–77.

[57]Janice F. Madden, *The Economics of Sex Discrimination* (Lexington, MA: Lexington Books, 1973). See also Alan Manning, "The Equal Pay Act as an Experiment to Test Theories of the Labour Market," *Economica* 63, no. 250 (May 1996): 191–212.

[58]We draw heavily here on Dan A. Black, "Discrimination in an Equilibrium Search Model," *Journal of Labor Economics* 13, no. 2 (April 1995): 309–34.

[59]A problem with the monopsony explanations, however, is that they require that women's labor supply to the *firm* be less sensitive to wages than men's. Yet, as we know from Chapter 4, women's labor supply to the *market* tends to more sensitive than men's. Although proponents of the monopsony view do suggest plausible reasons why women's mobility at the firm level may be reduced, these explanations may or may not be sufficient to outweigh women's greater overall wage elasticity of labor supply to the market. In fact, after reviewing results from three studies of the quit behavior of men and women, Francine D. Blau and Lawrence M. Kahn find no evidence that men's labor supply is more sensitive to wages than women's at the firm level; see "Institutions and Laws in the Labor Market," in *Handbook of Labor Economics,* edited by Orley Ashenfelter and David Card (The Netherlands: Elsevier Science, B.V., 1999), chap. 25, pp. 3A: 1399–461.

Another possible reason (not originally considered by Becker) for the persistence of discrimination in the labor market is that the employers' motivation for discriminating against women is not simply personal prejudice but is related to actual or perceived differences between male and female workers in productivity or behavior. We consider such models of **statistical discrimination** later in this chapter. A major contribution of Becker's, however, is the realization that, even if employers themselves have no tastes for discrimination against women, their profit-maximizing behavior may result in gender discrimination in the labor market if employees or customers have such tastes. No conflict arises here with profit maximization by employers. Hence, there is no economic reason why this type of discrimination cannot continue.[60] We now consider the possibility of discriminating employees and customers.

Employee Discrimination

If a male employee has tastes for discrimination against women, he will act as if there were nonpecuniary costs of working with women equal to his discrimination coefficient, d_e. This is the premium he must be paid to induce him to work with women. Thus, if a discriminating male worker would receive w_m if he did not work with a woman, he would only be willing to work with a woman at a higher wage $(w_m + d_e)$. This higher wage is analogous to the compensating wage differential that economists expect workers to be offered for unpleasant or unsafe working conditions.[61]

What will be the profit-maximizing employer's response to this situation? One solution would be for the employer to hire a sex-segregated workforce and thereby eliminate the necessity of paying a premium to male workers for associating with female workers. If all employers responded in this way (but had no taste for discrimination themselves), male and female workers would be paid the same wage rate, although they would work in segregated settings.

However, complete segregation may not be profitable when substantial costs of adjustment arise from the previous situation.[62] For example, the hiring of new workers entails recruitment and screening costs for the firm. Further, for jobs in which firm-specific training is important, the firm must incur the costs of these investments as well. Where such costs are involved in changing from the current situation, history matters. Given rising female participation rates over time, women, as relatively new entrants, will find men already in place in many sectors. Further, as we saw in Chapter 2, women were heavily concentrated in a few female-dominated activities even when they constituted a small proportion of the labor force. Regardless of the various factors initially causing

---

[60]Lawrence M. Kahn presents a model that shows that customer discrimination can produce persistent discriminatory wage differentials in "Customer Discrimination and Affirmative Action," *Economic Inquiry* 29, no. 3 (July 1991): 555–71.

[61]Two recently proposed models of discrimination suggest alternative motivations for male employees to discriminate against female coworkers than the personal prejudices assumed in the Becker model, particularly for resisting the introduction of women into traditionally male occupations. In one, occupations are associated with societal notions of "male" and "female," leading men to resist the entry of women due to the loss in male identity (or sense of self); see George A. Akerlof and Rachel E. Kranton, "Economics and Identity," *Quarterly Journal of Economics* 115, no. 3 (August 2000): 715–53. In the second, the entry of women would reduce the prestige of the occupation, based on perceptions that women are, on average, less productive; see Claudia Goldin, "A Pollution Theory of Discrimination: Male and Female Differences in Occupations and Earnings," National Bureau of Economic Research Working Paper 8985 (June 2002).

[62]Arrow, "The Theory of Discrimination."

this segregation, adjustment costs in conjunction with employee tastes for discrimination could help to perpetuate it.

Given employee tastes for discrimination and adjustment costs, marketwide wage differences between male and female workers may result. Again, the size of the wage differential depends on the distribution and intensity of, in this case, *employees'* discriminatory tastes, as well as the relative number of women seeking employment. If employees with no taste for discrimination against women represent a large proportion or relatively few women are seeking jobs, then it may be possible for all the women to work with nondiscriminatory men; and no pay differential would occur.

However, if discriminatory tastes are widespread or relatively large numbers of women are seeking jobs, some of the women will have to work with discriminating male workers. Those males will require higher compensation to induce them to work with women. The result will be a wage differential between male and female workers, on average, because some males will receive this higher pay, and women may be paid less to compensate. More variation will also occur in male workers' wage rates than would otherwise be the case. Discriminating male workers who do not work with women do not need to be paid a wage premium, nor do nondiscriminating males, regardless of whether they are employed with women.

In an empirical test of this prediction, one study compared the wages of men and women (within the same narrowly defined white-collar occupations) in sex-integrated and sex-segregated firms.[63] The study found that, contrary to what was expected on the basis of the employee discrimination model, men earned *more* in sex-segregated than in integrated firms, and women earned *more* when they worked with men than when they worked only with other women. These findings are more consistent with a situation in which high-wage (e.g., monopolistic or unionized) employers are better able to indulge their preferences for hiring men than one in which the pay differential is due to employee discrimination. There may, however, be other cases in which employee discrimination has played an important role.

If such employee tastes for discrimination do in fact exist, and if they vary by occupation, employee discrimination may be a factor causing occupational segregation as well as pay differentials. For example, one reason why women may not be not hired for supervisory and managerial positions may be that even male employees who do not mind working with women do not like being supervised by them. As we have seen, there is some evidence of this. This could create a barrier to the employment of women in such jobs.[64]

Barbara Bergmann and William Darity have suggested that employee discrimination may also adversely affect the morale and productivity of discriminating male workers who are forced to work with women, a possibility not initially considered by Becker.[65]

---

[63]Blau, *Equal Pay in the Office.*

[64]However, one study found that both male and female employees earned *less* when they worked under a female supervisor, which is inconsistent with employee discrimination against female supervisors and suggests that the presence of a female supervisor is associated with less favorable characteristics of the job. See Donna S. Rothstein, "Supervisor Gender and the Early Labor Market Outcomes of Young Workers," in *Gender and Family Issues in the Workplace,* edited by Francine D. Blau and Ronald G. Ehrenberg (New York: Russell Sage, 1997): 210–55.

[65]Barbara R. Bergmann and William A. Darity Jr., "Social Relations in the Workplace and Employer Discrimination," *Proceedings of the Thirty-Third Annual Meetings of the Industrial Relations Research Association* (Madison: University of Wisconsin, 1981), pp. 155–62.

This possibility would make employers reluctant to hire women, especially when their male employees require considerable firm-specific training and are hard to replace. Further, if employers did hire women under such circumstances, they would pay them less to compensate for the reduction in the productivity of the discriminating male employees. In a sense, a woman's marginal productivity is lower than a man's because adding her to the workforce causes a decline in the productivity of previously employed male workers. Adding an additional male worker causes no such decline in output.

Another way in which employee discrimination could affect worker productivity, also not initially considered by Becker, is that it can directly reduce the productivity of women in comparison to men. This is most likely to be a problem in traditionally male fields where the majority of workers are male. For example, on-the-job training frequently occurs informally as supervisors or coworkers demonstrate how things are done and give advice and assistance. When male employees have tastes for discrimination against women, they may be reluctant to teach them these important skills, and, as a result, women may learn less and be less productive.

Customer Discrimination

Customers or clients who have tastes for discrimination against women will act as if there were a nonpecuniary cost associated with purchasing a good or a service from a woman, equal to their discrimination coefficient, d_c. That is, they behave as if the full price of the good or service is $p + d_c$ if provided by a women, but only p if sold by a man. Then, at the going market price, women will sell less. Alternatively, in order to sell as much as a comparable male, a woman would have to charge a lower price $(p - d_c)$. Again, discrimination, this time on the part of possible customers or clients, can result in potentially equally productive women being less productive (in terms of revenue brought in) than comparable males. They are, thus, less desirable employees and receive lower pay. If, as we speculated earlier, such customer discrimination exists in some areas but not in others, occupational segregation may also result.

Subtle Barriers

It is important to recognize that discrimination against women by employers, fellow employees, customers, or clients is not always or even usually conscious and overt. In Chapter 6, we outlined subtle barriers that may limit women's acquisition of formal schooling. Such subtle barriers may also operate in the labor market, as suggested in our discussion of the glass ceiling. For instance, as in educational institutions, women in the workplace may participate less in the beneficial *mentor-protégé* relationships that often develop between senior and junior workers and may be excluded from the *informal networks* that tend to arise among peers at the workplace. As a result, they will be denied access to important job-related information, skills, and contacts, as well as the informal support systems that male workers generally enjoy. In these cases, although women are *potentially* equally productive, discrimination, in effect, reduces both their productivity and their pay.

Discrimination may also result from the perception that a woman would not "fit in" with the group as well as a man would and evaluations of a female employee's competence may be tainted by gender stereotypes of appropriate female behavior. Discrimination by employers, employees, and customers may also be reinforced by habitual behavior that has the effect of disadvantaging women, even though its link to discriminatory outcomes may not be apparent at first. A good example of this is the role that all-male clubs traditionally played for business executives, high-level professionals, and civic leaders.[66] Some mistakenly perceive such clubs as "social" in their orientation. However, as the significant business and professional relevance of such places is increasingly recognized, many, under legal pressure or voluntarily, have opened their doors to women. Although no federal law prohibits gender discrimination by private clubs, a number of major cities and several states, including New York, Florida, Michigan, and Minnesota, have banned the exclusion of women by business-oriented private clubs.[67] However, this issue is by no means entirely one of the past. In 2002, a firestorm of negative media attention surrounded the male-only membership restriction of the exclusive Augusta National Golf Club, which hosts the Masters Tournament. Yet, as of the 2004 Masters, it still did not allow women members.[68]

Statistical Discrimination

As noted earlier, models of statistical discrimination developed by Edmund Phelps and others[69] attribute a different motivation to employers for discrimination, one that is potentially more consistent with profit maximization and, thus, with the persistence of discrimination in the long run. In this view, employers are constantly faced with the need for decision making under conditions of incomplete information and uncertainty. Even if they carefully study the qualifications of applicants, they never know for certain how individuals will perform on the job or how long they will stay with the firm after being hired. Mistakes can be costly, especially when substantial hiring and training costs are involved. Promotion decisions entail similar risks, although in this case employers have additional firsthand information on past job performance with the firm.

Perceptions of Average Gender Differences Can Result in a Pay Gap

In light of these uncertainties, it is not surprising that employers often use any readily accessible information that may be correlated with productivity or job stability in making difficult personnel decisions. If they believe that, *on average,* women are less productive or less stable employees, *statistical discrimination* against *individual* women may result. That is, employers may judge the individual woman on the basis of their beliefs about group averages. The result may be discrimination against women in pay or in hiring and promotion.

For example, suppose an employer is screening applicants for an entry-level managerial position and that the two major qualifications considered are level of education and grades. Assume further that the employer believes that at the same level of qualifications (e.g., an MBA with an A– average), women as a group will be less likely to remain with the firm than men. Then, for a given level of qualifications, the employer would hire a woman only at a lower wage or, perhaps, simply hire a man rather than a woman for the job. More

---

[66]For further discussion of this issue, see Robin L. Bartlett and Timothy I. Miller, "Executive Earnings by Gender: A Case Study," *Social Science Quarterly* 69, no. 4 (December 1988): 892–909.

[67]Tom McNichol, "Is There a 'Glass Ceiling'?" *USA Weekend,* November 16, 1997, p. 8; and Cailin Brown, "Private Clubs Less Restrictive," *Times Union,* May 14, 1995, p. B1.

[68]Alex Kuczynski, "It's Still a Man's, Man's, Man's World," *New York Times,* July 21, 2002, sec. 9, pp. 1–2; and Clifton Brown, "Sports Desk: Golf; Game, Not Membership, Is Hot Topic at Masters," *New York Times,* April 6, 2004, sec. D, p. 2.

[69]See, for example, Edmund S. Phelps, "The Statistical Theory of Racism and Sexism," *American Economic Review* 62, no. 4 (September 1972): 659–61; and Dennis J. Aigner and Glen G. Cain, "Statistical Theories of Discrimination in Labor Markets," *Industrial and Labor Relations Review* 30, no. 2 (January 1977): 175–87.

careful screening of applicants might enable the employer to distinguish more from less career-oriented women (e.g., a consideration of the candidate's employment record while a student or of extracurricular activities while in school), but it may not be cost-effective for the employer to invest the additional resources necessary for this screening.

Judged on the basis of statements employers themselves make, such beliefs regarding differences in average ability or behavior by sex are quite common. For example, employers are often concerned that women do not take their careers as seriously as men and fear that they will quit their jobs when they have children. Other perceptions of average differences in behavior or performance of men and women were noted in our consideration of issues related to the glass ceiling.

If such employer beliefs are simply incorrect or exaggerated or reflect time lags in adjusting to a new reality, actions based on them are clearly unfair and constitute labor market discrimination as we define it. That is, they generate wage and occupation differences between men and women that are not accounted for by (potential) productivity differences. If such views are not simply rationalizations for personal prejudice, it might be expected that, over time, they will yield to new information. However, this process may be more sluggish than one would like and, in the meantime, employers make less than optimal choices. Moreover, as noted previously, some discrimination may not be conscious and thus, that much less susceptible to change by new information.[70]

The situation is different, and a bit more complicated, if the employer views *are* indeed correct *on average*. Employers make the best choices possible with imperfect knowledge, and, in a sense, labor market discrimination does not exist in this case: Any resulting wage and employment differences between men and women, on average, would be accounted for by *average* productivity differences.

Yet the consequences for *individual* women are far from satisfactory. A particular woman who would be as productive and as stable an employee as her male counterpart is denied employment or paid a lower wage. It seems fairly clear from a *normative* perspective that basing employment decisions on a characteristic such as sex—a characteristic that the individual cannot change—is unfair. Indeed, the practice of judging an *individual* on the basis of *group* characteristics rather than upon his or her own merits seems the very essence of stereotyping and discrimination. Such behavior is certainly not legal under the antidiscrimination laws and regulations that we discuss later in this chapter. Yet it most likely still plays a role in employer thinking. Moreover, statistical discrimination, which is based on employers' *correct* assessment of average gender differences, is not likely to be eroded by the forces of competition.

Statistical Discrimination and Feedback Effects

As Kenneth Arrow pointed out, the consequences of statistical discrimination are particularly pernicious when accompanied by *feedback effects*.[71] For example, if

---

[70]Social cognition theory developed by social psychologists suggests that people tend to automatically categorize others and treat them in a manner consistent with the stereotypes they hold about the social category to which the individuals belong. They also tend to remember evidence that is consistent with their preexisting stereotypes and ignore, discount, or forget evidence that undermines them. See Barbara F. Reskin, "The Proximate Causes of Employment Discrimination," *Contemporary Sociology* 29, no. 2 (March 2000): 319–28; Susan T. Fiske, "Stereotyping, Prejudice, and Discrimination," in *Handbook of Social Psychology*, ed. D.T. Gilbert, S.T. Fiske, and G. Lindzey (New York: McGraw-Hill: 1998), pp. 357–411; and Francine D. Blau, Mary C. Brinton, and David B. Grusky, "The Declining Significance of Gender?" Unpublished Working Paper (December 2004).

[71]Arrow, "The Theory of Discrimination."

employers' views of female job instability lead them to give women less firm-specific training and to assign them to jobs where the costs of turnover are minimized, women experience little incentive to stay and may respond by exhibiting exactly the unstable behavior that employers expect. Employers' perceptions are confirmed, and they see no reason to change their discriminatory behavior. Yet if employers believe women to be stable workers and hire them into positions that reward such stability, they might well be stable workers!

Hence, where statistical discrimination is accompanied by feedback effects, employer behavior that is based on *initially* incorrect assessments of average gender differences may persist in the long run and be fairly impervious to competitive pressures.

Empirical Evidence on Gender Differences in Quitting

Some indication that such feedback effects are important is provided by studies of male and female quitting. This possibility is especially important because employer views that women are more likely to quit their jobs than men tend to be fairly widespread. A number of studies find that although women are on average more likely to quit their jobs than men, *most of this difference is explained by the types of jobs women are in and other individual characteristics.*[72] These findings suggest that, when a woman worker is confronted with the same incentives to remain on the job in terms of wages, advancement opportunities, and so on, a woman is no more likely to quit than a comparable male worker. Moreover, while some research suggests that the quit behavior of women was more difficult to predict than the quit behavior of men for earlier cohorts, this was not found to be the case for women born after 1950. Indeed, for college-educated workers, little difference was found between men and women even in overall turnover rates.[73]

Even though these studies of gender differences in turnover offer little justification for employers to practice statistical discrimination against women based on presumed differences in quit rates, this does not necessarily mean that gender differences in quit behavior are unrelated to the pay gap. Women are more likely than men to quit their jobs for family-related reasons or to exit the labor force entirely and less likely than men to quit in order to move to another job. Such behavioral differences and the resulting workforce interruptions will contribute to the gender pay gap, although, interestingly, even in this aspect of quitting, college women's behavior now appears more similar to their male counterparts.[74]

The Overcrowding Model

In the models discussed to this point, gender segregation in employment (by firm or occupation) is a possible consequence of discrimination against women in hiring and

---

[72]See, for example, Francine D. Blau and Lawrence M. Kahn, "Race and Sex Differences in Quits by Young Workers," *Industrial and Labor Relations Review* 34, no. 4 (July 1981): 563–77; W. Kip Viscusi, "Sex Differences in Worker Quitting," *Review of Economics and Statistics* 62, no. 3 (August 1980): 388–98; Nachum Sicherman, "Gender Differences in Departures from a Large Firm," *Industrial and Labor Relations Review* 49, no. 3 (April 1996): 484–505; and Anne Beeson Royalty, "Job-to-Job and Job-to-Nonemployment Turnover by Gender and Education Level," *Journal of Labor Economics* 16, no. 2 (April 1998): 392–443.

[73]Audrey Light and Manuelita Ureta, "Panel Estimates of Male and Female Job Turnover Behavior: Can Female Nonquitters Be Identified?" *Journal of Labor Economics* 10, no. 2 (April 1992): 156–81; and Royalty, "Job-to-Job."

[74]Sicherman, "Gender Differences in Departures from a Large Firm"; Royalty, "Job-to-Job"; and Kristin Keith and Abagail McWilliams, "The Wage Effects of Cumulative Job Mobility," *Industrial and Labor Relations Review* 49, no. 1 (October 1995): 121–37.

job assignments, as are pay differentials. Both wage and employment differences are believed to result either from tastes for discrimination against women (among employers, employees, or customers) or from (real or perceived) gender differences in average productivity or job stability. We now consider an analysis of the pay gap, developed by Barbara Bergmann, that gives a more central role to employment segregation.[75]

Bergmann's overcrowding model demonstrates that, regardless of the reason for segregation (e.g., socialization, personal preferences, or labor market discrimination), the *consequence* may be a male-female pay differential. This differential will occur if demand (job opportunities) in the female sector is small relative to the supply of women available for such work. The overcrowding model is consistent with the evidence presented earlier that, all else being equal, earnings tend to be lower in predominantly female than in predominantly male jobs. The fact that men in predominantly female occupations also receive low wages is not necessarily inconsistent with the overcrowding hypothesis. Although men as a group are obviously not excluded from the male sector, some of them may, nonetheless, enter female occupations because they have a strong preference or particular skills for this type of work. Or they may be simply unlucky or poorly informed about alternative opportunities. They will accept the lower wages paid in female jobs. However, this lower pay is primarily caused by the many women who "crowd" into these jobs due to their preferences for the work or a lack of alternative opportunities.

This model is illustrated in Figure 7-1. F jobs and M jobs are considered. As in the previous models of discrimination, it is assumed that male and female workers are perfect

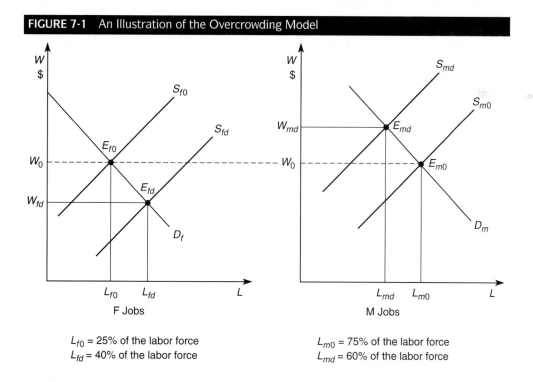

FIGURE 7-1   An Illustration of the Overcrowding Model

F Jobs

L_{f0} = 25% of the labor force
L_{fd} = 40% of the labor force

M Jobs

L_{m0} = 75% of the labor force
L_{md} = 60% of the labor force

[75]Barbara R. Bergmann, "Occupational Segregation, Wages and Profits When Employers Discriminate by Race or Sex," *Eastern Economic Journal* 1, nos. 1–2 (April–July 1974): 103–10.

substitutes for each other (i.e., they are potentially equally productive). The hypothetical situation of no discrimination is represented by demand curves D_f and D_m and supply curves S_{f0} and S_{m0}. The nondiscriminatory equilibrium points in the two markets (E_{f0} and $\dot{E}_{m0}$) are determined so that the wage rate (W_0) is the same for both types of jobs.

To see why, in the absence of discrimination, the wage rate will be the same for both types of jobs, recall that we assumed all workers are equally well qualified for F and M jobs and that employers are indifferent between hiring male and female workers. Suppose that, by chance, the equilibrium wage in F jobs is higher than the equilibrium wage in M jobs. Then workers attracted by the higher wage rates would transfer from M jobs to F jobs. This process would continue until wages in F jobs were bid down to the level of wages in M jobs. Similarly, if by chance wages in M jobs were set above those in F jobs, workers would move from F jobs to M jobs until the differential was eliminated. Thus, in the absence of discrimination, worker mobility ensures that the wages paid for both types of work are the same, at least after allowing time to make adjustments. This outcome, of course, assumes that no *nonpecuniary* differences exist in the relative attractiveness of the two jobs that would result in a compensating wage differential.

In the hypothetical example given in Figure 7-1, demand conditions are such that, in the nondiscriminatory equilibrium, L_{f0} workers (25 percent of the labor force) are employed in F jobs and L_{m0} workers (75 percent of the labor force) work in M jobs. F and M jobs have no sex labels associated with them and both women and men are randomly divided between the two sectors.

How does the situation differ when discrimination occurs against women in "male" occupations or when, for a variety of reasons, women choose to concentrate in typically female jobs? The consequences of such segregation may be ascertained by comparing this situation to the hypothetical situation of no segregation. In our example, the restriction of M jobs to men results in an inward shift of the supply curve to M jobs from S_{m0} to S_{md}, causing wages to be bid up to W_{md}. At this higher wage, only L_{md} workers (60 percent of the labor force) are employed in M jobs. The exclusion of women from M jobs means that all the women must (or choose to) "crowd" into the F jobs. The expanded supply of labor in F jobs, represented by an outward shift of the supply curve from S_{f0} to S_{fd}, depresses wages there to W_{fd}. Now L_{fd} workers (40 percent of the labor force) are employed in F occupations.

The overcrowding model shows how gender segregation in employment may cause a wage differential between otherwise equally productive male and female workers. This differential will occur if the supply of women seeking employment is large relative to the demand for labor in the F jobs. This may well be what actually takes place in the labor market. Nevertheless, the analysis also shows that gender segregation in employment need not always result in a wage differential between men and women. If it so happens that the wage rate that equates supply and demand in the F sector is the same as the wage that equates supply and demand in the M sector, no wage differential will result (i.e., if the F sector is not overcrowded). However, this will happen only by chance. Labor market discrimination (or some other barrier) eliminates the free mobility of labor between the two sectors that would otherwise ensure wage equality between M and F jobs.

Returning to the more likely situation illustrated in Figure 7-1, in which segregation does lower women's pay, we may examine its impact on the *productivity* of women relative to men. Employers of women in F jobs accommodate a larger number of workers (L_{fd} rather than L_{f0}) by substituting labor for capital. The relatively low wages of the women, W_{fd}, make it profitable to use such labor-intensive production methods. On the other hand, the higher wage in the male sector, W_{md}, encourages employers to substitute capital for labor to economize on relatively high-priced labor. In the overcrowding model, women earn less than men, but both are paid in accordance with their productivity. Discrimination causes differences in both wages and productivity between *potentially* equally productive male and female labor—women are less productive than men because, due to segregation and crowding, they have less capital to work with.

The claim that the supply of labor to a particular occupation (or industry) helps to determine the wage rate is relatively noncontroversial. But the crowding hypothesis, in and of itself, does not explain why so many women are employed in typically female sectors. Controversy centers on the question of whether this segregation and crowding result because men and women have inherently different talents or preferences for different types of work; because, due to differences in socialization or in household responsibilities, women are willing to trade higher wages and steeper lifetime earnings profiles for more favorable working conditions and lower penalties for discontinuous labor force participation; or because employers, coworkers, or customers discriminate against women in some occupations but not in others.

Institutional Models

The idea that the male-female pay gap is closely related to employment segregation is echoed in institutional models of discrimination.[76] Such explanations emphasize that labor markets may not be as flexible as the simple competitive model assumes. Rigidities are introduced both by the institutional arrangements found in many firms and by various barriers to competition introduced by the monopoly power of firms in the product market or of unions in the labor market.

The Internal Labor Market

Institutionalists point out that the job structure of many large firms looks like the illustration in Figure 7-2a. Firms hire workers from the outside labor market for so-called entry jobs. The remaining jobs are internally allocated by the firm as workers progress along well-defined promotion ladders by acquiring job-related skills, many of which are firm specific in nature. When firm-specific skills are emphasized and a high proportion of jobs are filled from internal sources, the firm has an *internal labor market.* That is, it determines wages for each job category and the allocation of workers among categories and is insulated to some extent (although not entirely) from the impact of market forces.

To administer their personnel systems, larger firms often take the occupational category as the decision unit, establishing pay rates for each category (with some allowance

---

[76]See, for example, Peter B. Doeringer and Michael J. Piore, *Internal Labor Markets and Manpower Analysis* (Lexington, MA: D.C. Heath and Co., 1971); Michael J. Piore, "The Dual Labor Market: Theory and Implications," in *Problems in Political Economy: An Urban Perspective,* edited by David M. Gordon (Lexington, MA: D.C. Heath and Co., 1971), pp. 90–94; Francine D. Blau and Carol L. Jusenius, "Economists' Approaches to Sex Segregation in the Labor Market: An Appraisal," *Signs: Journal of Women in Culture and Society* 1, no. 3 (Spring 1976, Part 2): 181–99; and Glen G. Cain, "The Challenge of Segmented Labor Market Theories to Orthodox Theory: A Survey," *Journal of Economic Literature* 14, no. 4 (December 1976): 1215–57.

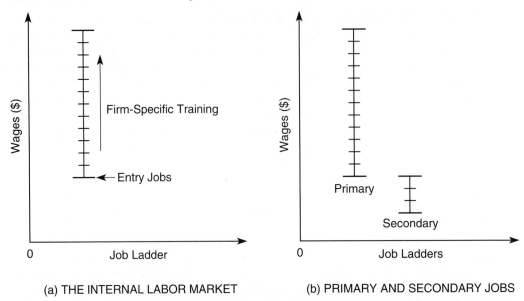

FIGURE 7-2 An Illustration of the Institutional Model

for seniority and merit considerations), and linking jobs together into promotion ladders. Thus, group treatment of individuals is the norm, and it will be to the employer's advantage to make sure that workers within each job category are as similar as possible. If it is believed that men and women (as well as, say, whites and nonwhites) differ in their productivity-related characteristics (like quit and absenteeism rates), statistical discrimination is likely to result in their being channeled into different jobs.

Primary and Secondary Jobs

The dual labor market model developed by Peter Doeringer and Michael Piore takes this analysis a step further and emphasizes the distinction between primary and secondary jobs.[77] Primary jobs emphasize high levels of firm-specific skills and, thus, pay high wages, offer good promotion opportunities, and encourage long-term attachment between workers and firms. In secondary jobs, firm-specific skills are not as important. Such jobs will pay less, offer relatively fewer promotion opportunities, and have fairly high rates of labor turnover. This situation is depicted in Figure 7-2b. Applying the dual labor market model to gender discrimination leads us to expect that men would be more likely to be in primary jobs and women in secondary jobs.

The distinction between primary and secondary jobs may occur within the same firm—say, between the managerial and clerical categories. In addition, it is believed that primary jobs are more likely to be located in monopolistic, unionized industries that are generally higher paying and have traditionally offered more stable employment and that secondary jobs are more likely to be found in lower-paying, competitive industries with more labor turnover. This is an additional reason for expecting women to be more concentrated in the competitive sector.

---

[77]Doeringer and Piore, *Internal Labor Markets;* and Piore, "The Dual Labor Market."

Radical economists further argue that employers as a group benefit from such segmentation of the labor force by gender and race because it prevents workers from seeing their common interests across gender and race lines. That is, capitalists (employers) practice "divide and rule" tactics to thwart unionization and other attempts by workers to share power. As we noted in Chapter 3, radical feminists add another element to this analysis. In their view, one must take into account the effects not only of capitalism, but also of patriarchy, which is defined as a system of male oppression of women. Thus, they point to the role of male workers and of their unions, as well as of employers, in maintaining occupational segregation.[78]

Segmentation of male and female workers into primary and secondary jobs is likely to produce both pay and productivity differences between them due to unequal access to on-the-job training. Institutionalists also point out that feedback effects are likely to magnify any initial productivity differences, as women respond to the lower incentives for employment stability in the secondary sector.

The institutional analysis also reinforces the point made earlier that labor market discrimination against women is not necessarily the outcome of conscious, overt acts by employers. Once men and women are channeled into different types of entry jobs, the normal, everyday operation of the firm—"business as usual"—will virtually ensure gender differences in productivity, promotion opportunities, and pay. This process is termed *institutional discrimination.*[79] Even gender differences in initial occupational assignment may be in part due to adherence to traditional policies that tend to work against women; for example, referrals from current male employees or an informal network of male colleagues at other firms, sexist recruitment materials picturing women in traditionally female jobs and men in traditionally male jobs, and lack of encouragement of female applicants to broaden their sights from traditional areas.

Feedback Effects

As noted several times already, labor market discrimination or unequal treatment of women in the labor market may adversely affect women's own decisions and behavior.[80] These feedback effects are illustrated in Figure 7-3. Human capital theory and other supply-side explanations for gender differences in economic outcomes tend to emphasize the role of the gender division of labor in the family in causing differences between men and women in labor market outcomes, and are indicated by the arrow pointing to the right in the figure.

This relationship undoubtedly exists; however, such explanations tend to neglect the impact of labor market discrimination in reinforcing the traditional division of labor (shown by the arrow pointing to the left). Even a relatively small amount of initial

---

[78]For the radical view, see David M. Gordon, Richard Edwards, and Michael Reich, *Segmented Work, Divided Workers: The Historical Transformation of Labor in the United States* (Cambridge: Cambridge University Press, 1982) ; and, for the radical feminist analysis, Heidi I. Hartmann, "Capitalism, Patriarchy and Job Segregation by Sex," *Signs: Journal of Women in Culture and Society* 1, no. 3, pt. 2 (Spring 1976): 137–69.

[79]See Roos and Reskin, "Institutional Factors," for a description of business practices that tend to adversely affect women.

[80]A number of authors emphasize the importance of feedback effects in analyzing discrimination in pay and employment. See, for example, Arrow, "The Theory of Discrimination"; Shelly J. Lundberg and Richard Startz, "Private Discrimination and Social Intervention in Competitive Labor Markets," *American Economic Review* 73, no. 3 (June 1983): 340–47; and Yoram Weiss and Reuben Gronau, "Expected Interruptions in Labour Force Participation and Sex-Related Differences in Earnings Growth," *Review of Economic Studies* 48, no. 4 (October 1981): 607–19.

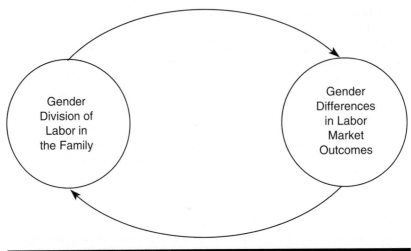

FIGURE 7-3   An Illustration of Feedback Effects

labor market discrimination can result in greatly magnified effects if it discourages women from making human capital investments, weakens their attachment to the labor force, and provides economic incentives for the family to place priority on the husband's career. Although it is unlikely that labor market discrimination is responsible for initially causing the traditional division of labor in the family, which clearly predates modern labor markets, it may well help to perpetuate it by inhibiting more rapid movement toward egalitarian sharing of household responsibilities today.

The net result is what might be viewed as a vicious circle. Discrimination against women in the labor market reinforces traditional gender roles in the family, while adherence to traditional roles by women provides a rationale for labor market discrimination. However, this also means that effective policies to end labor market discrimination can have far-reaching effects, particularly when combined with simultaneous changes in social attitudes toward women's roles. A decrease in labor market discrimination will have feedback effects as the equalization of market incentives between men and women induces further changes in women's supply-side behavior. These changes would in turn further encourage employers to reduce statistical discrimination against women. In addition, as more women enter previously male-dominated fields, the larger number of female role models for younger women is likely to induce still further increases in the availability of women for such jobs. Thus, demand-side policies can be expected to play an important role in sustaining a process of cumulative change in women's economic status.

POLICY ISSUE: THE GOVERNMENT AND EQUAL EMPLOYMENT OPPORTUNITY

Government policies to combat labor market discrimination against women can potentially be justified on at least two grounds. One is equity or fairness—"a matter of simple justice."[81] Thus, government intervention may be rationalized to assure equal

---

[81]This phrase provided the title of the Report of the President's Task Force on Women's Rights and Responsibilities (Washington, DC: U.S. Government Printing Office, April 1970).

treatment for all participants in the labor market, regardless of gender (or race, ethnic origin, etc.).

As well as being unfair, unequal treatment on the basis of gender may result in an inefficient allocation of resources. This inefficiency provides a second rationale for government intervention. Consider the case where equally productive men and women are hired for different jobs and women's jobs are lower paid (as in the over-crowding model). Under these circumstances, prices do not serve as accurate indicators of social costs. In comparison to the nondiscriminatory situation, society produces "too little" of the outputs that use "overpriced" male labor, given that equally productive female labor is available at a lower price to expand production. Society produces "too much" of the outputs that use "underpriced" female labor, given that the contribution of equally productive labor is valued more highly in the male sector (as measured by its price).

The inefficiency caused by discrimination is even greater when we take into account feedback effects. If women are deterred from investing in their human capital because of discrimination, society loses a valuable resource. Thus, opening doors previously closed (or only slightly ajar) to women potentially benefits society as well as individual women by bringing their talents and abilities to bear in new areas. As Nobel laureate Paul A. Samuelson commented, "To the degree that women are getting an opportunity they didn't have in the past, the economy is tapping an important and previously wasted resource."[82]

Weighed against these potential gains are the costs of the increased government intervention in society that may be necessary to produce this result. These costs loom large indeed to those who are skeptical of the evidence of labor market discrimination against women presented earlier. Some may also fear what they regard as the possible excesses of such policies in the form of reverse discrimination or preferential treatment for women and minorities. However, research to date provides no evidence that the increased employment of women and minorities encouraged by legislation entailed such efficiency costs.[83] We examine the record of government intervention in this area next.[84]

Equal Employment Opportunity Laws and Regulations

There is a long history of government involvement in shaping conditions encountered by women in the labor market. During the period following the Civil War, in response to concern and agitation by workers and their sympathizers, a number of states passed protective labor laws limiting hours and regulating other terms of employment for all

---

[82]*Business Week,* January 28, 1985, p. 80.

[83]Leonard, "Antidiscrimination or Reverse Discrimination"; and Harry Holzer and David Neumark, "Are Affirmative Action Hires Less Qualified? Evidence from Employer-Employee Data on New Hires," *Journal of Labor Economics* 17, no. 3 (July 1999).

[84]For excellent summaries of the legal situation, see Mack A. Player, *Federal Law of Employment Discrimination*, 5th ed. (St. Paul, MI: Thomson/West, 2004); and Susan Deller Ross, Isabelle Katz Pinzler, Deborah A. Ellis, and Kary L. Moss, *The Rights of Women: The Basic ACLU Guide to a Woman's Rights,* 3rd ed. (Carbondale: Southern Illinois University Press, 1993). For a useful description of the legal setting, including a discussion of how lawyers and economists view discrimination and the role of economists in employment litigation, see Joni Hersch, "Employment Discrimination, Economists and the Law," in *Women, Family and Work: Writings on the Economics of Gender,* edited by Karine S. Moe (Oxford: Blackwell Publishers, 2003), pp. 217–333.

workers. At first, the Supreme Court struck down these laws as unconstitutional on the basis that they interfered with the freedom of workers to enter contracts. Subsequently, in its 1908 decision in *Muller v. Oregon,*[85] the Court upheld such laws when they were confined to women alone, arguing that individual rights may be abridged because the state has a legitimate interest in the possible social effects of women's work. Louis Brandeis, later to become a Supreme Court Justice known for his support of individual human rights, wrote the following about the case:

> The two sexes differ in structure of body, in the functions performed by each, in the amount of physical strength, in the capacity for long-continued labor, particularly when done standing, the influence of vigorous health upon the future well-being of the race, the self-reliance which enables one to assert full rights, and in the capacity to maintain the struggle for subsistence. The difference justifies a difference in legislation, and upholds that which is designed to compensate for some of the burdens which rest upon her.

In time, however, the concern shifted from protection to equal opportunity. Indeed, protective laws came eventually to be viewed as undesirable impediments to the advancement of women. Supreme Court Justice Brennan expressed this view well in a 1973 case: "Traditionally, discrimination was rationalized by an attitude of romantic paternalism which in practical effect put women not on a pedestal but in a cage."[86]

As early as 1961, President Kennedy issued an Executive Order calling for a Presidential Commission on the Status of Women. Two years later, the **Equal Pay Act** of 1963 was passed, which requires employers to pay the same wages to men and women who do substantially equal work, involving equal skill, effort, and responsibility, and performed under similar conditions in the same establishment. In 1964, **Title VII** of the Civil Rights Act was enacted. The legislation was originally written to prohibit discrimination in employment on the basis of race, religion, and national origin, but was changed at the last minute to include the word *sex.*[87] Title VII prohibits sex discrimination in virtually all aspects of employment, including hiring and firing, training, promotions, wages, fringe benefits, or other terms and conditions of employment. As amended, it covers all businesses employing 15 or more workers, including federal, state, and local governments and educational institutions. It also prohibits discrimination by employment agencies and labor organizations. The **Equal Employment Opportunity Commission (EEOC)** is the federal agency charged with enforcing the Equal Pay Act and Title VII.

Executive Order 11246 issued in 1965, and amended in 1967 to include sex, bars discrimination in employment by all employers with federal contracts and subcontracts. It also requires affirmative action for classes of workers disadvantaged by past discrimination. Contractors are required to analyze their own employment patterns to determine where women and minorities are underrepresented. Whenever such deficiencies are found, they are to set up "goals and timetables" for the hiring of women and minorities

---

[85]*Muller v. Oregon,* 208 U.S. 412 (1908).
[86]*Frontiero v. Richardson,* 411 U.S. 677 (1973).
[87]Because it was Howard Smith, a conservative congressman from Virginia, who proposed this amendment, it is widely believed that his purpose in doing so was to increase opposition to the bill, and reduce the chances of its passage.

and to make good faith efforts to reach their goals in the specified period. The Executive Order is enforced by the Office of Federal Contract Compliance. Violators face possible loss of their government contracts, although this sanction is seldom invoked.

In the years since their passage and implementation, the federal antidiscrimination laws and regulations have been interpreted and clarified by the courts, with the final arbiter being the U.S. Supreme Court. This process proved especially important for Title VII of the Civil Rights Act, the broadest law and the centerpiece of the federal government's antidiscrimination enforcement effort. In some cases, the Court's interpretations of the law changed as the membership on the Court shifted, which is likely to continue to be the case in the future. Bearing this likelihood in mind, in order to better understand what activities are currently prohibited under Title VII, we turn to a brief summary of some of the more important Court decisions.

Title VII permits exceptions to its ban on gender discrimination when sex is found to be a bona fide occupational qualification (BFOQ). When the law was passed in the mid-1960s, it was not entirely clear what this exemption would mean as a practical matter. At that time, social views widely accepted the notion that a considerable number of jobs were particularly suitable for women and a goodly number of others especially appropriate for men. Indeed, newspapers routinely divided portions of their help wanted sections into "help wanted male" and "help wanted female." The former might include openings for such jobs as manager or construction worker, while the latter might include "girl friday" (i.e., administrative assistant) or receptionist. Thus, the interpretation of the bona fide occupational qualification exemption by the courts is extremely important. If interpreted broadly, to match the social views of the day, considerable gender discrimination would have been permissible under Title VII in that sex might have been viewed as a valid qualification for a host of traditionally male and traditionally female jobs. However, both the EEOC and the courts took the position that this exception should be interpreted narrowly. That is, men and women are entitled to consideration on the basis of their individual capabilities, rather than on the basis of characteristics generally attributed to the group. The Court, for example, rejected the BFOQ exemption for predominately male jobs in which heavy lifting is required as well as for the predominately female position of flight attendant where it was argued by the employer that airline passengers preferred women in the job. Also, the Court ruled that it is discriminatory to bar all women of childbearing age from jobs where they would work with substances that might be hazardous to unborn children.[88] In the only major case to date in which gender was found to be a bona fide occupational qualification, the 1977 *Dothard v. Rawlinson* case, the Supreme Court allowed the hiring of males only for the position of guard in Alabama's maximum security male prisons. The Court reasoned that due to the nature of the prison population, as well as the atmosphere of the prison, women would be particularly subject to sexual assault, which would interfere with their job performance. Regardless of whether one agrees with this reasoning, this case

---

[88]The Court found such exclusionary policies to be discriminatory because "fertile men, but not fertile women, are given a choice as to whether they wish to risk their reproductive health for a particular job." It clarified that the bona fide occupational qualification exemption of Title VII "must relate to ability to perform the duties of the job" rather than to any danger or risk to the woman herself. The Court also concluded that the risk of employer liability was slight given that "Title VII bans sex-specific fetal-protection policies, the employer fully informs the woman of the risk, and the employer has not acted negligently...." See Bureau of National Affairs, *Daily Labor Report,* no. 55 (March 21, 1991), pp. A1–A3 and D1–D11.

has not resulted and is not likely to result in substantially greater acceptance by the courts of the BFOQ exception for other jobs, given its unusual circumstances.[89]

The Court also found that sex cannot be used in combination with some other factor as a legal basis for discrimination under Title VII. The Court held, for example, that an employer cannot refuse to hire women with preschool-age children while men with preschool-age children are hired.[90] Furthermore, it is illegal to pay women lower monthly pension benefits than men.[91] In the past, this practice was justified on the basis that, on average, women live longer and, thus, it would be more costly to provide them with the same monthly benefit. The courts ruled that each woman is entitled to be treated as an individual, rather than as a group member.

Disparate treatment of women and minorities, that is, differential treatment of these groups with the intention to discriminate, is a clear violation of Title VII. A more complex issue addressed by the courts in interpreting Title VII concerns unintentional discrimination. This type of discrimination arises when a firm's apparently neutral hiring or promotion practices result in a **disparate impact**, or disproportionately adverse effects, on women or minorities. An example of disparate impact might be a minimum height and weight requirement for the position of police officer that screens out a higher proportion of women than men. Based on a 1971 Supreme Court decision in *Griggs*, apparently neutral practices resulting in a disparate impact on women and minorities may be illegal even if the discrimination is not intentional. Once the plaintiffs show that the practice creates a disparate impact, the burden of proof shifts to the employer to show that the practice is a matter of "business necessity" or that the requirement is job related; otherwise the practice is discriminatory.[92]

A later 1989 Supreme Court decision[93] held that even after a disparate impact was demonstrated, the burden of proof remained with the plaintiffs to show that the employer had no business necessity justification for the practice. This decision was widely criticized by civil rights advocates. The original interpretation of the law that places the burden of proof on the *employer* was reestablished in November 1991, when a new civil rights law was enacted. In addition to this provision, the new law permits women to obtain compensatory and punitive damages for intentional discrimination, although the amounts are limited. (Racial minorities had such rights under existing law.)

An issue at the center of considerable attention in recent years is sexual harassment.[94] Sexual harassment potentially encompasses a broad range of objectionable behaviors ranging from the making of sexual demands where a refusal results in an

---

[89]*Dothard v. Rawlinson,* 433 U.S. 321 (1977); see Ross et al., *The Rights of Women* for a consideration of this and other cases.

[90]*Philips v. Martin Marietta Corp.,* 400 U.S. 542 (1971).

[91]*City of Los Angeles, Dept. of Water v. Manhart,* 435 U.S. 702 (1978).

[92]*Griggs v. Duke Power Co.,* 401 U.S. 424 (1971).

[93]*Wards Cove Packing Co. v. Atonio,* 490 U.S. 642 (1989).

[94]This issue attracted particular attention during the 1991 confirmation hearings of Supreme Court Justice Clarence Thomas, when charges of sexual harassment were made against the nominee by Anita Hill, a law professor who had formerly worked as his assistant. Although Justice Thomas was confirmed, the airing of this issue in a national forum greatly heightened public awareness of the problem. Kaushik Basu provides an overview of the extent of and trends in sexual harassment and discusses the rationale for government intervention in this area in "The Economics and Law of Sexual Harassment in the Workplace," *Journal of Economic Perspectives* 17, no. 3 (Summer 2003):141–57; see also Heather Antecol and Deborah A. Cobb-Clark, "The Changing Nature of Employment-Related Sexual Harassment: Evidence from the U.S. Federal Government (1978–1994)," *Industrial and Labor Relations Review* 57, no. 3 (April 2004): 443–61.

adverse action (e.g., dismissal, the loss of a promotion, reduced benefits, etc.), generally called "quid pro quo" harassment, to various actions that are sufficiently offensive to result in a hostile work environment. Deciding whether sexual harassment was indeed covered under Title VII and demarcating the conditions under which the behavior was egregious enough to be illegal has proved challenging for the courts. A major step forward was the Supreme Court's 1986 decision in *Meritor*, which held that sexual harassment is illegal under Title VII if it is unwelcome and "sufficiently severe or pervasive to alter the conditions of the victim's employment and create an abusive working environment."[95] Some controversy followed the Court's ruling over what constituted evidence of a hostile environment, with some lower courts requiring evidence of severe psychological injury or diminished job performance. In its 1993 *Harris*[96] case, the Supreme Court clarified this issue, overturning a lower court ruling that an employee who was subjected to the company president's repeated offensive and demeaning comments of a sexual nature was not entitled to redress under the law because she had not suffered sufficient psychological damage. The standard put forth by the Court in its decision is essentially that a hostile environment is one that a *reasonable person* would perceive to be "hostile or abusive." Writing for the majority, Justice Sandra Day O'Connor said that the protection of federal law "comes into play before the harassing conduct leads to a nervous breakdown." The Court has since ruled that Title VII prohibits sexual harassment between members of the same sex under the same legal standards as those used to evaluate claims of sexual harassment by a member of the opposite sex.[97]

Because sexual harassment generally results from interactions between employees, the question arises as to when employers are held liable for the actions of their employees. This issue is important because employers represent the "deep pockets"; that is, they can potentially pay financial compensation to individuals who are the victims of harassment. The stakes involved may be considerable. In 1998, in the largest sexual harassment settlement negotiated up to that point, Mitsubishi Motor Corporation agreed to pay $34 million to end a government lawsuit charging that hundreds of female employees at its automobile assembly plant in Normal, Illinois, had been sexually harassed.[98] Prior to two 1998 Supreme Court decisions,[99] it was believed based on a lower court ruling that employers could only be held liable for sexual harassment if they knew or should have known that the harassment had taken place. In its recent decisions, the Supreme Court extended the employer's liability

---

[95]*Meritor Savings Bank v. Vinson*, 477 U.S. 57 (1986); the quotation was cited in "Ending Sexual Harassment: Business Is Getting the Message," *Business Week*, March 18, 1991, p. 99.

[96]*Harris v. Forklift Systems Inc.*, ___ U.S. ___, No. 92–1168, 11/9/93. The summary of the case and quotation from the opinion are from Linda Greenhouse, "Court, 9–0, Makes Sex Harassment Easier to Prove," *New York Times*, November 10, 1993, pp. A1–A14; see also "Psychological Injury Not Needed to Prove Sex Harassment, Unanimous Supreme Court Rules," Bureau of National Affairs, *Daily Labor Report*, no. 216, November 10, 1993, pp. AA1–AA2.

[97]This ruling came in the 1998 case of *Oncale v. Sundowner Offshore Services, Inc.*; see Charles J. Muhl, "The Law at Work: Sexual Harassment," *Monthly Labor Review* 121, no. 7 (July 1998): 61–62.

[98]Barnaby J. Feder, "$34 Million Settles Suit for Women at Auto Plant," *New York Times*, June 12, 1998, at www.nytimes.com.

[99]The two cases, both decided in 1998, are *Faragher v. City of Boca Raton* and *Burlington Industries, Inc. v. Ellerth*. The quotations are from Linda Greenhouse, "The Supreme Court: The Workplace; Court Spells Out Rules for Finding Sex Harassment," *New York Times*, June 27, 1998, at www.nytimes.com. See also Muhl, "The Law at Work"; and Steven Greenhouse, "Companies Set to Get Tougher on Harassment," *New York Times*, June 28, 1998, at www.nytimes.com.

well beyond this situation, making it clear that employers bear the fundamental responsibility for preventing and eliminating sexual harassment from the workplace. The Court ruled that when sexual harassment results in "a tangible employment action, such as discharge, demotion or undesirable assignment" (as in the quid pro quo type of case described earlier), the employer's liability is absolute. In cases of no tangible action (including hostile environment cases), an employer could still be liable but can defend itself by establishing that it took "reasonable care to prevent and correct promptly any sexually harassing behavior" and that the employee "unreasonably failed to take advantage of any preventive or corrective opportunities" provided. It is widely believed that a strong, well-publicized employer policy against harassment coupled with an effective grievance (complaint) procedure are the best tools currently available to employers to combat sexual harassment at the workplace and to safeguard themselves from liability. Such a policy cannot simply be "on the books." The employer must make sure that the policy is effectively communicated to employees, complaints are promptly investigated, and corrective action, where merited, is promptly taken.

A final issue also featured in recent public debate is employment discrimination based on sexual orientation. Title VII has not been interpreted to prohibit employment discrimination against individuals due to their sexual orientation. However, 15 states do prohibit such discrimination in private employment, and, in an additional 10 states, state employees are protected from such discrimination by executive order or civil service rule. Further, a number of cities and counties prohibit discrimination on the basis of sexual orientation.[100]

Effectiveness of the Government's Antidiscrimination Effort

Much remains to be learned about the functioning of these laws and regulations. Questions have been raised both about their effectiveness in improving opportunities for protected groups and about the possibility that they might result in reverse discrimination against groups not covered.

It is highly likely that the impact of the Equal Pay Act is minimal. The major reason is that men and women rarely do exactly the same kind of work in the same firm. However, the protection offered by this law may be growing more important as occupational segregation continues to decline.

Considerably less agreement exists on the effects of Title VII and the Executive Order. Although some empirical work looks at their effectiveness, the results are not entirely conclusive, in large part because it is difficult to isolate the effect of legislation from other changes that occurred.

A review of the trends in the male-female pay gap was presented in Chapter 5. It gave no indication of a notable improvement in women's economic status in the post-1964 period that might be attributable to the effects of the government's antidiscrimination

---

[100]Discrimination in private employment is prohibited in California, Connecticut, District of Columbia, Hawaii, Maryland, Massachusetts, Minnesota, Nevada, New Hampshire, New Jersey, New Mexico, New York, Rhode Island, Vermont, and Wisconsin; discrimination is prohibited in state employment in Alaska, Colorado, Delaware, Illinois, Indiana, Kentucky, Montana, Pennsylvania, and Washington. See, "Laws Prohibiting Job Discrimination Based on Sexual Orientation and/or Gender Identity," June 9, 2003, from www.aclu.org.

effort, at least through the late 1970s or early 1980s. During this time period, however, blacks experienced considerable increases in their earnings relative to whites that many ascribe, at least in part, to the impact of the antidiscrimination laws.

On the other hand, some detailed studies do find positive effects of the government's policies on women's earnings and occupations.[101] Studies focusing specifically on the impact of affirmative action also suggest modest employment gains for women attributable to this program. Such programs also appear to boost the relative wages of women, both because establishments using affirmative action are higher paying, controlling for the characteristics of workers employed in them, and because sex differences in wages are smaller in such establishments.[102] It might also be argued that the improvement in women's economic position that began around 1980 could be due at least in part to the opportunities created by the government's antidiscrimination laws and regulations. This influence would potentially include both the direct effect of improving the treatment of women in the labor market and, in response to that, the indirect effect of increasing the incentives for women to train for nontraditional jobs.

Beginning in the 1980s, it appears that the government scaled back its antidiscrimination enforcement efforts. Its enforcement of affirmative action in the contract sector was reportedly reduced at that time.[103] Also notable was the decline in class action cases brought by the EEOC under Title VII, alleging a pattern and practice of discrimination against women or minorities on the part of an employer. The resolution of such suits on behalf of the plaintiffs potentially results in a much larger labor market impact than the resolution of individual complaints. Interestingly, however, the number of class action and other employment discrimination suits is again on the increase, due to a rising number brought by employees themselves, either individually or banding together and being represented by private law firms. The 76 federal class action claims in 2003 represent a substantial increase from 32 in 1991. This development may be related to the incentives established by the 1991 federal law, discussed previously, which makes it more lucrative for private law firms to represent employees alleging discrimination. Under the original antidiscrimination legislation, monetary redress was generally limited

---

[101]For studies finding that antidiscrimination legislation improved women's earnings (relative to men's), see Ronald Oaxaca, "The Persistence of Male-Female Earnings Differentials" in *The Distribution of Economic Well-Being,* edited by Thomas F. Juster (Cambridge, MA: Ballinger Publishing Company, 1977), pp. 303–44; and Andrea H. Beller, "The Impact of Equal Employment Opportunity Laws on the Male/Female Earnings Differential," in *Women in the Labor Market,* edited by Cynthia B. Lloyd, Emily Andrews, and Curtis L. Gilroy (New York: Columbia University Press, 1979), pp. 304–30. Other research suggests that the antidiscrimination legislation and regulations resulted in positive employment effects for women and minorities; see, for instance, William J. Carrington, Kristin McCue, and Brooks Pierce, "Using Establishment Size to Measure the Impact of Title VII and Affirmative Action," *Journal of Human Resources* 35, no. 3 (Summer 2000): 503–23; or increased women's probability of being employed in a male occupation; see Andrea H. Beller, "Occupational Segregation by Sex: Determinants and Changes," *Journal of Human Resources* 17, no. 3 (Summer 1982): 317–92. Evidence was more mixed in a study by David Neumark and Wendy A. Stock, which found that sex discrimination/equal pay laws increased the relative earnings of black and white women, but reduced their relative employment; see "The Effects of Race and Sex Discrimination Laws," National Bureau of Economic Research Working Paper No. 8217 (April 2001).

[102]Harry Holzer and David Neumark, "Assessing Affirmative Action," *Journal of Economic Literature* 38 no. 3 (September 2000): 483–568; see also Holzer and Neumark, "What Does Affirmative Action Do?"; and Jonathan S. Leonard, "Women and Affirmative Action," *Journal of Economic Perspectives* 3, no. 1 (Winter 1989): 61–75.

[103]Leonard, "Women and Affirmative Action."

to back pay. Now, in cases of intentional discrimination, it is possible to sue for distress, humiliation, and punitive damages. In addition, the new law allows discrimination cases to be argued before juries as well as judges, rather than only before judges as was previously the case. In 1994, workers won 43.3 percent of all employment discrimination cases heard by juries compared to 22.1 percent of those heard by judges.[104]

Affirmative Action

Just as there is disagreement on the effectiveness of the government's antidiscrimination effort, so there is controversy about the form it should take. Debate particularly centers on the desirability of affirmative action to remedy past underrepresentation of women and minorities. Affirmative action may be defined as "...pro-active steps...to erase differences between women and men, minorities and nonminorities, etc." in the labor market, and contrasts with laws and regulations that simply require employers not to discriminate against these groups.[105] Thus, affirmative action refers to a broad array of possible activities ranging from efforts to more vigorously recruit women and minorities for job openings to some sort of preferences for women and minorities.

Affirmative action plans are legally mandated in only two cases. First, the Executive Order requires affirmative action by government contractors who are found to underutilize women or minorities. Such employers are required to set goals based on estimates of the availability of protected groups for similar types of positions and to set reasonable timetables for meeting those goals. Thus, contrary to popular belief, the government contract compliance program does not impose hiring quotas on employers. Second, affirmative action may be imposed by the courts in cases where employers are found guilty of discrimination or settlements are reached in discrimination suits. Although quotas may sometimes be ordered in such instances, quotas remain extremely rare in the labor market. In addition to these legal requirements, some employers have voluntarily adopted affirmative action programs. They may be motivated by a sincere desire to expand their utilization of protected groups, the hope of heading off potential lawsuits by women and minorities, the potential public relations benefits of such efforts, or some combination of all of these factors.

A variety of different views is held about affirmative action. First, some argue that there is no conclusive evidence that serious discrimination (still) exists and that, even if there were, removing it would be sufficient and affirmative action is not needed. Second, others accept the need for some form of affirmative action but oppose the use of goals and timetables for fear that they will be too rigidly enforced and become de facto quotas. A difference of opinion, even among strong proponents of affirmative action,

---

[104]Statistics on class action suits are from Brooke A. Masters and Amy Joyce, "Costco Is the Latest Class-Action Target: Lawyers' Interest Increases in Potentially Lucrative Discrimination Suits," *Washington Post*, August 18, 2004, at www.washingtonpost.com; see also, Allen Myerson, "As U.S. Bias Cases Drop, Employees Take Up Fight," *New York Times*, January 12, 1997, at www.nytimes.com. A 1999 Supreme Court ruling may, however, make it less likely that employees who bring successful discrimination suits against their employers will be able to collect punitive damages. In *Kolstad v. American Dental Association,* the Court ruled that when a company makes "good faith efforts" to comply with the civil rights law, it cannot be required to pay punitive damages for the discriminatory actions of managers who violate company policy; see Linda Greenhouse, "Ruling Raises Hurdle in Bias-Award Cases," *New York Times,* June 23, 1999, at www.nytimes.com.

[105]Holzer and Neumark, "Assessing Affirmative Action," p. 484. The Holzer and Neumark article, as well as Barbara R. Bergmann, *In Defense of Affirmative Action* (New York: Basic Books, 1996), provide extremely useful treatments of the issues surrounding affirmative action and assessments of the empirical evidence.

focuses on whether it should take the form of sincere efforts to find and encourage fully qualified candidates from the protected groups or go so far as to hire them preferentially. Some believe that preferential treatment may at times be needed to overcome the effects of past discrimination, while others do not believe such steps are warranted.

Although affirmative action programs that include preferences for women or minorities in employment are controversial in the public debate, such programs have generally been found by the courts to be legitimate approaches to remedying past discrimination in the labor market. The legal status of court-mandated affirmative action plans that include employment preferences is not in question. Similarly, those required by the Executive Order have generally not been challenged.[106]

The Supreme Court has also found that voluntary programs incorporating employment preferences are legal under certain circumstances. Specifically, employers can give employment preferences to women and minorities as a temporary measure to remedy manifest imbalances in traditionally segregated job categories.[107] A recent court ruling upholding affirmative action in admission to the University of Michigan Law School was interpreted by some experts as possibly providing (through extension) an additional rationale for affirmative action in the employment arena, namely, achieving diversity. Specifically, the court's majority opinion, written by Justice Sandra Day O'Connor, cited the views put forward by a number of major companies in "friend of the court" briefs in finding that the educational benefits of diversity are "not theoretical but real, as major American businesses have made clear that the skills needed in today's increasingly global marketplace can only be developed through exposure to widely diverse people, cultures, ideas, and viewpoints."[108]

At the same time, the Court has stressed the need for affirmative action plans to be flexible, gradual, and limited in their adverse effect on men and whites; it has also tended to disapprove of strict numerical quotas except where necessary to remedy demonstrated cases of severe past discrimination. Furthermore, although the Court has ruled that employers may give preference to women and minorities in hiring and promotion under certain circumstances, it has rejected the use of such preferences to protect women and minorities from layoffs.[109] This distinction may be due to a concern over the rights of third parties, that is, members of nonprotected groups who are adversely affected by the affirmative action program. Being denied a potential benefit such as being hired for a particular job, gaining admittance to a training program, or securing a promotion may be viewed as a less serious cost than being laid off from a job, especially after accumulating considerable seniority.

---

[106]The Supreme Court's ruling in the 1995 *Adarand* case placed significant limits on federal government programs that favor racial minorities (and presumably women). However, that case dealt with preferences for minority-owned firms in awarding contracts rather than with employment.

[107]*Steelworkers v. Weber,* 443 U.S. 193 (1979) and *Johnson v. Santa Clara County Transportation Agency*, 480 U.S. 616 (1987).

[108]Cited in Lisa E. Chang, "*Grutter v. Bollinger*, et al.: Affirmative Action Lessons for the Private Employer," *Employee Relations Law Journal* 30, no. 1 (Summer 2004): 3–15. This article includes a useful appraisal of the impact of the *Grutter* decision on employers. See also, Steven Greenhouse and Jonathan D. Glater, "Companies See Court Ruling as Support for Diversity," *New York Times*, June 24, 2003, at www.nytimes.com. Note that the Court struck down the affirmative action program used for undergraduate admissions at Michigan for giving too much weight to race, in contrast to the law school which considered race as one factor among many. This ruling was interpreted in the employment arena as reinforcing the Court's negative stance on quotas, as discussed in following text.

[109]Stuart Taylor, "Court's Change of Course," *New York Times,* March 27, 1987, p. 1; and Steven A. Holmes, "Quotas: Despised by Many, but Just What Are They?" *New York Times,* June 2, 1991, p. 20.

It is important to recognize, however, that most affirmative action programs do not require employment preferences. Indeed, affirmative action programs may improve human management systems because, in the face of affirmative action pressures, many companies have implemented wider and more systematic search procedures and developed more objective criteria and procedures for hiring and promotion.[110] Not only are such changes likely to make human resource management systems more effective, but they should also help to create more objective evidence when considering women and minority candidates for promotions or other employment opportunities.

In recent studies comparing workers in firms using affirmative action and firms that did not, little evidence indicated that women or minorities hired under affirmative action performed worse. Where affirmative action was used in *recruitment only* (as compared to hiring), the results indicated that women and minorities, if anything, performed better than white males. When affirmative action was used in the hiring process, it was again found that new female hires possessed similar qualifications and job performance. Some evidence of lesser qualifications was found "on paper" for minorities, but once hired, most minority groups performed at a level equivalent to their white male peers.[111] These findings are consistent with empirical research, which strongly suggests that rigid employment quotas and reverse discrimination are not the norm in the labor market. One study found that the employment goals of government contractors covered under the Executive Order were not filled with the rigidity one would expect if they were really quotas. That is, firms tended to fall short of their employment goals for women and minorities. Nonetheless, the setting of goals had a positive effect on the employment of these groups in that establishments that promised to employ more women and minorities in the future tended to do so in subsequent years.[112]

As in the case of affirmative action, it has been found, with respect to the broader issue of antidiscrimination policy as a whole, that the increased employment of women was achieved without substantial reverse discrimination. Specifically, no evidence at the industry level indicates that the productivity of women fell relative to men as their employment increased—as would be expected if there were substantial reverse discrimination. Direct tests at the company level of the effect of affirmative action pressure, Title VII litigation, and changing proportions of women and minorities on profits also failed to show any adverse effect.[113] Indeed, rather than having produced an epidemic of reverse discrimination, as noted previously, research suggests that the government's enforcement of the Executive Order was in fact scaled back in the 1980s.[114]

Given that the government's efforts to enforce affirmative action in the contract sector have declined considerably and there is little evidence that affirmative action produced ill effects in any event, one may wonder why the program has excited so much public opposition. One reason may be that it is unclear who the "victims" of affirmative action efforts are and, hence, it is easy to form exaggerated views of their numbers. So, for example,

[110]Holzer and Neumark, "What Does Affirmative Action Do?"

[111]Holzer and Neumark, "Are Affirmative Action Hires Less Qualified?"; and Holzer and Neumark, "What Does Affirmative Action Do?"

[112]Jonathan S. Leonard, "What Promises Are Worth: The Impact of Affirmative Action Goals," *Journal of Human Resources* 20, no. 1 (Winter 1985): 3–20.

[113]Leonard, "Antidiscrimination or Reverse Discrimination"; see also Holzer and Neumark, "Are Affirmative Action Hires Less Qualified?"

[114]Leonard, "Women and Affirmative Action."

when a woman or minority gets a position, observers may leap to the conclusion that the individual is an "affirmative action hire," which may or may not be true in the first place. Then, since it is generally not known who would have otherwise been hired, all those who did not get the job may feel that it was "because" of affirmative action. Of course, in reality, no more than one of the rejected applicants would have been hired. A second reason for the upsurge of public opinion against affirmative action is that, as we shall see in greater detail in Chapter 8, despite vigorous employment growth at least through the 1990s, these have been in some respects difficult and uncertain times in the labor market, especially for the less skilled. Affirmative action becomes a ready scapegoat for those who feel adversely affected by what are in truth broader economic trends that are unrelated to the government's antidiscrimination effort.

Exaggerated public perceptions of the negative effects of affirmative action and other government antidiscrimination programs constitute a serious concern, because they may adversely affect attitudes toward women and minorities in the workplace. A related problem is that women and minorities may, as noted earlier, be branded as affirmative action hires and stigmatized as less competent. Such perceptions could sap their confidence and make it difficult for them to function effectively in their jobs. On the other hand, if the alternative to affirmative action is greater discrimination against women and minorities, the absence of good advancement opportunities could, through feedback effects, discourage these groups from investing in job skills.

Comparable Worth

In the latter half of the 1970s, impatience with the slow progress in closing the male-female earnings gap, as well as some reluctance to accept the movement of women into different occupations as a necessary component of the solution, led to great interest in a possible alternative approach to increasing women's wages. The new idea, in simple terms, amounts to extending the notion of equal pay for equal work to the broader concept of equal pay for work of comparable worth within the firm.[115] Proponents argue this is a reasonable interpretation of Title VII and a feasible way of achieving a more rapid reduction in the male-female pay gap. Opponents point to the difficulties involved in determining exactly what comparable worth means in practical terms. They are also concerned about interfering with the working of the market and the possibility of bringing about a substantial imbalance in the supply of and demand for female workers.

Comparing the value to the firm of workers employed in different jobs is a difficult task that involves the establishment of equivalences for various fields of education, different types of skill, and varying work environments. Nonetheless, job evaluation is widely used to determine pay scales, not only by governments, but also by many larger firms. This wide usage certainly shows that the approach is feasible. However, it should

---

[115]For an early article articulating the legal basis for this approach, see Ruth G. Blumrosen, "Wage Discrimination, Job Segregation, and Title VII of the Civil Rights Act of 1964," *University of Michigan Journal of Law Reform* 12, no. 3 (Spring 1979): 399–502. For examinations of the economic and social issues involved, see, for example, Barbara R. Bergmann, *The Economic Emergence of Women* (New York: Basic Books, 1986), chap. 8; Mark R. Killingsworth, *The Economics of Comparable Worth* (Kalamazoo, MI: W.E. Upjohn Institute for Employment Research, 1990); Paula England, *Comparable Worth: Theories and Evidence* (New York: Aldine De Gruyter, 1992); Robert T. Michael, Heidi Hartmann, and Brigid O'Farrell, eds., *Pay Equity: Empirical Inquiries* (Washington, DC: National Academy Press, 1989); and Mark R. Killingsworth, "Comparable Worth and Pay Equity: Recent Developments in the United States," *Canadian Public Policy* 28, no. s1 (May 2002): S171–86.

be noted that such a procedure is generally used in conjunction with information about market wage rates, rather than as a completely separate alternative to the market. Moreover, existing job evaluation schemes have themselves been criticized for undervaluing the skills and abilities that are emphasized in female jobs. Finally, when unions are involved in determining and implementing comparable worth or pay equity adjustments, alterations in pay rates across jobs may in part be determined through the negotiation process rather than solely through job evaluation.

Turning to the issue of setting wages at a level other than that determined by the market, the strongest opposition to such a policy comes primarily from those who believe that the existing labor market substantially resembles the neoclassical competitive model. In such a market, only the person's qualifications and tastes limit access to jobs, and all workers are rewarded according to their productivity. In this view, raising women's wages is not only unnecessary but would lead to excess supply, hence, unemployment and a misallocation of resources.

On the other hand, many of those in favor of the comparable worth approach begin with a view of a segmented labor market, where workers' access to highly paid positions is often limited by discriminating employers, restrictive labor organizations, entrenched internal labor markets, and differences in the prelabor market socialization of men and women. Under such circumstances, the crowding of women into traditional occupations is believed to represent a misallocation of resources, which is permitted to continue by societal and labor market discrimination against women. Mandating higher wages would bring the earnings of those who remain in women's jobs closer to the level of comparably qualified men.

However, raising women's wages without changing the underlying conditions that produced them could still result in job loss. This is illustrated in Figure 7-1. Suppose we begin with the discriminatory situation. The relevant supply curves are S_{fd} and S_{md}, and wages are W_{fd} and W_{md}, in the female and male sectors, respectively. Suppose further that a comparable worth system set wages in female jobs at W_0, the rate that would prevail in the absence of discrimination. At that wage, only L_{f0}, rather than L_{fd} workers, would be demanded by employers. The remainder, $L_{fd} - L_{f0}$, would be displaced from their jobs.

If such shifts were major and abrupt, which of course need not be the case, the transition period might be quite protracted. To the extent that not only new entrants but experienced workers were involved, it would be disruptive and painful. Female unemployment rates might well be increased. The costs associated with this policy depend crucially on how many workers are displaced, how quickly, and what happens to them.

It is also worth noting that the alternative approach of raising women's pay through the principles of equal pay for equal work and equal employment opportunity also offers the potential for increasing the wages even of women who remain in female jobs. This scenario may also be illustrated in Figure 7-1. Suppose that we again begin with the discriminatory situation. If the barriers to entry into male jobs are reduced, women will transfer from F jobs to M jobs. The supply curve in F jobs will shift inward toward S_{f0} while the supply curve in M jobs shifts outward toward S_{m0}. Wages in the female sector are increased by the reduction of overcrowding there. A completely successful antidiscrimination policy would result in a wage of W_0 being established for both types of jobs. Proponents of comparable worth contend, however, that existing policies have not achieved notable success as yet and that a new strategy is called for.

Thus far, we have emphasized the economic issues relevant to the subject of comparable worth—issues that are paramount in concluding whether, and for whom, such a policy would be beneficial. However, the courts are making decisions concerning the issue on purely legal grounds. Currently, the status of comparable worth as a legal doctrine under Title VII is unclear because the matter has not been definitively addressed by the Supreme Court.[116] Nor is there much evidence of the adoption of comparable worth in the private sector, although many state and local governments have implemented or are in the process of implementing some version of comparable worth.[117] In addition, some unions, particularly those in the public sector, have pressed for pay equity as a collective bargaining demand.

Empirical evidence on the potential impact of comparable worth in the United States is based on analyses of its implementation for state and municipal government employees, since the private sector has little experience with comparable worth. Such studies tend to find positive effects on women's relative wages. When employment effects are also examined, adverse effects on the growth of women's relative employment are usually found, although such effects are generally small.[118] Some additional light can be shed on these issues by examining what happened in Australia when wages in female occupations were abruptly raised by introducing a comparable worth policy. The experience of that country is described in Chapter 11, but overall it tends to be relatively positive in that a considerable narrowing of the pay gap was achieved with relatively modest negative employment effects.

However, it may be difficult to extrapolate the results of studies that focus on government employees to the impact of the adoption of a nationwide comparable worth policy that includes the private sector. Even studies of comparable worth as implemented in Australia may be less than fully instructive because the labor market in that country tends to be highly centralized with a large role for government tribunals and unions in setting wage rates. This contrasts strongly with the highly decentralized U.S. labor market, which relies much more heavily on the market and generally gives firms considerable autonomy in setting wages. In this respect a recent study, which focused

---

[116]In *County of Washington v. Gunther*, 452 U.S. 161 (1981), the Supreme Court removed a major legal stumbling block to the comparable worth doctrine by ruling that it is not required that a man and woman do "equal work" in order to establish pay discrimination under Title VII. However, many other issues remain unresolved, and the Court stopped short of endorsing the comparable worth approach. See Ross et al., *The Rights of Women*, pp. 26–29. A major legal victory for proponents of comparable worth was attained in September 1983 when a federal court ruled in favor of the American Federation of State, County, and Municipal Employees (AFSCME) and found that the State of Washington had violated Title VII by paying employees in traditionally female job classifications less than employees in traditionally male occupations. A 1974 comparable worth study, commissioned by the state, found that women received 20 percent lower pay than men for jobs requiring equal skill and responsibility. When Washington failed to eliminate the disparity, AFSCME filed suit. The ruling in favor of the plaintiffs was later overturned on appeal (see *American Federation of State, County and Municipal Employees v. State of Washington*, 770 F.2d 1401 [1985]). In 1986, the parties settled out of court. Thus, the Supreme Court issued no definitive ruling on the comparable worth issue. See Bureau of National Affairs, *Daily Labor Report*, no. 181 (September 16, 1983); and "Washington State Settles Dispute Over Pay Equity," *New York Times*, January 2, 1986, p. A15.

[117]Susan E. Gardner and Christopher Daniel, "Implementing Comparable Worth/Pay Equity: Experiences of Cutting-Edge States," *Public Personnel Management* 27, no. 4 (Winter 1998): 475–89.

[118]See, for example, Killingsworth, *The Economics of Comparable Worth*; Peter F. Orazem and J. Peter Mattila, "The Implementation Process of Comparable Worth: Winners and Losers," *Journal of Political Economy* 98, no. 1 (February 1990): 134–52; and June O'Neill, Michael Brien, and James Cunningham, "Effects of Comparable Worth Policy: Evidence from Washington State," *American Economic Review* 79, no. 2 (May 1989): 305–09.

on the consequences of a pay equity initiative in one Canadian province, Ontario, beginning in the early 1990s, may be more relevant, because the Canadian labor market is more similar to the United States in being relatively decentralized. The results of this study suggest some caution in implementing comparable worth in such circumstances. Substantial lapses in compliance and implementation of the law were found. These lapses tended to center on small firms that lacked the resources to undertake the necessary job evaluation programs and often did not have a sufficient sample of male and female jobs to make meaningful comparisons. Because such small firms employed the majority of both male and female workers in Ontario, little evidence was found of a positive impact of the policy on women's relative pay overall. Even among large firms, where compliance was fairly complete, estimated positive effects on women's pay in female jobs were modest and typically statistically insignificant.[119] It is also possible that the ineffectiveness of pay equity legislation in this case reflects additional factors specific to the situation in Ontario, such as the particular law implemented there or a change in the governing party that occurred a few years after the passage of the law.

Job Evaluation

The implementation of comparable worth requires an evaluation of the contribution of the many different jobs within an enterprise.* At present, formal job evaluation procedures are already used by the federal government, a number of state governments, and many large private firms as an aid in determining pay rates. Employers rely on such evaluations because many positions are filled entirely from within the firm itself through promotion and upgrading of the existing workforce. Job evaluation may be useful in setting pay rates in such jobs, especially since some of them are unique to a particular enterprise. This means that "going rates" for all jobs are not always available in local labor markets. Thus, employers may find it necessary to establish wages for such jobs, rather than simply to accept those determined by the market. It is important to bear in mind that, when wages are set in this way, it does not mean that market forces are ignored. In setting wages, most firms and governmental units that use job evaluation try to take into account whatever information is available on prevailing wages for different types of labor. At the same time, the existence of job evaluation and other procedures for setting wages tends to make wages less responsive to short-term shifts in market conditions than they would otherwise be.

The actual methods used differ in detail but share the same basic rationale and approach. The first step is always a description of all the jobs within the given organization. The next step is to rate each job according to all the various features that are believed to determine pay differences across jobs. Last, these ratings are combined to create a score for each job, which may then be used to help determine wages.

Among the factors used to construct job scores are such characteristics as level of education, skills, and responsibility, as well as the environment in which the work is

[119]Michael Baker and Nicole M. Fortin, "Comparable Worth Work in a Decentralized Labor Market: The Case of Ontario," *Canadian Journal of Economics* 37, no. 4 (November 2004): 850–78.

performed. Commonly, multiple regression is used to link these to the existing pay structure. At other times, weights are assigned according to the judgment of the experts constructing the scale. In theory, various jobs can be assigned values objectively, presumably not influenced by irrelevant factors such as the gender and race of the incumbent, and quite different jobs may be assigned equal values, if warranted.

It would be a mistake, however, to take the objectivity of such procedures for granted. Both prevailing wage structures and the judgments of individuals may be tainted by existing inequalities in the economy and in society. An additional problem with the job evaluation approach is that it is most readily implemented in large firms.

* Job evaluation is discussed in Donald J. Treiman and Heidi I. Hartmann, eds., *Women, Work and Wages: Equal Pay for Jobs of Equal Value* (Washington, DC: National Academy Press, 1981), pp. 71–74. Institutional models, discussed earlier, emphasize the importance of job evaluation and other administrative procedures for determining wages. See Peter B. Doeringer and Michael J. Piore, *Internal Labor Markets and Manpower Analysis* (Lexington, MA: D. C. Heath and Co., 1971).

Conclusion

Economists define labor market discrimination as a situation where two equally qualified individuals are treated differently on the basis of gender (race, age, etc.). Such discrimination against a particular group is likely to be detrimental, both directly and indirectly through feedback effects on their accumulation of human capital. Empirical studies have used available evidence on differences in the characteristics of male and female workers to explain the pay gap and the differences in occupational distributions between the two groups. Productivity-related factors have not been able to account for all of the gender differences in economic outcomes, suggesting that discrimination does play a part, accounting for perhaps 40 percent of the male-female earnings differential.

As much attention as has been focused on the issue of whether discrimination exists, there has been almost equal interest in the question of who discriminates, why, and how. We reviewed theories that suggested the following:

- Employers, coworkers, or customers have tastes for discrimination against women.
- Employers judge individual women in terms of the average characteristics of the group (statistical discrimination).
- Women's wages are depressed because they are crowded into a few sectors.
- Women are concentrated in dead-end jobs with few opportunities for on-the-job training and promotion.

Last, we examined the government's equal employment opportunity policies and considered the pros and cons of comparable worth.

Each of the models of discrimination that we considered contributes to our understanding of a complex reality, where factors keeping women in segregated and poorly paid jobs, rather than being mutually exclusive, are likely to reinforce each other. By the same token, however, we pointed out that any improvements in women's labor market outcomes are likely to have feedback effects. By rewarding women more highly for their human capital, they are encouraged to accumulate more human capital on which they can gather rewards.

APPENDIX 7A

Regression Analysis and Empirical Estimates of Labor Market Discrimination

In Table 7-1, we presented empirical estimates of labor market discrimination. In this appendix,[120] we explain in more detail how economists arrive at such estimates. The goal is to be able to "decompose" the gender wage gap into a portion due to measured productivity-related characteristics and a portion that cannot be explained by differences in characteristics and is, therefore, potentially due to labor market discrimination.

The starting point of such analyses is the estimation of a wage regression, which expresses wages as a function of such factors as experience and education. For simplicity, let's begin with the case in which there is only one explanatory variable, experience. Figure 7-4 shows a hypothetical scatter of points, "observations," for individual women with each point representing one woman's wage rate and experience.

To better understand how wages are determined, we would like to use this information to estimate the effect of an additional year of work experience on wages. As can be seen, if

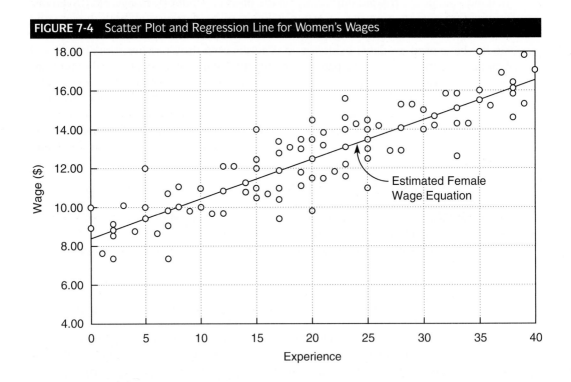

FIGURE 7-4   Scatter Plot and Regression Line for Women's Wages

---

[120]In formulating this section we benefited from reviewing Ronald G. Ehrenberg and Robert S. Smith, *Modern Labor Economics,* 8th ed. (Reading, MA: Addison Wesley, 2003), Appendix 1A, pp. 15–23; and Mark Killingsworth, "Where Does the Pay Gap Come From?" Class Handout for Economics 375, Women in the Economy, Rutgers University. For a more detailed treatment of regression analysis, see a statistics or econometrics text.

we were to fit a straight line to the points in Figure 7-4, it would be an upward sloping line, suggesting that wages increase with additional years of labor market experience.

Before considering the technique that we would use to estimate the line shown in the figure, let's begin with the following equation that models the general relationship between wages and experience.

$$WAGE_i = a_0 + a_1 X_i + e_i$$

In this equation WAGE represents the wage rate of individual i and is called the **dependent variable**. The **independent** or **explanatory variable** is X, which represents the individual's level of experience. The regression coefficients, a_0 and a_1, specify the relationship between the dependent and independent variable: a_0 is the intercept of the line on the y-axis and a_1 is the slope of the line. The intercept gives the wage rate corresponding to zero years of work experience, that is, for a new entrant into the labor market. The slope of the line tells us by how much wages increase for each additional year of experience. The last term, e, is a random error term. It is included because we do not expect each observation to lie along the straight line; random factors unrelated to experience are also likely to influence wages. (We shall see below that systematic factors such as education, which also affect wages, can be incorporated in multiple regression analysis.)

How do we find the straight line that best fits the points in the figure? This amounts to estimating a_0 and a_1. The statistical technique generally used is called **least squares regression analysis**. It is estimated by finding the line that minimizes the sum of the squared deviations (vertical differences) of each point from the line.

If we estimate a least squares regression using the points in Figure 7-4 we obtain the following estimated line:

$$WAGE_i = 8.5 + 0.2X_i$$

The estimate of $a_0 = 8.5$ and the estimate of $a_1 = 0.2$ mean that a new entrant into the labor market is expected to earn $8.50 per hour and an individual's wages are expected to increase by $0.20 with each additional year of experience.

At least two potential problems arise with this estimate. First, the hypothetical and the actual earnings profiles we showed in Chapter 6 were not straight lines but rather curved lines, which suggests that even though earnings rise with experience, the rate of increase tends to fall over time. Such a relationship can readily be estimated using regression analysis and in fact most studies by economists allow for this.[121] We, however, will stick to a straight line as in Figure 7-4 to simplify our exposition.

Second, economic theory tells us that a number of other explanatory variables are potentially important determinants of wages. These additional explanatory variables can be incorporated by using **multiple regression analysis**. We illustrate multiple regression analysis by adding education as an additional explanatory variable. Our wage equation now becomes:

$$WAGE_i = a_0' + a_1' X_i + a_2' ED_i + e_i'$$

ED is a variable measuring years of schooling completed. Each regression coefficient now tells us the impact of a unit change in each explanatory variable on the dependent variable, *holding the other independent variables constant*. So, for example, a_1' gives the effect of an additional year of experience on wages, holding education constant. Thus, the regression coefficients a_0' and a_1' are not necessarily equal to a_0 and a_1, because their interpretation has changed.

---

[121]To do this we include experience squared (X^2), in addition to X, as an explanatory variable in the regression.

This new relationship estimated by multiple regression analysis is found to be:

$$\text{WAGE}_i = 2 + 0.3X_i + 0.5Ed_i$$

That is, we find that, holding education constant, each additional year of experience raises wages by $0.30; and, holding experience constant, each additional year of education raises wages by $0.50.

Note that including education changed our estimate of the effect of experience. This change occurs because education is *correlated* with experience: Given the trend toward rising educational attainment, younger women have higher levels of education, on average, but less experience than older women. The estimated experience coefficient in the simple regression (the one that includes only experience) is *smaller* than in the multiple regression because the positive effect of experience on earnings is offset somewhat by the tendency of older people (with higher

levels of experience) to be less well educated. Thus, education is an important *omitted variable* and not taking it into account results in a *biased* estimate of the effect of experience; specifically, the estimated effect of experience is *biased downward* when education is omitted from the regression.

The results obtained with multiple regression analysis for the relationship between wages and experience can still be summarized in a simple diagram if we evaluate them at a specific level or specific levels of education, as shown in Figure 7-5 for *ED* = 12 (high school graduates) and *ED* = 16 (college graduates).

Now that the basics of regression analysis are clear, we can consider how it may be used to obtain statistical estimates of the extent of labor market discrimination. We do this first in terms of a diagram and then present a general formula.

FIGURE 7-5   The Estimated Relationship between Wages and Experience for Women Evaluated at 12 and 16 Years of Education

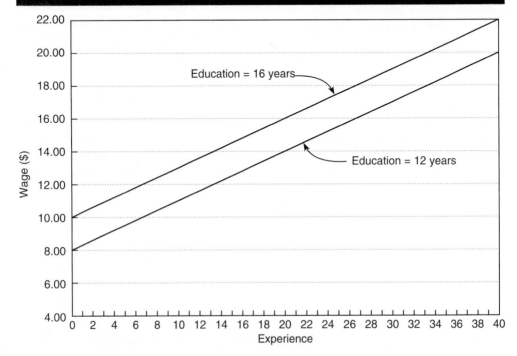

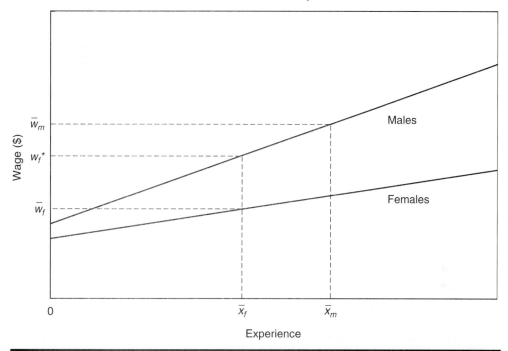

FIGURE 7-6 Hypothetical Regression Lines for Male and Female College Graduates

Figure 7-6 shows hypothetical male and female wage regression lines for college graduates. By focusing on one education group, we can proceed in terms of simple regression with one explanatory variable, experience. As may be seen in the figure, women's average wages, $\overline{w}_f$, are lower than men's, $\overline{w}_m$. At the same time, women have less experience on average, $\overline{x}_f$, than men do, $\overline{x}_m$. How much of the difference in average wages between men and women, $\overline{w}_m - \overline{w}_f$, is due to the gender difference in average levels of experience, $\overline{x}_m - \overline{x}_f$, and how much cannot be explained by this difference in qualifications? This "unexplained" portion is our estimate of discrimination.

We begin by observing that the female regression line lies below the male line and that it is also flatter. This comparison shows that women earn less than men with the same experience both because they earn less at the outset of their careers than men

do (the intercept of the female line is below the intercept of the male line) and because they receive a smaller return than men for each additional year of experience (the female line is flatter than the male line). We would like our estimate of discrimination to capture these differences.

To estimate how much of the gender wage gap is due to gender differences in experience, we ask what women's wages would be if they were rewarded the same way as men for their experience. Reading off of the male regression line, we see that a man with $\overline{x}_f$ years of experience would receive a wage of w_f^*. Thus, the portion of the gender wage gap attributable to women's lower average level of experience is $\overline{w}_m - w_f^*$. The remainder, $w_f^* - \overline{w}_f$, is unexplained and potentially due to discrimination. The unexplained portion of the gender gap is due to gender differences in the estimated coefficients of the wage regression (a_0 and a_1).

We can express this relationship mathematically as follows:

Gender wage difference	=	Difference due to qualifications	+	Unexplained difference

$$= \overline{w}_m - \overline{w}_f = \left(\overline{w}_m - w_f{}^*\right) + \left(w_f{}^* - \overline{w}_f\right)$$

where

$$\overline{w}_m = a_{0m} + a_{1m} \times \overline{x}_m$$
$$\overline{w}_f = a_{0f} + a_{1f} \times \overline{x}_f$$
$$w_f{}^* = a_{0m} + a_{1m} \times \overline{x}_f$$

In the preceding equations, a_{0m} and a_{1m} are the intercept and slope of the male regression and a_{0f} and a_{1f} are the intercept and slope of the female regression.

The portion of the wage difference that is due to differences in qualifications, in this case experience, $(\overline{w}_m - w_f{}^*)$, is obtained by evaluating both men's and women's average levels of experience using the male regression coefficients. The unexplained portion of the gender difference is estimated by the difference between what women's wages are when their average experience is evaluated using the male regression versus when they are evaluated using the female regression. This approach can readily be applied in the multiple regression context and underlies estimates such as those presented in Table 7-1.[122]

Questions for Review and Discussion

1. How do economists generally measure the extent of labor market discrimination against women statistically? What important qualifications need to be noted about such estimates? Do such studies indicate that discrimination against women in the labor market continues to exist? Is there any evidence that there is now reverse discrimination as a general pattern in the labor market?

2. What factors explain why some researchers conclude that labor market discrimination against women is small while others come to a different conclusion? [*Hint:* You may also want to consult the inset on the gender pay gap in Chapter 5.]

3. Suppose you are given data about a firm, indicating that the average wage of male employees is $15.00/hour and the average wage of female employees is $10.50/hour. Define "labor market discrimination" against women. Do the preceding data prove that the firm discriminates against women? What kind of additional information would you need to determine whether such discrimination exists?

4. Prohibition of discrimination, affirmative action, and comparable worth are all possible means of reducing the wage gap. Which, if any, are likely to be effective? Why or why not? Do you see them as substitutes or as complements and why?

5. To the extent that it is true that women earn less because they spend less time in the labor market and that they spend less time in the labor market because they are paid less, how can this vicious circle be broken?

---

[122]Our ability to perform this decomposition is aided by the property of least squares regression that the regression line passes through the means of the dependent and explanatory variables. Thus, the point $(\overline{w}_f, \overline{x}_f)$ will lie on the female regression line and the point $(\overline{w}_m, \overline{x}_m)$ will lie on the male regression line. This analysis is sometimes known as a "Oaxaca Decomposition," after the economist who was one of the first to use it; he provides a detailed description in Ronald Oaxaca, "Male-Female Wage Differentials in Urban Labor Markets," *International Economic Review* 14 (October 1973): 693–709.

6. Given the discussions in Chapters 6 and 7, why do you think the income ratio for black females to black males is so much higher than for all women relative to all men, as shown by data presented in Chapter 5?

7. "Excluding women from occupations that require physical strength is justified because men tend to be stronger than women." Evaluate the validity of this argument.

Suggested Readings

Akerlof, George A., and Rachel E. Kranton. "Economics and Identity." *Quarterly Journal of Economics* 115, no. 3 (August 2000): 715–53.

Altonji, Joseph G., and Rebecca M. Blank. "Race and Gender in the Labor Market." In *Handbook of Labor Economics,* edited by Orley C. Ashenfelter and David Card. pp. 3143–259. Amsterdam: North-Holland, 1999.

Basu, Kaushik. "The Economics and Law of Sexual Harassment in the Workplace." *Journal of Economic Perspectives* 17, no. 3 (Summer 2003):141–57.

Becker, Gary S. *The Economics of Discrimination,* 2nd ed. Chicago: University of Chicago Press, 1971.

Bergmann, Barbara R. *In Defense of Affirmative Action.* New York: Basic Books, 1996.

Blau, Francine D. "Discrimination Against Women: Theory and Evidence." In *Labor Economics: Modern Views,* edited by William A. Darity Jr., pp. 53–89. Boston: Kluwer-Nijhoff, 1984.

Blau, Francine D., and Lawrence M. Kahn. "Gender Differences in Pay." *Journal of Economic Perspectives* 14, no. 4 (Fall 2000): 75–99.

Darity, William A. Jr., and Patrick L. Mason. "Evidence on Discrimination in Employment: Codes of Color, Codes of Gender." *Journal of Economic Perspectives* 12 no. 2 (Spring 1998): 63–90.

Fiske, Susan T. "Stereotyping, Prejudice, and Discrimination," in *Handbook of Social Psychology,* edited by D. T. Gilbert, S. T. Fiske, and G. Lindzey, pp. 357–411, New York: McGraw-Hill: 1998.

Goldin, Claudia. "A Pollution Theory of Discrimination: Male and Female Differences in Occupations and Earnings," National Bureau of Economic Research Working Paper No. 8985 (June 2002).

Gunderson, Morley. "Male-Female Wage Differentials and Policy Responses." *Journal of Economic Literature* 27, no. 1 (March 1989): 46–72.

Hersch, Joni. "Employment Discrimination, Economists and the Law," in *Women, Family and Work: Writings on the Economics of Gender,* edited by Karine S. Moe, pp. 217–333, Oxford: Blackwell Publishers, 2003.

Holzer, Harry, and David Neumark. "Assessing Affirmative Action." *Journal of Economic Literature* 38, no. 3 (September 2000): 483–568.

Madden, Janice F. *The Economics of Sex Discrimination.* Lexington, MA: Lexington Books, 1973.

Reskin, Barbara F. "The Proximate Causes of Employment Discrimination." *Contemporary Sociology* 29, no. 2 (March 2000): 319–28.

Reskin, Barbara F., and Patricia A. Roos. *Job Queues, Gender Queues: Explaining Women's Inroads into Male Occupations.* Philadelphia: Temple University Press, 1990.

Valian, Virginia. *Why So Slow? The Advancement of Women.* Cambridge MA: MIT Press, 1998.

8

RECENT DEVELOPMENTS IN THE LABOR MARKET: THEIR IMPACT ON WOMEN AND MEN

Chapter Highlights

■ Trends in Female and Male Wages

■ The Declining Gender Pay Gap

■ The Rising Payoff to Education

■ Changing Labor Market Dynamics

■ The Rise of the Nonstandard Workforce

■ The Growth in Women's Self-Employment

■ The Changing Face of Labor Unions

In previous chapters we examined historic developments and long-term trends in the status of women and discussed various explanations for them. We chronicled dramatic changes in women's participation in the labor force and their roles within the family. We also documented substantial improvements in women's labor market outcomes, notably the significant decrease in the gender pay gap that occurred beginning in the 1980s. This is only one of a number of dramatic labor market shifts that have taken place in recent years. Other changes include a flattening of the growth in real wages that American workers long took for granted, and a widening wage gap between high- and low-skilled workers that is associated with a rising payoff to education. In addition workers face increased concerns about job security in the wake of corporate restructuring and downsizing, growth in nonstandard employment arrangements, and a continued decline in the share of the workforce that is unionized. Women also benefit from new opportunities and confront new challenges as their self-employment rates increase. In this chapter we focus on these important developments and examine their impact on women and men.

TRENDS IN FEMALE AND MALE WAGES

One of the most notable labor market trends in recent years is the dramatic increase in **wage inequality** that occurred among both male and female workers since 1970. The rise in inequality was especially pronounced over the 1980s. By increasing wage inequality, we mean a widening dispersion in the distribution of earnings within each group (men and women), so that the wage gap between those at the bottom and those at the top widened considerably. Male workers also experienced stagnating **real wages**. Real wages are wages that have been adjusted for changes in the cost of living or price inflation. In the presence of constant or falling real wages for males overall, rising wage inequality means substantial declines in the real wages of less-educated men who are at the lower end of the wage distribution.[1]

The declining relative labor market position of the less skilled is believed to reflect an increase in demand for skilled workers relative to the demand for unskilled workers, which raised the **returns to skill** or the rewards that the labor market gives for various worker skills or qualifications. The reasons for this increase in demand are not fully understood, but most studies point to the importance of technological change and increasing international competition, both of which are believed to negatively affect the relative demand for less skilled workers. In addition, institutional factors including the decline in unionism, which we discuss at the end of this chapter, and the decreasing real value of the minimum wage also played a role.[2]

The trends in real earnings for men and women since 1960 are summarized in Table 8-1 and Figure 8-1, which show trends in the median annual earnings of year-round, full-time workers after adjustment for inflation. Although male real earnings rose substantially during the 1960s and moderately during the 1970s, they declined over the 1980s and then increased only slightly in the 1990s and early 2000s. Indeed, as may be seen in the table and the figure, male real earnings actually peaked in 1973 and fell 6.7 percent since then. The real earnings trends for women are fairly similar to men's, decade by decade, with the important exception of the 1980s. During the 1980s,

---

[1]For summaries of these trends, see, for example, Frank Levy, *The New Dollars and Dreams: American Incomes and Economic Change* (New York: Russell Sage Foundation, 1998); Francine D. Blau, "Trends in the Well-Being of American Women: 1970–95," *Journal of Economic Literature* 36, no. 1 (March 1998): 112–65; and David H. Autor, Lawrence F. Katz, and Melissa S. Kearney, "Trends in U.S. Wage Inequality in the 1990s: Re-Assessing the Revisionists," Working Paper, Massachusetts Institute of Technology (August 2004).

[2]For an excellent summary of the evidence, see Lawrence F. Katz and David H. Autor, "Changes in the Wage Structure and Earnings Inequality," in *Handbook of Labor Economics,* edited by Orley C. Ashenfelter and David Card (Amsterdam: Elsevier, 1999), pp. 3A:1463–555. Some of the better known studies include Chinhui Juhn, Kevin M. Murphy, and Brooks Pierce, "Wage Inequality and the Rise in Returns to Skill," *Journal of Political Economy* 101, no. 3 (June 1993): 410–42; Lawrence F. Katz and Kevin M. Murphy, "Changes in Relative Wages, 1963–87: Supply and Demand Factors," *Quarterly Journal of Economics* 107, no. 1 (February 1992): 35–78; and John DiNardo, Nicole M. Fortin, and Thomas Lemieux, "Labor Market Institutions and the Distribution of Wages, 1973–1992: A Semiparametric Approach," *Econometrica* 64, no. 5 (September 1996): 1001–44.

TABLE 8-1   Change in Real Median Earnings of Men and Women, Year-Round, Full-Time Workers, 1960–2003

Period	Men (%)	Women (%)
1960–1970	30.2	27.4
1970–1980	4.2	5.6
1980–1990	–6.4	11.5
1990–2000	2.2	5.2
2000–2003	2.2	4.7
1973–2003	–6.7	24.4
1960–2003	32.6	65.1

Notes: Persons 15 years old and over beginning in 1980, and persons 14 years old and over for previous years. Adjusted for inflation using the Consumer Price Index for All Urban Areas.

Sources: 1960–2000: U.S. Census Bureau, *Current Population Reports*, Historical Tables, Series P-60, Table P-36 from www.census.gov/hhes/income/histinc/p36.html; and 2003: CPS Annual Demographic Survey March Supplement, PINC-05 Tables, from ferret.bls.census.gov/macro/032004/perinc/toc.htm.

FIGURE 8-1   Median Earnings of Year-Round, Full-Time Workers by Sex, 1960–2003 (2003 dollars)

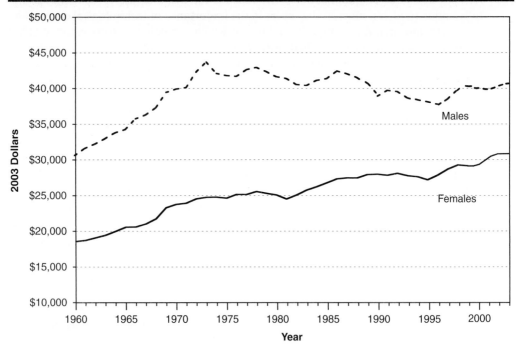

the period of major convergence in the gender wage gap, women's real earnings increased by 11.5 percent while men's real earnings fell by 6.4 percent. In addition, over the 1990s and early 2000s, while both men and women experienced some real earnings increases, female gains were larger than those of males. Overall, in stark contrast to the experience of men, women's real earnings increased by 24 percent since 1973. Thus, the decline in the gender gap since 1973 reflects not only women's real earnings growth, but also men's weak real earnings trends.[3]

THE DECLINING GENDER PAY GAP

As we saw in Chapter 5, starting in the late 1970s or early 1980s, the gender pay ratio began to increase. Between 1978 and 2003, for example, the weekly earnings of women full-time workers rose from 61 to 79 percent of men's weekly earnings. The pace of change was most rapid over the 1980s, slowed considerably over the 1990s, and rebounded in the early 2000s. In order to fully understand the reasons for the progress in narrowing the gender gap (i.e., increasing the gender ratio), it is important to consider the labor market context in which this change took place, most importantly the fact that overall wage inequality increased. This consideration raises the question of how women, who are disproportionately represented at the bottom of the wage distribution, succeeded in narrowing the gender pay gap in the face of overall labor market trends that were unfavorable for low-wage workers in general.

We begin our analysis of the trends in the gender pay gap with a consideration of the determinants of the pay gap based on economic theory. We then apply these concepts to understanding the trends in the pay gap and review empirical results for the 1980s and 1990s. We also briefly consider what is known about the reasons for the trends in the race pay gap during this same period.

Determinants of Trends in the Gender Pay Gap

In analyzing the reasons for the decline in the gender pay gap, it makes sense to start with the two major explanations for the pay gap as developed by economists, which we reviewed in previous chapters:

- **Differences in human capital investments** or other gender differences in qualifications (considered in Chapter 6)
- **Labor market discrimination** or differences in the treatment of equally qualified men and women (considered in Chapter 7)

These two explanations are not necessarily mutually exclusive. Both may play a role in explaining the gender pay gap, and, in addition, feedback effects may occur if discrimination in the labor market lowers women's incentives to invest in their qualifications and women's lower qualifications reinforce statistical discrimination against them. The empirical research reviewed in previous chapters provides considerable support for each set of factors—differences in qualifications and discrimination—in explaining the gender pay gap.

Following this reasoning, we would expect the pay gap to decline if (1) women increased their qualifications relative to men's, or (2) labor market discrimination against women decreased. The evidence provides some reason to believe that both

---

[3]Estimated trends in real earnings vary to some extent depending on the earnings measure and price deflator used, the data set employed, and the starting and ending years selected. Although the trends reported here, based on government data, are broadly consistent with the findings in the literature, we note that, in recent years, considerable controversy centers around the measurement of price changes. See, for example, Michael J. Boskin, "The CPI Commission: Findings and Recommendations," *American Economic Review* 87, no. 2 (May 1997): 78–83; and Katharine Abraham, John S. Greenlees, and Brent R. Moulton, "Working to Improve the Consumer Price Index," *Journal of Economic Perspectives* 12, no. 1 (Winter 1998): 27–36.

these developments occurred. As we saw in Chapter 6, women narrowed the gap in work experience with men and increased their share of college and professional degrees, as well as their representation in traditionally male fields of study at all levels. At the same time, women's increasing commitment to market work may have induced employers to reduce the extent of statistical discrimination against them. That is, employers may judge individual women less negatively than in the past for being members of a group they view as less committed to the labor market, on average.

Recent research suggests that explaining trends in the gender pay differential requires that we also consider a third factor, one not mentioned in earlier chapters—overall trends in wage structure:[4]

- **Wage structure** refers to the returns that the labor market offers for various skills and for employment in higher-paying industries or occupations.

Both the human capital and discrimination explanations of the pay gap suggest an important role for trends in wage structure in determining how women fare over time. For example, despite important recent gains, women still have less experience than men, on average. If the market return to experience (i.e., the increase in wages associated with each additional year of experience) rises over time, then women will be increasingly disadvantaged by their lesser amount of experience. In addition, both the human capital and discrimination models suggest reasons why women are likely to be employed in different occupations and perhaps in different industries than men. This factor implies that an increase in the rewards for employment in "male" occupations or industries will also place women at an increasing disadvantage. In fact, the patterns of rising overall wage inequality found for both men and women in the labor market, particularly in the 1980s, resulted from precisely such increases in the market rewards to skill and to employment in high-paying male sectors. During that time, then, women as a group were essentially "swimming upstream" in a labor market growing increasingly unfavorable for workers with below-average skills—in this case, below-average experience—and for workers employed in disproportionately female occupations and industries.

Empirical Results for the 1980s

How can we explain the decrease in the gender pay gap in the 1980s in the face of overall shifts in labor market returns that worked against women as a group? Recent studies by Francine Blau and Lawrence Kahn shed light on this question.[5] We especially

---

[4]Francine D. Blau and Lawrence M. Kahn, "Rising Wage Inequality and the U.S. Gender Gap," *American Economic Review Papers and Proceedings* 84, no. 2 (May 1994): 23–28; Francine D. Blau and Lawrence M. Kahn, "Swimming Upstream: Trends in the Gender Wage Differential in the 1980s," *Journal of Labor Economics* 15, no. 1, pt. 1 (January 1997): 1–42; and Francine D. Blau and Lawrence M. Kahn, "The U.S. Gender Pay Gap in the 1990s: Slowing Convergence," National Bureau of Economic Research Working Paper No. 10853 (October 2004).

[5]Blau and Kahn, "Swimming Upstream"; and Blau and Kahn, "The U.S. Gender Pay Gap in the 1990s." We draw heavily on the results of these studies. Other research on the convergence of the gender gap includes June O'Neill and Solomon W. Polachek, "Why the Gender Gap in Wages Narrowed in the 1980s," *Journal of Labor Economics* 11, no. 1, pt. 1 (January 1993): 205–28; Elaine Sorensen, *Exploring the Reasons Behind the Narrowing Gender Gap in Earnings* (Washington, DC: Urban Institute Press, 1991); Alison J. Wellington, "Changes in the Male/Female Wage Gap, 1976–85," *Journal of Human Resources* 28, no. 2 (Spring 1993): 383–411; Finis Welch in "Growth in Women's Relative Wages and in Inequality Among Men: One Phenomenon or Two?" *American Economic Review* 90, no. 2 (May 2000): 444–49; Nicole M. Fortin and Thomas Lemieux, "Are Women's Wage Gains Men's Losses? A Distributional Test," *American Economic Review* 90, no. 2 (May 2000): 456–60; and Casey B. Mulligan and Yona Rubinstein, "The Closing Gender Gap as a Roy Model Illusion," National Bureau of Economic Research Working Paper No. 10892 (November 2004).

focus our discussion on the 1980s because it was the period of the greatest narrowing of the gender gap. In the next subsection we examine explanations for the slower progress of women over the 1990s.

In their research, Blau and Kahn examined the effect of changes in women's and men's measured characteristics—experience, education, occupation, industry and union status—and changes in wage structure on trends in the gender wage gap. The part of the change in the gender gap that cannot be explained by these factors is referred to as "unexplained." As discussed in Chapter 7, the "unexplained" gap is often attributed, at least in part, to labor market discrimination, though it is acknowledged that it may reflect other factors, such as unmeasured skills, as well. It appears that women were able to overcome the effect of adverse shifts in overall wage structure (i.e., rising labor market returns to skills and to employment in high-paying male sectors) on their relative wages in the 1980s, in part, by improving their qualifications relative to men. So, although women continued to have lower skills than men, on average, particularly less labor market experience, they *narrowed the gender difference in skills.* Of particular importance was the decline in the experience difference between men and women: the gender gap in full-time experience fell from 6.6 to 4.3 years over this period. Shifts in women's occupations played a significant role too, as the employment of women as professionals and managers rose relative to men's, while their relative employment in clerical and service jobs fell. Women's wages also increased relative to men's because of deunionization (the decline of unions). Deunionization had a larger negative impact on male than female workers because men, who traditionally were more likely than women to be unionized, experienced a larger decrease in unionization than women. Another factor that worked to increase the gender pay ratio substantially was a decrease in the "unexplained" portion of the gender differential, that is, a decline in the pay difference between men and women with the same measured characteristics (i.e., experience, education, occupation, industry, and union status).

Taken together, changes in qualifications and in the unexplained gap worked to increase the gender wage ratio substantially. Working in the opposite direction, however, were changes in wage structure (or returns to characteristics) that favored men over women during this period. Of particular importance were a rise in the return to experience (since women have less of it) and increases in returns to employment in occupations and industries where men are more highly represented. The effect of these adverse shifts in labor market returns by themselves would reduce the gender ratio substantially. Thus, in order for the wage gap to decline, the factors favorably affecting women's wages needed to be large enough to more than offset the impact of unfavorable shifts in returns. This was indeed the case, so the gender pay gap did decline over the 1980s.

What can we say about the reasons for the decline in the unexplained gender wage gap that occurred over the 1980s? Such a shift may reflect a decline in labor market discrimination against women, but also an upgrading of women's *unmeasured* labor market skills, a shift in labor market demand favoring women over men, or changes in the composition of the labor force due to the pattern of labor force entries or exits. Indeed all of these factors perhaps played a role, and all appear credible during this period.

First, because women improved their relative level of measured skills, as shown by the narrowing of the gap in full-time job experience and in occupational differences between men and women, it is plausible that they also enhanced their relative level of unmeasured skills. For example, women's increasing labor force attachment may have encouraged them to acquire more on-the-job training or encouraged their employers to offer them more training. And, as we saw in Chapter 6, gender differences in college major—found to be strongly related to the gender wage gap among college graduates—decreased over the 1970s and 1980s. Thus, the marketability of women's education probably improved. As we also saw in Chapter 6, the male-female difference in SAT math scores declined as well, which could be a sign of improved quality of women's education.

Second, the argument that discrimination against women declined in the 1980s may seem less credible than that their unmeasured human capital characteristics improved, because the federal government scaled back its antidiscrimination enforcement effort during the 1980s.[6] However, as women increased their commitment to the labor force and improved their job skills, the rationale for statistical discrimination against them diminished; thus it is plausible that this type of discrimination decreased. Further, in the presence of feedback effects, employers' revised views can generate additional increases in women's wages by raising women's returns to investments in job qualifications and skills. To the extent that such qualifications are not fully controlled for in the statistical analysis used to explain the change in the gender wage gap, it may also help to account for the decline in the "unexplained" gap. Another possible reason for a decline in discrimination against women is that changes in social attitudes made such discriminatory tastes increasingly less acceptable.

Third, the underlying labor market demand shifts that widened wage inequality over the 1980s appeared to favor women relative to men in certain ways, and thus likely also contributed to a decrease in the unexplained gender gap. Overall, manufacturing employment declined. In addition, some evidence indicates that technological change produced within-industry demand shifts that favored white-collar relative to blue-collar workers in general. Given the traditional male predominance in manufacturing and in blue-collar jobs, these shifts might be expected to benefit women relative to men.[7] Moreover, one aspect of technological change, increased computer use, favors women both because they have been found to be more likely than men to use computers at work and because computers restructure work in ways that deemphasize physical strength.[8]

Finally, another factor contributing to the considerable narrowing of the "unexplained" gender wage gap in the 1980s was favorable shifts in the composition of the female labor force. Specifically, Blau and Kahn found that, controlling for the measured characteristics mentioned earlier, the women who entered the labor force over this period tended to be those with relatively high (unmeasured) skills. These skills improved the quality of the female labor force and thus contributed to the narrowing of the gender wage gap.[9]

---

[6]Jonathan S. Leonard, "Women and Affirmative Action," *Journal of Economic Perspectives* 3, no. 1 (Winter 1989): 61–75.

[7]Eli Berman, John Bound, and Zvi Griliches, "Changes in the Demand of Skilled Labor within U.S. Manufacturing Industries: Evidence from the Annual Survey of Manufacturing," *Quarterly Journal of Economics* 109, no. 2 (May 1994): 367–97; and Blau and Kahn, "Swimming Upstream." Such demand shifts probably helped to offset the effects of the large increase in female labor supply that also occurred during this time.

[8]Alan B. Krueger, "How Computers Have Changed the Wage Structure: Evidence from Microdata, 1984–1989," *Quarterly Journal of Economics* 108, no. 1 (February 1993): 33–60; and Bruce Weinberg, "Computer Use and the Demand for Female Workers," *Industrial and Labor Relations Review* 53, no. 2 (January 2000): 290–308. The growing importance of "brains" relative to "brawn" as a factor narrowing the gender pay gap is particularly emphasized by Welch in "Growth in Women's Relative Wages and in Inequality Among Men."

[9]Blau and Kahn, "The U.S. Gender Pay Gap in the 1990s: Slowing Convergence"; see also Mulligan and Rubinstein, "The Closing Gender Gap as a Roy Model Illusion."

So far we considered the effects of changes in wage structure and rising wage inequality on the gender pay gap. Such an approach assumes that estimates of changing labor market returns are a useful indicator of the market rewards facing both men and women. Consistent with this assumption is evidence that widening wage inequality in the 1980s and 1990s was affected by the economy-wide forces discussed previously, including technological change, international trade, the decline in unionism, and the falling real value of the minimum wage.[10] Moreover, increases in wage inequality during this period were similar for men and women, suggesting that both groups were fairly similarly affected by these trends. However, it should be pointed out that under some circumstances, the gender pay gap could influence male inequality. For example, suppose the overall hierarchy of jobs is fixed and that jobs determine wages. In this case, as women succeed in increasing the gender pay ratio by moving up in the overall distribution of jobs (and wages), men who are displaced move down resulting in widening male inequality. One view argues that recent trends in the gender pay gap and male wage inequality are consistent with such a model.[11] In this view, women's gains, to some extent, come at the expense of men's losses.

The experience of blacks in the 1980s stands in sharp contrast to that of women. As we saw in Chapter 5, even though the gender pay gap narrowed considerably, there was little evidence of further reductions in the race gap during the 1980s, and only moderate signs of further wage convergence since then. Some research suggests that changes in the wage structure over the 1980s may provide at least a partial explanation for the lack of progress of blacks during that period. Blacks, on average, have lower educational attainment than whites and, as a consequence, are more adversely affected than whites by declining relative wages for less-educated workers. In addition, although blacks continued to reduce the race gap in education over the 1980s, their rate of progress was slower during that period than in previous decades. Some evidence also indicates that the decline in blue-collar jobs in manufacturing particularly negatively affected black males. Further, although the exit of black women from extremely low-paying, private household employment was an important factor in their narrowing the race gap in earlier years, this process pretty much played itself out by the 1980s as black women's representation in these jobs approached levels for whites. Despite these interesting insights, the full explanation for the unfortunate stalling of progress in narrowing the race gap in earnings since the 1980s remains elusive.[12]

---

[10]See, for example, Katz and Autor, "Changes in the Wage Structure."

[11]Fortin and Lemieux, "Are Women's Wage Gains Men's Losses?"

[12]For studies of black-white trends, see Francine D. Blau and Andrea H. Beller, "Black-White Earnings over the 1970s and 1980s, Gender Differences in Trends," *Review of Economics and Statistics* 74, no. 2 (May 1992): 276–86; John Bound and Richard B. Freeman, "What Went Wrong? The Erosion of Relative Earnings and Employment Among Young Black Men in the 1980s," *Quarterly Journal of Economics* 107, no. 1 (February 1992): 201–32; Chinhui Juhn, Kevin M. Murphy, and Brooks Pierce, "Accounting for the Slowdown in Black-White Wage Convergence," in *Workers and Their Wages,* edited by Marvin Kosters (Washington, DC: AEI Press, 1991), pp. 107–43. As noted in Chapter 5, the issue of selection bias has received considerable attention in analyzing the male trends. For studies that include the 1980s see Chinhui Juhn, "Labor Market Dropouts, Selection Bias, and Trends in Black and White Wages," *Industrial and Labor Relations Review* 54, no. 4 (July 2003): 643-62; James J. Heckman, Thomas M. Lyons, and Petra E. Todd, "Understanding Black-White Wage Differentials, 1960–1990," *American Economic Review* 90, no. 2 (May 2000): 344–49; and Amitabh Chandra, "Labor-Market Dropouts and the Racial Wage Gap: 1940–90," *American Economic Review* 90, no. 2 (May 2000): 333–38.

The data presented in Chapter 5 also indicated that the wages of Hispanic women and men fell relative to those of whites. Education gaps between Hispanics and whites are considerably larger than those between blacks and whites, so it is likely that they were especially negatively affected by the declining relative wages of less-educated workers and the decrease in blue-collar and manufacturing employment. In addition, as noted in Chapter 5, a large and growing proportion of Hispanics are recent immigrants to the United States, hence their earnings are reduced because they tend to be relatively young, may not speak English well, and are likely to face other difficulties in adjusting to their new environment. Some additional evidence shows that the economic status of immigrants deteriorated relative to the native born in recent years.[13]

Empirical Results for the 1990s

Why did convergence in female and male wages slow over the 1990s? Again we turn to recent research by Francine Blau and Lawrence Kahn.[14] They find that human capital trends cannot account for the slowdown: women improved their relative human capital by about the same amount in both the 1980s and the 1990s. In the 1980s this upgrading consisted of rising relative experience while in the 1990s it consisted of rising relative experience and (especially) increasing educational attainment of women. Nor did changes in the wage structure in the 1990s affect women more adversely than changes in the previous decade—in fact the impact of changing wage structure was actually more negative for women in the 1980s. Slowing convergence in men's and women's occupations and unionization in the 1990s was found to account for some of the slowdown, but only a small portion.

Blau and Kahn found that the major reason for the slowdown in wage convergence in the 1990s was the considerably smaller narrowing of the "unexplained" gender pay gap in the 1990s compared to the 1980s. As our earlier discussion suggests, this smaller narrowing could be due to slower improvement in women's unmeasured qualifications relative to men's in the 1990s than in the 1980s; a smaller decline in discrimination against women in the 1990s than in the 1980s; or less favorable demand shifts for women in the 1990s than in the 1980s. Each of these factors apparently plays a role in explaining the observed trends. In addition, controlling for the measured characteristics mentioned earlier, female labor force entrants were less skilled during the 1990s, perhaps as a result of the entry of many relatively low-skilled, female single-family heads. Indeed, differences between the two decades in such shifts in labor force composition were found to explain as much as 25 percent of the apparent slowdown in convergence in the unexplained gender pay gap in the 1990s.[15]

---

[13]For analyses of Hispanic and immigrant earnings, see Maury B. Gittleman and David R. Howell, "Changes in the Structure and Quality of Jobs in the United States: Effects by Race and Gender, 1973–1990," *Industrial and Labor Relations Review* 48, no. 3 (April 1995): 420–40; Gregory DeFreitas, *Inequality at Work: Hispanics in the U.S. Labor Force* (Oxford: Oxford University Press, 1991); George J. Borjas, "Assimilation and Changes in Cohort Quality Revisited: What Happened to Immigrant Earnings in the 1980s?" *Journal of Labor Economics* 13, no. 2 (April 1995): 201–45; and Barry R. Chiswick, "Speaking, Reading, and Earnings Among Low-Skilled Immigrants," *Journal of Labor Economics* 9, no. 2 (April 1995): 149–70.

[14]Blau and Kahn, "The U.S. Gender Pay Gap in the 1990s."

[15]See also, Mulligan and Rubinstein, "The Closing Gender Gap as a Roy Model Illusion," who give a larger role to selection—shifts in labor force composition due to labor force entry—in explaining the trends.

THE RISING PAYOFF TO EDUCATION

The more favorable real earnings experience of women and the rising gender pay ratio over the past 25 years point to significant gender differences in earnings trends. However, when we compare how the less educated fared relative to the more highly educated, the experiences of men and women are more similar. Among both women and men, the less educated are increasingly falling behind others, as earnings disparities by education grow. Among men, these disparities are associated with substantial declines in real wages for the less educated, while among women, real wages either declined slightly or at least grew considerably more slowly for the less educated.

These trends are seen in Tables 8-2 and 8-3. Table 8-2 gives the mean earnings of year-round, full-time workers in each educational category relative to those of high school graduates for 1974 and 2003. It is clear that the earnings of those who did not complete high school fell relative to high school graduates, while the relative earnings of college graduates increased considerably. For instance, in 2003, women and men with a college degree or more earned about twice as much as high school graduates, compared to about 50 percent more in 1974.[16] Those with some college also increased their earnings relative to high school graduates, but to a lesser extent than college graduates did. Interestingly, the ratios of each educational category's earnings relative to high school graduates are quite similar for men and women in both years, indicating that the extent of earnings differentials by education is about the same for both. Thus, the increase in earnings inequality over this period, as measured by the widening disparities across educational groups, was similar for men and women.

Table 8-3 shows the consequences of widening inequality in earnings by education for trends in real earnings over the 1974 to 2003 period. For both men and women,

TABLE 8-2	Mean Earnings of Education Groups Relative to High School Graduates, 1974 and 2003 (%)			
	1974		*2003*	
Education	*Men (%)*	*Women (%)*	*Men (%)*	*Women (%)*
High school				
1–3 years	88.9	85.3	75.9	76.6
4 years	100.0	100.0	100.0	100.0
College				
1–3 years	113.6	112.6	122.8	119.5
4 or more years	155.0	147.2	211.3	190.4

Notes: Data refer to year-round, full-time workers 18 years of age and older. Definitions of educational categories are not exactly comparable for the two years. In 2003, median income for 1–3 years of college is computed as a weighted average of the medians for "some college, no degree" and "associate degree."

Sources: 2003: PINC04 Tables of the U.S. Census Bureau, Current Population Survey, 2004 Annual Social and Economic Supplement, from ferret.bls.census.gov/macro/032004/perinc/new04_000.htm; 1974: U.S. Census Bureau, Historical Income Tables - People, Table P-35, from www.census.gov/hhes/income/histinc/p35.html.

---

[16]Of course, the costs of going to college rose as well, but even taking this cost increase into account, the figures suggest an increase in the return to a college education.

TABLE 8-3   Change in Real Mean Earnings of Men and Women by Education for Year-Round, Full-Time Workers, 1974–2003

Education	Men (%)	Women (%)
High school		
1–3 years	−27.7	−3.5
4 years	−15.3	7.5
College		
1–3 years	−8.4	14.1
4 or more years	15.5	39.0

Notes: Data refer to workers 18 years of age and older. Definitions of educational categories are not exactly comparable for the two years. In 2003, median income for 1–3 years of college is computed as a weighted average of the medians for "some college, no degree" and "associate degree."

Sources: 2003: PINC04 Tables of the U.S. Census Bureau, Current Population Survey, 2004 Annual Social and Economic Supplement, from ferret.bls.census.gov/macro/032004/perinc/new04_000.htm; 1974: U.S. Census Bureau, Historical Income Tables - People, Table P-35, from www.census.gov/hhes/income/histinc/p35.html.

more highly educated workers did considerably better in terms of real earnings changes. Among men, only college graduates experienced an increase in real earnings; for others real earnings decreased. The largest decline was for high school dropouts: Their real earnings fell by 28 percent over the period, while the real earnings of men with some college decreased by 8 percent. In contrast, male college graduates experienced an *increase* in their real earnings of 16 percent. Women fared better than their male counterparts within each educational category. However, here too the more highly educated did a great deal better: Real earnings declined by 4 percent among female dropouts but rose by 39 percent among female college graduates. Note that real wage changes for men and women overall are determined not just by the wage trends for each education group but also by changes in the relative size of each education group. In this respect, rising educational attainment helped to boost the real earnings of both men and women, although male real earnings have nonetheless continued to stagnate since the early 1970s.

These trends indicate a rising payoff to a college education for both men and women. They also mean that, among both men and women, the earnings of the less educated fell compared to others. The deteriorating earnings situation of less educated women and men tell only part of the story of the declining economic status of the less educated. To be included in these tabulations, an individual must not only be employed, but work year-round and full-time. As we saw in Chapter 4, less educated women and men are increasingly less likely to be in the labor force than the more highly educated over the past 30 years. Among women, this reflects considerably smaller increases in participation rates for those with less than four years of high school in comparison to substantial increases for those with higher levels of education. Among men, decreases in participation rates occurred among all education groups, but the declines were especially precipitous among those who did not complete high school. A final piece of the story is the rising incidence of mother-only families that we will examine in the next chapter; the increase, particularly pronounced among the less educated, places them and their families at even greater economic disadvantage.[17]

CHANGING LABOR MARKET DYNAMICS

The High-Churning U.S. Labor Market

Individuals may lose jobs involuntarily at any point in the business cycle. Layoffs occur even during major upswings, such as the period during the late 1990s through 2000, when the national unemployment rate fell to a low of 3.9 percent. Of course, when the economy weakens, job losses are more frequent. Although the corporate downsizing that contributes to such job loss may reflect decreases in demand in particular sectors, more often than in the past it represents an effort by firms to streamline their operations and increase efficiency.[18] Less-educated workers with fewer skills, who cannot take advantage of the new opportunities available, as well as older workers, who find it difficult to "retool" and who may also face age discrimination, are at a particular disadvantage when such downsizing occurs.

Job loss imposes real costs on workers, which cannot be masked by recent "layoff-speak" reminiscent of George Orwell's *1984* such as "downsizing," "separation," "being unassigned," or notification that a job "is not moving forward." Displaced workers may suffer subsequent unemployment, underemployment in full-time jobs or movement into part-time jobs, and income losses.[19] Even workers who retain their positions may be assailed by a sense of insecurity and the thought that "next time it could be me." The loss of coworkers also leads to increased workloads and greater work-related pressures for those who remain. One recent study finds that men's and women's perceptions of job insecurity are fairly similar, but perceptions do vary substantially by race; blacks, who do in fact have higher unemployment rates, are twice as likely to expect that they will lose their jobs as whites.[20] Not surprisingly, those with higher levels of schooling tend to be less concerned about job security, on average, than those who have less education.

The economic and emotional toll of job loss depends, in large part, on workers' ability to find new jobs and the wages they can earn in these jobs. For families, the economic consequences of job loss also depend on the presence of more than one wage earner. Dual-earner families, as compared with traditional families with a single (male) wage earner, are more likely to be buffered from the consequences of unemployment of one spouse, especially if the husband and wife work in different industries or at least for

---

[17]This development is particularly emphasized in Blau, "Trends in the Well-Being of American Women."

[18]Peter Cappelli, "Examining the Incidence of Downsizing and Its Effect on Establishment Performance," in *On the Job: Is Long-Term Employment a Thing of the Past?* edited by David Neumark (New York: Russell Sage Foundation, 2000), pp. 463–516; Henry S. Farber and Kevin F. Hallock, "The Changing Relationship between Job Loss Announcements and Stock Prices: 1970–1999," unpublished working paper, Princeton University and University of Illinois (February 2004); Ryan T. Helwig, "Worker Displacement in a Strong Labor Market," *Monthly Labor Review* 124, no. 6 (June 2001): 13–28; and Henry S. Farber, "Job Loss in the United States, 1981–2001," Working Paper No. 471 (Princeton University: Industrial Relations Section), May 2003.

[19]Lori G. Kletzer, "Job Displacement," *Journal of Economic Perspectives* 12, no. 1 (Winter 1998): 115–36; and Henry S. Farber, "Alternative and Part-Time Employment Arrangements as a Response to Job Loss," *Journal of Labor Economics* 17, no. 4, pt. 2 (October 1999): 142–69.

[20]Charles F. Manski and John D. Straub, "Worker Perceptions of Job Insecurity in the Mid-1990s," *Journal of Human Resources* 35, no. 3 (Summer 2000): 447–79.

different firms. Consequently, one might speculate that the risk of marital dissolution as a result of layoffs is likely to be particularly high for single-earner families. For them, layoffs not only mean financial hardship but also may cause increased stress due to the job loss of the sole breadwinner. Job loss may also destabilize marriage to the extent that it signals future labor market difficulties.[21] Nonetheless, it is valuable to consider U.S. job loss in a larger context. The U.S. economy generated a tremendous number of new jobs in the 1990s and, even since that time, the United States continues to experience substantially lower unemployment rates than many other economically advanced nations.[22]

Unemployment

As we saw in Chapter 4, the official definition of **unemployment** includes all individuals not currently working for pay but actively looking for work and persons temporarily laid off from a job to which they expect to return.[23] The overall unemployment rate includes four types of unemployment: frictional, seasonal, structural, and cyclical. **Frictional unemployment** occurs when new entrants and reentrants enter the labor force, as well as when workers are between jobs, either having quit or lost their last job. Given imperfect information, it will often take such individuals some time to find a job, even when enough appropriate job openings are available.[24] **Seasonal unemployment** occurs due to variations in employment over the course of the year, such as a lack of jobs for construction workers in the snowbelt during the winter and for ski instructors during the summer. A more serious type of unemployment is **structural unemployment**, when those looking for work do not have the right skills or are not in the right location to fill the vacancies that exist. It is likely to be more persistent because these difficulties are not easily or quickly remedied. **Cyclical unemployment**, associated with an overall deficiency in demand, is created by an excess of workers relative to available positions. Because the first three types of unemployment will exist to a greater or lesser degree even during times of no deficiency in overall demand, some amount of unemployment is present even in an economy that achieves full employment. This level of unemployment is typically called the **full-employment unemployment rate** or the **natural rate of unemployment**.

For a long time the natural rate of unemployment was estimated to be about 5.5 percent, but the low unemployment rates of the late 1990s through 2000, which were not accompanied by a surge of inflation, suggest it is now considerably lower.[25] Economists

---

[21]Kerwin Kofi Charles, and Melvin Stephens, Jr., "Job Displacement, Disability, and Divorce," *Journal of Labor Economics* 22, no. 2 (April 2004): 489–522.

[22]For international evidence, see Lawrence M. Kahn, "Labour Market Institutions and Unemployment in OECD Countries," *DICE Report* (Munich: Center for Economic Studies and the IFO Institute for Economic Research) 1, no. 4 (Winter 2003): 25–32. It is also the case that unemployment insurance, among other safety net programs, is much more generous in West European countries.

[23]For a formal definition, see U.S. Department of Labor, "How the Government Measures Unemployment," Report 864 (February 1994; last revised July 2001), at www.bls.gov.

[24]The majority of those who change jobs do not, however, experience unemployment because most workers search while holding on to the old job until they have found a new one. See J. Peter Mattila, "Job Quitting and Frictional Unemployment," *American Economic Review* 64, no.1 (March 1974): 235–39. Similarly, many labor market entrants never experience a period of unemployment; see Ronald G. Ehrenberg, "The Demographic Structure of Unemployment Rates and Labor Market Transition Probabilities," in *Research in Labor Economics,* vol. 3, edited by Ronald G. Ehrenberg (Greenwich, CT: JAI Press, Inc., 1980), p. 253.

[25]Ronald G. Ehrenberg and Robert S. Smith, *Modern Labor Economics: Theory and Public Policy,* 7th ed. (Reading, MA: Addison-Wesley, 2000), p. 595.

offer a number of explanations as to why the natural rate decreased. The workforce is older and more educated, and both these factors reduce employment transitions. Also, incarceration rates increased, particularly among the less skilled, resulting in fewer less-skilled individuals (who tend to encounter greater difficulties finding jobs) in the labor force than there would otherwise be. Furthermore, a number of changes in the labor market, including the rise of the temporary help industry and job postings on the Internet, likely reduced time spent searching for a job and facilitated better matches between workers and jobs.[26]

As noted earlier, the ranks of the unemployed include new entrants into the labor market, reentrants, job losers, and job leavers. New entrants are likely to be young people who recently left school or women entering the labor force after caring for their children full-time. Reentrants might be persons who left the labor market to get additional education, or women who did so in order to take care of their children. Job losers are workers whose jobs were terminated for whatever reason. Finally, job leavers are those who voluntarily terminate employment and immediately begin (or perhaps continue) looking for another job.

Table 8-4 shows unemployment rates by gender, age, race, and Hispanic origin for 2003. These data indicate that, among both men and women, unemployment rates are about twice as high among blacks of all ages as for whites. Possible explanations include lower levels of education and fewer skills of blacks, a lack of jobs located near communities where blacks live, regional shifts in the demand for workers that have been unfavorable to blacks, and employment discrimination.[27] Other recent research points to the employment difficulties of ex-offenders, and because incarceration rates are higher for young black men, this factor may also contribute to their greater employment difficulties.[28] Black unemployment has also been found to be especially responsive to local labor market conditions, with black men and women benefiting much more from tighter labor markets than do whites.[29] Thus, a strong and growing economy is especially important for African Americans.

Hispanics of all ages also tend to have higher unemployment rates than whites, although the difference is generally less than between blacks and whites. The unemployment

---

[26]Congressional Budget Office, "The Effect of Changes in Labor Markets on the Natural Rate of Unemployment" (April 2002), at www.cbo.gov; and Lawrence F. Katz and Alan B. Krueger in "The High-Pressure U.S. Labor Market of the 1990s," *Brookings Papers on Economic Activity,* no. 1 (1999): 1–65.

[27]See Harry Holzer, for example, "Black Employment Problems: New Evidence, Old Questions," *Journal of Policy Analysis and Management* 13, no. 4 (Fall 1994): 699–722; and Robert W. Fairlie and William A. Sundstrom, "The Emergence, Persistence, and Recent Widening of the Racial Unemployment Gap," *Industrial and Labor Relations Review* 52, no. 2 (January 1999): 252–70. Also of concern, as we saw in Chapter 4, a much higher fraction of black as compared to white men are not included in the labor force at all because they have given up on job search or are incarcerated and hence not included in workforce statistics.

[28]See Chandra, "Labor-Market Dropouts"; and Harry J. Holzer, Paul Offner, and Elaine Sorensen, "Declining Employment Among Young Black Less-Educated Men: The Role of Incarceration and Child Support," Institute for Research on Poverty Discussion Paper No. 1281-04 (May 2004). This study also suggests that greater child support enforcement caused some noncustodial fathers to drop out of formal employment altogether.

[29]Cordelia W. Reimers, "The Effect of Tighter Labor Markets on Unemployment of Hispanics and African Americans: The 1990s Experience"; and Richard B. Freeman and William M. Rodgers III, "Area Economic Conditions and the Labor-Market Outcomes of Young Men in the 1990s Expansion," in *Prosperity for All? The Economic Boom and African Americans,* edited by Robert Cherry and William M. Rodgers III (New York: Russell Sage Foundation, 2000), pp. 3–49, 50–87; and Katharine Bradbury, "How Much Do Expansions Reduce the Black-White Unemployment Gap?" *Regional Review* (Federal Reserve Bank of Boston), 10, no. 3 (Third Quarter 2000).

TABLE 8-4   Unemployment Rates by Sex, Age, Race, and Hispanic Origin, 2003[a]

	All	*White*	*Black*	*Asian*	*Hispanic*
Age 16 and over					
Men	6.3	5.6	11.6	6.2	7.2
Women	5.7	4.8	10.2	5.7	8.4
Age 25 and over					
Men	5.0	4.5	8.8	5.4	5.9
Women	4.6	4.0	7.9	5.2	7.2
Age 16–19					
Men	19.3	17.1	36.0	20.3	21.9
Women	15.6	13.3	30.3	13.8	17.7

[a]Civilian labor force
Notes: Race refers to those who selected this race group only on the 2003 CPS survey. Persons whose ethnicity is Hispanic may be of any race.
Source: U.S. Bureau of Labor Statistics, *Employment and Earnings* (January 2004), Tables 3, 4 and 24. Available at www.bls.gov/cps.

rate of Hispanic men and women shows greater responsiveness to local labor market conditions than that of whites, but less so than that of blacks.[30] Asian women and men have lower unemployment rates than the other minority groups, though their rates are still above those of whites.

Table 8-4 also shows that all groups of teens had unemployment rates that were considerably above the overall national rate of 6.3 percent. Black teens had the highest rates, with more than one-third of young black men and nearly one-third of young black women unemployed. Whether comparing Asian, black, white, or Hispanic teens, in all cases, male teens have higher rates of unemployment than their female counterparts. These figures also clearly show that young black men are at the greatest disadvantage in the labor market as compared to all other groups. In fact, even in 2000, when the overall national unemployment rate reached a recent low of 3.9 percent, their unemployment rate was still over 26 percent.[31]

Finally, as seen in Table 8-4 and in Figure 8-2, for the population as a whole, gender differences in the unemployment rate have tended to be fairly small compared to differences between whites and minorities or teens and adults.

Other Indicators of Employment Problems

Although the unemployment rate provides an important indicator of the health of the economy, it is an incomplete tool for fully assessing either economic hardship for workers or the loss of output for the economy. For one thing, unemployment rates fail to provide information about underemployed workers. **Underemployment** occurs when workers have to take jobs for which they are clearly overqualified, or when they work

---

[30]Reimers, "The Effect of Tighter Labor Markets"; however, Reimers finds that although blacks benefit more from labor market tightness than whites, even controlling for industry, occupation, education, and age, Hispanic unemployment, especially of men, tends to be less sensitive to local unemployment rates than that of whites once these controls are added.
[31]U.S. Bureau of Labor Statistics, *Employment and Earnings* (January 2001), table 3.

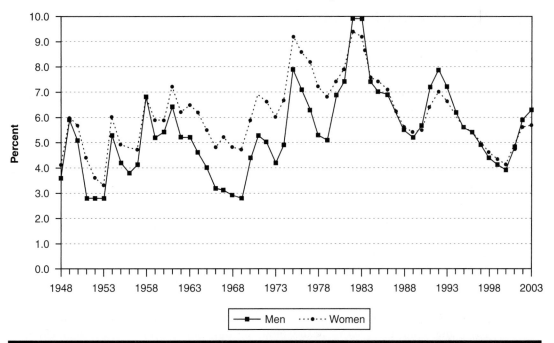

FIGURE 8-2 Unemployment Rates of Men and Women, 1948–2003 (16 years and older)

fewer hours than they would prefer. Examples of the former would be an MBA taking a job as a sales clerk or a skilled automobile mechanic harvesting fruit. Examples of the latter are persons who would prefer to work full-time but can only find part-time work. They are classified as **part-time for economic reasons** or sometimes called **involuntary part-time workers**.[32] These problems tend to arise more often in a slack labor market, when the recorded unemployment rate is also high.

Second, measured unemployment rates fail to include individuals who would like a job, but did not look for work during the prior four weeks, because they believe their search would be futile. Thus, they are not classified as currently looking for work and are not included among the unemployed nor in the labor force. Individuals who fit this description but searched some time in the last year (though not in the last four weeks) are referred to by the Bureau of Labor Statistics as **marginally attached workers**. As this term suggests, these individuals are the most likely to resume search, and hence reenter the labor market, when the economy picks up. The Bureau of Labor Statistics defines **discouraged workers** as the subset of marginally attached workers who have specifically stated that their reason for being out of the labor force is that they do not think labor market opportunities are available for them given their skills, or express concerns about labor market discrimination. The recent brief recession, which technically lasted only from March 2001 to November of the same year, provides an example

---

[32]Specifically, this measure only counts those who worked part-time in the survey week *and* who usually work part-time for economic reasons, as discussed in Leslie S. Stratton, "Reexamining Involuntary Part-Time Employment," *Journal of Economic and Social Measurement* 20 (1994): 95–115.

of these concepts. Following this recession, relatively few new jobs were created for the next couple of years, a period characterized as a "jobless recovery." Nonetheless, the overall unemployment rate only rose to 6.3 percent as of June 2003. One explanation for why unemployment rates did not rise further is that some individuals gave up searching, joining the ranks of the marginally attached or discouraged workers, and thus were no longer counted as part of the labor force.[33] Because the unemployment rate is so sensitive to the definition of who is counted in the labor force, many economists also rely on broader measures of joblessness that include marginally attached or discouraged workers, in addition to those officially classified as unemployed.

Trends in the Gender Difference in Unemployment

As seen in Figure 8-2, the gender difference in the overall unemployment rate for men and women has fluctuated over time. Although women traditionally had higher unemployment rates than men, in recent years, this differential virtually disappeared. The small and changing gender gap in unemployment rates shown in the figure is the net result of various factors working in opposing directions. It appears that, over time, the balance of these forces shifted.

The first major factor affecting unemployment is *labor force attachment.* On average, women are less firmly attached both to the labor force as a whole and to particular jobs than men, although, as discussed in Chapter 4, the difference continues to decline. The higher labor force turnover of women in comparison to men results in an ambiguous effect on their relative unemployment rates.

On the one hand, the larger proportion of entrants or reentrants among women in the labor force tends to increase female relative to male unemployment rates because many will experience a period of frictional unemployment as they search for jobs. Hence it is not surprising that in 2003, for example, 36 percent of unemployed women were entrants or reentrants, as compared to only 22 percent of unemployed men.[34] On the other hand, unemployed women are considerably more likely than unemployed men to exit the labor force. This tendency results in their being counted as "out of the labor force" rather than unemployed. This factor is particularly important during recessions and helps to explain why the female rate of measured unemployment tends to rise less than the male unemployment rate during economic downturns. In fact, during recent recessions, the male unemployment rate actually exceeded the female unemployment rate.

The second major factor that contributes to differences in male and female unemployment rates is that men and women tend to be employed in different occupations and industries. Like gender differences in labor force attachment, gender differences in *employment by occupation and industry* have an ambiguous effect on the gender gap in unemployment rates. On the one hand, men are more heavily represented in blue-collar jobs and in durable manufacturing, sectors with above-average layoff and unemployment rates. Women are more likely to be employed in white-collar jobs, which experience lower layoff and unemployment rates. On the

---

[33]See, for instance, David Leonhardt, "The Nation: Help Wanted; Out of a Job and No Longer Looking," *New York Times* (September 29, 2002), p. 1; and Robert Gavin, "U.S. Employers Continue to Cut Jobs; Unemployment Rate Falls as More Drop Job Search," *The Boston Globe* (August 2, 2003): C1.

[34]The 2003 figures on the reasons for unemployment cited here and later are from U.S. Department of Labor, *Employment and Earnings* (January 2004), p. 238.

other hand, women are also disproportionately represented in service occupations, which have above-average unemployment rates. On balance, occupational distribution appears to lower the female unemployment rate relative to the male rate as suggested by the higher proportion of men than women who tend to be unemployed because they lost their last job. For example, in 2003, 69 percent of unemployed men compared to 53 percent of unemployed women were job losers.[35] The fact that blue-collar jobs and durable-goods manufacturing industries, with their larger proportion of male workers, are subject to greater cyclical variations in employment also helps to explain why the difference in male and female unemployment rates changes over the business cycle. Men's unemployment rate tends to rise more in downturns than women's, but also declines more during upswings.

Prior to the 1980s, the net result of these opposing forces was that women's unemployment rates were higher than men's. As an added factor, during this earlier period, women faced considerable competition for entry jobs from the growing number of young workers, both male and female, who were also seeking employment, as the large baby boom cohort entered the job market.

Beginning in the 1980s, women's unemployment rates tended to be about the same as men's, or, during recessions, even lower. One reason may be the increase in women's labor force attachment, which reduced their labor force turnover relative to men's. In addition, demand shifts benefited women relative to men, as service industries, with a traditionally high concentration of women, expanded relative to manufacturing industries, which disproportionately employ men. In addition, as the baby bust cohort entered the job market, a declining number of young people were competing with women for entry-level jobs.

Future Labor Market Prospects

Looking toward the future, it is likely that workers of both sexes will continue to face the prospect of job loss as the economy continues to adapt to changing technology, globalization, and other developments. Workers with less education, who have fewer transferable skills, and older workers will likely have the greatest difficulties finding reemployment. In light of these concerns, some have proposed programs to enhance workers' education and job skills to keep pace with advances in technology and computerization.[36] Another concern for workers is that access to affordable health insurance is typically tied to full-time employment, and so job loss makes them vulnerable to a loss of health insurance. The federal government enacted a law that partly addresses this concern. Since 1996, workers who suffer a job loss or change jobs and previously had health insurance through their employer can remain covered for some period of time. This law helps workers, especially those with preexisting conditions, in coping with job loss, as well as facilitating voluntary job moves. It does not, however, ensure that coverage will be affordable or provide assistance for those workers not currently insured.

---

[35]See also Francine D. Blau and Lawrence M. Kahn, "Causes and Consequences of Layoffs," *Economic Inquiry* 19, no. 2 (April 1981): 270–96.

[36]Robert B. Reich, "Rescuing Castoff Workers," *St. Louis Post-Dispatch,* March 8, 1996, p. 7B; see also, Christopher J. O'Leary, Robert A. Straights, and Stephen A. Wandner, eds., *Job Training Policy in the United States* (Kalamazoo, MI: Upjohn Institute for Employment Research, 2004).

THE RISE OF THE NONSTANDARD WORKFORCE

Evidence indicates that the proportion of people in the labor force who do not have "regular" full-time jobs increased over time, though in recent years the figure appears to be holding fairly steady, at about 25 percent of the workforce when part-time workers, as well as workers in various alternative employment arrangements, are included.[37] This section defines the nonstandard workforce, examines recent data, and then looks at the consequences of the rise in nonstandard work for American workers and their families.

Definition and Characteristics of the Nonstandard Workforce

Nonstandard workers are those who do not hold "regular" full-time jobs. They include workers defined by the Bureau of Labor Statistics (BLS) as having "alternative" or nontraditional employment arrangements; that is, "individuals whose employment is arranged through an employment intermediary such as a temporary help firm, or individuals whose place, time, and quantity of work are potentially unpredictable."[38] Four major categories of workers in alternative arrangements are identified by the BLS: *temporary help agency workers ("temps"), on-call workers, contract workers,* and *independent contractors.* Many of these workers, particularly among those employed as temps and on-call workers, would be classified as holding "contingent" jobs, that is, jobs in which an individual "does not have an explicit or implicit contract for long-term employment."[39] Our definition of the nonstandard workforce also includes **part-time workers**, those who work fewer than 35 hours per week.

Temporary help agency workers are employed by agencies and sent out to other businesses as they are needed. **On-call workers** or limited duration hires are only employed as needed, generally for a short time; they include, for instance, substitute teachers and construction workers supplied by a union hiring hall. **Contract workers** are employed by a firm that contracts out employees or services to other companies; they supply such services as cleaning, security, landscaping, or computer programming.[40] **Independent contractors** or freelance workers are individuals who obtain customers on

---

[37]See, for instance, Marianne A. Ferber and Jane Waldfogel, "The 'Contingent' Labor Force," in *The Elgar Companion to Feminist Economics*, edited by Janice Peterson and Margaret Lewis, (Cheltenham, UK: Edward Elgar, 1999); Steven Hipple, "Contingent Work in the Late 1990s," *Monthly Labor Review* 124, no. 3 (March 2001): 3–27; and the contributions in Francoise Carré, Marianne A. Ferber, Lonnie Golden, and Steve Herzenberg, eds., *Nonstandard Work Arrangements and the Changing Labor Market: Dimensions, Causes, and Institutional Responses,* Industrial Relations Research Association Volume (2000). Other evidence also points to a decline in the duration of jobs in the 1990s, though it is not yet clear whether this trend will continue into the 2000s. See contributions in David Neumark, ed., *On the Job: Is Long-Term Employment a Thing of the Past?* (New York: Russell Sage Foundation, 2000).

[38]Anne E. Polivka, "Contingent and Alternative Work Arrangements, Defined," *Monthly Labor Review* 119, no. 10 (October 1996): 3–9.

[39]Polivka, "Contingent and Alternative Work Arrangements, Defined," p. 4. A recent government report estimated that 55 percent of temps, 24 percent of on-call workers, and 17 percent of contract workers were contingent, which was true of only 4 percent of independent contractors. In contrast, just under 3 percent of workers in traditional employment arrangements were classified as contingent. See U.S. Department of Labor, Bureau of Labor Statistics, "Contingent and Alternative Employment Arrangements: February 2001," *News,* USDL 01-153, May 24, 2001.

[40]To be included under alternative employment arrangements, contract workers had to report that they usually had only one customer and worked at the customer's worksite. These requirements distinguish contract workers from those employed by companies that obtain contracts to carry out work assignments, such as advertising agencies, equipment manufacturers, lawyers, or employees of economic "think tanks." See Polivka, "Contingent and Alternative Work Arrangements, Defined," p. 8.

their own to whom they provide a product or service. Management consultants, free-lance writers, and textbook editors are all examples of occupations in which some individuals work on a freelance basis. These workers are most often self-employed. Individuals who are self-employed business operators, however, such as shop owners or restaurateurs, are not included among independent contractors.[41]

The status of part-time workers is less clear because many are employed by a single employer for an extended period of time, and so, perhaps from this perspective, should not be included. They are, however, included in our estimates of the nonstandard workforce on the basis that they share a number of the same problems as others in this category, such as often having limited training and promotion opportunities and receiving few if any benefits.

Table 8-5 gives a breakdown of the employment arrangements included in our definition of nonstandard work.[42] In all, more than 9 percent of employed workers were in alternative employment arrangements as temps, on-call workers, independent contractors, and contract workers.[43] Including part-timers in otherwise traditional employment arrangements brings the total to 25 percent. Part-time workers are a longtime feature of the labor market. In the 1950s, they comprised 12 percent of employed workers.

TABLE 8-5   Nonstandard Workers in the Labor Force, 2001

		Percent Female	*Percent of All Employed*
I.	Alternative Employment Arrangements		
	On-call workers	47.0	1.6
	Temporary help agency workers	58.9	0.9
	Independent contractors	35.5	6.4
	Workers provided by contract firm	29.5	0.5
	Subtotal	39.3	9.4
II.	Part-Time Workers (not included above)	67.5[a]	15.3
III.	Total Nonstandard Workers (sum of I and II)	57.6[a]	24.8

[a]Percentage female for "Part-Time Workers (not included above)" is based on all part-time workers.

Sources: U.S. Department of Labor, Bureau of Labor Statistics, "Contingent and Alternative Employment Arrangements, February 2001," *News*, USDL 01-153 (May 2001); and U.S. Department of Labor, Bureau of Labor Statistics, *Employment and Earnings* (January 2002).

---

[41]See section titled "concepts and definitions" in Bureau of Labor Statistics, "Contingent and Alternative Employment Arrangements: February 2001."

[42]In academia, a large and growing number of faculty are employed in nontenure track jobs, typically as instructors or lecturers. These individuals are not included in the table but are in fact nonstandard workers. For instance, from academic year 1980–1981 to 1999–2000, the percentage of full-time faculty with tenure fell from nearly 65 to 62.4 percent. Moreover, in 1999–2000 only 51 percent of women in academe held full-time tenured or tenure-track positions, as compared to 69 percent of men. See National Center for Education Statistics, *Digest for Education Statistics*, 2002, Table 242, at nces.ed.gov.

[43]Focusing on contingent workers, that is, workers without an implicit or explicit contract for long-term employment, the Bureau of Labor Statistics estimates that 1.7 to 4.0 percent of workers are contingent; see U.S. Department of Labor, Bureau of Labor Statistics, "Contingent and Alternative Employment Arrangements: February 2001." Additional workers who might be considered to have alternative employment arrangements are **direct-hire temporaries** who were hired into a temporary job directly by their employer rather than through a temporary agency. The BLS does not provide information on this category.

That number rose to 18 percent by 2003. Some individuals who work part time do so involuntarily, because they cannot find full-time jobs, while others voluntarily choose this schedule. As might be expected, the proportion of involuntary part-time workers rises considerably in recessions and falls in more prosperous times.[44] Regardless of the business cycle, the proportion of voluntary part-time workers always remains quite large, especially among women, often homemakers; young people, often students; and older people, often retired or in transition to retirement.

As shown in Table 8-5, women are overrepresented among nonstandard workers; it is estimated that 58 percent of such workers were women, as compared to 46 percent of all employed workers. However, the representation of women varies considerably by employment arrangement. Women comprise the vast majority of part-time workers, and are overrepresented among temps and on-call workers. They are, however, underrepresented among independent contractors and contract workers. In terms of labor market outcomes, contract workers and independent contractors tend to earn more than similar workers in traditional positions, while on-call and temporary workers earn less. Similarly, although workers in all alternative arrangements were less likely than those in traditional ones to be covered by health insurance and pensions, contract workers and independent contractors were most likely to be covered while on-call and temporary workers were least likely to be covered. Part-time workers also tend to receive fewer benefits.[45] Because women are overrepresented among part-timers, on-call workers, and temps, as a group, they are likely to have lower average earnings and fewer benefits.

Explanations Behind the Rise of Nonstandard Workers

There is little agreement about the extent to which the growth in nonstandard jobs is caused by an increase in demand on the part of employers or an increase in the supply of workers who prefer such arrangements.

On the demand side, recent studies point to a variety of reasons why firms make use of nonstandard workers. Small and medium-size firms, for instance, especially benefit from the use of contracted services in specialized areas such as computer support, because it may not be cost-effective for them to hire a full computer support staff if skills, such as programming, are needed only occasionally. Also, if production is characterized by peak and off-peak periods or demand for the product is variable, firms may find it cost effective to hire temporary help workers during peak periods in order to dispense

---

[44]Chris Tilly, "Reasons for the Continuing Growth of Part-Time Employment," *Monthly Labor Review* 114, no. 3 (March 1991): 10–18; and U.S. Department of Labor, *Employment and Earnings.*

[45]Gideon Kunda, Stephen R. Barley, and James Evans, "Why Do Contractors Contract? The Experience of Highly Skilled Technical Professionals in a Contingent Labor Market" *Industrial and Labor Relations Review* 55, no. 2 (January 2002): 234–61; and Steven Hipple and Jay Stewart, "Earnings and Benefits of Workers in Alternative Arrangements," *Monthly Labor Review* 119, no. 10 (October 1996): 46–54. For instance, 58 percent of workers with traditional employment arrangements and nearly the same percentage of contract workers had employer-provided health insurance, but the same was true of only 21 percent of on-call workers and 9 percent of temps. (No information was available for independent contractors.) See U.S. Department of Labor, Bureau of Labor Statistics, "Contingent and Alternative Employment Arrangements." It has also been pointed out there are both "good" and "bad" part-time jobs; see Rebecca M. Blank, "Are Part-Time Jobs Bad Jobs?" in *A Future of Lousy Jobs?* edited by Gary Burtless (Washington, DC: Brookings Institution, 1990), pp. 123–55; and Chris Tilly, "Two Faces of Part-Time Work: Good and Bad Part-Time Jobs," in *Working Part-Time: Risks and Opportunities,* edited by Barbara D. Warme, Katherina L.P. Lundy, and Larry A. Lundy (New York: Praeger, 1992).

with the need to carry surplus workers in slow times or avoid the costs of repeated hiring and firing of workers. In addition, the use of nonstandard workers provides a way to screen future employees. Losses of regular jobs also occur when businesses abolish them or shift them to nonstandard positions in an attempt to cut costs. Indeed, after downsizing, some firms may subsequently hire back former workers on a contingent basis. Further, some high-wage companies contract out for services rather than use their regular workforce because they want to pay lower wages or reduced benefits, but do not want to create inequities within the ranks of their own workers.[46]

From the supply-side perspective, various types of nonstandard work undoubtedly attract men and women, whether they are students, young people exploring career options, adults reentering the labor market, homemakers in need of flexibility because of family responsibilities, or older people in transition to retirement. Also, as noted, some nonstandard jobs can be attractive and, on occasion, pay higher wages to compensate for the uncertainty and lower benefits. In fact, more than four-fifths of independent contractors and just under one-half of on-call and temporary workers stated in a 2001 survey that they preferred nonstandard work arrangements.[47]

Although the reasons just offered explain why firms and workers might choose to make use of nonstandard arrangements, they do not explain the reasons for increases in such employment. Among the possible explanations may be that job growth was greater in industries where nonstandard work arrangements are more common, although, for temporary help, practically all of the growth in such jobs between 1977 and 1997 was due to the fact that more firms employed these types of workers.[48] Another factor may be that the cost of benefits, health insurance especially, rose so substantially and increased the incentive for firms to hire nonstandard workers in order to avoid these expenses. In addition, a growing number of states now limit the right of employers to terminate employment "at will," which makes hiring permanent workers riskier and thus increases the advantage to employers who use nonstandard employment arrangements.[49] Finally, the number of small firms is growing, and these firms are most likely to benefit from the purchase of specialized skills from outside sources.

Consequences for Workers and Their Families

Nonstandard work is likely to result in a variety of consequences for workers and their families. Most obviously, such workers will tend to experience less job security because the average duration of their jobs is relatively short as compared with regular full-time

---

[46]Katherine G. Abraham and Susan K. Taylor, "Firms' Use of Outside Contractors: Theory and Evidence," *Journal of Labor Economics* 14, no. 3 (July 1996): 394–424; Katherine G. Abraham, "Restructuring the Employment Relationship: The Growth of Market-Mediated Work Arrangements," in *New Developments in the Labor Market,* edited by Katherine G. Abraham and Robert B. McKersie (Cambridge, MA: MIT Press, 1990), pp. 85–118; Dale Belman and Lonnie Golden, "Contingent and Nonstandard Work Arrangements in the United States: Dispersion and Contrasts by Industry, Occupation and Job Type," in *Nonstandard Work Arrangements,* edited by Carré et al. pp. 167–212; and Susan N. Houseman, "Why Employers Use Flexible Staffing Arrangements: Evidence from an Establishment Survey," *Industrial and Labor Relations Review* 55, no. 1 (October 2001): 149–70.

[47]See U.S. Department of Labor, Bureau of Labor Statistics, "Contingent and Alternative Employment Arrangements: February 2001," Table 11.

[48]Marcello Estavao and Saul Lach, "The Evolution of the Demand for Temporary Help Supply Employment in the United States," in Carré et al., eds., *Nonstandard Work Arrangements,* pp. 123–44.

[49]David H. Autor, "Outsourcing at Will: The Contribution of Unjust Dismissal Doctrine to the Growth of Employment Outsourcing," *Journal of Labor Economics* 21, no. 1 (January 2003): 1–42.

jobs.[50] Part-time workers may be more attached to their employers than others in nonstandard jobs, but even they have shorter tenure on average than those who work full-time, are more likely to be assigned to routine jobs, and often receive less training as well as fewer promotions. In addition, nonstandard workers generally lack the protection provided by labor unions, in part because they are especially difficult to organize and because unions for a long time opposed part-time employment. Perhaps most importantly, although it is not clear whether nonstandard workers earn lower wages than regular workers with *comparable* qualifications, they usually receive substantially fewer benefits, including sick pay, holidays, health insurance, and unemployment coverage; nor do most of them accumulate pension rights, and they generally accumulate fewer Social Security benefits.

Because some workers desire these employment arrangements and others may be unsuccessful in obtaining regular jobs, it would be counterproductive to advocate restrictions on such jobs. However, as such arrangements continue to expand, policy makers must consider how important benefits such as health care and pensions may be provided to the growing numbers of workers who do not receive them from their employers.

THE GROWTH IN WOMEN'S SELF-EMPLOYMENT

In recent years, notable changes occurred in self-employment, especially for women. As shown in Table 8-6, women's self-employment rate (the percentage of women workers who are self-employed) increased from 5.1 to 6.8 percent between 1979 and 2003. Most of this increase happened during the 1980s, though the most recent figures for 2003 suggest that women's self-employment rate may again be on the rise after declining a bit in the late 1990s. Men's self-employment rate is considerably higher than women's, at 12.4 percent in 2003, but because it increased only slightly since the late 1970s, the "self-employment" gender gap continues to narrow.[51] Patterns similar to those identified in Table 8-6—men's higher rates of self-employment along with larger increases in women's rate of self-employment—also hold for an extensive set of race and ethnic groups. However, self-employment rates for women (and men) vary considerably by group; for instance, the rate for Korean women was 9 times higher than the rate for African American women. More generally, rates of self-employment among

---

[50]Susan N. Houseman and Anne E. Polivka, "The Implications of Flexible Staffing Arrangements for Job Security," in *On the Job: Is Long-Term Employment a Thing of the Past?* ed. David Neumark (New York: Russell Sage Foundation, 2000), pp. 427–62.

[51]Self-employment is defined here to include both those individuals who identify themselves as mainly self-employed in their own unincorporated businesses, typically sole proprietorships with no employees, as well as those running their own, typically larger, incorporated businesses. The figures reported here were calculated from Current Population Survey data by Robert W. Fairlie; see econ.ucsc.edu/~fairlie. In contrast, the U.S. Bureau of Labor Statistics includes only individuals in an unincorporated business as self-employed and counts those running an incorporated business as wage and salary workers. The BLS definition indicates a decline in both men's and women's self-employment rates from the mid 1990s through 2002; see U.S. Bureau of Labor Statistics, *Women in the Labor Force: A Databook,* Report 973 (Feb. 2004), table 32. See also, Theresa J. Devine, "Characteristics of Self-Employed Women in the United States," *Monthly Labor Review* 117, no. 3 (March 1994): 20–34; and Marilyn E. Manser and Garnett Picot, "The Role of Self-Employment in U.S. and Canadian Job Growth," *Monthly Labor Review* 122, no. 4 (April 1999):10–25.

TABLE 8-6	Self-Employment Rates of Women and Men in the Nonagricultural Sector for Selected Years, 1979–2003		

| | *Self-Employment Rate (%)* | | |
Year	*Total*	*Women*	*Men*
1979	9.3	5.1	12.1
1985	10.2	6.4	13.0
1990	10.3	6.9	13.1
1995	10.1	7.1	12.7
2000	9.4	6.5	11.9
2003	9.8	6.8	12.4

Notes: Includes individuals 16 years of age and older who work 15+ hours per week. Figures were calculated by Robert W. Fairlie of University of California, Santa Cruz, using data from the Current Population Survey. The self-employed include workers in both unincorporated and incorporated businesses. Due to a change in the underlying survey design, the series is not perfectly comparable before and after 1994.

Source: Data are electronically available at Robert W. Fairlie's home page, econ.ucsc.edu/~fairlie/ (accessed September 1, 2004).

African Americans, both men and women, remain among the lowest of any group, in part due to fewer assets and less access to credit.[52]

A number of factors likely contribute to the growth in women's self-employment. Perhaps a reasonable starting place is to inquire what motivates people to enter self-employment in the first place. The ability to set one's own hours, at least to some extent, is likely to be attractive, especially to women seeking to combine family and work responsibilities. In addition, the presence of a spouse already covered by health insurance would also make the choice of self-employment more attractive.[53] Further, an increase in the labor market return to self-employment, all else equal, should increase entry into self-employment. Notably, one study found that the increase in women's self-employment earnings largely contributed to the substantial rise in women's self-employment rate during the 1980s,[54] suggesting that women's move into self-employment represents a desirable expansion in their opportunities.

---

[52]Robert W. Fairlie and Bruce D. Meyer, "Ethnic and Racial Self-Employment Differences and Possible Explanations," *Journal of Human Resources* 31, no. 4 (Fall 1996): 757–93; Robert W. Fairlie, "The Absence of the African-American Owned Business: An Analysis of the Dynamics of Self-Employment," *Journal of Labor Economics* 17, no. 1 (January 1999): 80–108; David G. Blanchflower, Phillip B. Levine, and David J. Zimmerman, "Discrimination in the Small-Business Credit Market," *The Review of Economics and Statistics* 85, no. 4 (Nov. 2003): 930–43; and Timothy Bates, *Race, Self-Employment and Upward Mobility* (Baltimore, MD: Johns Hopkins Press, 1997), pp. 261–68.

[53]Karen V. Lombard finds evidence for each of these explanations for married women's self-employment decision; see "Female Self-Employment and the Demand for Flexible, Nonstandard Work Schedules," *Economic Inquiry* 39, no. 2 (April 2001): 214–37. For evidence on the attractiveness to women of the greater flexibility offered by self-employment, see Greg Hundley, "Male/Female Earnings Differences in Self-Employment: The Effects of Marriage, Children, and the Household Division of Labor," *Industrial and Labor Relations Review* 54, no. 1 (October 2000): 95–114. Regarding the role of health insurance coverage, see Allison J. Wellington, "Health Insurance Coverage and Entrepreneurship," *Contemporary Economic Policy* 19, no. 4 (October 2001): 465–78.

[54]Lombard, "Female Self-Employment." Consistent with this, Devine, "Characteristics of Self-Employed Women in the United States," reports that earnings of female self-employed workers rose relative to those of wage and salary workers between 1975 and 1990.

Nonetheless, some women (like some men) may end up in self-employment as a last resort, when they are displaced from their jobs and encounter difficulty finding wage and salary employment.[55] In addition, some of the growth in self-employment likely reflects the increase in independent contractors, discussed in the previous section, who comprise one component of the nonstandard workforce.[56] Also, some women may seek to enter self-employment to escape from a glass ceiling that limits their advancement in the wage and salary sector.[57] For poor women, self-employment may be a route out of poverty. In fact, some financial and technical assistance is available through Microenterprise Assistance Programs, funded by the federal government, nonprofit, and private organizations. However, the success of these programs in raising incomes remains mixed, as discussed further in Chapter 10.[58]

Research suggests that female self-employed workers receive lower earnings than their wage and salary counterparts, even those with the same qualifications, and recent evidence suggests that it may be true for self-employed men as well.[59] In addition, some evidence indicates that self-employed women who subsequently move into wage and salary positions experience lower wage growth than women who continuously held wage and salary positions.[60] One possible explanation is that self-employment causes them to lose out on valuable firm- and industry-specific human capital, though it does not explain why men do not bear the same self-employment penalty. All told, the available evidence suggests that women and possibly men as well may forgo some income in exchange for greater freedom in determining their own hours and working conditions. Hence the lower earnings may be considered to be a compensating differential. In fact, this differential is likely to be even larger when total compensation, including benefits, are considered because self-employed workers are less likely than wage and salary workers to have health care coverage in their own right, and are likely to have lower retirement benefits, if any, as well.[61]

---

[55]Richard E. Mueller, "The Transition from Paid to Self-Employment in Canada: The Importance of Push Factors," *Applied Economics* 34, no. 6 (March 2002):791–801.

[56]In many cases, the ranks of independent contractors and the self-employed overlap. The Bureau of Labor Statistics estimates that one-half of all self-employed workers are independent contractors. (They also find that 88 percent of independent contractors are self-employed). See "Concepts and Definitions" in Bureau of Labor Statistics, "Contingent and Alternative Employment Arrangements: February 2001."

[57]See, for example, Dorothy P. Moore and E. Holly Buttner, *Women Entrepreneurs Moving Beyond the Glass Ceiling* (Thousand Oaks, CA: Sage Publications, 1997). On the other hand, Theresa J. Devine provides evidence suggesting that a glass ceiling for women wage and salary workers does not explain the rise in female self-employment in "Changes in Wage-and-Salary Returns to Skill and the Recent Rise in Female Self-Employment," *American Economic Review* 84, no. 2 (May 1994): 108–13.

[58]See, for instance, Mark Schreiner, "Self-Employment, Microenterprise, and the Poorest Americans," *Social Service Review* 73, no. 4 (December 1999): 496–523.

[59]Ferber and Waldfogel, "The Long-Term Consequences of Nontraditional Employment," find that self-employed women earn less than their wage and salary counterparts but the reverse is true for men. Other studies also found that self-employed men have higher earnings, with an important recent exception. Using a detailed set of controls as well as accounting for selection into self-employment, a study by Barton H. Hamilton finds evidence of lower earnings for self-employed men; see "Does Entrepreneurship Pay? An Empirical Analysis of the Returns to Self-Employment," *Journal of Political Economy* 108, no. 3 (June 2000): 604–31.

[60]Donald R. Williams, "Consequences of Self-Employment for Women and Men in the United States," *Labour Economics* 7, no. 5 (September 2000): 665–87.

[61]Devine, "Characteristics of Self-Employed Women"; Ferber and Waldfogel, "The Long-Term Consequences of Nontraditional Employment"; and Wellington, "Health Insurance Coverage and Entrepreneurship."

THE CHANGING FACE OF LABOR UNIONS

Over the past 30 years, union membership has undergone a major transition; many fewer workers are union members than in the past and women comprise a growing proportion of union membership. This section discusses these trends, their impact, and prospects for the future.

Trends in Labor Union Membership

Overall union membership, which reached a high of more than one-quarter of the U.S. labor force in the mid-1950s (a figure far lower than in most other economically advanced countries), has declined steadily, especially since the 1970s. As may be seen in Table 8-7, by 2003 only 14.3 percent of workers were in unions. One reason for this overall decline was the shift in industrial structure away from more heavily unionized sectors such as manufacturing. Because these sectors were largely the bastions of men, men's overall unionization rate fell most dramatically, from just over 32 percent in 1956 to 15.6 percent in 2003. Women's overall rate, historically much lower, declined far more modestly, from just 15.7 percent in 1956 to 12.9 percent in 2003. In fact, unionization rates stayed constant or even increased in some sectors in which women are heavily

TABLE 8-7   Representation of Women in Labor Organizations for Selected Years, 1956–2003

Year	Women's Share of — All Employed Workers	Women's Share of — Membership in Labor Organizations	Union Membership as a Percent of Employed Workers — Men	Union Membership as a Percent of Employed Workers — Women	Union Membership as a Percent of Employed Workers — Total
Unions only:					
1956	32.0	18.5	32.2	15.7	27.0
1966	35.6	19.3	30.7	13.1	24.4
Unions and associations:					
1970	37.7	23.9	32.9	16.9	26.8
1980	42.4	30.1	25.1	14.7	20.7
1990	47.2	36.9	19.3	12.6	16.1
2000	48.0	42.3	16.5	13.1	14.9
2003					
All	48.3	43.6	15.6	12.9	14.3
Whites	47.5	42.1	15.2	12.2	13.8
Blacks	54.8	50.8	19.8	16.9	18.2
Asians	47.0	47.5	12.8	13.1	12.9
Hispanics	40.5	39.4	12.1	11.6	11.9

Notes: Race refers to those who selected this race group only on the 2003 CPS survey. Persons whose ethnicity is Hispanic may be of any race.

Sources: U.S. Department of Labor, Bureau of Labor Statistics, "Earnings and Other Characteristics of Organized Workers," Bulletin 2105 (May 1980), Table 2, p. 2; Linda H. LeGrande, "Women in Labor Organizations: Their Ranks Are Increasing," *Monthly Labor Review* 101, no. 8 (August 1978), Table 1, p. 9; U.S. Department of Labor, *Employment and Training Report of the President* (1981), Table A-16, pp. 144–46; U.S Department of Labor, Bureau of Labor Statistics, *Employment and Earnings* (January issues, 1991 and 2001); and U.S. Department of Labor, Bureau of Labor Statistics, "Union Members in 2003," USDL 04-53 (January 2004).

represented, such as the public sector, and among white-collar and service workers, including hotel, food service, and health care workers.[62] One consequence of these recent developments is that the gender difference in unionization rates narrowed considerably. Another consequence is that women's share of union membership is rapidly approaching their share of the labor force as a whole. As of 2003 they comprised 44 percent of all union members, up from less than 20 percent in the mid-1950s.

Benefits of Union Membership for Workers and the Impact of Deunionization

Unions confer a range of benefits on their members, with the most-cited benefit being a wage advantage, though its size tends to vary by occupation and industry. Overall, the union relative wage advantage remained fairly constant from the mid-1950s to at least the mid-1990s, at about 15 percent, but then declined somewhat in more recent years.[63] Past research generally found that the union wage gain for women and men was about the same, with some researchers finding that women received a relatively higher premium, though a recent study suggests that men may now enjoy a relative advantage.[64] In evaluating the economic gains of unionization to workers, it should also be noted that the gains typically increase with labor force attachment, because unions tend to provide generous benefits to workers with more seniority.[65] As women's labor force attachment continues to grow, the benefits to women of union membership may be expected to increase as well.

Women's and men's participation rates in unions and changes in these rates are watched closely, in part, because they directly affect the size of the male-female pay gap. A higher unionization rate for men than for women contributes to the male-female pay gap because men then benefit from the union wage premium to a greater extent than women. And, in the past, the gender gap in unionization was quite substantial. In more

---

[62]See Richard B. Freeman and Jonathan S. Leonard, "Union Maids: Unions and the Female Work Force," in *Gender in the Workplace,* edited by Clair Brown and Joseph A. Pechman (Washington, DC: The Brookings Institution, 1987), pp. 189–216; and Kate Bronfenbrenner, "Organizing Women: The Nature and Process of Union Organizing Efforts among U.S. Women Since the Mid-1990s," unpublished working paper, Cornell University (2003). Regarding the overall decline of unions, see Henry S. Farber and Bruce Western, "Accounting for the Decline of Unions in the Private Sector, 1973–1998," *Journal of Labor Research* 22, no. 3 (Summer 2001): 459–85.

[63]David G. Blanchflower and Alex Bryson, "Changes Over Time in Union Relative Wage Effects in the U.K. and the U.S. Revisited," in *International Handbook of Trade Unions*, edited by John T. Addison and Claus Schnabel (Cheltenham, England: Edward Elgar, 2003). One difficulty in precisely identifying the union wage premium is that union status is not exogenously determined, but rather, firms that become organized are likely to exhibit characteristics that increase this likelihood. For instance, if high-wage firms are more likely to be organized, a higher wage might be observed, but not because of the union's presence. In a recent attempt to disentangle these factors, John DiNardo and David S. Lee compared wages in newly organized firms and firms in which the effort lost by just one vote and thus had virtually the same likelihood of being successfully organized. Contrary to the vast empirical literature, they find no difference in wages paid. See Dinardo and Lee, "Economic Impacts of Unionization on Private Sector Employers: 1984–2001," National Bureau of Economic Research Working Paper No. 10598 (June 2004).

[64]Recent evidence from Blanchflower and Bryson, "Changes Over Time," suggests that the union advantage for women diminished relative to men's since the mid 1990s, but earlier evidence provided in their paper, as well as earlier work, suggests that women had a relative advantage in the past. See for instance, Freeman and Leonard, "Union Maids," and Heidi Hartmann, Roberta Spalter-Roth, and Nancy Collins, "What Do Unions Do for Women?" *Challenge* 37, no. 4 (July–August 1994): 11–18.

[65]William E. Even and David A. Macpherson, "The Decline of Private Sector Unionism and the Gender Wage Gap," *Journal of Human Resources* 28, no. 2 (1993): 279–96.

recent years, the far greater decline in unionism for men than for women contributed to a reduction in the male-female wage gap.[66]

The extent to which workers are unionized also has profound effects on wage inequality, more generally. Because unions provide relatively high-paying job opportunities for many less-skilled workers, their presence tends to reduce wage inequality while deunionization creates the opposite effect. Thus, the dramatic decline in men's unionization in recent years contributed to rising male wage inequality in the United States. For women, this factor had little effect, most likely because unionism fell far more modestly for them.[67] Further, unions tend to increase the fringe benefits of their members relative to their nonunion counterparts. Thus, it is not surprising that one of the serious consequences of deunionization is the loss of access to health insurance.[68]

Finally, some argue that unions provide important nonpecuniary benefits to their members, chiefly by giving them a greater opportunity to shape their work environment by communicating their preferences to employers through the collective bargaining process and by providing for grievance procedures.[69] In addition, unions offer the potential to help reduce the tension between work and family by negotiating for such benefits as family leave, on-site day care, and flexible schedules. These benefits are not only particularly important for women workers, but also increasingly for men, as they share more household responsibilities.

Even though unions offer many potential advantages to workers, including higher wages and greater fringe benefits, to the extent that the demand for labor is responsive to cost, unionization is also associated with lower employment. Hence, the gains of those who get greater rewards are in part at the expense of those who are not hired, or are displaced, due to unionization.

Reasons for the Historic Underrepresentation of Women in Unions

In light of the advantages to workers of union membership, how do we explain the historic underrepresentation of women in unions? Interestingly, the evidence does not show that women exhibit a lesser "taste" or preference for unionism. In fact, considerable evidence indicates that currently unorganized women have tended to be more supportive of collective action to achieve their goals than men and are more likely to vote for union representation.[70] Women, however, have tended to be concentrated in

---

[66]Even and Macpherson, "The Decline of Private Sector Unionism"; Blau and Kahn, "Rising Wage Inequality and the U.S. Gender Gap"; and Blau, "Trends in the Well-Being of American Women." In the latter paper, Blau reports that the decline in unionism lowered the real wages of men by 2.8 percent and of women by 1.6 percent, thereby narrowing the gender gap.

[67]David Card, "The Effect of Unions on Wage Inequality in the U.S. Labor Market," *Industrial and Labor Relations Review* 54, no. 2 (January 2001): 296–315; and Richard B. Freeman, "How Much Has De-Unionization Contributed to the Rise in Male Earnings Inequality?" in *Uneven Tides: Rising Inequality in America,* edited by Sheldon Danziger and Peter Gottschalk (New York: Russell Sage Foundation, 1993), pp. 133–64.

[68]Thomas C. Buchmeuller, John E. Dinardo, and Robert G. Valletta, "Union Effects on Health Insurance Provision and Coverage in the United States," *Industrial and Labor Relations Review* 55, no. 4 (July 2002): 610–27. The evidence on fringes is from Richard B. Freeman and James L. Medoff, *What Do Unions Do?* (New York: Basic Books, 1984).

[69]Richard B. Freeman termed this process the "voice effect" of unions; see "Individual Mobility and Union Voice in the Labor Market," *American Economic Review* 66, no. 2 (May 1976): 361–68.

[70]Freeman and Medoff, *What Do Unions Do?*; and Kate Bronfenbrenner, "Organizing Women: The Nature and Process of Union Organizing Efforts among U.S. Women Since the Mid-1990s," working paper (Cornell University, 2003).

industries and occupations where, for whatever reason, unionization was below average. As already noted, traditionally, unionization was highest among blue-collar workers in manufacturing, while women were concentrated in clerical and service occupations and in service industries, which experience lower rates of unionization. Moreover, within the manufacturing sector, women are concentrated in the more competitive industries, while unionization occurs more frequently in monopolistic industries. One study finds that three-fourths of the difference in unionization between men and women is explained by the underrepresentation of women in highly organized occupations and sectors. This finding also explains why the economy-wide shift away from blue-collar and manufacturing jobs worked to decrease the gender gap in unionization in recent years.[71]

Historically, the policies of unions themselves also contributed to women's underrepresentation among their ranks. Male craft unions did not begin to admit women until the late 1800s[72] and failed to be hospitable to women (or blacks) long after they no longer formally excluded them. Also, unions faced criticism for their less than vigorous efforts to organize women workers and lack of support for women's own efforts to unionize. Moreover, the tendency of unions to emphasize issues of greater concern to male workers, while neglecting women's concerns, likely decreased the appeal of unions for women.[73] For example, fringe benefits such as health insurance would perhaps be of less value to women workers because many of them are members of two-earner families and are frequently already covered under their husbands' plans. On the other hand, benefits such as parental leave and day care are likely to be of greater interest to women than to men.

The Glass Ceiling in Union Leadership

Although women now comprise nearly 44 percent of all union members, they appear to face a glass ceiling here, as in corporate America, when it comes to leadership positions, especially top posts at both the national and local level. For instance, in 2004 only 12 percent of AFL-CIO executive council members were women.[74] The Coalition of Labor Union Women (CLUW), an advocacy group, was formed in 1974 with the express goal of moving women into such positions, but its impact at that level appears fairly modest to date. Women have found somewhat more success in attaining middle-level positions at the local union level such as union steward or member of the local executive board, and some have even reached top-level positions in union locals.[75]

---

[71]Even and Macpherson, "The Decline of Private Sector Unionism."

[72]Barbara M. Wertheimer and Anne H. Nelson, " 'Union Is Power': Sketches from Women's Labor History," in *Women: A Feminist Perspective,* 4th ed., edited by Jo Freeman (Palo Alto, CA: Mayfield, 1989), pp. 312–28. See also Margaret S. Coleman, "Undercounted and Underpaid Heroines: The Path to Equal Opportunity Employment During the Twentieth Century," *Working USA* 3, no. 5 (January–February 2000): 37–65.

[73]For further discussion, see Anne Forrest, "Connecting Women with Unions: What Are the Issues?" *Industrial Relations* (Canadian) 56, no. 4 (Autumn 2001): 647–77.

[74]"About AFL-CIO," at www.aflcio.org, accessed September 2004.

[75]Lois S. Gray, "The Route to the Top: Female Union Leaders and Union Policy," in *Women and Unions: Forging a Partnership,* edited by Dorothy Sue Cobble (Ithaca, NY: ILR Press, 1987). See also Helen Elkiss, "Training Women for Union Office: Breaking the Glass Ceiling," *Labor Studies Journal* 19, no. 2 (Summer 1994): 25–41; and Dale Melcher, Jennifer L. Eichstedt, Shelley Eriksen, and Dan Clawson, "Women's Participation in Local Union Leadership: The Massachusetts Experience," *Industrial and Labor Relations Review* 45, no. 2 (1992): 267–80.

Women are also underrepresented among union organizers (those seeking to unionize currently unorganized workers), which is particularly striking in light of the fact that the majority of recently organized workers are women.[76]

The reasons for the lack of women in key leadership roles are not entirely clear, but most likely reflect the same types of barriers encountered by women in other organizations, from corporations and foundations to elective positions in government. First, because women generally hold the primary responsibility in the home, most employed women must juggle family and job responsibilities, leaving little time available for union activities. Such participation can require as much as 20 to 40 hours of work per week and, at the local level, is often unpaid. A second and related factor is that election to top leadership positions often takes years of working with rank and file members. Many men begin these activities in their twenties, while many women find it particularly difficult to participate at that age, which coincides with their childbearing years. Third, studies show that women tend to underestimate their abilities and are thus less likely to place themselves on a leadership "career track."[77]

As is true in other organizations, the existing underrepresentation of women in union leadership positions itself also hinders women's advancement because it reduces the opportunities for women to receive informal mentoring and to find role models, and also makes them more likely to be perceived as outsiders. Also, women frequently lack the crucial education and experience required for leadership positions, such as negotiating skills and institutional knowledge about union offices. Finally, women must often contend with the perception that they are not "tough" enough to negotiate contracts or participate in bargaining, and at times may even face overt sexual harassment.[78]

Prospects for Women in Unions

In spite of all these problems, important recent efforts at the national level in the AFL-CIO and among international unions are opening up leadership positions to women. Under the auspices of its president, John Sweeney, the AFL-CIO created the position of executive vice president to be filled by a woman trade union activist. In addition, the executive council was expanded to allow for greater female representation, and one position was designated for a representative from the Coalition of Labor Union Women, signaling the importance of this group. Another step was to create a Working Women's Department in an effort to reach out to current and potential women union members. Also, to promote grass roots change, the national AFL-CIO is helping local unions with outreach and training for women.

Individual unions are also expanding opportunities for women. Many have formed women's committees to take greater account of women workers' needs. Although taking this approach runs the risk of marginalizing women's issues, such committees provide women with the opportunity to actively participate in the union and gain leadership experience. Further, an increasing number of unions are reserving seats on executive committees for women, and some guarantee them proportional representation on executive boards. Such a policy, however, carries the risk that women will be viewed as mere tokens, especially if they are appointed to such posts rather than elected. Nonetheless,

---

[76]Bronfenbrenner, "Organizing Women."
[77]See Helen Elkiss, "Training Women for Union Office"; and Gray, "The Route to the Top."
[78]These and other factors are discussed in Gray, "The Route to the Top."

these positions do provide them with an up-close view of the decision-making process. Finally, international unions are directing specific efforts toward women's education and building their self-confidence, including emphasis on public speaking and negotiating in an effort to develop women's leadership skills.[79]

Some routes to leadership positions for women do not require special efforts by unions. Founders of new unions typically end up as leaders. Consider, for example, Karen Nussbaum, who was a founder of 9 to 5 (a union of clerical workers), which subsequently became affiliated with the SEIU. A more likely route that may help women reach the top is working for a union in an area of technical expertise, such as in human resources, pensions, occupational safety and health, education, or the legal department.[80]

Since the decline in unionism has proceeded more rapidly among men than women, women's share of union membership has increased considerably. To halt further declines in membership, it is in unions' interests to increase their efforts to make unions attractive to women, including bringing women into leadership positions.

Conclusion

In this chapter we began by emphasizing that the gender wage gap narrowed considerably since the late 1970s. During these years women's real wages continued to rise while those of men stagnated, and real wages of low-skilled men declined considerably as earnings inequality rose rapidly. Relative wage gains were especially dramatic during the 1980s. In the face of rising returns to skill during that decade, women, who on average still had lower qualifications than men, managed to overcome this disadvantage by substantially upgrading their qualifications, especially their experience and occupations. They also benefited from a decrease in the unexplained gender gap, which may represent a decline in discrimination, an improvement in women's qualifications that we are not able to measure using conventional data sources, or demand shifts that favored women more than men. Progress in narrowing in the gender pay gap slowed in the 1990s. The main factor accounting for this change was slower convergence in the unexplained gender pay gap over the 1990s than in the previous decade. This may mean that, during the 1990s, the gender gap in unmeasured qualifications narrowed more slowly, that discrimination decreased less, or that demand shifts were less favorable to women. The evidence also indicates that, controlling for the measured characteristics, female labor force entrants were less skilled during the 1990s than they had been in the 1980s, resulting in a less favorable shift in the composition of the labor force in the 1990s.

Next we examined a number of other developments in the labor market, including corporate downsizing, the growth of nonstandard work, women's rising self-employment, and the decline and changing role of labor unions, and considered the impact of each. Although women's rising self-employment, for instance, appears to be a favorable development, other changes, such as the growth of nonstandard work, raise concerns for both women and men. Men suffered the greatest consequences of deunionization because they had the highest rates of unionization and their rates declined most dramatically. Among both men and women, individuals with few educational credentials experienced

---

[79]Anne Trebilcock, "Strategies for Strengthening Women's Participation in Trade Union Leadership," *International Labour Review* 130, no. 4 (1991): 407–26.

[80]Gray, "The Route to the Top"; and Michelle Hoyman, "Working Women: The Potential of Unionization and Collective Action in the United States," *Women's Studies International Forum* 12, no. 1 (1989): 51–58.

the greatest labor market difficulties in recent years. Among men, they are more likely to be out of the labor force than in years past and, among women, their participation rates decreased relative to the more highly educated. Further, real earnings trends were much less favorable for the less educated, and, among men, this group experienced a precipitous decline in real earnings over the last 30 years. Moreover, a growing proportion of less-educated women head single-parent families. The difficulties faced by single-parent families is one of the subjects discussed in Chapter 9. Chapter 10, in turn, discusses recent changes in welfare and other government policies that affect these families.

Questions for Review and Discussion

1. Discuss the advantages and disadvantages of our "high-churning" economy. How does your answer differ when you focus on women? Less-skilled workers? Older women? Older men? Minority workers?
2. Explain why economists, especially in times of recession, try to keep track of marginally attached workers, discouraged workers, as well as those who are unemployed. How do these groups differ?
3. It is said various factors either "push" or "pull" individuals into self-employment. Provide an example or two of each.
4. Explain why teen unemployment rates are so much higher than for workers who are age 20 and over.
5. What factors caused the gender earnings ratio in the United States to increase substantially over the 1980s, according to the study by Blau and Kahn cited in the text? Based on these results, can you conclude that discrimination against women in the labor market actually declined? Why or why not? What differences did they identify for the 1990s?
6. What are the pros and cons of nonstandard employment for workers?
7. For many individuals in the United States, health insurance depends on their employment. Consider this situation in light of the recent employment trends discussed in the text.

Suggested Readings

Bennett, James T., and Bruce E. Kaufman, eds. *The Future of Private Sector Unionism in the United States*. Armonk, NY: M. E. Sharpe, 2002.

Blau, Francine D., and Lawrence M. Kahn. "Swimming Upstream: Trends in the Gender Wage Differential in the 1980s." *Journal of Labor Economics* 15, no. 1, pt. 1 (January 1997): 1–42.

Blau, Francine D., and Lawrence M. Kahn. "Gender Differences in Pay." *Journal of Economic Perspectives* 14, no. 4 (Fall 2000): 75–99.

Carré, Francoise, Marianne A. Ferber, Lonnie Golden, and Steve Herzenberg, eds. *Nonstandard Work Arrangements and the Changing Labor Market: Dimensions, Causes, and Institutional Responses*. Industrial Relations Research Association Research Volume, 2000.

Cobble, Dorothy Sue, ed. *Women and Unions: Forging a Partnership*. Ithaca, NY: ILR Press, 1987.

Fortin, Nicole M., and Thomas Lemieux. "Are Women's Wage Gains Men's Losses? A Distributional Test." *American Economic Review* 90, no. 2 (May 2000): 456–60.

Freeman, Richard B., and Peter Gottschalk. *Generating Jobs: How to Increase Demand for Less-Skilled Workers*. New York: Russell Sage Foundation, 1998.

Freeman, Richard B., and James L. Medoff. *What Do Unions Do?* New York: Basic Books, 1984.

Holzer, Harry. "Black Employment Problems: New Evidence, Old Questions." *Journal of Policy Analysis and Management* 13, no. 4 (Fall 1994): 699–722.

Houseman, Susan, and Machiko Osawa, eds. *Nonstandard Work in Developed Economies.* Kalamazoo, MI: W.E. Upjohn Institute, 2003.

Juhn, Chinhui, Kevin M. Murphy, and Brooks Pierce. "Wage Inequality and the Rise in Returns to Skill." *Journal of Political Economy* 101, no. 3 (June 1993): 410–42.

Katz, Lawrence F., and David H. Autor. "Changes in the Wage Structure and Earnings Inequality." In *Handbook of Labor Economics,* edited by Orley C. Ashenfelter and David Card, pp. 3A:1463–555. Amsterdam: Elsevier, 1999.

Katz, Lawrence F., and Kevin M. Murphy. "Changes in Relative Wages, 1963–87: Supply and Demand Factors." *Quarterly Journal of Economics* 107, no. 1 (February 1992): 35–78.

Kruse, Douglas, and Joseph Blasi. "The New Employee-Employer Relationship." In *A Working Nation: Workers, Work, and Government in the New Economy,* edited by David T. Ellwood, Rebecca M. Blank, Joseph Blasi, Douglas Kruse, William A. Niskanen, and Karen Lynn-Dyson, chap. 2, pp. 42–91. New York: Russell Sage Foundation, 2000.

Levy, Frank. *The New Dollars and Dreams: American Incomes and Economic Change.* New York: Russell Sage Foundation, 1998.

Levy, Frank, and Richard J. Murnane. "U.S. Earnings Levels and Earnings Inequality: A Review of Recent Trends and Proposed Explanations." *Journal of Economic Literature* 30, no. 3 (September 1991): 1222–381.

Neumark, David, ed. *On the Job: Is Long-Term Employment a Thing of the Past?* New York: Russell Sage Foundation, 2000.

O'Neill, June, and Solomon W. Polachek. "Why the Gender Gap in Wages Narrowed in the 1980s." *Journal of Labor Economics* 11, no. 1, pt. 1 (January 1993): 205–28.

U.S. Department of Labor, Bureau of Labor Statistics. "Contingent Workers and Alternate Work Arrangements." *Monthly Labor Review* 119, no. 10 (October 1996): 3–83.

9

CHANGING WORK ROLES AND THE FAMILY

Chapter Highlights

- Economic Explanations for Family Formation

- Marriage

- Divorce

- Cohabitation: Opposite-Sex and Gay and Lesbian Couples

- Fertility

- Changing Family Structure and Economic Well-Being

In earlier chapters, we discussed the family as an economic institution and the allocation of time of husband and wife between the household and the labor market. We now turn our attention to the impact a woman's employment has on her family and also consider a number of issues associated with changing family structure. One important difference between our approach here and in Chapter 4 is that there we accepted marital status and fertility as given, exogenous to our models, and focused on the effects of these factors on women's labor force participation. In this chapter, we turn the tables and examine the impact of economic factors, including women's labor force participation, on demographic outcomes.

The first sections of this chapter deal with the effect of economic factors on the incidence of marriage, divorce, cohabitation by opposite-sex and gay and lesbian couples, and fertility. Next, we look at the effect of changing family structure on economic well-being, focusing on dual-earner families and single-parent families. One of the most important issues associated with changing family structure and increased labor market activity of women that we consider is their consequences for the well-being of children. Thus, we review the literature on the effect of maternal employment on children's development and then examine the effect of family structure on measures of children's future success.

ECONOMIC EXPLANATIONS FOR FAMILY FORMATION

What is the expected effect of economic factors, including women's increased labor force participation, on family formation? From the viewpoint of neoclassical economics, the determining factor in decisions concerning family issues such as marriage, divorce, and fertility is whether the benefits exceed the costs.[1] Thus, the question arises as to the effect of women's increasing labor force participation and other economic factors on the costs and benefits associated with these decisions—do more or fewer couples choose to marry, divorce, or bear children? The answer to this question is not obvious from a theoretical point of view. That is, forces operate both to reduce and to increase the benefits and costs of these decisions.

Marriage

Marriage is encouraged by a number of factors, though perhaps the one most emphasized by neoclassical economists is that it makes possible the specialization and exchange that potentially increase the couple's productivity and economic well-being. In general, the more the comparative advantage in producing home and market goods *differs* between the two partners, the larger the potential gain, for each may then specialize mainly or entirely in his or her area of higher relative productivity. As women have been acquiring more job-oriented education and training, and perhaps encountering less discrimination in the labor market, their market productivity has increased relative to their home productivity. This leads to smaller gains from specialization and exchange than in the days when women prepared for the traditional role of homemaker in a family with only a male breadwinner. From this perspective, rising female labor force participation is expected to result in lower marriage rates. Working hand in hand with this, women's improved opportunities for earning their own living are expected to reduce their incentives to marry because they present women with a viable alternative to marriage, making it economically feasible to postpone or altogether forgo such a commitment. For all these reasons women's increasing labor force participation is expected to lower marriage rates, but the matter is not quite that simple.

The much greater acceptability of market work for married women today may encourage marriage by reducing its opportunity cost. That is, women are no longer pressured to choose between employment on the one hand and marriage on the other. Although many women continue to accommodate their paid work to what are still perceived to be their household responsibilities, they are far less likely than in the past to

[1]Seminal work by neoclassical economists on the economics of the family was first done by Gary S. Becker and is summarized by him in *A Treatise on the Family* (Cambridge, MA: Harvard University Press, 1991). See also Robert Willis, "What Have We Learned from the Economics of the Family?" *American Economic Review* 77, no. 2 (May 1987): 68–81; Shoshana Grossbard-Shechtman, *On the Economics of Marriage* (Boulder, CO: Westview Press, 1993); and Mark R. Rosenzweig and Oded Stark, eds., *Handbook of Population and Family Economics,* vol. 1A and 1B (Amsterdam: Elsevier, 1997). For a recent review of theory and evidence, see Robert T. Michael, "An Economic Perspective on Sex, Marriage, and the Family in the United States," in *The Modern Family in Interdisciplinary Perspective,* edited by Steven Tipton and John Witte Jr., (Berkeley: University of California, forthcoming).

cut short their education or leave the labor market entirely at the time they get married. Working in the same direction, some sociologists argue that some men may prefer women who can make a larger contribution to family income.[2] In sum, women's rising labor force participation may negatively or positively affect marriage rates.

As we saw in Chapter 3, several other economic factors, unrelated to comparative advantage and changes in women's labor force participation, may also work to encourage marriage.[3] Marriage provides a benefit in the form of economies of scale. That is, the cost of housing and food is much less on a per person basis if shared. In addition, marriage makes possible the consumption of public goods such as a well-tended garden or a newly mowed lawn. Even though many of these advantages can also be reaped by unmarried couples, roommates, or those living with extended families, given prevailing tastes and norms, these other alternatives are often less desirable or less socially acceptable. Also, the contractual relationship of marriage encourages marriage-specific investments. And, some evidence suggests that married couples enjoy better health. Thus, even as the rewards to specialization based on the traditional division of labor diminish, marriage remains the norm and is likely to continue to do so, especially when we take into account noneconomic considerations such as affection and companionship. Further, two-earner couples are particularly likely to benefit from marriage to the extent that they have more similar tastes and shared experiences than traditional couples, which should enhance their mutual enjoyment. In addition, though such couples have less time, they have more money than those with only one paycheck. Not only does their higher income permit them to consume more of the market goods and services they desire, it also presumably reduces at least one potential area of stress and friction—conflicts over the use of scarce dollars. Also, sharing both market work and housework might be expected to create greater understanding and empathy between husband and wife. Finally, having two wage earners reduces the economic risks for families because they are not entirely dependent on one income.

Marriage rates are also affected by men's economic prospects. In recent years, the labor market position of less educated men has substantially weakened. One consequence is a reduced supply of "marriageable men," which provides another possible explanation for declining marriage rates.[4] A low ratio of men to women in the marriageable population due, for example, to demographic trends or high incarceration

---

[2]See, for instance, Valerie Kincade Oppenheimer, "Women's Rising Employment and the Future of the Family in Industrial Societies," *Population and Development Review* 20, no. 2 (June 1994): 293–342.

[3]For a comprehensive discussion of the benefits of marriage, see David C. Ribar, "What Do Social Scientists Know About the Benefits of Marriage? A Review of Quantitative Methodologies," IZA Discussion Paper No. 998 (January 2004).

[4]The declining supply of marriageable men was originally proposed as an explanation by William J. Wilson and Kathryn Neckerman, "Poverty and Family Structure: The Widening Gap Between Evidence and Public Policy Issues," in *Fighting Poverty: What Works and What Doesn't,* edited by Sheldon Danziger and Daniel Weinberg (Cambridge, MA: Harvard University Press, 1986), pp. 232–59. For further discussion on the role of men's economic prospects, see Robert A. Moffitt, "Female Wages, Male Wages, and the Economic Model of Marriage," in *The Ties That Bind: Perspectives on Marriage and Cohabitation,* edited by Linda Waite (New York: Aldine de Gruyter, 2000), pp. 302–19; and Valerie Kinkaide Oppenheimer, "The Continuing Importance of Men's Economic Position in Marriage Formation," in *The Ties that Bind,* edited by Waite, pp. 283–301.

rates of males may further contribute to insufficient supply.[5] Recent economic trends, which adversely affected less educated men, are expected to disproportionately affect marriage rates of African Americans and Hispanics because they tend to attain less education, on average, than whites, and may also face discrimination. In addition as seen in Chapter 5, the gender differential in wages for these groups is much smaller than among whites, which means that the gains to marriage from specialization and exchange are also smaller, all else equal.

Another factor receiving quite a bit of attention as possibly affecting trends in marriage rates is the role of income support available outside of marriage, such as welfare. This concern influenced the policy debate about redesigning welfare in the mid-1990s because welfare largely provided government support for single mothers and was thought to discourage women from getting married. As discussed further in Chapter 10, a large body of research supports the view that, contrary to popular perception, welfare cannot explain the large shift in family structure away from marriage toward single-parent families that began in the 1970s, even among low-income women.[6] Other government policies, including tax policies, also potentially affect marriage rates and are discussed at length in Chapter 10.

Economic considerations are not, however, the only ones that play a role in demographic decisions, including marriage. Another factor that undoubtedly contributed to the growing number of unmarried people is the dramatic liberalization in attitudes toward divorce, cohabitation, and sex outside of marriage beginning in the 1960s and 1970s.[7] As a result, marriage and sex are no longer as closely linked together as they once were.

Taken together, these factors create an ambiguous effect, some serving to increase marriage rates and others to reduce them. However, the evidence suggests the dominance of the factors causing marriage rates to fall, principally the rapid entry of women into the labor market and the liberalization of social attitudes. Indeed, as Table 9-1 shows, the marriage rate fell from 10.6 marriages per 1,000 population in 1970 to 8.4 by 2002. Some of these changes reflect postponement of marriage by young men and women rather than their forgoing it completely. This may be seen in Table 9-1 in the rising median age of first marriage for women and men, along with the dramatic increase in the fraction of young women and men who have never been married. In 1970, for example, only 36 percent of women age 20 to 24 had never been married as compared with fully 74 percent in 2002.

---

[5]Shoshana Grossbard-Shechtman, *On the Economics of Marriage,* chaps. 4 and 5; and Joshua Angrist, "How Do Sex Ratios Affect Marriage and Labor Markets? Evidence from America's Second Generation," *Quarterly Journal of Economics* 117, no. 3 (August 2002): 997–1038.

[6]Robert A. Moffitt, "Welfare Benefits and Female Headship in U.S. Time Series," *American Economic Review* 90, no. 2 (May 2000): 373–77; and for a review, Robert A. Moffitt, "The Effect of Welfare on Marriage and Fertility" in *Welfare, the Family, and Reproductive Behavior: Research Perspectives,* edited by Robert A. Moffitt (Washington, DC: National Research Council, 1998), pp. 50–97. Also, changes to welfare programs to promote marriage do not appear to have been successful. For instance, see Marianne P. Bitler, Jonah B. Gelbach, Hilary W. Hoynes, and Madeline Zavodny, "The Impact of Welfare Reform on Marriage and Divorce," *Demography* 41, no. 2 (May 2004): 213–36; as well as a meta-analysis of findings from 14 welfare programs in Lisa A. Gennetian and Viginia Knox, "Staying Single: The Effects of Welfare Reform Policies on Marriage and Cohabitation," MDRC Working Paper No. 13 (April 2003).

[7]Arland Thornton and Linda Young-DeMarco, "Four Decades of Trends in Attitudes Toward Family Issues in the United States: The 1960s Through the 1990s," *Journal of Marriage and the Family* 63 (November 2001): 1009–37.

TABLE 9-1	Trends in Family Structure, 1970–2002			
	1970	*1980*	*1990*	*2002*
Marriage				
Marriage rate per 1,000 population	10.6	10.6	9.8	8.4[a]
Median age at first marriage				
Men	23.2	24.7	26.1	26.9
Women	20.8	22.0	23.9	25.3
% Never-married men				
Age 20–24	54.7	68.8	79.3	85.4
Age 30–34	9.4	15.9	27.0	34.0
Age 40–44	6.3	7.1	10.5	16.7
% Never-married women				
Age 20–24	35.8	50.2	62.8	74.0
Age 30–34	6.2	9.5	16.4	23.0
Age 40–44	4.9	4.8	8.0	11.5
% Married adults	71.7	65.5	61.9	55.3
Whites	72.6	67.2	64.0	58.1
Blacks	64.1	51.4	45.8	35.6
Asians	n.a.	n.a.	n.a.	56.7
Hispanic origin[b]	71.8	65.6	61.7	50.6
Divorce				
Divorce rate per 1,000 population	3.5	5.2	4.7	4.0[a]
Cohabitation				
Cohabitors (unmarried, opposite-sex couples) per 100 married couples	1.2	3.2	5.5	8.6

[a]Figure is from 2001.
[b]Person of Hispanic origin can be of any race.
n.a. = Not available.

Source: U.S. Census Bureau, "Children's Living Arrangements and Characteristics: March 2002," *Current Population Reports,* Series P20-547. Detailed tables available at www.census.gov: Table A1, "Marital Status of People Age 15 Years and Over"; Table MS-2, "Estimated Median Age at First Marriage"; Table UC-1, "Unmarried-Couple Households by Presence of Children"; and Table HH-1, "Households by Type: 1940–Present; and U.S. Census Bureau, *Statistical Abstract of the United States: 2002,* Table 66.

These trends likely reflect increased economic opportunities for women, which encouraged them to stay in school longer and, in many cases, to subsequently pursue careers.[8] Claudia Goldin and Larry Katz also point to the pivotal role of the birth control pill, which became widely available to single women starting in the late 1960s and

---

[8]Evidence that women's improved labor market opportunities have lead to a decline in marriage is provided by T. Paul Schultz, "Marital Status and Fertility in the United States," *Journal of Human Resources* 29, no. 2 (Spring 1994): 637–69; and Francine D. Blau, Lawrence M. Kahn, and Jane Waldfogel, "Understanding Young Women's Marriage Decisions: The Role of Labor Market and Marriage Market Conditions," *Industrial and Labor Relations Review* 53, no. 4 (July 2000): 624–47. However, Valerie Kincade Oppenheimer and Vivian Lew question the emphasis placed on this factor in explaining recent trends; see "American Marriage Formation in the 1980s: How Important Was Women's Economic Independence?" in *Gender and Family Change in Industrialized Countries,* edited by Karen Oppenheim Mason and An-Magitt Jensen (Oxford: Clarendon Press, 1995).

early 1970s, in fostering this delay because it allows young women to postpone child-bearing without the cost of abstinence.[9]

As marriage rates fell, cohabitation rates increased. Table 9-1 shows that the ratio of unmarried to married couples increased from 1:100 in 1970 to almost 9:100 in 2002 and many more individuals undoubtedly cohabited at some point, if only briefly. Even so, most individuals eventually marry; the proportion of people who never marry in their lifetime, in recent years about 5 percent, is not expected to increase to more than 10 percent in the foreseeable future.[10] One important difference from past patterns, however, is that more children are now being born to unmarried mothers.

As may be seen in Table 9-1, the largest decline in marriage occurred among blacks. This shift appears to reflect black women's rising economic opportunities combined with black men's often poor job prospects.[11] In inner cities, especially, high rates of homicide and incarceration have further reduced the supply of "marriageable" men.

In conclusion, despite the decline in the marriage rate in the United States since the 1970s, marriage remains the norm and the U.S. marriage rate remains among the highest of the economically advanced nations. Furthermore, most people who get divorced do eventually remarry, though the remarriage rate has also declined, no doubt for the same reasons that caused marriage rates to fall.[12] Nonetheless, the fact that marriage and remarriage rates continue to be so high suggests that, in spite of all the changes, marriage remains central to the lives of many Americans.

Divorce

A related set of economic and social factors affects marital dissolution—that is, separation or divorce.[13] Among traditional married couples, the interdependence of husband and wife due to specialization and exchange is probably the single most important economic deterrent to divorce. In the case of the breadwinner husband and homemaker wife, the wife generally has relatively few market skills that would enable her to earn enough money on her own to buy whatever she requires of market goods and services, while the husband has little training for household tasks and needs someone to look after home and children. Investments in marriage-specific human capital by the couple further cement this relationship.

As the traditional division of labor breaks down, the economic incentives for remaining married are reduced. Therefore, women's improved economic opportunities

---

[9]Claudia Goldin and Lawrence F. Katz, "Career and Marriage in the Age of the Pill," *American Economic Review* 90, no. 2 (May 2000): 461–65.

[10]U.S. Census Bureau, "Number, Timing, and Duration of Marriages and Divorces: 1996," *Current Population Reports* P70-80 (February 2002).

[11]T. Paul Schultz finds that black women's marriage rates are more greatly affected by their husband's economic prospects than by their own in "Eroding the Economic Foundations of Marriage and Fertility in the United States," *Structural Change and Economic Dynamics* 9, no. 4 (December 1998): 391–413. See also William J. Wilson and Kathryn Neckerman, "Poverty and Family Structure," *Structural Change and Economic Dynamics* 9, no. 4 (December 1998): 391–414. On the other hand, Robert G. Wood finds weaker evidence for this explanation in "Marriage Rates and Marriageable Men," *Journal of Human Resources* 30, no. 1 (Winter 1995): 163–93.

[12]See Department of Health and Human Services, Centers for Disease Control and Prevention, "Cohabitation, Marriage, Divorce, and Remarriage in the United States," Series 23, no. 22 (July 2002); and Pamela J. Smock, "Remarriage Patterns of Black and White Women: Reassessing the Role of Educational Attainment," *Demography* 27, no. 3 (August 1990): 467–73.

[13]Gary S. Becker, Elisabeth M. Landes, and Robert T. Michael, "An Economic Analysis of Marital Instability," *Journal of Political Economy* 85, no. 6 (December 1977): 1141–87.

will tend to increase the propensity to divorce, although divorce remains costly, even when the wife is employed. For instance, although the generally higher income of two-earner couples gives them the opportunity to acquire more assets, dividing them, especially such illiquid assets as a house or a car, often creates problems. Also, as mentioned earlier, considerable economic benefits to marriage are not related to comparative advantage, and these benefits may be even greater for high-income couples with two earners.

In considering divorce, it is also important to keep in mind that all marriages are not good ones, and in some cases, a divorce may be an improvement for all concerned. Women who are in difficult marriages may be more likely to seek employment to provide the potential for economic independence. In such instances, we would observe a positive relationship between women's employment and divorce, but it is not a *causal* relationship; that is, women's employment facilitated the divorce, but it did not cause it.

Other factors also influence the probability of divorce. One is that unexpected events, such as a sudden increase or decrease in the earnings ability of one or both partners, may create frictions in the marriage.[14] Another is that individuals' preferences and needs may change as time passes, especially during times of rapid shifts in long-accepted standards and norms, such as those that occurred since the 1960s and 1970s. Similarly, changes in the rules governing legal termination of marriage, whether concerning alimony and child support or the introduction of no-fault divorce laws, might be expected to affect divorce. Child support enforcement, for instance, intensified in recent years. The effect of this policy change on divorce, however, is not clear a priori. On the one hand, if the expected payment increases, the spouse who expects to get the payments would presumably be more willing to terminate a marriage because these payments provide a financial cushion; at the same time the partner who must make such payments would be less likely to favor breaking up the marriage. Some research found that the latter effect dominates—that is, stronger child support enforcement discourages divorce—while other research found no net effect.[15] Another factor, the liberalization of the divorce laws, which occurred in many states during the 1970s, might be expected to increase the likelihood of marital dissolution by making divorce easier to obtain. Some, but not all studies, found such an effect.[16] Welfare generosity may also affect divorce rates. For instance, concern was frequently expressed that welfare not only reduced incentives to marry, but also increased incentives to divorce. The research evidence, however, suggests a minor effect, at most.[17]

---

[14]Kerwin Kofi Charles and Melvin Stephens, Jr., "Job Displacement, Disability, and Divorce," *Journal of Labor Economics* 22, no. 2 (April 2004): 489–522; and Yoram Weiss and Robert Willis, "Transfers Among Divorced Couples: Evidence and Interpretation," *Journal of Labor Economics* 11, no. 4 (October 1993): 629–79.

[15]Lucia Nixon finds that the latter effect dominates, leading stronger child support enforcement to discourage divorce in "The Effect of Child Support Enforcement on Marital Dissolution," *Journal of Human Resources* 32, no. 1 (Winter 1997): 159–81; while Bradley T. Heim finds no effect in "Does Child Support Enforcement Reduce Divorce Rates? A Reexamination," *Journal of Human Resources* 38, no. 4 (Fall 2003): 773–91.

[16]For evidence that no-fault divorce did not increase the divorce rate, see H. Elizabeth Peters," Marriage and Divorce: Informational Constraints and Private Contracting," *American Economic Review* 76, no. 3 (June 1986): 437–54; and Jeffrey S. Gray, "Divorce-Law Changes and Married Women's Labor Supply," *American Economic Review* 88, no. 3 (June 1998): 628–42. For evidence on the other side, see Leora Friedberg, "Did Unilateral Divorce Raise Divorce Rates?" *American Economic Review* 88, no. 3 (June 1998): 608–27.

[17]See, for instance, Saul D. Hoffman and Greg J. Duncan, "The Effect of Incomes, Wages, and AFDC Benefits on Marital Disruption," *Journal of Human Resources* 30, no. 1 (Winter 1995): 19–41.

Further, divorce is also influenced by religious beliefs and broad social attitudes. One recent study, for instance, presents evidence that divorce in the United States occurs less frequently in families with sons, suggesting some preference for male children.[18]

For some time, the factors that serve to increase divorce appeared to dominate those that encourage the continuation of marriage. The divorce rate, which stood at 2.2 divorces per 1,000 population in 1960, increased considerably thereafter. As shown in Table 9-1, the divorce rate rose to 3.5 divorces per 1,000 population in 1970, and then increased very sharply to 5.2 in 1980. As noted earlier, women's rising economic opportunities likely help to account for the upward trend because they reduce economic interdependence between husbands and wives. The research evidence on this relationship, however, is mixed, perhaps because similar lifestyles of husbands and wives enhance the quality of some marriages.[19] Interestingly, one recent study finds that the relationship between women's increased labor force participation and divorce depends on whether the spouses were happily married. The wife's labor force participation has no effect on the likelihood of divorce for couples with a fulfilling marriage, but increases the likelihood of divorce for unhappy couples, perhaps because the wife's paid work makes it more economically feasible for the spouses to set up separate households.[20]

Since 1980, the divorce rate leveled off and even declined somewhat from 5.2 divorces per 1,000 population to 4.0 in 2001, though at the current rate an estimated one-half of all marriages will end in divorce.[21] One possible explanation for the leveling off and decline of the divorce rate is that the decreasing economic and social pressures to marry, associated with women's rising labor force participation, leads young people to postpone marriage. These changes may promote marital stability to the extent that couples who get married at older ages are less likely to break up.[22] One recent study, however, found no relationship between the rising age at marriage and recent trends in divorce rates. Another possibility is that increases in cohabitation explain recent trends, to the extent that breakups of these unions are not counted in the divorce statistics. However, the same study found that this factor played only a minor role, at most, leaving the question open as to what caused the leveling off and modest decline in divorce rates.[23] Looking ahead, even though the divorce rate may continue to decline a bit, whatever the reason,

---

[18]Nonetheless, the observed preference for sons in the United States is far less pronounced than in many East Asian countries, as discussed in Chapter 11. For evidence on the United States, see Gordon B. Dahl and Enrico Moretti, "The Demand for Sons: Evidence from Divorce, Fertilty, and Shotgun Marriage," National Bureau of Economic Research Working Paper No. 10281 (January 2004).

[19]For papers that support the hypothesis that women's increased employment or rising wages caused a higher divorce rate, see Steven Ruggles, "The Rise of Divorce and Separation in the United States, 1890–1990," *Demography* 34, no. 4 (November 1997): 455–566; and Robert Michael, "Why Did the U.S. Divorce Rate Double Within a Decade?" *Research in Population Economics* 6 (1988): 367–99. For papers that come to a different conclusion, see Valerie Kincade Oppenheimer, "Comment on 'The Rise of Divorce and Separation in the United States, 1880–1990'," *Demography* 34, no. 4 (November 1997): 467–72; and Hoffman and Duncan, "The Effect of Incomes, Wages, and AFDC Benefits on Marital Disruption."

[20]Robert Schoen, Nan Marie Astone, Kendra Rothert, Nicola J. Standish, and Joung J. Kim, "Women's Employment, Marital Happiness, and Divorce," *Social Forces* 81, no. 2 (December 2002): 643–62.

[21]This projection is provided in Michael, "An Economic Perspective on Sex, Marriage, and the Family in the United States."

[22]Alan Booth and Lynn White, "Thinking About Divorce," *Journal of Marriage and Family* 42, no. 3 (August 1980): 605–16; and Julie DaVanzo and M. Omar Rahman, "American Families: Trends and Correlates," *Population Index* 59, no. 3 (Fall 1993): 350–86.

[23]Joshua R. Goldstein, "The Leveling of Divorce in the United States," *Demography* 36, no. 3 (August 1999): 409–14.

it is not likely to fall to the levels that prevailed when traditional marriages were the norm and social attitudes toward divorce were extremely negative.

One problem associated with divorce is that it leaves full-time homemakers and their children particularly vulnerable. Full-time homemakers are dependent on their husbands not only for money income but also for their social status and even, at times, for much of their circle of friends. For children, family disruption creates potentially unfavorable effects on their future development, including educational attainment, wages, and teen pregnancy, in part because family disruption leads to reduced incomes but likely for other reasons as well. These issues will be discussed shortly.

Custody Battles: It Would Take a Solomon[*]

As more and more women are increasingly committed to their work, and as fathers continue to become more involved with their children, legal battles that arise when both parents want custody of their children, or when the noncustodial parent does not want to permit the children to move out of their community, become increasingly common. Such cases raise serious and complicated issues.

Traditionally, the mother was routinely awarded custody, barring overwhelming evidence that she was unfit and, in general, this outcome remains most common. However, increasingly more fathers are aggressively seeking custody. One well-justified concern, prompted by this change, centers on the usual presumption that the mother should automatically be given preference, and that the father, especially when not married to the mother of the child, has few rights. Another equally justified concern is that courts appear to look askance at mothers who have a career, or aspire to one, but fail to show the same reservations about "career fathers." Further, inevitable difficulties arise when contestants and their respective supporters make charges and countercharges that are difficult to verify with any degree of certainty. A brief summary of two high-profile cases and recent court rulings concerning permission for the custodial parent to move illustrate the problems involved.

The first case attained celebrity status in part because Sharon Prost, the mother of two boys, worked as counsel to conservative Senator Orrin G. Hatch of Utah. Kenneth Greene, the father, was assistant executive director of the American Federation of Television and Radio Artists. They were married in 1984 and separated eight years later. The judge awarded custody of the children to Mr. Greene in a sharply worded opinion that cited his friends and relatives who described his former wife as a driven workaholic, while claiming that he was a playful and affectionate parent. Partisans of Prost, including Senator Hatch, on the other hand, claimed that this picture was distorted and ignored the maximum efforts she made to be a responsible parent, while her husband chose not to take care of the children full-time even while he was unemployed. They objected to the fact that the judge gave the father credit for any time he participated in activities at the children's kindergarten, and for coming home first in the evening, but ignored the teacher's description of Ms. Prost as "surrogate room mom" as well as the fact that she regularly got up at 5:30 A.M. to play with the children before she left for work at 8:00. In sum, they charged that the judgment involved sex bias. The judge, a mother herself, who had worked part-time while her children were young, explained that a woman was entitled to put her career ahead of other demands in her life but, having made that decision, she must live with the consequences. Whether one agrees with the judge's decision, it must be expected to make some professional women fearful that courts may use a double standard, because they are likely to compare them to other mothers, who often are employed only part-time, or not at all, while fathers will be compared to other men with children, who almost invariably are employed full-time. Such comparisons would tend to make career mothers look bad as compared to similarly positioned fathers.

The second case involved different circumstances but also raised issues with implications for the role of women as mothers, albeit somewhat more indirectly. The mother had given birth to a daughter in 1991, when both she and the defendant were 16 years old and unmarried. She first agreed to give the baby up for adoption, but three weeks later changed her mind and decided to raise the child herself. Both mother and father lived with their respective families, continued to go to high school, and eventually graduated. The father had no contact with the infant during the first year of her life, but after that visited her regularly. In the fall of 1993 the plaintiff and her child moved to Ann Arbor, where she attended the University of Michigan on a scholarship. They lived in university family housing and the child attended university-approved day care. Expenses were covered by the maternal grandmother, while the child received occasional gifts from the father and his family. At no time were any charges made that the child was less than adequately cared for, or that the relationship between mother and child was anything less than warm and satisfactory. The child enjoyed a strong emotional attachment to both parents.

No problems occurred until the mother filed an action for child support. Only then did the father claim that he should obtain custody of his daughter because it would be better for her to be looked after by his mother (the child's paternal grandmother) rather than in a day care center. The court sided with the father, but the child was not removed from the mother's custody because she appealed the case. The decision was later reversed in a higher court. This reversal clearly stated that a party's arrangements for the child's care while a parent worked or went to school are not an appropriate consideration.

The implications of the issue at stake in this instance go well beyond custody cases. The initial decision, which was explicitly made on the grounds that it is preferable for a child to be cared for by a blood relative (her paternal grandmother) than by strangers (day care center workers), ignored the substantial amount of contact parents and children have, and the substantial amount of parental care children receive even when they spend eight hours a day, five days a week, at a day care center. Furthermore, this decision, which overruled the recommendations of two impartial child welfare groups, obviously implies that day care is always second best to having children taken care of by their own parents or, in this instance, even grandparents. Realistically, that assumption suggests that a woman who really cares about her children should stay home and give up, or at least interrupt, her career; it also means that if she does not, it might one day be held against her if anyone chooses to question her fitness as a mother. Wide acceptance of this view, even though it is contrary to the evidence of the great preponderance of research, could prove to be an obstacle in the path of women's further progress toward equality in the labor market.

A question related to custody that can be as difficult to resolve as the questions involved in custody cases themselves is whether and under what circumstances the custodial parent, most often the mother, should be permitted to move out of state. Growing numbers of divorced parents confront this issue, as American society grows increasingly mobile. On the one hand, the father will find it more difficult to see his children regularly if they live further away; on the other hand, not being able to move may impose serious constraints on a woman who needs to find a job or is offered better opportunities elsewhere, or who wants to marry someone who lives in another state. And, the best interests of the children must be considered. In the past, a woman in this situation was permitted to move only under "exceptional" circumstances. In recent years courts have become somewhat more permissive, though rulings vary considerably from case to case.

* These descriptions draw on Susan Chira, "Custody Fight in Capital: A Working Mother Loses," *New York Times*, September 20, 1994, sec. A, p. 1; Anna Quindlen, "Sometimes You Just Can't Win for Losing. Particularly If You're a Single Mother in America," *New York Times*, July 10, 1994, sec. 1, p. 19; Raymond Hernandez, "Court Ruling Gives Divorced Parents Right to Leave the State," *New York Times*, March 27, 1996, sec. A, p. 1; Leslie Eaton, "Divorced Parents Move, and Custody Gets Trickier," *New York Times*, August 8, 2004, p. 1; *Jennifer Ireland, Plaintiff-Appellant, Cross Appellate v. Steve Smith a/k/a Steven J. Smith, Defendant-Appellee, Cross-Appellant*, Nos. 177431, 182369, Court of Appeals of Michigan, 214 Mich. App. 235; 1995 Mich. App. LEXIS 478, May 3, 1995, Submitted; November 7, 1995, Decided; and Sanford L. Braver, Ira M. Ellman, and William V. Fabricius, "Relocation of Children After Divorce and Children's Best Interests: New Evidence and Legal Considerations," *Journal of Family Psychology* 17, no. 2 (2003): 206–19.

Cohabitation: Opposite-Sex, Unmarried Couples[24]

Opposite-sex cohabitation represents an increasingly common living arrangement, in large part due to changing attitudes about premarital sex. As previously mentioned, since the 1970s, the ratio of unmarried to married couples increased considerably. In some instances, women and men cohabit prior to their first marriage, while others cohabit after one or both is divorced or widowed. Studies on cohabitation were once rare, but now a good deal of research focuses on the economic and social explanations for the rise in cohabitation, and its role vis-à-vis marriage.

Like marriage, cohabitation involves two individuals living together in a single household. Here again, the situation presents possibilities for specialization and economies of scale as well as other gains derived from couples living together as discussed earlier.

[24]Although the term *mixed-sex* or *different-sex* is used by some researchers to distinguish men-women couples from gay and lesbian couples, we use the term *opposite-sex* couple here because of its usage by the U.S. Census Bureau and the general public.

Why then, might some couples choose to cohabit while others marry? One important consideration is the current financial and economic resources of the two partners. Because current employment provides important information about long-term economic security, individuals may choose to cohabit rather than marry until one or both partners have good job prospects. Also, as discussed in Chapter 3, marriage establishes property rights between the two individuals regarding any assets brought into or acquired after setting up a joint household. Thus, one would expect individuals who want to live together to be more likely to cohabit rather than marry if little or no legal protection of property is at issue. Other major factors influencing the decision are likely to include the degree of commitment to the relationship, as well as the desire for and presence of children. The propensity to cohabit is also strongly influenced by social attitudes, which, except among the very religious, have grown increasingly more liberal.[25]

We expect cohabitors to remain together for a shorter period of time than married couples. One reason for this expectation is that cohabitation does not provide legal guarantees for a partner who specializes in homemaking and forgoes the opportunity to maintain and increase labor market skills to the same extent marriage does. Consequently, cohabitors are less likely to become as economically interdependent. In addition, the fact that cohabitation creates few, if any, legal commitments makes it more likely that any personal problems or economic setbacks that arise will lead to breakups.

Consistent with expectations, the median length of time couples spend cohabiting is short—as brief as a year or so, with the cohabitation ending either in marriage or the breakup of the couple. Indeed, overall, more than 50 percent of cohabiting couples eventually get married, suggesting that cohabiting is often not so much an alternative to marriage as a prelude to it.[26] It might be expected that premarital cohabitation would stabilize marriage by providing the partners with more information about each other. Surprisingly, however, little evidence indicates that premarital cohabitation provides this stabilizing effect.[27]

Rates of cohabitation increased substantially among all cohorts but especially among the young. As of the mid 1990s, an estimated 40 percent of the population 15 to 44 years of age cohabited at some time in their lives.[28] For many, cohabitation, albeit brief, serves as part of a larger "family building" process that often includes nonmarital childbearing as well as marriage.[29] One consequence of rising rates of cohabitation is

---

[25]For evidence, see Pamela J. Smock and Sanjiv Gupta, "Cohabitation in North America," in *Just Living Together: Implications for Children, Families and Public Policy*, edited by Alan Booth and Ann C. Crouter (Lawrence Erlbaum Assoc., March 2002), pp. 53–84; Deborah Roempke Graefe and Daniel T. Lichter, "Life Course Transitions of American Children: Parental Cohabitation, Marriage, and Single Motherhood," *Demography* 36, no. 2 (May 1999): 205–17; and Marcia Carlson, Sara McLanahan, and Paula England, "Union Formation in Fragile Families," *Demography* 41, no. 2 (May 2004): 237–61.

[26]Larry L. Bumpass and James A. Sweet, "The Role of Cohabitation in Declining Rates of Marriage," *Journal of Marriage and the Family* 53, no. 4 (November 1991): 913–27; and Larry Bumpass and H.-H. Lu, "Trends in Cohabitation and Implications for Children's Family Context in the United States," *Population Studies* 54, no. 1 (March 2000): 29–41.

[27]Lee A. Lillard, Michael J. Brien, and Linda J. Waite suggest that one reason cohabitors may be less successful at marriage is that they have average unmeasured characteristics, such as a lower average level of commitment, that are more likely to lead to a breakup. Still, even after they account for this "selectivity" issue, they do not find that cohabitation reduces marital dissolution in "Pre-Marital Cohabitation and Subsequent Marital Dissolution: Is It Self-Selection?" *Demography* 32, no. 3 (August 1995): 437–58.

[28]U.S. Census Bureau, *Statistical Abstract of the United States: 1999*, table 66.

[29]See Michael J. Brien, Lee A. Lillard, and Linda J. Waite, "Interrelated Family-Building Behaviors: Cohabitation, Marriage and Nonmarital Conception," *Demography* 36, no. 4 (November 1999): 535–51.

that increasing numbers of children are living with cohabiting parents. For instance, in 2003, just over 40 percent of cohabiting couples included at least one child under age 18, a figure that is only slightly lower than the percent of married-couple families with children under 18 present.[30] Moreover, it is projected that 40 percent of *all* children will spend at least some of their childhood in a cohabiting family.[31]

Increasing rates of cohabitation raise some concerns. For one, cohabiting families are considerably more likely to break up than married-couple families, which puts children at greater risk of the often negative consequences of family disruption.[32] In addition, when cohabitors break up, they are treated differently by the legal system than married couples. For instance, even if they have been together for a long time, neither partner is legally entitled to a spousal benefit under Social Security. Also, cohabiting couples, on average, have considerably lower levels of income than married couples and a much larger fraction live in poverty.[33] As discussed in Chapter 10, these economic difficulties would not be fully remedied by simply having these couples marry; even if they were to do so, they would still have lower earnings, on average, than married couples mainly because they tend to have less education and work experience. Moreover, marriage, per se, would not be likely to equalize the breakup rate, because cohabiting couples appear to be more susceptible to breakup in the first place.

Looking toward the future, it is expected that cohabitation rates will continue to rise, although it is not yet clear to what extent cohabitation will replace marriage rather than remain a prelude to it. One reason for expecting a further increase is that rates are even higher in a number of other economically advanced countries, particularly Sweden, where as many as one in five couples are unmarried. However, one important difference is that cohabitation tends to be of longer duration in Sweden and the other Scandinavian countries.[34]

Cohabitation: Gay and Lesbian Couples

Like traditional marriage and opposite-sex cohabitation, same-sex relationships offer the partners not only companionship and affection, but economic benefits, including the ability to share economic resources and to realize economies of scale. However, even though same-sex partners may also differ in terms of their comparative advantage in the home and in the market to some degree,[35] neither partner is likely to specialize in home production to the same degree as the average married woman. First, as

---

[30]Jason Fields, "America's Families and Living Arrangements: 2003," *Current Population Reports* P20-553 (Washington, DC: U.S. Census Bureau, November 2004).

[31]Bumpass and Lu, "Trends in Cohabitation."

[32]Wendy D. Manning, Pamela J. Smock, and Debarun Majumdar, "The Relative Stability of Cohabiting and Marital Unions for Children," *Population and Research Review* 23, no. 2 (April 2004): 135–59.

[33]Gregory Acs and Sandra Nelson, "The Kids Are Alright? Children's Well-Being and the Rise in Cohabitation," *New Federalism National Survey of America's Families*, Series B, No. B-48 (Washington, DC: Urban Institute, July 2002).

[34]Constance Sorrentino, "The Changing Family in International Perspective," *Monthly Labor Review* 113, no. 3 (March 1990): 41–58.

[35]See Lisa A. Giddings, "Political Economy and the Construction of Gender: The Example of Housework Within Same-Sex Households," *Feminist Economics* 4, no. 2 (Summer 1998): 97–106; M. V. Lee Badgett, "Gender, Sexuality, and Sexual Orientation," *Feminist Economics* 1, no. 1 (Spring 1995): 121–39; and Julie Matthaei, "The Sexual Division of Labor, Sexuality, and Lesbian/Gay Liberation: Toward a Marxist-Feminist Analysis of Sexuality in U.S. Capitalism," in *Homo Economics: Capitalism, Community, and Lesbian and Gay Life*, edited by Amy Gluckman and Betsy Reed (New York: Routledge, 1997), pp. 135–64.

in the case of unmarried opposite-sex couples, same-sex couples have far fewer legal protections than married couples, which makes investment in homemaking skills particularly costly in the event that the couple breaks up.[36] Second, to the extent that young women know they are not likely to enter an opposite-sex relationship, they will have little incentive to specialize in homemaking skills. Specifically, those expecting to have partnerships with other women are more likely, all else equal, to accumulate human capital useful for the labor market as compared with those expecting to be members of a more traditional household. For the same reason, they are also likely to choose more career-oriented, male-dominated occupations. At the same time, young gay men are also likely to acquire mainly skills useful for the labor market because men have traditionally held the role of breadwinner.[37]

Several surveys provide some information about the number of gay men and lesbians, but there are difficulties in obtaining reliable estimates. One difficulty is that gay men and lesbians may be reluctant to identify themselves given prevailing attitudes. Counts also vary considerably depending on the definition used.[38] According to one recent study, about 2.5 percent of men are gay and 1.4 percent of women are lesbians.[39] It is further estimated that about 29 percent of gay men and 44 percent of lesbians were living with a same-sex partner at the time of the survey. As would be expected, the percentage of gays and lesbians who have ever had a same-sex live-in partner is considerably higher, 68 percent and 94 percent, respectively.

Although a smaller fraction of same-sex couples than opposite-sex couples have children, it has nonetheless been estimated that around 5 percent of gay couples and nearly 22 percent of lesbian couples have children. Estimates that include gays and lesbians who do not currently have partners indicate that as many as 14 percent of gay men and 28 percent of lesbians have children, many of them from a prior marriage. These figures suggest that children's living arrangements are far more diverse than

---

[36]Opposite-sex couples in the United States have the option of marrying if they choose, whereas same-sex couples generally do not. Recent exceptions are Massachusetts, where same-sex marriage became legal in 2004, and Vermont, which has permitted civil unions since 2000.

[37]Also, gay men are not expected to reap the same benefits from specialization as married men. This reason, perhaps along with possible employer bias, and the possibility that gay men may trade off higher wage jobs for those that are more open to gays, likely explains why they are found to earn less than heterosexual men, both married and unmarried. Conversely, recent evidence suggests that lesbians earn more than married and unmarried heterosexual women. This is likely due to the fact that they may be more career-oriented than women who are married or expect to marry and may even benefit to the extent that employers view unmarried women as more career-minded. Of course, some lesbians, just like gay men, may trade off higher wages for jobs where they are more accepted. See Dan A. Black, Hoda R. Makar, Seth G. Sanders, and Lowell Taylor, "The Effects of Sexual Orientation on Earnings," *Industrial and Labor Relations Review* 56, no. 3 (April 2003): 449–69; and John M. Blandford, "The Nexus of Sexual Orientation and Gender in the Determination of Earnings," *Industrial and Labor Relations Review* 56, no. 4 (July 2003): 622–42. In earlier work, however, M.V. Lee Badgett found a wage penalty for lesbians in "The Wage Effects of Sexual Orientation Discrimination," *Industrial and Labor Relations Review* 48, no. 4 (July 1995): 726–39.

[38]M.V. Lee Badgett, *Money, Myths and Change: The Economic Lives of Lesbians and Gay Men* (Chicago: University of Chicago Press, 2001), chap. 2.

[39]These estimates are based on survey data pooled from 1989 through 1996. Gays and lesbians are defined as those who reported having had exclusively same-sex relationships during the prior year. These figures, as well as those that follow, are from Dan A. Black, Gary Gates, Seth G. Sanders, and Lowell Taylor, "Demographics of the Gay and Lesbian Population in the United States: Evidence from Available Systematic Data Sources," *Demography* 37, no. 2 (May 2000): 139–55. Considerable regional variation is evident as well; see Jason Ost and Gary Gates, *The Gay and Lesbian Atlas* (Washington, DC: Urban Institute Press, 2004).

Census Bureau categorizations suggest. Moreover, "family" for these children tends to be more broadly defined than for many of those living in heterosexual families.[40]

As for future trends, it is expected that the fraction of same-sex couples, including those with children, will increase to the extent that societal attitudes toward them become more tolerant and other states follow the lead of Massachusetts and permit gay marriage or at least allow for civil unions, as in Vermont. Like marriage, civil unions establish legal rights of gay and lesbian couples, such as rights regarding adoption, pensions, and inheritance. However, civil unions are not generally viewed as having the same social standing as marriage. Further, to the extent that alternative reproductive technologies become less expensive and more acceptable, the fraction of children raised in nontraditional households is likely to further increase.

Fertility

Neoclassical economic theory sheds considerable light on people's decisions about whether to have children, how many to have, and to what extent they should allocate scarce resources to them. According to the economic approach suggested by Gary Becker, parents' demand for children critically depends not only on the benefits they expect to derive from having children but also on the costs of raising them, including the "opportunity cost of time," and the family income available.[41] Fertility is also likely to be affected by the availability and reliability of contraceptive technology, access to abortion, and government tax and transfer policies.

With respect to the demand for children, one obvious economic consideration is the cost of clothing, housing, and education. In 2002, the U.S. Department of Agriculture estimated that the expenditures required for an average married couple to raise a child through age 17 amounted to $173,880.[42] However, a large part of parents' contribution to raising children is the time they devote to childrearing. Even when a great deal of child care is purchased, parents, most often mothers, still devote a good deal of time to finding suitable caregivers, taking care of emergencies, and helping with school work, as well as providing recreation and other enrichment. The time and energy parents devote to these purposes could otherwise be used to obtain more education or training and thus advance their careers, to work longer hours to earn more income, or to enjoy more leisure. Giving up some or all of these constitutes the opportunity cost of rearing children.

---

[40]Nancy E. Rose and Lynn Bravewomon, "Family Webs: A Study of Extended Families in the Lesbian/Gay/Bisexual Community," *Feminist Economics* 4, no. 2 (Summer 1998): 107–9.

[41]Richard A. Easterlin offers a different explanation for changes in fertility and female labor force participation. In his model, the driving force behind changes in these outcomes is that people aspire to achieve at least the same income their parents had when they were growing up. If members of a particular birth cohort are worse off than their parents were, female labor force participation will rise to compensate and fertility will decline. If, on the other hand, their income is higher than what their parents' achieved, the effect on fertility will be positive. See Richard A. Easterlin, "On the Relation of Economic Factors to Recent and Projected Fertility Changes," *Demography* 3 (August 1966): 131–53. For a recent review of Easterlin's work and influence, see Diane J. Macunovich, "Fertility and the Easterlin Hypothesis: An Assessment of the Literature," *Journal of Population Economics* 11, no. (1998): 53–111. For a discussion of other ways to broaden the economic model of fertility, see Robert Pollak and Susan Cotts Watkins, "Cultural and Economic Approaches to Fertility: Proper Marriage or Mesalliance?" *Population and Development Review* 19, no. 3 (September 1993): 467–96.

[42]Mark Lino, *Expenditures on Children by Families, 2002* (U.S. Department of Agriculture, Center for Nutrition Policy and Promotion. Miscellaneous Publication no. 1528-2002, 2002), Table ES-1.

Higher income enables a family to meet the money costs of raising more children, and so one might expect to see a positive relationship between income and fertility. In fact, however, fertility tends to decline with income. One reason is that parents with higher incomes tend to spend more income on what has been called child *"quality"* rather than on the *quantity* of children.[43] Child quality may be enhanced by expenditures on piano lessons, a spot at soccer camp, or advanced classes in science, and for older children, paying for college and perhaps graduate school and supporting them while they are students. Because education and skills are particularly valued in today's labor market, parents who make these kinds of expenditures provide their children with considerable advantages. Another dimension of child quality is children's health, which also requires expenditures, either through paying insurance premiums or out-of-pocket costs. Parents with strong preferences for child quality are likely to have fewer children because higher expenditures on child quality increase the costs of child quantity (i.e., such expenditures increase the costs of having additional children). For instance, parents who are committed to providing a college education for each of their children will find an additional child more costly than those solely focusing on getting their children through high school.

Because women continue to be the primary caregivers for children, changing economic opportunities of women and men tend to result in different effects on the fertility decision. As women's wages rise, the opportunity cost of the time they spend with children increases, leading to a negative substitution effect on fertility. In other words, as children become more expensive, the individual is likely to substitute away from children toward the consumption of other goods or services that provide utility. Even though a higher wage is expected to also have a positive income effect encouraging fertility, the substitution effect of the wage increase is likely to dominate for women. Similarly, because women's wages are a key determinant of their labor force participation, we would expect to observe a negative association between fertility and women's labor market activity. Over the long term, the relationship between women's wages (or labor force participation) and fertility depends on the relative strength of competing factors. On the one hand, as women become better educated and more career-oriented, this raises the opportunity cost of childrearing, thereby reducing the demand for children.[44] On the other hand, the availability of high-quality child care, at least for those who can afford it, as well as the increasing acceptance of using it, probably reduce the opportunity cost of child rearing to some extent. In principle, access to child care makes it easier for women to combine employment with having a family.

For men, the income effect of a wage increase is likely to dominate the substitution effect because they generally do not give up as much of their time to provide child care. Therefore, as men's wages increase we would expect to see a rise in fertility, all else equal, though as discussed, families are also likely to use the added income to increase spending per child, rather than just increase their family size.

---

[43]Becker, *A Treatise on the Family*; Gary Becker and Nigel Tomes, "Child Endowments and the Quantity and Quality of Children," *Journal of Political Economy* 84, no. 4, part 2 (August 1976): S143–S162; and Robert Willis, "What Have We Learned from the Economics of the Family?"

[44]For instance, McKinley L. Blackburn, David E. Bloom, and David Neumark found that late childbearers tend to invest more heavily in human capital than early childbearers in "Fertility Timing, Wages and Human Capital," *Journal of Population Economics* 6, no. 1 (1993): 1–30. Late childbearing would also be expected to reduce the number of children per woman, all else equal. See also Ronald R. Rindfuss, S. Philip Morgan, and Kate Offutt, "Education and the Changing Age Pattern of American Fertility: 1963–1989," *Demography* 33, no. 3 (August 1996): 277–90.

In addition to women's wages and family income, a number of other factors may affect fertility rates. For instance, the introduction of new and more effective methods of birth control, such as the birth control pill, allows couples to limit their fertility more easily and effectively. These methods, along with reproductive technologies that facilitate births to women at older ages, also permit more control over the timing of births. Evidence also indicates that access to abortion affects fertility rates.[45]

Table 9-2 and Figure 9-1 show the considerable fluctuation in the fertility rate since the 1940s. From the end of World War II until the early 1960s—the period known as the "baby boom"—the fertility rate reached a peak of 3.7 children per woman (3,690 children per 1,000 women) between 1955 and 1959, far above the replacement rate of 2.1 children per woman. By 1976, however, during the "baby bust," the rate declined to as low as 1.7 children per woman. The cohort that was born after the baby boom and includes the baby bust period is referred to in the media as "Generation X." After a number of years of relatively low fertility, the fertility rate rose modestly starting in the

TABLE 9-2 Total Fertility Rates, 1940–2002	
Years	*Total Fertility Rate*[a]
1940–1944	2,523
1945–1949	2,985
1950–1954	3,337
1955–1959	3,690
1960–1964	3,449
1965–1969	2,622
1970–1974	2,094
1975–1979	1,774
1980–1984	1,819
1985–1989	1,899
1990–1994	2,042
1995–1999	2,022
2000	2,056
2001	2,034
2002	2,013

[a]The number of births that a cohort of 1,000 women would have if they experienced the age-specific birthrates occurring in the current year throughout their childbearing years. Dividing by 1,000 provides a measure of births per woman.

Source: U.S. Census Bureau, *Statistical Abstract of the United States*, 1984, 1999; U.S. Department of Health and Human Services, "Births: Final Data for 2002," *National Vital Statistics Reports* 52, no. 10 (December 17, 2003), at www.cdc.gov/nchs.

---

[45]See, for instance, Goldin and Katz, "Career and Marriage in the Age of the Pill"; and Elizabeth Oltmans Anant, Jonathan Gruber, and Phillip B. Levine, "Abortion Legalization and Life Cycle Fertility," National Bureau of Economic Research Working Paper 10705 (August 2004).

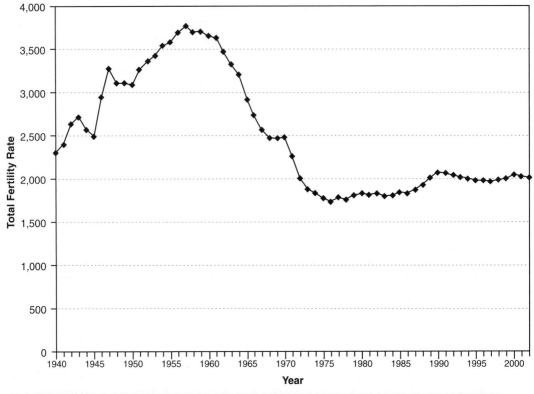

FIGURE 9-1   Total Fertility Rates, 1940–2002

mid 1980s, and reached the replacement rate level by 1990, where it remains today. Apart from the fertility rate, the total number of births is also related to the absolute number of women in their childbearing years. The baby boomers produced a large cohort of children starting in the early to mid-1980s referred to as the "echo of the baby boom," the "baby boomlet," and, more recently, "Generation Y."

These fluctuations in the fertility rate occurred, in substantial part, as a result of variations in the strength of the factors discussed earlier. The baby boom took place during a time of prosperity and rising real wages of men and women. Because relatively few married women of childbearing age were employed in those days, the main effect was an increase in fertility due to the income effect of husbands' rising wages. A recent study also points to the role of falling prices of labor-saving appliances, such as the vacuum cleaner and clothes dryer, in spurring their adoption, and, in turn likely reducing the burden of larger families.[46] Nonetheless, the magnitude of the baby boom probably cannot be fully explained without taking into account the postponement of births during the Great Depression of the 1930s and World War II, as well as a variety of social and cultural factors.

---

[46]"Jeremy Greenwood, Ananth Seshadri, and Guillaume Vandenbroucke, "The Baby Boom and Baby Bust," *American Economic Review* 95, no. 1 (March 2005): 183–207.

The subsequent sharp drop in fertility beginning in the early 1960s coincided with both rapid increases in the labor force participation rate of young women and advances in contraceptive techniques. The downward trend can also be explained in part by the higher cost of dropping out of the labor force to bear and raise children for women who found their labor market opportunities substantially increased and became increasingly committed to their careers. Such women were also more likely to find their work absorbing and fulfilling. The modest rise in fertility from the mid-1980s to the early 1990s may reflect a "catching up" phenomenon, as women who did not have children earlier chose to have them at a later time.[47] It may also, in part, reflect the decision of some couples to start their families earlier in light of publicity about the difficulties that some older women face in becoming pregnant.[48] Since then, the level has fluctuated only modestly at about 2.1 children per woman.

Future trends in fertility are difficult to predict, but it is unlikely that the overall fertility rate will rise significantly from its present level, especially given women's continuing high levels of education and commitment to market work. One might even project that fertility rates will fall somewhat given the recent experience of West European countries, including Spain and Italy, as well as the experience of Japan. Rates in these countries steadily declined and are now close to 1 child per woman as discussed in Chapter 11. At the same time, the negative effect of these factors on fertility may be mitigated, at least to some extent, by the increasing involvement of fathers with their children, and by the greater availability of good child care, as well as any new tax provisions or subsidies reducing the financial burden of raising and educating children that may be enacted in the future.

In the remainder of this section, we review recent trends in fertility for various subgroups. For instance, despite sizable fluctuations in the overall fertility rate, the share of births to unmarried mothers increased markedly since the 1970s, though it shows an apparent leveling in recent years. Table 9-3 indicates that births to unmarried mothers rose from 11 percent of all births in 1970 to just over one-third by 2002. Several factors contributed to this increase. First, there was a decline in births to married women. Hence, even if births to unmarried women had not increased, the proportion of such births would have risen. Second, this figure depends on both the number of unmarried women as well as their probability of giving birth. As shown in Table 9-3, between 1980 and 2002, the birthrate among unmarried women actually declined among blacks, and remains relatively low among whites, though it increased for this group. What changed most is the number of unmarried women, which increased substantially as a result of delays in marriage.[49]

Births to unmarried mothers are related to many of the same factors that tend to reduce incentives to marry. For instance, women's increased labor market opportunities

---

[47]DaVanzo and Rahman, "American Families." Blackburn, Bloom, and Neumark, "Fertility Timing, Wages and Human Capital," suggest that this postponement was associated with women's greater investment in human capital.

[48]For recent discussions, see Karen Springen, Julie Scelfo and Ellise Pierce, "Should You Have Your Baby Now?" *Newsweek* (August 13, 2001), pp. 40–49; and Sylvia Ann Hewlett, *Creating a Life: What Every Woman Needs to Know About Having a Baby and Career* (New York: Hyperion, 2003).

[49]Rebecca Blank, "Teen Pregnancy: Government Programs Are Not the Cause," *Feminist Economics* 1, no. 2 (Summer 1995): 47–58.

TABLE 9-3   Selected Birth Rates, 1970–2002

	1970	1980	1990	2002
Birth Rates (Births per 1,000 Women in Specified Group)[a]				
Overall birth rate, ages 15–44	87.9	68.4	70.9	64.8
Teen birth rate, ages 15–19	68.3	53.0	59.9	43.0
Older mother birth rate				
Ages 35–39	31.7	19.8	31.7	41.4
Ages 40–44	8.1	3.9	5.5	8.3
Unmarried Birth Rates (Births per 1,000 Unmarried Women in Specified Group)[b]				
Unmarried birth rate, ages 15–44	26.4	29.4	43.8	43.7
Whites	13.9	18.1	32.9	38.9
Blacks	95.5	81.1	90.5	66.2
Unmarried teen birth rate, ages 15–19	22.4	27.6	42.5	35.4
Whites	10.9	16.5	30.6	30.4
Blacks	96.9	87.9	106.0	64.8
Unmarried older mother birth rate				
Ages 35–39	13.6	9.7	17.3	20.8
Ages 40–44	3.5	2.6	3.6	5.4
Types of Births				
Unmarried births as % of all births	10.7	18.4	28.0	34.0
Whites	5.7	11.2	20.4	28.5
Blacks	37.6	55.5	66.5	68.2
Unmarried teen births as % of all teen births	31.9	48.3	67.6	80.0
Unmarried teen births as % of all unmarried births	50.1	40.8	31.0	24.9

Notes: For data stratified by race, race refers to child's race for 1970; data refer to mother's race for other years.
[a]For instance, overall birth rate for ages 15–44 refers to births to women ages 15–44 per 1,000 women in that age group.
[b]For instance, unmarried birth rate for ages 15–44 refers to births to unmarried women ages 15–44 per 1,000 unmarried women in that age group.

Sources: U.S. Department of Health and Human Services, "Births: Final Data for 2002," *National Vital Statistics Reports* 52, no. 10 (December 17, 2003); and U.S. Department of Health and Human Services, *Nonmarital Childbearing in the United States, 1940–99,* 48, no. 16 (October 18, 2000), Table 4.

provide them with greater financial means to support a family. In addition, men's ability to support a family declined among the less educated, and welfare also likely played a role, albeit a small one.[50] Finally, premarital sex and unmarried childbearing are more widely accepted than in the past and unmarried women who become pregnant are now far less

---

[50]For evidence on the poor job prospects of low-skilled workers, see Chinhui Juhn, "Decline of Male Labor Market Participation: The Role of Declining Market Opportunities," *Quarterly Journal of Economics* 107, no. 1 (February 1992): 79–122. Regarding the effect of welfare, see Moffitt, "The Effect of Welfare on Marriage and Fertility." Robert J. Willis also suggests that unmarried fertility may be a result of an imbalance in the sex ratio in "The Economics of Fatherhood," *American Economic Review* 90, no. 2 (May 2000): 378–82.

likely to get married before the baby's birth.[51] In fact, in many cases, unmarried mothers are living with their child's father. Estimates suggest that as many as 40 percent of all non-marital births in the United States in the early 1990s occurred to cohabiting couples, rather than to women living alone.[52] Moreover, a recent study found that whether or not the child's parents are living together, the fathers are often around at the time of the birth, want to help raise their children, and more often than not are romantically involved with the mother. These couples are termed *fragile families*, because, quite often, the parents have low levels of educational attainment, unstable employment histories, and low earnings, and are quite susceptible to breakup.[53]

The figure that continues to receive perhaps the greatest attention is the rate of teen births in the United States, which is considerably higher than in other economically advanced countries, including Canada and the United Kingdom.[54] Although the U.S. rate still remains quite high, it is rather encouraging that it declined substantially since the early 1990s, from a high of 62 births per 1,000 teens in 1991 to a historical U.S. low of 43 births per 1,000 in 2002. Nonetheless, teen births remain a particular concern in that a growing share of them are to unmarried mothers (fully 80 percent in 2002, up from only one-third in 1970). This shift is in large part due to the significant decline in the rate of teen marriage. Another striking recent trend shown in Table 9-3 is that the birthrate for unmarried teens declined most markedly for African American teens, though their rate remains substantially higher than that for white teens.

Teen pregnancy and births to unmarried teens may be related to poor labor market prospects for less-educated young people, which lower the opportunity cost of pregnancy for young women and reduce the availability of young men with good economic prospects. Other factors, including the availability of welfare, access to contraceptives, public support for family planning, as well as the availability and affordability of abortion, may also affect trends in teen pregnancy and childbearing.[55] Notably, evidence indicates that the recent reduction in the overall teen birth rate, for the most part, resulted from a decline in teen pregnancy, due to reduced sexual activity and increased use of contraceptives, and not the result of an increase in abortions.[56]

---

[51]George A. Akerlof, Janet L. Yellen, and Michael L. Katz argue that the availability of the birth control pill and legal abortion reduced the cost of premarital sex as well as unmarried women's ability to "bargain" for marriage in the event of pregnancy. These changes, in turn, lead to a reduction in the number of marriages following pregnancy and a rise in nonmarital fertility; see "An Analysis of Out-of-Wedlock Childbearing in the United States," *Quarterly Journal of Economics* 111, no. 2 (May 1996): 277–317.

[52]Bumpass and Lu, "Trends in Cohabitation."

[53]Sara McLanahan and Irwin Garfinkel, "The Fragile Families and Child Well-Being Study: Questions, Design, and a Few Preliminary Results" (University of Wisconsin–Madison: Institute for Research on Poverty), Discussion Paper No. 1208–00 (May 2000).

[54]Susheela Singh and Jacqueline E. Darroch, "Adolescent Pregnancy and Childbearing: Levels and Trends in Developed Countries," *Family Planning Perspectives* 32, no. 1 (Jan./Feb. 2000):14–23; and UNICEF, "A League Table of Teenage Births in Rich Nations, *Innocenti Report Card*, no. 3 (Florence, Italy: Innocenti Research Centre, July 2001).

[55]See Barbara Wolfe, Kathryn Wilson, and Robert Haveman, "The Role of Economic Incentives in Teenage Nonmarital Childbearing Choices," *Journal of Public Economics* 81, no. 3 (September 2001):473–511; Shelly Lundberg and Robert D. Plotnick, "Adolescent Premarital Childbearing: Do Economic Incentives Matter?" *Journal of Labor Economics* 13, no. 2 (April 1995): 177–200; Daniel T. Lichter, Diane K. McLaughlin, and David C. Ribar, "State Abortion Policy, Geographic Access to Abortion Providers and Changing Family Formation," *Family Planning Perspectives* 30, no. 6 (December 1998): 281–87; and Moffitt, "The Effect of Welfare on Marriage and Fertility."

[56]For details by race and ethnicity, see Alan Guttmacher Institute, *U.S. Teenage Pregnancy Statistics: Overall Trends, Trends by Race and Ethnicity and State by State Information* (New York and Washington: The Allen Guttmacher Institute, February 19, 2004), Table 1.

Delays of childbearing by young women should lead to several positive outcomes. For instance, the health of children would be expected to improve, because babies born to teens tend to have more health problems, beginning with premature birth and low birth weight. For the young women themselves, deferring the birth of their first child enables them to spend more time acquiring an education and job skills that will ultimately place them and the children they have later in a much better economic position.

Recent evidence also points to an increasing divergence in women's timing of childbearing, depending on their level of educational attainment. A long-standing pattern is that college-educated women delay childbearing somewhat more than less-educated women, principally because they tend to be more career-oriented, and the opportunity cost of having children early in their careers is likely to be quite substantial. However, in recent years, although the average age of first birth rose for all women, it increased substantially more for college-educated women.[57] The net result is that by 2002, among women ages 25 to 34, 24 percent of women who completed just high school remained childless as compared to 55 percent of those with a bachelor's degree.[58] In addition to rising educational attainment, increased availability of reproductive technologies also likely encouraged delays in childbearing.

Table 9-3 also shows that birthrates among women age 35 and older rose substantially since 1980 and are now even higher than in 1970. The important difference, however, between 1970 and the current situation is that, in the 1970s, women generally started their childbearing in their twenties, and because family size was larger, many continued to have children even into their early forties. In more recent years, many college-educated women delayed childbearing, and it is now much more likely that births to older mothers are first births. The figures in Table 9-3 also reflect the previously mentioned surge in motherhood among unmarried women since the 1980s, especially among those ages 35 to 39, but even among those ages 40 to 44. Still, given the low numbers of such births, they remain the exception.

CHANGING FAMILY STRUCTURE AND ECONOMIC WELL-BEING

The U.S. labor force was once composed almost entirely of workers with few if any responsibilities for homemaking. The majority were married men with wives who were full-time homemakers, while most of the others were single. Today the labor force includes a growing proportion of workers from **dual-earner families**, in which both husbands and wives participate in the paid labor force, and from **single-parent families**. As we shall see, the structure of workers' families presents substantial implications for the well-being of workers and their families. The policy issues raised by these changes will be discussed in Chapter 10.

Dual-Earner Families

As shown in Table 9-4, over the period 1976 to 2001 dual-earner families emerged as the predominant structure among married couples, rising from 50 to nearly 60 percent

---

[57]See, for instance, David T. Ellwood and Christopher Jencks, "The Spread of Single-Parent Families in the United States Since 1960," mimeo, Harvard University (October 2002), Table 2; and Steven P. Martin, "Delayed Marriage and Childbearing: Implications and Measurement of Diverging Trends in Family Timing," in *Social Inequality*, edited by Kathryn Neckerman (New York: Russell Sage Foundation, forthcoming).
[58]"Fertility of American Women: June 2002," *Current Population Reports* P20-548 (October 2003).

TABLE 9-4 Dual-Earner Couples, 1976–2001				
	1976	*1980*	*1990*	*2001*
Dual-Earner Couples				
As % of all married couples	50.1	53.5	59.4	59.4
As % of all married couples with employed husband	59.4	64.5	73.4	74.6
% where both spouses employed full-time, full-year	33.0	36.0	44.1	52.3
% where wife has higher annual earnings than husband	n.a.	15.9	21.0	24.1
Median Income of Married Couples ($2001)				
All married couples	n.a.	n.a.	$52,394	$60,335
Husband only employed	n.a.	n.a.	$46,651	$50,926
Dual earners	n.a.	n.a.	$62,164	$73,407
Both spouses employed full-time, full-year	n.a.	n.a.	$72,321	$81,136
Ratio of median income of dual earners to those with husband only employed	n.a.	n.a.	1.3	1.4

Notes: Dual-earner couple is defined as married couple with both spouses employed. Figures are for given or adjacent year.

n.a. = Not available.

Sources: U.S. Census Bureau, Historical Income Tables, "Work Experience of Husband and Wife—Married-Couple Families (All Races), by Median and Mean Income, 1976 to 2001"; and "Married-Couple Families with Wives' Earnings Greater than Husbands' Earnings: 1981 to 2001," at www.census.gov.

of all such families. Even more striking, in 2001, dual-earner families constituted 75 percent of all couples with an employed husband, and in over 50 percent of dual-earner families, both spouses worked full-time, full-year. As would be expected, the explanations for the rise in dual-earner families are much the same as those offered for women's increased labor force participation discussed in Chapter 4. In large part, the increase is a result of women's increased education, training, and experience as well as women's response to their own increased labor market opportunities. This view is consistent with the fact that increases in labor force participation are most pronounced among women who earn high wages who are also married to high-wage men.[59] As we saw in Chapter 3, women who completely specialize in homemaking face considerable risk, especially in the event of divorce. Most likely, some married women work for pay to mitigate these risks. Another explanation is that many families cannot achieve an acceptable standard of living unless both partners are employed.

In any case, married women's earnings are an important source of family income today. As shown in Table 9-4, the incomes of dual-earner married couples, on average, are 40 percent higher than those with just an employed husband. One consequence of women's improved qualifications and increasing labor market opportunities, in conjunction with declines in the real earnings of less-educated men, is that the earnings of

---

[59]For a detailed discussion of trends in earnings and employment among spouses, see Chinhui Juhn and Kevin M. Murphy, "Wage Inequality and Family Labor Supply," *Journal of Labor Economics* 15, no. 1, pt. 1 (January 1997): 72–97.

employed wives rose relative to their husbands, on average,[60] and the percentage of wives with higher annual earnings than their husbands also increased, from only 16 percent in 1981 to 24 percent by 2001.[61] These trends, both women's increased earnings and the increase in the fraction of wives who earn more than their husbands, would be expected to increase women's bargaining power within marriage.

In dual-earner couples, whose career takes precedence—whether it is the wife's or husband's—is likely to affect the wages of the spouse. More often than not, husbands have the primary career in the family, which tends to benefit them, but tends to negatively affect the level and growth of their wives' wages. One reason is that those with secondary careers are less able to determine their place of residence so as to maximize their wages and opportunities for advancement. Further, wives' "secondary" earnings position in the family reduces their bargaining power with their current employer because they cannot make as credible a threat as people who can readily move to further their careers.[62] Even if spouses pursue equal careers, they may both bear a wage penalty to the extent that their joint location decision limits their job opportunities and potential for career advancement.

Considerable evidence shows that women also suffer a wage penalty if they have children.[63] Estimates of the "motherhood penalty" vary, but lesser levels of labor market experience, resulting from time out of the labor force, appear to explain much, but by no means all, of it. Another factor may be the loss of the reward to firm-specific training if women permanently leave their current employers when they have a child. Although some of these mothers may choose to stay home with their children, others may leave the labor force due to insufficient access to job-protected maternity leave. As discussed in Chapter 10, adequate family leave policies should reduce these negative consequences and help "level the playing field" for mothers and others who provide care for family members.

What continues to raise particular attention is that mothers earn less than other women, even those with the same labor market experience and human capital. At least part of the explanation for this remaining wage penalty is that mothers' greater household and child care responsibilities may leave them with less available effort or time for their jobs, thereby negatively affecting wages. Also, inflexible work schedules of some employed mothers may make it difficult to juggle paid work and family, leading to

---

[60]Francine D. Blau, "Trends in the Well-Being of American Women, 1970–1995," *Journal of Economic Literature* 36, no. 1 (March 1998): 112–65.

[61]Anne E. Winkler, Timothy D. McBride, and Courtney Andrews find that in the majority of couples in which the wife earns more than her husband, this pattern persists for some period of time; see "Wives Who Outearn Their Husbands: A Transitory or Persistent Phenomenon for Couples?" *Demography* (forthcoming).

[62]For further discussion, see Anne E. Winkler and David C. Rose, "Career Hierarchy in Dual-Earner Families," *Research in Labor Economics*, edited by Solomon Polachek (Greenwich, Connecticut: JAI Press, 1999), pp. 147–72; Joyce Jacobsen and Laurence M. Levin, "Marriage and Migration: Comparing Gains and Losses from Migration for Couples and Singles," *Social Science Quarterly* 78, no. 3 (September 1997): 688–709; and Kristin Keith and Abagail McWilliams, "Job Mobility and Gender-Based Wage Growth Differentials," *Economic Inquiry* 35, no. 2 (April 1997): 320–33.

[63]For theory and evidence, see for instance, Jane Waldfogel, "Understanding the 'Family Gap' in Pay for Women with Children," *Journal of Economic Perspectives* 12, no. 1 (Winter 1998): 137–56; Michelle J. Budig and Paula England, "The Wage Penalty for Motherhood," *American Sociological Review* 66 (April 2001): 204–25; and Deborah J. Anderson, Melissa Binder and Kate Krause, "The Motherhood Wage Penalty Revisited: Experience, Heterogeneity, Work Effort and Work-Schedule Flexibility," *Industrial and Labor Relations Review* 56, no. 2 (January 2003): 273–94.

greater absenteeism, and, in turn, lower wages.[64] Mothers may also bear a wage penalty as compared to nonmothers with the same labor market experience if they are not able to return to their original employer after childbirth, but instead must change firms. This situation might occur, for instance, if their employer does not provide adequate job-related maternity leave. In such a case, these women lose out on the benefits of firm-specific training along with any potential rewards from an especially good job match.[65] A further explanation for mothers' lower earnings, based on some evidence, is that women who are especially career-oriented, with a higher potential wage, are more likely to remain childless. In this case, although the presence of children is associated with lower wages, children do not *cause* lower wages.[66] Researchers point to other possible explanations as well. For instance, mothers with a choice among a range of jobs may deliberately choose those that offer more flexibility but pay lower wages, though one recent study does not find this factor to be an important one.[67] It is also possible that employers discriminate against women with children.

For men, marriage is generally associated with an increase in their wages, most likely due to the benefits of specialization in the family.[68] Wages are also higher for fathers than other men, presumably because fatherhood increases the incentive to work harder to support the family. This effect appears to be greater for male children, suggesting some preference for boys.[69] Among married couples, some evidence indicates that husbands with employed wives bear a wage penalty, as compared to their counterparts who are the sole earners in their families.[70] For a number of reasons, men with employed wives may not do as well. Employers may still look askance at men not in a "traditional" family, particularly if the wife is employed full-time, or they may believe these men do not need as much income. As noted previously, the wife's employment

---

[64]Gary Becker first theorized that household responsibilities may reduce available effort on the job in "Human Capital, Effort, and the Sexual Division of Labor," *Journal of Labor Economics* 3, no. 1, pt. 2 (January 1985): 33–58. For evidence on this and other theories, see Joni Hersch and Leslie Stratton "Housework, Fixed Effects, and Wages of Married Workers," *Journal of Human Resources* 32, no. 2 (Spring 1997): 285–307; Leslie S. Stratton, "Why Does More Housework Lower Women's Wages? Testing Hypotheses Involving Job Effort and Hours Flexibility," *Social Science Quarterly* 82, no. 1 (March 2001): 67–76; and Anderson, Binder and Krause, "The Motherhood Wage Penalty Revisited."

[65]Jane Waldfogel, "Working Mothers Then and Now: A Cross Cohort Analysis of the Effects of Maternity Leave on Women's Pay," *Gender and Family Issues in the Workplace*, edited by Francine D. Blau and Ronald Ehrenberg (New York, Russell Sage Foundation, 1997), pp. 92–126.

[66]Shelly Lundberg and Elaina Rose, "Parenthood and the Earnings of Married Men and Women," *Labour Economics* 7, no. 6 (November 2000): 689–710.

[67]Budig and England, "The Wage Penalty for Motherhood."

[68]This explanation is also supported by evidence that cohabiting men, except for those who have cohabited a long time, do not receive a wage premium; see Leslie S. Stratton, "Examining the Wage Differential for Married and Cohabiting Men," *Economic Inquiry* 40, no. 2 (April 2002):199–212.

[69]For a comprehensive review of studies on the marriage premium for men, see Ribar, "What Do Scientists Know About the Benefits of Marriage?" Regarding the effects of fatherhood, see Shelly J. Lundberg and Elaina Rose, "The Effects of Sons and Daughters on Men's Labor Supply and Wages," *Review of Economics and Statistics* 84, no.2 (May 2002): 251–68; and Dahl and Moretti, "The Demand for Sons."

[70]For evidence that having an employed wife leads to a wage penalty see Hyunbae Chun and Injae Lee, "Why Do Married Men Earn More: Productivity or Marriage Selection?" *Economic Inquiry* 39, no. 2 (April 2001): 307–19. Julie L. Hotchkiss and Robert E. Moore, "Testing for and Decomposing the Working Spouse Effect: Accounting for Endogeneity of the Wife's Decision to Work," *Industrial and Labor Relations Review* 52, no. 3 (April 1999): 410–23; and Jeffrey S. Gray, "The Fall in Men's Return to Marriage: Declining Productivity Effects or Changing Selection?" *Journal of Human Resources* 32, no. 3 (Summer 1997): 481–504. On the other hand, Joyce P. Jacobsen and Wendy L. Rayack find no effect of wives' employment on husbands' wages in "Do Men Whose Wives Work Really Earn Less?" *American Economic Review* 86, no. 2 (May 1996): 268–73.

may also restrict the husband's mobility, or it may lower his productivity as a result of less spousal career support or greater home responsibilities.[71] On the other hand, the husband's lower earnings could be the cause rather than the result of the wife's employment. At any rate, although a wife's employment may negatively affect her husband's earnings, it is clear that, on balance, her paycheck increases total family income and frequently helps raise families above the poverty line.

Apart from considering the effect of the rise in dual-earner families on wives' and husbands' incomes, separate and combined, it is also instructive to consider the effect of this trend on income inequality among married couples. Over the past several decades, income inequality among married couples increased. On the one hand, the larger proportion of women in the labor force served to reduce income inequality among married couples because there are now fewer couples with wives who have zero earnings. On the other hand, the correlation between the earnings of husbands and wives increased. Although this positive relationship, which simply reflects the fact that men and women with higher earnings potential tend to be married to one another, always existed, it grew stronger.[72] To date, it is not clear whether, on net, the rising employment and earnings of wives increased income inequality or caused it to rise less than might have otherwise been the case.[73] In any case, it is clear that the primary factor causing family income inequality to rise is the large increase in earnings inequality among husbands.

Maternal Employment and Children's Outcomes

A particularly emotionally charged issue concerns the effect of maternal employment on children's development. In principle, the question should be asked about parental rather than just maternal employment; however, it is still commonly accepted that the father will be working for pay full-time and, as of now, that assumption is realistic. Even so, although most research in the past ignored the role of the father entirely, some limited attention is now being paid to the influence of fathers' employment on their children.[74]

Some decades ago, the increased labor force participation of married women with infants and small children prompted study of the effect of maternal employment on children's development. More recently, following the 1996 welfare legislation, single mothers are required to seek employment as a condition for receiving welfare benefits. Consequently, considerable interest now focuses on how this work requirement affects

---

[71]These reasons are cited in Hotchkiss and Moore, "Testing for and Decomposing the Working Spouse Effect."

[72]John Pencavel, "Assortative Mating by Schooling and the Work Behavior of Wives and Husbands," *American Economic Review* 88, no. 2 (May 1998): 326–29.

[73]For evidence that rising wives' employment did not increase married-couple inequality, see Maria Cancian, Sheldon Danziger, and Peter Gottschalk, "Working Wives and Family Income Inequality Among Married Couples," in *Uneven Tides: Rising Inequality in America*, edited by Sheldon Danziger and Peter Gottschalk (New York: Russell Sage Foundation, 1993); and Maria Cancian and Deborah Reed, "The Impact of Wives' Earnings on Income Inequality: Issues and Estimates," *Demography* 36, no. 2 (May 1999): 173–84. Lynn Karoly and Gary Burtless reach the opposite conclusion in "Demographic Changes, Rising Earnings Inequality, and the Distribution of Personal Well-Being, 1959–1989," *Demography* 32, no. 3 (August 1995): 379–406.

[74]See for instance, Toby L. Parcel and Elizabeth G. Meaghan, *Parents' Jobs and Children's Lives* (New York: Aldine de Gruyter, 1994); and Christopher J. Ruhm, "Parental Employment and Child Cognitive Development," *Journal of Human Resources* 39, no. 1 (Winter 2004): 155–92.

outcomes, both for preschoolers and for older children who are now less likely to have parental supervision when they get home from school.

Research clearly shows that children's development is determined by a great many factors in addition to mother's employment. These factors include the innate characteristics of the children themselves, their sex, the number of children in the family, the family's level of resources, parents' characteristics, such as their level of educational attainment and the mother's sensitivity and responsiveness to the children's needs, the role in their lives of their father, of other family members, and of close friends, the quality of their alternative care, and last but by no means least, the nature of the community where they live. In addition, many aspects of children's development merit consideration other than merely progress in cognition, educational attainment, and whether a girl becomes pregnant in her teens, the criteria most frequently employed by economists to gauge child outcomes. Social and emotional development is obviously important as well, as are such long-term outcomes as the stability of their marriages and their success in raising their own children. Again the evidence shows that many different factors influence these various outcomes as well.[75]

Another factor to consider, as discussed in Chapter 3, is that nonemployed women often engage in other household activities when at home with their children, so that the difference between the amount of time that employed and nonemployed mothers spend in one-on-one activities with their children is smaller than might initially be suspected. Also, many employed mothers work part-time. Further, as indicated in Chapter 3, fathers' time with children increased in many families, which should also serve to reduce any potential negative effects of mothers' employment on children's development.[76]

The general consensus among researchers is that children between ages two and four tend to do better in center day care both intellectually and socially than children cared for entirely at home. For infants, however, the evidence remains more mixed, with some recent studies, in particular, finding negative effects on their later cognitive development when their mother is employed.[77] Even though these studies do consider many relevant factors, an important qualification is that they are not able to fully account for the quality of nonmaternal care provided, which might attenuate any negative effects. Also, maternal employment provides additional resources to the families, which tend to benefit children. A particular challenge faced by researchers in this field and those interpreting these findings is that the factors affecting children's outcomes

---

[75]For a review of the issues, see Jack P. Shonkoff and Deborah A. Phillips, eds. *From Neurons to Neighborhoods: The Science of Early Child Development* (Washington, DC: National Research Council, 2000), especially chaps. 10 and 11.

[76]Suzanne M. Bianchi, "Maternal Employment and Time with Children: Dramatic Change or Surprising Continuity?" *Demography* 37, no. 4 (November 2000): 401–14; and Joseph H. Pleck, "Balancing Work and Family," *Scientific American Presents* 10, no. 2 (Summer 1999): 38–43.

[77]For recent evidence, see Ruhm, "Parental Employment and Child Cognitive Development"; Chalres L. Baum II, "Does Early Maternal Employment Harm Child Development? An Analysis of the Potential Benefits of Leave Taking," *Journal of Labor Economics* 21, no. 2 (April 2003): 409–48; and Jane Waldfogel, "Child Care, Women's Employment, and Child Outcomes," *Journal of Population Economics* 15, no. 3 (August 2002): 527–48.

are highly interrelated, making it extremely difficult to isolate the influence of a single factor.[78]

As already mentioned, a critical dimension of this issue is the extent to which the *quality* of nonmaternal child care affects children's development. Studies of specific child care programs provide evidence on this point. Quality is measured either in terms of institutional features of child care settings such as teacher training, group size, and child-teacher ratios, or in terms of children's experiences in child care, such as the amount of verbal interaction between children and teachers or whether "developmentally appropriate" activities are provided. As might be expected, settings that tend to be of high quality in one dimension tend to also be of high quality in others. Findings vary but evidence indicates that quality of care does matter. For instance, recent research found that the amount of verbal interaction between child care providers and children positively influences children's outcomes, though factors related to the child's own family environment are consistently stronger determinants of their development than attributes of day care. The conclusion that the quality of child care matters is supported, for instance, by the success of Head Start, a preschool program targeted at low-income children and funded by the federal government, as well as by positive results from other early intervention programs.[79] Even though children in low-income families are arguably in the greatest need of quality child care, regrettably, they are also the least able to access it because such care is expensive and tends to be in inadequate supply, as discussed further in Chapter 10.

The impact on school-aged and older children of mothers' employment is largely favorable, with positive effects on children's academic success and on daughters' self-esteem.[80] Nonetheless, some research conducted in the aftermath of welfare reform documented negative effects of maternal employment on older children's behavior, presumably due to a lack of supervision.[81]

Single-Parent Families

As the demographic trends reviewed earlier suggest, single-parent families are increasingly common in the United States, especially families maintained by mothers.[82] Table 9-5 indicates that, among families with a child or children under age 18 present, the percentage of mother-only families increased from slightly less than 12 percent to 26 percent between

---

[78]See, for instance, Tamar Lewin, "A Child Study Is a Peek. It's Not the Whole Picture," *New York Times*, July 21, 2002, p. 4; and Shonkoff and Phillips, eds. *From Neurons to Neighborhoods*, chap. 11. Moreover, causation between mothers' employment and children's outcomes may go either way. For instance, mothers of children with developmental delays may be slower to return to employment.

[79]For evidence that quality matters, see Shonkoff and Phillips, eds. *From Neurons to Neighborhoods: The Science of Early Child Development*, chapters 10 and 11; Janet Currie, "Early Childhood Education Programs," *Journal of Economic Perspectives* 15, no. 2 (Spring 2001): 213–38; and David Blau and Janet Currie, "Preschool, Day Care, and Afterschool Care: Who's Minding the Kids," National Bureau of Economic Research Working Paper No. 10670 (August 2004).

[80]Robert Haveman and Barbara Wolfe, "The Determinants of Children's Attainments: A Review of Methods and Findings," *Journal of Economic Literature* 33, no. 4 (December 1995): 1829–78; Robert Haveman and Barbara Wolfe, *Succeeding Generations: On the Effects of Investments in Children* (New York: Russell Sage Foundation, 1994), chap. 5 and 8; and Paul Amato and Alan Booth, *Generation at Risk: Growing Up in an Era of Family Upheaval* (Cambridge MA: Harvard University Press, 1997).

[81]See P. Lindsay Chase-Lansdale et al., "Mothers' Transitions from Welfare to Work and the Well-Being of Preschoolers and Adolescents," *Science* 299, no. 5612 (March 7, 2003): 1548–62. See also Blau and Currie, "Preschool, Day Care, and Afterschool Care."

[82]For an excellent discussion, see Ellwood and Jencks, "The Spread of Single-Parent Families in the United States Since 1960."

TABLE 9-5 Trends in Families with Own Children Under Age 18, 1970–2003

	As a % of All Families			
	1970	*1980*	*1990*	*2003*
Mother-Only Families				
All races	11.5	19.4	24.2	26.1
White	8.9	15.1	18.8	21.1
Black	33.0	48.7	56.2	55.5
Hispanic origin	n.a.	24.0	29.3	27.9
Father-Only Families				
All races	1.3	2.1	3.9	5.8
White	1.2	2.0	3.8	5.7
Black	2.6	3.2	4.3	6.4
Hispanic origin	n.a.	1.9	4.0	7.0
Married-Couple Families				
All races	87.1	78.5	71.9	68.1
White	89.9	82.9	77.4	73.1
Black	64.3	48.1	39.4	38.1
Hispanic origin	n.a.	74.1	66.8	65.1

Notes: Families include those heading their own households and those living in the households of others (subfamilies). Cohabitors may be included among single-parent families. White refers to those who reported race as white alone. Black includes those who reported this race alone or in combination with one or more other race groups. Persons of Hispanic origin may be of any race.
n.a. = Not available.

Sources: U.S. Census Bureau, "All Parent/Child Situations by Type, Race, and Hispanic Origin of Householder or Reference Person: 1970 to Present," Table FM-2, at www.census.gov.

1970 and 2003. In addition, just under 6 percent were father-only families, a figure that quadrupled since 1970. These figures include single-parent families who head their own household as well as those who live in someone else's household, whether with a parent or nonrelative. One point to keep in mind is that with the increase in cohabitation, the count of single-parent families based on the Census Bureau's definition increasingly includes families in which the parents of the child are cohabiting. Indeed, an estimated 12 percent of single mothers cohabit with a male partner.[83] The rise in cohabitation also likely explains at least part of the dramatic increase in father-only families since the 1970s; in many of these families the children's mother may well be present.[84]

Differences in family types by race are substantial. Historically, mother-only families are more common among African Americans, but as shown in Table 9-5 and Figure 9-2,

[83]Rebecca A. London, "Trends in Single Mothers' Living Arrangements, 1970–1995," *Demography* 35, no. 1 (February 1998): 125–31. From the perspective of children, 11 percent of children living with a single mother were in a cohabiting family, and as many as 33 percent of children living with a single father were in such a family in March 2002. See Jason Fields, "Children's Living Arrangements and Characteristics: March 2002," *Current Population Reports* P20-547 (Washington, DC: U.S. Census Bureau, June 2003), Figure 1.
[84]See Steven Garasky and Daniel R. Meyer, "Reconsidering the Increase in Father-Only Families," *Demography* 33, no. 3 (August 1996): 385–93.

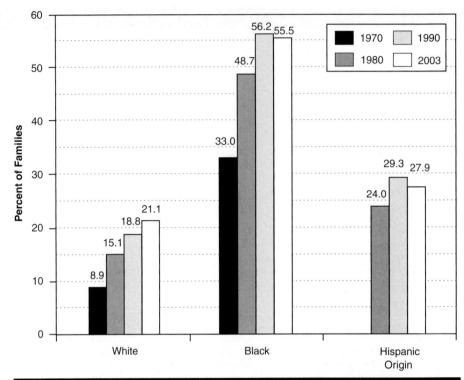

FIGURE 9-2   Mother-Only Families by Race and Ethnicity, 1970–2003 (Percent)

the proportion of these families among whites increased considerably since 1970.[85] As of 2003, nearly 56 percent of black families with children were maintained by mothers as compared with 21 percent of white families and 28 percent of families of Hispanic origin.

Single-parent families raise considerable concerns, particularly in relation to child well-being. First, such families, especially those maintained by women, experience a high incidence of poverty. Second, it is believed that growing up in a family with only one adult may result in long-term negative consequences for children, both economic and social.

Table 9-6 shows the income and poverty status of families with children in 2003. Most strikingly, the median income of female-headed families was less than half that of married couples. Nearly 36 percent were poor, compared to 7 percent of married couples. Families headed by women are also likely to have incomes below the poverty line for an extended period of time.[86] These statistics explain why the "feminization" of poverty is at the center of a great deal of discussion.

Poverty rates are particularly high for African American and Hispanic female-headed families with children, with approximately 43 percent of both living in poverty in

[85]Michael S. Rendall observes, however, that in contrast to black families, many white families still have two parents present, whether married or cohabiting, in "Entry or Exit? A Transition-Probability Approach to Explaining the High Prevalence of Single Motherhood Among Black Women," *Demography* 36, no. 3 (August 1999): 369–76.

[86]Mary Corcoran, "Mobility, Persistence, and the Consequences of Poverty for Children: Child and Adult Outcomes," in *Understanding Poverty,* edited by Sheldon H. Danziger and Robert H. Haveman (New York: Russell Sage Foundation, 2001), pp. 127–61.

TABLE 9-6 Income and Poverty Rates for Families with Children Under Age 18, 2003

	Percent in Poverty	*Median Income ($2003)*
All Families	14.8	51,342
White	12.1	55,659
Black	28.6	30,652
Asian	10.9	66,110
Hispanic origin	25.2	32,073
Type of Family		
Married-couple families	7.0	66,419
Male householder, no wife present	19.1	31,913
Female householder, no husband present	35.5	22,625
White	31.8	24,861
Black	42.7	19,346
Asian	28.2	30,884
Hispanic origin	43.0	19,301

Note: Figures are for families heading their own households, with related children under age 18. White refers to those who reported race as white alone. Black (Asian) includes those who reported this race alone or in combination with one or more other race groups. Persons of Hispanic origin may be of any race.

Sources: U.S. Census Bureau, Detailed Table POV04, "Families by Age of Householder, Number of Children, and Family Structure: 2003," from www.census.gov; and U.S. Census Bureau, Detailed Table FINC-03, "Presence of Related Children Under 18 Years Old—All Families by Total Money Income in 2003, Type of Family Experience in 2003, Race and Hispanic Origin of Reference Person," from www.census.gov.

2003, although these figures are well below the highs of 61 percent in the early 1990s. Even among white female-headed families, the poverty rate for 2003 was 32 percent. Inevitably, the high rates of poverty among single-parent families are a major factor behind the high rates of poverty for children, overall. In 2003, nearly 18 percent of all children, 14 percent of white, 30 percent of Hispanic, and 34 percent of black children lived in poverty.[87]

In interpreting poverty statistics, it is important to understand the way in which the official poverty rate is currently determined. On the one hand, income used to determine poverty status does not include such items as food stamps, Medicaid, housing subsidies, and the Earned Income Tax Credit, so that it understates real income. On the other hand, although the poverty threshold is updated for changes in inflation, it remains a fixed multiple of the amount of money needed to provide food for the family, established as long ago as the 1960s, ignoring the fact that expenditures on food increased substantially less than costs for other items such as housing, health insurance, and education. In view of these concerns, alternative measures of poverty are currently being calculated as well. These alternatives, for instance, modify income by including the value of in-kind benefits such as food stamps, and by deducting work-related expenses such as the cost of child care and out-of-pocket medical expenses. Some also include adjustments to the poverty threshold so that it better reflects regional differences

---

[87]U.S. Census Bureau, Detailed Poverty Tables for 2004, Table POV 01, at www.census.gov.

in housing costs. Nevertheless, the official poverty rate continues to serve as a major indicator of economic well-being.[88]

It is not difficult to understand why single-parent families have incomes so much lower than families with two parents. First, they have a lower ratio of adults to children, thus fewer potential earners as well as fewer caregivers per dependent. This double burden makes it far more difficult to do justice both to job and family, not to mention the reduction in leisure time. Second, a higher incidence of female-headed families occurs among the less educated, which further accounts for their lower income.[89] Third, women tend to earn considerably less than men with comparable qualifications, and mothers tend to accumulate less labor force experience than other workers.

As noted earlier, single mothers may live independently or in extended households, either with their parents (their children's grandparents), other relatives, or with an unmarried male partner.[90] Doubling up with parents, for instance, involves some loss of privacy, but also reduces costs, because of economies of scale. In addition, other household members can provide financial assistance and emotional support as well as in-house child care. When a single mother cohabits with a male partner, U.S. Census Bureau figures do not take into account the partner's income in determining the family's income or poverty status because unmarried partners are not counted as part of the family. The mother and her children may, nevertheless, benefit from some degree of income sharing with the partner, depending on factors such as the length of time the couple stays together and whether the partner is the children's biological father.[91] One study finds that the poverty rate for children would fall slightly, but that many would remain poor even if cohabitors' incomes were included because many cohabitors have low or no incomes.[92]

The economic circumstances of families maintained by women also vary considerably depending on the woman's age and marital status. Never-married mothers tend to have particularly low incomes, not only because they are less likely than divorced mothers to receive child support from absent fathers, but also because they are, on average, younger with less education. Women who become parents as teenagers, most of whom are not married, tend to be at a particular economic and social disadvantage throughout their lives. They tend to have low levels of educational attainment, and if they are

---

[88]The National Research Council offered a number of recommendations for revising the poverty measure, and several experimental measures are now being tested. See, for instance, Kathleen Short, "Experimental Poverty Measures: 1999," *Current Population Reports,* P60–216 (Washington, DC: U.S. Census Bureau, October 2001). For a detailed look at how poor single mothers keep their families afloat, see Kathryn Edin and Laura Lein, *Making Ends Meet: How Single Mothers Survive Welfare and Low-Wage Work* (New York: Russell Sage Foundation, 1997).

[89]Francine D. Blau, "Trends in the Well-Being of American Women, 1970–1995," *Journal of Economic Literature* 36, no. 1 (March 1998): 112–65; and Sara McLanahan, "Diverging Destinies: How Children Are Faring Under the Second Demographic Transition," *Demography* 41, no. 4 (November 2004): 607–28.

[90]See for instance, Wendy Sigle-Rushton and Sara McLanahan, "The Living Arrangements of New Unmarried Mothers," *Demography* 39, no. 3 (August 2002): 415–33. For recent evidence on the rising number of children living with grandparents, see Fields, "Children's Living Arrangements and Characteristics: March 2002."

[91]Anne E. Winkler, "Economic Decisionmaking Among Cohabitors: Findings Regarding Income Pooling," *Applied Economics* 29, no. 8 (August 1997): 1079–90.

[92]Marcia Carlson and Sheldon Danziger, "Cohabitation and the Measurement of Child Poverty," *Review of Income and Wealth* 45, no. 2 (June 1999): 179–91. See also Gregory Acs and Megan Gallagher, "Income Inequality Among America's Children," Assessing the New Federalism Series B, No. B-6 (Washington, DC: Urban Institute, January 2000).

employed, they generally earn low wages. At first, researchers assumed that it was early childbearing that led to these negative outcomes. More recently, however, studies suggest that many of these women would not have done well even if they delayed childbearing until their twenties, because many are, themselves, from economically and socially disadvantaged backgrounds. The research evidence is mixed, but it appears that early childbearing, per se, has some detrimental effect on young women and their children, though findings differ considerably regarding the magnitude of this effect.[93]

Divorced mothers tend to fare somewhat better than never-married mothers, in part because they are more likely to receive child support payments. Yet many struggle financially. One recent study found that after the first year of divorce, children's family income was 40 percent lower, on average, than if their parents stayed together. After six years, their economic situation was somewhat better, and their post-divorce family income was only 20 percent lower, on average, though the latter figure varies considerably depending on whether the mother remarries.[94]

A significant reason for the low income of both never-married and divorced mothers is that if noncustodial parents provide any child support at all, they tend to contribute less than what would generally be considered their fair share. In 2001, only 59 percent of custodial parents were awarded child support; of those who were supposed to receive payments the same year, fewer than half (45 percent) received the full amount they were awarded, 29 percent received partial payment, and the remaining 26 percent received no payment at all.[95] Nonetheless, child support payments provide a considerable supplement to income for parents who do receive them, especially those who are poor, and reduce reliance on welfare.[96]

A number of factors contribute to low rates of child support collection.[97] Some parents fail to pay child support they could well afford because they believe that the custodial parent does not spend the entire amount on their children. Of course, the question arises as to what extent they take into account a share of overhead items such

[93]For evidence that early childbearing has little effect, see Arline T. Geronimus and Sanders Korenman, "The Socioeconomic Consequences of Teen Childbearing Reconsidered," *Quarterly Journal of Economics* 107, no. 4 (November 1992): 1187–214; and Joseph Hotz, Susan McElroy, and Seth Sanders, "The Impact of Teenage Childbearing on the Mothers and the Consequences of Those Impacts for Government," in *Kids Having Kids*, edited by Rebecca Maynard (Washington, DC: The Urban Institute, 1997), pp. 55–94. For evidence of negative consequences, see Saul Hoffman, E. Michael Foster, and Frank F. Furstenberg, "Reevaluating the Costs of Teenage Childbearing," *Demography* 30, no. 1 (February 1993): 1–13; and Daniel Klepinger, Shelly Lundberg, and Robert Plotnick, "How Does Adolescent Fertility Affect the Human Capital and Wages of Young Women?" *Journal of Human Resources* 34, no. 3 (Summer 1999): 421–43.
[94]Marianne E. Page and Ann Huff Stevens, "The Economic Consequences of Absent Parents," *Journal of Human Resources* 39, no. 1 (Winter 2004): 80–107. For evidence on the gender gap in economic well-being between spouses following separation, see Suzanne M. Bianchi, Lekha Subaiya, and Joan R. Kahn, "The Gender Gap in the Economic Well-Being of Nonresident Fathers and Custodial Mothers," *Demography* 36, no. 2 (May 1999): 195–203.
[95]Figures are from U.S. Census Bureau, "Custodial Mothers and Fathers and Their Child Support: 2001," Table 4, at www.census.gov.
[96]Judi Bartfeld, "Child Support and the Postdivorce Economic Well-Being of Mothers, Fathers, and Children," *Demography* 37, no. 2 (May 2000): 203–13; Daniel R. Meyer and Mei-Chen Hu find more modest effects in "A Note on the Antipoverty Effectiveness of Child Support Among Mother-Only Families," *Journal of Human Resources* 34, no. 1 (Winter 1999): 225–34. Along with the booming economy of the 1990s and the 1996 welfare legislation, more vigorous child support enforcement likely contributed to the substantial decline in the welfare caseload. See Chien-Chung Huang, Irwin Garfinkel, and Jane Waldfogel, "Child Support Enforcement and Welfare Caseloads," *Journal of Human Resources* 39, no. 1 (Winter 2004): 108–34.
[97]For a formal treatment and discussion, see Andrea Beller and John W. Graham, *Small Change: The Economics of Child Support* (New Haven, CT: Yale University Press, 1993), chap. 3.

as the cost of housing, maintenance, and so on. Others may withhold payments in retaliation for limited visitation rights or simply because of resentment against the former spouse. In a few cases the other parent may be deceased. Far more frequently, however, absent parents are themselves poor and it would be genuinely difficult for them to pay more.[98] Unfortunately, it is most often the mothers, who are the least able to stand on their own, with little education, little or no labor market experience, and few other resources, who are also the least likely to receive any support from their children's father(s).

This review makes clear that single-parent families are at a particular economic disadvantage. In Chapter 10 we review government policies intended to raise their incomes, pointing to both the successes and limitations of these policies.

Family Structure and Children's Outcomes

As evident from the statistics, the share of single-parent families increased considerably. Consequently, an increasing fraction of children are being raised in these families. For instance, in 2002, only 69 percent of children under age 18 lived in a married couple family, and even fewer of these children lived with both biological or adoptive parents (in the remainder a stepparent was present).[99] Children's living arrangements as well as the transitions they experience may affect their economic and social well-being. Studies, such as those cited here, looked at effects on family income, as well as a number of outcomes for children, including their educational attainment, labor force participation, and likelihood of teen pregnancy.

A study by Sara McLanahan and Gary Sandefur, which received considerable attention, found that children in married-couple families with both biological or adoptive parents present do better in these respects than those from single-parent families.[100] For instance, they report that children in single-parent families have a higher high school dropout rate and a higher rate of teen birth than those from two-parent families, even after taking account of differences in parents' educational levels, race, and income.[101]

Children in single-parent families are also at disadvantage because their parents have less income, and often have little money for after-school care, let alone enrichment programs. Another disadvantage is that such families tend to move more often, and so tend to form fewer connections to their local communities. Community ties are valuable because a community network can help with schooling decisions and getting a job, as well as with solving personal problems that may arise. Finally, children in single-parent families tend to receive less parental attention and supervision at home. This study also found that a number of outcomes are not as favorable for children in stepparent families as for those living with both biological parents.

Despite this evidence, researchers continue to debate whether, and to what extent, growing up in a single-parent family is the real cause of children performing

---

[98]See, for instance, Maureen Waller and Robert Plotnick, *Child Support and Low-Income Families: Perceptions, Practices and Policies* (San Francisco, CA: Public Policy Institute of California, 1999).

[99]Fields, "Children's Living Arrangements and Characteristics: March 2002," at www.census.gov.

[100]Sara McLanahan and Gary Sandefur, *Growing Up With a Single Parent: What Hurts, What Helps?* (Cambridge, MA: Harvard University Press, 1994).

[101]McLanahan and Sandefur observe that parents' education is an important determinant of children's future educational attainment in *Growing Up With a Single Parent*. David M. Blau finds that family background, including parental education, has a far greater impact on children's development than income in "The Effect of Income on Child Development," *Review of Economics and Statistics* 81, no. 2 (May 1999): 261–76. For other evidence on the role of parental education, see Haveman and Wolfe, "The Determinants of Children's Attainments."

poorly in school, among other negative outcomes. Some argue that other factors might lead to both children's poor school performance and parents' divorce, such as a parent's substance abuse problem or a high degree of family conflict. In these cases, the child might well perform poorly in school even if the parents did not separate. As a result, researchers continue to make efforts to disentangle causation from correlation.[102] Some of this research tends to confirm McLanahan and Sandefur's findings that living in single-parent families or living with one stepparent rather than with both biological parents results in unfavorable effects on educational outcomes, but others find no such effect.[103] In interpreting the research findings, it is important to keep in mind that even if growing up in a single-parent family has negative effects, this only means that the risk of less desirable outcomes is increased, *not* that it is assured or nonexistent for children in families with both biological parents.

Conclusion

This chapter considered the effect of a woman's labor force participation and other factors on the formation, functioning, and possible breakup of families. It is clear that dual-earner families and female-headed families are becoming far more common, rapidly replacing the traditional married-couple family of the breadwinner husband and homemaker wife. Dual-earner families earn considerably more income, on average. In addition, women's increased earnings most likely increase their bargaining power in the family. Nevertheless, some concern centers on whether maternal employment during a child's first year may negatively affect children's cognitive development. In evaluating this finding it is important to keep in mind that maternal employment is only one factor, of many, that affects children's well-being and achievement and, moreover, researchers cannot fully account for the quality of non-parental care, which may attenuate any negative effects. Effects for preschoolers, on the other hand, are generally found to be beneficial. We also looked at the difficulties faced by women who head families. In Chapter 10, we examine policies designed to raise incomes of these and other low-income families. Some evidence also indicates that children growing up in single-parent families do not, on average, fare as well as those raised in married-couple families with both biological parents present, though again it is an area of active research.

---

[102]For reviews of the methodological challenges, see Donna K. Ginther and Robert A. Pollak, "Family Structure and Children's Educational Outcomes: Blended Families, Stylized Facts, and Descriptive Regressions," *Demography* 41, no. 4 (November 2004): 671–96: and Ribar, "What Do Social Scientists Know About the Benefits of Marriage?"

[103]For further evidence that family structure influences educational attainment see Gary D. Sandefur and Thomas Wells, "Does Family Structure Really Influence Educational Attainment?" *Social Science Research* 28 (December 1999): 331–57; Gary Painter and David I. Levine, "Family Structure and Youths' Outcomes: Which Correlations Are Causal?" *Journal of Human Resources* 35, no. 3 (Summer 2000): 524–49; Anne Case, I-Fen Lin, and Sara McLanahan, "Household Resource Allocation in Stepfamilies: Darwin Reflects on the Plight of Cinderella," *American Economic Review* 89, no. 2 (May 1999): 234–38; and Eirik Evenhouse and Siobhan Reilly, "A Sibling Study of Stepchild Well-Being," *Journal of Human Resources* 39, no. 1 (Winter 2004):248–76. For evidence on the other side see Ginther and Pollak, "Family Structure and Children's Educational Outcomes."

Questions for Review and Discussion

1. Describe the main changes in the typical family in the United States over the past 30–40 years and explain their causes.
2. Women's rising labor force participation might either increase or reduce marriage rates. Explain why the effect could go either way.
3. A negative relationship is observed between women's labor force participation and fertility. Is higher labor force participation the cause of the lower birthrate, or vice versa? Discuss.
4. Increasing numbers of children are being raised in families in which mothers are cohabiting, either with the child's father or with a boyfriend. Consider the pros and cons for children of these arrangements versus living with a single parent.
5. In what ways are marriage and cohabitation similar and in what ways do they differ?
6. Explain why child support enforcement might encourage some married couples to stay together while it might encourage others to break up.
7. What are the advantages and disadvantages of the rising age of marriage?
8. Women who become mothers when they are teenagers are less likely to obtain a college degree than those who delay their childbearing until at least their mid twenties. Discuss why this outcome is generally the case and what the consequences for these women and their families are likely to be. [*Hint*: Refer back to the human capital model in Chapter 6.]
9. Explain why the distinction between causation and correlation is so important in understanding the relationship between family structure and children's well-being. Suggest another factor that may affect both children's outcomes and family structure.

Suggested Readings

Badgett, M. V. Lee. *Money, Myths and Change: The Economic Lives of Lesbians and Gay Men.* Chicago: University of Chicago Press, 2001.

Beller, Andrea H., and John W. Graham. *Small Change: The Economics of Child Support.* New Haven, CT: Yale University Press, 1993.

Bianchi, Suzanne. "The Changing Demographic and Socioeconomic Characteristics of Single Parent Families." *Marriage and Family Review* 20, nos. 1–2 (Spring 1995): 71–97.

Blau, Francine D. "Trends in the Well-Being of American Women, 1970–1995." *Journal of Economic Literature* 36, no. 1 (March 1998): 112–65.

DaVanzo, Julie, and M. Omar Rahman. "American Families: Trends and Correlates." *Population Index* 59, no. 3 (1993): 350–86.

Edin, Kathryn, and Laura Lein. *Making Ends Meet: How Single Mothers Survive Welfare and Low-Wage Work.* New York: Russell Sage Foundation, 1997.

Ellwood, David T., and Christopher Jencks. "The Spread of Single-Parent Families in the United States Since 1960." Unpublished working paper, Harvard University, October 2002.

Gluckman, Amy, and Betsy Reed, eds. *Homo Economics: Capitalism, Community, and Lesbian and Gay Life.* New York: Routledge, 1997.

McLanahan, Sara. "Diverging Destinies: How Children Are Faring Under the Second Demographic Transition." *Demography* 41, no. 4 (November 2004): 607–28.

McLanahan, Sara, and Gary Sandefur. *Growing Up With a Single Parent: What Hurts, What Helps?* Cambridge, MA: Harvard University Press, 1994.

Moffitt, Robert A., ed. *Welfare, the Family, and Reproductive Behavior: Research Perspectives.* Washington, DC: National Research Council, 1998.

Rosenzweig, Mark R., and Oded Stark, eds. *Handbook of Population and Family Economics.* Vol. 1A and 1B. Amsterdam: Elsevier, 1997.

Shonkoff, Jack P., and Deborah A. Phillips, eds. *From Neurons to Neighborhoods: The Science of Early Child Development.* Washington, DC: National Research Council, 2000.

Smith, Tom W. "The Emerging 21st Century American Family." GSS Social Change Report no. 42. University of Chicago: National Opinion Research Center, 1999.

Tucker, M. Belinda, and Claudia Mitchell-Kernan. *The Decline in Marriage Among African-Americans.* New York: Russell Sage Foundation, 1995.

Waite, Linda, ed. *The Ties That Bind: Perspectives on Marriage and Cohabitation.* New York: Aldine de Gruyter, 2000.

CHAPTER

10 | POLICIES AFFECTING PAID WORK AND THE FAMILY

Chapter Highlights

■ Policies to Alleviate Poverty

■ Taxes, Specialization, and Marriage

■ The Competing Demands of Work and Family

■ Who Is Responsible for Children?

■ Family-Friendly Policies

A host of programs and policies have emerged and evolved over time that influence the well-being of individuals and their families. This chapter begins where Chapter 9 left off, by discussing government policies to alleviate poverty, especially those that affect mother-only families, because these families often face the greatest difficulties. Next, we review some major features of the U.S. federal income tax and Social Security systems and point to some of their potential effects on paid work and family formation decisions. The remainder of the chapter discusses the competing demands of paid work and family faced by more and more individuals as single-parent and dual-earner families swiftly replace the traditional family of a breadwinner husband and homemaker wife. We discuss the potential role for government and employers in alleviating these conflicts and review family-friendly policies, including family and medical leave and child care.

POLICIES TO ALLEVIATE POVERTY

This section examines a number of policies designed to help raise the incomes of people living in poverty in the United States, with emphasis on policies that assist mother-only families. We begin by describing Aid to Families with Dependent Children (AFDC), the federal program that, for more than 60 years, guaranteed cash assistance to poor children and their families, and then turn to the program that replaced it in 1996, Temporary Assistance for Needy Families (TANF).[1] We next examine government employment programs, the Earned Income Tax Credit (EITC), and policies designed to increase child support paid by noncustodial parents. In light of pending legislation, we also review marriage promotion initiatives intended to improve economic well-being.

AFDC: Our Former Welfare Program

AFDC, initiated in 1935 as part of the Social Security Act, was a federal entitlement program that provided all eligible families, principally those headed by single mothers, with cash assistance. As the program evolved, AFDC recipients also generally qualified for in-kind benefits including food stamps and Medicaid, which is effectively government-provided health insurance. Many were eligible for housing subsidies as well.

AFDC came to be one of the most hotly debated government transfer programs, despite the fact that it made up only about 1 percent of the federal budget. One concern was that if AFDC mainly provided benefits to single mothers, it created an incentive for couples not to get married or to break up, in order for the mother and her children to be eligible for welfare.[2] Public concern was heightened when it became clear that the program, originally intended to help families of poor widows, in fact mainly served divorced women and, more recently, increasing numbers of never-married mothers. This trend can be seen in Table 10-1, which provides data on AFDC for 1970 and 1993 (the latter, when caseloads were at their peak level), and for TANF for 2002. Table 10-1 shows that from 1970 to 1993 the percentage of families on AFDC headed by never-married mothers increased from 28 to 53 percent. It was, therefore, argued that this program discouraged marriage and encouraged unmarried women to have children. Recent evidence suggests, however, that even though AFDC appears to affect these decisions, it cannot explain the dramatic rise in female headship or in births to unmarried women since the 1970s.[3]

AFDC also created potential disincentives for paid work because it provided the maximum benefit, termed the "AFDC guarantee," for recipients who where not employed. As we saw in Chapter 4, the availability of nonlabor income increases the reservation wage, thereby reducing the probability of labor force participation. Furthermore, in the later years of AFDC, if a recipient entered the labor force, the AFDC guarantee

---

[1]For overviews of the AFDC and TANF programs, see Robert A. Moffitt, "The Temporary Assistance for Needy Families Program," in *Means-Tested Transfer Programs in the United States*, edited by Robert A. Moffitt (Chicago: University of Chicago Press, 2003), pp. 291–363; and Rebecca M. Blank, "Fighting Poverty: Lessons from Recent U.S. History," *Journal of Economic Perspectives* 14, no. 2 (Spring 2000): 3–19.

[2]Although single mothers always made up the majority of the caseload, since 1961 states could offer two-parent families with an unemployed spouse benefits through the AFDC-UP program. Further, starting in 1988, all states were mandated to do so. For discussion and evidence, see Anne E. Winkler, "Does AFDC-UP Encourage Two-Parent Families?" *Journal of Policy Analysis and Management* 14, no. 1 (Winter 1995): 1–24.

[3]See Robert A. Moffitt, "Temporary Assistance to Needy Families Program," and Robert A. Moffitt, "The Effect of Welfare on Marriage and Fertility," in *Welfare, the Family, and Reproductive Behavior: Research Perspectives,* edited by Robert A. Moffitt (Washington, DC: National Research Council, 1998), pp. 50–97. For evidence that AFDC also may have encouraged cohabitation, see Robert A. Moffitt, Robert Reville, and Anne E. Winkler, "Beyond Single Mothers: Cohabitation, Marriage and the U.S. Welfare System," *Demography* 35, no. 3 (August 1998): 359–78.

TABLE 10-1   Selected Statistics on the AFDC/TANF Program, 1970, 1993, and 2002

	1970	*1993*	*2002*
Benefits			
AFDC/TANF guarantee for three-person family[a]			
In current dollars	$194	$414	$454
In 2002 dollars	$861	$517	$454
AFDC/TANF tax rate (rate at which benefits are reduced)	67.0%	100.0%	varies
Recipient Characteristics			
Average monthly number of recipients (in thousands)	7,415	14,143	5,654
AFDC/TANF recipients as % of population	4.1%	5.4%	1.9%
AFDC/TANF adults with earnings (%)[b]	n.a.	7.4%	21.8%
AFDC/TANF adults who are never-married (%)[c]	27.9%	53.1%	66.6%
Average AFDC/TANF family size	4.0	2.9	2.5

[a] Weighted average monthly benefit computed as the benefit for each state weighted by that state's share of total AFDC/TANF families.
[b] The 1970 and 1993 figures indicate percentage of AFDC families with earnings.
[c] For 1970 and 1993, figures indicate percentage of AFDC children with never-married parent.
n.a. = Not available.
Source: U.S. Department of Health and Human Services, *Indicators of Welfare Dependence,* Annual Report to Congress (2000 and 2004 editions), available at aspe.hhs.gov.

was reduced by a dollar for each dollar earned on the job. In other words, recipients faced a 100 percent tax rate on their earnings.[4] Needless to say, for any individual, on welfare or not, a 100 percent tax rate provides a considerable disincentive to work. Evidence shows that AFDC reduced labor supply, but again the effects found were relatively small. Further, altering the tax rate has not been found to have much impact on recipients' propensity to work.[5]

AFDC also discouraged paid work because, by keeping their hours low, recipients could retain access to Medicaid, which would be lost once they were no longer receiving AFDC benefits. However, changes starting in the late 1980s reduced this disincentive.[6] Another concern was that AFDC promoted welfare dependency because benefits were not time-limited. The evidence indicates, however, that most recipients used AFDC for transitory assistance, though others did rely on it for long periods of time.[7]

Finally, AFDC and other transfer programs were the subject of a great deal of criticism because they produced only modest success in alleviating poverty. Part of the reason that AFDC and other programs were not more successful is that the amount of money

---

[4] Starting in 1981, the AFDC tax rate was set at 67 percent for four months and then rose to 100 percent thereafter.
[5] Robert A. Moffitt, "The Temporary Assistance for Needy Families Program."
[6] Anne E. Winkler, "The Incentive Effects of Medicaid on Women's Labor Supply," *Journal of Human Resources* 26, no. 2 (Spring 1991): 308–37; Robert A. Moffitt and Barbara Wolfe, "The Effect of the Medicaid Program on Welfare Participation and Labor Supply," *Review of Economics and Statistics* 74, no. 4 (November 1992): 615–26; and Aaron S. Yelowitz, "The Medicaid Notch, Labor Supply, and Welfare Participation: Evidence from Eligibility Expansions," *Quarterly Journal of Economics* 110, no. 4 (November 1995): 909–39.
[7] See, for instance, Peter Gottschalk, Sara McLanahan, and Gary Sandefur, "Dynamics of Poverty and Welfare Participation," in *Confronting Poverty: Prescriptions for Change,* edited by Sheldon H. Danziger, Gary D. Sandefur, and Daniel H. Weinberg (New York: Russell Sage Foundation, 1994), pp. 85–108.

available became increasingly inadequate. As the figures in Table 10-1 show, the value of the AFDC guarantee provided by states fell by 45 percent between 1970 and 1993 in inflation-adjusted terms. Although the impact of this decline was cushioned somewhat by an increase in the real value of food stamps, as of 1993, the combined value of the two benefits for a family of three still provided only two-thirds of the amount needed to reach the poverty threshold. The stagnation of real wages for less educated individuals since the early 1970s, discussed earlier in Chapter 8, served to further compound the difficulty of raising low-income households out of poverty.

The Iron Triangle of Welfare

Redesigning welfare is made particularly difficult by the fact that three often-sought policy goals are in conflict: alleviating poverty, providing incentives to work, and limiting costs by keeping down the number of recipients. This conflict is sometimes referred to as the "iron triangle of welfare." It is impossible to simultaneously have a low tax rate on additional earnings of welfare recipients to encourage work, a high welfare guarantee to provide an adequate safety net, and still maintain a low break-even level of income—the maximum income level at which benefits are available—in order to limit the number of eligible individuals and thus program costs.

Table 10-2 illustrates this dilemma. Consider a hypothetical case in which benefits under the program are computed as the guarantee minus taxable earnings. If the annual welfare guarantee is set at $10,000 and the tax rate on welfare benefits is 100 percent, families are eligible for assistance provided their earnings are below $10,000.[8] However, the incentive to work is low because benefits are reduced dollar for dollar with labor market earnings.

Next, suppose the government reduces the tax rate to 50 percent to encourage people to work. That is, benefits are now reduced by only $.50 for each dollar of labor market earnings. In this case, the earnings threshold for eligibility will increase from $10,000 to $20,000, meaning that a much larger percentage of the population will be eligible for the program. Although work incentives for welfare recipients will increase, as will the number of individuals helped by the program, so will program costs. Finally, suppose the tax rate remains at 50 percent but the welfare guarantee is cut in half from $10,000 to

TABLE 10-2 Illustration of the Iron Triangle of Welfare		
Annual Welfare Guarantee	*Welfare Tax Rate (in percent)*	*Break-even Earnings*
$10,000	100	$10,000
$10,000	50	$20,000
$ 5,000	50	$10,000

Definitions:

Benefit formula: Benefits received = Guarantee – (tax rate × earnings).

Guarantee: Maximum welfare benefit (available if earnings are zero).

Break-even income: Maximum earnings level that qualifies for benefits.

---

[8]This tax rate only applies to the earnings of *welfare recipients;* it differs from the federal income tax rates, which will be discussed shortly.

$5,000. In this case, the incentives to work remain, but the earnings threshold and the number of eligible individuals are reduced; thus, many more families will be in poverty.

These conflicts were present in AFDC. As we will see, the TANF program differs from this earlier welfare program by using mandatory work requirements, with sanctions for those who don't comply, to create work incentives. These features also keep down the number of recipients. Unlike AFDC, however, TANF does not function as a true "safety net" because failure to comply fully with program rules can lead to a loss of benefits.[9]

Employment Strategies

Another problem is that employment, in and of itself, is often insufficient to lift families out of poverty. What is needed is a job that pays enough to live on, covers work-related expenses, including child care, transportation, and such additional clothing as may be needed, and provides access to health insurance. The employment outlook for welfare recipients tends to be especially bleak because, as a rule, they have little education and few job skills. Many also face other barriers to employment, including discrimination and often physical or mental health problems. In addition they may encounter problems getting to work due to lack of transportation.

Thus, the government could simply assist people in finding jobs, which tends to be quite inexpensive to do, but jobs alone are not likely to help many of them escape poverty. The alternative is to provide education and skills that raise the earnings of both welfare recipients and those who are poor but not on welfare. However, such investments involve considerable costs in the short run, as compared with merely maintaining welfare payments, and it takes some time for them to pay off. Unfortunately, resources for this purpose from state and local governments have tended to be scarce, not only during times when obtaining additional funds would require raising taxes, but even in the late 1990s and 2000, when many state governments, as well as the federal government, experienced budget surpluses.

The federal government has to some extent been active in providing training and employment programs for at least some disadvantaged and unemployed workers since the 1960s. The most important initial program that was designed to help people prepare for better jobs was the Manpower Development and Training Act (MDTA) of 1962, which emphasized a rather centralized approach to these problems. It was replaced by the Comprehensive Employment and Training Act (CETA) of 1973, which gave a greater role in decision making and program implementation to local governments. In 1982, CETA was followed by the Job Training Partnership Act (JTPA), and, in 1998, the latter policy was superceded by the Workforce Investment Act (WIA). The WIA builds on earlier efforts and provides funds for job training and job support services at the local level.

Beginning in the 1980s, states also initiated some education and training programs explicitly designed to move AFDC recipients from welfare to work. Subsequently, in 1988 Congress passed the Family Support Act, which mandated that states expand the skills and training of AFDC recipients through JOBS—the Job Opportunities and Basic Skills program. This program required recipients, except those with an infant or disability, to engage in activities such as job search, training, and education. To ease the transition to work, the Family Support Act also provided for child care and transitional Medicaid benefits. Analysis of a number of these welfare-to-work programs indicated

---

[9]See Moffitt, "The Temporary Assistance for Needy Families Program," p. 341.

that, in some cases, such programs increased earnings, but not enough to lift individuals out of poverty.[10]

Most recently, following the passage of the 1996 welfare legislation, the federal government largely shifted the emphasis of its employment strategy for welfare recipients away from job training and education as routes to self-sufficiency to a focus on employment. Many states are now pursuing a "work first" strategy, which emphasizes job search and tries to get welfare recipients into paid employment as quickly as possible. If this effort is unsuccessful, states may place welfare recipients in unpaid work or subsidized employment. Alternatively, they may offer them limited opportunities for education and training. The success of a "work first" approach depends on a number of factors, most notably a sustained healthy economy that creates sufficient jobs for lower-skilled workers. Also, this approach must be sufficiently flexible to assist individuals who lack adequate qualifications or face any of the other types of employment barriers mentioned earlier.[11] Another key ingredient for success is the presence of complementary policies that raise incomes, such as the Earned Income Tax Credit, because many of the jobs obtained are likely to be low-paying.

Self-employment, instead of working for someone else, is another employment strategy. However, access to credit often poses a substantial barrier, and even those with a promising idea may lack the financial and management skills needed to be successful. Microenterprise Assistance Programs, funded by the federal government, foundations, and private organizations, have been developed in the United States to meet these needs following efforts in developing countries, such as the Grameen Bank in Bangladesh. These programs provide start-up funds, training, and mentoring to assist low-income individuals in becoming entrepreneurs. Notably, however, Microenterprise Assistance Programs in the United States have failed to show the same promise as in developing countries. Among the explanations, developing countries tend to have a large "informal" sector that provides self-employment opportunities for those with relatively few skills. Also, such employment is subject to few regulations, so it does not tend to require as much business "know-how."[12]

TANF: Our Current Welfare Program

The 1996 welfare legislation replaced AFDC with a new program called Temporary Assistance to Needy Families (TANF), which altered the federal provision of welfare transfers in a number of important ways. For one, it changed welfare from a federal entitlement program to a program of fixed dollar block grants administered by states and gave states much more discretion than in the past to set eligibility and program rules. States can even use a portion of the block grant funds for support services such as transportation or child care instead of cash benefits. The main reason for shifting to block grants was the claim on the part of advocates of the new policy that states would

---

[10]The most-often cited example of success is the Riverside California GAIN program. See, Moffitt, "The Temporary Assistance to Needy Families Program."

[11]See David E. Card and Rebecca M. Blank, eds., *Finding Jobs: Work and Welfare Reform* (New York: Russell Sage Foundation, 2000).

[12]See, for instance, Mark Schreiner, "Self-Employment, Microenterprise, and the Poorest Americans," *Social Service Review* 73, no. 4 (December 1999): 496–523; and Mark Schreiner, "Microenterprise Development Programs in the United States and in the Developing World," *World Development* 31, no. 9 (September 2003): 1567–80.

be better able to tailor aid to their population based on their knowledge of their residents' needs. The legislation also required that, starting in 2002, 50 percent of single parents (and 90 percent of two-parent families) receiving welfare must be employed in some capacity for a minimum of 30 hours (more for two-parent families). Work requirements are likely to be further increased when Congress passes legislation to reauthorize TANF, action that was still pending as of late 2004. Part of the argument for the work requirement is that most married women, including those with small children, are now employed so that it is not unreasonable to require women maintaining families to also be employed. To put "teeth" into these rules, the legislation gave states the authority to impose sanctions, such as eliminating benefits for those recipients who do not comply with program rules. The new legislation also attempted to reduce welfare dependency by mandating a five-year cumulative time limit on receiving federally funded welfare, albeit with exemptions possible for up to 20 percent of families. In addition, it restricted eligibility for teen parents, so that only those who stay in school and live with their parents can receive benefits, and it stepped up enforcement of child support by noncustodial parents, most often fathers. Further, it limited eligibility for food stamps for some adults, and cut the tie that had long-existed between Medicaid and AFDC.[13]

Pressure to restructure welfare grew, beginning in the 1980s, as reflected in the emphasis on work in the 1988 Family Support Act, and President Clinton's promise during the 1992 campaign to "end welfare as we know it." In the early days of his presidency, he encouraged states to experiment with welfare reform. In response, more than two-thirds of the states sought and received waivers from the federal government, which allowed them to try alternative approaches to welfare, including time limits for welfare receipt, requiring recipients to work after a certain period, limiting AFDC benefit increases for those who had additional children while receiving aid, providing sanctions or bonuses to encourage completion of high school, and cutting off benefits to teen mothers who did not live with their parents. The 1996 welfare legislation embodies the main features of this earlier wave of reform. Nonetheless one fundamental difference is that the 1996 legislation ended the federal guarantee of assistance. Under TANF, states provide benefits to needy families only if they are willing and able to do so.

As might be expected, states (and the District of Columbia) took advantage of the greater latitude given to them by the federal government and are now essentially running 51 different welfare experiments. For instance, in calculating welfare benefits, states now differ greatly as to how much of recipients' earnings they disregard, with some choosing to disregard a substantial fraction in an effort to increase work incentives.[14] States also made different choices regarding eligibility for two-parent families, and whether benefits are reduced if recipients bear additional children. Because the policies generally include both "carrots" and "sticks" in an effort to encourage or discourage certain behaviors, it is virtually impossible to classify individual states as harsh or generous across the board. This fact also makes program evaluation rather difficult, because it is hard to isolate the influence of individual policies.

Though TANF was only fully implemented by 1997 and much remains to be learned, some conclusions about the initial success of welfare reform are possible. Most

---

[13]U.S. House of Representatives, *2004 Green Book.*
[14]Barbara L. Wolfe, "Incentives and Challenges of TANF Design: A Case Study," *Journal of Policy Analysis and Management* 21, no. 4 (Fall 2002): 577–86.

dramatically, as shown in Table 10-1, it resulted in more than a 50 percent reduction in the national welfare caseload from 1993, when numbers were at or near their most recent peak, to 2002. The decrease in the caseload size was unprecedented in the history of the program, and far larger than policymakers anticipated. Overall, by 2002, just 1.9 percent of the U.S. population received welfare benefits, as compared with 5.4 percent in 1993. This dramatic decline was a result of three major factors: (1) changes in welfare, which began with the waivers in the early 1990s; (2) the expansion of the EITC (to be discussed shortly); and (3) the booming U.S. economy of the late 1990s.[15] These factors contributed to a considerable reduction in the rate of families entering welfare, along with an increase in the rate of families exiting the program.[16]

A critical issue is whether the welfare changes are associated with increased employment, earnings, and income, and hence reductions in poverty rates of the target population. In addition, a full analysis should also consider the effects of welfare reform on a broader array of outcomes such as homelessness and children's well-being, including whether they are properly nourished and have adequate child care.[17] Another set of issues concerns what is likely to happen when the economy experiences a substantial downturn.

TANF and the other changes do appear to be successful at moving individuals from welfare to work. As discussed in Chapter 4, since the mid-1990s employment among single mothers with children increased considerably more rapidly than among married women with children. In fact, single mothers' high rate of employment even continued through the 2001 recession.[18] Further, the employment rate for single mothers receiving welfare, though still low, increased substantially, as was intended by the "work first" strategy. This trend can be seen in Table 10-1, which shows that nearly three times as many welfare recipients had earnings in 2002 as in 1993, prior to the new welfare legislation.[19]

Recent welfare changes also appear to have led to increases in family earnings and reductions in poverty. However, some evidence indicates that the economic well-being of women on the lowest rungs of the economic ladder may have worsened.[20] One difficulty in drawing definitive conclusions from available data is that there are a number of serious methodological challenges in identifying the impact of TANF, in part because it

---

[15]Numerous studies have sought to untangle the role of each factor. For reviews, see Moffitt, "Temporary Assistance to Needy Families Program"; and Rebecca A. Blank, "Evaluating Welfare Reform in the United States," *Journal of Economic Literature* 60, no. 4 (December 2002): 1105–66.

[16]Jeffrey Grogger, Steven J. Haider, and Jacob Klerman, "Why Did the Welfare Rolls Fall During the 1990s? The Importance of Entry," in *The American Economic Review* 93, no. 2 (May 2003): 288–92; and Jeffrey Grogger, "Welfare Transitions in the 1990s: The Economy, Welfare Policy, and the EITC," *Journal of Policy Analysis and Management* (forthcoming).

[17]Christina Paxson and Jane Waldfogel, "Work, Welfare, and Child Maltreatment," *Journal of Labor Economics* 20, no. 3 (July 2002): 435–74.

[18]Robert I. Lerman, "Single Mothers Retain Nearly All Their Employment and Wage Gains in the Current Economic Slowdown," *Single Parents' Earnings Monitor* (Washington, DC: Urban Institute, January 2003). For data, see Chapter 4 and U.S. Census Bureau, *U.S. Statistical Abstract: 2003,* Table 597.

[19]See also Brian J. O'Hara, "Work and Work-Related Activities of Mothers Receiving Temporary Assistance to Needy Families: 1996, 1998, and 2000," *Current Population Reports*, P70–85 (May 2002).

[20]Robert F. Schoeni and Rebecca M. Blank, "What Has Welfare Reform Accomplished? Impacts on Welfare Participation, Employment, Income, Poverty, and Family Structure," National Bureau of Economic Research Working Paper No. 7627 (2000); Blank, "Evaluating Welfare Reform in the United States"; and Moffitt, "The Temporary Assistance for Needy Families Program." For an interesting critique of the research to date, see Karen Christopher, "Welfare as We [Don't] Know It: A Review and Feminist Critique of Welfare Reform Research in the United States," *Feminist Economics* 10, no. 2 (July 2004): 143–71.

was instituted during a period of economic expansion.[21] Questions about the effects of welfare changes over a longer time horizon are also important. For instance there is concern about the long-term wage prospects of recipients who leave welfare, given the types of jobs they tend to find. Also, states are required to find employment for a growing fraction of welfare recipients, many of whom will likely encounter greater employment difficulties than those initially placed into jobs.[22] In addition, as we move into the mid-2000s, more families will reach the time limit for federally funded welfare benefits. The degree to which states will continue providing assistance by using their own funds or provide extensions remains to be seen. Furthermore, the gap in access to affordable, quality child care that already exists is not likely to be closed any time soon. Finally, the extent to which welfare recipients flood the low-skilled labor market may depress wages and perhaps displace some workers already employed.[23]

Other concerns center on how states will respond and how individuals will fare in a prolonged economic downturn. This issue is particularly serious because in times of people's greatest economic need, states will have the least financial ability to provide economic assistance. Notably, in the 2001 recession, although effects on TANF caseloads varied from state to state, the national caseload, as a whole, did not rise as compared with past recessions. This difference may in part be due to the fact that the unemployment rate increased by a relatively modest amount, along with the fact that families were perhaps deterred from entering TANF as a result of the work requirements and the time-limited nature of the benefits. Although the national caseload size did not increase during the recession, a majority of states faced fiscal crises, in many cases leading to cuts in TANF benefits and related support programs targeted at needy families. The impact would have likely been greater, if not for the fact that states were able to draw upon TANF fund surpluses that accumulated during the boom years of the 1990s. The difficulties faced by states, even during this rather mild recession, point to the much graver difficulties that would likely arise during a more prolonged, serious recession. In addition, they point to the importance of a continuation of the federal contingency fund, originally established in the 1996 legislation, which could provide additional reserves in such a situation.[24]

Looking to the future, it is likely that welfare rules will become even stricter than in the original 1996 legislation. As of 2004, both the U.S. House of Representatives and the Senate had proposals pending that would increase the fraction of TANF recipients who must be employed, from 50 to 70 percent, and would increase the required number of hours worked. In fact, the pending House bill would increase this figure from 30 to 40 hours per week for single parents. Critics, however, question whether 40 hours of work per week is realistic because many individuals will likely find it difficult to

---

[21]Blank, "Evaluating Welfare Reform"; and Robert A. Moffitt and Michelle Ver Ploeg, eds., *Evaluating Welfare Reform in an Era of Transition* (Washington, DC: National Research Council, 2001).

[22]LaDonna Pavetti, "How Much More Can Welfare Mothers Work?" *Focus* 20, no. 2 (Spring 1999): 16–19.

[23]For a review of the evidence, see Blank, "Evaluating Welfare Reform."

[24]This discussion is drawn from Jeffrey Grogger, "Welfare Transitions in the 1990s: The Economy, Welfare Policy, and the EITC," National Bureau of Economic Research Working Paper No. 9472 (January 2003); Howard Chernick and Andrew Reschovsky, "State Fiscal Responses to Welfare Reform During Recessions: Lessons for the Future," Institute for Research on Poverty Discussion Paper No. 1270-03 (July 2003); and Sharon Parrott and Nina Wu, "States Are Cutting TANF and Child Care Programs: Supports for Low-Income Working Families and Welfare-to-Work Programs Are Particularly Hard Hit," (Washington, DC: Center on Budget and Policy Priorities, June 2003).

hold full-time jobs given their family responsibilities combined with a lack of adequate support services, principally child care. Moreover, employers may prefer to hire recipients for part-time work so they can avoid paying costly premiums for health insurance. Another controversial feature of these proposals is that they explicitly provide funds for marriage promotion activities, as discussed in the following inset.[25]

Beyond Traditional Income and Work Support Policies: Marriage Promotion

Efforts to alleviate poverty among families and improve children's well-being have long relied on welfare programs including AFDC and, most recently, TANF. As discussed further shortly, these efforts were buttressed by expansions in the federal Earned Income Tax Credit (EITC), a tax credit that supplements the income of families with low earnings, as well as by policies to strengthen child support enforcement. Most recently, considerable attention has focused on another strategy—promoting and supporting healthy marriages. As discussed in an inset in Chapter 3, the 1996 welfare legislation explicitly mentioned marriage promotion and a substantial number of states started such efforts. In addition, welfare reauthorization proposals, pending as of late 2004, include as much as $1.5 billion over 5 years for initiatives to promote healthy marriages.*

Proponents point to a range of benefits of marriage,** including the fact that married-couple families are, on average, on considerably better financial footing than single-parent families, as shown earlier in Table 9-6. Married couples also have considerably higher incomes than cohabiters. In addition, Chapter 9 pointed to some evidence that suggests that children tend to do better in married families with both biological parents present than when raised with a single parent.

However, an important factor that complicates comparisons of the economic well-being of married and unmarried couples is that they have very different characteristics, on average. For instance, parents in married-couple families tend to be older and more highly educated. Thus, it is not reasonable to assume that if all cohabiting couples were to marry that they would achieve the same economic well-being as married couples. One study finds that when marriage is "simulated" among cohabiting couples, the poverty rate of children in these families falls from over three to two times the rate for children in married-couple families. Nonetheless, this improvement would still leave a considerable fraction of children in poverty because of their parents' characteristics (except that their work hours might increase to some extent).†

While there is a considerable pro-marriage constituency, concerns have been raised about such an emphasis, even by some of those favoring marriage promotion.†† One concern is that a focus on marriage promotion may divert government funds from traditional assistance programs for lower-income families. Also,

[25]For details and assessments, see Shawn Fremstad and Sharon Parrott, "The Senate Finance Committee's TANF Reauthorization Bill," (Washington, DC: Center on Budget and Policy Priorites, May 2004); and Douglas J. Besharov and Peter Germanis, *Toughening TANF: How Much? And How Attainable?* (Washington, DC: Department of Health and Human Services, March 2004).

if marriage were more actively promoted, what might be the implications for the success of these marriages? At worst, it might even lead to an increase in domestic violence. Further, as discussed in Chapter 9, some research finds negative effects associated with growing up with a stepparent, suggesting that all marriages may not be equally beneficial for children. Finally, another worry is that marriage promotion may distract attention from other policy priorities. In this view, policymakers should actively address the decline in job opportunities and real earnings for less-skilled men and take measures to reduce the number of unwed births, especially among the very young, because unmarried mothers are less likely to marry.

In light of the various reservations expressed, one proposed approach, which might be regarded as a "middle" course, suggests that the government encourage marriage *alongside* efforts to expand employment opportunities, provide income support to those in need, and reduce unwed births. Such marriage policies might include but not be limited to eliminating marriage disincentives in TANF and the EITC, along with local programs to promote and support healthy marriages. Whether these various efforts result in the intended effect, however, remains to be seen.

*Information on the pending bills is from Shawn Fremsted and Sharon Parrott, "The Senate Finance Committee's TANF Reauthorization Bill" (Washington, DC: Center on Budget and Policy Priorities, May 12, 2004). For the Bush administration's perspective, see a speech by Wade F. Horn, Assistant Secretary for Children and Families in the Administration for Children and Families, U.S. Department of Health and Human Services, given at the conference, "Marriage and Family Formation Among Low-Income Couples," sponsored by the National Poverty Center as excerpted in *Poverty Research Insights* (University of Michigan: National Poverty Center, Winter 2004); and Wade F. Horn, "Wedding Bell Blues: Marriage and Welfare Reform," *The Brookings Review* 19, no. 3 (Summer 2001): 3–42.

**For a review, see Robert Lerman, "Marriage and the Economic Well-Being of Families with Children: A Review of the Literature" (Washington, DC: U.S. Department of Health and Human Services, July 2002); and David C. Ribar, "What Do Social Scientists Know About the Benefits of Marriage? A Review of Quantitative Methodologies," IZA Discussion Paper No. 998 (January 2004).

†Gregory Acs and Sandi Nelson, "Should We Get Married in the Morning?" Discussion Paper (Washington, DC: Urban Institute, 2004). See also Adam Thomas and Isabel Sawhill, "For Richer or Poorer: Marriage As an Antipoverty Strategy," *Journal of Policy Analysis and Management* 21, no. 4 (Fall 2002): 587–99.

††The remainder of the inset draws from discussions by Theodora Ooms, "Marriage and Government: Strange Bedfellows?" *Policy Brief,* No 1, Center for Law and Social Policy (August 2002); Daniel T. Lichter, "Marriage as Public Policy," Progressive Policy Institute (September 2001); and Daniel Lichter, Deborah Roempke Graefe, and J. Brian Brown, "Is Marriage a Panacea?" *Social Problems* 50, no. 1 (February 2003): 60–86.

The Earned Income Tax Credit

The **Earned Income Tax Credit** (EITC) is a federal program that both raises income and encourages individuals with low potential wages to seek employment. The EITC is a refundable tax credit based on household earnings. In contrast to many tax credits, which benefit only households with an income high enough to pay taxes, the government provides a refund if the amount of the credit exceeds taxes owed, thereby particularly benefiting low-income households. Further, unlike the minimum wage, it targets only low-wage workers living in poor and near-poor households.[26]

The EITC was originally established in 1975 to offset the Social Security payroll tax for low-earner households with children, and was expanded considerably in the early 1990s. It has become the largest cash transfer program for low-income families in the United States, dwarfing the size of TANF. The amount of the credit varies according to the presence of children as well as the level of earnings.[27] For example, in 2003, for a family with two children and up to $10,510 in earnings, their earnings were subsidized at a rate of 40 percent. A similar family with earnings between $10,510 and $13,730 received $4,204, the maximum amount available. Beyond $13,730 the credit was reduced by 21 cents for every additional dollar earned until it was fully phased out at $33,692.

The impact of the EITC on raising families out of poverty is substantial.[28] For instance, as shown in Table 10-3, the income of an employed single parent with two children who works full-time, full-year at the minimum wage was increased from $10,300 to $14,504, just below the amount of the relevant poverty threshold. This family is also eligible for food stamps, which increases net income, but must pay federal payroll taxes on earnings. In addition, such a family may also receive some federal child care assistance, though not enough to fully cover child care costs. One study found that these factors, taken together, nearly offset one another, leaving income at about the level reported in Table 10-3 (for "Earnings plus EITC").[29] Another benefit, however, is not reflected in the simple calculation reported in Table 10-3. Children under age 15 may also receive federally funded health care, either through Medicaid or via the Children's Health Insurance Program (CHIP) enacted in 1997, though their parents may or may not have health care coverage, depending on their employer.

TABLE 10-3 Making Ends Meet for a Low-Earner Single-Parent Family with Two Children, 2003	
Earnings (assume employed at minimum wage job full-time, full-year)[a]	$10,300
EITC (maximum credit)	$4,204
Earnings plus EITC	$14,504
Poverty threshold[b]	$14,680
Ratio of earnings plus EITC to poverty threshold	0.99

[a] Earnings are computed as $5.15 multiplied by 40 hours per week multiplied by 50 weeks per year.
[b] This figure, calculated by the Census Bureau, is for a three-person family for 2003. See www.census.gov.

---

[26]See, for instance, Saul D. Hoffman and Laurence S. Seidman, *Helping Working Families: The Earned Income Tax Credit* (Kalamazoo, MI: W.E. UpJohn Institute for Employment Research, 2003); and V. Joseph Hotz and John Karl Scholz, "The Earned Income Tax Credit," in *Means-Tested Transfers in the United States*, edited by Moffitt, pp. 141–97.
[27]Since 1994, low-income households without children have also been eligible, though only for a small credit.
[28]For recent evidence, see Craig Gunderson and James P. Ziliak, "Poverty and Macroeconomic Performance Across Space, Race, and Family Structure," *Demography* 41, no. 1 (February 2004): 61–86.
[29]David T. Ellwood, "The Plight of the Working Poor," Children's Roundtable Report #2 (Washington, DC: Brookings Institution, November 1999).

In contrast to AFDC, which provided maximum payments to those not employed and imposed a high marginal tax rate on earnings, the EITC encourages individuals to seek employment by subsidizing earnings.[30] For individuals in the low income range, the amount of the EITC increases with additional hours worked. At the same time, however, the EITC may cause some workers to reduce the number of hours worked. The provision of a fixed credit over the middle income range, for instance, provides these workers with a pure increase in income. As discussed in Chapter 4, with higher nonlabor income, individuals tend to work fewer hours.

For individuals in the highest income range among those eligible, the credit and thus the net wage are reduced as earnings increase. In this range, individuals tend to substitute toward nonmarket time and away from paid work because of the decrease in the opportunity cost of nonmarket time. At the same time, total income is still higher than it would otherwise be without the EITC program, also providing an incentive for individuals to work less. Hence, in this range, both the substitution and income effects operate to reduce hours worked.

The effect of the EITC program thus varies depending on which phase of the schedule individuals face. Overwhelming evidence indicates that the EITC provides a strong incentive for single mothers to enter the paid labor force. In fact, one study finds that nearly 60 percent of the increase in single mother's employment from 1984 to 1996 was due to the expansion of the EITC alone.[31] On the other hand, the design of the EITC also causes some secondary earners in married-couple families, typically wives, to leave the labor force.[32] Wives' additional earnings often place the family's income in the phase-out range of the credit, thereby leading to receipt of a lower EITC or none at all. The EITC's secondary earner penalty was eased slightly in recent years as a result of tax changes made by the Bush administration in 2003, though by no means was eliminated.[33] These changes increase the income range over which the maximum credit is available for married-couples by $3,000, before the onset of the phase-out range. As will be discussed shortly, the EITC may also affect family structure to the extent that people take its earnings criteria into account in their decisions to marry or get divorced.

Child Support Enforcement

Child support enforcement is another strategy for aiding single-parent families. Over the last 25 years, child support enforcement in the United States changed considerably, shifting from a "complaint-driven, court-enforced system" subject to considerable

---

[30]Most discussions on incentive effects, such as the one here, assume that the EITC is received on a regular basis throughout the year. However, virtually all recipients receive it as a lump sum, which may affect their response; see Timothy Smeeding, Katherine Ross Philips, and Michael O'Connor, "The EITC: Expectation, Knowledge, Use and Economic and Social Mobility," *National Tax Journal* 53, no. 4, pt. 2 (December 2000): 1187–209.

[31]Bruce D. Meyer and Dan T. Rosenbaum, "Welfare, the Earned Income Tax Credit, and the Labor Supply of Single Mothers," *Quarterly Journal of Economics* 116, no. 3 (August 2001): 1063–114. See also Nada Eissa and Jeffrey B. Liebman, "Labor Supply Response to the Earned Income Tax Credit," *Quarterly Journal of Economics* 111, no. 2 (May 1996): 606–37.

[32]Nada Eissa and Hilary Williamson Hoynes, "Taxes and the Labor Market Participation of Married Couples: The Earned Income Tax Credit," *Journal of Public Economics* (forthcoming).

[33]For possible solutions, see Saul D. Hoffman, "The EITC Marriage Tax and EITC Reform," University of Delaware (January 2003).

discretion to a system guided by state and federal laws and regulations.[34] The first major child support legislation enacted in 1975 was aimed at enforcing payments by noncustodial parents. Additional legislation in 1984 and 1988 considerably strengthened this law by requiring states to adopt numerical guidelines in setting child support awards and allowing them to collect income withheld from employers (garnish wages) or retain income tax refunds from noncustodial parents who do not make the required payments. The 1996 welfare legislation further instituted rules that make the establishment of paternity faster and easier, added a national registry system that makes tracking down delinquent parents across state lines possible, and set forth tough new penalties for non-payment, including revoking professional licenses and seizing assets. Subsequently, a law passed in 1998 toughened the sanctions, including penalties of up to 2 years in prison, for "deadbeat" parents.

Mothers who receive welfare are required to pursue child support as one of the conditions for receiving cash benefits. Until the 1996 welfare legislation, all states allowed a small portion of child support monies received to directly "pass-through" to welfare recipients, while the rest was kept by the states to cover the costs of public assistance. The pass-through provided an incentive for noncustodial parents to make child support payments because they could assume that their children would get some of the benefits of their payments. Since 1996, however, states have new latitude in deciding the amount of the pass-through, if any, and a majority of states eliminated it altogether. One notable exception is Wisconsin, where welfare families may keep all child support monies received.[35]

Recent evidence indicates that the government policies outlined here (in the case of the pass-through, a policy that retains it) do lead to higher rates of child support receipt by families, especially those on welfare. Not surprisingly, these effects are even stronger when combined with greater state expenditures on enforcement. Even so, the success of recent enforcement efforts is not apparent in aggregate statistics on child support received, which show that the proportion of single-mother families who received child support remained remarkably steady from the late 1970s to 1997, at just over 30 percent. This figure changed so little, in part, because at the same time that enforcement efforts increased, the composition of single-parent families changed as well. Specifically, the proportion of never-married mothers increased and they are much less likely to get awards, let alone actual payments, as compared with divorced women.[36] Nevertheless, child support award rates for never-married mothers, while still quite low, continue to rise, no doubt as a result of the many new policies targeted at this group.[37]

---

[34]This characterization is from Elaine Sorensen and Ariel Halpern, "Child Support Reforms: Who Has Benefited?" *Focus* 21, no. 1 (Spring 2000): 38–41. For a concise review of the major changes in federal laws and empirical evidence on the effects, see "Child Support Enforcement Policy and Low-Income Families," *Focus* 21, no. 1 (Spring 2000): 3. See also Andrea H. Beller and John W. Graham, *Small Change: The Economics of Child Support* (New Haven, CT: Yale University Press, 1993), chap. 6.

[35]See Judith Cassety, Maria Cancian, and Daniel R. Meyer, "Child Support Disregard and Pass-Through Policies," *Focus* 21, no. 1 (Spring 2000): 64–66.

[36]Figure is from Sorensen and Halpern, "Child Support Reforms." See also, Richard B. Freeman and Jane Waldfogel, "Dunning Delinquent Dads: The Effects of Child Support Enforcement Policy on Child Support Receipt by Never-Married Women," *Journal of Human Resources* 36, no. 2 (Spring 2001): 207–25; and Elaine Sorensen and Ariel Hill, "Single Mothers and Their Child Support Receipt," *Journal of Human Resources* 39, no. 1 (Winter 2004): 135–54.

[37]Freeman and Waldfogel, "Dunning Delinquent Dads."

At the same time, there is increasing concern that the current system is not sufficiently flexible to deal with the diverse economic status of noncustodial parents, typically fathers. The current guidelines are designed for those with stable employment and adequate incomes, while many face a different economic reality of little education, unstable employment, and consequently low earnings. These fathers, sometimes labeled "dead-broke" dads, may simply not be able to financially support their children, and, for them, existing policies may well promote counterproductive outcomes. For instance, they may shift from legal employment to "under-the-table" work, with all its attendant disadvantages, or may give up employment altogether. In addition, such policies may lead some fathers to avoid social contact with their children.[38] To address these concerns, the federal government has funded a variety of initiatives to improve the labor market opportunities of young unmarried fathers.[39]

One alternative to the patchwork of child support policies in the United States is to establish a Child Support Assurance System, similar to the one that already exists in Sweden.[40] Under this system, both parents and government would be responsible for the support of children. Awards from nonresident parents would be a percentage of their income, set by a court, and would be withheld from earnings, much as taxes are. If the parent cannot meet this obligation, the government would provide the minimum assured benefit. New York tried a modest version of this program, which showed positive results. Such a program, however, faces little chance of being adopted nationwide given the reluctance of many to see the role of federal government expanded from merely setting guidelines and rules to encourage private child support payments to providing actual child support monies.

TAXES, SPECIALIZATION, AND MARRIAGE

Up to this point we largely ignored the role of the federal income tax system, but it is in fact quite important in this context. First, it helps to finance federal programs, including those discussed here. At the same time it means that individuals do not retain all their labor market earnings. Hence, the structure of the federal income tax system affects take-home pay and consequently decisions regarding whether and how much to work, as well as decisions about family formation. Similarly, payroll taxes and the Social Security payments they fund also affect these decisions. Both federal income taxation and Social Security face criticism for being biased in favor of the traditional, one-earner family.[41] Both these programs, which evolved when this type of family was the norm, in

---

[38]These impacts are cited in Maureen Waller and Robert Plotnick, "A Failed Relationship? Low-Income Families and the Child Support Enforcement System," *Focus* 21, no. 1 (Spring 2000): 12–17; Anu Rangarajan and Philip Gleason, "Young Unwed Fathers of AFDC Children: Do They Provide Support?" *Demography* 35, no. 2 (May 1998): 175–86; Irwin Garfinkel, Sara McLanahan, Daniel Meyer, and Judith Seltzer, eds. *Fathers Under Fire: The Revolution in Child Support Enforcement* (New York: Russell Sage Foundation, 1998); and Harry J. Holzer, Paul Offner, and Elaine Sorensen, "Declining Employment Among Young Black Less-Educated Men: The Role of Incarceration and Child Support," Institute for Research on Poverty Discussion Paper No. 1281-04 (May 2004).
[39]U.S. Department of Health and Human Services, "Promoting Responsible Fatherhood," *HHS Fact Sheet* (April 26, 2002).
[40]For a discussion of child support systems elsewhere, see Anne Corden and Daniel R. Meyer, "Child Support Policy Regimes in the United States, United Kingdom, and Other Countries: Similar Issues, Different Approaches," *Focus* 21, no. 1 (Spring 2000): 72–79.
[41]Here we focus on two major federal programs only, but it should be noted that most states assess their own income tax, and an array of other taxes are imposed at the federal, state, and local levels.

effect, subsidize married women who stay home. Therefore it can be argued that they need to be modified in light of the changing structure of American families.

One of the primary rules proposed by economists for fair taxation is **horizontal equity**, which simply means that those in similar circumstances should be treated the same.[42] We specifically consider the question of whether the current income tax and Social Security systems violate this rule in their treatment of one-earner and two-earner families.[43]

Income Taxation Policy

First and foremost, the present income tax system may be considered inequitable because the value of goods and services produced in the home is not taxed, whereas money income is subject to taxation. As a result, two couples with different levels of economic well-being may have the same taxable incomes. Suppose, for instance, that Ellen and Ed earn $25,000 each and produce $10,000 worth of goods and services in the household. Suppose too that Jim earns $50,000 and Jane, a full-time homemaker, produces $30,000 worth of goods and services in the home. Although Jim and Jane produce a total income of $80,000, including the value of home production, while Ellen and Ed only produce an income of $60,000, taxable income is $50,000 for both.

One of the concerns with such a policy is that it provides incentives for families to adopt the traditional division of labor and creates a disincentive for married women to participate in the labor force. The disincentive to work for pay additionally stems from the fact that the family is the unit of taxation and the tax structure is progressive, meaning that higher levels of family income are taxed at a higher *rate* than lower levels. As shown in panel a of Table 10-4, this means that if a married couple's earnings are $50,000, part of this amount is subject to a 10 percent tax rate and the remainder is subject to a 15 percent rate, assuming they file jointly. In general, progressive tax rates are considered to be desirable because they result in wealthier families paying a proportionately larger share of their incomes in taxes. The degree of progressivity in the tax system has varied considerably in recent years. The Tax Reform Act of 1986 reduced the number of tax brackets from 15 brackets, with a top rate of 50 percent, to only two brackets, with stated rates of 15 and 28 percent. Under President Clinton, the top tax rate was 39.6 percent. Most recently, in 2001 President Bush introduced a 10 percent bracket, and lowered all other rates, including the top rate, which now stands at 35 percent, as shown in Table 10-4.[44]

The current tax structure means that a married woman, still generally considered to be the secondary earner by most families, will often face a high marginal tax rate on her potential income, should she decide to enter the labor market. The first dollar of her earnings is taxed at her husband's top marginal tax rate, thereby reducing the incentive

---

[42]The view that "there is a generally accepted standard of equity or fairness with respect to public finance measures: equal treatment of those equally circumstanced," was first expressed by Carl S. Shoup, *Public Finance* (Chicago: Aldine Publishing Company, 1969), p. 23, and has been widely shared ever since.

[43]These topics have been discussed by economists for some time, from Nancy R. Gordon, "Institutional Responses: The Federal Income Tax System" and "Institutional Responses: The Social Security System," in *The Subtle Revolution*, edited by Ralph E. Smith (Washington, DC: Urban Institute, 1979), pp. 201–21, 223–55; to Edward J. McCaffery, *Taxing Women* (Chicago: University of Chicago Press, 1997).

[44]Many of the 2001 tax changes were to be phased in over the 2000s, but were instituted much earlier as part of a 2003 tax stimulus package.

TABLE 10-4 Federal Individual Income Tax Rates and Calculation of Marriage Penalty/Bonus

(a) 2003 Federal Individual Income Tax Rate Schedules[a]

Single Schedule

Taxable Income	Tax Rate
$0–$7,000	10.0%
$7,000–$28,400	15.0%
$28,400–$68,800	25.0%
$68,800–$143,500	28.0%
$143,500–$311,950	33.0%
$311,950+	35.0%

Married Filing Jointly Schedule

Taxable Income	Tax Rate
$0–$14,000	10.0%
$14,000–$56,800	15.0%
$56,800–$114,650	25.0%
$114,650–$174,700	28.0%
$174,700–$311,950	33.0%
$311,950+	35.0%

(b) Calculation of Marriage Penalty/Bonus Using 2003 Tax Rate Schedule[b]

Couple	Value of Home Production (not taxable)	Husband's Income (taxable)	Wife's Income (taxable)	Combined Income (taxable)	Tax Liability if: Married Couple	Tax Liability if: Both Single	Marriage Penalty or Bonus
Ellen and Ed	$10,000	$ 25,000	$25,000	$ 50,000	$ 6,800	$ 6,800	$ 0 penalty
Jane and Jim	$30,000	$ 50,000	$ 0	$ 50,000	$ 6,800	$ 9,310	$2,510 bonus
Gina and Greg	$10,000	$ 60,000	$60,000	$120,000	$23,781	$23,620	$ 161 penalty
Debra and Dave	$30,000	$120,000	$ 0	$120,000	$23,781	$28,346	$ 4,565 bonus

[a]Two other schedules are not shown here: the head of household schedule for single individuals with a dependent child and a married filing separately schedule for couples who are separated.

[b]This table makes several simplifying assumptions. It assumes no children and that taxable income equals gross income. In actual practice, taxable income is calculated as gross income less personal exemptions and less the standard deduction.

for her to enter the labor market. In the case of Jane and Jim, if Jane decides to work for pay, the first dollar she receives is taxed at a 15 percent rate. This is because her income will be added on to Jim's and their tax liability will be determined using the married filing jointly tax schedule. This disincentive increases considerably with couples' income. For instance, consider a couple in which the husband, Dave, has $120,000 in earnings and his wife, Debra, is presently a full-time homemaker. If Debra were to enter the labor market, her first dollar of pay would be taxed at a 28 percent rate, not at the bottom tax rate of 10 percent. As noted earlier, the EITC, which is part of the federal tax code, also discourages participation by a secondary earner in low-earning families, because the value of the EITC eventually declines as family earnings rise.

In addition to these potential disincentives to participate in the paid labor force, the so-called marriage penalty has received considerable attention. A marriage penalty refers to the additional taxes a couple must pay if they are married as compared to the taxes they would pay if they remained single, while a marriage subsidy refers to possible tax savings due to marriage. A marriage penalty results when the income brackets for married couples are less than twice as wide as the brackets for singles. Marriage penalties originated with a policy change initiated in 1969 to provide some relief to single taxpayers relative to their married-couple counterparts. However, the process of reducing the relative tax liability of single taxpayers inevitably increased the relative tax liability for some married couples. In President Bush's 2001 tax changes, he eliminated the marriage penalty for some and reduced it for other couples by making the new 10 percent bracket for married couples twice as wide as for singles and gradually phasing in the same change for the existing 15 percent bracket. President Bush also reduced the marriage penalty by increasing the value of the standard deduction for married couples so that it is now twice the value for singles.[45]

Even with President Bush's changes, our current tax structure imposes penalties on being married for some couples, while it provides subsidies for others. For instance, consider again Jim and Jane and Ellen and Ed, but now suppose that they are unmarried, as shown in panel b of Table 10-4, which provides an illustrative example using the 2003 tax rates. If Jim earns $50,000 and marries Jane, who has no earnings, their combined tax liability declines by $2,510, providing a marriage bonus of this amount. Conversely, if Ellen and Ed each earn $25,000, with President Bush's tax changes, they face no marriage penalty because their top tax rate is 15 percent. Marriage penalties remain, however, for couples whose income is taxed in brackets higher than 15 percent. For instance, Gina and Greg, who each earn $60,000, face a marriage penalty of $161. In general, the tax system favors single-earner married couples over two-earner married couples; those couples with fairly equal incomes tend to be at the greatest disadvantage.[46] The reason for this difference is that the tax system essentially "splits" joint income between two married individuals and treats them as if they were two individuals with equal income. This treatment lowers the tax liability for Jim and Jane because, as a result of the progressive tax system, part of Jim's income would be subject to a higher rate if he was single. Gina and Greg do not benefit from this provision. On the

---

[45]Edward J. McCaffery, "Marriage Penalty Relief in the New Tax Law," (Washington, DC: National Center for Policy Analysis, June 2003); and Adam Carasso and C. Eugene Steurle, "How Marriage Penalties Change Under the 2001 Tax Bill," Discussion Paper (Washington, DC: Urban Institute, May 2002).
[46]Couples cannot get around this "penalty" by filing separate returns. The tax rates for married filing separately are higher than the rates for single individuals.

contrary, when the wife is employed, many couples such as those like Gina and Greg end up paying more in taxes than they would if they were single.

The way in which the 2001 tax changes provided tax relief to married couples has substantial revenue implications. For instance, by making the width of the 10 and 15 percent married couple brackets and the standard deduction twice as large as those for singles, these changes not only reduced the penalty for some, but increased the size of the marriage bonus for others. A less costly alternative, which would exclusively target those bearing a marriage penalty, is to restore the two-earner deduction that was in place in the early 1980s. The design of the income tax results in other consequences, apart from effects on revenue. For instance, various features of the tax system influence the rate and timing of marriage, as well as the probability of divorce, although the effect on the latter appears to be small.[47]

The marriage penalty tends to be larger not only for two-earner couples with high incomes but also those with low incomes. In fact, as a percent of income, low-income couples face the most severe penalty, and thus, the greatest disincentive to marry. One study found that the marriage penalty could be nearly 20 percent of combined earnings for some low-earner couples.[48] The reason that the penalty is so severe for these couples is that the EITC, for which low-earner couples are eligible, is based on family income. For instance, if a low-earner single mother with children currently receiving the EITC marries a low-earning man, it may well push family earnings high enough to make them ineligible for any credit. On the other hand, if a nonemployed woman with children who is ineligible for the EITC marries a low-earner male, the amount of their total credit will rise. President Bush's tax changes also somewhat reduced marriage penalties in the EITC. As noted earlier, in 2003 the income level at which the EITC phases out for married couples was increased somewhat. Also, changes made to the child tax credit, which both increased its value and made it partially deductible, reduced the marriage penalty for low-income workers.[49] These various changes, nevertheless, substantially increased the complexity of the tax code.

Even though recent policy changes focused exclusively on reducing or eliminating the marriage penalty, other biases affect the tax system. A proposal that would eliminate the work disincentives faced by a secondary earner (as well as the marriage penalty) would be to tax each person as an individual, as Canada, Sweden, and the United Kingdom do, and as the United States did prior to 1948. This approach, which would equalize tax rates for individuals with equal incomes, regardless of their marital status, has not received much support in this country. Such a policy would clearly be to the advantage of two-earner couples but would increase the tax liability of one-earner families, even though these families would still benefit because in-kind income is not taxed. Whether it is viewed as more equitable in its treatment of money income than the current arrangement (in the sense of establishing horizontal equity) depends on whether the individual or the family is viewed as the appropriate tax unit.[50] A flat tax, which

---

[47]James Alm, Stacy Dickert-Conlin, and Leslie A. Whittington provide a useful summary of recent research findings in "Policy Watch: The Marriage Penalty," *Journal of Economic Perspectives* 13, no. 3 (Summer 1999): 193–204.

[48]Daniel R. Feenberg and Harvey S. Rosen, "Recent Developments in the Marriage Tax," *National Tax Journal* 48, no. 1 (March 1995): 91–101.

[49]Carasso and Steurle, "How Marriage Penalties Change Under the 2001 Tax Bill."

[50]For instance, some argue that the family should be the unit of taxation because it is a basic economic unit in society and because husbands and wives pool income. However, recent empirical evidence weakens the latter argument. See McCaffery, *Taxing Women,* chap. 1.

imposes the same rate on all incomes, would also meet the goal of horizontal equity and surfaces periodically in discussions about tax reform. Still, even with a large personal exemption such a tax would be much less progressive than the current system.

Finally, the possibility of taxing household production receives almost no attention. It is doubtful that such a proposal would garner much popular support. Moreover, it would be extremely difficult to implement because of the great difficulties involved in obtaining reliable estimates of the value of household production, as discussed in Chapter 3.

The Social Security System

The Social Security system also poses problems of equity between one-earner married couples, on the one hand, and two-earner married couples, unmarried couples, and single people, on the other hand.[51] The problem arises because payroll taxes are based on each individual's employment history, while Social Security benefits received are family based. As of 2004, individuals in jobs covered by Social Security (and Medicare) faced a 15.3 percent tax rate on earnings up to a specified maximum level, half to be paid by the employer, half by the worker. To receive benefits, individuals must obtain a threshold level of pay from jobs covered by Social Security for 40 calendar quarters. Spouses of covered workers are entitled to receive Social Security benefits equal to 50 percent of the amount received by the covered worker, and survivor benefits of 100 percent if the covered worker dies, even if they have never paid payroll taxes.[52] Alternatively, the spouse may receive benefits based on his or her own earnings record if that amount is greater. Among married couples, it is almost invariably the husband who is either the sole wage earner or has the greater earnings, if both are employed. These cases are considered in turn.

The current Social Security system clearly favors families with a full-time homemaker over all others. In such a family, only the husband pays payroll taxes while the family receives 150 percent of his Social Security benefit.

Next, consider the case of the wife who is employed, but who earns substantially lower wages over a shorter worklife than her husband. In this case, the wife pays payroll taxes into the system too but the family still receives precisely the same benefits as they would if she had not been employed and had paid no payroll taxes. Nevertheless, the husband and wife together receive more benefits than they would if they were single.

Finally, consider the case of the wife who earns enough to receive larger benefits in her own right than she would receive as a spouse.[53] The family will receive somewhat larger benefits than they would in the other cases. However, in this case the wife gets

---

[51] Useful overviews of these issues are provided in Melissa M. Favreault, Frank J. Sammartino, and C. Eugene Steurle, "Social Security Benefits for Spouses and Survivors: Options for Change," in *Social Security and the Family: Addressing Unmet Needs in an Underfunded System*, edited by Melissa M. Favreault, Frank J. Sammartino, and C. Eugene Steurle (Washington, DC: The Urban Institute, 2002), pp. 177–228; McCaffery, *Taxing Women;* and Marianne A. Ferber, "Women's Employment and the Social Security System," *Social Security Bulletin* 56, no. 3 (Fall 1993): 33–55.

[52] Since 1977, spouses divorced after at least 10 years of marriage are entitled to the same benefit as current spouses.

[53] Phillip B. Levine, Olivia S. Mitchell, and John W. Phillips find that two-thirds of wives nearing retirement who have 40 calendar quarters of employment will receive benefits based on their own work history in "A Benefit of One's Own: Older Women's Retirement Entitlements Under Social Security," *Social Security Bulletin* 63, no. 3 (2000): 47–53.

no benefit from being a spouse. She and her husband receive exactly the same amount in benefits as if they were both single.

The inconsistencies in the preceding descriptions obviously violate the cardinal rule of horizontal equity, namely that equal contributions should secure equal returns. Each employed wife pays in as much as she would if she were single, but only the one who earns considerably less than her husband receives additional benefits as a spouse, and a wife who is not employed receives benefits as a spouse without making any tax payments at all. Clearly this system provides secondary earners, typically wives, with yet another disincentive to work for pay. Not only do they pay income taxes on their earnings, while the value of home production is not taxed, but they get a much lower return on the payroll taxes they are required to pay than full-time homemakers.

One way to bring about equity among couples would be through "earnings sharing."[54] This approach, which assigns an equal share of total household earnings to each spouse, recognizes that the division of labor in the home represents a joint decision and that both spouses contribute to family welfare through their market and/or non-market work. Unlike the present system, earnings sharing would not penalize dual-earner couples. In addition, the Social Security system would move in the direction of greater horizontal equity, in that equal contributions to Social Security would yield equal benefits.[55] No couple would have an advantage as compared to any other couple or unmarried individual. Such a change would, however, create problems for traditional couples who, it might be argued, made their labor supply decisions under the existing rules. This difficulty could, however, be overcome by giving couples who married before a certain date the option of remaining under the current system. A change to earnings sharing might also raise concerns about the adequacy of benefit levels for single-earner families. Although such issues remain to be addressed, continued growth of the two-earner family is likely to increase support for policies that eliminate the existing advantages of single-earner families, whether for individual taxation in the federal income tax system or earnings sharing in the Social Security system.

Under the current system, the adequacy of Social Security benefits for never-married, divorced, and widowed women causes concerns because these groups have the highest poverty rates among the elderly. This high poverty level is in part due to the fact that women, on average, earn lower wages, work fewer hours per week, and are much more likely to have spent time out of the labor market to raise children or take care of other family members.[56] For this reason, they are also much less likely to have pensions from employers and are thus much more likely to rely on Social Security as their major source of income. Widows, for instance, receive just 50 to 75 percent of the combined benefit of a married couple, which results in a considerable drop in their standard of living because the cost of maintaining a one-person household is considerably more than half of

---

[54]For further discussion, see Ferber, "Women's Employment and the Social Security System."

[55]No Social Security taxes are paid on the value of what is produced in the household, but neither does the family accumulate benefits.

[56]See, for instance, Timothy J. Smeeding, "Social Security Reform: Improving Benefit Adequacy and Economic Security for Women," Policy Brief No. 16 (Syracuse University: Aging Studies Program, 1999); Steven H. Sandell and Howard M. Iams, "Reducing Women's Poverty by Shifting Social Security Benefits from Retired Couples to Widows," *Journal of Policy Analysis and Management* 16, no. 2 (Spring 1997): 279–97; and Favreault, Sammrantino, and Steurle, "Social Security Benefits for Spouses and Survivors."

the cost of maintaining a household of two.[57] Never-married women, and divorced women who were married fewer than 10 years receive benefits based on their own earnings record only. Elderly women at greatest risk of poverty are those who spent a good deal of time on welfare in earlier years. Their shorter work lives and most often low earnings lead to extremely low Social Security benefits. Even though they are likely to be eligible for Supplemental Security Income (SSI), which provides cash benefits for the low-income elderly, even the combined benefits are generally insufficient to lift them out of poverty.[58] One way to address these problems would be to increase the value of the minimum Social Security benefit. Others advocate increasing the size of the spousal and survivor benefit or perhaps giving women "credit" for time spent out of the labor force to raise children, though these latter changes would further increase the advantage of one-earner over two-earner families and increase incentives for women to stay out of the labor force.[59]

Recently, the majority of reform proposals for Social Security have focused on ensuring that the program will be financially solvent to meet the demands of the baby boom cohort, which is quickly nearing retirement. Payroll taxes could be raised, the cap on the maximum amount of earnings that are subject to Social Security taxes could be increased or even removed, benefits could be cut, or some combination of these reforms could be instituted. In addition to such reforms, a number of proposals include a "two-tier" system with a traditional Social Security program that would provide a safety net, similar to the design of the present program, coupled with a second tier of private investments.[60] The merits of this specific reform are the subject of a lively debate, particularly because it is such a substantial departure from the status quo. Part of the discussion focuses on the implications of such a change for women.[61] Among the concerns is that women who spend time out of the labor market to rear children, and especially those who were never employed, will be disadvantaged because they will accumulate little in the investment program. Even women in paid employment would likely accrue smaller amounts because of their lower earnings levels. On the other hand, if women did make individual contributions into their investment funds, they would be able to keep them, while under the present system they do not benefit from additional contributions to Social Security as long as they are entitled to greater benefits as a spouse. It might also be possible to combine this type of reform with earnings sharing to address some of the equity issues raised earlier.

---

[57]Another inequity of the current system is that widows from one-earner families receive a survivor benefit of 75 percent of the couple's previous benefit while widows from dual-earner families in which the spouses had fairly similar earnings, only receive 50 percent of the couple's previous benefit.

[58]Sheila R. Zedlewski and Rumki Saha, "Social Security and Single Mothers," in *Social Security and the Family,* edited by Favreault, Sammartino Steurle, pp. 89–121.

[59]See, for instance, Smeeding, "Social Security Reform."

[60]For details on one possible proposal, see John F. Cogan and Olivia S. Mitchell, "Perspectives from the President's Commission on Social Security Reform," *Journal of Economic Perspectives* 17, no. 2 (Spring 2003): 149–72. For a critique of this and other similar proposals, see Marianne Ferber, Vanessa Rouillon, and Patricia Simpson, "The Aging Population and Social Security: Must We Destroy It to Save It?" Working paper (University of Illinois at Urbana–Champaign, Summer 2004).

[61]Theresa J. Devine, "Women and Social Security Reform," Paper presented at American Economic Association Meetings (January 2000); and U.S. General Accounting Office, "Social Security Reform: Implications for Women," Report T-HEHS-99-52 (Washington, DC: U.S. General Accounting Office, February 1999). Although many concerns have been raised, a simulation by Rudolph G. Penner and Elizabeth Cove suggests that women might actually benefit from such a change. See "Women and Individual Accounts," in *Social Security and the Family*, edited by Favreault, Sammartino, and Steurle, pp. 229–70.

THE COMPETING DEMANDS OF WORK AND FAMILY

As described in Chapter 9, today a growing share of the workforce has family responsibilities. There are greater numbers of two-earner families, including those with small
children, and more single-parent families than in earlier days. Although the burden of
balancing the competing demands of work and family is still largely borne by individuals, this section considers new and expanding programs provided by government and
employers to help individuals in such families better balance the demands of their dual
responsibilities.

Problems of balancing family demands and paid work can occur throughout the
life cycle. Young workers often need to care for small children. As workers grow older,
some may need to assist their teenage children in solving behavioral problems or to
help grown children establish themselves. Frequently, they also must meet the needs of
aging relatives and perhaps close friends as well.

Because of their limited amount of time and energy, individuals confront a trade-
off between doing full justice to their job and fully meeting family responsibilities.
Balancing these demands is generally most difficult for employed women with families because they typically do most of the housework, as well as child and elder care,
thus in effect facing a "second shift."[62] As seen in Chapter 3, employed wives do twice
as much housework as their husbands. As discussed in Chapter 9, time spent in such
activities appears to reduce wages, perhaps by limiting the effort or time workers are
able to expend for market work. In addition, the need for elder care, mainly provided
by women, is likely to place increasing demands on women's time in the coming years.
The Census Bureau projects that by 2050, the U.S. population age 65 and older will increase by 80 percent, a figure substantially greater than the expected increase in the
population of working-age adults. In addition, as a result of improved health care and
nutrition, the size of the "old old" population, typically defined as those age 85 and
older, is increasing and these individuals are even more likely to require care.[63] Demands are especially great on women whose age places them in what has been called
the "sandwich generation," those responsible for both the care of their parents and
their children at the same time, often women who delayed childbearing until their mid
thirties to forties.[64]

Some women respond to these competing demands by taking part-time rather than
full-time jobs, in many cases putting their careers on hold. Indeed, as Table 10-5 shows, in
2003 less than one-half of all married mothers with children under 18 years of age were
employed full-time; this was true of only 35 percent of married mothers with a child
under age 3. Those who do work full-time are more securely attached to the labor force
and earn higher incomes, but they are also likely to face a considerable time squeeze.

---

[62]Arlie Hochschild, *The Second Shift* (New York: Viking Press, 1989). See also Glenna Spitze and Karyn
Loscocco, "Women's Position in the Household," *Quarterly Review of Economics and Finance* 39, no. 5
(Special Issue 1999): 647–61.
[63]U.S. Census Bureau, "Census Bureau Frames U.S. in Global Context; Identifies Aging, Fertility Trends,"
CB02-CN53 (February 2002). For evidence on elder care responsibilities see, for instance, Richard W. Johnson
and Anthony T. Lo Sasso, "The Employment and Time Costs of Caring for Elderly Parents," *Joint Center for
Poverty Research Newsletter* (September–October 2001); and Susan L. Ettner, "The Impact of 'Parent Care'
on Female Labor Supply Decisions," *Demography* 32, no. 1 (February 1995): 63–108.
[64]See, for instance, Leslie B. Hammer and Margaret B. Neal, "Sandwiched Generation Caregivers: Prevalence, Characteristics, and Outcomes," Presented at the University of Maryland Population Research Center Conference on "Workforce/Workplace Mismatch: Work, Family, Health, and Well-Being" (June 2003).

TABLE 10-5 Work Experience of Mothers, by Age of Youngest Child, 2003		
	All Mothers	*Married Mothers*
With child under age 18		
% employed	67.0	65.9
% employed full-time[a]	49.6	46.8
With child under age 3		
% employed	54.1	54.0
% employed full-time[a]	36.3	35.3

[a]Full-time refers to usually works 35 hours or more per week at all jobs.

Source: Bureau of Labor Statistics, "Employment Characteristics of Families in 2003," *News*, USDL 04-719 (April 20, 2004), Tables 5 and 6.

It is, however, low-income single mothers who are likely to face the most serious time squeeze. Those on welfare are required to work for pay for no less than 30 hours per week as of 2004, and their earnings, even supplemented by the EITC, are often inadequate to pay all bills. In addition, their jobs are likely to offer little flexibility, limiting their ability to do such things as tend to sick children or go to parent-teacher conferences, and they are unlikely to be able to afford help with house cleaning and often even child care.[65]

In the absence of adequate provisions for maternity leave, women in the labor force who bear children face unique challenges. For instance, as a general rule, pregnant women must be careful to avoid heavy lifting and excessive physical exertion. At the same time, in recent years larger fractions of women are engaged in occupations that require such activities. If firms do not accommodate the needs of pregnant women in such jobs by assigning them to alternative duties, the women may have to leave their jobs or may be terminated.[66] Also, breastfeeding, a practice strongly encouraged by the American Academy of Pediatrics, poses yet another potential work-family conflict, with women often choosing feeding practices that best accommodate their situation in the workplace.[67]

Given women's primary role as caregivers, they would be the main beneficiaries of more family-friendly policies. Adoption of such policies would make it easier for them to remain attached to the labor force and to succeed on the job, while also meeting what many still regard as their family obligations. Such accommodations would, in turn, increase the incentives both for women themselves and for their employers to invest in women's human capital. Of course, those men who already shoulder sizable housework and child care responsibilities would benefit as well,[68] and others would

[65]Randy Albeda, "Welfare-to-Work, Farewell to Families? U.S. Welfare Reform and Work/Family Debates," *Feminist Economics* 7, no. 1 (March 2001): 119–135.

[66]Sue Shellenbarger, "Pregnant Workers Clash with Employers Over Job Inflexibility," *Wall Street Journal*, February 10, 1999, p. B1.

[67]Brian Roe, Leslie A. Whittington, Sara Beck Fein, and Mario F. Teisl, "Is There Competition Between Breast-Feeding and Maternal Employment?" *Demography* 36, no. 2 (May 1999): 157–71. These authors find that mothers who have leaves of longer duration breastfeed their infants for a longer period of time, but they also find that many mothers who return to the workplace manage to do both, with key factors being access to a private area and break time.

[68]For a discussion of men's difficulties in balancing work and family, see Joseph H. Pleck, "Balancing Work and Family," *Scientific American Presents* 10, no. 2 (Summer 1999): 38–43.

find it easier to do a larger share. Thus, family-friendly policies would also be expected to promote a more equal division of labor in the household.

WHO IS RESPONSIBLE FOR CHILDREN?

In all economically advanced countries, though with considerable variation, government plays some role in child care through such policies as mandated parental leave, public provision of day care, or financing of day care. However, in contrast to most other economically advanced countries, the government's role in the United States remains quite limited.[69] The U.S. government did not mandate that firms provide unpaid family leave to workers until the Family and Medical Leave Act (FMLA) was passed in 1993, while all other economically advanced nations provide *paid* leave, and most have been doing so for a considerable period of time. The U.S. government does to some extent subsidize child care for poor families and offers tax deductions to others, but does not generally provide day care itself. Consequently, families must make their own private arrangements or take advantage of benefits offered voluntarily by some firms such as on-site child care or help in finding child care. In comparison, France, Sweden, and Denmark, among others, provide free or heavily subsidized day care through the government sector.

The question of how the costs of raising children should be shared between parents, the government, and employers is quite complex.[70] One economic argument for government to play a role is that there are externalities associated with bearing and raising children. For instance, children's parents undoubtedly receive a direct benefit from their own children and thus bear a special responsibility for their care; the nation also benefits when children grow up to be healthier, better-educated, and better-trained adults. They are more likely to be more productive, contribute more both as workers and as taxpayers, and less likely to be a burden on the public. In other words, significant positive externalities result when children are better cared for, which benefits not only their parents, but the whole community. Employers also benefit when their employees have dependable child care arrangements in that it should reduce workers' absenteeism and increase the likelihood that they will not leave their current position. These benefits suggest that government and employers, to some extent, should help finance the costs of raising children.

Issues of equity and redistribution provide another rationale for government to play a role. Government support for young children through such policies as subsidies for day care, parental leave, and infant nutrition serve to ensure that all children have a more equal chance at life, regardless of the economic status of the family into which they are born. Currently, various levels of government in the United States subsidize primary, secondary, and, to some extent, higher education. Arguably, it makes little sense to help educate youngsters from age five or six on, but not to help ensure that they will be ready

---

[69]Council of Economic Advisers, "The First Three Years: Investments That Pay" (Washington, DC: Council of Economic Advisers, April 1997).

[70]For excellent discussions of these issues, see Arleen Leibowitz, "Child Care: Private Cost or Public Responsibility?" in *Individual and Social Responsibility: Child Care, Education, Medical Care, and Long-Term Care in America,* edited by Victor R. Fuchs (Chicago: University of Chicago Press, 1996), pp. 33–57; and Nancy Folbre, "Children as Public Goods," *American Economic Review* 84, no. 2 (May 1994): 86–90.

to benefit from that education. Family leave, when taken by fathers as well as mothers, and subsidized day care also serve to enhance equity because they place female and male workers on a more equal footing, by reducing the potentially negative employment consequences associated with having to take time out for raising children.

An argument for government rather than employers playing a major role in providing benefits such as family leave and health insurance relates to a phenomenon called **adverse selection**. Adverse selection occurs if only some but not all firms offer such policies. It arises as a result of the fact that those workers who expect to benefit most from these policies are most likely to seek employment with firms that provide them. To understand the problem adverse selection poses, consider the following example. Suppose no federal family leave policy exists and instead only one firm offers it, basing its estimate of costs on the percentage of the total workforce that might use it. It could then provide the benefit and offer its workers a somewhat lower wage that would cover its costs. Given the scarcity of this benefit, however, this firm would be prone to attract workers with a higher probability of using family leave than the workforce at large. Hence, it would face higher costs than anticipated, and would be expected to try, to the extent it could, to pass along the cost increase in the form of still lower wages. This would further aggravate the adverse selection problem because those willing to work for these lower wages would increasingly consist of those who were most likely to take advantage of leaves, further increasing costs and thereby placing additional downward pressure on wages. In the end, the firm might well stop offering this benefit because it is too costly. More generally, adverse selection is likely to result in too few firms offering family leave relative to the optimal number, given workers' preferences. This suggests that a government mandate requiring all firms to offer such leave could eliminate the adverse selection problem and might be desirable on these grounds.[71]

The preceding discussion provides important efficiency and equity reasons as to why the government should play a role in raising children. However, in fully assessing the issue, potential costs should be considered too. For instance, government financing of any program, including subsidized day care and paid family leave, requires tax collection. Some research suggests that taxes cause individuals to work and save somewhat less than they would otherwise, thus reducing output.[72] For this reason, employer-mandated leave may be more efficient than leave paid for by the government, especially if the group that potentially benefits from the mandate bears the cost of the leave benefit in the form of lower wages. At least one study provides some evidence that wages do adjust and, thus, the policy is efficient.[73] Mandates would also boost economic efficiency to

---

[71]This example is drawn from Christopher J. Ruhm and Jackqueline L. Teague, "Parental Leave Policies in Europe and North America," in *Gender and Family Issues in the Workplace,* edited by Francine D. Blau and Ronald G. Ehrenberg (New York: Russell Sage Foundation, 1997), pp. 133–56. For a discussion of the adverse selection problem in general, see Harvey Rosen, *Public Finance,* 4th ed. (Chicago: Irwin, 1995).

[72]For evidence of the negative effect of taxes on labor supply, see, for instance, Jerry A. Hausman, "The Effect of Taxes on Labor Supply," in *How Taxes Affect Economic Behavior,* edited by Henry Aaron and Joseph Pechman (Washington, DC: Brookings, 1981), pp. 27–84.

[73]Jonathan Gruber, "Incidence of Mandated Maternity Benefits," *American Economic Review* 84, no. 3 (June 1994): 622–41. Note, however, that if mandates are efficient, then they are not effective from a redistributive or equity standpoint because the group who benefits from the policy also bears the cost of the policy. For further discussion, see Susan N. Houseman, "The Effects of Employer Mandates," in *Generating Jobs: How to Increase Demand for Less-Skilled Workers,* edited by Richard B. Freeman and Peter Gottschalk (New York: Russell Sage Foundation, 1998), pp. 154–91.

the extent that they encourage women to stay in the labor force, thereby raising the firm-specific human capital of the labor force.[74] On the other hand, mandates for unpaid leave, financed through wage reductions of the affected groups, eliminate any subsidy for parents. Recall that such subsidies are advocated by some because of the benefits that society as a whole derives from children who become the next generation of productive citizens and workers. In addition, the lower wages, by reducing the incentive of these women to stay in the labor force, might even serve to counter the effects such policies would otherwise have on increasing women's labor force attachment. Finally, such a policy is particularly burdensome for low-income workers whose wages would be reduced further.

This discussion shows that the issues regarding family leave and subsidized day care are complex. It is therefore not surprising that the extent of government's involvement differs considerably across countries, as do the manner in which policies are instituted and the generosity of these policies.

FAMILY-FRIENDLY POLICIES

U.S. families bear much of the burden of balancing work and family, but they do, as already noted, receive some voluntary assistance from firms. Employers may institute family-friendly benefits in lieu of wage increases and other benefits. Alternatively, they may introduce them because they expect the gains to outweigh the costs. Possible benefits for employers include improved recruitment and retention of workers and greater productivity as a result of better morale and reductions in tardiness and absenteeism. It is often much less costly to provide workers with such benefits than to train new employees. Popular programs may also improve public relations, and announcement of a firm's new work-family policy has even been found to increase the value of its stock.[75] On the other hand, firms are likely to incur additional costs because they may need to hire replacements and also deal with scheduling problems. In addition, costs of such policies tend to rise to the extent that more workers take advantage of them. On balance, however, we would expect that employers' incentives to adopt policies of this type will increase as a larger portion of the workforce, both men and women, must cope with the difficulties of combining market work with home responsibilities.

It is becoming increasingly clear that family-friendly policies lead to many positive results for employees. Such policies can dramatically increase workers' satisfaction with the firm and they may also reduce work-family conflict by lowering stress.[76] For a number of reasons, family-friendly policies are, nonetheless, being introduced only at a rather slow pace. First, their adoption requires a change in corporate "culture." Currently, family issues are seen as separate from the work sphere. For example, workers may be

---

[74]Christopher J. Ruhm, "The Economic Consequences of Parental Leave Mandates: Lessons from Europe," *Quarterly Journal of Economics* 113, no. 1 (February 1998): 285–318.

[75]Harry J. Holzer, "Work and Family Life: The Perspective of Employers," presented at the University of Maryland Population Research Center conference on "Workforce/Workplace Mismatch: Work, Family, Health, and Well-Being" (June 2003). Regarding the effect of such policies on a company's stock price, see Michelle M. Arthur and Alison Cook," Taking Stock of Work-Family Initiatives: How Announcements of 'Family Friendly' Human Resource Decisions Affect Shareholder Value," *Industrial and Labor Relations Review* 57, no. 4 (July 2004): 599–613.

[76]See, for instance, James T. Bond, Ellen Gallinsky, and E. Jeffrey Hill, *When Work Works: Summary of Families and Work Institute Research Findings* (New York: Families and Work Institute, 2004).

deemed unprofessional if they say they are delayed due to child care problems rather than car problems. Second, in many firms, workers are evaluated on the basis of "face time" (i.e., the number of hours spent at the office or plant) rather than on output per se. The concern is that with more flexible policies, including family leave, job sharing, home-based work, and flextime, it may be harder to monitor employees. Thus, work may have to be organized differently to accommodate substantial increases in the adoption of such policies.[77]

Large firms are generally at the forefront of implementing family-friendly policies. Perhaps the main reason is that they can reap the advantages of economies of scale in setting up programs because the number of workers who can potentially take advantage of them is so great. Needless to say, it is particularly true of firms with a high proportion of women, and hence, these firms are the ones most likely to adopt such policies. Small firms have lagged behind, not only because they cannot take advantage of economies of scale in benefit provision, but also because even the short-term loss of a single highly trained individual may have a substantial impact on the operation of a small business.

Some of the most common policies to assist individuals in juggling their family and paid work are examined in detail next: family leave, child care, alternative work schedules, flexible benefit plans, and policies to assist couples.

Family Leave

Family leave allows workers to take time off from their job for such reasons as pregnancy if there are complications or if the nature of the work creates a hazard for the mother or fetus, for childbirth, infant care, and tending to ill family members. Without such a policy, workers may have to deal with these problems by giving up their jobs, with loss not only of earnings, but of accrued benefits and seniority. The availability of family leave, even a relatively short and unpaid one, with provisions for job security and some other entitlements, is often helpful in enabling workers, particularly women workers, to avoid these high costs. It also increases incentives for women to invest in firm-specific training and for employers to provide them with opportunities to do so.

The government mandates two specific policies regarding leave.[78] The Pregnancy Discrimination Act of 1978 (an amendment to Title VII of the Civil Rights Act of 1964) prohibits employers from discriminating against workers on the basis of pregnancy. An employer may not, for example, terminate or deny a job to a woman because she is pregnant. Employers who have a short-term disability program must provide paid disability leave for pregnancy and childbirth on the same basis as for other medical disabilities.[79]

The second is the Family and Medical Leave Act of 1993 (FMLA), which allows eligible workers to take up to 12 weeks of unpaid leave for birth or adoption; acquiring a

---

[77]Charlene Marmer Solomon, "Work/Family's Failing Grade: Why Today's Initiatives Aren't Enough," *Personnel Journal* 73, no. 5 (May 1994): 72–87; and Olivia Mitchell, "Work and Family Benefits," in *Gender and Family Issues in the Workplace,* edited by Francine D. Blau and Ronald G. Ehrenberg (New York: Russell Sage Foundation, 1997), pp. 269–76.

[78]For a review, see Eileen Trzcinski and William T. Alpert, "Pregnancy and Parental Leave Benefits in the United States and Canada," *Journal of Human Resources* 29, no. 2 (Spring 1994): 535–54.

[79]Employers who do not have a short-term disability program, however, are not required to provide paid disability for pregnancy and childbirth.

foster child; illness of a child, spouse, or parent; or their own illness.[80] The worker may also take shorter leaves intermittently, pending the firm's approval. During the leave, the firm must continue health insurance coverage and, afterwards, the employee must be given the same or an equivalent position, with the same benefits, pay, and other conditions of employment. The FMLA applies to public- and private-sector workers employed with the same employer for at least one year and who worked at least 1,250 hours. However, the act only applies to firms with at least 50 workers. To the extent that some states mandate more generous benefits, they supersede the federal law.

The Family and Medical Leave Act was hotly debated. Opponents of the measure were particularly concerned about the costs imposed on them, because they must continue to pay for health insurance for workers on leave and also bear the costs of training replacement workers. (Pay for replacement workers, however, is not an added cost because workers on leave do not draw a paycheck.) However, employers also benefit from providing family leave, as already pointed out. Family leave reduces the costs of turnover, which can be quite substantial when training expenses are considered. Also, it may enhance workers' commitment to the firm and hence their productivity. A 1995 bipartisan Commission on Leave, as well as a more recent 2000 study commissioned by the Department of Labor, found that providing short, unpaid leaves has not been unduly onerous for business in terms of profitability or growth.[81] Evidence from other countries also indicates that parental leave does not cause the severe problems for firms anticipated by some critics.[82] Nonetheless, in a recent U.S. survey, firms reported an increase in the administrative burden of complying with the FMLA, citing difficulties ranging from determining what qualifies as a "serious health problem" to coordinating with rules for the Americans with Disabilities Act (ADA).[83]

The overall effect of family leave on women's labor force attachment and wages is ambiguous a priori. On the one hand, availability of leave is likely to increase labor force attachment by enabling workers to return to the same employer following an absence, and thus to maintain job continuity. It would be expected to result in a positive effect on wages and allow for longer job tenure and associated investments in firm-specific training, the maintenance of a good "job match," and provide the opportunity to continue climbing the firm's career ladder. On the other hand, to the extent that leave allows women to stay out of the labor market longer than they would without such a policy, leave or the extension of leave time might have a negative effect due to the depreciation of human capital. This concern is particularly important in some other countries where leave time is considerably longer, often as much as 12 months or more, rather than in the United States where mandated leave is quite short. Even so, as previously suggested,

---

[80]From the late 1980s to the time the legislation passed, approximately one-half of states adopted some form of their own legislation. See Jacob Klerman and Arleen Leibowitz, "Labor Supply Effects of State Maternity Leave Legislation," in *Gender and Family Issues in the Workplace*, edited by Francine D. Blau and Ronald G. Ehrenberg (New York: Russell Sage Foundation, 1997), pp. 65–85. The debate over federal family leave is described in Andrew E. Scharlach and Blanche Grosswald, "The Family and Medical Leave Act of 1993," *Social Service Review* 71, no. 3 (September 1997): 335–59.

[81]Commission on Leave, *A Workable Balance: Report to Congress on Family and Medical Leave Policies* (Washington, DC: U.S. Department of Labor, 1996); and David Cantor et al., *Balancing the Needs of Families and Employers: The Family and Medical Leave Surveys: 2000 Update* (Rockville, MD: Westat, 2001), available at www.dol.gov.

[82]Organisation for Economic and Cultural Development (OECD), "Long-Term Leave for Parents in OECD Countries," *OECD Employment Outlook*, (July 1995): 171–202.

[83]David Cantor et al., *Balancing the Needs of Families and Employers.*

widespread use of paid leave might reduce women's relative wages to finance the benefit, although this negative effect will be considerably mitigated to the extent that men as well as women avail themselves of leave. Finally, it is possible that employers might respond to increased costs by cutting back on employment.

Empirical evidence thus far indicates that the FMLA resulted in, if anything, a modest positive effect on employment, with no effect on wages.[84] Other studies that looked at the availability of employer-provided leave found it to have a positive effect on both the wages and employment of women who become mothers.[85] These findings of no effect or a positive effect of leave based on U.S. data may reflect that leave in the United States is generally unpaid and of short duration. Looking across countries, leave of short duration has been found to have few, if any, negative effects, but where leave is paid and of medium or long duration, some evidence indicates negative effects on employment and earnings.[86]

From a broader perspective, family leave, if taken by both fathers and mothers, likely promotes greater gender equality by encouraging both parents to share the job of caring for infants and meeting family emergencies. Another benefit of family leave is that it provides children with increased parental time, especially during infancy. At the same time, the FMLA offers the advantage of allowing parents to return to their previous job after taking it. Thus, some women who would remain with their employers in any case may stretch their leave time a bit longer, and others who would likely quit their jobs rather than return to work immediately postbirth will now stay with their employer.[87]

From the point of view of workers, a major problem with the FMLA is that it provides limited coverage. It does not cover workers in establishments with fewer than 50 employees, workers who fail to meet the 1,250 hours per year requirement, or workers employed for less than one year. Hence, it is estimated that the FMLA covers just 47 percent of private-sector workers.[88] For the remainder, coverage is much more sporadic, depending on state and firm-specific parental leave policies. One promising development is that one study found that an increasing number of firms not covered by the FMLA voluntarily offered such policies over the period 1995 to 2000, perhaps to be

---

[84]Jane Waldfogel, "The Impact of the Family and Medical Leave Act," *Journal of Policy Analysis and Management* 18, no. 2 (Spring 1999): 281–302. On the other hand, Katherin E. Ross found the FMLA had no effect on employment (she did not look at wages) in "Labor Pains: The Effect of the Family and Medical Leave Act on the Return to Paid Work After Childbirth," *Focus* 20, no. 1 (Winter 1998–99): 34–36. For discussions of the effects of this and other leave policies, see Christopher J. Ruhm, "Policy Watch: The Family and Medical Leave Act," *Journal of Economic Perspectives* 11, no. 3 (Summer 1997): 175–86.

[85]For evidence of positive effects of leave, see Jane Waldfogel, "The Family Gap for Young Women in the U.S. and Britain: Can Maternity Leave Make a Difference?" *Journal of Labor Economics* 16, no. 3 (July 1998): 505–45; and Masanori Hashimoto, Rick Percy, Teresa Schoellner, and Bruce A. Weinberg, in "The Long and Short of It: Maternity Leave Coverage and Women's Labor Market Outcomes." IZA Discussion Paper No. 1207 (July 2004). For a summary of the issues, see Francine D. Blau and Ronald G. Ehrenberg, "Gender and Family Issues in the Workplace," in *Gender and Family Issues in the Workplace,* edited by Francine D. Blau and Ronald G. Ehrenberg (New York: Russell Sage Foundation, 1997).

[86]Ruhm and Teague, "Parental Leave Policies"; and Ruhm, "The Economic Consequences."

[87]For instance, Charles L. Baum II finds that leave policy, whether provided by states or the FMLA, increases women's likelihood of returning to their original firm after the birth of a child and also increases the length of leave taken in "The Effects of Maternity Leave Legislation on Mothers' Labor Supply After Childbirth," *Southern Economic Journal* 69, no. 4 (April 2003): 772–99. See also, "Maternity Leave and Employment Patterns: 1961–1995," *Current Population Reports* P70–79 (November 2001).

[88]Jane Waldfogel, "Family and Medical Leave: Evidence from the 2000 Surveys," *Monthly Labor Review* 124, no. 9 (September 2001): 17–23.

able to better compete for workers against firms that were covered by FMLA.[89] Still, leave remains less common in smaller firms and less likely for those working part-time.

Another problem with the present Family and Medical Leave is that it is unpaid, which limits the ability of some covered workers, particularly those with low incomes, to take advantage of its provisions. Most firms do not offer paid leaves, though, in the case of pregnancy and childbirth, some workers have access through their employers' short-term disability plan. Others must use vacation time or sick leave. Even though paid leave is not mandated at the federal level, several states, including California, provide paid leave for pregnancy under the state's short-term disability program.[90] Moreover, in 2004, California expanded the availability of this leave to include those who must care for an ill family member, including a spouse, parent, or domestic partner, as well as following birth or adoption. The leave, covered by the State Disability Insurance program, is financed by an additional payroll deduction. The program replaces 55 percent of earnings, up to a specified maximum, and leave can be taken for up to six weeks per year.[91] This significant policy development will no doubt be watched closely by state and federal policy makers. Since June 2000, states could also use funds from their unemployment insurance (UI) programs to provide paid leave to parents at the time of a birth or adoption, but no state had yet done so as of December 2004.[92]

Apart from these changes, recommendations have been made to change federal family leave policy. These include proposals to expand FMLA coverage to firms with 25 to 49 workers, though serious opposition from small business continues. Another proposal makes leave policy more flexible by including 24 hours of unpaid time for essential family matters such as participating in a child's school activities and accompanying children and elderly relatives to medical appointments. Massachusetts, for instance, put into effect its own "Small Necessities Leave Act" in 1998.[93] As of the end of 2004, neither change had been made at the federal level.

Child Care

Finding affordable, quality day care is a critical concern for most single parents and dual-earner couples with children.[94] In fact, a substantial fraction of such families face this problem shortly after their child's birth, given that 55 percent of all women with infants (and presumably virtually all fathers) were in the labor force as of 2002.[95] In making their

---

[89]Cantor et al., *Balancing the Needs of Families and Employers*.
[90]Rhode Island, New Jersey, New York, and Hawaii (also Puerto Rico) had such a program in 2004.
[91]Ruth Milkman and Eileen Appelbaum, "Paid Leave in California: New Research Findings," (University of California: Institute of Industrial Relations, June 2004).
[92]Steven K. Wisensale, "Two Steps Forward, One Step Back: The Family and Medical Leave Act as Retrenchment Policy," *Review of Policy Research* 20, no 1 (Spring 2003): 135–51; and Bruce D. Philips, "The Economic Cost of Expanding the Family and Medical Leave Act to Small Business," *Business Economics* 37, no. 2 (April 2002): 44–54.
[93]"State Law Grants Leave for Families' 'Small Necessities'," *Boston Herald*, May 7, 1998, p. 20.
[94]A thorough discussion of these issues is found in Myra H. Strober, "Formal Extrafamily Child Care—Some Economic Observations," in *Sex, Discrimination and the Division of Labor*, edited by Cynthia B. Lloyd (New York: Columbia University Press, 1975); Leibowitz, "Child Care"; and David M. Blau, "Child Care Subsidy Programs," in *Means-Tested Programs*, edited by Robert Moffitt (Chicago: University of Chicago Press, 2003), pp. 443–516.
[95]Figure is from U.S. Census Bureau, "Women 15–44 Years Old Who Have Had a Child in the Last Year and Their Percentage in the Labor Force by Selected Characteristics," Table H6 (October 2003), available at www.census.gov. See also, Jacob A. Klerman and Arleen Leibowitz, "The Work-Employment Distinction Among New Mothers," *Journal of Human Resources* 29, no. 2 (Spring 1994): 277–303.

decision to continue working or go back to their job, parents must decide how much they value the earnings compared to the value of time at home. The value of home time includes the leisure they would have enjoyed as well as goods and services they would have produced themselves if they had remained at home; among these, child care is generally foremost.

In the United States most of the costs of raising children are borne by parents, though the federal government does provide some subsidies for purchased day care for employed parents through the tax system and grants. The government presumably does so because, as discussed earlier, children provide benefits for society at large as well as for their parents and because subsidies make the playing field more equal for all children at an early age, regardless of their families' income. Given that higher-income families are better able to purchase higher-quality care, this suggests that the highest priority for government should be to provide subsidies for low-income families so that they may obtain good care.[96]

As long as women are the primary caregivers, child care subsidies benefit mothers as compared to fathers. Such subsidies make it easier for mothers to take and remain in jobs that offer valuable experience and on-the-job training opportunities that increase their human capital. Child care benefits also enable some mothers to leave welfare for employment. Beyond all these factors, as long as child care occupations remain some of the most female dominated, greatly expanded day care facilities would help to provide jobs for many women, not only for trained teachers, but also for relatively unskilled women, including those in transition from welfare to work, who would often make excellent teacher's aides and day care workers.[97]

Still, despite the substantial potential benefits to children and families, some concern still remains about government subsidies. One common argument against public subsidies for day care is that they benefit families with employed mothers at the expense of those with stay-at-home mothers. In evaluating this argument it is useful to recall from the earlier discussion on taxes that without such subsidies, the federal tax system heavily favors traditional families because home production is untaxed, and because income splitting favors one-earner couples. Thus, the subsidies may be seen as a way to offset this imbalance. Furthermore, even though these subsidies may encourage some mothers to work outside the home who might not otherwise do so, many are already employed and will remain employed in any case. In fact, as noted earlier, recent changes in welfare rules require that recipients take a job; child care subsidies are essential to enable them to do so.[98]

There is also some concern that, by reducing parents' costs of raising children, subsidies will encourage people to have more of them. However, as already discussed, providing

---

[96]For a discussion of the issues, see Leibowitz, "Child Care."

[97]Although these occupations are among the lowest paid, increased demand for day care providers would be expected to raise wages.

[98]See, for instance, Patricia M. Anderson and Philip B. Levine, "Child Care and Mothers' Employment Decisions," in *Finding Good Jobs: Work and Welfare Reform,* edited by David E. Card and Rebecca M. Blank (New York: Russell Sage Foundation, 2000), pp. 420–62; Jean Kimmel, "Child Care Costs as a Barrier to Employment for Single and Married Mothers," *Review of Economics and Statistics* 80, no. 2 (May 1998): 287–99; and Robert J. Lemke, Robert Witt, and Ann Dryden Witte, "Child Care and the Welfare to Work Transition," unpublished paper, Wellesley College (June 2003). For a review, see David M. Blau, "Child Care Subsidy Programs," in *Means-Tested Programs,* edited by Robert Moffitt (Chicago: University of Chicago Press, 2003), pp. 443–516.

subsidized day care also encourages mothers to enter the labor market. To the extent that women acquire more—and more market-oriented—education in anticipation of this and accumulate more work experience as a consequence, they will have higher earnings. Hence, the opportunity cost of additional children will also increase. Further, it may be that women who work develop stronger preferences for market goods, and perhaps for having their own income, which gives them a greater feeling of independence. Therefore, it is not possible to determine a priori which set of forces is likely to be stronger.

Finally, a concern frequently voiced by opponents of publicly subsidized day care involves children's well-being. As discussed in Chapter 9, even though some recent studies found a negative effect of maternal employment on child outcomes, particularly nonparental care in the first year of life, these studies are generally not able to control fully for child care quality, which may attenuate or even negate any such effects. And, children between ages 2 and 4 tend to do better in center day care both intellectually and socially than children cared for entirely at home. Moreover, as noted earlier, children's development is affected by a host of other factors, most importantly, family characteristics.

One way that the federal government subsidizes purchased day care is through a set of block grants. One of these, the Child Care and Development Block Grant (CCDBG), provides states with funds to expand day care services for low-income families, including those on welfare, as well as to improve the overall quality and supply of day care. The principal aim of these funds is to support parents' employment. States may also use funds from the TANF block grant and Social Services block grant for the same purposes. How the funds are disbursed varies substantially. States might provide funds to child care providers, who can then allow families to pay for child care on a sliding-scale basis, depending on their income. Alternatively they might give vouchers to low-income families, which would allow them to buy child care from an eligible provider or even from a friend or relative living outside of their home. A smaller but important amount of federal support goes to Head Start, which is explicitly designed to provide early childhood education for low-income preschoolers.[99]

In addition to grants and direct expenditures, the federal government provides a number of tax subsidies for child care. Through the Dependent Care Tax Credit, employed parents receive a tax credit of 35 percent of expenses up to $3,000 for the care of one child, and $6,000 for the care of two or more children, provided their adjusted income is below $15,000. The credit falls to 20 percent of actual expenses for families with adjusted incomes above $43,000. However, this credit is nonrefundable, so low-income families who do not pay taxes do not benefit.

Another subsidy is the Child Tax Credit introduced in 1998. Starting in 2003, it provides up to a $1,000 tax credit to families for each child under age 17. For married couples, this credit is phased out when their income reaches $110,000. Tax changes in 2001 made the credit partly refundable so that the credit is of some benefit to families with lower earnings. Families might also use funds from the Earned Income Tax Credit (EITC) for child care. Recall that this program provides a fully refundable tax credit, up

---

[99]The various government subsidies for child care are described in U.S. House of Representatives, *2004 Green Book*. Regarding Head Start see Ron Haskins and Isabel Sawhill, "The Future of Head Start," *Welfare Reform and Beyond Brief #27* (Washington, DC: Brookings Institution, July 2003); and Janet Currie, "Early Childhood Education Programs *Journal of Economic Perspectives* 15, no. 2 (Spring 2001): 213–38.

to a maximum of $4,204 in 2003, to low-income working families with two or more children. These two credits differ substantially from the Dependent Care Tax Credit in that families may receive them whether child care is purchased or not.[100]

Another subsidy consists of flexible spending accounts, which are available to some employees. These accounts allow employees to take money out of their paychecks for dependent care expenses on a pretax basis, thereby reducing the costs of such care.

Beyond the programs and tax subsidies provided by the government, a small but growing number of firms are assisting workers with their child care needs. In 2003, 5 percent of private employees had access to on-site or off-site day care at their firm, 3 percent were able to receive funds from their employers to pay for child care, and 10 percent had access to referral services to assist them in finding child care. Perhaps not surprisingly, these benefits are more likely to be provided by larger establishments, and are more often provided to white-collar workers.[101]

As noted, some firms provide on- or near-site day care. This service has both advantages and drawbacks for employees, who must typically pay for at least part of the costs. On the one hand, parents do not have to make a separate trip to take children elsewhere, they are nearby in case of emergencies, and the children receive care during whatever hours the parent works.[102] On the other hand, children often are taken out of their own neighborhood, perhaps travel long distances, and must change caregivers when parents change jobs.

In recent years, the use of purchased day care has grown in part due to increases in the percentage of employed mothers with children and, no doubt, also as a result of the federal subsidies discussed earlier.[103] As Table 10-6 shows, the proportion of families with employed mothers using organized child care rose, from 13 percent in 1977 to a high of 30 percent in 1993 (not shown in the table), though it subsequently fell to 22 percent in 1999. Still, the largest percentage of families, 47 percent, continue to use child care provided by the child's father or other relatives, either in their own home or in a relative's home. An additional 20 percent used the services of a nonrelative, either in their own home or at the home of the day care provider. The remainder cared for their children at work or did not have a regular arrangement.

The type of child care utilized differs, in part, depending on the financial situation of the family. Poor families are much less likely to use center care and more likely to have their children cared for by relatives at no cost.[104] Among those families that purchase

---

[100]C. Eugene Steuerle points out that it may make sense to have both policies, because the child credit adjusts for differences in family size, while the child care credit adjusts for the costs of employment in "Systematic Thinking About Subsidies for Child Care, Part Three: Application of Principles" (Washington, DC: Urban Institute, February 1998). For another useful discussion, see Barbara R. Bergmann, "Subsidizing Child Care by Mothers at Home," *Feminist Economics* 6, no. 1 (March 2000): 77–88.

[101]U.S. Bureau of Labor Statistics, "Employee Benefits in Private Industry, 2003," USDL 03-489 (September 2003).

[102]Many such day care centers are at hospitals, where large numbers of women of childbearing age who have to work nonstandard hours are employed. A few innovative employers are combining care for children and for the elderly, such as the Stride Rite Intergenerational Center. See Ferber, O'Farrell, and Allen, *Work and Family.*

[103]William Goodman, "Boom in Day Care Industry the Result of Many Social Changes," *Monthly Labor Review* 118, no. 8 (August 1995): 3–12.

[104]Jeffrey Capizzano, Gina Adams, and Freya Sonenstein, "Child Care Arrangements for Children Under Five: Variation Across States," *Assessing the New Federalism*, Series B, No. B-7 (Washington, DC: Urban Institute, March 2000).

TABLE 10-6   Child Care Arrangements Used by Employed Mothers of Preschoolers, Selected Years (Percent Distribution)

	1977[a]	1985	1995	1999
Parents	25.8	23.8	22.0	21.5
Mother cares for child at work	11.4	8.1	5.4	3.1
Father	14.4	15.7	16.6	18.5
Relatives	30.9	24.1	21.4	28.8
Grandparent	n.a.	15.9	15.9	20.8
Sibling or other relative	n.a.	8.2	5.5	8.0
Organized child care facilities	13.0	23.1	25.1	22.1
Other nonrelative care	29.4	28.2	28.5	20.3
In child's home	7.0	5.9	4.9	3.3
In provider's home	22.4	22.3	23.6	16.9
Other[b]	0.6	0.8	0.7	2.7
No regular arrangement[c]	n.a.	n.a.	2.2	4.6

[a]Data only for the two youngest children under age 5; relatives not broken out separately.
[b]Other includes school-based activity, child cares for self, and children in kindergarten/grade school.
[c]Starting in 1995, the survey added a new category called "no regular arrangement."
n.a. = Not available.

Sources: U.S. Census Bureau, Historical Time Series Tables, "Primary Child Care Arrangements Used for Preschoolers by Families with Employed Mothers: Selected Years, 1977 to 1994," at www.census.gov; and U.S. Census Bureau, Historical Table. "Primary Child Care Arrangements Used by Employed Mothers of Preschoolers: 1985 to 1999" at www.census.gov/population/socdemo/child/ppl-168/tabH-1.pdf (accessed January 17, 2005).

day care, poor families pay less because of the type of care they use, whether it be provided at low cost by relatives or via subsidized programs targeted at the low-income population like Head Start. Nonetheless, poor families that purchased care spent as much as 18 percent of their income on day care on average, as compared with only 7 percent for high-income families.[105]

Another factor that affects the type of child care chosen is the child's age. A much smaller percentage of infants are in organized group day care as compared with preschool children.[106] Parents of infants who can afford to do so may hire a nanny or find some other way to have their children cared for in their own home because there the children generally receive more one-on-one attention and their exposure to infectious diseases is limited. For preschoolers, group care provides the advantages of contact with other children and it teaches them to share and cooperate. For school-age children, the question of after-school care arises. A reported 7 percent of children ages 6–9 and 12 percent of children ages 10–12 are regularly left unsupervised.[107] Even though "self-care" can build self-esteem and independence for older children, it is generally a poor and even a dangerous alternative for younger children. In response to this

[105]Linda Giannarelli, Sara Adelman, and Stefanie Schmidt, *Getting Help with Child Care Expenses,* (Washington, DC: Urban Institute, February 2003). *Poor* refers to below the poverty line and *higher-income* refers to greater than 200 percent of the poverty line.
[106]Capizzano, Adams, and Sonenstein, "Child Care Arrangements for Children Under Five."
[107]Sharon Vandivere et al., "Unsupervised Time: Family and Child Factors Associated with Self-Care," Assessing the New Federalism, Occasional Paper No. 71, (Washington, DC: Urban Institute, 2003).

concern, along with an effort to improve school outcomes, after-school programs that allow students to engage in supervised educational and recreational activities received some funding at the federal and state level.[108]

Quality of care, which has important consequences for children's development, varies considerably across different settings—center-based care, family day care (in the home of a nonrelative), and relative care, as well as within settings. Quality is typically measured in terms of structural characteristics of the child care arrangement, and also in terms of children's experiences in that setting. Structural characteristics include level of teachers' education and training, group size, and the child-teacher ratio. Measures of children's experiences in child care include the way caregivers relate to children, such as the child's exposure to language, and the continuity of care with the same caregiver. Even though some high-quality child care is available, especially for those who can afford it, much of what is currently available tends to be of poor quality, suggesting considerable room for improvement.[109]

In recent years, child care has become an especially high priority issue for families and society at large as a greater fraction of women are employed full-time, full-year, and as more low-income women move from welfare to work. A pressing concern is that federal child care funds are insufficient to cover all eligible children; a 1999 government report indicated that only 10 percent of children eligible for federal child care assistance received it.[110] Funds earmarked for child care in the TANF reauthorization are not likely to adequately address this gap. In addition, as economic activity continues to shift to 24 hours per day, seven days per week, there is increasing need for child care that is available in the evenings, on weekends, and in the early morning.[111] Another concern is that the Child Development Block Grant, which provides child care funds to assist low-income workers, focuses solely on supporting parents' paid work, not on providing early childhood education like Head Start, though many of the children in these families are also at considerable "risk."[112]

Suggested solutions to the child care problem range from sweeping to more modest, and address concerns about affordability, accessibility, quality, or all three. The most ambitious proposal, which is unlikely to be adopted in the United States anytime soon, would be universal government-provided child care, as is the case in a number of west European countries. Another option would be to combine private provision with substantial government subsidies and more regulation to ensure quality.[113] More modest

---

[108]For evidence on effects of unsupervised care, see Anna Aizer, "Home Alone: Supervision After School and Child Behavior," *Journal of Public Economics* 88, no. 9–10 (August 2004): 1835–48. Regarding policies, the federal program, the 21st Century Learning Center Program, centers on academics, but other programs have a nonacademic focus. See Rob Hollister, "The Growth in After-School Programs and Their Impact," *Brookings Institution* (February 2003).

[109]Barbara Wolfe and Deborah Lowe Vandell, "Welfare Reform Depends on Good Child Care," *The American Prospect* 13, no. 13 (July 2002): 19–21.

[110]Department of Health and Human Services, "Only 10 Percent of Eligible Families Get Child Care Help, New Report Shows," news release, October 19, 1999.

[111]U.S. Department of Labor, "Care Around the Clock: Developing Child Care Resources Before Nine and After Five," Women's Bureau Special Reports, 1995. For an example of the difficulties faced in finding such care, see Barbara Carton, "In 24-Hour Workplace, Day Care Is Moving to the Night Shift," *Wall Street Journal*, July 6, 2001, pp. 1, 4.

[112]Ron Haskins and Isabel Sawhill, "The Future of Head Start," *Welfare Reform and Beyond Brief* #27 (Washington, DC: Brookings Institution, July 2003).

[113]Suzanne Helburn and Barbara Bergmann, *America's Child Care Problem: The Way Out* (New York: Palgrave, St. Martin's Press, 2002).

proposals focus on government training for child care workers or expanding information on choosing high-quality, independently accredited, child care. The government might also create financial incentives for families to use and for providers to offer high-quality care.[114] For instance, child care centers that are deemed high-quality might receive government subsidies.

Alternative Work Schedules

Alternative work schedules can provide greater flexibility for workers to take care of family responsibilities and to arrange their personal lives more conveniently. They include flextime, nonstandard work schedules, part-time employment, job sharing, and home-based work.

A policy often known as **flextime** permits some degree of variation in work schedules at the discretion of the employee, ranging from modest changes in starting and quitting times to variation in the number of hours worked per day, week, or pay period. For 2001, an estimated 29 percent of wage and salary workers employed full time worked flexible schedules, most often an informal arrangement rather than part of a formal employer-provided program.[115] Such flexibility can be quite advantageous for many workers, especially for those with young children or other family members who depend on their care.[116] Another potential advantage of flextime is a reduction in commuting time. In fact, if enough workers are on flextime, rush-hour traffic is reduced, benefiting even those not on flextime. The degree of flexibility that can be offered depends on the nature of the enterprise and the type of work. Some employers may be reluctant to offer this benefit because they need key employees to be present during standard hours, perhaps to be available to handle customers or to meet work flow demands. They may also be concerned about the potential for abuse.

Other workers have **nonstandard work schedules**, where they are employed on alternating shifts, nights, or weekends. These schedules have expanded considerably as economic activity has moved to virtually 24/7 (24 hours a day, 7 days a week). The availability and widespread adoption of technologies such as the fax, computer, cell phone, and beeper explains at least part of this change. Another factor is the rise in the number of dual-earner and single-parent families, who must buy groceries and make other purchases on weekends and evenings.[117] For instance, in 1997, only 60 percent of full-time workers over age 18 regularly worked a fixed schedule, say 9 to 5, Monday through Friday, with the rest working a nonstandard schedule of some sort, and since that time, this figure likely fell further. Like flextime, nonstandard work schedules potentially provide some flexibility for workers juggling child care, perhaps schooling, and the

---

[114]For these proposals, among others, see David M. Blau, "Child Care Subsidies"; and Barbara Bergmann, "Thinking about Child Care Policy," in *The Economics of Work and Family*, edited by Jean Kimmel and Emily Hoffman (Kalamazoo, MI: W.E. Upjohn Institute for Employment Research, 2002), pp. 43–70.

[115]U.S. Bureau of Labor Statistics, "Workers on Flexible and Shift Schedules in 2001," USDL 02-225 (April 18, 2002).

[116]This flexibility appears to be so valuable that some workers may be working longer hours in exchange for it. See Lonnie Golden, "Flexible Work Schedules: What Are We Trading Off to Get Them?" *Monthly Labor Review* 124, no. 3 (March 2001): 50–67.

[117]The term *nonstandard* used here refers to work schedules, rather than to the type of worker or employment, as in Chapter 8. This section and the figure cited are drawn from Harriet B. Presser, "Toward a 24-Hour Economy," *Science* 284 (June 11, 1999): 1778–79; and Harriet B. Presser, *Working in a 24/7 Economy: Challenges for American Families* (New York: Russell Sage Foundation, 2003). See also U.S. Bureau of Labor Statistics, "Workers on Flexible and Shift Schedules in 2001" *News*, USDL 02-225, April 18, 2002.

need to earn a living. However, unlike flextime, these schedules are typically set by employers rather than at the discretion of employees. To the extent that workers are not able to choose their schedules, those with young children may face considerable difficulties finding child care on weekends and at night. In addition, in two-parent families with such schedules, adults tend to spend less time together, potentially leading to negative consequences for the marriage, even including divorce. Biological difficulties for workers in adjusting to night work may also be a factor.

Another alternative is **part-time employment**. This arrangement is especially common among women (as well as young people going to school and older workers retired from their full-time jobs) and does offer some flexibility as compared to a strict 9 to 5, five days a week schedule. Nearly 26 percent of employed women and nearly 11 percent of employed men worked less than full-time (defined as at least 35 hours per week) in 2003.[118] As discussed earlier in Chapter 8, the main problems with much of part-time work as a solution to difficulties in combining work and family responsibilities are few fringe benefits (such as health care and pensions), frequently poor compensation, and few opportunities for promotion. Some firms may also offer the possibility of **job sharing**, where two individuals share one position. For individuals seeking less than full-time work, this arrangement may be a good way to obtain a more challenging part-time position, while employers may find that this option helps them retain valuable employees. One potential concern, as with all part-time work, is that workers who share a job may receive only partial benefits or none at all.

Finally, an increasing number of workers are choosing **home-based employment**.[119] Estimates of the extent of home-based work vary widely depending on the definition used. For example, it has been estimated that in 2001, 15 percent of workers did at least some work for their primary job at home.[120] On the other hand, just under 5 percent of workers were classified as working entirely at home in 1997, the most recent year for which such data are available.[121] Regardless of the definition used, the percentage of home-based workers increased since the 1980s. This increase is, no doubt, partly the result of improvements in computers and communications technology, but also due to the rise in women's labor force participation, the increasing number of two-earner couples, and the growing number of small individual- and family-owned businesses. Home-based employment likely encourages paid work, especially by women, because the fixed costs associated with this type of employment tend to be lower. Parents may be able to keep a closer eye on teens as well. Further, the many home-based workers who are self-employed can often set their own schedules and do not have to answer to an employer about the way they allocate their time. For those telecommuting with an employer based elsewhere, however, significant issues may arise related to how the firm measures workers' productivity. Beyond these factors, it is important to be realistic

[118]U.S. Department of Labor, *Employment and Earnings,* January 2004, p. 204.
[119]The discussion that follows is drawn from William G. Deming, "Work at Home: Data from the Current Population Survey," *Monthly Labor Review* 117, no. 2 (February 1994): 14–20; Linda N. Edwards and Elizabeth Field-Hendry, "Home-Based Workers? Data from the 1990 Census of Population," *Monthly Labor Review* 119, no. 11 (November 1996): 26–34; and Linda N. Edwards and Elizabeth Field-Hendry, "Home-Based Work and Women's Labor Force Decisions," *Journal of Labor Economics* 20, no. 1 (January 2002):170–200.
[120]U.S. Bureau of Labor Statistics, "Work at Home in 2001," *News,* USDL 02-107, 1 March 2002.
[121]U.S. Census Bureau, "Home-Based Workers in the United States: 1997," *Current Population Reports* P70–78 (December 2001).

about other drawbacks as well as benefits. Whether the home-based worker is self-employed or works for someone else, one issue is how much work can really be accomplished when an infant, toddler, school-age child, or infirm parent is present and requires attention during work time. Another is the isolation the individual may experience when working at home.

Flexible Benefits

As the workforce becomes more diverse, with some workers who are members of traditional families, some who have employed spouses, some who are single, and others who live with partners they are not married to, flexible benefit plans (often known as cafeteria plans) are increasingly important as an alternative to standard or fixed benefit packages. These plans allow employees to select from a specified assortment of benefits worth up to an amount predetermined by the employer. They increase the value of fringe benefits to workers and may also provide a further inducement to individuals to enter or to remain attached to the labor market and even to the firm because they can choose the set of benefits that best meet their particular needs.[122] For example, two-earner couples derive no benefit from double health insurance coverage (which occurs when one or both are covered under their own employer's health insurance program and under their spouse's), but with a cafeteria plan, one of the spouses could instead choose to receive child care benefits if the couple has young children, or perhaps payments into a pension fund, if they don't have children or their children are older.

Policies to Assist Couples

Dual-earner couples, married as well as unmarried, whether same or opposite sex, face particular problems in the workplace. Such couples, especially those with two professionals, must deal with the often daunting task of finding two jobs commensurate with their respective skills in the same location, or having a "commuting relationship," if both are to successfully pursue their careers. As discussed in Chapter 9, heterosexual couples are still considerably more likely to give priority to the husband's career, often leading the wife's career to suffer, although evidence shows that increasingly husbands are making sacrifices too.

Employers can assist two-career couples and, in particular, reduce the negative consequences for the "trailing partner" in a number of ways. For example, firms, either acting alone or with others, can actively help partners find employment. This assistance might take the form of sending out a spouse's resume to an employer network or to a number of specific employers, as well as making use of personal contacts.

Many universities as well as some other establishments set up programs for hiring couples, or offer jobs to partners of employees, whenever suitable positions can be found.[123] Businesses can also reduce difficulties for such couples by not penalizing

---

[122]Federal and state tax policy can encourage the growth of many employer-paid benefits in general by excluding them from taxable employee income, while permitting businesses to treat them as a normal business expense. See Marianne A. Ferber and Brigid O'Farrell, with La Rue Allen, eds., *Work and Family: Policies for a Changing Workforce* (Washington, DC: National Academy Press, 1991).

[123]Jane W. Loeb, "Programs for Academic Partners: How Well Can They Work?" in *Academic Couples: Problems and Promises,* edited by Marianne A. Ferber and Jane W. Loeb (Champaign, IL: University of Illinois Press, 1997), pp. 270–98.

employees who decline a promotion because they have family responsibilities or decline a transfer to branch in a different location because their partner might find it difficult to locate a satisfactory job there. Antinepotism rules, once widely used to restrict the hiring or retention of relatives of employees, but most particularly spouses of employees, virtually disappeared in academia and are less common elsewhere as well. These rules not only prevented couples from being hired, but if two employees married, one—usually the wife—would have to go. The most common forms of restriction today are less severe. Some employers restrict two family members, unmarried partners, and in some cases even couples with romantic attachments from working in the same department, or at least avoid having one partner directly supervising the other. In these cases, the concern is that a partner who has influence may use it to have the other hired or promoted or that the couple would form a working alliance that may be resented by their coworkers.

Such abuses undoubtedly take place, but evidence does not indicate that they are any greater than when people simply are or become close friends. In fact, one might expect couples to be somewhat more circumspect because favoritism would be so obvious. In any case, the risk that such problems may occur must be weighed against the disadvantage of not being able to hire and retain the best-qualified people regardless of their relationship. One problem with even the remnants of antinepotism rules is that as long as husbands are most often senior to their wives and in higher positions, it is the woman who will be viewed as more expendable. Further, employment of the partner by a competitor may well create its own set of problems. For instance, the employee may inadvertently share confidential business information such as trade secrets with the partner, putting the firm at risk.

Policies that are helpful to married couples, with and without children, raise questions about fairness to those who do not have a family.[124] For instance, such singles are at a disadvantage to the extent that employers pay lower wages to all employees as a result of providing benefits such as family leave, on-site day care, or subsidized spousal health care and pensions. Also, singles may be far less interested in flexible schedules and may regret the reduction in "face time" with coworkers. In addition, some single individuals claim that they are often called upon to shoulder extra responsibilities at work when a coworker's child becomes sick, and at times are expected to work weekends, nights, or holidays so that others can spend time with their families. Regarding benefits, one solution is for firms to offer cafeteria plans, so that workers can choose the benefits they want. Another solution, recently adopted by some larger firms, is to extend benefits to a broader set of household members, including workers' grown children, parents, or unmarried partners.[125] A far more radical alternative would be to level the playing field by scaling back all such benefits, but if it is recognized that people's situations change—singles marry, adults have children or adopt, married people get divorced or become widowed, and parents get ill—most workers are likely to benefit from even the existing set of policies at some point in their lives.

Unmarried couples, whether opposite sex or same sex, also tend to be at a disadvantage relative to married couples because they are generally not eligible for the substantial

[124]See Barbara Bergmann, "Work-Family Policies and Equality Between Women and Men," in *Gender and Family Issues in the Workplace,* edited by Francine D. Blau and Ronald G. Ehrenberg (New York: Russell Sage Foundation, 1997), pp. 277–79; and Michelle Conlin, "Unmarried America," *BusinessWeek,* October 20, 2003, pp. 106–16.
[125]Conlin, "Unmarried America."

fringe benefits that are usually available to spouses. These benefits frequently include dental and medical insurance, parental leave, life insurance, and leave in case of a family member's illness. However, since the early 1980s, a growing number of employers have extended such benefits to unmarried couples as a result of the domestic partnership movement.[126] Further, as discussed previously in Chapters 3 and 9, same-sex marriage, permitted in Massachusetts, and civil unions, permitted in Vermont, extend spousal rights available under state law to same-sex couples. Also, New Jersey, California, and Hawaii extend additional rights to domestic partners. Nevertheless, these couples still do not have the same federal benefits as their opposite-sex married counterparts.

How to Handle a Job Interview

How much should you tell a potential employer during a job interview about your current or expected family responsibilities in order to learn about the employer's willingness to accommodate your family concerns?* This question is not easy to answer. On the one hand, mentioning that you plan to marry or have children, or that you currently have young children or perhaps other family members who need care, or that you have a spouse who would also need to relocate, may reduce your chances of being offered a position for which you are fully qualified. On the other hand, in order for you to be sure that you and the firm will be a good "match," you may need to get sufficient information about items such as whether the potential employer will make it easier for you to handle possible family emergencies, or whether your progress would be impeded if you were reluctant to move. The question may even arise as to whether you would want to work for an organization that looks askance at anyone who has a life outside the workplace.

At the same time it is likely that because of the high costs of hiring and training workers, employers who interview you are also interested in making a good long-term match and therefore want to learn as much as possible about you. They too, however, face challenges and constraints. On the one hand, employers need to learn about your degree of commitment to the job. On the other hand, they are not allowed by law to ask directly about your family situation, including current or intended pregnancies, whether any family members have disabilities, or even your marital status.† One problem is that some employers may nevertheless ask questions that are illegal, fall into a gray area, or are at least "unwise," depending on how they are asked. Their questions confront you with the difficult decision of how to handle the situation.

Although it is impossible to offer suggestions on precisely what to say and do under all circumstances that may arise, some general recommendations should help you to elicit the information that you need and send the message that you want, while avoiding a discussion about your current or expected family responsibilities, per se. For instance, you might ask your potential employer to describe

---

[126]"Domestic Partner Benefits: Facts and Background" (Washington, DC: Employee Benefit Research Institute, March 2004).

a "typical day" or a "typical week" for a person who would hold your job or for your coworkers, more generally. This answer would give you a sense of whether you are likely to be expected to work late hours during the week or on weekends, without your asking the question directly and thus perhaps giving the appearance that you are not willing to work hard. Also, at a later stage in the interview process, you could ask for materials regarding conditions of employment, which may include information about options for flextime and various paid and unpaid fringe benefits, such as on-site child care. In addition, discrete conversations with potential coworkers may serve to answer questions you would be reluctant to raise with the employer directly. You might even "mount an offensive" concerning family responsibilities, by stating what kind of employee you expect to be, and emphasizing your reliability and commitment to work.[††]

Concerns about family responsibilities will remain especially problematic for women as long as they continue to bear primary responsibility for the family and household. Under these circumstances, employers have the option of hiring men who tend to have few if any family responsibilities that will interfere with their devotion to their jobs. Even though public policies emphasizing equal opportunity may facilitate change to some extent, it is probably the case that only when women and men more fully share these responsibilities will we see fundamental change.

[*] This inset is drawn from Sue Shellenbarger, "What You Should Say About Family Duties in a Job Interview," *Wall Street Journal*, April 10, 1996, sec. B1, p. 1; "Advice to Help You Get Ahead from the Experts: Business Newsletters, Magazines and Books; Job Seekers Should Beware," *Atlanta Constitution*, June 20, 1999; Kirsten Downey Grimsley, "Awkward Queries in Interviews," *San Francisco Chronicle*, February 25, 2000, p. B3; and Michael Barrier, "Hire Without Fear," *Nation's Business* (U.S. Chamber of Commerce), May 1999, p. 16.
[†] "Advice to Help You Get Ahead from the Experts," p. 1R.
[††] Shellenbarger, "What You Should Say."

Conclusion

This chapter began by examining the major changes that occurred in the last few years in the U.S. welfare system. At present, it remains difficult to provide a firm assessment of the success of these changes because the policy is still relatively new, and it was implemented at a time of unprecedented economic prosperity. Clear evidence does show a drop in welfare caseloads and a rise in the employment of single mothers. Other indications are that changes in welfare led to increased earnings and reduced poverty for many, though not all families. Many questions remain, nonetheless, as to the future effects of time limits, and how needy families will fare in a serious economic downturn. Also, although the final details of the TANF reauthorization legislation are yet to be determined, it will likely impose substantially higher work requirements on welfare recipients.

Even though the full effects of welfare changes remain to be sorted out, it is clear that the expansion of the Earned Income Tax Credit played an important role in reducing poverty. In addition, child support awards increased for many single-parent families, particularly never-married mothers, as a direct result of recent changes in federal child support rules. These programs, however, have limitations. For instance, the EITC reduces some married women's incentive to seek employment and it may discourage some unmarried couples from marrying or encourage some married couples to get divorced. Perhaps most serious, stepping up child support enforcement without sufficient recognition that many noncustodial parents have low incomes themselves may further increase the distance, both geographic and emotional, between them and their children. The consequences of marriage promotion policies, both those underway and being proposed, remain to be seen.

This chapter also identified a number of important ways in which both federal income taxes and Social Security affect the work and family decisions of individuals. Tax policies often favor families with full-time homemakers as compared to those with two earners, despite the fact that the latter are now the norm among married-couple families. We noted that it is critical for policy makers to consider the effects of such policies on incentives for secondary earners to work for pay, especially when evaluating proposals to restructure Social Security or revamp the income tax system.

We also looked at how government and some employers implemented a number of new policies in recent years to help people meet the dual demands of paid work and family. These policies received increasing attention as women joined the paid labor force in record numbers and men took on more household responsibilities, including child care and elder care. Nevertheless, several points of concern arise. First, many people gain little from the new programs, especially part-time workers and workers in small establishments, as well as the growing numbers of nonstandard workers (workers who do not have "regular" full-time jobs), discussed in Chapter 8. In addition, there continues to be a serious shortage of affordable, quality child care, not just for infants, but for school-age children as well as poor children of all ages. These problems have increased, particularly as more low-income women have been leaving welfare for work and as a greater fraction of businesses operate 24 hours a day, seven days a week. It is in the interest of firms that want a focused, committed workforce now and in the future as well as society at large to find solutions to these problems. Increased funding for before- and after-school programs, increased flextime, and additional child care subsidies would be useful steps in that direction.

A further issue of growing importance is that *family* is rather narrowly defined as it pertains to various policies. This problem must be addressed because living arrangements other than the traditional family of a husband, wife, and their own biological children residing in the same home are increasingly common. Often members of the same family live in different homes, as parents split up, remarry, or live with other partners, perhaps more than once. In such cases, the question arises as to whose policy covers a given child.[127] The growing number of unmarried couples also is reason for governments and employers to adjust their policies in this respect as well.

Questions for Review and Discussion

1. In what fundamental ways does TANF differ from the former AFDC program?
2. The Earned Income Tax Credit received bipartisan support, while AFDC was far less widely accepted. What are the key differences in these programs that led one to be popular and the other (now defunct and replaced by TANF) to have received so much less support?

---

[127]Mitchell, "Work and Family Benefits."

3. Consider a married couple in which the husband and the wife each has $70,000 in taxable earnings. Assume they have no children and all income is from earnings. Using the information in Table 10-4:
   a. Compute their tax liability as a married couple.
   b. Compute their tax liability if they live together but are not married.
   c. Assuming they are married, compute their marriage bonus or penalty. Is this outcome what you would have expected based on the discussion in the text? Explain.
   d. Answer the prior questions again, but this time assume that the husband has $140,000 in taxable earnings and the wife has no earnings. Do your findings differ? If so, explain why.
   e. Suppose the wife in part d is deciding whether to enter the labor force. What income tax rate affects this decision? Explain your answer.
4. In recent years, child support enforcement was stepped up considerably. What are the pros and cons of this policy change?
5. When the Family and Medical Leave Act was passed in the United States in 1993, it was attacked as overly generous by some and as inadequate by others. Discuss the pros and cons of the FMLA.
6. Suppose you work for a "singles" lobby group. Point to the various policies that "work against singles." What sort of policies would be useful to families but would be more neutral with respect to family structure?
7. Discuss the pros and cons of taxing each spouse as an individual without regard to marital status.
8. Make the best case you can for:
   a. Parents being entirely responsible for the care of their children.
   b. Employer-financed day care.
   c. Government-financed day care.
9. Discuss the pros and cons of mandating that employers provide relatively long paid parental leaves of, say, one year.

Suggested Readings

Beller, Andrea H., and John W. Graham. *Small Change: The Economics of Child Support.* New Haven, CT: Yale University Press, 1993.

Blank, Rebecca M. "Fighting Poverty: Lessons from Recent U.S. History." *Journal of Economic Perspectives* 14, no. 2 (Spring 2000): 3–19.

_____. *It Takes a Nation: A New Agenda for Fighting Poverty.* Princeton, NJ: Princeton University Press, 1996.

Blau, David M. *The Child Care Problem: An Economic Analysis.* New York: Russell Sage Foundation, 2001.

Blau, Francine D., and Ronald G. Ehrenberg, eds. *Gender and Family Issues in the Workplace.* New York: Russell Sage Foundation, 1997.

Card, David E., and Rebecca M. Blank, eds. *Finding Jobs: Work and Welfare Reform.* New York: Russell Sage Foundation, 2000.

Danziger, Sheldon H., ed. *Economic Conditions and Welfare Reform.* Kalamazoo, MI: W.E. Upjohn Institute for Employment Research, 1999.

Danziger, Sheldon and, Robert Haveman, eds. *Understanding Poverty.* Cambridge, MA: Harvard University Press, and New York: Russell Sage Foundation, 2002.

Edin, Kathryn, and Laura Lein. *Making Ends Meet: How Single Mothers Survive Welfare and Low-Wage Work.* New York: Russell Sage Foundation, 1997.

Fredriksen-Goldsen, Karen I., and Andrew E. Scharlach. *Families and Work: New Directions in the Twenty-First Century.* Oxford: Oxford University Press, 2001.

Garfinkel, Irwin, Sara McLanahan, Daniel Meyer, and Judith Seltzer, eds. *Fathers Under Fire: The Revolution in Child Support Enforcement.* New York: Russell Sage Foundation, 1998.

Hochschild, Arlie. *The Second Shift.* New York: Viking Press, 1989.

Jacobs, Jerry A., and Kathleen Gerson. *The Time Divide: Balancing Work and Family in Contemporary Society.* Cambridge, MA: Harvard University Press, 2004.

Leibowitz, Arleen. "Child Care: Private Cost or Public Responsibility?" In *Individual and Social Responsibility: Child Care, Education,*

Medical Care, and Long-Term Care in America, edited by Victor R. Fuchs, pp. 33–57. Chicago: University of Chicago Press, 1996.

McCaffery, Edward J. *Taxing Women.* Chicago: University of Chicago Press, 1997.

Moffitt, Robert A., ed. *Means-Tested Transfer Programs in the United States.* Chicago: University of Chicago Press, 2003.

_____, ed. *Welfare, the Family, and Reproductive Behavior: Research Perspectives.* Washington, DC: National Research Council, 1998.

Presser, Harriet B. *Working in a 24/7 Economy.* New York: Russell Sage Foundation, 2003.

Rank, Mark. *Living on the Edge: The Realities of Welfare in America.* New York: Columbia University Press, 1994.

CHAPTER

11

GENDER DIFFERENCES
IN OTHER COUNTRIES

Chapter Highlights

■ The Economic Status of the World's Women: Overview

■ A Comparison of the United States to Other Economically Advanced
   Countries

■ Developing Countries

■ Countries of the Former Soviet Bloc

U p to this point we focused almost entirely on the situation in the United
States. Throughout, we emphasized the influence of economic factors in
determining the status of women. This focus is not to suggest that nothing
else matters, but rather that, everything being the same, economic considerations
play an important role. Of course, in the real world, everything else is generally
not the same. Societies differ in their political systems, economic and social policies, cultures, and religions. In this chapter, we turn to a consideration of women in
other countries both to shed light on the causes of the substantial diversity in their
status and to see what we can learn about institutions and policies elsewhere that
have retarded or enhanced improvements in the position of women.

We begin with a broad description of the economic status of women as compared to men throughout the world, with special attention paid to women's
labor market activity and the forces that influence it. Next, we turn to a more
detailed consideration of the economically advanced countries that, in many
ways, are most similar to the United States, focusing particularly on Sweden
and Japan, the former because women have made great progress there and the
latter because in that country women have made far less headway toward equality. Last, we briefly examine some of the issues of special concern in developing
countries and in the countries of the former Soviet bloc, with their past history of
more than four decades of regimes that officially subscribed to Marxist ideology.

THE ECONOMIC STATUS OF THE WORLD'S WOMEN: OVERVIEW

A number of measures are, by general agreement, regarded as useful indicators of women's economic status: women's labor force participation, the degree of occupational segregation by sex, the female-male earnings ratio, women's educational attainment, the fertility rate, the allocation of housework, and women's role in government as well as their standing before the law. These factors not only are themselves direct indicators of women's economic status but also are causally intertwined with one another.

Labor Force Participation

Labor force participation is arguably the most important indicator of women's economic status. Although it is true that women perform a great deal of work in all economies, the total amount and the allocation between household and paid work differ substantially. Paid work is deemed to be particularly important because it provides women with status in their own right, allows for greater power and influence in decision making within the family, and raises the family's standard of living overall.[1] This is true not only in economically advanced countries but also in many developing countries, even though the burden of women's work in the household is particularly onerous there; water and fuel are often carried for long distances, clothes have to be washed by hand, food must be procured and prepared on a daily basis for lack of refrigeration, and many other goods and services that are generally purchased in economically advanced countries are produced at home.[2]

Table 11-1 provides figures on women's labor force participation and women's share of the labor force by broad regional grouping and for selected countries in these regions. The labor force participation rate is the more familiar concept and the one we emphasized in previous chapters. However, each measure has its advantages and disadvantages in international comparisons. Labor force participation is influenced not only by the age range of the population that is included, but also by the age distribution of the population, the typical school leaving and retirement ages, and the prevalence of market work itself versus family-based activities, for example, which may not be counted. Using share of the labor force that is female largely mitigates these problems. However, it may be influenced by the sex ratio in the general population and also gives less direct information about the extent that women are involved in work outside the home. Note that in Table 11-1 we also present the ratio of women's to men's participation where available; this measure also addresses the problems of comparing the female participation rate across countries and is not affected by the sex ratio.

The data in Table 11-1 indicate considerable variation in both measures, across regions and selected countries. Among developing countries, women's labor force participation rates range from about 60 percent in Sub-Saharan Africa and East Asia to 29 percent in the Middle East and North Africa. In addition we can see from Table 11-1

---

[1]Ester Boserup, *Women's Role in Economic Development* (New York: St. Martin's Press, 1970). For discussions on women's work in the world economy, see Susan P. Joekes, *Women in the World Economy, an INSTRAW Study* (New York: Oxford University Press, 1987); and Allen Tuovi, "Economic Development and the Feminization of Poverty," in *Women's Work in the World Economy,* ed. Nancy Folbre, Barbara Bergmann, Bina Agarwal, and Maria Floro (New York: New York University Press, 1992), pp. 107–19.

[2]Debra Ann Donahoe, "Measuring Women's Work in Developing Countries," *Population and Development Review* 25, no. 3 (September 1999): 543–76.

that women's labor force participation rates and share of the labor force are strongly and positively related; in countries in which women's participation rates were 50 percent or higher, women typically comprised 40 percent or more of the labor force, while in the areas with the lowest participation rates, women comprised less than 30 percent of the total labor force.

Table 11-2 provides data on *trends* in labor force participation for a number of more economically advanced countries, as well as for several countries of the former Soviet bloc.[3] (Note that Tables 11-1 and 11-2 are based on different age ranges—15 and over and 15 to 64, respectively—so that levels of participation are not fully comparable across tables.) This table also shows considerable variation in women's in labor force participation rates across countries, ranging from just over 48 percent in Italy, to 70 percent in the United States, and more than 75 percent in Denmark, Sweden, Norway, and Switzerland. Interestingly, Russia historically had female participation rates well in excess of those in economically advanced countries, but the current rate is reported to be just 63.9 percent.[4] Trends in labor force participation rates for Russia and other countries of the former Soviet bloc are discussed further in a later section.

Part of the explanation for differences in labor force activity by gender is that countries and, more generally, regions, are in various stages of economic development, ranging from agricultural to industrial and postindustrial. As discussed in Chapter 2, one hypothesis that receives some support from the evidence is that the relationship between economic development and women's labor force participation rates tends to be U-shaped. That is, female labor force participation is high in the stage of subsistence agriculture, when women tend to be heavily involved as family workers, but then declines during the early stages of economic development as the nature of agricultural work changes and the locus of much production moves out of the household and into factories and offices. One argument for much lower labor force participation at this stage, which is effectively the "bottom" of the U, is that societal norms often work against women performing manual, factory-type work. Then, as countries become more developed and women's education and opportunities in white-collar employment rise, their labor force participation once again increases.[5] Consistent with this pattern, we see in Table 11-1 relatively high rates of participation in countries that only recently moved from the horticultural to the agricultural stage, such as those in Sub-Saharan Africa, but lower rates at the next stage of development, as is true of countries in Latin America, particularly those in

---

[3]The Soviet bloc, which broke apart in 1989, refers to the countries of the former Union of Soviet Socialist Republics (USSR)—including Russia, the Ukraine, Armenia, Uzbekistan, and others—the former Czechoslovakia (now the Czech Republic and Slovakia), East Germany, Poland, Hungary, Bulgaria, and Romania.

[4]Even in transition countries where data are available, it is often difficult to draw meaningful inferences about trends because of changes in survey methods. UNICEF, "Women in Transition," Regional Monitoring Reports No. 6 (Florence, Italy: UNICEF International Child Development Centre, 1999), chap. 2.

[5]For a discussion and evidence, see Claudia Goldin, "The U-Shaped Female Labor Force Function in Economic Development and Economic History," in *Investment in Women's Human Capital*, edited by T. Paul Schultz (Chicago: University of Chicago Press, 1995), pp. 61–90; Kristin Mammen and Christina Paxson, "Women's Work and Economic Development," *Journal of Economic Perspectives* 14, no. 4 (Fall 2000): 141–64; and Louise A. Tilly and Joan W. Scott, *Women, Work and Family,* 2nd ed. (New York: Routledge, 1987).

TABLE 11-1   Indicators of Women's Economic Status, by World Regions and Selected Countries[a]

	GNP per Capita 2001	Female Labor Force Participation Rate (15+) 2000	Ratio of Female-to-Male Labor Force Participation 2000
Low-Income Economies	$430	n.a.	n.a.
Middle-Income Economies	1,860	n.a.	n.a.
Low- and Middle-Income Economies	1,160	n.a.	n.a.
Sub-Saharan Africa	460	62.0	72.1
Côte d'Ivoire	630	43.5[d]	49.6[d]
Ethiopia	100	71.9	80.2
South Africa	2,820	43.9	76.1
East Asia and Pacific	900	60.0	75.0
China	890	73.7[d]	86.1[d]
Korea	9,460	48.8	66.3
Thailand	1,940	65.0	79.9
South Asia	450	45.0[b]	53.6[b]
India	460	41.3[d]	48.4[d]
Pakistan	420	16.3	19.6
Europe and Central Asia	1,970	59.0	78.7
Russia	1,750	51.8	77.2
Middle East and North Africa	2,220	29.0	37.7
Egypt	1,530	20.2	29.4
Saudi Arabia	8,460	14.5[d]	18.1[d]
Latin America and Caribbean	3,580	45.0[c]	57.7[c]
Mexico	5,530	38.6	47.2
High-Income Economies	26,510	n.a.	n.a.
Japan	35,610	49.2	65.0
Sweden	25,400	66.6	90.7
United States	34,280	60.1	80.5
European Monetary Union	20,670	n.a.	n.a.

[a]All figures and regional definitions are from the World Bank, *World Development Indicators*, except for columns 2 and 3. Country figures in columns 2 and 3 are from ILO, *Yearbook of Labour Statistics*, 2002 or 2003, and ILO, *Key Indicators of the Labour Market 2001–2002*. Source that provides most recent data was used. Figures are within two years of 2000, except where otherwise indicated. Regional figures in columns 2 and 3 are for 1997 and from U.N., *The World's Women 2000*. Regional definitions used by the United Nations do not perfectly match definitions used by the World Bank.
[b]Figure is for Southern Asia. For Southeastern Asia, women's participation rate is 62 and ratio to men's is 73.8.
[c]Figure excludes Caribbean. For Caribbean, women's participation rate is 53 and ratio to men's is 70.7.

Female Share of Labor Force (%) 2001	Adult Illiteracy Rate (%)				Total Fertility Rate [f]	
	Female		Male			
	1980	2001	1980	2001	1970	2001
37.9	60	46	35	28	6.0	3.6
42.1	22	18	15	9	4.6	2.2
40.2	48	30	29	17	5.6	2.8
42.0	72	46	51	30	6.5	5.2
33.5	87	62	66	40	7.4	4.7
40.9	89	68	72	52	5.8	5.6
37.9	25	15	22	14	5.7	2.8
44.5	43	19	20	7	5.7	2.1
45.2	48	21	22	7	5.8	1.9
41.6	11	3	3	1	4.3	1.4
46.3	17	6	8	3	5.5	1.8
33.5	75	56	48	34	6.0	3.3
32.4	74	54	45	31	5.8	3.0
29.0	86	71	59	42	7.0	4.6
46.3	8	4	3	1	2.5	1.6
49.2	2	1	1	0	2.0	1.2
28.1	72	46	44	25	6.8	3.4
30.7	75	55	47	33	5.9	3.2
16.9	67	32	33	16	7.3	5.4
35.0	23	12	18	10	5.2	2.6
33.5	22	11	14	7	6.5	2.5
43.3	e	e	e	e	2.4	1.7
41.6	e	e	e	e	2.1	1.4
48.0	e	e	e	e	1.9	1.6
46.1	e	e	e	e	2.5	2.1
41.3	n.a.	e	n.a.	e	n.a.	1.5

[d]Figure for South Africa is for 1992; figures for China and Côte d'Ivoire are for 1995.
[e]Illiteracy is less than 5 percent.
[f]The total fertility rate is defined as the number of births that a cohort of 1,000 women would have if they experienced the age-specific birthrates occuring in the current year throughout their childbearing years (see Table 9.2). Here it is divided by 1,000 to measure births per woman.
n.a. = Not available.

TABLE 11-2 Trends in Labor Force Participation Rates for Women and Men, Ages 15–64, for Selected Countries, 1982–2002

	Women		Men	
	1982	*2002*	*1982*	*2002*
Australia	52.0	66.7	86.7	84.2
Austria	50.3	62.8	83.2	79.8
Belgium	48.3	58.1[a]	77.7	72.1[a]
Canada	59.2	71.7	84.9	83.2
Czech Republic*	69.1[b]	64.3	78.0[b]	80.5
Denmark	72.6	75.6	87.9	84.0
Finland	72.4	73.1	82.6	78.0
France	55.4	63.8	80.0	76.3
Germany**	52.9	65.0	83.3	79.5
Greece	36.4	50.4[a]	81.6	75.0[a]
Hungary*	57.6[b]	52.0	72.9[b]	66.1
Ireland	37.6	57.9	87.8	80.5
Italy	39.8	48.4	81.4	75.8
Japan	55.7	64.0	88.8	92.0
Korea	46.9	56.5	73.6	77.4
Netherlands	39.0	67.3	80.8	84.4
Norway	64.3	76.8	87.9	84.0
Poland*	63.6[b]	59.6	76.5[b]	71.3
Portugal	54.1	68.9	83.8	84.8
Russia*	70.7[c]	63.9[a]	78.2[c]	74.2[a]
Spain	32.6	52.9	83.4	79.4
Sweden	76.3	75.6	86.6	79.4
Switzerland	55.4	77.4	95.9	97.2
United Kingdom	57.1	67.7	89.2	82.5
United States	61.5	70.1	85.2	83.0

Note: All figures are within two years of stated figure except where noted.
*Former country of the Soviet bloc.
**For 1982, figure is for West Germany (only).
[a]1999
[b]Figure is for late 1980s to early 1990s.
[c]Figure is for 1989, for the Soviet Union.
n.a. = Not available.
Sources: OECD, *Labour Force Statistics,* 1982–2002; International Labour Organization, *Yearbook of Labour Statistics;* International Labour Organization, *Key Indicators of Labour Market Statistics 2003* (for Russia); U.S. Bureau of Labor Statistics, at www.bls.gov (for U.S.).

Central America, that are in the early stages of industrialization. Higher rates are found once again in more economically advanced countries.

Apart from stage of development, women's labor market activity is also determined by demand and supply factors that vary from place to place, as well as over time. The demand for women workers is influenced by such factors as the industrial mix of the economy and relative size of the market and nonmarket sectors, which help to determine the nature of the jobs available in the labor market, and the preferences of employers for male versus female workers.[6] Factors that influence the supply of female labor include the relative value of market earnings as compared to time spent in household production, which is itself strongly influenced by fertility rates, the availability of goods and services for purchase, perceptions of what type of work is appropriate for each sex, general attitudes toward the appropriate roles for women and men, and tastes for market goods as compared to commodities mainly produced at home.

Social forces such as religion, ideology, and culture also influence women's status, especially through their effect on women's labor market activity.[7] For instance, women's labor force participation is considerably lower in countries dominated by religious faiths that particularly emphasize women's traditional roles as wives and mothers, such as in Latin America with its predominantly Catholic population and in the Middle East, which is largely Moslem. Marxist ideology, which strongly advocates women's entry into the workforce, surely helps to explain why women's participation came to be extremely high in many of the former Soviet bloc countries. Similarly, concern for gender equality in the Scandinavian countries was one of the reasons for the introduction of policies that encouraged female labor force participation such as tax schedules favorable to two-earner couples, family leave, and subsidized day care. Apart from their direct effect, these policies in turn likely influenced attitudes about women's role in the economy. Women's economic role may also be related to other aspects of society, such as the practice of polygamy. Although polygamy is rare elsewhere, it is practiced in at least 26 Sub-Saharan African countries, and in seven of these countries, more than 40 percent of women have husbands with one or more other wives.[8] It has been argued that one reason men take on several wives in these countries is because these wives perform an important economic function in traditional agricultural production, beyond the usual household responsibilities.[9] This reasoning would suggest that as economic development proceeds and modern methods of production are introduced, polygamy should decline. It is also likely that polygamy is related to the sex ratio in the population, as well as to women's own education and labor market opportunities.[10]

Occupations

In considering women's economic status, it is interesting to go beyond examining to what extent women participate in the labor market, and also consider what jobs they have. When making comparisons between different countries, there are two serious difficulties. First, many do not provide detailed data on the occupational distribution

---

[6]For instance, Richard Freeman and Ronald Schettkat suggest that the reason that labor force participation rates are higher in the United States as compared with Germany is a result of the fact that goods like meals are more often produced in the market rather than at home in the United States, thereby increasing the demand for lower-skilled workers; see "Marketization of Production and the U.S.–Europe Employment Gap," *Economic Policy* 20, no. 41 (January 2005): 6–50.

[7]See, for instance, World Bank, "Removing Social Barriers and Building Social Institutions," *World Development Report 2000/2001: Attacking Poverty.*

[8]United Nations, *The World's Women 2000: Trends and Statistics* (New York: United Nations, 2000). Polygamy is legal in some Moslem countries as well but is now rarely practiced.

[9]For instance, see Hanan G. Jacoby, "The Economics of Polygyny in Sub-Saharan Africa: Female Productivity and the Demand for Wives in Cote d'Ivoire," *Journal of Political Economy* 103, no. 5 (October 1995): 938–71.

[10]Shoshana Grossbard-Shectman, *On the Economics of Marriage* (Boulder, CO: Westview Press, 1993), chap. 11.

of men and women, and those that do tend to use various classification schemes. Second, the degree of segregation is affected by the distribution of all workers across the occupational structure. Thus, if, at the extreme, the majority of people in the labor force in one country were employed in a single occupation like agriculture, while in another they are distributed among a considerably larger number of occupations, the indexes of segregation would surely differ. One study completed in the mid-1990s largely overcame the first of these limitations and examined occupational sex segregation for more than 40 countries around the world using data on 75 consistent occupations. Table 11-3 shows the index of occupational segregation for each of these countries, which, as discussed in Chapter 5, is defined as the percentage of women (or men) that would have to change jobs in order for the occupational distribution of men and women to be the same. These figures indicate that occupational segregation by sex remains "very extensive in each and every country,"[11] but the extent of segregation varies, particularly across regions. For instance, the index tends to be substantially higher in countries in the Middle East and North Africa, and in "Other Developing Countries," as compared with elsewhere. Other evidence indicates that occupational segregation declined in recent decades, albeit not in all countries or all regions.[12]

It appears that across all cultures and at all times, occupations have been sex segregated to a greater or lesser extent. One study, which looked at more than 200 cultures over time, found that metal working and hunting were, with few exceptions, exclusively male activities, while activities such as cooking, laundering, and spinning were predominately female. However, with the exception of certain occupations such as these, the more general pattern is that while occupations tend to be sex segregated, they vary as to whether they are dominated by men or women.[13] For instance, while in the United States women are overrepresented in the clerical sector, this is not the case in a number of countries, including Pakistan, Haiti, and Nigeria. This discussion suggests that occupational differences cannot be explained simply by inherent differences between women and men or by differences in their human capital investment decisions alone. Factors such as social norms, traditions, and religious beliefs also appear to play an important part in the varied patterns of the distribution of men and women by occupation. Despite this variation, one common feature of women's employment is that it tends to be in lower-paying jobs.

Earnings

The available evidence indicates that women everywhere earn less than men, although large variations occur in the extent to which this is the case. For instance, in 2002, the female-male earnings ratio in economically advanced countries ranged from a low of .65

---

[11]The study cited is Richard Anker, *Gender and Jobs: Sex Segregation of Occupations in the World* (Geneva: International Labour Office, 1998). The quote is from p. 407. See especially chap. 9 (main evidence) and chap. 16 (summary and conclusion).

[12]Anker, *Gender and Jobs.*

[13]This conclusion is from Joyce P. Jacobsen, "Sex Segregation at Work: Trends and Predictions," *Social Science Journal* 31, no. 2 (1994): 153–69, based on data from George P. Murdock and Caterina Provost, "Factors in the Division of Labor by Sex: A Cross-Cultural Analysis," in *Ethnology* 12, no. 2 (April 1973): 203–25. See also William Rau and Robert Wazienski, "Industrialization, Female Labor Force Participation, and the Modern Division of Labor by Sex," *Industrial Relations* 38, no. 4 (October 1999): 504–21; and Anker, *Gender and Jobs,* chaps. 8 and 16.

TABLE 11-3 Occupational Segregation by Sex for Selected Countries, 1980s/1990s[a]

Region/Country/Area	Occupational Segregation Index	Region/Country/Area	Occupational Segregation Index
Economically Advanced		**Other Developing**	
Australia	58.1	Angola	65.6
Canada	54.1	Costa Rica	59.8
Finland	61.6	Ghana	71.0
France	55.6	Haiti	66.9
Germany (West)	52.3	Senegal	57.3
Italy	44.9		
Netherlands	56.7	**Transition Economies**	
New Zealand	58.2	Bulgaria	54.1
Norway	57.3	Hungary	55.8
Spain	56.9	Poland	59.2
Sweden	63.0	Former Yugoslavia	54.0
Switzerland	58.1		
United Kingdom	56.7		
United States	46.3		
		Middle East and North Africa	
Asia/Pacific			
China	36.3	Bahrain	62.7
Hong Kong	49.3	Egypt	58.7
India	44.6	Iran	68.1
Japan	50.2	Jordan	77.6
Korea	43.2	Kuwait	73.3
Malaysia	48.9	Tunisia	69.5

[a]Index is computed using 75 similar occupations. Years of data vary, but the majority are from 1985 to 1991.

Source: Richard Anker, *Gender and Jobs: Sex Segregation of Occupations in the World*, 1998, Table 9.1, column 3, pp.176–177. Copyright © International Labour Organization 1998. Reprinted by permission of the International Labour Organization.

in Japan to a high of .90 in Australia.[14] We cannot be as specific about developing countries because of problems with data availability and reliability, but considerable variability appears to be the case among these countries as well. A number of factors explain the observed variation, including differences among countries in the extent of occupational segregation, gender differences in educational attainment and labor force attachment, labor market discrimination, and government policies. In addition, general rewards for skills, such as education or labor market experience, or for employment in male-dominated occupations and industries are also a factor.

Educational Attainment

Women's educational attainment is also important as an indicator of their economic status, in that it influences women's occupations and earnings, which are themselves indicators

---

[14]Data are presented later in Table 11-4.

of women's status. Also, it allows women to make better-informed decisions about affairs in their own household, their community, and their nation. Gender differences in educational attainment are fairly small among economically advanced countries, but vary considerably across all countries, as a result of, and related to, differences in levels of affluence, as well as differences in fertility, social customs, and government policy.

One recent study estimated years of schooling for the average woman and man (age 15 and over) in various world regions for the years 1960 to 2000.[15] For 2000, they found that these two figures were close to parity for economically advanced countries and those of the former Soviet bloc. The average woman in South Asia, Sub-Saharan Africa, and the Middle East and North Africa, however, had only 60 to 76 percent as much schooling as the average man in the same region, though even these figures are considerably higher than they were in 1960. As might be expected, they also found that both women and men in these regions had the lowest average levels of schooling.

Illiteracy rates provide another useful measure of educational attainment. As shown in Table 11-1 and Figure 11-1, female illiteracy rates in 2001 stood at 56 percent in South Asia, and 46 percent in Sub-Saharan Africa as well as in the Middle East and North Africa. The rates for men were considerably lower in each region. For example, in South Asia the male illiteracy rate was 34 percent, and in Sub-Saharan Africa and in the Middle East and North Africa, the male rates were 30 and 25 percent, respectively.

An important factor that contributes to low levels of educational attainment for both men and women in the poorest countries is that large numbers of children do not even attend school because many of them, especially girls, are helping out at home, while others are employed (see the discussion of child labor). Hence, much progress in this respect is unlikely unless parents are able to earn enough to support their families without assistance from their children.

Although illiteracy rates for both women and men remain high in some regions, Table 11-1 also shows that they declined quite a bit since 1980. The relatively high rates of female illiteracy that persist reflect, in part, the lower average levels of schooling in these regions as well as disparities in the treatment of girls and boys. They are, however, very likely to decrease further in the coming years because enrollment of girls in primary and secondary schools has increased substantially over the last couple of decades in many of the countries in these regions. This progress is expected to continue given heightened international attention to gender disparities in education at recent U.N. and international conferences. Hence, even though a sizable gender difference in average levels of schooling and illiteracy rates is likely for the foreseeable future, the situation is expected to improve.[16]

Fertility

There is also a strong relationship between fertility, educational attainment, and labor market activity. Fertility rates are an important indicator of women's economic status

---

[15]Robert J. Barro and Jong-Wha Lee, "International Data on Educational Attainment: Updates and Implications," *Oxford Economic Papers* 53, no. 3 (July 2001): 541–63. See also, OECD, "Women at Work: Who Are They and How Are They Faring?" *OECD Employment Outlook* (2002), pp. 71–76.

[16]United Nations Development Fund for Women (UNIFEM), "Progress of the World's Women 2002: Gender Equality and the Millennium Development Goals," (2002), pp. 1–53. For an example of the difficulties still faced, see Somini Sengupta, "African Girls' Route to School Is Still Littered with Obstacles," *New York Times*, December 14, 2003.

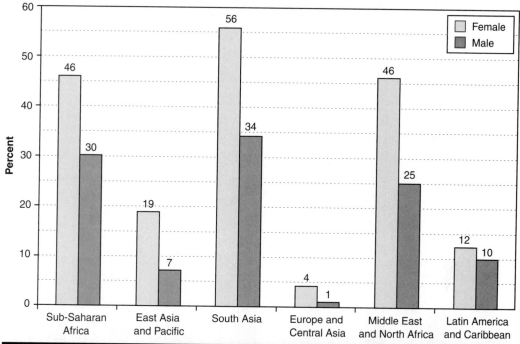

FIGURE 11-1   Illiteracy Rates, World Regions, 2001

because with fewer children, women have greater opportunities to engage in production for pay. Conversely, if birthrates are high, women have more incentive to remain full-time homemakers. As noted in earlier chapters, however, causation runs in the other direction as well. As women invest more in education and increase their participation in market work, particularly when it is away from the household, the opportunity cost of bearing children rises, thereby providing an incentive to reduce the number of children. In addition, fertility is at times related to explicit government policy, as well as religion and ideology. For instance, in recent history, some governments implemented pronatalist policies or policies that may have pronatalist effects, such as relatively generous child allowances, paid parental leaves, and subsidized day care. Some also introduced laws prohibiting various types of family planning, often justifying them on the grounds of religious strictures. Other countries, however, have sought to control population growth; many have done so by making birth control information available, while China, for example, went so far as to impose severe economic penalties for having more than one child. Its policy, however, has eased since it was first implemented.

Given the various factors mentioned here, it is not surprising that fertility rates differ dramatically across regions. As shown in Table 11-1 and Figure 11-2, in 2001, fertility rates were as high as 5.2 births per woman in Sub-Saharan Africa, followed by the Middle East and North Africa and South Asia, with rates of just under 3.5 births per woman. In sharp contrast, the U.S. rate was 2.1, just at replacement level, and the average rate among all high-income economies was 1.7. Figure 11-2 further points to the fact that current fertility rates for regions including South and East Asia as well as the Middle East and North Africa, are substantially lower than in past decades. Indeed, in

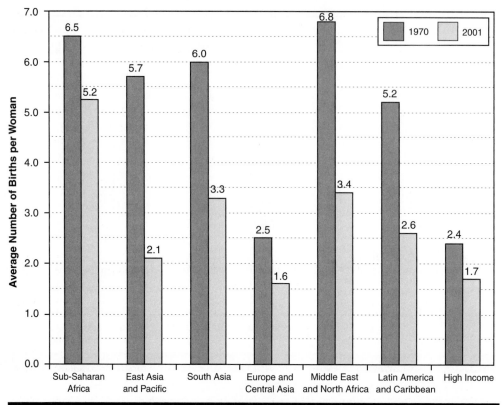

FIGURE 11-2   Total Fertility Rates, World Regions, 1970 and 2001

light of these trends, Ronald Lee observes: "The question about their fertility transition is no longer 'whether,' but rather 'how far' and 'how fast.'"[17] As indicated in Figure 11-2, Sub-Saharan Africa remains the one region where fertility declines are thus far quite modest.

Housework

As was discussed at some length in earlier chapters, the roles of women and men in the labor market are interrelated with their roles in the household. Nonetheless, we found that in the United States, although women's participation in the labor market increased rapidly for some time, participation of men in housework began to increase only more recently and that the continued unequal division of household responsibilities potentially influences both the amount of men's and women's leisure time and their achievements on the job. This unequal division of housework is also true across other economically advanced countries, as discussed in greater detail later. It is also important to recall that women in developing countries, especially in poor rural areas, often do an especially large amount of unpaid work needed for their families' subsistence, including carrying water and firewood and growing agricultural products, in addition to the usual housework.

---

[17]Ronald Lee, "The Demographic Transition: Three Centuries of Fundamental Change," *Journal of Economics* Perspectives 17, no. 4 (Fall 2003): 167–90. Quote is from p. 175.

Women's Role in Government and Their Standing Before the Law

Finally, women's roles in government and their standing before the law also serve as important indicators of their status. Greater representation of women among public officials is widely thought to increase the extent to which women's issues receive attention from the government, and greater equality before the law affects, among other things, women's right to inherit and own property, as well as their rights within the family and in case of divorce. Although women today have the right to vote in virtually all countries with representative institutions, they continue to be substantially underrepresented in public positions. For instance, as of 2000, only 17 women had ever been elected heads of state[18] and only 25 women had served as prime minister. There are, once again, considerable differences between countries and regions. Of the six female heads of state who were in office in 2000, four were in Europe and none were in North America. Also, women occupied one-third or more of all parliamentary seats in the Scandinavian countries and 13 percent in East Asia, but 5 percent or less in South Asia and in North Africa and the Middle East.[19] The distribution of ministerial positions followed a similar pattern. Women remain underrepresented in U.S. government as well. In 2004, only 14 percent of representatives and 14 percent of senators were women. Women also continue to be underrepresented in U.S. presidential cabinet and cabinet-level appointments, though recent administrations have included substantially more women than in the past.[20] More encouraging is the fact that in the majority of countries that provide such information, women's representation increased considerably at the local level. To the extent that such positions are stepping-stones to higher offices, this increase portends well for the future.

Similarly, women's progress toward equality before the law has been slow and uneven. In some countries, only men can inherit or only husbands have the right to dispose of their wives' earnings.[21] As of 2004, 179 countries (90 percent of members of the United Nations) had ratified an "international bill of rights for women" known as the Convention for the Elimination of All Forms of Discrimination Against Women (CEDAW). The United States remains one notable exception.[22] Further, "even when legal discrimination is removed, it can take generations for practice to catch up with the revised law."[23]

Interpretations and Implications

The evidence presented here and later in this chapter shows that there is substantial variation in the status of women among different regions and even across countries

---

[18]This figure excludes the tiny Republic of San Marino, where a number of women served as head of state.
[19]United Nations, *The World's Women 2000*, chap. 6; and UNIFEM, *Progress of the World's Women*. See also *World Bank, World Development Report 2000/2001: Attacking Poverty*, chap. 7.
[20]For more details, go to the Center for American Women and Politics, Eagleton Institute of Politics, Rutgers University, www.cawp.rutgers.edu.
[21]Ester Boserup, "Obstacles to Advancement of Women During Development," in *Investments in Women's Human Capital*, edited by T. Paul Schultz (Chicago: University of Chicago Press, 1995), pp. 51–60; World Bank, "Removing Social Barriers and Building Social Institutions," *World Development Report 2000/2001: Attacking Poverty;* and United Nations, *Human Development Report 1995*.
[22]United Nations at www.un.org.
[23]United Nations, *Human Development Report 1995*, pp. 42–43. In addition, as Diane Elson points out, legal equality often means little for poor rural women as long as they are concentrated in the informal sector, or in female ghettoes of the formal sector, and intrahousehold distribution is not necessarily affected by these changes. See her "Introduction" in *Male Bias in the Development Process* (Manchester: Manchester University Press, 1991), pp. 1–28.

within the same region, as measured by any of the indicators discussed, whether it be labor force participation, female-male earnings ratios, educational attainment, distribution of housework, or women's role in government. This suggests that while economic factors influence the status of women as compared to men, the situation is very complex, and that noneconomic influences play an important role as well. The picture is further complicated by the fact that women may be doing well in a country in terms of some criteria but not in terms of others.[24]

An additional factor that affects women's status in some countries, including China and India, is the longstanding cultural preference for sons, which has resulted in bias against daughters and women in general. This preference is reflected in the very high sex ratio—the ratio of men to women—in these countries as well as by the sizeable estimates of what Amartya Sen has referred to as "missing women."[25]

Some evidence indicates that in regions where women work for pay, there is a higher ratio of women to men. For example, in Sub-Saharan Africa the ratio of women's economic activity to men's is high and the ratio of men to women in the population is low while in southern Asia (including India), just the opposite is observed.[26] This pattern of findings suggests that girls are more highly valued and better treated—as reflected by higher survival probabilities—when girls and women make an economic contribution outside the home. It may be the case that girls are more highly valued when women are more economically active, in part because they are viewed as potential providers of financial assistance to parents in old age. In addition, they may be seen as a source of a "bride-price," rather than as a financial drain on the family, that is, as requiring a dowry in order to get married.

China is a notable exception to the pattern described, with its high female activity ratio but still a high sex ratio. This situation illustrates that how girls fare relative to boys also likely depends on a number of historical and cultural factors. For instance, in China, the custom has long been that it is the obligation of just sons, not all children, to support their parents in their old age, which makes sons more valuable.

An interesting line of research also suggests that girls' outcomes improve when mothers have more resources because mothers tend to devote somewhat more resources to girls, while fathers tend to favor sons.[27] Further, mounting evidence indicates that mothers tend to spend a larger share of their resources on children, whether

---

[24]A similar conclusion that the relation between economic development and women's status is at least to a degree erratic and cannot readily be explained was reached by Shirley Nuss and Larraine Majka, "The Economic Integration of Women: A Cross National Investigation," *Work and Occupations* 10, no. 1 (February 1983): 29–48.

[25]Amartya Sen, "More than 100 Million Women Are Missing," *The New York Review of Books* 37, no. 20 (December 1990). For recent evidence, see Stephan Klasen and Claudia Wink, "Missing Women: Revisiting the Debate," *Feminist Economics* 9, no. 2–3 (July–November 2003): 263–99. Even in the United States, some slight preference for sons is evident, though by no means to the same extent. See Gordon B. Dahl and Enrico Moretti, "The Demand for Sons: Evidence from Divorce, Fertility, and Shotgun Marriage," National Bureau of Economic Research Working Paper No. 10281 (January 2004).

[26]Jean Dreze and Amartya Sen, *Hunger and Public Action* (Oxford: Clarendon Press, 1989), chap. 4. See also Mammen and Paxson, "Women's Work and Economic Development"; and Marianne A. Ferber and Helen M. Berg, "Labor Force Participation of Women and the Sex Ratio: A Cross-Country Analysis," *Review of Social Economy* 48, no. 1 (Spring 1991): 2–19; and Klasen and Wink, "Missing Women."

[27]For evidence on the United States, Brazil, and Ghana, see Duncan Thomas, "Like Father, Like Son: Like Mother, Like Daughter: Parental Resources and Child Height," *Journal of Human Resources* 29, no. 4 (Fall 1994): 950–88. See also, Bina Agarwal, " 'Bargaining' and Gender Relations: Within and Beyond the Household," *Feminist Economics* 3, no. 1 (March 1997): 1–51.

boys or girls, than do fathers.[28] Taken together, these findings suggest that advances in women's economic status, as measured by higher rates of labor force participation, better jobs, and greater educational attainment, should benefit children generally, as well as reduce the considerable imbalance in the allocation of resources to girls and boys in countries that traditionally favored boys.

In recent decades, women from around the world, in spite of their wide cultural differences, joined in international efforts to improve women's status. A prime example is that, in 1995, women from nearly 190 nations attended the United Nations Fourth World Conference on Women in Beijing and put together a "Plan for Action" that focused on education as a key to women's progress, in addition to addressing a wide range of other issues, from violence against women to economic development. Some evidence suggests that this platform, though not legally binding, resulted in improvements in women's status in some countries. For instance, a growing number of African countries subsequently passed laws to limit or ban altogether the practice of ritual genital mutilation of girls, though by no means eliminated it (see inset), and a large number of governments formulated plans to increase women's rights.[29]At the same time, women's status continues to remain low in many countries, and in addition, women face some new and growing difficulties. In Jordan, Pakistan, and India, women continue to be victims of "honor killings," in retaliation for being suspected of an extramarital affair or premarital sex. Though illegal, girls continue to be forced into child marriages in India. In addition, in civil wars in Bosnia, Sierra Leone, and most recently in Sudan, women were systematically raped as a part of "warfare."[30]

At a follow-up conference at the United Nations called "Beijing Plus Five," held in 2000, women representatives from around the world came together again to take stock of the progress made since 1995, to press for additional rights, and to reaffirm each government's commitment to change. Apart from preserving the rights originally decided upon in 1995, after some heated debate, the final document went beyond earlier ones and declared that women have the right to decide freely all matters related to their sexuality and childbearing.[31] The document also added strong wording against "honor killings," trafficking in girls, genital mutilation, and other forms of violence against girls and women. These declarations should place increased pressure on countries to outlaw these types of violence and should serve to improve women's position. Also in 2000, at the U.N. Millennium Summit, world leaders set forth a number of development goals, among these to "promote gender equality and empower women." Among the specific

---

[28]Duncan Thomas, "Intra-Household Resource Allocation: An Inferential Approach," *Journal of Human Resources* 25, no. 4 (Fall 1990): 635–64; and Shelly J. Lundberg, Robert A. Pollak, and Terence J. Wales, "Do Husbands and Wives Pool Their Resources? Evidence from the U.K. Child Benefit," *Journal of Human Resources* 32, no. 3 (Summer 1997): 463–80.

[29]See "A World of Rights for Women," *Boston Globe,* June 7, 2000, p. A18; and Barbara Crossette, "Women See Key Gains Since Talks in Beijing," *New York Times,* March 8, 1998.

[30]Minh T. Vo, "World's Women Get a Bit Safer," *Christian Science Monitor,* June 8, 2000, p. 1; John F. Burns, "Child Marriages, Though Illegal, Persist in India," *New York Times,* May 11, 1998; Colum Lynch, "Sierra Leone Seeks Aid on Tribunal; U.N. Weighs Requests on War Crime Trials," *Washington Post,* June 16, 2000, p. A24; and Maggie Farley, "The World; Annan Urges the U.N. to Pressure Sudan to Disarm Militias," *Los Angeles Times* July 8, 2004, p. 3.

[31]Barbara Crossette, "Rights Gains Are Preserved at U.N. Forum on Women," *New York Times,* June 11, 2000, p. A4.

charges to countries, they must take measures to eliminate gender difference in educational attainment, increase women's labor force participation, and augment women's political representation.[32]

Perhaps the most serious threat to the people of many developing countries, men and women alike, is the HIV/AIDS epidemic. The nations of Sub-Saharan Africa have among the highest rates of infection in the world; in Botswana and Swaziland, for example, an estimated 40 percent of the adult population has the HIV infection. Moreover, in Sub-Saharan Africa rates of HIV infection are more than twice as high among young women as among young men. Although the situation is most dire in Sub-Saharan Africa, a 2003 U.N. report points to the rapid globalization of the epidemic, including recent dramatic increases in HIV infection among people living in Eastern Europe and Asia. International monies to battle the expanding epidemic are failing to keep pace.[33]

A COMPARISON OF THE UNITED STATES TO OTHER ECONOMICALLY ADVANCED COUNTRIES

The same trends that occurred in the United States since the 1970s—women's rising labor force participation; improvements in the female-male wage ratio; a modest reallocation of housework among men and women; declining marriage rates; rising rates of divorce, cohabitation, and births to unmarried mothers—also occurred in other economically advanced countries, although in some, particularly Japan, to a more limited extent. For the most part, the explanations for these trends are similar to those offered for the United States in earlier chapters, such as changes in fertility, educational attainment, labor market opportunities, and social attitudes. However, other factors, including differences in government policies (e.g., the availability and amount of family leave and whether it is with pay, the availability of publicly funded day care, the design of tax policy, and variations in wage structures), are particularly important in explaining cross-country differences in outcomes.[34]

This section provides some comparisons of policies relevant to the status of women and the well-being of their families among economically advanced countries, then goes on to examine labor market outcomes and changes in the division of housework, as well as some demographic trends, in greater detail. As previously noted, special attention is paid to Sweden and Japan because Sweden made notable progress toward greater equality between men and women in the home as well as in the labor market, while Japan experienced much slower change.

The goal of Swedish policy has been to treat women and men, as far as possible, in the same way. Efforts were made to discourage gender-based stereotypes at all levels

---

[32]United Nations, *Progress of the World's Women 2002,* discusses the Millennium Summit and provides a useful summary table of international goals set at the Beijing, Beijing +5, and other conferences; see also United Nations, *Human Development Report 2003: Millennium Development Goals.*

[33]UNAIDS, *"Sub-Saharan Africa,"* Fact Sheet (December 2003); and Lawrence K. Altman, "U.N. Report Shows Concern Over Rise of H.I.V. in Asia," *The New York Times,* July 7, 2004.

[34]Constance Sorrentino, "The Changing Family in International Perspective," *Monthly Labor Review* 113, no. 3 (March 1990): 41–58; Siv Gustafsson, "Public Policies and Women's Labor Force Participation: A Comparison of Sweden, West Germany and the Netherlands," in *Investment in Women's Human Capital,* edited by T. Paul Schultz (Chicago: University of Chicago Press, 1995), pp. 91–112; and Francine D. Blau and Lawrence M. Kahn, "Wage Structure and Gender Earnings Differentials: An International Comparison," *Economica* 63 (supplement 1996): 29–62.

of the educational system. All gender differences in public aid were removed. Legislation was introduced to make marriage an equal partnership; a husband is no longer required to support his wife. Full participation of women and men in the labor market became the established goal. To encourage married women to enter the labor force, the joint income tax for spouses was eliminated (except for nonwage income) and replaced by a system of individual taxation. As discussed in Chapter 10, a joint income tax can have a considerable negative impact on work incentives, especially for wives, who are often perceived to be secondary workers. This is less true of individual taxation because the applicable marginal tax rate a married woman faces upon entering the labor market is lower than the rate she would have to pay as the second earner.[35]

As discussed in Chapter 7, antidiscrimination legislation is also expected to affect labor market outcomes. Since the 1970s, legislation has been enacted throughout the OECD countries, including Sweden in 1980 and 1992, and Japan in 1985 and 1997, to ensure women's rights to equal opportunity in employment.[36] It is interesting to note, however, that in this respect all the OECD countries lagged considerably behind the United States, which adopted similar measures in the early 1960s.[37]

On the other hand, all economically advanced countries, with the exception of the United States, provide mandated paid leave for mothers or for both parents, though most are less generous than in Sweden. Only in 1993 did the United States mandate that firms must provide workers with unpaid family leave of 12 weeks, and even still the mandate is restricted to firms with more than 50 employees. The Swedish government provides 12 months of paid leave, which may be taken by either parent at 80 to 90 percent replacement pay, and an additional three months with a flat-rate payment. Workers are guaranteed their jobs when they return, and may work part-time (6 hours per day) until the youngest child is age 8. Similarly, in other industrialized countries, the duration of leave is often 10 to 12 months and wage replacement is often in excess of 80 percent. In addition, employers in these countries frequently go beyond compliance with government mandates in accommodating workers with dual responsibilities; many not only provide opportunities for part-time work, but also the option of flexible schedules and alternative work arrangements. Even Japan's policy is somewhat more generous than that of the United States. Mothers are entitled to 14 weeks leave at 60 percent replacement pay and either parent may take unpaid leave for up to a year.[38] Following the birth of a child, workers may also opt to work part-time, and in Japan, part-time work in general has expanded considerably.[39]

As we noted in Chapter 10, the opportunity to take parental leave can be quite important to women in maintaining their attachment to the labor force and to the firm. Indeed, relatively short leaves have been found to increase women's labor force attachment

---

[35]See Diane Sainsbury, "Taxation, Family Responsibilities, and Employment," in *Gender and Welfare State Regimes,* edited by Diane Sainsbury (Oxford: Oxford University Press, 1999), pp. 185–210.
[36]Sweden's 1992 Equal Opportunity Act superseded the 1980 Act. One of its provisions is that employers must try to obtain a well-balanced sex distribution in various jobs and must make it easier for workers to combine job and family. For a brief overview, see Helina Melkas and Richard Anker, *Gender Equality and Occupational Segregation in Nordic Labour Markets* (Geneva: ILO, 1998), chap. 4.
[37]For a list of the laws passed, see OECD, *Women and Structural Change: New Perspectives* (1994).
[38]Janet C. Gornick and Marcia K. Meyers, *Families That Work* (New York: Russell Sage Foundation, 2003), chap. 5; and OECD, *Women and Structural Change.*
[39]Susan Houseman and Machiko Osawa, "Part-Time and Temporary Employment in Japan," *Monthly Labor Review* 118, no. 10 (October 1995): 10–18.

and wages. However, the situation may be more ambiguous for longer leaves. Such leaves (more than 3 months in one study) were found to have a modest negative effect on women's wages.[40] Moreover, because leaves tend to be disproportionately taken by mothers, even when available to both parents, they may reinforce traditional gender roles in the family and thus help to perpetuate differences in labor market outcomes between men and women. Also, as noted earlier, part-time work frequently provides less opportunity for upward mobility than full-time employment.[41]

Only a few countries provide subsidized child care, but some of these have committed a large amount of resources for this purpose. For instance, in Sweden, heavily subsidized day care is available for nearly half of children ages 1 to 2 and four-fifths of children ages 3 to 5. France subsidizes child care even more generously. There, all children ages 3 to 5 are eligible for free preschool, and virtually all of them do attend even if the mother is not employed. In addition, 20 percent of children ages 1 to 2 are in day care. By way of contrast, in Germany out-of home care for children ages 1 to 2 is rare, and even though 77 percent of children ages 3 to 5 are in preschool, the majority of this care is part-time.[42]

Wage-setting institutions also differ considerably by country. These differences affect wage structures and, hence, workers' standard of living, wage inequality, and the gender earnings ratio. The manner in which wages are determined may be highly centralized, as is true in many European countries, including Sweden. These countries have strong unions, and wages are largely determined by a collective bargaining process.[43] On the other hand, the process can be quite decentralized, as in the United States, where only a small proportion of the labor force belongs to labor unions and wages are largely determined by employers. Only 14 percent of workers in the United States are covered by collective bargaining agreements as compared with rates of 83 to 93 percent in the Scandinavian countries and 33 percent in Britain.[44] Wage structure refers to the relative wages paid for various labor market qualifications, such as the proficiency of a qualified crafts worker compared to an untrained laborer, or a college graduate compared to someone who only finished high school. In the United States

[40]Christopher J. Ruhm, "The Economic Consequences of Parental Leave Mandates: Lessons from Europe," *Quarterly Journal of Economics* 113, no. 1 (1998): 285–317.

[41]See, for instance, Elena Bardasi and Janet C. Gornick, "Women and Part-Time Employment: Workers' 'Choices' and Wage Penalties in Five Industrialized Countries," in *A Researcher's Guide to the National Statistics Socioeconomic Classification,* edited by David J. Pevalin and David Rose (London: Sage Publications, 2003), pp. 209–44; and OECD, "Women at Work."

[42]Gornick and Meyers, *Families That Work,* chap. 10; and Siv Gustafsson and Frank P. Stafford, "Three Regimes of Child Care: The United States, the Netherlands, and Sweden," in *Social Protection Versus Economic Flexibility,* edited by Rebecca M. Blank (Chicago: University of Chicago Press, 1994), pp. 333–61; Sheila B. Kamerman and Alfred J. Kahn, *Child Care, Parental Leave and the Under 3s: Policy Innovation in Europe* (New York: Auburn House, 1991); Eileen Trzcinski, "Family Policy in Germany: A Feminist Dilemma?" *Feminist Economics* 6, no. 1 (March 2000): 21–44; and Anita Nyberg, "From Foster Mothers to Child Care Centers: A History of Working Mothers and Child Care in Sweden," *Feminist Economics* 6, no. 1 (March 2000): 5–20.

[43]Where unions are strong, collective bargaining agreements are often extended to nonunion workers and may also cause nonunion firms to voluntarily imitate union pay structures. See, for instance, Francine D. Blau and Lawrence M. Kahn, "International Differences in Male Wage Inequality: Institutions Versus Market Forces," *Journal of Political Economy* 104, no. 4 (August 1996): 791–837.

[44]Figures are from OECD, *Employment Outlook 2004,* chap. 3. For discussion, see Francine D. Blau and Lawrence M. Kahn, *At Home and Abroad: U.S. Labor Market Performance in International Perspective* (New York: Russell Sage Foundation, 2002); and Blau and Kahn, "International Differences in Male Wage Inequality."

today, less-skilled workers tend to receive lower relative pay than in most other economically advanced countries, at least in part because they are less likely to have their pay boosted by union wage scales. As a relatively low-wage group in all countries, women disproportionately benefit from wage policies to "bring up the bottom" of the wage distribution.

Finally, most of these countries, with the exception of the United States, provide child benefits or a child allowance to families based on the number of children, without regard to income. In the United States, the tax system provides child exemptions but these exemptions reduce taxes for higher-income families more than for those in lower tax brackets, and are of no help to families whose income is so low that they pay no income tax. Although a child tax credit was introduced in 1997 and its value was increased in the early 2000s, low-income families either receive no credit or just a partial credit, depending on their earnings. Further, most of these countries, unlike the United States, offer either national health insurance or a national health care system. Such programs reduce the cost of rearing children and potentially improve the health and, thus, the productivity of the present as well as future workforce.

Labor Force Participation

Table 11-2 shows that between 1982 and 2002 women's labor force participation increased appreciably, while men's participation decreased somewhat in all of the economically advanced countries included in the table. (As noted earlier, the table also includes some countries of the former Soviet bloc for comparison purposes.) Nevertheless, substantial cross-country differences are notable, especially in women's participation rates. In 2002, participation rates were highest in Sweden and the other Scandinavian countries, with rates of 75 percent or more, followed closely by the United States at 70 percent.[45] Labor force participation rates were somewhat lower in countries such as Japan, Germany, and Austria, and considerably lower in southern Europe, including Greece, Spain, and especially Italy, where the rate was only 48 percent. Part of the reason for the particularly low rates in these latter countries may be their emphasis on the traditional family, related to their religious orientation, which would be expected to reduce labor force participation.[46]

The high labor force participation rate in Sweden is not surprising in view of all their policies intended to encourage women to enter and remain in the labor force.[47]

---

[45]Surprisingly, Sweden was hardly a leader in this respect in earlier days; married women there were not granted the legal right to enter into work contracts and to control their own earnings until 1920, as discussed in Christina Jonung and Inga Persson, "Combining Market Work and Family," in *Population, Economy and Welfare in Sweden,* edited by Tommy Bengtsson (New York: Springer-Verlag, 1994), pp. 37–64. For further discussion of cross-country trends, see Dora L. Costa, "From Mill Town to Board Room: The Rise of Women's Paid Labor," *Journal of Economic Perspectives* 14, no. 4 (Fall 2000): 101–22.

[46]For Italy, Daniela Del Boca also points to a "mismatch" between the type of jobs married women with children would prefer and those that are available in "Environmental Effects on the Participation and Fertility Decisions of Married Women," C.V. Starr Center for Applied Economics Working Paper No. 98-28, New York University (1998).

[47]Finland and Denmark follow similar policies, with correspondingly high rates of labor force participation. For international comparisons, see OECD, "Female Labour Force Participation: Past Trends and Main Determinants in OECD Countries," in *Economic Policy Reforms: Going for Growth* 2005, no. 1 (March 2005): pp. 161–174. Gustafsson and Stafford, "Three Regimes of Child Care"; Gustafsson, "Public Policies and Women's Labor Force Participation"; and Janet C. Gornick, Marcia K. Meyers, and Katherin E. Ross, "Public Policies and the Employment of Mothers: A Cross National Study," *Social Science Quarterly* 79, no. 1 (March 1998): 35–54.

At the same time, it should be noted that women at home caring for their young children, who are covered by Sweden's generous parental leave policy, are considered to be in the labor force. If these women were excluded, the female participation rate would be more in line with that of the United States. Further, a larger proportion of women in Sweden work part-time.[48] Nonetheless, the official labor force participation rate does provide a useful measure of women's attachment to the labor force because the leave policy gives mothers the right to return to their former job and to retain their seniority.

As noted earlier, Japan's female participation rate lies in the middle of the OECD countries included in Table 11-2. However, the nature of women's employment is different there in important respects from other economically advanced countries, including the United States. For instance, as of 2002, in the United States fewer than 1 percent were unpaid family workers, while in Japan, as many as 10 percent were unpaid workers in a family enterprise.[49] The drawback to this type of employment is that these women earn no independent income they personally control.

Lifetime participation patterns of women in Japan differ from those of high-participation countries such as Sweden and the United States. As evident in Figure 11-3, the pattern is M-shaped in Japan; labor force participation decreases during the childbearing years but increases to a second peak later. This pattern also prevailed in the United States between World War II and the early 1970s. Today, however, there is an inverted U pattern in the United States and especially in Sweden; labor force participation rises during the early years, reaches a plateau, and eventually declines as retirement age approaches.[50] Some researchers suggest that Japan is merely lagging behind these other countries and will eventually "catch up." It may be, however, that for historical and cultural reasons, the same factors operative in the United States and in Sweden are not operative in Japan, so that extrapolation based on their experience may be inappropriate.[51] In addition, as we will see, the nature of women's employment in Japan differs in that far fewer women have opportunities for career advancement within their firms.

Occupations

As previously noted, Table 11-3 shows that considerable sex segregation by occupation continues in the more economically advanced countries. Nonetheless, progress is being made by at least some groups. For instance, younger workers, particularly those who are college-educated, are experiencing less occupational sex segregation. Still, sex segregation appears to be more firmly entrenched for less-educated workers. These findings, which indicate diverging trends in sex segregation by educational group among a number of

---

[48]Christina Jonung and Inga Persson, "The Misleading Tale of Participation Rates in International Comparisons," *Work, Employment and Society* 7, no. 2 (1993): 259–74; Marit Ronsen and Marianne Sundstrom, "The Choice Between Full-Time Work for Norwegian and Swedish Mothers," in *Economics of the Family and Family Policies*, edited by Inga Persson and Christina Jonung (London: Routledge, 1997), pp. 159–77; and Janet C. Gornick, "Gender Equality in the Labor Market," in *Gender and Welfare State Regimes*, edited by Diane Sainsbury (Oxford: Oxford University Press, 1999), pp. 210–42.

[49]Data are computed from the International Labour Organization, *Yearbook of Labour Statistics*, 2003. For a discussion of women's labor force participation in Japan, see Yoshi-Fumi Nakata and Ryoji Takehiro, "Employment and Wages of Female Japanese Workers: Past, Present, and Future," *Industrial Relations* 41, no. 4 (October 2002): 521–47; and Mary Brinton, *Women and the Economic Miracle: Gender and Work in Postwar Japan* (Berkeley: University of California Press, 1993).

[50]For age-participation profiles for 30 countries, see OECD, "Women at Work," pp. 72–73.

[51]Brinton, *Women and the Economic Miracle*, p. 43.

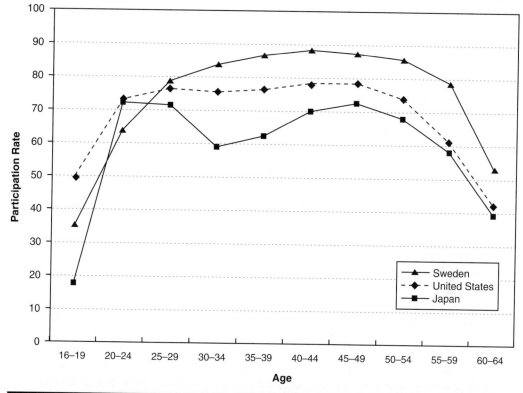

FIGURE 11-3 Labor Force Participation Rates of Women by Age for Selected Countries, 2001

Source: International Labour Organization, *Yearbook of Labour Statistics.*

economically advanced countries, mirror recent trends for the United States described earlier in Chapter 5.[52]

In looking at specific countries, one might expect the index of segregation for Sweden to be relatively low because its policies quite successfully raised not only women's labor force participation, but also increased their attachment to the labor force. In fact, its index is the highest of the economically advanced countries included in the table and quite a bit higher than that for the United States.[53] Women in Sweden continue to be disproportionately employed in traditionally female clerical and white-collar jobs, most notably in the government sector, and in health care, education, and child care. Moreover, although women are well represented in medicine as well as in diplomacy, few hold degrees in other traditionally male fields such as engineering, the natural sciences, and mathematics.[54] Evidence on the trend in occupational segregation in Sweden is mixed, with one study finding a modest decline, and another finding that it has

[52]OECD, "Women at Work."

[53]See Melkas and Anker, *Gender Equality and Occupational Segregation*, chap. 5–8; Juan J. Dolado, Florentino Felgeuroso, and Juan F. Jimeno, "Recent Trends in Occupational Segregation by Gender: A Look Across the Atlantic," IZA Discussion Paper No. 524 (Bonn, Germany: Institute for the Study of Labor, July 2002); and OECD, "Women at Work," pp. 85–91.

[54]Sherwin Rosen, "Public Employment and the Welfare State in Sweden," *Journal of Economic Literature* 34, no. 2 (June 1996): 729–40; and "Strindberg's Nightmare," *Economist,* June 8, 1996, p. 55.

not changed appreciably since the 1960s.[55] This stands in marked contrast to the United States, where the index decreased substantially over the same period.

Part of the explanation for so little change in occupational segregation in Sweden is that women are relatively well paid in predominantly female occupations. In addition, for a long time Sweden put far more emphasis on policies that encourage women to enter the labor market than on opening up new careers for them.[56] It has also been suggested that because of laws that permit long stretches of part-time work after childbirth, a high percentage of women are in jobs where part-time work is acceptable, and these often tend to be "women's jobs." However, others argue that working part-time is likely to be less disruptive to maintaining and accumulating market skills than dropping out entirely.

Equally surprising as the high index of occupational segregation in Sweden is the low index for Japan. Part of the explanation is that a larger share of the labor force in Japan is still employed in agriculture and blue-collar jobs, which happen to be occupations that employ a relatively large percentage of women in that country. It should also be noted that the low representation of women in white-collar positions in Japan is a disadvantage for them because many of these jobs are among the most prestigious and well paid, and are also most likely to be associated with permanent employment.[57]

Japan's lack of concern with gender equality is well illustrated by the fact that the government did not promulgate an equal opportunity employment law until 1985, when it became more acceptable to business as a consequence of internal labor shortages that made the hiring of women advantageous, and when external forces, including pressure from the United Nations, became difficult to ignore. Even then, employers were only asked to comply voluntarily and the government was not given the right to impose sanctions or financial penalties. Therefore it is not surprising that segregation *within* broad occupational categories remains high in Japan. This continued segregation may be a result of the weak enforcement mechanisms associated with the legislation, and may change as a result of important modifications that were made in 1997 revisions to the EEO law. The revised law explicitly prohibits discrimination in hiring, training, and promotion, and imposes stricter rules regarding sexual harassment in the workplace. Since the new EEO law was first implemented in 1999, women have sued over discriminatory practices in the workplaces and won in court, showing that the new law has "teeth." In one such suit, a woman was fired for refusing to serve tea, and in another, women failed to be promoted because their firm placed them on a lower job "track" that did not allow for upward mobility.[58]

The EEO law is quite new and its effects on women's position, as whole, will not be known for some time but some evidence suggests how well women fared since the 1985 law. More university-educated women were subsequently hired as clerical and technical

---

[55]Britta Hoem finds virtually no change in "The Way to the Gender-Segregated Swedish Labour Market," in *Gender and Family Change in Industrialized Countries,* edited by Karen O. Mason and An-Magritt Jensen (Oxford: Clarendon Press, 1995), pp. 279–96, while Anker finds a modest decline for the 1970s and 1980s in *Gender and Jobs,* chap. 13.

[56]Jane Lewis and Gertrude Astrom, "Equality, Difference, and State Welfare: Labor Market and Family Policies in Sweden," *Feminist Studies* 18, no. 1 (Spring 1992): 59–87; and Jonung and Persson, "Combining Market Work and Family."

[57]Brinton, *Women and the Economic Miracle;* and Anker, *Gender and Jobs,* chap. 9.

[58]For details on the revised law, see Takashi Araki, "Recent Legislative Developments in Equal Employment and Harmonization of Work and Family Life in Japan," *Japan Labor Bulletin,* 37, no. 4 (April 1998). The court cases are discussed in Bayan Rahman, "Japanese Women Push at the Door of Change," *The Financial Times* (London), April 19, 2002, p. 13; and Yasue Aio, "The 'Office Lady' Who Wouldn't Serve Tea," *The Christian Science Monitor,* November 26, 1999.

workers, but largely assigned to lower status, mommy-track type of positions and were rarely offered "core employment," which not only provides job security but also is typically associated with regular wage increases and steady promotions. Women's experience sharply differs from that of their male counterparts, even those who perform the same work.[59] In fact, one recent Japanese government survey of more than 200 firms estimated that women held only a little over 2 percent of all "core" employment positions.[60]

Some part of the gender inequality in Japan's multiple-track system may be caused by the decision of many women themselves to remain in the less demanding tracks, in anticipation of having a family. This preference would be understandable because in Japan, core employment positions are tailored for men in traditional families, who do extremely little housework. These positions require a degree of commitment that would be hard for women with families to manage. This system makes it difficult for women to take maternity leave and maintain their status in the firm, so that they are, in effect, faced with the choice of family or career. Moreover, husbands' employment in these positions means that they would find it difficult to share in household tasks and child care, even if they wanted to do so.

Looking toward the future, firms are likely to experience considerable pressure to modify the multiple-track system, as a result of both the revised EEO law and Japan's low fertility rate. In the years to come, the Japanese economy will need to rely on more women workers, but to do so, it will also need policies and practices in place that enable employed women to combine marriage and family. At present, this dual role is made difficult by the fact that not only do men do little housework, but little private child care is available. Moreover, in Japan the long-standing custom is that that wives are responsible for their own family and their in-laws, which adds to their caregiving responsibilities.[61]

The Gender-Wage Gap

Table 11-4 compares the ratio of women's to men's earnings in nonagricultural employment for the period from 1970 to 2002 in a number of economically advanced countries. It offers a useful overview, although a number of qualifications must be borne in mind. The data used are for hourly earnings, with the exception of Japan and the United States, for which only monthly and weekly earnings are available, respectively. Because weekly and monthly earnings are influenced by the number of hours and days worked, the earnings differential is likely to be larger than if hourly wages were compared. Also, data for the United States are reported for full-time workers, which is not the case for all countries, and the data are not precisely comparable in other respects either. In some cases they are for subgroups of workers, such as employees in manufacturing in Germany and nonsupervisory workers in Australia. There are also differences in the definition of wages among various countries; they may or may not include income in kind, family allowances,

---

[59]Kathleen Cannings and William Lazonick, "Equal Employment Opportunity and the 'Managerial Woman' in Japan," *Industrial Relations* 33, no. 1 (January 1994): 44–69; Helen A. Goff, "Glass Ceilings in the Land of the Rising Sons: The Failure of Workplace Gender Discrimination Law and Policy in Japan," *Law and Policy in International Business* 26, no. 4 (Summer 1995): 1147–68; and Linda N. Edwards, "The Status of Women in Japan: Has the Equal Employment Opportunity Law Made a Difference?" *Journal of Asian Studies* 5, no. 2 (Summer 1994): 217–40.

[60]Rahman, "Japanese Women Push at the Door of Change."

[61]For a discussion of low fertility and late marriage, see Robert D. Retherford, Naohiro Ogawa, and Rikiya Matsukura, "Late Marriage and Less Marriage in Japan," *Population and Development Review* 27, no. 1 (March 2001): 65–102.

TABLE 11-4   Ratio of Women's to Men's Hourly Earnings, Nonagricultural Workers, for Selected Years, 1970–2002

	1970	*1975*	*1980*	*1985*	*1990*	*1995*	*2002*
Australia	0.65	0.84	0.86	0.87	0.88	0.90	0.90
France	n.a.	0.79	0.79	0.81	0.81	0.81	n.a.
Japan, Series I	0.51	0.56	0.54	0.52	0.50	n.a.	n.a.
Japan, Series II	n.a.	n.a.	n.a.	n.a.	n.a.	0.62	0.65
Germany[a]	0.69	0.72	0.72	0.73	0.73	0.74	0.74
Norway[b]	0.75	0.78	0.82	0.84	0.86	0.87	0.88
Sweden[b]	0.80	0.85	0.90	0.90	0.89	0.87	0.88
Switzerland, Series I	0.66	0.67	0.68	0.67	0.68	n.a.	n.a.
Switzerland, Series II	n.a.	n.a.	n.a.	n.a.	n.a.	0.73	0.75
United Kingdom, Series I	0.60	0.68	0.70	0.69	0.70	n.a.	n.a.
United Kingdom, Series II	n.a.	n.a.	n.a.	0.74	0.76	0.80	0.82
United States	0.62	0.62	0.64	0.68	0.72	0.75	0.79

Notes: Japan, Switzerland and the United Kingdom have two series listed to indicate that the data presented are not continuous. Figures are for given or adjacent year.
[a]Manufacturing sector 1995 and after.
[b]Manufacturing sector before 1995.
n.a. = Not available.

Source: International Labour Organization, *Yearbook of Labour Statistics* (various issues), U.S. Bureau of Labor Statistics, *Handbook of Labor Statistics*; and Francine D. Blau and Lawrence M. Kahn, "The Gender Earnings Gap: Some International Evidence," in *Differences and Change in Wage Structure*, edited by Richard B. Freeman and Lawrence F. Katz (Chicago: University Chicago Press, 1995). The latter paper draws on the same sources cited here.

and so on. In addition, in the 1990s, some substantial changes were made to several earnings series. For this reason, both old and new earnings series are provided for Japan, the United Kingdom, and Switzerland. In interpreting these data, it is important to keep in mind that one can only be confident about trends *within* each given series.

As shown in the table, in all these countries women are paid less than men, but also the ratio of women's to men's earnings rose at least since the mid-1960s in all of them. Interestingly, however, the most rapid increases did not occur at the same time, nor did the ratios reach the same level in each of these countries.[62] As discussed in Chapter 5, the ratio of usual median weekly earnings of full-time workers in the United States increased substantially from .64 in 1980 to .77 in 1993. For several years afterwards the ratio fell, but by 1999 it rebounded to .77 and by 2003, the ratio climbed to .79.

In the case of Sweden, on the other hand, most of the gains occurred by the early 1980s and the ratio remained virtually unchanged since then at just under .90, which is among the highest for any country. In a number of other countries, including the United Kingdom, the ratio also increased substantially early on, then stagnated for some time, only to show recent evidence of a renewed increase.[63] As seen in Table 11-4, a new

---

[62]See also, OECD, "Women at Work," pp. 96–100.
[63]For evidence on the pay gap in the United Kingdom, see, for instance, Peter Dolton, Donal O'Neill, and Olive Sweetman, "Gender Differences in the Changing Labor Market," *Journal of Human Resources* 31, no. 3 (Summer 1996): 549–65; and Gerald Makepeace, Pierella Paci, Heather Joshi, and Peter Dolton, "How Unequally Has Equal Pay Progressed Since the 1970s? A Study of Two British Cohorts," *Journal of Human Resources* 34, no. 3 (Summer 1999): 534–56.

earnings series for the United Kingdom (UK Series II), indicates a steady rise from .74 in 1985, when the new series began, to .82 in 2002.

In Australia, the ratio increased sharply from 1970 to 1975, as a result of the introduction of comparable worth (see the inset on Australia), and has risen somewhat further to .90. The earnings ratio in Japan, historically lower than in other economically advanced countries, actually declined from .56 in 1975 to .50 in 1990. However, a newly available series, which cannot be directly compared with the earlier one, indicates that the gender-wage ratio in Japan increased from .62 in 1995 to .65 in 2002, offering at least some preliminary evidence of a recent upward trend.

In sum, the overall trend for the selected countries provides some indication of relative wage gains for women in all countries, and it appears that after a period of stagnation, women's wages relative to those of men are again rising. It is difficult to sort out the reasons for the trends in these series, and they need not be the same for all countries. It is, however, likely that changing wage structures within countries, the degree of enforcement of antidiscrimination laws, and changes in the relative qualifications of women workers play a greater or lesser role.

Another issue that deserves attention is the relationship between the female-male earnings ratio and occupational segregation by sex. On the one hand, for the reasons discussed in Chapter 7, one might expect a negative relationship; the higher the degree of segregation, the lower the female–male earnings ratio. On the other hand, if earnings for women are relatively high in women's fields, they may have less incentive to enter men's occupations so that one could observe both a high degree of segregation and a relatively high earnings ratio.[64] This might occur in countries with strong union policies that serve to compress the overall wage structure, as experienced in Sweden, or where "comparable worth" policies are adopted.

It is also worthy of note that the earnings ratio in the United States falls in the middle of the selected countries, rather than closer to the top. This is surprising because the United States was among the first to promulgate antidiscrimination laws, beginning in the early 1960s, and U.S. women tend to have similar, if not higher, levels of human capital relative to men as compared to women in these other countries. The answer to this puzzle lies in the fact that the size of the gender gap is determined not only by differences across countries in women's qualifications and in the extent of discrimination against them but also by international differences in wage structure or the returns that the labor market sets for skills and employment in higher-wage occupations and industries.[65] Because women tend to have less experience than men, on average, and to be concentrated in low-wage sectors, the gender-wage gap will be greater when the return to experience or the reward to employment in higher-wage occupations and industries is especially large.

---

[64]This relationship is consistent with findings by Donald J. Treiman and Patricia A. Roos, "Sex and Earnings in Industrial Society: A Nine-Nation Comparison," *American Journal of Sociology* 89, no. 3 (April 1984): 612–46. They found almost no effect of occupational distribution on earnings but quite substantial and complicated effects of rates of return for men and women within major occupational groups.

[65]For a more detailed discussion, see Francine D. Blau and Lawrence M. Kahn, "Gender Differences in Pay," *Journal of Economic Perspectives* 14, no. 4 (Fall 2000): 75–100; and Blau and Kahn, "Wage Structure and Gender Earnings Differentials." For additional recent evidence, see Francine D. Blau and Lawrence M. Kahn, "Understanding International Differences in the Gender Pay Gap" *Journal of Labor Economics* 21, no. 1 (January 2003): 106–44.

A comparison with Sweden is particularly instructive. As discussed earlier, the gender-wage ratio is much higher in Sweden than in the United States. One recent study suggests this is due to differences between the two countries in wage structure, with Sweden's reward structure being considerably more compressed than that in the United States.[66] This compression is largely caused by the role unions play in Sweden in determining wages. With women disproportionately represented among lower-paid workers, wage compression in Sweden raises women's wages relative to men's. In contrast, U.S. wage setting is highly decentralized and characterized by considerable wage differences between lower-skilled and higher-skilled workers. This study suggests that the United States would have as high a gender-wage ratio as Sweden if it had the same compressed wage structure. In fact, the high level of U.S. wage inequality raises the gender gap in the United States compared to many other economically advanced countries. In contrast, the even larger gender gap in Japan (which was not included in this study) likely reflects factors specifically related to gender, including the high degree of segregation of women within broad occupational categories there.

Thus, the international evidence suggests that wage structure is an important factor influencing differences across countries in the size of the gender pay gap. This finding implies that changes over time in the extent of wage inequality are likely to have an impact on trends in the gender pay gap within countries as well. As you will recall from Chapter 8, the U.S. labor market experienced a dramatic increase in wage inequality over the 1970s and 1980s, driven to a great extent by rising returns to labor market skills and rewards for employment in predominantly male occupations and industries. This poses a question as to how the sizable reduction in the gender pay gap during that time was achieved because women remain less skilled than men, on average, and are still concentrated in female sectors. Women were able to counter the unfavorable effects of the changes in overall wage structure by improvements in "gender-specific" factors: women's qualifications increased relative to men's and the unexplained portion of the pay difference between men and women with similar qualifications declined.[67]

The U.S. experience raises the question of to what extent wage gains for women in other countries were influenced by shifts in overall wage inequality versus changes in their qualifications and labor market treatment. Studies of this issue for Sweden and the United Kingdom provide an interesting comparison. Notably, in both cases, gender-specific factors were found to be of most importance in explaining the trends in the gender-wage gap over time within each country, even in Sweden where that country's solidarity wage policy did result in a dramatic narrowing of wage inequality. Although wage compression plays an important role in explaining the reduction in the gender-wage gap between 1968 and 1974 (a period of particularly large reductions in wage inequality),

---

[66]Blau and Kahn, "Wage Structure and Gender Earnings Differentials"; Francine D. Blau, "Where Are We in the Economics of Gender? The Gender Pay Gap," in *Women's Work and Wages,* edited by Christina Jonung and Inga Persson (New York: Routledge, 1998), pp. 15–35; and Francine D. Blau and Lawrence M. Kahn, "The Gender Earnings Gap: Some International Evidence," in *Differences and Changes in Wage Structures,* edited by Richard B. Freeman and Lawrence F. Katz (Chicago: University of Chicago Press, 1995), pp. 105–43.

[67]Francine D. Blau and Lawrence M. Kahn, "Rising Wage Inequality and the U.S. Gender Gap," *American Economic Review* 84, no. 2 (May 1994): 23–28; and Francine D. Blau and Lawrence M. Kahn, "Swimming Upstream: Trends in the Gender Wage Differential in the 1980s," *Journal of Labor Economics* 15, no. 1, pt. 1 (January 1997): 1–42.

taking the 1968 to 1981 period as a whole, gender-specific factors were nonetheless found to be critically important.[68]

In sum, it appears that international differences in wage structure are an important factor in explaining differences across countries in the gender pay gap and, especially, for explaining the surprisingly large pay gap in the United States. However, within given countries for which this question has been considered, gender-specific factors were found to be the primary determinant of changes in the pay gap over time. The reason wage inequality is so important in explaining international differences in the gender gap but not in explaining changes over time within a country may be because differences in the extent of wage inequality across countries are considerably larger than any changes in wage inequality that occurred within countries. It is also the case that, as noted in Chapter 8, rising wage inequality was associated with demand shifts that favored white-collar workers in general. Given the traditional male predominance in blue-collar jobs, this shift likely benefited women relative to men, as did increased computer use, both because women are more likely than men to use computers at work and because computers restructure work in ways that deemphasize physical strength.

Comparable Worth in Australia

Australia has the distinction among economically advanced countries of having one of the highest female-to-male earnings ratios. As described here, the implementation of equal pay and, particularly, of comparable worth in Australia in the 1970s, played a major role in raising the relative earnings of women.*

Australia's wage determination system is markedly different from that in the United States. In Australia, minimum wage rates for occupations are determined by government wage tribunals and unions play a larger role, though the wage system has become somewhat more decentralized in recent years, as discussed shortly.

Up to 1969, the Australian pay structure explicitly discriminated against women. Until 1950, female award rates were set at 54 percent of male rates; that year they were raised to 75 percent. In 1969, the concept of equal pay for equal work was implemented, and the award rate was raised to 100 percent. In 1972, the federal tribunal moved toward "comparable worth" by deciding that the "equal pay for equal work" concept should be expanded to "equal pay for work of equal value" in order to cover employees in predominantly female jobs.

As shown in Table 11-4, the result of the implementation of these policies, particularly of comparable worth, was a 19 percentage point increase in the gender earnings ratio among nonsupervisory workers, from 65 percent in 1970 to 84 percent by 1975. Moreover, during these years, the unemployment rate of women in Australia continued to fall relative to that of men, and employment continued to grow faster

---

[68]For Sweden, see Per-Anders Edin and Katarina Richardson, "Swimming with the Tide: Solidarity Wage Policy and the Gender Earnings Gap," *Scandinavian Journal of Economics* 104, no. 1 (March 2002): 49–67; and for the United Kingdom, see Dolton, O'Neill, and Sweetman, "Gender Differences in the Changing Labor Market."

for women than for men. Critics nevertheless suggested that implementation of comparable worth caused women's employment to increase less rapidly than would have been expected if their wages had not risen.† One explanation for the fairly small negative impact of comparable worth on women's employment is thought to be that the persistent high degree of occupational segregation constituted a substantial barrier to the replacement of women by men as the wage gap declined.

Clearly, the Australian institutional structure, with its reliance on wage tribunals to determine occupational pay rates, facilitated implementation of pay equity. This policy substantially reduced the gender-wage gap, while apparently having little effect on women's employment. Nevertheless, an overall gender pay gap in Australia remained through the mid-1990s, even with their highly centralized system of wage determination.

Since 1996, Australia's wage determination system has grown more decentralized than in years past; individual firms can now negotiate wage agreements, unions possess less bargaining power, and government wage tribunals play a much more modest role in determining wages, effectively serving as a "safety net." These recent changes have prompted concerns about possible negative effects on women's employment and earnings. As shown in Table 11-4, the female-male earnings ratio has not declined since that time, but it is important to keep in mind that these figures are only broad averages, and, moreover, they only reflect one dimension of what is happening in the labor market.

*This account of comparable worth is based on Robert G. Gregory and Vivian Ho, "Equal Pay and Comparable Worth: What Can the U.S. Learn from the Australian Experience?" The Australian National University, Centre for Economic Policy Research, Discussion Paper No. 123, July 1985; R. G. Gregory and A. E. Daily, "Can Economic Theory Explain Why Australian Women Are So Well Paid Relative to Their United States Counterparts?" in *Women's Wages: Stability and Change in Six Industrialized Countries, International Review of Comparative Public Policy, Research Annual,* edited by Steven L. Willborn (Greenwich, CT: JAI Press, 1991), pp. 3:81–125; Mark Killingsworth, *The Economics of Comparable Worth* (Kalamazoo, MI: Upjohn Institute for Employment Research, 1990); Bob Gregory, "Labour Market Institutions and the Gender Pay Ratio," *Australian Economic Review* 32, no. 3 (September 1999): 273–78; Jeff Borland, "The Equal Pay Case—Thirty Years On," *Australian Economic Review* 32, no. 3 (September 1999): 265–72; and Glenda Strachan and John Burgess, "Will Deregulating the Labor Market in Australia Improve the Employment Conditions of Women?" *Feminist Economics* 7 no. 2 (July 2001): 53–76. See also, Francine D. Blau and Lawrence M. Kahn, "The Gender Earnings Gap: Some International Evidence," in *Differences and Changes in Wage Structures,* edited by Richard B. Freeman and Lawrence F. Katz (Chicago: University of Chicago Press, 1995), pp. 105–43.
†See Killingsworth, *The Economics of Comparable Worth.*

Demographic Trends

Table 11-5 provides data on trends in various demographic indicators, including fertility, births to unwed mothers, marriage, and divorce for selected economically advanced countries for 1980 to 2001, though many of these trends started quite a bit earlier. As would be expected in view of the increasing labor force participation rate of women in all these countries, presumably at least in part in response to increased economic opportunities outside the home, the table shows that fertility rates declined in most of them. With the exception of the United States, most countries' rates are well below the replacement rate of 2.1 births per woman.[69] In fact, in Italy, the rate was as low as 1.2 births per woman in 2001. The fertility rate was even low in Sweden, at 1.6, which is particularly surprising in light of the fact that it provides generous policies of paid family leave and subsidized day care, which would be expected to increase fertility, along with labor force participation, by reducing the private cost of having children.[70] For the countries of the European Union (EU), the fertility rate was estimated to be 1.5 as of 2001 (see Table 11-1). The low fertility rates for Europe, as well as Japan, are expected to lead to substantial declines in population in the years to come. Governments in these countries are paying close attention to fertility trends because reductions in population size will likely reduce the international power of these regions, especially in light of the fact that populations in other parts of the world are fast-increasing. The declines could be moderated,

TABLE 11-5 Demographic Trends for Selected Countries, 1980–2001[a]

	Total Fertility Rate[b]		Births to Unmarried Women (as % of all births)		Marriage Rate per 1,000 Population Age 15–64		Divorce Rate per 1,000 Population Age 15–64		Single-Parent Households (as % of all Households with Children)[c]	
	1980	2001	1980	2000	1980	2000	1980	2000	1980	2001
Canada	1.7	1.6	12.8	28.3	11.5	7.4	3.7	3.4	12.7	19.3
Denmark	1.6	1.7	33.2	44.6	8.0	10.8	4.1	4.0	13.4	18.4
France	2.0	1.9	11.4	42.6	9.7	7.5	2.4	3.1	11.9[d]	17.1
Germany	n.a.	1.3	n.a.	23.4	n.a.	7.5	n.a.	3.5	15.2[d]	21.2
Italy	1.6	1.2	4.3	9.6	8.7	7.2	0.3	1.0	n.a.	n.a.
Japan	1.8	1.4	0.8	1.6	9.8	9.3	1.8	3.1	4.9	8.3
Netherlands	1.6	1.7	4.1	24.9	9.6	8.2	2.7	3.2	9.6[d]	13.0
Sweden	1.7	1.6	39.7	55.3	7.1	7.0	3.7	3.8	11.2[d]	23.1
United Kingdom	1.9	1.6	11.5	39.5	11.6	7.8	4.4	4.0	13.9	20.7
United States	1.8	2.1	18.4	33.2	15.9	12.8	7.9	6.2	19.5	26.5

[a] Data are for stated year or an adjacent year unless otherwise noted.
[b] Total fertility rate has same definition as in Table 9.2, but is divided by 1,000 here.
[c] The definition of children differs slightly across countries. See source listed here.
[d] For France and the Netherlands, data are for 1988. For Germany data are for 1991 and for Sweden data are for 1985.
n.a. = Not available.

Source: Adapted from Gary Martin and Vladimir Kats, "Families and Work in Transition in 12 Countries, 1980–2001," *Monthly Labor Review,* 126, no. 9 (September 2003): 4–31.

---

[69]It has, however, been argued that the present total fertility rate may understate the actual rate of childbearing of women in the United States and other industrialized countries because it does not adequately account for the continuing rise in the age of childbearing. See John Bongaarts, "Fertility Decline in the Developed World: Where Will It End?" *American Economic Review* 89, no. 2 (May 1999): 256–60.
[70]Family leave in Sweden and some other Western European nations was intended to encourage fertility. See Gustaffson and Stafford, "Three Regimes of Child Care."

however, if immigration were encouraged, or perhaps if countries were to adopt policies that better enable women to combine employment and childrearing.[71]

Marriage rates began declining in all the selected countries in the 1970s and continued their decline from 1980 to 2000, as shown in Table 11-5.[72] One striking finding is that the marriage rate in the United States remained among the highest in 2000, at 12.8 per 1,000 population aged 15 to 64. In Japan, on the other hand, the marriage rate fell considerably from 14 in 1970 (data not shown in table) to 9.3 by 2000.[73] Among the explanations for the trend in Japan is not only the growing economic independence of women, but also the especially low status of married women; husbands spend considerable time working for their employer and do little housework. Further, as noted earlier, wives in Japan have a particularly strong cultural obligation to care for both their own and their husbands' elderly parents. Interestingly, Sweden's marriage rate remained at a low level for a long period of time, perhaps because getting married there continues to offer few tax or other advantages in this highly secular society.

In many economically advanced countries, while marriage rates declined, rates of cohabitation continued to rise. The increase in cohabitation is a major factor in explaining the dramatic rise in births to unmarried mothers, although the degree to which these factors are associated varies considerably across countries.[74] For the mid-1990s, it is estimated that about 30 percent of Swedish women ages 25 to 29 were cohabiting as compared with about 10 percent of U.S. women of the same age, and 7 percent of U.S. women overall.[75] As shown in Table 11-5, the proportion of births to unwed mothers in 2000 was as high as 55 percent in Sweden and 33 percent in the United States. In Sweden, virtually all of the babies born to unmarried mothers were actually brought home to live with cohabiting fathers. For the United States, a recent study found that the comparable figure was 40 percent.[76] The high rates of cohabitation in Sweden, in the rest of the Nordic countries, and increasingly elsewhere, suggest that most men and women continue to choose to live with partners, even as marriage rates decline, albeit without long-term legal (or religious) commitments. Undoubtedly such couples, much like those who do marry, are seeking companionship, but they probably also want to reap gains from economies of scale, and, to an extent, specialization and exchange.

---

[71]Paul Demeny, "Population Policy Dilemmas in Europe at the Dawn of the Twenty-First Century," *Population and Development Review* 29, no. 1 (March 2003): 1–28; Lee, "The Demographic Transition"; and T. Paul Schultz, "The Fertility Transition: Economic Explanations," Yale University Economic Growth Center Discussion Paper No. 833 (August 2001).

[72]Quite a few European countries provide alternatives to marriage that offer some of the same legal protections. See Sarah Lyall, "For Europeans, Love, Yes; Marriage, Maybe," *The New York Times,* March 24, 2002.

[73]For 1970 figures for all countries, see Constance Sorrentino, "The Changing Family in International Perspective," *Monthly Labor Review* 113, no. 3 (March 1990): 41–60.

[74]For instance, Kathleen Kiernan observes that in The Netherlands and Germany, the rate of unwed births is lower than would be expected based on cohabitation rates, while the reverse is true for the United Kingdom and Ireland in "Cohabitation in Western Europe: Trends, Issues and Implications," in *Just Living Together: Implications of Cohabitation on Families, Children and Social Policy,* edited by Alan Booth and Ann C. Crouter, (Lawrence Erlbaum Assoc., March 2002), pp. 3–31.

[75]Figures discussed but not reported in Table 11-5 are from Kiernan, "Cohabitation in Western Europe"; U.S. Census Bureau, *U.S. Statistical Abstract: 1999,* Table 66; and Table 9.3. See also Sorrentino, "The Changing Family in International Perspective."

[76]The figures for Sweden and the United States, respectively, are from Sorrentino, "The Changing Family in International Perspective"; and Larry Bumpass and H.-H. Lu, "Trends in Cohabitation and Implications for Children's Family Context in the United States," *Population Studies* 54, no. 1 (March 2000): 29–41.

Rates of cohabitation for Japan are not known, but are likely to be low, given the fact that births to unwed mothers, which tend to increase with cohabitation, are negligible.

Family structure also changed since the 1970s because of rising divorce rates, though trends vary considerably by country. In the case of the United States, the divorce rate increased considerably from the mid-1960s to the early 1980s, but fell somewhat since then.[77] Nonetheless, in 2000 the United States' divorce rate of 6.2 divorces per 1,000 population was the highest of the countries shown in Table 11-5. In comparison, rates in Canada, the United Kingdom, and Sweden were quite a bit lower, ranging from 3.4 to 4 divorces per 1,000 population. The divorce rate in Japan, historically quite low, increased from 1.8 to 3.1 from 1980 to 2000, a sign of change in family marriage patterns. In Italy, the divorce rate continues to be extremely low, at 1 divorce per 1,000 population, most likely a result of the strong influence of the Vatican, though it also increased somewhat over the same period.

Families headed by single parents, most often mothers, are most common in the United States, but single-parent families also increased in a number of other economically advanced countries. Regrettably, statistics for different countries are not entirely comparable because some include cohabitors with children among married couples while others do not, and age limits for children differ. In the United States and most of these other countries, women most often become single mothers as a result of divorce or marital separation, but the proportion of never-married mothers continues to grow. As shown in Table 11-5, in 2001, single parents maintained 26.5 percent of households with dependent children in the United States, but rates in Sweden, Germany, and the United Kingdom were not all that far behind. Consistent with what we already saw, the figure for Japan was only about 8 percent.[78]

In all these countries, single-parent families, especially those headed by women, are among the most economically vulnerable. Social policies to assist them vary considerably.[79] On the one hand, in Sweden, single mothers, like all adults, are encouraged to work for pay and are given sufficient support to do so, including parental leave and day care. In addition, Sweden provides a child support "advance" system, which provides awards to custodial parents when the other parent fails to pay the agreed-upon amount of support. On the other hand, as we saw in Chapters 9 and 10, the United States provides considerably less support for single-parent families. One consequence of these differences, along with the fact that Sweden has a more highly compressed wage structure, leading to a small proportion of single women earning below-poverty

---

[77]A measure of divorces per 1,000 married persons is preferred, especially in international comparisons, because the measure reported here, divorces per 1,000 population, is influenced by the incidence of marriage—where marriage rates are lower, this rate is also lower. Figures were not available for this measure, however.

[78]See also, Majella Kilkey and Jonathan Bradshaw, "Lone Mothers, Economic Well-Being and Policies," in *Gender and Welfare State Regimes,* edited by Diane Sainsbury (Oxford: Oxford University Press, 1999), pp. 147–84. Notably, the relatively high rate of single parenthood in Sweden is not due to high rates of cohabitation because cohabitors are counted as married couples, not single-parent families. On the other hand, in the United States, some "single-parent" families may be cohabitors with children. See Sorrentino, "The Changing Family in International Perspective."

[79]For a discussion of these issues, see Siv Gustafsson, "Single Mothers in Sweden: Why Is Poverty Less Severe?" in *Poverty, Inequality, and the Future of Social Policy,* edited by Katherine McFate, Robert Lawson, and William Julius Wilson (New York: Russell Sage Foundation, 1995), pp. 291–325; K. Vleminckx and T. Smeeding, eds., *Child Well-Being, Child Poverty and Child Policy in Modern Nations: What Do We Know?* (Toronto: University of Toronto Press, 2001).

wages, is that poverty rates for mother-only families are considerably lower in Sweden than in the United States.[80]

Housework

Comparable international data on gender differences in time spent on housework are limited but a number of sources provide at least some information. As noted earlier, one consistent finding is that men do considerably less housework than women. As would be expected in view of women's high rates of labor force participation and the egalitarian policies in Sweden, the number of hours that women spend in housework compared to men is somewhat more equal in Sweden than in the United States. For instance, in Sweden employed women spent 1.5 as much time in housework as employed men in the late 1990s, while the figure for the United States reported in Chapter 3, though not perfectly comparable, was closer to 2. Nonetheless, even in Sweden, women still do a greater share of the housework.[81] Part of the reason for the gender difference in Sweden may be the availability of part-time schedules for workers caring for younger children—often women. In sharp contrast, Japanese men spend substantially less time in housework than men in these as well as other economically advanced countries, consistent with women's more traditional role in Japanese society. Surveys find that only 10 percent of Japanese husbands feel an obligation to share in housework.[82] Indeed, even among young Japanese families in which the wife is well-educated, holds a full-time job, and has children, three-fourths of the wives do most, and often virtually all, of the housework. On the other hand, a more equal sharing of household responsibilities occurs in such families in the United States, with only one-third of wives doing most of the household tasks.[83] Thus, there has yet been little progress toward more egalitarian marriages in Japan.

Summary on Economically Advanced Countries

This discussion indicates real progress toward economic equality made by women in economically advanced countries over the last several decades, but it also highlights the very different experiences of specific countries and the challenges that remain. For instance, in Sweden, with its high rate of labor force participation and high female-to-male earnings ratio, women still hold different jobs than men. In Japan, women are entering the labor market, but do not fare as well in other respects, and the gender earnings ratio has only increased slightly. In the United States, large numbers of single mothers continue to live in poverty. Government policies, along with distinctive cultural and historical differences, no doubt help to explain the considerable differences among countries. Much must still be learned about these factors, and also about ways to ensure the continuation of progress.

---

[80]Karen Christopher, Paula England, Katherin Ross, Timothy Smeeding, and Sara McLanahan, "The Gender Gap in Poverty in Modern Nations: Single Motherhood, the Market, and the State," *Sociological Perspectives* 45, no. 3 (2002): 219–42.

[81]Figure for Sweden is from Eurostat, "How Is the Time of Europeans Distributed? Differences Between Women and Men," news release 93/2004 (July 27, 2004). For other supporting evidence see Thomas Juster and Frank P. Stafford, "The Allocation of Time: Empirical Findings, Behavioral Models, and Problems of Measurement," *Journal of Economic Literature* 29 (June 1991): 477; and Janeen Baxter, "Gender Equality and Participation in Housework: A Cross-National Perspective," *Journal of Comparative Family Studies* 28 (Autumn 1997): 220–47.

[82]T.R. Reid, "Male, Mid 20's Desperately Seeks Mate," *Washington Post Weekly Edition*, September 27–October 3, 1993, p. 19.

[83]Myra H. Strober and Agnes Miling Kaneko Chan, *The Road Winds Uphill All the Way: Gender, Work, and Family in the United States and Japan* (Cambridge, MA: MIT Press, 1999), p. 108.

DEVELOPING COUNTRIES

Women in developing countries merit special attention because they face major challenges and difficulties as a result of the extremely low income level of these countries.[84] The poorest two-fifths of the world's population receives only 3 percent of the income, while the wealthiest 15 percent receives 80 percent of the income.[85] Not surprisingly, then, developing countries are generally characterized by an extremely low standard of living, high rates of infant mortality, short life expectancy, and high rates of illiteracy. In many instances, their high rates of fertility rates tend to exacerbate some of the other problems. Thus, most individuals in developing countries live in extremely difficult circumstances. In addition, most often women bear a disproportionate share of the burdens of economic and social deprivation.[86]

It is not possible here to fully cover women's situation in the Third World. To do so would require a book considerably larger than this one because of the great variation in many respects among the different countries, as shown by Table 11-1 and the accompanying discussion. Some can only euphemistically be called "developing," while others are soon likely to be reclassified as "economically advanced." There are also great differences in their religions, customs, geographic locations, and economic resource bases, among other factors.[87] Perhaps the two most dramatic cases in recent years are India and China, which experienced considerable average income growth. Even in these countries, the changes have been quite uneven, with the creation of modern central cities, even as rural populations were left behind.[88] In this section we take a fairly modest approach and focus on four issues of great importance to women in developing countries. The first is education, which potentially offers the promise of raising women's economic status, as well as enhancing prospects for development. Second is the controversial question of public policies intended to influence the birth rate. These policies can be extremely problematic, whether they restrict access to information about means for controlling family size or attempt to force women to limit the number of children they have. Third is the issue of child labor, which has received considerable attention in the United States and internationally. Finally, we consider the potential role of microcredit in improving women's economic status.

Education as the Pathway to Empowerment

The days when it was widely accepted that it was unnecessary to send daughters to school are long behind us. In affluent countries, and in a growing number of developing countries, virtually all girls and boys attend primary schools and, increasingly, secondary schools as well. Nonetheless, in many of the poorest countries, where even primary education is still far from universal, it is generally girls who are least likely to obtain even a

---

[84]A number of useful books and many interesting articles on women in developing countries have been published since the 1970s. The pioneering work among them was Ester Boserup, *Women's Role in Economic Development*. More recently, see, for instance, Ester Boserup, *Economic and Demographic Relationships in Development* (Baltimore: Johns Hopkins University Press, 1990); T. Paul Schultz, ed., *Investment in Women's Human Capital* (Chicago: University of Chicago Press, 1995); and papers in *World Development* 20, no. 11 (November 1992).

[85]World Bank, *World Development Indicators*, 2005.

[86]Tuovi, "Economic Development and the Feminization of Poverty."

[87]Boserup, "Obstacles to Advancement of Women."

[88]United Nations, *Human Development Report 2003*.

minimal amount of education, and illiteracy rates among women in these countries continue to be substantially higher than among men. As Figure 11-1 shows, the illiteracy rate for adult women in South Asia is 56 percent, and rates in Sub-Saharan Africa and the Middle East and North Africa are 46 percent, substantially higher than the comparable rates for men.

Women's educational attainment has been historically lower than men's for several reasons. From a purely economic standpoint, the opportunity cost of sending daughters to school is often greater in terms of productive output forgone because, in many cases, girls do more household work and market work than boys. Even more important, sons will become the breadwinners and in most cultures are expected to support their parents in their old age, while girls marry into another family and have no independent means to support their parents. In addition, customs and religion play an important role. In some cultures, education, beyond a minimal level, may actually reduce a woman's chance of marrying. In any case, education is likely to postpone marriage, which could defer and possibly reduce the bride-price (still common in many countries) when she does marry.[89] Finally, as we noted in the case of economically advanced countries, to the extent that girls receive a smaller return on their educational investments than boys due to a shorter expected work life, it may be that they opt for less of it.

The low level of women's education in the developing countries, and particularly in the poorest among them, is most unfortunate. This situation, however, appears to be changing. There is growing awareness that education is not only the key to independence and empowerment for women, but that it gives them both the incentive and ability to reduce their fertility, as well as the opportunity to better contribute to their families. Further, there is growing recognition of the substantial links between women's education and a country's standard of living and general well-being. Indeed, as noted earlier, world conferences, including the 1995 conference in Beijing and the U.N.'s 2000 Millennium Summit, made women's education a centerpiece of policy.[90]

Education enhances women's potential for entry into the labor force and raises their potential earnings. It also benefits families and children in a number of other ways. For instance, women will be able to read labels and instructions, and are thus likely to be better informed about nutrition, proper hygiene, and health care, including birth control. Indeed, one recent study finds that mother's numeracy and literacy skills learned in school improve their children's health outcomes.[91] In addition, parental education significantly influences children's schooling, with some evidence that mother's schooling particularly affects her daughters.[92] Finally, because the education of women increases the opportunity cost of raising children, they are likely to have fewer of them, allowing parents to devote more of their limited resources to each child.

From a societal perspective, education of women is an effective means of encouraging voluntary family planning that is vastly preferable to government policies such as

---

[89]M. Anne Hill and Elizabeth M. King, "Women's Education and Economic Well-Being," *Feminist Economics* 1, no. 2 (Summer 1995): 21–46.

[90]Seth Faison, "Women of the World Disperse: To What?" *New York Times,* September 17, 1995, sec. 4, p. 3.

[91]Paul Glewwe, "Why Does Mother's Schooling Raise Child Health in Developing Countries?" *Journal of Human Resources* 34, no. 1 (Winter 1999): 124–59.

[92]Hill and King, "Women's Education and Economic Well-Being"; and Thomas, "Like Father, Like Son." See also T. Paul Schultz, "Investments in the Schooling and Health of Women and Men: Quantities and Returns," in *Investments in Women's Human Capital,* edited by T. Paul Schultz (Chicago: University of Chicago Press, 1995), pp. 15–50.

those pursued in China, which penalized families for having additional children. Furthermore, as already suggested, it makes for a healthier, better-trained, and hence a more productive workforce.[93] Greater literacy among women in developing countries may also be one way to stem the rapid spread of the HIV/AIDS virus, which has already infected millions of teens and adults there; literacy would enable them to learn more about the vital importance of practicing safe sex, information they can pass on to the rest of their family. Even so, education is certainly not a panacea for this epidemic; HIV/AIDS is a problem among educated people in industrialized countries as well. Last but not least, education is necessary for a better informed citizenry, so crucial to the achievement and functioning of a healthy democracy. As also discussed earlier, women's education and economic empowerment not only shift more resources toward children but reduces the considerable imbalance between resources devoted to boys as compared to girls.

Governments throughout the developing world, as well as women's organizations, are beginning to take note of the societal benefits of women's education.[94] For instance, in Thailand, successive governments emphasized the importance of women's health and education, with the result that female illiteracy in that country was only 6 percent in 2001, well below the rate for its region (East Asia and the Pacific) of 19 percent. In addition, Thailand's fertility rate fell from 5.5 births per woman in 1970 to 1.8 in 2001.

Fertility and Population Control

As already noted, fertility and population control in developing countries are critically linked not only to women's economic status but to the economic viability of these countries, especially the poorest among them.[95] The methods developing countries use to control fertility range from encouraging the voluntary use of contraceptives and other methods of family planning to coercive population control enforced by the government. China, for instance, combined policies encouraging contraception and sex education, with limits on the number of children couples are permitted to have. The policies adopted by India have been less coercive but at times the government's tactics have not been far from compulsion.[96] In many other developing countries, family planning is entirely voluntary and increasingly common, while in yet others, family planning, including contraceptive use, is quite rare. Among the reasons may be a lack of adequate information about contraceptives, lack of availability or high cost of contraceptives, concerns about their side effects, or, in some cases, religious strictures that specifically discourage their use.

Expanding women's education is an exceptionally promising solution to controlling population growth because it enhances women's economic status while also reducing fertility, without using any form of compulsion. As already discussed, it is effective

---

[93]Hill and King, "Women's Education and Economic Well-Being."

[94]Ihsan Bouabid, "Women-Education: Nothing Less than a Human Right," Inter Press Service, September 8, 1995.

[95]For a more theoretical treatment, see T. Paul Schultz, "Demand for Children in Low-Income Countries," in *Handbook of Population and Family Economics,* edited by Mark R. Rosenzweig and Oded Stark (Amsterdam: Elsevier, 1997), pp. 1A:349–430.

[96]Regarding China, see Ansley J. Coale and Judith Bannister, "Five Decades of Missing Females in China," *Demography* 31, no. 3 (August 1994): 459–79; and on India, see Amartya Sen, "Fertility and Coercion," *University of Chicago Law Review* 63, no. 3 (Summer 1996): 1035–61.

in large part because the opportunity cost of raising children is greater for more highly educated women, and also because it gives women greater access to information about methods of birth control, at least where the established religion or government policy does not offer strong resistance.

The data in Table 11-1 and Figure 11-2 provide evidence that considerable strides have been made in much of the developing world over the last 20 years in reducing fertility. Only in Sub-Saharan Africa countries do rates remain at five children per woman. Clearly, these high rates are a major point of concern.

A second concern is that in a handful of countries efforts to control fertility, whether voluntary or coercive, appear to have substantially increased the ratio of men to women in the population. The increase in this ratio is especially pronounced in countries in East and South Asia, where there is a strong preference for boys over girls. This preference is evident in the historically lopsided sex ratio, particularly in China and India, which indicates the presence of considerably more men than women, as compared to what would be expected based on normal rates of infant mortality and subsequent survival rates.[97] In some cases, this was the result of outright infanticide and, in other cases, of girls being given less food and medical care than boys, amounting to what has been termed *passive infanticide,* so that the family would have more resources for present or future sons. In recent years, the major factor leading to the high sex ratios in these countries, as well as in South Korea and Taiwan, is the availability of sex-determination tests and use of sex-selective abortion as a form of birth control. In China, and perhaps elsewhere as well, another contributing factor is that births of girls tend to be underreported. Although about 105 to 106 boys would normally be expected to be born for every 100 girls, recent estimates put this figure at 117 in China, 110 in South Korea and in Taiwan, and somewhat lower at 108 for India as a whole, though in some provinces the rate is as high as 126.[98] Moreover, these high sex ratios prevail despite the fact that sex-determination tests were officially banned in all these countries in the 1990s, with the exception of Taiwan. The impact appears especially pronounced in second and higher-order births, suggesting that if a couple already has a girl, they are much less willing to accept another. The bias is also much more pronounced in rural areas, where sons, according to custom, must support parents in old age. Urban couples are more likely to receive pensions, lessening the importance of having a son.[99]

Fewer baby girls translates into a shortage of marriageable women—a phenomenon already observed in China, for example.[100] Ironically, the declining supply of women, which resulted from a bias against women, may eventually increase their value in the "marriage market" and girls who are only children may benefit from greater parental

---

[97]See, for instance, Fred Arnold, Minja Kim Choe, and T. K. Roy, "Son Preference, the Family-Building Process and Child Mortality in India," *Population Studies* 52 (November 1998): 301–15.
[98]Figures for China, India, and South Korea are from Dugger, "Modern Asia's Anomaly"; and figure for Tawain is from Sheila Tefft, "A Rush to Rob the Cradle—of Girls," *Christian Science Monitor,* August 2, 1995. See also Coale and Bannister, "Five Decades of Missing Females in China"; Chu Junhong, "Prenatal Sex Determination and Sex-Selective Abortion in Rural Central China," *Population and Development Review* 27, no. 2 (June 2001): 259–81; Erik Eckholm, "Desire for Sons Drives Use of Prenatal Scans in China," *The New York Times*, June 21, 2002.
[99]Elisabeth Rosenthal, "Bias for Boys Leads to Sale of Baby Girls in China," *The New York Times,* July 20, 2003.
[100]"China's Mania for Baby Boys Creates Surplus of Bachelors," *New York Times,* August 16, 1994, pp. A1, A8.

investments than would have been the case if they grew up with brothers.[101] This policy may result in larger social consequences as well. Among the dire predictions, the large numbers of unmarried men may substantially increase crime rates and perhaps even foment social unrest.[102]

It is particularly interesting to take a closer look at China, with just over 20 percent of the world's population, and thus the distinction of being the most populous country in the world. Around 1980, it instituted a particularly rigid policy of "one couple, one child" for urban residents unless the first child was incapacitated or died. In rural areas, couples were allowed to try again if their first child was a daughter. The one-child policy was pursued through political and social pressure, as well as by creating powerful economic incentives. Couples with a single child were entitled to such perks as cash bonuses, longer maternity leave, better child care, and preferential housing. However, couples who had more than the number allowed, particularly in the city, could face steep fines or the loss of their jobs or other benefits.

This policy was rigorously administered until 1983, when it became clear that it was not accepted by the public and was thus eased somewhat. Greater emphasis was placed on other ways of reducing fertility such as later marriage and education about contraception. Also, more control was given to autonomous regions and provinces in setting their own policies, with exemptions for minority groups.[103] By the late 1990s, the rule was less aggressively enforced and lower monetary penalties were imposed in smaller cities, leading some residents to pay fines in exchange for permission to have additional children.[104] In recent years, the Chinese government even relaxed the one-child policy for urban residents living in the largest cities. For instance, since 2000, married men and women living in urban areas who are both "only" children are permitted to have two children. The language used by the government softened as well. Starting in 2002, urban couples choosing to have more than one child (who do not have a special exemption) must pay a "social compensation fee," which ranges from one to 10 times local income, instead of a "fine." In addition to social pressure, these changes were prompted by the fact that the current fertility rate in China, as is the case in many economically advanced countries, is now below replacement level.[105]

---

[101]Vanessa L. Fong, "China's One-Child Policy and the Empowerment of Urban Daughters," *American Anthropologist* 104, no. 4 (2002): 1098–109; and Ming Tsui and Lynne Rich, "The Only Child and Educational Opportunity for Girls in Urban China," *Gender & Society* 16, no. 1 (February 2002): 74–92. It is also argued that another possible effect of parents' preference for sons, along with a preference for children who eventually marry, is that it may lead to a society in which upper-class families have boys because they have a good chance in life and a good chance to marry, while lower-income parents tend to choose daughters, who would have a good chance to marry men who are as well or better off than they are. See Lena Edlund, "Son Preference, Sex Ratios, and Marriage Patterns," *Journal of Political Economy* 107, no. 6, pt. 1 (December 1999): 1275–304. See also Arnold, Choe, and Roy, "Son Preference."

[102]Valerie M. Hudson and Andrea M. den Boer, *Bare Branches: Security Implications of Asia's Surplus Male Population* (Cambridge, MA: MIT Press, 2004).

[103]Christina Wu Harbaugh, "Geographic and Demographic Setting," in *China: A Country Study,* edited by Robert L. Worden and Andrea Matles Savada (Washington, DC: GPO, forthcoming). For a more general discussion on China, see Ray Bowen, "China: A Nation in Transition," *Congressional Quarterly, Inc.* (Washington, DC: Congressional Quarterly, Inc., 1995), pp. 155–86.

[104]Seth Faison, "Chinese Happily Break the 'One-Child' Rule," *New York Times,* August 17, 1997, pp. 1, 6.

[105]Seth Faison, "China Moves Quietly to Ease Its Strict One-Child-Per-Family Rule," *St. Louis Post-Dispatch,* May 3, 2000, p. A10; and Philip P. Pan, "China's One-Child Policy Now a Double Standard: Limits and Penalties Applied Unevenly," *The Washington Post,* August 20, 2002, p. 1; and Jim Yardley, "Fearing Future, China Starts to Give Girls Their Due," *The New York Times,* January 31, 2005.

As Table 11-1 shows, family planning policies in China, initially introduced in the 1970s, reduced fertility substantially from 5.8 children per woman in 1970 to 1.9 in 2001.[106] The greatest decline occurred in urban areas, where about one-third of the population lives, presumably because of tighter government control and greater penalties.[107] Fertility declined much less in rural areas, where the majority of the population lives, in part because families there are more economically dependent on their children, particularly their sons, as is the case in many traditional societies. In addition, unlike most urban residents, they are not entitled to old-age pensions or heavily subsidized housing.

Even though the one-child policy in China probably increased discrimination against girls in the short run, and women are far from achieving equality either in the household or the public sphere, some progress toward gender equality is evident. Women's labor force participation is high compared with other countries in the region such as India and Japan. Moreover, the existing gender imbalances in higher education and in the occupational distribution, although substantial, appear to be an improvement over the rather lowly position of women in the past.[108] On the other hand, the evidence concerning the earnings gap between women and men is mixed, with some studies finding only a minor gap and others finding a substantial difference.[109] Also, as noted earlier, the one-child policy may improve women's value in the future when they will be more scarce.

Child Labor

As discussed earlier, girls often face particular challenges in developing countries because of gender bias in parental investments in education and, in some cases, even bias in the basic nutrition they receive. Compounding these difficulties, many girls as well as boys in developing countries are engaged in economic activity, defined as doing work on a regular basis for which they receive pay or that results in output the family sells in the market. The International Labour Organization (ILO) estimates that in 2002, 210 million boys and girls ages 5 to 14 engaged in such economic activity worldwide. A greater fraction of child laborers are boys according to the official statistics, but these figures tend to undercount female child laborers, many of whom are employed as domestic workers in other people's homes, and hence "invisible."[110] If they were counted,

---

[106]For a quantitative analysis, see Marjorie McElroy and Dennis Tao Yang, "Carrots and Sticks: Fertility Effects of China's Population Policies," *American Economic Review* 90, no. 2 (May 2000): 389–92.

[107]Harbaugh, "Geographic and Demographic Setting"; and Rosemary Santana Cooney and Jiali Li, "Household Registration Type and Compliance with the 'One Child' Policy in China, 1979–1988," *Demography* 31, no. 1 (February 1994): 21–32.

[108]C. Montgomery Broaded and Chongshun Liu, "Family Background, Gender and Educational Attainment in Urban China," *China Quarterly* 145 (March 1996): 53–86.

[109]For a review of the evidence on both sides, see Margaret Murer-Fazio, Thomas G. Rawski, and Wei Zhang, "Inequality in the Rewards for Holding Up Half the Sky: Gender Wage Gaps in China's Urban Labour Market, 1988–1994," *China Quarterly* no. 41 (January 1999): 55–88.

[110]The 210 million figure is the number of "economically active" children as counted by the ILO. Their count of "child laborers" is 186 million, somewhat lower, because it excludes those ages 12–14 who do "light work." These terms are used interchangeably in the discussion here. See International Labour Office, *Every Child Counts: New Global Estimates on Child Labour* (Geneva: ILO, 2002). Regarding girl domestic workers, see International Labour Organization, "The Girl Child Labourer: ILO-IPEC's Response," Unit 2: Gender Issues in the World of Work, ILO/SEAPAT's OnLine Gender Learning & Information Module, at www.ilo.org; and International Labour Organization, *IPEC Action Against Child Labour: Achievements, Lessons Learned and Indications for the Future 1998–1999* (Geneva: ILO, 1999).

the total child labor force would be even higher. Child labor is not considered a problem to the extent that it involves performing light tasks after school such as helping with the farm or family business or doing household chores. Rather, international attention is focusing on labor that prevents children from going to school or that involves potential physical or mental harm.

The ILO classifies cases in which children work under forced labor conditions or in bondage, face hazardous working conditions, and where children are "vulnerable," such as those under age 12, as the worst forms of child labor.[111] More often than not, children end up in these situations because their families are in a dire economic situation, not because their parents are indifferent or seek to exploit them.

Estimates of girls employed as domestic workers, many starting as young as six years old, are high. The ILO estimates that 20 percent of all Brazilian, Colombian, and Ecuadorian girls between ages 10 to 14 in urban areas are domestic workers, with much higher figures in rural areas. In many cases, these arrangements are "akin to slavery"; the girls often work long hours, are at the mercy of the family for whom they work, and may receive no compensation apart from room and board. Helping girl domestic workers is a difficult task because the prevailing norm is that domestic work is women's work, regardless of the working conditions or the individual's age. Nevertheless, programs sponsored by the ILO instituted in a number of developing countries help to inform these girls of their rights and raise awareness about abuse. In addition, these programs may provide assistance in the form of education, skills training, and counseling services.[112]

With regard to the larger issue of child labor, suggested policy solutions abound, but in order for them to be successful, alternative ways to solve the problem of dire poverty must be found and each country's specific cultural and economic conditions must be considered. For instance, proposals to ban imports to the United States that were produced in developing countries using child labor may merely cause children's employment to shift from export-related industries to other sectors where conditions may be even more harmful. In one instance, just the anticipation of such policies caused many girls in Bangladesh to be forced out of work stitching carpets and into prostitution.[113] Another possibility is for developing countries to ban child labor of any form in all sectors and seriously enforce the policy. However, any one country may well be reluctant to adopt such a policy if others do not take similar actions, because doing so unilaterally would likely make its producers less competitive and lead to a decline in employment. Further, such a policy ignores the harsh reality that, more often than not, children are employed out of economic necessity.

Under former President Clinton's administration, the United States proposed the establishment of a set of minimal labor standards, such as protections for workers and the right to organize, that would be universally adopted by all countries.[114] However,

---

[111]ILO, *Every Child Counts*.

[112]UNICEF, "Child Domestic Work," *Innocenti Digests* 5 (1999): 1–20; and International Labour Organization, *Helping Hands or Shackled Lives? Understanding Child Domestic Labour and Responses to It* (Geneva: ILO, 2004).

[113]Kaushik Basu, "International Labor Standards and Child Labor," *Challenge* 42, no. 5 (September–October 1999): 80–93; and Miriam Wasserman, "Eliminating Child Labor," *Regional Review* 10, no. 2 (Second Quarter 2000): 8–17.

[114]International Labour Organization, "President Clinton Addresses International Labour Conference," press release, June 16, 1999; and Druscilla K. Brown, "Labor Standards: Where Do They Belong on the International Trade Agenda?" *Journal of Economic Perspectives* 15, no. 3 (Summer 2001): 89–112.

this type of policy faces considerable opposition in many developing countries, partly due to concern that it is strongly favored by protectionist lobbies in the United States whose goal is to limit competition from abroad. An additional concern is who would enforce such standards, what sort of punitive measures would be taken if they were violated, and, as mentioned earlier, fear that their adoption might leave children and their families in developing countries worse off.[115] Another strategy is to make schooling compulsory, though in the poorest countries, an intermediate policy that encourages a combination of school and work, or one that encourages schooling by providing economic incentives such as free lunch or a payment to the family, may be more realistic. Such policies would help the family to survive and also help to end the cycle of poverty because the children would at least get some education. Another complementary strategy is to improve access to credit so that families can weather difficult economic times without needing their children's help. Finally, government policies that improve the adult labor market or increase families' incomes would be expected to reduce families' dependence on child labor.[116] Thus, no simple solution is readily available, but ongoing international efforts lead by the ILO may help at least to eliminate the worst forms of child labor.

Microcredit for Women: Lifeline or Mirage?

Most people are well aware that in a modern economy, businesses, large and small, are heavily dependent on credit. Funds are needed to keep an enterprise going, and even more so to expand it or to start a new one. In developing countries the amounts needed are often rather small, but have nonetheless been beyond the reach of millions of poor people, and particularly poor women, who frequently lack any contacts with potential lenders, have no collateral, and are generally regarded as poor credit risks. At the same time, demand for labor in large-scale agriculture continues to decline as a result of mechanization, and demand in the emerging modern sectors is frequently entirely inadequate to absorb the rapidly growing populations. It is not surprising, therefore, that interest in self-employment has been growing as one solution to this problem, and in the role credit can play in facilitating it. In recent years, both governments and nongovernmental organizations are recognizing the contribution that the extension of even small loans could make toward increasing the earnings and raising the standard of living of the poor.[117]

Microcredit loans started with the Grameen Bank of Bangladesh in 1976, and subsequently similar institutions were founded in other developing countries, including

---

[115]For a discussion of the issues, see Kaushik Basu, "Child Labor: Cause, Consequence, and Cure, with Remarks on International Labor Standards," *Journal of Economic Literature* 37, no. 3 (September 1999): 1083–119.

[116]Rajeev Dehejia and Roberta Gatti, "Child Labor: The Role of Income Variability and Access to Credit Across Countries," National Bureau of Economic Research Working Paper No. 9018 (June 2002); and Kaushik Basu and Zafiris Tzannatos, "The Global Child Labor Problem: What Do We Know and What Can We Do?" *The World Bank Economic Review* 17, no. 2 (2003): 147–73; Basu, "Child Labor"; and Eric V. Edmonds, "Does Child Labor Decline With Improving Economic Status?" *Journal of Human Resources* 410, no. 1 (Winter 2005): 77–99.

[117]Interestingly, there are historic precedents in nineteenth-century Europe of similar organizations that lasted for many decades. Aidan Hollis and Arthur Sweetman found that organizations that obtained funds from depositors, especially if they were also able to adjust interest rates, were more long lasting than those that relied on charity in "Microcredit: What Can We Learn from the Past?" *World Development* 26, no. 10 (1999): 1875–89.

Indonesia, India, and Peru. Such programs now even operate in depressed areas of economically advanced countries, including the United States, as discussed earlier in Chapter 10.

In developing countries, one of the distinctive features of the microcredit institutions that make small loans to the poor is that they mainly extend credit to women. Even though the proportion of women among those obtaining loans from commercial banks is rarely above 20 percent, it is about 70 percent among those who borrow from the poverty-centered development banks, and some of them make loans only to women. Borrowers in local groups guarantee one another's loans, so that no one receives a second loan until all the first loans are repaid. This arrangement has led to high repayment rates, often an astonishing 90 percent, which enabled these banks not only to continue, but to expand.[118] Furthermore, because they lend at regular market rates, there is little pressure from affluent members of the community to extend loans to them, resulting in the largest share of the loans going to the poor, many of them illiterate and unskilled women. Most recently, there is a push to channel funds to some of the "poorest of the poor" in these countries, those living on less than $1 per day. For instance, starting in 2000, one-half of U.S. funds for international microenterprise programs are focused on this group.[119]

In addition to the loans, the microcredit institutions provide other useful services. These include sending agents to villages to collect payments and assist customers with necessary paperwork, or helping villagers organize and choose a representative who can make the trip to the bank to take care of these matters for everyone. Many microcredit institutions provide initial advice on what kind of business to start and how to run it, although they do not continue to do so once the businesses are established. The activities of the recipients of these loans range from the processing and sale of food, brewing of beer, and production of a variety of crafts, to petty trade in other items and the provision of services to affluent households as well as larger businesses.

Advocates of microcredit point to substantial evidence that the income of the women who were able to borrow these meager amounts rose perceptibly. Not only does this credit provide needed resources to their families, the fact that it is the wives' income that is increased should help to increase their decision-making power in the family, thus helping to improve their lives.[120] Additional evidence shows that other family members did a larger share of housework. Most important, perhaps, aspirations for children's education increased considerably.[121]

Even so, it would be a mistake to exaggerate the favorable effects or to ignore the reservations of critics. One critic points out that "most studies of microfinance programs have drawn their conclusions exclusively from successful borrowers in large, mature,

[118]Rosintan D. M. Panjaitan-Driodisuryo and Kathleen Cloud, "Gender, Self-Employment and Microcredit Programs: An Indonesian Case Study," *The Quarterly Review of Economics and Finance* (Special Issue, 1999): 769–79.
[119]Emmy Simmons, "The Role of Microenterprsie in U.S. Development Policy," *Economic Perspectives* (An Electronic Journal of the U.S. Department of State) 9, no. 1 (February 2004).
[120]Myra Buvinic, Myra Valenzuela, and J. P. Valenzuela, "Investing in Women" (Washington, DC: International Center for Research on Women, Policy Series, 1992); Daisy Dwyer and Judith Bruce, "Introduction," in *Home Divided: Women and Income in the Third World,* edited by Daisy Dwyer and Judith Bruce (Stanford: Stanford University Press, 1988), pp. 1–19; and B. Elavia, "Women and Rural Credit," in *Capturing Complexity: An Interdisciplinary Look at Women, Households, and Development,* edited by Romy Borooah, Kathleen Cloud, Subadra Seshadri, T. S. Saraswathi, Jean T. Peterson, and Amitra Verma (New Delhi, India: Sage, 1994), pp. 151–62.
[121]Panjaitan-Driodisuryo and Cloud, "Gender, Self-Employment and Microcredit Programs."

and successful programs."[122] Also, a surprisingly large proportion of eligible women do not choose to participate in such programs,[123] and those who do participate rarely achieve more than a modest rise in their standard of living. Observers also questioned whether shifting some microcredit funds toward the poorest is the best allocation of limited resources because members of this group are likely to have greater difficulties in starting a successful enterprise than those in "near" poverty.[124] Finally, the same group pressures that have been so successful in assuring high repayment rates can create serious hardships for the women who are subjected to them, especially when in some instances husbands or other family members exploit women's success for their own purposes.[125] Therefore, microcredit should not be viewed as a panacea for either poverty or for women's inferior status. At the same time, any program that succeeds in mitigating the dire destitution and powerlessness of many women and helps to give their children a start toward a better life should not be heedlessly discarded, but should rather be seen as a useful first step toward solving these serious problems.

Genital Mutilation and Patriarchal Traditions

For some years, a rising tide of condemnation of the age-old practice of genital cutting has echoed from the podiums of United Nations assemblies in Vienna, Cairo, and Beijing. Recently the United States joined the chorus. This practice, frequently referred to as *female circumcision,* but in fact far more drastic than that term implies, dates back about 2,000 years, and continues to be widespread. It is, undoubtedly, one more indication of the strength of patriarchal tradition and of women's subservient status in the 28 countries where it is practiced.* It is most prevalent among Muslims but is also common among Christians and followers of traditional African religions; it most generally occurs among the illiterate, but by no means is unknown among those with some education, nor is it unknown among emigrants from countries where cutting was traditionally practiced. The proportion of women subjected to cutting ranges from 5 in 100 in Niger to 9 out of 10 in Somalia and Mali. In these countries, the practice is deeply entrenched and even accepted by a substantial number of women.

At the same time, awareness is increasing that women who are cut suffer excruciating pain, because the operation is usually performed without any kind of anesthetic and that they are deprived of normal sexual pleasure for the remainder of their lives. Other reports suggest that they frequently experience complicated deliveries, and that some die as a result of this cruel procedure.

Public interest in the United States was aroused by the story of Fauzija Kassindja, who arrived on these shores December 17, 1994.† She fled her native

---

[122]Michael J. V. Woolcock, "What Unsuccessful Cases Tell Us About How Group-Based Programs Work," *American Journal of Economics and Sociology* 58, no. 1 (January 1999): 17–42. Quote is from p. 36.

[123]Timothy G. Evans, Alayne M. Adams, Rafi Mohammed, and Alison H. Norris, "Demystifying Nonparticipation in Microcredit: A Population-Based Analysis," *World Development* 27, no. 12 (1999): 419–30.

[124]Celia W. Dugger, "Debate Stirs Over Tiny Loans for World's Poorest," *The New York Times,* April 29, 2004.

[125]Aminur Rahman, "Microcredit Initiatives for Equitable and Sustainable Development: Who Pays?" *World Development* 27, no. 1 (1999): 67–82.

Togo in order to avoid forced genital cutting and sought asylum in the United States. As it turned out, she spent more than a year in prison before a precedent-setting decision by the highest administrative tribunal in the immigration system reversed the decision of an immigration judge who had dismissed her story because he did not believe it and considered it irrational. As a result of publicity about this case and growing social awareness of the problem, support for action on this matter grew, and in 1995 the Immigration and Naturalization Service (INS) introduced guidelines that advise asylum officers that gender-based persecution is an additional ground for asylum. Further, in 1996 Congress outlawed the practice of genital cutting in the United States. Still, this issue is not fully resolved. Advocates for refugees and some members of Congress remain adamant that current INS guidelines for those seeking asylum in the United States are insufficient because judges still hold the discretion over whether to grant asylum.

One particularly vocal opponent of genital cutting is supermodel Waris Dirie, who spent her early life as a nomad in Somalia and was herself subjected to genital mutilation. In addition to serving as a Special U.N. Ambassador on this issue, she coauthored a book on her horrifying experience. Indeed, a growing awareness that genital mutilation is a form of violence against women led 10 African countries to ban the practice, though it remains to be seen whether these governmental actions will substantially reduce the practice itself. Another critical step is for economically advanced countries to follow suit and ban this practice, so that it is not further perpetuated. Genital mutilation is banned in the United States and Canada and condemned by the European Union, though not all EU countries specifically ban the practice.[††]

*The figures in this inset are from United Nations, *The World's Women 2000: Trends and Statistics* (New York: United Nations, 2000), chap. 6; and Press Conference by United Nations Population Fund (New York: United Nations, June 2000). For more details regarding this practice, see Tina Rosenberg, "Mutilating Africa's Daughters: Laws Unenforced, Practices Unchanged," *The New York Times,* July 5, 2004; and Waris Dirie and Catherine Miller, *Desert Flower: The Extraordinary Journey of a Desert Nomad* (New York: William Morrow & Co, 1998).

†Celia W. Dugger, "A Refugee's Body Is Intact but Her Family Is Torn," *New York Times,* September 11, 1996, pp. A1, B6–B7; and Celia W. Dugger, "Woman Betrayed by Loved Ones Mourns a Double Loss," *New York Times,* September 11, 1996, p. B7.

††Data on countries banning genital cutting are from United Nations Population Fund (UNFPA), "Frequently Asked Questions About Genital Cutting," at www.unfpa.org/gender (accessed July 19, 2004).

Summary on Women in Developing Countries

Given all their serious problems, the near-term outlook for women in developing countries may not seem overly bright. At the same time, it would be a mistake to overlook the tremendous progress made over the last several decades.[126] As we emphasized, the gender gap in schooling continues to decline with the growing recognition, both by individual governments and international organizations, that resources devoted to the

---

[126]United Nations, *Human Development Report 1995,* p. 13.

advancement of women have a greater payoff than many other types of investments, and that growth is more rapid when gender inequality is reduced. Therefore, the emphasis of development policies may be expected to further shift in this direction. Further, by and large, women now have greater control over their own fertility. However, it is important to keep in mind that women's empowerment will help little without overall economic development. Everyone tends to benefit when governments invest more in infrastructure and transportation systems and encourage the development of business and industry. If, however, women are to share fully in the benefits of economic progress, it is also important to remove any existing barriers to their participation in the labor force.

COUNTRIES OF THE FORMER SOVIET BLOC

The economies of the former Union of Soviet Socialist Republics (USSR) and its satellites in Central and Eastern Europe have been undergoing a major transition since the fall of the Berlin Wall in 1989 and the dissolution of the USSR shortly thereafter. They shifted from an economic system of central planning and public ownership of resources, to a market system with private ownership. Specific countries, however, experienced considerable variation in the speed and manner in which changes have been implemented.[127] Individuals in these countries face challenges that are more or less unique to them, much as individuals in developing countries do many years after colonialism ended.

During the time of the dominance of the USSR, its government and those of its satellites officially subscribed to Marxist ideology, including its views about the role of women.[128] The leaders who successfully carried out the revolution in Russia at the end of World War I and shaped the ideas that dominated the USSR during its early years viewed the relationship between men and women as inextricably entwined with the revolutionary reconstruction of society. They essentially espoused the notion that the abolition of private property and class structure is both necessary and sufficient for achieving equality between women and men. Consistent with these views, they initially struck down all legal discrimination against women, mandated equal treatment in the educational system and in the labor market, and introduced liberal family laws making the marriage contract egalitarian and legalized abortion readily available. Although some of this legislation was later modified,[129] the dominant ideology of the Soviet bloc remained unchanged as long as the USSR lasted.

Because there was, generally, not only full employment but often a labor shortage, doctrinal belief in labor force participation of women was reinforced by the need for them to help with the rapid industrialization that was the main goal of the regime. For the same reason, little progress was made in "socializing housework," the Soviet solution for women's "double burden."

---

[127]The former Soviet Bloc refers to the USSR, Czechoslovakia (now the Czech Republic and Slovakia), Bulgaria, Romania, Hungary, East Germany, and Poland. For more information on the economic transition, see Jan Svenar, "Transition Economies: Performance and Challenges," *Journal of Economic Perspectives* 16, no. 1 (Winter 2002): 3–28.

[128]Marxist views on the role of women are briefly discussed in the section on "Marxist and Radical Feminist Views of the Family" in Chapter 3.

[129]This was particularly true during the Stalinist period when, for instance, abortions were made illegal, and again during later years when, in response to the low birth rates, pronatalist policies were introduced.

Housework was to be made unnecessary by the provision of public services, from communal dining rooms to day care centers. In practice, however, much housework still needed to be done. Although good child care was provided, at least for children 3 years of age and older, there were frequently long lines in stores where necessities had to be purchased, and the appliances middle-class households in the economically advanced countries have long taken for granted were often not available. Women were told that all these goods and services would be provided as soon as higher-priority goals were achieved. In the meantime, however, housekeeping continued to be a major burden and responsibility that rested squarely on the shoulders of women. Although women were now expected to be workers as well as homemakers, there was no equivalent recognition that men could be homemakers as well as workers. Sharing of household responsibilities was never part of the official ideology. Data from the 1980s, for instance, illustrate the considerable inequality in time spent on household tasks among men and women in the USSR. Despite women's high rates of labor market activity, women still spent 2.3 times as much time on housework as men, a figure that was slightly higher than the figure for the United States for the same period.[130]

The results of this mixed situation were, inevitably, also mixed. On the one hand, the status of women was clearly better than it had been in earlier days, and in some respects it compared favorably with that of women in the economically advanced countries in the West. For instance, women's labor force participation rate of nearly 80 percent was well in excess of the rates in many economically advanced countries.[131] Also, occupational segregation declined, and both the amount and the kind of education women received more nearly approximated that of men. On the other hand, women continued to be concentrated in low-status, low-paying occupations, as well as in lower levels of the hierarchies within occupations. Moreover, the earnings gap appeared to be within the same range as that in market economies.[132] Nor did women succeed in penetrating the top echelons of the powerful government hierarchy.

Thus, the Marxist solution to "the woman question" left something to be desired, even in principle, and was far from satisfactory in practice. Consequently, most women in the Soviet orbit came to see their greater participation in paid work not as a right but rather as an obligation dictated by an oppressive regime and, in the satellite countries, one that was imposed by a foreign power. By the same token, women came to have an idealized view of the family as a refuge from the harsh realities of a world that was not of their own making.

The fall of the Berlin Wall, the velvet "revolution" in Czechoslovakia, and the dissolution of the USSR ushered in a new political and economic era. It was widely assumed that many women would retreat to their more traditional roles as homemakers and, in turn, women's labor force participation would decline substantially. This retreat was expected to be reinforced by higher unemployment rates, cuts in public child care,

---

[130]Figures are from Juster and Stafford, "The Allocation of Time: Empirical Findings, Behavioral Models, and Problems of Measurement," p. 477.

[131]Elizabeth Brainerd, "Women in Transition: Changes in Gender Wage Differentials in Eastern Europe and the Former Soviet Union," *Industrial and Labor Relations Review* 54, no. 1 (October 2000): 138–62.

[132]For a comparison of women's earnings and labor market activity before and shortly after the economic transition, see UNICEF, "Women in Transition," chap. 2 and 3. For earlier evidence, see Jacob Mincer, "Inter-Country Comparisons of Labor Force Trends and of Related Developments: An Overview," in *Trends in Women's Work, Education, and Family Building,* ed. Richard Layard and Jacob Mincer, *Journal of Labor Economics* 3, no. 1, pt. 2 (January 1985).

and in many cases, governments' failure to enforce women's right to have their jobs held open during maternity and child care leaves. Even so, data from the late 1990s indicate that although women's labor force participation rates declined by more than men's in some of these countries, no "tectonic shift" occurred in the gender ratio in participation rates. Further, the proportion of women who work part-time remains very low compared to rates elsewhere, although it is not clear to what extent women prefer working full-time or if few part-time jobs available.[133]

The effects of economic restructuring on the gender-wage ratio varied widely in the countries of the former Soviet Bloc. Women in Russia and Ukraine experienced a decline in their wages relative to men's, largely as a result of widening wage inequality in these countries. At the same time, women in the Central and East European countries (e.g., Hungary, Poland, the Czech Republic) fared better. Wage inequality also widened in these countries, but it appears that the gender earnings ratio increased because of the rise in the return to women's labor market skills.[134] Regrettably, in East Germany, it appears that the increase in the gender earnings ratio came at the expense of women's reduced employment.[135] In sum, this varied evidence points to the pitfalls of trying to generalize about how women are faring over the course of the economic transition.

To date, feminist movements have fared poorly in these countries, though this situation appears to be changing. The fact that equality in the labor market, one of the main goals of feminist movements, was also an official goal of the Communist regimes helps to explain why the various women's movements that emerged in these countries during the Soviet era were generally small, single-issue organizations that were, for the most part, explicitly nonfeminist. Thus, "feminism, which got short shrift under communism (supposedly because it weakened the class struggle), has also been under attack in post-communist Eastern Europe. Distaste for feminism is about the only thing on which there is great continuity between communism and capitalism."[136] Even so, women in these countries are pursuing a number of the same goals sought by feminist movements elsewhere.

Notably, many women's groups are agitating against abolishing the right to abortions and are putting up stiff resistance against the elimination of such family-friendly policies as child care and generous paid maternity leave. Thus it appears that Barbara Einhorn was right when she suggested some time ago that "women's consciousness was affected by their experience of the identity of working woman as the norm: that they have greater self-esteem as a result, and are more outspoken. Such a view implies that it will be only a matter of time before they defend or attempt to regain the right to work, the right to reproductive choice, the right to political representation, the right to be

---

[133]UNICEF, "Women in Transition," chaps. 2 and 3. Quoted phrase is from p. 26; Marni Lazreg, ed., *Making the Transition Work for Women in Europe and Central Asia* (Washington, DC: World Bank, 2000); and Pierella Paci, *Gender in Transition* (Washington, DC: World Bank, 2002).

[134]Brainerd, "Women in Transition: Changes in Gender Wage Differentials."

[135]Jennifer Hunt, "The Transition in East Germany: When Is a Ten-Point Fall in the Gender Wage Gap Bad News?" *Journal of Labor Economics* 20, no. 1 (January 2002): 148–68.

[136]Lynn Turgeon, "Afterword," in *Democratic Reform and the Position of Women in Transitional Economies*, ed. Valentine M. Moghadam (Oxford: Clarendon Press, 1993), pp. 353–57. See also Marianne A. Ferber and Phyllis Hutton Raabe, "Women in the Czech Republic: Feminism, Czech Style," in *Women in the Age of Transformation: Gender Impact of Reforms in Post-Socialist and Developing Countries,* edited by Nahid Aslanbeigui, Steven Pressman, and Gale Summerfield (London: Routledge, 1994).

heard."[137] In fact, recently an increasing number of women, particularly highly educated professional women, are recognizing to what extent they share the same problems that feminists struggle with in the rest of the world, and particularly in the Western countries.[138] And this is likely to become even more true as growing numbers of the transition countries join the European Union.[139]

Conclusion

In this chapter, we found that women generally have lower educational attainment than men, though these differentials are smallest in the economically advanced countries and many of the countries of the former Soviet bloc and largest in developing countries. Women also tend to earn less, be segregated into different occupations, and hold fewer government positions. International differences in these outcomes are the result of government policies, social custom, ideology, and religion, as well as a variety of economic factors. Women's status is particularly precarious in many of the developing countries, but almost everywhere there has been some degree of improvement.

We also discussed how government can play a crucial role in promoting education and women's participation in the labor market. In most of the developing countries, governments are making efforts to expand educational opportunity. In a number of economically advanced countries, notably the Scandinavian countries and particularly Sweden, governments have, with considerable success, used a variety of policies to encourage women's labor force participation, while also making it possible for them to take care of their families. Even there, the situation is far from perfect, mainly because occupational segregation remains high and housework continues to be divided quite unequally. Nonetheless, our review leads us to be cautiously optimistic about the outlook for women throughout the world, and also specifically about the possibility of government playing a constructive role in advancing their status.

Questions for Review and Discussion

1. To what extent are comparisons of women's labor force participation among various countries a reliable indicator of women's contributions to the standard of living in those countries?
2. As seen in Table 11-2, women's labor force participation rates in economically advanced countries vary considerably. What economic and noneconomic factors might help to explain this disparity?
3. What are some specific policies that might improve women's well-being in the poorest countries? What are the difficulties and challenges entailed in undertaking them?
4. How does the experience of women living in the United States, Sweden, and Japan compare in terms of the following?
   a. Labor force participation

---

[137]Barbara Einhorn, *Cinderella Goes to Market: Citizenship, Gender and Women's Movements in East Central Europe* (London: Verso, 1993), p. 15.

[138]See articles on "Feminist and Economic Inquiry in Central and Easter Europe," edited by Marianne A. Ferber and Edith Kuiper, *Feminist Economics* 10, no. 3 (November 2004): 81–118.

[139]In May 2004, the Baltic countries (Estonia, Latvia, Lithuania), Poland, the Czech Republic, and Slovakia joined the EU.

    b. Occupational segregation
    c. Gender-wage ratio
    d. Housework

5. Occupational segregation in Sweden is very high and yet it has the smallest gender earnings gap of any economically advanced country in the world. "This proves that occupational segregation does not reduce women's earnings relative to the earnings of men." Evaluate the validity of this statement.

6. A number of countries have policies intended to encourage people to have larger families, while others offer inducements to reduce family size. Would you favor either policy for the United States? Why or why not?

7. It is widely believed that government investments in women's education result in societal as well as private benefits. Discuss each. Such investments are particularly important in developing countries. Why?

8. Some occupations are predominantly female in some countries and predominantly male in others. What factors might help to explain these differences?

Suggested Readings

Aslanbeigui, Nahind, Steven Pressman, and Gale Summerfield, eds. *Women in the Age of Transformation: Gender Impacts of Reforms in Post-Socialist & Developing Countries.* London: Routledge, 1994.

Blau, Francine D. "Gender and Economic Outcomes: The Role of Wage Structure." *Labour* 7, no. 1 (1993): 73–92.

Blau, Francine D., and Lawrence M. Kahn, "Gender Differences in Pay." *Journal of Economic Perspectives* 14, no. 4 (Fall 2000): 75–100.

———. "Wage Structure and Gender Earnings Differentials: An International Comparison." *Economica* 63 (Supplement 1996): 29–62.

Boserup, Ester. *Women's Role in Economic Development.* New York: St. Martin's Press, 1970.

Brainerd, Elizabeth. "Women in Transition: Changes in Gender Wage Differentials in Eastern Europe and the Former Soviet Union." *Industrial and Labor Relations Review* 54, no. 1 (October 2000): 138–62.

Brinton, Mary. *Women and the Economic Miracle: Gender and Work in Postwar Japan.* Berkeley: University of California Press, 1993.

Gornick, Janet C., and Marcia K. Meyers. *Families That Work: Policies for Reconciling Parenthood and Employment.* New York: Russell Sage Foundation, 2003.

Hill, M. Anne, and Elizabeth M. King. "Women's Education and Economic Well-Being." *Feminist Economics* 1, no. 2 (Summer 1995): 21–46.

Houseman, Susan, and Alice Nakamura, eds. *Working Time in Comparative Perspective: Volume II–Life-Cycle Working Time and Nonstandard Work.* Kalamazoo, MI: Upjohn Institute for Employment Research, 2001.

Mammen, Kristin, and Christina Paxson. "Women's Work and Economic Development." *Journal of Economic Perspectives* 14, no. 4 (Fall 2000): 141–64.

Mason, Karen Oppenheim, and An-Magritt Jensen. *Gender and Family Change in Industrialized Countries.* Oxford: Clarendon Press, 1995.

McFate, Katherine, Robert Lawson, and William Julius Wilson, eds. *Poverty, Inequality, and the Future of Social Policy: Western States in the New World Order.* New York: Russell Sage Foundation, 1995.

Melkas, Helina, and Richard Anker. *Gender Equality and Occupational Segregation in Nordic Labour Markets.* Geneva: International Labour Organization, 1998.

Persson, Inga, and Christina Jonung, eds. *Economics of the Family and Family Policies.* London: Routledge, 1997.

———, eds. *Women's Work and Wages.* London: Routledge, 1998.

Sainsbury, Diane, ed. *Gender and Welfare State Regimes*. Oxford: Oxford University Press, 1999.

Schultz, T. Paul, ed. *Investment in Women's Human Capital*. Chicago: University of Chicago Press, 1995.

Strober, Myra H., and Agnes Miling Kaneko Chan. *The Road Winds Uphill All the Way: Gender, Work, and Family in the United States and Japan*. Cambridge, MA: MIT Press, 1999.

UNICEF. "Women in Transition." *Regional Monitoring Reports*, No. 6. Florence, Italy: UNICEF International Child Development Centre, 1999.

Wong, Ging, and Garnett Picot, eds. *Working Time in Comparative Perspective: Volume 1–Patterns, Trends, and Policy Implications of Earnings Inequality and Unemployment*. Kalamazoo, MI: Upjohn Institute for Employment Research, 2001.

Author Index

A

Aaron, Henry, 351n
Abbott, Edith, 22n
Abraham, Katherine G., 189n, 259n, 277n
Acs, Gregroy, 301n, 320n, 336n
Adams, Alayne M., 412n
Adams, Gina, 359n, 360n
Addison, John T., 282n
Adelman, Sara, 360n
Agarwal, Bina, 50n, 52n, 372n, 384n
Aigner, Dennis J., 226n
Aio, Yasue, 392n
Aizer, Anna, 361n
Akerlof, George A., 223n, 255, 309n
Albeda, Randy, 349n
Allen, La Rue, 359n, 364n
Allen, Mike, 183n
Allgeier, Elizabeth Rice, 17n, 18n
Allison, Paul, 147n
Alm, James, 344n
Alpert, William T., 353n
Altman, Lawrence K., 386n
Altonji, Joseph G., 191n, 204n, 255
Amato, Paul, 316n
Anders, K. A., 179n
Anderson, Deborah J., 145n, 146n, 312n, 313n
Anderson, Patricia M., 117n, 129n, 357n
Andreoni, James, 52n
Andrews, Courtney, 312n
Andrews, Emily, 241n
Angier, Natalie, 16n
Angrist, Joshua D., 106n, 292n
Anker, Richard, 378n, 387n, 391n, 392n, 418
Antecol, Heather, 210n, 238n
Appelbaum, Eileen, 356n

Araki, Takashi, 392n
Ardrey, Robert, 15n
Arnold, Fred, 406n, 407n
Arrow, Kenneth, 218n, 227n, 233n
Arthur, Michelle M., 352n
Ashenfelter, Orley C., 204n, 218n, 221n, 222n 255, 288
Aslanbeigui, Nahid, 416n, 418
Astone, Nan Marie, 296n
Astrom, Gertrude, 392n
Autor, David H., 129n, 257n, 263n, 277n, 288

B

Babcock, Linda, 177n
Badgett, M.V. Lee, 59n, 301n, 302n, 324
Baker, Michael, 248n
Bannister, Judith, 405n, 406n
Bardasi, Elena, 388n
Barley, Stephen R., 276n
Barrett, Jennifer, 70n
Barrier, Michael, 367n
Barro, Robert J., 380n
Barron, John M., 191n, 207n, 213n
Bartfeld, Judi, 321n
Bartlett, Robin L., 226n
Basu, Kaushik, 238n, 255, 409n, 410n
Bates, Timothy, 279n
Baum, Charles L., II, 315n, 355n
Baxter, Janeen, 402n
Bayard, Kimberly, 139n, 212n
Bebel, August, 54n
Beck, Melinda, 48n
Becker, Gary S., 35, 35n, 36n, 43n, 50n, 58–59, 75n, 83, 96n, 100n, 134, 160,

160n, 184n, 195n, 201, 203n, 218, 218n, 220–25, 223n, 224, 255, 290n, 294n, 304n, 313n
Beller, Andrea H., 145n, 149n, 154n, 241n, 263n, 321n, 324, 339n, 369
Belman, Dale, 277n
Bengtsson, Tommy, 389n
Bennett, James T., 287
Berg, Helen M., 175n, 181n, 384n
Bergmann, Barbara R., 61n, 68n, 224, 224n, 229, 229n, 242n, 245n, 255, 359n, 361n, 362n, 365n, 372n
Bergstrom, Theodore, 50n
Berman, Eli, 262n
Bertrand, Marianne, 215n
Besharov, Douglas J., 335n
Betz, Nancy E., 181n
Bianchi, Suzanne M., 56n, 60, 60n, 61n, 62n, 83, 315n, 321n, 324
Binder, Melissa, 312n, 313n
Birnbaum, Bonnie G., 36n, 83
Bitler, Marianne P., 292n
Bittman, Michael, 59n
Black, Dan A., 191n, 204n, 207n, 213n, 222n, 302n
Black, Sandra E., 221n
Blackburn, McKinley L., 304n, 307n
Blakemore, Arthur F., 173n
Blanchflower, David G., 279n, 282n
Blandford, John M., 302n
Blank, Rebecca M., 108n, 117n, 128n, 134, 204n, 217n, 255, 276n, 288, 307n, 327n, 331n, 333n, 334n, 357n, 369, 388n
Blank, Roy J., 208n

Blasi, Joseph, 288
Blau, David M., 60n, 117n, 316n, 322n, 356n, 357n, 362n, 369
Blau, Francine D., 7n, 33n, 48n, 56n, 57n, 65n, 83, 94n, 111n, 126n, 131n, 139n, 143n, 144n, 145n, 146n, 149n, 154n, 181n, 185n, 189n, 197n, 201, 204n, 205n, 212n, 215n, 222n, 224n, 227n, 228n, 231n, 255, 257n, 260–64, 260n, 262n, 263n, 264n, 267n, 273n, 283n, 287, 293n, 312n, 313n, 320, 324, 351n, 353n, 354n, 355n, 365n, 369, 386n, 388n, 394n, 395n, 396n, 398n, 418
Blinder, Alan, 207n
Bloch, Farrell E., 154n
Bloom, David E., 304n, 307n
Blum, Deborah, 16n, 17n, 18n, 34
Blumberg, Rae L., 18n, 47n, 52n
Blumrosen, Ruth G., 245n
Blumstein, Philip, 47n
Bodie, Z., 185n
Bond, James T., 352n
Bongaarts, John, 399n
Booth, Alan, 296n, 300n, 316n, 400n,
Borass, Stephanie, 65n
Borjas, George J., 162n
Borland, Jeff, 398n
Borooah, Romy, 411n
Boserup, Ester, 372n, 383n, 403n, 418
Boskin, Michael J., 259n
Bouabid, Ihsan, 405n
Bound, John, 262n, 263n
Bowen, Ray, 407n
Bradbury, Katharine, 269n
Bradshaw, Jonathan, 401n
Brainerd, Elizabeth, 415n, 416n, 418
Braunstein, Elissa, 28
Braver, Sanford L., 299n
Bravewoman, Lynn, 303n
Brewer, Dominic J., 181n
Brien, Michael J., 247n, 300n
Brill, Steven, 70n
Brines, Julie, 59n
Brinton, Mary C., 174n, 227n, 390n, 392n, 418
Broaded, C. Montgomery, 408n
Bronfenbrenner, Kate, 282n, 283n, 285n

Broschak, Joseph P., 214n
Brown, Cailin, 226n
Brown, Charles, 154n, 163n
Brown, Clair, 53n, 102n, 122n, 282n
Brown, Clifton, 226n
Brown, Druscilla K., 409n
Brown, Eleanor, 52n
Brown, James, 189n
Brown, J. Brian, 336n
Brown, Murray, 50n
Browning, Martin, 106n
Bruce, Judith, 411n
Bryant, W. Keith, 56n
Bryson, Alex, 282n
Buchmeuller, Thomas C., 283n
Budig, Michelle J., 147n, 312n, 313n
Bullough, Bonnie, 17n
Bullough, Vern L., 17n
Bumpass, Larry L., 71n, 300n, 301n, 309n, 400n
Burgess, John, 398n
Burns, John F., 385n
Burtless, Gary, 276n, 314n
Butcher, Kristin, 175n
Butler, Richard, 154n
Buttner, E. Holly, 280n
Buvinic, Myra, 411n

C

Cain, Glen G., 226n, 231n
Call, Kathleen Thiede, 59n
Campenni, C. Estelle, 177n
Cancian, Maria, 314n, 339n
Canes, Brandice, 181n
Cannings, Kathleen, 393n
Cantor, David, 354n, 356n
Cantor, Milton, 23n, 26n, 87n
Capizzano, Jeffrey, 359n, 360n
Cappelli, Peter, 267n
Carasso, Adam, 343n, 344n
Card, David E., 117n, 167n, 204n, 222n, 255, 283n, 288, 331n, 357n, 369
Carlson, Marcia, 300n, 320n
Carré, Francoise, 274n, 277n, 287
Carrington, William J., 214n, 241n
Carter, Bill, 175n
Carton, Barbara, 361n
Case, Anne, 175n, 323n
Cassety, Judity, 339n
Chafe, William H., 124, 124n
Chan, Agnes Miling Kaneko, 402n, 418

Chan, Anna Y., 56n
Chandra, Amitabh, 130n, 154n, 263n
Chang, Kenneth, 16n
Chang, Lisa E., 243n
Charles, Kerwin Kofi, 184n, 268n, 295n
Chase-Lansdale, P. Lindsay, 316n
Chernick, Howard, 334n
Cherry, Robert, 130n, 269n
Chiappori, Pierre-Andre, 50n
Chira, Susan, 299n
Chiswick, Barry R., 264n
Choe, Minja Kim, 406n, 407n
Christopher, Karen, 333n, 402n
Chun, Hyunbae, 313n
Clark, Kim B., 116n
Clawson, Dan, 284n
Cloud, Kathleen, 411n
Coale, Ansley J., 405n, 406n
Cobb-Clark, Deborah A., 213n, 238n
Cobble, Dorothy Sue, 124n, 284n, 287
Cogan, John F., 347n
Cohen, Lisa E., 214n
Cohen, Philip N., 62n
Coleman, Margaret S., 284n
Coleman, Mary T., 95n
Collins, Nancy, 282n
Conlin, Michelle, 365n
Connelly, Rachel, 117n
Cook, Alison, 352n
Cooney, Rosemary Santana, 408n
Cooney, Teresa M., 59n
Corcoran, Mary E., 163n, 208n, 318n
Corden, Anne, 340n
Costa, Dora L., 22n, 34, 134, 389n
Courant, Paul, 208n
Cove, Elizabeth, 347n
Crispell, Diane, 47n
Crossette, Barbara, 385n
Crouter, Ann C., 300n, 400n
Cullen, Julie Berry, 116n
Cunningham, James, 247n
Currie, Janet, 60n, 316n, 358n

D

Dahl, Gordon B., 108n, 296n, 313n, 384n
Dahlberg, Frances, 19n
Daily, A. E., 398n

Daniel, Christopher, 247n
Dank, Stephen, 177n
Danziger, Sheldon H., 283n, 291n, 314n, 318n, 320n, 328n, 369
Dardis, Rachel, 62n
Darity, William A., Jr., 224, 224n, 255
Darroch, Jacqueline E., 309n
DaVanzo, Julie, 72n, 296n, 307n, 324
Davies, Margery, 30n
Day, Kathleen M., 65n
Deford, Frank, 182n
DeFreitas, Gregory, 264n
Degler, Carl N., 23n
De Gruyter, Aldine, 72n
Dehejia, Rajeev, 410n
Del Boca, Daniela, 389n
Demeny, Paul, 400n
Deming, William G., 363n
Den Boer, Andrea M., 407n
Depperschmidt, Thomas O., 70n
Devereux, Paul, 129n
Devine, Theresa J., 278n, 279n, 280n, 347n
Devlin, Rose Anne, 65n
Dickert-Conlin, Stacy, 344n
DiNardo, John, 257n, 282n, 283n
Dirie, Waris, 413n
Doeringer, Peter B., 231n, 232, 249n
Dolado, Juan J., 391n
Dolton, Peter, 394n, 397n
Donahoe, Debra Ann, 372n
Downs, Barbara, 94n
Dreze, Jean, 384n
Duggan, Mark G., 129n
Dugger, Celia W., 406n, 412n, 413n
Duncan, Beverly, 141n
Duncan, Greg J., 191n, 207n, 213n, 295n, 296n
Duncan, Otis Dudley, 141n
Dwyer, Daisy, 411n

E

Eagly, Alice H., 215n
Easterlin, Richard A., 303n
Easton, Barbara, 26n
Eaton, Leslie, 299n
Eatwell, John, 7n
Eckholm, Erik, 406n
Eckstein, Zvi, 118n

Edin, Kathryn, 320n, 324, 369
Edin, Per-Anders, 397n
Edlund, Lena, 407n
Edmonds, Eric V., 410n
Edwards, Linda N., 363n, 393n
Edwards, Richard C., 30n, 233n
Ehrenberg, Ronald G., 33n, 181n, 224n, 250n, 268n, 313n, 351n, 353n, 354n, 355n, 365n, 369
Eichstedt, Jennifer L., 284n
Eide, Eric, 174n
Einhorn, Barbara, 416n, 417n
Eissa, Nada, 116n, 128n, 338n
Elavia, B., 411n
Elkiss, Helen, 284n, 285n
Ellis, Deborah A., 235n
Ellman, Ira M., 299n
Ellwood, David T., 288, 310n, 316n, 324, 337n
Elson, Diane, 383n
Engels, Friedrich, 54n
England, Paula, 36n, 50n, 59n, 147n, 198n, 201, 213n, 245n, 300n, 312n, 313n, 402n
Engleberg, Laurie, 179n, 180n
Epstein, Cynthia F., 15n, 174n
Eriksen, Shelley, 284n
Estavao, Marcello, 277n
Estioko-Griffin, Agnes, 19n
Ettner, Susan L., 348n
Evans, James, 276n
Evans, Timothy G., 412n
Evans, William N., 106n
Even, William E., 221n, 282n, 283n, 284n
Evenhouse, Eirik, 323n

F

Fabricius, William V., 299n
Fairlie, Robert W., 269n, 278n, 279n
Faison, Seth, 404n, 407n
Farber, Henry S., 189n, 267n, 282n
Farkas, George, 50n
Farley, Maggie, 385n
Farley, Reynolds, 72n
Farmer, Amy, 48n, 49n
Favreault, Melissa M., 345n, 346n, 347n
Feder, Baranby J., 239n
Feenberg, Daniel R., 344n
Fein, Sara Beck, 349n
Feinberg, Kenneth, 70n
Feiner, Robert, 54n
Feiner, Susan, 54n

Felgeuroso, Florentino, 391n
Ferber, Marianne A., 33n, 36n, 47n, 53n, 56n, 83, 84, 131n, 175n, 181n, 216n, 217n, 222n, 274n, 280n, 287, 345n, 346n, 347n, 359n, 364n, 384n, 416n, 417n
Field-Hendry, Elizabeth, 363n
Fields, Jason, 301n, 317n, 322n
Figart, Deborah M., 95n
Fishman, Michael E., 74n
Fiske, Susan T., 227n, 255
Fitch, Catherine A., 72n
Fitzgerald, Louise F., 181n
Floro, Maria, 372n
Folbre, Nancy, 21n, 23n, 28, 53n, 54n, 59n, 67n, 68n, 84, 102n, 350n, 372n
Fong, Vanessa L., 407n
Forrest, Anne, 284n
Fortin, Nicole M., 248n, 257n, 260n, 263n
Foster, E. Michael, 321n
Fox, Bonnie J., 25n
Fox, Mary Frank, 18n
Fox, Robin, 15n, 34
Fraad, Harriet, 55n
Frank, Levy, 288
Fredriksen-Goldsen, Karen I., 369
Freeman, Catherine E., 164n, 201
Freeman, Jo, 180n, 284n
Freeman, Richard B., 59n, 63n, 263n, 269n, 282n, 283n, 287, 339n, 351n, 377n, 394n, 396n, 398n
Fremstad, Shawn, 335n, 336n
Friedberg, Leora, 295n
Friedl, Ernestine, 15n, 18n, 34
Fuchs, Victor R., 84, 140n, 195n, 220n, 350n, 370
Furchtgott-Roth, Diane, 155–56
Furstenberg, Frank F., 321n

G

Gager, Constance T., 59n
Gallagher, Megan, 320n
Gallinsky, Ellen, 352n
Garasky, Steven, 317n
Gardiner, Karen, 74n
Gardner, Susan E., 247n
Garfinkel, Irwin, 309n, 321n, 340n, 369
Gates, Gary, 302n
Gatti, Roberta, 410n
Gavin, Robert, 272n
Geddes, Rick, 27–28

Gelbach, Jonah B., 292n
Gelles, Richard J., 48n
Gennetian, Lisa A., 292n
Germanis, Peter, 335n
Geronimus, Arline T., 321n
Gerson, Kathleen, 95n,
    135, 370
Giannarelli, Linda, 360n
Giddings, Lisa A., 59n, 301n
Gilbert, D. T., 227n, 255
Gilroy, Curtis L., 241n
Ginther, Donna K., 217n, 323n
Gittleman, Maury B., 264n
Glater, Jonathan D., 243n
Gleason, Philip, 340n
Glewwe, Paul, 404n
Glosser, Asaph, 74n
Gluckman, Amy, 301n, 324
Godbey, Geoffrey, 56n, 57n, 84
Goff, Helen A., 393n
Goldberg, Matthew, 219n, 221n
Goldberger, Arthur, 207n
Golden, Lonnie, 95n, 274n, 277n,
    287, 362n
Goldhaber, Daniel D., 181n
Goldin, Claudia, 23n, 28, 28n, 29n,
    30n, 31–33, 31n, 34, 88n,
    91n, 94n, 118n, 119n,
    120n, 124, 124n, 125n,
    127n, 134, 139n, 184n,
    185n, 208n, 209n, 223n,
    255, 293, 294n, 305n, 373n
Goldstein, Joshua R., 296n
Goodman, William, 359n
Gordon, David M., 30n,
    231n, 233n
Gordon, Linda, 26n
Gordon, Michael, 26n, 34
Gordon, Nancy R., 341n
Gornick, Janet C., 387n, 388n,
    389n, 390n, 418
Gottschalk, Peter, 283n, 287, 314n,
    328n, 351n
Graefe, Deborah Roempke,
    300n, 336n
Graham, John W., 321n, 324,
    339n, 369
Granger, Clive W., 126n
Gray, Jeffrey S., 53n, 121n,
    295n, 313n
Gray, Jerry, 74n
Gray, Lois S., 284n, 285n, 286n
Green, Carole, 33n
Greenblatt, Bernard, 123n
Greenhouse, Linda, 183n,
    239n, 242n
Greenhouse, Steven, 239n, 243n

Greenlees, John S., 259n
Greenwood, Daphne, 53n
Greenwood, Jeremy, 25n,
    120n, 306n
Gregory, Robert G., 398n
Griffin, P. Bion, 19n
Griliches, Zvi, 262n
Grimsley, Kirsten
    Downey, 367n
Grogger, Jeffrey, 333n, 334n
Gronau, Reuben, 96n, 233n
Groshen, Erica L., 139n, 212n
Gross, Edward, 144n
Grossbard-Schectman, Shoshana,
    126n, 290n, 292n, 377n
Grossberg, Adam J., 126n
Grosswald, Blanche, 354n
Gruber, Jonathan, 116n,
    305n, 351n
Grusky, David B., 227n
Gunderson, Craig, 337n
Gunderson, Morley, 213n, 255
Gupta, Sanjiv, 300n
Gustafsson, Siv, 59n, 386n, 388n,
    389n, 399n, 401n
Gustman, Alan L., 129n

H

Haider, Steven J., 333n
Hallock, Kevin F., 215n, 267n
Halpern, Ariel, 339n
Hamilton, Barton H., 280n
Hammer, Leslie B., 348n
Hammond, B., 185n
Hannan, Timothy, 221n
Harbaugh, Christina Wu,
    407n, 408n
Harkess, Shirley, 25n, 179n
Harris, Ann Sutherland, 180n
Hartmann, Heidi, I., 53n, 84,
    201, 213n, 233n, 245n,
    249n, 282n
Hashimoto, Masanori, 195n, 355n
Haskins, Ron, 358n, 361n
Hausman, Jerry A., 351n
Haveman, Heather, 214n
Haveman, Robert H., 309n, 316n,
    318n, 322n, 369
Hayes, Kathy J., 217n
Hecker, Daniel E., 173n
Heckman, James J., 96n, 113n,
    134, 151n, 154n, 263n
Heim, Bradley T., 295n
Helburn, Suzanne, 361n
Hellerstein, Judith K., 139n, 209n,
    212n, 221n

Helwig, Ryan T., 267n
Hendricks, Wallace E., 144n
Hernandez, Raymond, 299n
Hersch, Joni, 195n, 213n, 235n,
    255, 313n
Herz, Diane, 56n
Herzenberg, Steve, 274n, 287
Hewlett, Sylvia Ann, 307n
Hill, Ariel, 339n
Hill, E. Jeffrey, 352n
Hill, M. Anne, 404n, 405n, 418
Himmelweit, Susan, 68n
Hipple, Steven, 274n, 276n
Hirsch, Barry T., 145n, 199n, 211n
Ho, Vivian, 398n
Hochschild, Arlie, 348n, 370
Hoem, Britta, 392n
Hofferth, Sandra L., 60n, 61n
Hoffman, Emily, 362n
Hoffman, Saul D., 191n, 207n,
    213n, 295n, 296n, 321n,
    337n, 338n
Hollis, Aidan, 410n
Hollister, Rob, 361n
Holmes, Steven A., 162n, 243n
Holzer, Harry J., 130n, 235n, 241n,
    242n, 244n, 255, 269n,
    287, 340n 352n
Horn, Wade F., 74n, 336n
Horney, Mary Jean, 50n
Horrigan, Michael, 56n
Hotchkiss, Julie L., 313n, 314n
Hotz, Joseph, 321n, 337n
Houseman, Susan N., 277n, 278n,
    287, 351n, 387n, 418
Howard, Dick, 54n
Howell, David R., 264n
Hoyman, Michelle, 286n
Hoynes, Hilary W., 292n, 338n
Hu, Mei-Chen, 321n
Huang, Chien-Chung, 321n
Hubbard, Ruth, 16n, 17n
Huber, Joan, 18n, 25n, 216n
Hudson, Valerie M., 407n
Hundley, Greg, 279n
Hunt, Jennifer, 416n

I

Iams, Howard M., 346n
Ingrassia, Michele, 48n
Ireland, Thomas R., 70n

J

Jacobs, Jerry A., 95n, 135, 143n,
    145n, 146n, 164n,
    181n, 370
Jacobsen, Joyce P., 106n, 126n,
    140n, 145n, 172n, 196n,
    312n, 313n, 378n
Jacoby, Hanan G., 377n

Jaeger, David A., 161n
Jarrell, Stephen B., 204n
Jefferson, Therese, 53n, 84
Jencks, Christopher, 310n, 316n
Jensen, An-Magritt, 293n, 392n, 418
Jimeno, Juan F., 391n
Joekes, Susan P., 372n
John, Daphne, 56n
Johnson, George, 211n
Johnson, William R., 121n
Jonung, Christina, 389n, 390n,
    392n, 396n, 418
Joshi, Heather, 394n
Joyce, Amy, 242n
Juhn, Chinhui, 107n, 111n, 122n,
    126n, 129n, 130n, 135,
    154n, 170n, 257n, 263n,
    288, 308n, 311n
Junhong, Chu, 406n
Jusenius, Carol, 231n
Juster, F. Thomas, 62n, 84, 241n,
    402n, 415n

K

Kahn, Alfred J., 388n
Kahn, Joan R., 321n
Kahn, Lawrence M., 94n, 185n,
    189n, 197n, 201, 204n,
    205n, 215n, 222n, 223n,
    228n, 255, 260–64, 260n,
    262n, 263n, 264n, 268n,
    273n, 283n, 287, 293,
    293n, 386n, 388n, 394n,
    395n, 396n, 398n, 418
Kahn, Shulamit, 217n
Kamerman, Sheila B., 388n
Kang, Hyojin, 56n
Kaplan, Gisela, 16n, 17n
Karau, Steven J., 215n
Karoly, Lynn, 314n
Kats, Vladimir, 399n
Katz, Lawrence F., 122n, 127n,
    170n, 184n, 257n, 263n,
    269n, 288, 294n, 305n,
    394n, 396n, 398n
Katz, Michael L., 309n
Kaufmann, Bruce E., 287
Kearney, Melissa S., 257n
Keith, Kristen, 195n, 228n, 312n
Kessler-Harris, Alice, 21n, 26n
Kiernan, Kathleen, 400n
Kilkey, Majella, 401n
Killingsworth, Mark R., 96n,
    115n, 135, 245n, 247n,
    250n, 398n
Kim, Joung J., 296n

Kimmel, Jean, 117n, 357n, 362n
Kimura, Doreen, 16n
King, Elizabeth M., 404n, 405n, 418
King, John E., 53n, 84
King, Ronette, 210n
Klasen, Stephen, 384n
Klepinger, Daniel, 321n
Klerman, Jacob A., 107n, 127n,
    135, 333n, 354n, 356n
Kletzer, Lori G., 267n
Kniesner, Thomas J., 95n
Knox, Virginia, 292n
Konner, Melwin, 16n, 17n
Korenman, Sanders, 321n
Kosters, Marvin, 263n
Kranton, Rachel E., 223n, 255
Krause, Kate, 312n, 313n
Kreps, Juanita M., 22n
Krueger, Alan B., 262n, 269n
Kruse, Douglas, 288
Kuczynski, Alex, 226n
Kuhn, Peter, 210n
Kuiper, Edith, 417n
Kunda, Gideon, 276n

L

Lach, Saul, 277n
Lamphere, Louise, 15n, 19n, 34
Landefeld, J. Steven, 68n
Landes, Elisabeth M., 294n
Laschever, Sara, 177n
Laud, Stephanie, 74n
Laurie, Bruce, 23n, 26n, 87n
Lauzen, Martha M., 175n
Lawson, Robert, 401n, 418
Layard, Richard, 415n
Lazear, Edward P., 47n, 84, 189n
Lazonick, William, 393n
Lazreg, Marni, 416n
Lee, David S., 282n
Lee, Felicia R., 175n
Lee, Injae, 313n
Lee, Jong-Wha, 380n
Lee, Ronald, 382, 382n
LeGrande, Linda H., 281n
Lehrer, Evelyn L., 50n, 199n
Leibowitz, Arleen, 107n, 127n,
    135, 350n, 354n, 356n,
    357n, 370
Lein, Laura, 320n, 324, 369
Lemieux, Thomas, 257n, 260n,
    263n, 287
Lemke, Robert J., 357n
Leonard, Jonathan S., 209n,
    235n, 241n, 244n,
    262n, 282n

Leonhardt, David, 272n
Lerman, Robert I., 333n, 336n
Levin, Laurence M., 172n,
    196n, 312n
Levin, Sharon G., 217n
Levine, David I., 323n
Levine, Phillip B., 117n, 163n, 185n,
    279n, 305n, 345n, 357n
Lew, Vivian, 293n
Lewin, Tamar, 316n
Lewis, H. Gregg, 35n, 96n, 135
Lewis, Jane, 392n
Lewis, Margaret, 274n
Li, Jiali, 408n
Li, Su, 147n
Lichter, Daniel T., 300n,
    309n, 336n
Liebman, Jeffrey B., 128n, 338n
Light, Audrey, 197n, 228n
Lillard, Lee A., 300n
Lin, I-Fen, 323n
Lindzey, G., 227n, 255
Lino, Mark, 303n
Liu, Chongshun, 408n
Lloyd, Cynthia B., 241n, 356n
Loeb, Jane W., 216n, 222n, 364n
Lombard, Karen V., 279n
London, Rebecca A., 317n
Long, Sharon K., 48n
Lopata, Helena, 56n
Loscocco, Karyn, 348n
Low, Stuart A., 173n
Lowenstein, Mark A., 207n, 213n
Lu, H.-H., 71n, 300n, 301n,
    309n, 400n
Lueck, Dean, 27–28
Lundberg, Shelly J., 18n, 50n,
    51n, 52n, 84, 97n, 108n,
    116n, 233n, 309n, 313n,
    321n, 385n
Lundy, Katherina L. P., 276n
Lundy, Larry A., 276n
Luoh, Ming-Ching, 184n
Luxemburg, Rosa, 54n
Lyall, Sarah, 74n, 400n
Lynch, Colum, 385n
Lynch, Lisa M., 191n
Lynn-Dyson, Karen, 288
Lyons, Thomas M., 154n, 263n

M

Maccoby, Eleanor, 16n, 17n
Macpherson, David A., 145n,
    199n, 211n, 221n, 282n,
    283n, 284n

Macunovich, Diane J., 303n
Madden, Janice F., 196n, 222n, 255
Majka, Larraine, 384n
Majumdar, Debarun, 301n
Makar, Hoda R., 204n, 302n
Makepeace, Gerald, 394n
Mammen, Kristin, 373n, 418
Manning, Alan, 222n
Manning, Wendy D., 301n
Manser, Marilyn E., 50n, 278n
Manski, Charles F., 267n
Marini, Margaret M., 174n
Mark, Noah, 147n
Martin, Gary, 399n
Martin, Steven P., 310n
Mason, Karen Oppenheim, 293n, 392n, 418
Mason, Patrick L., 255
Masters, Brooke A., 242n
Matheson, George, 59n
Matsukura, Rikiya, 393n
Matthaei, Julie A., 19n, 34, 54n, 301n
Mattila, J. Peter, 247n, 268n
Maynard, Rebecca, 321n
McBride, Timothy D., 312n
McCaffery, Edward J., 341n, 343n, 344n, 345n, 370
McCue, Kristin, 213n, 241n
McCulla, Stephanie H., 68n
McDowell, John M., 217n
McElroy, Marjorie B., 50n, 51n, 408n
McElroy, Susan, 321n
McFate, Katherine, 401n, 418
McGeehan, Patrick, 209n
McKersie, Robert B., 277n
McLanahan, Sara, 26n, 300n, 302n, 304n, 309n, 322–23, 322n, 323n, 324, 328n, 369, 402n
McLaughlin, Diane K., 309n
McNichol, Tom, 226n
McWilliams, Abagail, 195n, 228n, 312n
Meaghan, Elizabeth G., 314n
Medoff, James L., 189n, 283n, 287
Melcher, Dale, 284n
Melkas, Helina, 387n, 391n, 418
Meulders, Danièle, 59n
Meyer, Bruce D., 108n, 128n, 279n, 338n
Meyer, Daniel R., 317n, 321n, 339n, 340n, 369
Meyerowitz, Joanne, 124n
Meyers, Marcia K., 387n, 389n, 418
Michael, Robert T., 47n, 84, 245n, 290n, 294n, 296n

Milgate, Murray, 7n
Milkie, Melissa A., 56n, 62n
Milkman, Ruth, 356n
Miller, Catherine, 413n
Miller, Timothy I., 226n
Mincer, Jacob, 35, 96n, 115, 122n, 135, 160, 160n, 161n, 172n, 184n, 189n, 196n, 197n, 201, 415n
Mitchell, Olivia S., 185n, 345n, 347n, 353n, 368n
Mitchell-Kernan, Claudia, 325
Moe, Karine S., 36n, 83, 235n, 255
Moffitt, Robert A., 291n, 292n, 308n, 309n, 324, 327n, 328n, 329n, 331n, 333n, 334n, 357n, 370
Moghadam, Valentine M., 416n
Mohammed, Rafi, 412n
Mokyr, Joel, 25n
Moore, Dorothy P., 280n
Moore, Robert E., 313n, 314n
Moore, Robert L., 220n
Moretti, Enrico, 108n, 296n, 313n, 384n
Morgan, S. Philip, 304n
Morris, Desmond, 15n
Moss, Kary L., 235n
Moulton, Brent R., 259n
Mroz, Thomas, 97n
Muelleer, Marnie W., 65n
Mueller, Richard E., 280n
Muhl, Charles J., 239n
Mulligan, Casey B., 260n, 262n, 264n
Murdock, George P., 378n
Murer-Fazio, Margaret, 408n
Murnane, Richard J., 288
Murphy, Kevin M., 107n, 111n, 122n, 126n, 135, 170n, 257n, 263n, 288, 311n
Musick, Marc, 65n
Myerson, Allen, 242n

Nakamura, Alice, 418
Nakata, Yoshi-Fumi, 390n
Navarro, Mireya, 182n
Neal, Derek, 205n
Neal, Margaret B., 348n
Neckerman, Kathryn, 291n, 294n, 310n
Nelson, Anne H., 284n
Nelson, Julie A., 2n, 36n, 53n, 67n, 83, 84, 102n

Nelson, Sandi, 336n
Nelson, Sandra, 301n
Neumark, David, 122n, 139n, 201, 208n, 209n, 212n, 219n, 221n, 235n, 241n, 242n, 244n, 255, 267n, 274n, 278n, 288, 304n, 307n
Newburger, Eric C., 164n
Newman, Peter, 7n
Nielsen, Joyce M., 19n, 34
Nikolov, Plamen, 74n
Niskanen, William A., 288
Nixon, Lucia, 295n
Norris, Alison H., 412n
Norton, Kevin I., 177n
Nuss, Shirley, 384n
Nyberg, Anita, 388n

O

Oaxaca, Ronald, 207n, 210n, 241n, 254n
O'Connell, Martin, 94n
O'Connor, Michael, 338n
O'Farrell, Brigid, 245n, 359n, 364n
Ofek, Haim, 172n
Offner, Paul, 130n, 269n, 340n
Offutt, Kate, 304n
Ogawa, Naohiro, 393n
O'Hara, Brian J., 333n
Oi, Walter, 184n
O'Kelly, Charlotte G., 34
Olds, Timothy S., 177n
Olive, Scott, 177n
Olsen, Reed Neil, 191n
Oltmans, Elizabeth, 305n
O'Neill, Donal, 394n, 397n
O'Neill, June, 94n, 147n, 149n, 156n, 185n, 189n, 197n, 201, 247n, 260n, 288
Oooms, Theodora, 336n
Oppenheimer, Valerie Kincade, 119n, 120n, 291n, 293n, 296n
Orazem, Peter F., 247n
Oropesa, R. S., 62n
Osawa, Machiko, 287, 387n
Ost, Jason, 302n
Owen, Robert, 54n

P

Paci, Pierella, 394n, 416n
Page, Marianne E., 321n
Paglin, Morton, 173n

Painter, Gary, 323n
Pan, Philip P., 407n
Panjaitan-Driodisuryo, Rosintan D. M., 411n
Parcel, Toby L., 314n
Parrott, Sharon, 334n, 335n, 336n
Parsons, Donald, 129n
Patterson, Michelle, 179n, 180n
Pavetti, LaDonna, 334n
Paxon, Christina, 333n, 373n, 418
Pearce, James Wishart, III, 106n, 126n
Pechman, Joseph A., 53n, 282n, 351n
Pencavel, John, 95n, 314n
Penner, Rudolph G., 347n
Percy, Rick, 195n, 355n
Perlmann, Joel, 72n, 84
Persson, Inga, 389n, 390n, 392n, 396n, 418
Peters, H. Elizabeth, 121n, 295n
Peterson, Janice, 274n
Peterson, Jean T., 411n
Pevalin, David J., 388n
Pezzin, Lilliana E., 50n
Phelps, Edmund S., 226n
Philips, Bruce D., 356n
Philips, Katherine Ross, 338n
Phillips, Deborah A., 315n, 316n, 324
Phillips, John W., 185n, 345n
Picot, Garnett, 278n
Pierce, Brooks, 122n, 170n, 241n, 257n, 263n, 288
Pierce, Ellise, 307n
Pigou, A. C., 66n
Pinzler, Isabelle Katz, 235n
Piore, Michael J., 231n, 232, 249n
Player, Mack A., 235n
Pleck, Joseph H., 56n, 61n, 315n, 349n
Plotnick, Robert D., 309n, 321n, 322n, 340n
Polachek, Solomon W., 94n, 161n, 167n, 173n, 185n, 189n, 191n, 194n, 197n, 199n, 201, 213n, 260n, 288, 312n
Polivka, Anne E., 274n, 278n
Pollak, Robert A., 18n, 36n, 43n, 48n, 50n, 51n, 52n, 53n, 75n, 84, 303n, 323n, 385n
Postlewaite, Andrew, 122n
Powell, Gary N., 145n
Presser, Harriet B., 362n, 370
Pressman, Steven, 416n, 418

Provost, Caterina, 378n
Psacharopoulos, George, 167n

Q

Quindlen, Anna, 299n
Quinn, Diane M., 177–79

R

Raabe, Phyllis Hutton, 416n
Rahman, Aminur, 412n
Rahman, Bayan, 392n, 393n
Rahman, M. Omar, 72n, 296n, 307n, 324
Raley, Sara, 60n
Rangarajan, Anu, 340n
Rank, Mark, 370
Ransom, Michael R., 210n
Rau, William, 378n
Rawski, Thomas G., 408n
Rayack, Wendy L., 313n
Reed, Betsy, 301n, 324
Reed, Deborah, 314n
Rees, Albert, 218n
Reich, Michael, 30n, 233n
Reich, Robert B., 273n
Reid, T.R., 402n
Reilly, Siobhan, 323n
Reimers, Cordelia W., 269n, 270n
Remick, Helen, 213n
Rendall, Michael S., 318n
Reschovsky, Andrew, 334n
Reskin, Barbara F., 147n, 174n, 201, 212n, 213n, 219n, 227n, 233n, 255
Resnick, Stephen, 55n
Retherford, Robert D., 393n
Reville, Robert, 327n
Ribar, David C., 195n, 291n, 309n, 313n, 323n, 336n
Rich, Lynne, 407n
Richardson, Katarina, 397n
Rindfuss, Ronald R., 304n
Rischall, Isaac, 52n
Ritzke, D., 179n
Robins, Philip K., 117n
Robinson, Joan, 13, 13n
Robinson, John P., 56n, 57n, 61n, 62n, 84
Robst, John, 199n
Rodgers, William M., III, 130n, 269n
Roe, Brian, 349n
Rogers, Lesley J., 16n, 17n

Ronsen, Marit, 390n
Roos, Patricia A., 147n, 213n, 219n, 233n, 255, 395n
Rosaldo, Michelle Z., 15n, 19n, 34
Rose, David, 388n
Rose, David C., 194n, 312n
Rose, Elaina, 108n, 313n
Rose, Nancy E., 303n
Rosen, Harvey S., 181n, 344n, 351n
Rosen, Sherwin, 391n
Rosenbaum, Dan T., 108n, 126n, 128n, 338n
Rosenberg, Tina, 413n
Rosenbloom, Joshua L., 106n
Rosenfeld, Megan, 177n
Rosenthal, Elisabeth, 406n
Rosenzweig, Mark R., 290n, 324, 405n
Rosoff, Betty, 15n, 16n
Ross, Katherin E., 355n, 389n, 402n
Ross, Susan Deller, 235n, 237n, 247n
Rothausen, Teresa J., 71n
Rothert, Kendra, 296n
Rothstein, Donna S., 181n, 224n
Rouillon, Vanessa, 347n
Rouse, Cecilia, 208n
Roy, T. K., 406n, 407n
Royalty, Anne Beeson, 192n, 195n, 207n, 228n
Rubinstein, Yona, 260n, 262n, 264n
Rufolo, Anthony M., 173n
Ruggles, Steven, 72n, 296n
Ruhm, Christopher J., 314n, 315n, 351n, 352n, 355n, 388n
Russett, Cynthia, 17n
Rytina, Nancy, 149n

S

Saha, Rumki, 347n
Sainsbury, Diane, 387n, 390n, 401n, 418
Sammartino, Frank J., 345n, 346n, 347n
Samuelson, Paul A., 50n, 235
Sandberg, John F., 60n, 61n
Sandefur, Gary D., 322–23, 323n, 322n, 324, 328n
Sandell, Steven H., 196n, 197n, 346n
Sanders, Seth G., 204n, 302n, 321n
Saraswathi, T. S., 411n
Sartwell, Crispin, 177n
Savada, Andrea Matles, 407n

Sawhill, Isabel, 336n, 358n, 361n
Sayer, Liana C., 56n, 59n, 61n
Scelfo, Julie, 307n
Scharlach, Andrew E., 354n, 369
Schemo, Diana Jean, 183n
Schettkat, Ronald, 377n
Schmidt, Stefanie, 360n
Schnabel, Claus, 282n
Schoellner, Teresa, 195n, 355n
Schoen, Robert, 296n
Schoeni, Robert F., 333n
Scholz, John Karl, 337n
Schone, Barbara Steinberg, 50n
Schreiner, Mark, 280n, 331n
Schultz, Theodore W., 160n, 160
Schultz, T. Paul, 29n, 34, 52n, 293n,
        294n, 383n, 386n, 400n,
        403n, 404n, 405n, 418
Schwartz, Pepper, 47n
Scott, Joan W., 26n, 34, 373n
Seidman, Laurence S., 337n
Seltzer, Judith, 340n, 369
Sen, Amartya, 384, 384n, 405n
Sengupta, Somini, 380n
Seshadri, Ananth, 25n, 120n, 306n
Seshadri, Subadra, 411n
Sexton, Edwin A., 191n
Shapiro, David, 127n, 197n
Shaw, Lois, 127n
Shellenbarger, Sue, 61n,
        349n, 367n
Shelton, Beth Anne, 56n
Shipley, Amy, 182n
Shonkoff, Jack P., 315n, 316n, 324
Short, Kathleen, 320n
Shoup, Carl S., 341n
Sicherman, Nachum, 228n
Sigle-Rushton, Wendy, 320n
Silbaugh, Katharine B., 74n
Simmons, Emmy, 411n
Simon, Herbert, 3n
Simpson, Patricia, 145n,
        146n, 347n
Singell, Larry D., Jr., 217n
Singh, Susheela, 309n
Skinner, Jonathan, 121n
Smeeding, Timothy, 338n, 346n,
        347n, 401n, 402n
Smith, Howard, 236n
Smith, James P., 94n, 106n,
        135, 185n
Smith, Kristin, 94n
Smith, Ralph E., 21n, 33n, 341n
Smith, Robert S., 250n, 268n
Smith, Tom W., 325
Smock, Pamela J., 294n,
        300n, 301n

Soberon-Ferrer, Horacio, 62n
Solnick, Sara J., 183n
Solomon, Charlene Marmer, 353n
Solon, Gary, 211n
Sonenstein, Freya, 359n, 360n
Sorensen, Elaine, 130n, 199n,
        211n, 212n, 260n, 269n,
        339n, 340n
Sorrentino, Constance, 301n,
        386n, 400n
South, Scott J., 59n
Spalter-Roth, Roberta, 282n
Spence, Michael, 170
Spencer, Steven J., 177–79
Spitze, Glenna, 18n, 59n, 216n, 348n
Spletzer, James R., 191n
Springen, Karen, 307n
Stafford, Frank P., 62n, 84, 388n,
        389n, 399n, 402n, 415n
Standish, Nicola J., 296n
Stanley, T. D., 204n
Stark, Oded, 290n, 324, 405n
Startz, Richard, 233n
Steele, Claude M., 177–79
Steinmeier, Thomas L., 129n
Steinpreis, R. E., 179n
Stephan, Paula E., 217n
Stephens, Melvin, Jr., 268n, 295n
Steurle, C. Eugene, 343n, 344n,
        345n, 346n, 347n, 359n
Stevens, Ann Huff, 321n
Stevenson, Betsey, 48n
Stewart, Jay, 276n
Stock, Wendy A., 241n
Stokes, Houston, 199n
Stolba, Christine, 155–56
Strachan, Glenda, 398n
Strahan, Philip E., 221n
Straights, Robert A., 273n
Stratton, Leslie S., 195n,
        271n, 313n
Straub, John D., 267n
Strauss, Gary, 177n
Strauss, Murray A., 48n
Strober, Myra H., 219n, 356n,
        402n, 418
Stromberg, Ann H., 25n, 179n
Subaiya, Lekha, 321n
Suggs, Welch, 182n
Summerfield, Gale, 416n, 418
Summers, Lawrence H., 116n
Sun, Han, 147n
Sundstrom, Marianne, 390n
Sundstrom, William A., 269n
Svenar, Jan, 414n
Sweet, James A., 22n, 300n
Sweetman, Arthur, 410n
Sweetman, Olive, 394n, 397n

T

Taeuber, Karl E., 22n
Takehiro, Ryoji, 390n
Tauchen, Helen V., 48n
Tawa, Renee, 156
Taylor, Lowell J., 204n, 302n
Taylor, Stuart, 243n
Taylor, Susan K., 277n
Teague, Jackqueline L.,
        351n, 355n
Tefft, Sheila, 406n
Teiman, Michelle L., 217n
Teisl, Mario F., 349n
Thomas, Adam, 336n
Thomas, Duncan, 52n, 384n, 385n,
        404n
Thompson, Jennifer, 147n
Thorne, Barrie, 102n
Thornton, Arland, 292n
Tiefenthaler, Jill, 48n, 49n
Tierney, Helen, 7n
Tiger, Lionel, 14n, 15n, 34
Tilly, Chris, 276n
Tilly, Louise A., 26n, 34, 373n
Tindall, Blair, 208n
Tipton, Steven, 290n
Tobach, Ethel, 15n, 16n
Tobias, Sheila, 164n, 201
Todd, Petra E., 154n, 263n
Toossi, Mitra, 131n
Topel, Robert, 189n
Trebilcock, Anne, 286n
Treiman, Donald J., 249n, 395n
Troske, Kenneth R., 139n, 209n,
        212n, 214n, 221n
Trzcinski, Eileen, 353n, 388n
Tsui, Ming, 407n
Tucker, M. Belinda, 325
Tuovi, Allen, 372n, 403n
Turgeon, Lynn, 416n
Tzannatos, Zafiris, 410n

U

Ureta, Manuelita, 197n, 228n

V

Valenzuela, J. P., 411n
Valenzuela, Myra, 411n
Valian, Virginia, 179n, 213n, 255
Valletta, Robert G., 283n
Vandell, Deborah Lowe, 361n
Vandenbroucke,
        Guillaume, 306n

Vandivere, Sharon, 360n
Vanek, Joann, 24n, 58n
VanGilder, Jennifer, 199n
Van Nort, Kyle D., 208n
Verma, Amitra, 411n
Ver Ploeg, Michelle, 334n
Viscusi, W. Kip, 213n, 228n
Vleminckx, K., 401n
Vo, Minh T., 385n

W

Wagman, Barnet, 67n
Waite, Linda J., 72n, 291n,
    300n, 325
Waldfogel, Jane, 33n, 195n, 201,
    274n, 280n, 293n, 312n,
    313n, 315n, 321n, 333n,
    339n, 355n
Wales, Terence J., 18n, 52n, 385n
Waller, Maureen, 322n, 340n
Wandner, Stephen A., 273n
Ward, John O., 70n
Ward, Michael P., 94n, 185n
Warme, Barbara D., 276n
Wasserman, Miriam, 409n
Waters, Mary C., 72n, 84
Watkins, Susan Cotts, 303n
Wazienski, Robert, 378n
Weinberg, Bruce A., 195n,
    262n, 355n

Weinberg, Daniel H.,
    291n, 328n
Weinberger, Catherine J., 208n
Weiss, Yoram, 233n, 295n
Welch, Finis, 260n
Wellington, Alison J., 185n,
    197n, 260n
Wells, Thomas, 323n
Welter, Barbara, 26n, 34
Wertheimer, Barbara A., 284n
Western, Bruce, 282n
White, Lynn, 296n
Whittington, Leslie A.,
    344n, 349n
Wiederman, Michael W.,
    17n, 18n
Wilkie, Janet R., 25n
Will, George, 155, 156n
Willborn, Steven L., 398n
Williams, Donald R., 280n
Willis, Robert J., 106n, 290n, 295n,
    304n, 308n
Wilson, Edward O., 15, 15n, 34
Wilson, John, 65n
Wilson, Kathryn, 309n
Wilson, William Julius, 291n, 294n,
    401n, 418
Wink, Claudia, 384n
Winkler, Anne E., 52n, 56n,
    131n, 194n, 312n, 320n,
    327n, 328n
Wirth, Linda, 214n

Wisensale, Steven K., 356n
Witt, Robert, 357n
Witte, Ann Dryden, 48n, 357n
Witte, John, Jr. 290n
Wolfe, Barbara, 309n, 316n, 322n,
    328n, 332n, 361n
Wolfers, Justin, 48n
Wolff, Richard, 55n
Wolpin, Kenneth I., 118n
Wong, Ging, 419
Wood, Robert G., 208n, 294n
Woolcock, Michael, J. V., 412n
Worden, Robert L., 407n
Wu, Nina, 334n

Y

Yardley, Jim, 407n
Yellen, Janet L., 309n
Yelowitz, Aaron S., 328n
Yorukoglu, Mehmet, 120n
Young-DeMarco, Linda, 292n

Z

Zavodny, Madeline, 292n
Zedlewski, Sheila R., 347n
Zetkin, Clara, 54n
Zhang, Wei, 408n
Zick, Cathleen D., 56n
Ziliak, James P., 217n, 337n
Zimmerman, David J., 163n, 279n

Subject Index

A

Abortion
fertility rates and, 305
sex-selective, 406
Absolute advantage, 39–40
Abstractions, 4
Academia
discrimination in, 179–80, 216–17
hierarchies in, 143
Adarand case, 243n
Added worker effect, 43, 115
Administrative support
occupations, 137, 138
Adult literacy rates, 375
Advanced countries. *See* United
States and advanced
countries comparison
Adverse selection, 351
Affirmative Action, 242–45
AFL-CIO, 284, 285
Africa, 385. *See also* North Africa;
South Africa; Sub-
Saharan Africa
African American, use of term, 7.
See also Blacks
Africans, enslavement of, 16
Age
child care and, 360–61
earnings ratios by, 149–51
education and, 151–52, 161
elderly women and poverty
risk, 347
males and participation
rates, 129
marriage rates, 293
of participation of
post-World War II
females, 90–92
participation rates,
worldwide, 376
teen pregnancies and births,
308, 309
unemployment rates, 269
of U.S. population, by 2050,
348–50

Age-earnings profiles, 168–69,
197–98
Aggregate indicators of economic
welfare, 5
Agricultural societies, 20
AIDS, 386, 405
Aid to Families with Dependent
Children (AFDC),
327–29, 332, 335, 338
Alaska, 240n
All-male clubs, 226
Alternative employment
arrangements, 274–75
Alternative work schedules,
362–64
Altruism, 65
Amendments. *See* U.S.
Constitution
American Academy of
Pediatrics, 349
American Express Financial
Advisors, 209
*American Federation of State,
County and Municipal
Employees v. State
of Washington*
(1985), 247n
American Medical Association, 179
Americans with Disabilities Act
(ADA), 354
American Time Use Survey
(ATUS), 56
Amex, 209
Analysis
least squares regression
analysis, 251
multiple regression analysis, 251
regression analysis of labor
market discrimination,
250–54
Angola, 379
Animal behavior, 15
Annual earnings, 149n
Annual work hours, 95
Anthropologists, gender studies
by, 15, 18

Antidiscrimination efforts
in advanced countries, 387
equal employment opportunity
laws and regulations,
235–40
Equal Pay Act of 1963, 236, 240
Pregnancy Discrimination Act
of 1978, 353
in private employment, 240n
status of world's women, 383
Title IX, 182–83, 184
Title VII, 236–42, 244
United States as pioneer in, 395
Antinepotism rules, 365
Arithmetic mean, 147n
Arizona, 73
Arkansas, 73
Armenia, 373n
Asia, 384, 386
Asians
defined, prior to 2003, 152n
earnings ratios, 152–53
educational attainment, 154, 162
income and poverty rates
for families with
children, 319
in labor unions, 281
marriage rates, 293
median income, 152, 153, 154
occupational differences and,
139–40
participation rates, 89–90, 91
volunteer work statistics, 64
Asia/Pacific, 379
Assessment, human capital
model, 196–200
Assumptions, 4
Attachment, as labor force trend,
92–94, 261–62, 272
marginally attached workers,
271
Augusta National Golf Club,
Masters Tournament, 226
Australia, 21, 56, 247, 376, 379,
394, 395, 397–98
Austria, 376, 389

B

Baby boom, 305–6
Baby boomlet, 306
Baby bust, 125, 273, 305–6
Baby-sitting, 86n
Bahrain, 379
Bangladesh, 331, 409, 410
Bargaining power
    allocation of income and time
        and, 46–47
    of homemakers, 61
    housework and, 58
    in marriage, 49–53
Barriers, human capital model,
    180–81
Battered women, 48–49
Bebel, August, 54
Behavior
    animal, 15
    economic, 2
    chosen, voluntary, 17
    traditional gender roles, 14–15
Belgium, 73, 376
Benefit plans, 364
Berlin Wall, fall of, 415
Biased evaluation, 179
Biological nature, 14–15
Birth control, 25, 127, 305, 406
Birth rates, 307–8
Blacks
    birth rates, 308
    child support payments, 130
    defined, prior to 1970, 152n
    demographics of, 72
    discrimination. *See*
        Discrimination
    as domestic servants/farm
        laborers, 30
    earnings ratios, 152–53
    educational attainment
        by, 162, 263
    families with children under age
        18, 317
    incarceration rates, 130
    income and poverty rates for
        families with children, 319
    labor force participation,
        late nineteenth
        century, 23
    in labor unions, 281
    market substitutes and, 62
    marriage rates, 292, 293, 294
    mother-only families, 317–18
    occupational differences and,
        139–40
    participation rates, 89–90, 91,
        129–31
    pay gaps, 263–64
    use of term, 7
    volunteer work statistics, 64, 65

wives in labor market, necessity
    of, 24, 26
women in work force, 130–31
Blau-Kahn study, on gender pay
    gap, 260–64
Block grants, 358
Blue-collar occupations, 138, 139
    Asians in, 140
    blacks in, 263
    education as factor in, 146
    predominantly male, 146
Bona fide occupational
    qualification (BFOQ), 237
Bonuses, 149n
Bosnia, 385
Botswana, 386
Brandeis, Louis, 236
Brazil, 409
Breastfeeding, 349
Brennan, Supreme Court
    Justice, 236
Britain, 388
Budget constraints, 97, 98, 99, 116n
Bulgaria, 373n, 379
Burden of proof, 238
Bureau of Labor Statistics, 88,
    271, 274
Bush, George W., 73, 341, 343
Bush administration, support of
    same-sex schools, 183
Business necessity, 238

C

Cafeteria packages, 364
California, 240n, 356, 366
Canada, 21, 56, 73, 344, 376, 379,
    399, 401, 413
Capital
    human. *See* Human capital
    plant and equipment, 8–9
Capitalism
    defined, 53
    patriarchy and, 55
Caribbean countries, 373, 374–75,
    381, 382
Cash jobs, 86n
Cash transfer program, 337
Catholicism. *See* Vatican
Census Bureau, 144
Central Asia, 374–75, 381, 382
Central Europe, 414, 416
Child care
    in advanced countries, 388–89
    day care centers during and after
        World War II, 123–24
    employer policies, 356–62
    government subsidies for,
        116–18
    nonmarket work versus leisure
        and, 59–61

Child Care and Development Block
    Grant (CCDBG), 358
Child care costs
    block grants, 358–62
    policies, 356–58
    subsidies, 116–18, 357–58
    tax credits, 358–59
Child Development Block
    Grant, 361
Child labor, 408–10
Child labor laws, 24
Child quality, 304
Children. *See also* Families
    decline of, with
        industrialization, 25
    development of, 315
    effect on participation, 106–9
    family structure and outcomes,
        322–23
    housework issue and, 59
    living arrangements of, 71
    in married families, 73
    maternal employment and
        outcomes, 314–16
    as negative effect on wages of
        women, 195
    in nineteenth century single-
        parent homes, 26
    responsibility for, 350–52
    sex-stereotyping of toys, 175–77
    single-parent families, 316–22
Children's Health Insurance
    Program (CHIP), 337
Child support, 130
Child Support Assurance
    System, 340
Child support enforcement, 295,
    335, 338–40
Child Tax Credit, 358
China, 108, 374–75, 379, 381, 384,
    405–8
Circular reasoning, 38
Citadel, 183
Civil Rights Act of 1964, 182,
    236, 353
Civil unions, 43, 74, 303, 366
Clerical employment, 30
Clinton, Bill, 332, 341
Clinton Administration, 409
Coalition of Labor Union Women
    (CLUW), 284, 285
Cohabiting couples, 6n. *See also*
        Opposite-sex couples;
        Same-sex couples
    demographics of, 71
    gay and lesbian, 301–3
    housework and, 59
    increase in, 294
    opposite-sex, unmarried, 299–301
Collection of data, 4–5
College education. *See* Education

Colombia, 409
Colonialism, 16
Colonial America, 21–22
Colorado, 240n
Commission on Leave,
    Department of Labor, 354
Commodities
  goods and time intensive, 100
  marriage-specific investments
    and, 50
  production and selection of, 37
  utility from consumption of, 96
Communism, feminism and, 416
Community property law, 53
Commuting relationship, 364
Comparable worth, 245–48, 395,
    397–98
Comparative advantage, 37–38, 40
Comprehensive Employment and
    Training Act (CETA) of
    1973, 330
Conflict of interest, husband/wife
    bargaining power and, 47
Connecticut, 240n
Construction and extraction
    occupations, 138
Consumption
  of commodities, 96
  externalities in, 42
  substitution in, 100–101
Contingent workers, 274
Contraceptive techniques, 25,
    127, 184
Contract workers, 274
Convention for the Elimination of
    All Forms of
    Discrimination Against
    Women (CEDAW), 383
Corporate officers, 138
Costa Rica, 379
Costs
  direct and indirect, of
    education, 167
  of interdependence, 45–46
  market, 67
  opportunity, 67
  of raising children, 357
  of transaction, 49–53
Cost stream, 167n
Cote d'Ivoire, 374–75
County of Washington v. Gunther
    (1981), 247n
Couples, assistance policies for,
    364–66
Court-mandated affirmative
    action, 242–45
Covenant marriage, 73
Craft occupations, 138
Craft unions, 284
Cross-tabulation, 5
Cult of true womanhood, 25–26

Current Population Survey, 56, 88,
    138n, 145
Curtiss-Wright, 123n
Curves
  demand, 8–9
  indifference, 97, 98, 99–102
  supply, 9–10
Custody, 297–99
Customer discrimination, 225
Cyclical unemployment, 268
Czechoslovakia, 373n, 415
Czech Republic, 373n, 376, 416

D

Darwin, Charles, 15–16
Data collection, 4–5
Day care. *See also* Child care
    123–24
  on-site or near-site, of firms, 359
Decision making, husband/wife
    bargaining power and, 47
Declaration of Sentiments and
    Resolutions (1848), 27–28
Defense of Marriage Act (1996),
    73–74
Degrees. *See* Education
Delaware, 240n
Demand. *See also* Supply and
    demand
  determinations of, 6
  for female labor, 119–20
Demand curve, 8–9
  shifts in, 10–12
Demographics
  changes in families, 310–23
  children's living arrangements
    and, 71
  family trends, 293
  influence on preference for home
    versus market time, 121
  marriage rates, 291–92
  1960s-1980s, shifts in, 125–27
  status of world's women,
    398–402
  United States and other
    advanced countries,
    398–402
  of unmarried, opposite-sex
    couples, 71
  women and the labor force
    and, 71
Denmark, 73, 350, 373, 376, 399
Denunionization, 282–83
Department of Labor, 354
Dependent Care Tax Credit,
    358, 359
Dependent variable, 251
Developing countries
  child labor, 408–10
  education, 403–5

fertility and population control,
    405–8
genital mutilation and patriarchal
    traditions, 412–13
microcredit for women, 410–12
participation rates, 372–73
summary, 413–14
Different-sex couples, 299n. *See
    also* Opposite-sex
    couples
Diminishing marginal
    productivity, 8–9
Diminishing marginal utility, 44n
Direct costs, of education, 167
Direct-hire temporaries, 275n
Dirie, Waris, 413
Discouraged worker effect, 115, 271
Discrimination. *See also*
    Antidiscrimination
    efforts; Labor market
    discrimination
  customer, 225
  in educational institutions, 143,
    216–17
  EEO law prohibitions, 392
  government's role in combating,
    182–83
  in Hispanic-white income
    differences, 155
  human capital model, 192–93
  inefficiency caused by, 235
  institutional, 233
  labor market, 160, 193, 259–60
  prelabor market, 159
  premarket, 136
  by September 11th Victim
    Compensation Fund
    of 2001, 69
  sexual harassment, 238–240; 392
  sexual orientation and, 240
  societal, 136, 159
  sociologists' definition, 159n
  statistical, 192, 223
  status of world's women, 383
  against women in the labor
    market, 6, 38, 41, 156
Discrimination coefficient, 219
Disparate impact, 238
Disparate treatment, 238
District of Columbia, 240n
Division of labor. *See also*
    Specialization,
    disadvantages of
  in primitive societies, 19
  technology as determinant of, 18
  traditional, 36, 38, 47
Divorce, 401
  children's gender as influence
    on, 108n
  covenant marriage and, 73
  custody battles, 297–99

Divorce (*continued*)
demographics of, 121
displaced homemaker risk, 46
as economic explanation for
family formation, 294–99
job loss and, 268
laws concerning, 49
unilateral laws, domestic
violence and, 53
Divorce-threat bargaining
model, 51
Domestic violence, 48–49
unilateral divorce laws and, 53
Dothard v. Rawlinson (1977), 237
Downsizing, 267
Dowry, 20, 22
Drug trafficking, 86n
Dual-earner families
family structure, well-being,
and, 310–14
housework, child care, and, 61
job loss and, 267
joint decision-making by, 47
marriage benefits, 291
risk pooling, 43

E

Earned Income Tax Credit
(EITC), 128, 319, 331,
335, 336–38, 343, 344, 358
Earnings, 136–37. *See also*
Human capital model;
Wages
discrimination. *See*
Discrimination
education as factor in, 151–52
experience-earnings profiles,
165–70
female-male earnings ratio,
147–56
full-time, year-round, 147–49
labor market discrimination,
204–10
lost future potential, 69–70
real, 257–59
of self-employed women, 280
status of world's women, 378–79
of women, increase in, 31
East Asia, 372, 374–75, 381, 382,
383, 405, 406
Eastern Europe, 386, 414, 416
East Germany, 373n, 416
Echo of the baby boom, 306
Economic behavior, 2
Economic conditions, 115–16, 126
Economic incentives, women's
property rights
evolution, 27–28
"Economic man," 35
Economics

concerns and concepts, 3–4
scope of, 5–6
topics in, 1–2
women's roles in, 19–21
Economic status of the world's
women. *See also*
Developing countries;
United States and
advanced countries
comparison
countries of the former Soviet
blocs, 414–17
developing countries, 403–14
earnings, 378–79
educational attainment,
379–80
fertility, 380–82
housework, 382
interpretations and
implications, 383–86
labor force participation, 372–77
law and, 383
occupations, 377–78
political representation, 383
regional comparisons, 383–86
women's role in
government, 383
Economic theory, uses of, 4–5
Economies of scale, 42, 291
Ecuador, 409
Education, 26–27
Asians and, 154, 162
attainment by women, rise in,
183–84
of blacks, 130
college-educated women, 31–33
as determinant of participation,
111, 112
in developing countries, 403–5
direct costs, 167
discrimination by educational
institutions, 143, 179–80,
216–17
earnings influenced by, 151–52
effect on hours worked, 95
expected work life, 171–74
females employed in, 139
females' rise in, 119
gender differences in, 161–65
gender-separate
opportunities, 183
government's role in combating
discrimination in, 182–83
Hispanics, 162, 246
indirect costs, 167
as influence on wage
inequality, 111
investment decisions, 165–70
males and participation rates, 129
occupational segregation
reduced by, 146

productivity and, 170–71
rising payoff to, 265–67
self-selection and investment
in, 111
university faculty hierarchies, 143
whites, 154, 162, 263–64
women's wages and, 126
Educational Amendments, to
Civil Rights Act of
1964, 182
Educational attainment
by race, 162, 263–64
status of world's women, 379–80
Educational investment decision
barriers, 180–81
biased evaluations, 179
discrimination by educational
institutions, 179–80
expected work life, 171–74
gender-appropriate traits and
competencies, 177–79
gender differences in, human
capital analysis, 171–74
human capital model, 165–70
socialization, 174–77
EEO law, 392
Egypt, 374–75, 379
Elizabeth I of England, 20
Empirical evidence, income and
substitution effects,
113–15
Employed group, 86
Employee discrimination, 223–25
Employer discrimination, 219–23
Employment. *See also job-related
topics*; Occupations;
Unemployment
alternative work schedules,
362–64
home-based, 363
nonstandard workforce, 274–78
by occupation and industry,
272–73
part-time, 274, 275, 278, 363
prohibition of employment of
married women. *See*
Marriage bars
self-employment, 278–80
Empty nest syndrome, 46
Engels, Friedrich, 54
Entrants, 269, 272
Equal Employment Opportunity
Commission (EEOC),
236, 241
Equal employment opportunity
laws and regulations,
235–40
Equal Pay Act of 1963, 236, 240
Equilibrium, in supply and
demand, 10–12
Ethiopia, 374–75

Ethnicity. *See* Hispanics
  terminology, 7
Europe, 374–75, 381, 382, 383,
  389, 399
European Monetary Union,
  374–75
European Union, 56, 399, 413
Evaluation, jobs, 248–49
Exchange, neoclassical model,
  37–41
Executive occupations, 138
Executive Order 11246, 236
  affirmative action and, 242–45
  enforcement of, 236–37
  for Presidential Commission on
    the Status of Women, 236
Expected work life, 171–74,
  190–92
Experience. *See also* On-the-job
    training
  females' rise in, 119
  human capital model, 189–90
  as market earnings
    determinant, 94
Experience-earnings profiles,
  165–70
Explanatory variable, 251
Extended family, 6n, 320
Externalities in consumption, as
    advantage of family, 42
External shocks, 10

F

Factors of production, 5
Families. *See also* Market time
    (*w*); Market work
    (*w*)Marriage;
    Nonmarket time (*w**);
    Nonmarket work
  advantages, 42–43
  bargaining power in, 49–53
  biased toward white middle
    class reality, 71n
  choosing between work and
    family, 356–57
  decision making in, 50
  defined, 6, 6n, 37, 71
  demands of work and family,
    348–50
  demographic mix of changing
    structure, 72
  division of labor in, traditional, 36
  dual-earner, 43, 47, 61, 267, 291,
    310–14
  federal income tax, 341–45
  formation of, factors
    influencing, 36
  fragile, 309
  goal of, 37
  government definition of, 71

industrialization and evolution
    of, 23–27
  job loss and, 267
  labor force participation, late
    nineteenth century, 23
  Marxist views of, 53–55
  neoclassical analysis of, 37–41
  neoclassical model. *See*
    Specialization and
    exchange
  nonstandard work and, 277–78
  organization of, 50
  radical feminist views of, 53–55
  shrinking size, 27
  single-parent, worldwide, 401–2
  structure changes, worldwide, 401
  traditional, 23–24, 41
  transaction costs, 49–53
  twenty-first century shifts in,
    70–72
Family and Medical Leave Act of
    1993 (FMLA), 350,
    353–56
Family formation, economic
    explanations for
  changing structure and economic
    well-being, 310–23
  cohabitation: gay and lesbian
    couples, 301–3
  cohabitation: opposite-sex,
    unmarried couples,
    299–301
  divorce, 294–99
  dual-earner families, 310–14
  family structure and children's
    outcomes, 322–23
  fertility, 303–10
  marriage, 290–94
  maternal employment and
    children's outcomes,
    314–16
  single-parent families, 316–22
Family-friendly policies, 352–57
Family leave, 353–56
Family structure
  children's outcomes and, 322–23
  dual-earner families, 310–14
  maternal employment and
    children's outcomes,
    314–16
  single-parent families, 316–22
  trends in, 293
Family Support Act (1988), 330, 332
Family wage, 24
Fathers, child care by, 60–61
Federal Glass Ceiling
    Commission, 218
Feedback effects, of labor market
    discrimination, 203, 233–34
  statistical discrimination, 227–28
Female circumcision, 412–13

Females. *See also* Children;
    individual races
  in academia, 216–17
  age, earnings ratio and, 150–51
  attachment trends, 272
  barriers to employment, 214–18,
    225–26. *See also* Glass
    ceiling
  barriers to entry, 121
  biased evaluations, 179
  child care subsidies and, 116–18
  class structure and, 20, 26
  college-educated, 31–33
  comparative advantage in
    household production, 38
  corporate officers, 214–15
  demand for labor of, 119–20
  demands of work and family,
    348–50
  discrimination. *See*
    Discrimination
  earnings increase, 31
  economic development and
    roles of, 19–21
  economic status of world's
    women, 372–417
  educational attainment, rise
    in, 41, 119, 162–65,
    183–84, 266
  employment. *See* Participation
  expected work life, 171–74,
    190–92
  female-male earnings ratio,
    147–56
  firm-specific training, 191
  higher-education degrees, 162–65
  hours worked, 95
  housework by, 57–63
  immigrants, 23–24, 26
  industrialization and, 21
  industrialization and evolution
    of the family, 23–27
  labor force experience, 94, 119,
    189–90
  labor force participation,
    increase in, post-World
    War II, 136
  in the labor market, 28–31
  life cycle changes, and
    specialization, 45
  married and single mothers, 1990s
    and early 2000s, 127–28
  married mothers, 1960s–1980s,
    125–27
  Marxist ideology and, 54, 414–17
  maternal employment and
    children's outcomes,
    314–16
  math stereotype threat, 177–79
  microcredit, 280, 331, 410–12
  nature of, 14–15

Females (*continued*)
 as nonstandard workers, 275–76
 occupational differences
  between males and
  females, 137–44
 overtime pay and bonuses, 149n
 participation trends, 118–22
 pay gap, 259–64
 post-World War II, 89, 124–25
 preindustrial period, 21–22
 productivity increase, 46, 120
 qualifications, 119
 self-employment, 278–80
 socialization, 174–77
 sociobiology, 15–18
 subordination and subjugation
  of, 20
 training decisions, 186–89, 190–93
 traits and competencies, 177
 unemployment rates,
  269–70, 271
 unemployment trends, 272–73
 union membership, 281–86
 unpaid labor or, 54
 volunteer work statistics, 64, 65
 votes, 37–38
 wages. *See* Earnings
 women's property rights
  evolution, 27–28
 World War II participation
  rates, 88–89, 122–24
Feminism
 communism and, 416
 economic perspective of, 2–3
 radical feminist views of family,
  53–55
Fertility
 decline of, 25, 125, 126n
 defined, 375n
 in developing countries, 405–8
 family formation and, 303–10
 future trends, 307
 participation influenced by, 121
 status of world's women, 375,
  380–82
 twenty-first century shifts in, 72
 World War II to 2002, 305–6
Final Rules. *See* September 11th
  Victim Compensation
  Fund of 2001
Financial occupations, 138, 139
Finland, 373, 376, 379
Firm-specific training, 186, 187–89,
  192, 225
First transformation, 23n
Flat tax, 344–45
Flexible benefit plans, 364
Flexible spending accounts, 359
Flextime, 362, 363
Florida, 226
Food stamps, 319, 327
Fragile families, 309

France, 73, 350, 376, 379, 394, 399
Freelancing, 275
Frictional unemployment, 268
Full-employment unemployment
  rate, 268
Full-time, year-round
  employment, 147n,
  150–51
Full-time workweek, 95

G

Gains to specialization and
  exchange, 40–41
Gaps. *See* Gender earnings gap;
  Gender pay gap; Pay gaps
Gays. *See* Same-sex couples
Gender
 barriers, 180–81
 biased evaluations, 179
 characteristics of, difficulty of
  changing, 17
 comparable worth, 245–48, 395,
  397–98
 connotation of, 7
 discrimination by educational
  institutions, 179–80
 earnings ratios, 147–56
 educational attainment, 161–65
 female-male earnings ratio,
  147–56
 labor market experience, 185–86
 quitting, 228
 sex distinguished from, 7
 socialization, 174–77
 stereotypes in children's toys,
  175–77
 stereotype threat situations,
  177–79
 traditional roles, 14–15
 training investment decisions,
  190–93
 traits and competencies, 177
 unemployment rates,
  269–70, 271
 unemployment trends, 272–73
 use of term, 7
 wage gap in advanced countries,
  393–97
Gender earnings gap, 149
 education as factor in, 151–52
Gender-neutral toys, 176
Gender pay gap
 declining, 259–64
 examples, 155–56
 labor market discrimination,
  204–10
 1980s, empirical results, 260–64
 1990s, empirical results, 264
 trends in, determinants of,
  259–60

"unexplained," 207, 261–62
Gender-separate educational
  facilities, 183
General training, 186–87
Generation X, 305
Generation Y, 306
Genital mutilation, 385, 412–13
Germany, 73, 376, 377n, 379, 388,
  389, 394, 399, 401
Ghana, 379
Ginsburg, Ruth Bader, 183
Glass ceiling
 examples and analysis of,
  214–18
 self-employment as escape
  from, 280, 280n
 in union leadership, 284–85
Goods
 goods-intensive
  commodities, 100
 public, 42, 47
Goods and services, 5, 24, 37, 96
Government. *See also*
  Antidiscrimination
  efforts
 child care subsidies, 116–18
 collection of data, 4–5
 equal employment opportunity
  laws and regulations,
  235–40
 potential to promote outcomes,
  52–53
 role in child care, 350–52
 role in combating
  discrimination in
  educational institutions,
  182–83
 subsidies. *See* Subsidies
 taxes. *See* Taxes
 women's role in, worldwide, 383
Grameen Bank, 331, 410
Great Depression, 123–24
Greece, 376, 389
Griggs v. Duke Power Co.
  (1971), 238
Gross benefits, of education, 167
Gross domestic product
  (GDP), 5
 defined, 66
 nonmarket production and,
  66–68
Group bonds, 18

H

Haiti, 379
Harris v. Forklift System Inc.
  (1993), 239
Harvard Law School, 180
Harvard Medical School, 180
Hatch, Orrin G, 297–98
Hawaii, 73, 240n, 366

Head Start, 358, 360, 361
Health insurance, 43
Health services, 139
Heterodox Marxist views of family, 53–55
Heterosexuals. *See* Opposite-sex couples
Hierarchies, occupational, 143
High school education. *See* Education
Hispanics
  defined, 152n
  demographics of, 72
  discrimination. *See* Discrimination
  earnings ratios, 152–54
  educational attainment by, 162
  education gaps, 264
  families with children under age 18, 317
  income and poverty rates for families with children, 319
  in labor unions, 281
  marriage rates, 292, 293
  mother-only families, 318
  occupational differences and, 139–40
  participation rates, 89–90, 91
  pay gaps, 264
  unemployment rates, 269–70
  use of term, 7
  volunteer work statistics, 64, 65
HIV/AIDS, 386, 405
Home-based employment, 88, 363
Homemaking
  bargaining power and, 61
  comparative advantage and gender differences in, 38
  divorce and, 46
  high-risk undertaking, 49
  hours devoted to, 24–25
  leisure, life cycle and, 61
  market work compared to, 37–41
  survey questions about, 88
Home production, 37–41
Home time (w^*). *See* Nonmarket work (w^*)
Homosexuals. *See* Same-sex couples
Hong Kong, 379
Honor killings, 385
Horizontal equity, 341
Horticultural societies, 19–20
Hourly wage rate (w). *See* Market work (w)
Hours decision
  impact on market wages, 113
  participation, 102–4
Hours worked

alternative work schedules, 362–64
annual, 95
  education's effect on, 95
  measurement of, 95
Household, defined, 6
Housework
  under Marxist ideology, 414–15
  sharing of, and specialization, 44–45
  socializing of, 54, 414–15
  status of world's women, 382, 402
  throughout the world, 402
  trends in, 56–63
  United States, 402
  value of, by September 11th Victim Compensation Fund of 2001, 68–70
Human capital model, 158, 233. *See also* Educational investment decision
  analysis, 171–74
  assessment of, 196–200
  barriers, 180–81
  biased evaluations, 179
  defined, 160–61
  discrimination, 192–93
  discrimination, by educational institutions, 179–80
  earnings, 193–94
  education, 170–71
  educational investment decision, 165–70
  educational investment decision, gender differences in, 171–81
  education differences, 161–65
  expected work life, 171–74
  experience, 189–90
  female rise in education, 183–84
  gender-appropriate traits and competencies, 177–79
  gender pay gap and, 259–60
  government's role in combating discrimination, 182–83
  labor market discrimination, 160
  labor market experience, 185–86
  occupations, 193–94
  on-the-job training, 184–85
  on-the-job training investment decision, 186–89
  productivity, 170–71, 189–90
  socialization, 174–77
  societal discrimination, 159
  stereotypes, 175–79
  stereotype threat, 177–79
  supply-side factors, 159, 194–96
  training investment decisions, 190–93
  women's unmeasured labor market, 261–62
Human trafficking, 385

Hungary, 373n, 376, 379, 416
Hunting and gathering societies, 19
Husbands. *See also* Marriage
  husband/wife bargaining power and, 47
  increasing earnings, 46, 121–22
  traditional role, 47

I

Illegal activities, 86n
Illinois, 240n
Illinois State Bar, 179
Illiteracy rates, worldwide, 380, 381
Immigrants
  demographics of, 72
  Hispanics as, 155, 264
  labor force participation, late nineteenth century, 23
  wives in labor market, necessity of, 24, 26
Immigration and Naturalization Service (INS), 413
Imperialism, 16
Incarceration rates, unemployment and, 269
Income. *See also* Human capital model; Wages
  allocation of, and bargaining power, 46–47
  experience-earnings profiles, 165–70
  federal income tax, 341–45
  female-male earnings ratio, 147–56
  husband's rising income, 46, 121–22
  increased by specialization, 40
  nonlabor, 99
  present value, 167n
Income effect, 105, 113–15, 132–33
Income taxation policy, 341–45
Independent contractors, 274–75
Independent variable, 251
Index of segregation, 141–42, 144–45
India, 108, 374–75, 379, 384, 385, 406, 408, 411
Indiana, 240n
Indifference curves, 97, 98, 99–102
Indirect costs, of education, 167
Indonesia, 411
Industrialization
  families, 23–27
  females, 22–23
  middle class roles during, 26
  "subtle revolution" in gender roles, 21
  upper class roles during, 26
  women's property rights evolution, 27–28
  U.S., 21–33

Infanticide, 406
Informal network, 181, 216, 225
Installation, maintenance, and
        repair occupations, 138
Institutional advantages, of
        married couples, 43
Institutional discrimination, 233
Institutional models, in labor
        market discrimination
    internal labor market, 231–32
    primary and secondary jobs,
        232–33
Insurance industry, 147
Interdependence, costs of, 45–46
Internal labor market, 231–32
Internal rate of return, 167n
International bill of rights for
        women, 383
International Labour Organization
        (ILO), 408–10
Interviews. *See* Job interviews
Investments. *See also* Educational
        investment decision
    in education, 111
    marriage-specific, 43, 50
    training decisions, 186–89,
        190–93
Involuntary part-time workers, 271
Iran, 379
Ireland, 376
Iron triangle of welfare, 329
Italy, 376, 379, 389, 399

J

Japan, 374–76, 379, 386, 387,
        389–90, 392–95, 399, 400,
        402, 408
Job evaluation, 248–49
Job interviews, 366–67
Job losers/leavers, 269
Job loss, 267
Job Opportunities and Basic Skills
        (JOBS) program, 330
Job segregation, 55
Job sharing, 363
Jobs, primary and secondary,
        232–33
Job Training Partnership Act
        (JTPA) of 1982, 330
Jordan, 379, 385

K

Kaiser, 123n
Kassindja, Fauzija, 412–13
Kennedy, John F., 236
Kentucky, 240n
*Kolstad v. American Dental
        Association* (1999), 242n

Korea, 108, 374–75, 376, 379
Kuwait, 379

L

Labor. *See also* Discrimination;
        Females; Labor force
    child labor, 24, 408–10
    nonmarket work (w^*), 55–68
    nonstandard work force, 274–78
Laborer occupations, 138, 139, 140
Labor force. *See also* Child care;
        Labor supply decision;
        Nonstandard workforce;
        Participation
    attachment trends, 92–94,
        261–62
    blacks, 129–31
    budget constraints, 97, 98,
        99, 116n
    cash jobs excluded, 86n
    decreases, 94
    defined, 86–88
    economic conditions, 115–16, 126
    entrants, 94
    exits, 94
    female participation, 118–22
    hours worked, 95
    illegal activities excluded, 86n
    income effect, 132–33
    increases, 94
    married and single mothers,
        1990s and early 2000s,
        127–28
    married mothers,
        1960s-1980s, 125–27
    men's participation, 128–29
    participation trends, 88–92
    post-World War II baby boom,
        124–25
    segregation in, 55
    status of world's women,
        372–77, 389–90
    substitution effect, 132–33
    supply decision, 96–118
    terms regarding, 86–88
    turnover rates, 354
    whites, 129–31
    World War II, 122–24
Labor force attachment, 272
Labor force participation rate, 87
Labor market
    dynamics of, 267–73
    employment problem
        indicators, 270–72
    future prospects, 273
    internal, 231–32
    supply and demand in, 8–12
    unemployment, 268–70, 272–73
    U.S. market, 267–68
    women in, 28–31

Labor market discrimination, 160,
        193, 202
    affirmative action, 242–45
    antidiscrimination efforts,
        240–42
    comparable worth, 245–48
    customer discrimination, 225
    defined, 203–4
    earnings differences, 204–10
    empirical evidence of, 204–18
    employee discrimination,
        223–25
    employer discrimination,
        219–23
    equal employment opportunity
        laws and regulations,
        235–40
    feedback effects, 203, 227–28,
        233–34
    gender pay gap and, 259–60
    glass ceiling, 214–18
    government and, 234–49
    institutional models, 231–33
    internal labor market, 231–32
    job evaluation, 248–49
    models of, 218–34
    occupational differences, 211–18
    occupational segregation, 211–14
    over- and underestimation of, 207
    overcrowding model, 228–31
    pay gaps and gender
        differences, 226–27
    primary and secondary jobs,
        232–33
    quitting and gender
        differences, 228
    regression analysis and
        empirical estimates of,
        250–54
    statistical discrimination, 223,
        226–28
    subtle barriers, 225–26
    tastes for discrimination, 218–26
Labor supply decision, 96
    budget constraints, 97, 98, 99
    child care subsidies, 116–18
    economic conditions, 115–16
    hours decision, 102–4, 113
    income effect, 113–15
    indifference curves, 97, 98,
        99–102
    market time (w), 109–12
    nonmarket time (w^*), 104–9
    substitution effect, 113–15
    taxes and the decision to
        work, 116
    women's participation and,
        116–18
Labor unions, 281–86
Latin America, 373, 374–75, 377,
        381, 382
Latino, use of term, 7

Laws, equal employment opportunity, 235–40
Layoffs, 267
Least squares regression analysis, 251
Leisure time, 37
  changing, 122
  job enjoyment and, 62
  utilities derived from, 44–45
  volunteer work distinguished from, 63
Lesbians. *See* Same-sex couples
Life cycle changes, 45
  homemaking and, 61
  of post-World War II females, 90–92
Life expectancy, 119
Literacy rate. *See also* Illiteracy rates, worldwide, 375
Louisiana, 73
Lucky Stores, 210

M

Maidplots, 2100
Malaysia, 379
Males
  all-male clubs, 226
  children's impact on participation, 108
  child support enforcement, 340
  comparative advantage in market work, 38
  demands of work and family, 348–50
  discrimination. *See* Discrimination
  education, 161–65
  educational attainment, 265–67
  expected work life, 171–74, 190–93
  female-male earnings ratio, 147–56
  gender pay gap and, 259–64
  as "head of household," 25
  housework by, 57–63
  industrialization and evolution of the family, 23–27
  labor force participation, decline in, post World War II, 136
  literacy, 375
  nature of, 14–15
  occupational differences between males and females, 137–44
  overtime pay and bonuses, 149n
  participation, 128–29
  participation decline, 89
  preindustrial period, 21–22
  self-employment, 278–79

socialization, 174–77
sociobiology, 15–18
training investment decisions, 190–93
traits and competencies, 177
unemployment rates, 269–70, 271
unemployment trends, 272–73
volunteer work statistics, 64, 65
wages, 257–59
Management, business, and financial occupations, 138
Managerial occupations, 138, 140
Manpower Development and Training Act (MDTA) of 1962, 330
Manufacturing, 139
Marginally attached workers, 271
Marital status, effect on participation, 105–9
Market
  equilibrium, 10
  substitutes, 120–21
Market cost approach, to value of unpaid work, 67
Market economy, 5
Market goods, 96
  substitution in, 101–2
Market income, 96
Market production, 37–41
Market time, 99
  factors influencing, 118–20
  substitution effect, 110
  value of, 109–12
Market work, 87
  defined, 96n
Marriage. *See also* Cohabiting couples; Dowry; Families
  comparative advantage in, 41
  as contractual affiliation, 50, 291
  covenant marriage, 73
  declining rates, 292–94, 400
  declining significance of, 71
  as economic explanation for family formation, 290–94
  expectations of success, 49
  government promotion of, 335–36
  housework division of labor in, 57–63
  job loss stress on, 268
  stability of, as influence on participation, 121
  threat point in, 51–52
  of unmarried couples, on birth of a son, 108n
  U.S. government promotion of, 73–74
Marriage bars, 28, 119–20, 209
Marriage penalty (taxation), 341–45
Marriage-specific investments, 43, 50, 291

Marriage squeeze, 126n
Married women. *See also* Blacks; Immigrants
  labor force participation, late nineteenth century, 23
  labor force participation, twentieth century, 29
  women's property rights evolution, 27–28
Marx, Karl, 53–55
Marxist feminist view of family, 55
Marxist ideology
  role of women, 414–17
  family views, 53–55
  female participation in Soviet bloc countries, 377
Maryland, 240n
Massachusetts, 73, 240n, 302n, 303, 356, 366
Mass murder, 16
Masters Tournament, 226
Mean, calculation of, 147n
Medicaid, 319, 327, 330, 332, 337
Medicare, 345
Men. *See* Males
Mentor-protégé system, 181, 225
Meritor Savings Bank v. Vinson (1986), 239
Mexico, 374–75
Michigan, 226
Microcredit loans, 410–12
Microenterprise Assistance programs, 280, 331
Middle East, 372, 374–75, 377, 378, 379, 380, 381, 382, 404
Minnesota, 226, 240n
Minors. *See* Child labor laws; Children
Mitsubishi Motor Corporation, 239
Mixed races, classifying, 72
Mixed-sex couples, 299n
Models. *See also* Human capital model
  building, 4–5
  institutional, 231–33
  of labor market discrimination, 218–34
  overcrowding, 228–31
"Mommy-track" occupations, 156
Monopsony power, 221–22
Montana, 240n
Morgan Stanley, 209
Moslem traditions, 377
Mothers. *See also* Children
  benefits for, worldwide, 387
  demographics of, 71
  married, 1960s-1980s, 125–27
  married and single, 1990s and early 2000s, 127–28
  maternal employment and children's outcomes, 314–16

Mothers (*continued*)
nonmarket work versus leisure
and, 59–61
Muller v. Oregon, 236
Multiple regression analysis, 251
Muslim traditions, 412–13

N

National Association for Single
Sex Public Education
(NASSPE), 183
National Organization for Women
(NOW) Legal Defense
and Education Fund,
69–70
Natural rate of unemployment, 268
Natural selection, 15
Negotiation, in marriage, 51
Negroes, use of term, 7
Neoclassical economics, 2, 35
analysis of families, 35–41
role of, 3–4
Neoclassical model of the family
shortcomings, 49–50
specialization and exchange,
37–41, 75–83
Neo-Darwinist theory, 17
Net benefits, of education, 167
Netherlands, 73, 376, 379, 399
Networks, informal, 181, 216, 225
Nevada, 240n
New Hampshire, 240n
New Jersey, 240n, 366
New Mexico, 240n
New York, 226, 240n, 340
New Zealand, 379
9 To 5, 286
Noncooperative threat point, 51n
Nonlabor income, 99
Nonmarket labor. *See* Nonmarket
work
Nonmarket production, estimating
value of, 66–68
Nonmarket time, 96, 99
factors influencing, 120–22
income effect, 105
substitution in, 101–2
value of, 104–9
Nonmarket work, 55
commodities production and,
96–97
housework, 56–63
labor force participation rate
and, 87
value of, estimating, 66–68
volunteer work, 63–66
Nonstandard workforce
consequences for workers and
families, 277–78
definition and characteristics of,
274–76

explanations behind, 276–77
Nonstandard work schedules, 362
Nontenure track jobs, 275n
North Africa, 372, 374–75, 378,
379, 380, 381, 382, 404
North America, 383
Norway, 376, 379, 394
Nuclear family, 6n
Nussbaum, Karen, 286

O

Oberlin College, 179
Occupational segregation. *See also*
Labor market
discrimination
causes of, 212–14
consequences of, 211–12
education and, 146
extent of, 143–44
human capital model, 198
index of segregation, 141–43
real improvements, 146–47
by sex, for selected
countries, 379
sex composition of occupations
and, 145–46
trends in, 144–47
Occupations, 136–37. *See also*
Human capital model;
Occupational
segregation
differences between males
and females, 137–44,
211–18
discrimination. *See*
Discrimination
hierarchies in, 143
self-employment, 275, 278–80,
331, 364
sex composition of, 145–46
single-sex, 146
status of world's women,
377–78, 390–93
O'Connor, Sandra Day, 239, 243
OECD countries, 387
Office and administrative support
occupations, 137
Office of Federal Contract
Compliance, 237
"Old boys' network," 215
On-call workers, 274
On-the-job training, 184–85
investment decision, 186–89
Opportunity cost, 3
Opportunity cost approach, t
o value of unpaid
work, 67
Opposite-sex couples, 36
controversy over classification
as family, 72
demographics of, 71

discrimination against, by
September 11th Victim
Compensation Fund of
2001, 70
family formation and, 299–301
job benefits for, 43
marriage rights and, 73–74
unmarried, ineligibility for
fringe benefits, 365–66
Overcrowding model, 228–31
Overtime pay, 149n
Owen, Robert, 54

P

Pacific Islanders, 152n
Pacific region, 374–75, 381,
382, 405
Paid work, 37
Pakistan, 374–75, 385
Panel Study of Income Dynamics
(PSID), 204
Participation. *See also* Labor force
blacks, 89–90, 91, 129–31
black/white differentials, 129–31
child care subsidies, 116–18
children's impact on, 106–9
1890-2003, 88, 89
females, 118–22
hours decision, 102–4
hours worked, 95
late nineteenth century, 22–23, 28
less-educated women, 146
males, 89, 128–29
marital status impact on, 105–9
married and single mothers,
1990s and early 2000s,
127–28
married mothers,
1960s-1980s, 125–27
of men, by age, 91–92, 93
post-World War II, 89,
124–25, 136
by race and Hispanic origin,
89–90, 91
status of world's women,
372–77, 389–90
twentieth century, 29–33
undercounting of, 87n
whites, 129–31
of women, by age, 90–92
of women, ramifications of,
85–86
World War II experience, 122–24
World War II participation
rates, 88–89
Part-time employment, 363
Part-time for economic reasons, 271
Part-time work, 95
Part-time workers, 274, 275, 278
Passive infanticide, 406

Pastoral societies, 20
Patriarchal property rights, 28
Patriarchy
    defined, 54
    tradition of, 55, 412–13
Pay gaps
    gender earnings gap, 149,
        151–52, 155–56
    labor market discrimination,
        204–10
    race and, 263–64
    statistical discrimination and,
        226–27
Pennsylvania, 240n
Pension rights, for married
        couples, 43
Peru, 411
Piecework, 87n
"Pipeline" argument, 216–17
Poland, 373n, 376, 379, 416
Policies
    alternative work schedules,
        362–64
    child care, 350–52, 356–62
    couples assistance, 364–66
    Family and Medical Leave Act
        of 1993 (FMLA), 353–56
    family-friendly, 352–67
    flexible benefit plans, 364
    income taxation, 341–45
    labor market discrimination,
        234–49
    poverty. *See* Poverty policies
    Social Security, 345–47
    taxes, 340–45
Polygamy, 377
Population control, in developing
        countries, 405–8
Portugal, 376
Post-college education. *See*
        Education
Poverty policies, 326
    Aid to Families with Dependent
        Children (AFDC), 327–29
    child support enforcement,
        338–40
    Child Tax Credit, 358
    Earned Income Tax Credit
        (EITC), 336–38
    employment strategies, 329–31
    marriage promotion, 335–36
    Temporary Assistance to Needy
        Families (TANF), 331–35
    welfare, 329, 330
Preferences. *See also* Tastes
    bargaining power and, 51–52
    for different goods, 75–83
    for income, 102
    for male children, 108
Pregnancy
    family-work conflict, 349
    working during, 94

Pregnancy Discrimination Act of
        1978, 353
Preindustrial period (U.S.), 21–22
Prelabor market, 159
Present value, 167n
Presidential Commission on the
        Status of Women, 236
Primary jobs, 232–33
Production
    factors of, 5
    substitution in, 101
Production occupations, 138
Production possibility frontiers, 75
Production roles, 19
Productivity. *See also* Human
        capital model
    diminishing marginal, 8–9
    education and, 170–71
    of females, increase in, 120
    of homemakers, 46
Professional occupations, 137–38
Prohibition of employment of
        married women. *See*
        Marriage bars
Property rights, 27–28
Prost, Sharon, 297–98
Prostitution, 86n
Public goods, 42, 47
Publishing data, 4
Publix Super Markets of Florida, 210
Purdah, 20

Q

Quid pro quo harassment, 238–39
Quitting, gender differences
        and, 228

R

Race. *See also* Discrimination;
        individual groups
    demographics of, 72
    earnings ratios by, 152–55
    educational attainment by, 162
    families with children under age
        18, 317
    income and poverty rates for
        families with children, 319
    labor force participation by,
        89–90, 91, 129–31
    mixed, classifications of, 72
    occupational differences by,
        139–40
    pay gaps, 263–64
    terminology, 7
    unemployment rates, 269–70
    volunteer work statistics, 64, 65
Racism, 16
Radical feminist views of family,
        53–55
Rape, as warfare tactic, 385

Rationality, 3
Ratios
    female-male earnings ratio,
        147–56
    of value of time at home to time
        in the market, 38
Real wages, 118
    defined, 257
    rise of, for educated women, 126
Reasonable person standard, 239
Reasoning, circular, 38
Recession of 2001, 271–72
Redistribution, 24
Reentrants, 269, 272
Regression analysis and empirical
        estimates of labor market
        discrimination, 250–54
Religion, as effect on women's
        participation, 377
Repair occupations, 138
Resegregation, 147
Reservation wage, 104
Returns to skill, 257
Rhode Island, 240n
Risk pooling, 43
Role models, 180
Romania, 373n
Russia, 373, 373n, 374–75,
        376, 416

S

Sales occupations, 138
Same-sex couples, 6n, 36
    controversy over classification
        as family, 72
    discrimination against, by
        September 11th Victim
        Compensation Fund of
        2001, 70
    family formation and, 301–3
    ineligibility for fringe benefits,
        365–66
    job benefits for, 43
    marriage rights and, 73–74
    specialization and, 59
Satisfaction, 3, 3n
    maximization of, as family
        goal, 37
    maximization of, as individual
        goal, 96
Satisfice, 3
Saudi Arabia, 374–75
Scale effect, 9
Scandinavia, 377, 388, 389
Scarcity, 3
Screening device, education as, 170
Seasonal unemployment, 268
Seasonal work, 87n
Secondary jobs, 232–33
Second transformation, 23n

Segregation, occupational, 141–47. *See also* Discrimination
heirarchies within occupation, 143–44
trends in, 144–47
SEIU (Service Employees' International Union), 286
Self-care, by children, 360–61
Self-employment, 275, 278–80, 331, 364
Seneca Falls Convention (1848), 27–28
Senegal, 379
September 11th Victim Compensation Fund of 2001, 68–70
Service occupations, 137, 273
Sex composition of occupations, 145–46
Sex-determination tests, 406
Sex discrimination lawsuits, 209–10
Sex, gender distinguished from, 7. *See also* Females; Gender; Males
Sexism, 16
Sex-selective abortion, 406
Sex-stereotyping, of toys, 175–77
Sexual harassment, 238–40, 392
Sexual orientation, discrimination based on, 240
Sharing jobs, 363
Shocks, 10
Sierra Leone, 385
Signal, education as, 170
Simpson, Nicole Brown, 48
Simpson, O.J., 48
Single-parent families, 26, 310, 316–22
Single-sex educational opportunities, 183
Single-sex occupations, 146
Single women, 26–27
1990s-early 2000s, 127–28
labor force participation, twentieth century, 29
Slavery/slaves
lack of rights, 22
production roles and determination of status, 19
rationalization for, 16
women, 21
Slovakia, 373n
Small Necessities Leave Act (Massachusetts), 356
Social compensation fee (China), 407
Social Darwinism, 15–16
Social forces, 377
Socialism, 54

Socialization, human capital model, 174–77
Socializing housework, 54
Social Security, 340, 345–47
Social Security Act (1935), 327
Social Security benefits
for married couples, 43
one-earner families favored, 49
Social Services block grant, 358
Societal discrimination, 159
Sociobiology, 15–18
Sole proprietorships, 278n
Somalia, 413
South Africa, 374–75
South Asia, 374–75, 380, 381, 382, 383, 404, 406
South Korea, 406
Soviet Union, former, 54, 380, 389
participation rates, 373
status of world's women, 414–17
Spain, 376, 379, 389
Specialization
disadvantages of, 43–49
income increases and, 40
neoclassical model, 37–41
public policies and, 49
risks to unmarried cohabiting couples, 59
traditional, examples, 36
well-being of family and, 38n
Specialization and exchange
absolute advantage, 39–40
comparative advantage, 37–38, 40
gains to, 40–41
graphical analysis, 75–83
marriage and, 290
numerical examples, 38–40
in production, 37–41
Spousal abuse, 48–49
Stable equilibrium, 10–12
Stanton, Elizabeth Cady, 27–28
State Disability Insurance program (California), 356
State Farm Insurance, 209
Statistical discrimination, 192, 223
feedback effects, 227–28
pay gaps, 226–27
quitting, 228
Status, determination of, 19
Stereotype threat situations, 177–79
Stereotyping
in children's toys, 175–77
of homemakers, 88
Structural unemployment, 268
Sub-Saharan Africa, 372–75, 377, 380–82, 384, 386, 404, 406
Subsidies, child care, 116–18
Substitution
availability of, 120–22
in consumption, 100–101

between market goods and nonmarket time, 101–2
in production, 101
Substitution effect, 9, 110, 113–15, 132–33
Sudan, 385
Supplemental security income (SSI), 347
Supply
curve, 9–10
nonstandard work and, 277
shifts in, 10–12
worker productivity, 6
Supply and demand
for labor, 5
in the labor market, 8–12
Supply decisions
budget constraints, 97, 98, 99, 116n
child care, 116–18
hours, 102–4
income and substitution effect, 105, 110
tastes, 102
taxes, 116
Supply-side factors, human capital model, 159, 194–96, 233
Swaziland, 386
Sweden, 340, 344, 350, 373–76, 379, 386–92, 394, 396, 399, 400–2
Sweeney, John, 285
Switzerland, 373, 376, 379, 394

T

Tabulation, 5
Taiwan, 406
Tastes. *See also* Preferences
allocation of income and time and, 46–47
changing, 122
for discrimination, 218–26
indifference curves and, 102
for unionism, 283
Taxes, 116, 340–45
Tax Reform Act of 1986, 116, 341
Tax subsidies, 359
Technological change, 120–22
Temporary Assistance to Needy Families (TANF), 331–35, 358, 361
Temporary help agency workers, 274
Temporary help industry, 269
Tenure, 186, 189n
nontenure track jobs, 275n
Thailand, 374–75, 405
Theories, uses of, 4–5
Threat point, 51, 86

Tied mover/stayer, 196
Time, allocation of, 35. *See also*
        Market time (*w*);
        Nonmarket time (*w**)
Time-intensive commodities, 100
Time squeeze, 95, 348–49
Title VII, Civil Rights Act of 1964,
        236–42, 244, 353
Title IX, Civil Rights Act of 1964,
        182–83, 184
Togo, 413
Traditional family, 23–24
Trailing partner, 364
Training. *See also* Education
    gender differences in, 190–93
    on-the-job, 186–89
Traits and competencies,
        gender, 177
Transaction costs, 49–53
Transportation and material
        moving occupations, 138
Trends
    attachment, 92–94, 261–62, 272
    family structure, 293
    female labor force participation,
        118–22
    female-male earnings ratio,
        147–56
    fertility, 307
    labor force, 88–92
    occupational segregation, 144–47
    pay gaps, 259–60
Tunisia, 379
Turnover rates, 354

U

Ukraine, 373n, 416
Underemployment, 270–71
Underground economy, 86n
Unemployed group, 86, 88
    blacks in, 130
    whites in, 130
Unemployment
    cyclical, 268
    defined, 268
    frictional, 268
    by gender, age, race, and
        Hispanic origin, 269–70
    groups affected, 269
    seasonal, 268
Unemployment insurance
        (UI), 356
Unilateral divorce laws, 53
Union of Soviet Socialist Republics
        (USSR), 373n, 414
Unions, labor, 281–86
United Kingdom, 344, 376, 379,
        394, 396, 399, 401
United Nations
    Beijing Plus Five, 385

Convention for the
        Elimination of All
        Forms of
        Discrimination Against
        Women (CEDAW), 383
    Fourth World Conference on
        Women (Beijing), 385
    Millennium Summit, 385, 404
United States
    college-educated women, 31–33
    fertility rates, 381
    indicators of women's economic
        status, 374–75
    industrialization, 22–23
    industrialization and evolution
        of the family, 23–27
    occupational segregation, 379
    participation, by age, 376
    preference for male
        children, 108
    preindustrial period, 21–22
    women in the labor market,
        28–31
    women's property rights
        evolution, 27–28
United States and advanced
        countries comparison, 386
    antidiscrimination efforts, 387
    child care, 388, 389
    comparable worth, 395–98
    demographic trends, 398–402
    family structure, 401
    gender-wage gap, 393–98
    housework, 402
    labor force participation,
        389–90
    marriage rates, 400
    occupations, 390–93
    wage-setting, 388
Universities. *See* Education
University of Michigan Law
        School, 208, 243
Unpaid work. *See* Nonmarket
        work (*w**)
Urbanization, 24
U.S. Constitution, 19th
        Amendment, 27
U.S. Department of Agriculture, 303
U.S. government, collection of
        data, 4–5
U.S. Information Agency, 209
U.S. Supreme Court, 179, 183
    equal employment opportunity
        laws and regulations,
        235–40
Utility
    maximization of, as family
        goal, 37
    maximization of, as individual
        goal, 96
    specialization and, 44
Uzbekistan, 373n

V

Variables, in regression analysis, 251
Vatican, 401
Velvet revolution
        (Czechoslovakia), 415
Vermont, 74, 240n, 303, 366
Virginia Military Institute
        (V.M.I.), 183
Voice of America, 209–10
Voluntary chosen behavior, 17
Volunteer work, 63–66

W

Wage inequality, 111, 257
Wages. *See also* Human
        capital model
    Asian-white ratios, 153
    black-white ratios, 152–54
    defined, 97, 99
    experience-earnings profiles,
        165–70
    female-male earnings ratio,
        147–56
    Hispanic-white ratios, 152–54
    increase of, 118
Wage structure, 260
Washington, George, 26n
Washington State, 240n
Wealth, allocation of, 35
Weekly earnings, 149
Welfare, 329, 330
Welfare-to-work programs, 330–31
White-collar occupations, 146
Whites
    birth rates, 308
    discrimination. *See*
        Discrimination
    as domestic servants/farm
        laborers, 30
    earnings ratios with non-whites,
        152–55
    educational attainment, 154
    educational attainment by, 162,
        263–64
    expected work life, 171–74,
        190–92
    families with children under age
        18, 317
    incarceration rates, 130
    income and poverty rates
        for families with
        children, 319
    in labor unions, 281
    marriage rates, 293
    mother-only families, 318
    non-whites and occupational
        differences and, 139–40
    participation rates by, since the
        1950s, 129–31

Whites (*continued*)
  social Darwinism and, 15–16
  unemployment rates, 269–70
  volunteer work statistics, 64
Wisconsin, 240n, 339
Witte, John, Jr., 290n
Wives. *See also* Marriage
  husband/wife bargaining power
    and, 47
  traditional role, 47

Women. *See* Females
Women's Figures (Furchtgott-
    Roth and Stolba), 155
Women's property rights, 27–28
Work experience. *See*
  Experience
Work first strategy, 331
Work force. *See* Labor force
Workforce Investment Act (WIA)
  of 1998, 330

World War II
  females, 122–24
  participation rates, 88–89

Y

Year-round employment, 147n
Yugoslavia, former, 379